Zend Framework

The Official Programmer's Reference Guide
Volume 1 of 2

Zend, Inc.

Apress®

The Zend Press Series

Zend Framework: The Official Programmer's Reference Guide (Volume 1 of 2)

Volume 1   ISBN-13 (pbk): 978-1-4302-2883-7
Volume 2   ISBN-13 (pbk): 978-1-4302-2880-6
Volume 3   ISBN-13 (pbk): 978-1-4302-1906-4

Printed and bound in the United States of America 9 8 7 6 5 4 3 2 1

Trademarked names may appear in this book. Rather than use a trademark symbol with every occurrence of a trademarked name, we use the names only in an editorial fashion and to the benefit of the trademark owner, with no intention of infringement of the trademark.

President and Publisher: Paul Manning
Lead Editor: Jeffrey Pepper
Editorial Board: Clay Andres, Steve Anglin, Mark Beckner, Ewan Buckingham, Tony Campbell, Gary Cornell, Jonathan Gennick, Michelle Lowman, Matthew Moodie, Jeffrey Pepper, Frank Pohlmann, Ben Renow-Clarke, Dominic Shakeshaft, Matt Wade, Tom Welsh
Compositor: StanInfo Solutions and Zend Technologies USA, Inc
Cover Designer: Anna Ishchenko

Distributed to the book trade worldwide by Springer-Verlag New York, Inc., 233 Spring Street, 6th Floor, New York, NY 10013. Phone 1-800-SPRINGER, fax 201-348-4505, e-mail orders-ny@springer-sbm.com, or visit http://www.springeronline.com.

For information on translations, please e-mail info@apress.com, or visit http://www.apress.com.

Apress and friends of ED books may be purchased in bulk for academic, corporate, or promotional use. eBook versions and licenses are also available for most titles. For more information, reference our Special Bulk Sales—eBook Licensing web page at http://www.apress.com/info/bulksales.

The information in this book is distributed on an "as is" basis, without warranty. Although every precaution has been taken in the preparation of this work, neither the author(s) nor Apress shall have any liability to any person or entity with respect to any loss or damage caused or alleged to be caused directly or indirectly by the information contained in this work.

About Zend Press

Zend Press publishes books that are authored by leaders in the PHP community, PHP engineers & consultants, employees of Zend, and all those knowledgeable about PHP and its use to deliver powerful, scalable, and reliable web-based applications and infrastructure. Zend Press is a joint publishing relationship between Zend and Apress, the leading publisher on emerging technologies.

As the market leader in PHP related technology, Zend will utilize Zend Press to deliver books on Zend-related projects or products and also on thought leading topics in professional PHP as well. Zend Press will publish books at all levels to meet the needs of a diverse PHP community with relevant, cutting edge know-how. Regardless of the audience, we are committed to publishing books that best serve the needs of users at any targeted level.

Through this publishing program, we are committed to bringing you more and better information, to help you use our products more effectively, with the professionalism that you have come to expect from Zend, from the PHP community at large, and from Apress.

Zeev Suraski
Zend Technologies Co-founder and Chief Technology Officer

Foreword

These two volumes contain the full Zend Framework Reference Guide in a handy format for quick reference (this same material can also be viewed online at http://framework.zend.com/manual). You may want to keep it next to you while developing or invest your time in a more thorough review to improve your ZF expertise in general. Much like the framework itself, it can be read in a 'use-at-will' fashion; that is, you can read each section of the guide without having to read other sections in advance. As its name implies, typically this reference guide would not be read cover-to-cover, but if you are dedicated to learning about every component in ZF it will also lend itself well to this purpose.

One of Zend Framework's core strengths is the fact that all contributors to the project have to supply documentation along with their code. As a result, every feature is called out and documented in detail. And with over 500 code examples, this reference guide will show you exactly how to use these features in your applications.

The guide documents each feature and API in full, with plenty of examples to make easy work of adding ZF components to your applications. In particular, this guide features:

- A chapter dedicated to every component in Zend Framework
- Quick Starts for key components such as Zend_Controller and Zend_Form
- Over a thousand pages of Zend Framework material written by hundreds of ZF contributors
- Edited and reviewed by the Zend Framework team at Zend Technologies

We hope you find this guide as useful as the Zend Framework components themselves while writing the next generation of PHP applications. The Zend Framework community has invested countless hours to make this guide as helpful as possible, but if you find improvements to be made, please join us at http://framework.zend.com to add your voice to our growing community!

Matthew Weier O'Phinney
Project Lead, Zend Framework

List of Tables

List of Examples

Chapter 1. Introduction to Zend Framework

Overview

Zend Framework (ZF) is an open source framework for developing web applications and services with PHP 5. ZF is implemented using 100% object-oriented code. The component structure of ZF is somewhat unique; each component is designed with few dependencies on other components. This loosely coupled architecture allows developers to use components individually. We often call this a "use-at-will" design.

While they can be used separately, Zend Framework components in the standard library form a powerful and extensible web application framework when combined. ZF offers a robust, high performance MVC implementation, a database abstraction that is simple to use, and a forms component that implements HTML form rendering, validation, and filtering so that developers can consolidate all of these operations using one easy-to-use, object oriented interface. Other components, such as Zend_Auth and Zend_Acl, provide user authentication and authorization against all common credential stores. Still others implement client libraries to simply access to the most popular web services available. Whatever your application needs are, you're likely to find a Zend Framework component that can be used to dramatically reduce development time with a thoroughly tested foundation.

The principal sponsor of the Zend Framework project is Zend Technologies [http://www.zend.com], but many companies have contributed components or significant features to the framework. Companies such as Google, Microsoft, and StrikeIron have partnered with Zend to provide interfaces to web services and other technologies that they wish to make available to Zend Framework developers.

Zend Framework could not deliver and support all of these features without the help of the vibrant ZF community. Community members, including contributors, make themselves available on mailing lists [http://framework.zend.com/archives], IRC channels [http://www.zftalk.com], and other forums. Whatever question you have about ZF, the community is always available to address it.

Installation

See the requirements appendix for a detailed list of requirements for Zend Framework.

Installing Zend Framework is extremely simple. Once you have downloaded and extracted the framework, you should add the /library folder in the distribution to the beginning of your include path. You may also want to move the library folder to another- possibly shared- location on your file system.

- Download the latest stable release. [http://framework.zend.com/download/latest] This version, available in both `.zip` and `.tar.gz` formats, is a good choice for those who are new to Zend Framework.

- Download the latest nightly snapshot. [http://framework.zend.com/download/snapshot] For those who would brave the cutting edge, the nightly snapshots represent the latest progress of Zend Framework development. Snapshots are bundled with documentation either in English only or in all available languages. If you anticipate working with the latest Zend Framework developments, consider using a Subversion (SVN) client.

- Using a Subversion [http://subversion.tigris.org] (SVN) client. Zend Framework is open source software, and the Subversion repository used for its development is publicly available. Consider using SVN to get Zend Framework if you already use SVN for your application development, want to contribute back to the framework, or need to upgrade your framework version more often than releases occur.

Exporting [http://svnbook.red-bean.com/nightly/en/svn.ref.svn.c.export.html] is useful if you want to get a particular framework revision without the .svn directories as created in a working copy.

Check out a working copy [http://svnbook.red-bean.com/nightly/en/svn.ref.svn.c.checkout.html] if you want contribute to Zend Framework, a working copy can be updated any time with svn update [http://svnbook.red-bean.com/nightly/en/svn.ref.svn.c.update.html] and changes can be commited to our SVN repository with the svn commit [http://svnbook.red-bean.com/nightly /en/svn.ref.svn.c.commit.html] command.

An externals definition [http://svnbook.red-bean.com/nightly/en/svn.advanced.externals.html] is quite convenient for developers already using SVN to manage their application's working copies.

The URL for the trunk of the Zend Framework SVN repository is: http://framework.zend.com/svn /framework/standard/trunk [http://framework.zend.com/svn/framework/standard/trunk]

Once you have a copy of Zend Framework available, your application needs to be able to access the framework classes. Though there are several ways to achieve this [http://www.php.net/manual/en /configuration.changes.php], your PHP include_path [http://www.php.net/manual/en/ini.core.php #ini.include-path] needs to contain the path to the Zend Framework library.

Zend provides a QuickStart [http://framework.zend.com/docs/quickstart] to get you up and running as quickly as possible. This is an excellent way to begin learning about the framework with an emphasis on real world examples that you can build upon.

Since Zend Framework components are loosely coupled, you may use a somewhat unique combination of them in your own applications. The following chapters provide a comprehensive reference to Zend Framework on a component-by-component basis.

Chapter 2. Zend_Acl

Introduction

`Zend_Acl` provides a lightweight and flexible access control list (ACL) implementation for privileges management. In general, an application may utilize such ACL's to control access to certain protected objects by other requesting objects.

For the purposes of this documentation,

- a *resource* is an object to which access is controlled.

- a *role* is an object that may request access to a Resource.

Put simply, *roles request access to resources*. For example, if a parking attendant requests access to a car, then the parking attendant is the requesting role, and the car is the resource, since access to the car may not be granted to everyone.

Through the specification and use of an ACL, an application may control how roles are granted access to resources.

Resources

Creating a resource in `Zend_Acl` is very simple. `Zend_Acl` provides the resource, `Zend_Acl_Resource_Interface`, to facilitate creating resources in an application. A class need only implement this interface, which consists of a single method, `getResourceId()`, so `Zend_Acl` to recognize the object as a resource. Additionally, `Zend_Acl_Resource` is provided by `Zend_Acl` as a basic resource implementation for developers to extend as needed.

`Zend_Acl` provides a tree structure to which multiple resources can be added. Since resources are stored in such a tree structure, they can be organized from the general (toward the tree root) to the specific (toward the tree leaves). Queries on a specific resource will automatically search the resource's hierarchy for rules assigned to ancestor resources, allowing for simple inheritance of rules. For example, if a default rule is to be applied to each building in a city, one would simply assign the rule to the city, instead of assigning the same rule to each building. Some buildings may require exceptions to such a rule, however, and this can be achieved in `Zend_Acl` by assigning such exception rules to each building that requires such an exception. A resource may inherit from only one parent resource, though this parent resource can have its own parent resource, etc.

`Zend_Acl` also supports privileges on resources (e.g., "create", "read", "update", "delete"), so the developer can assign rules that affect all privileges or specific privileges on one or more resources.

Roles

As with resources, creating a role is also very simple. All roles must implement `Zend_Acl_Role_Interface`. This interface consists of a single method, `getRoleId()`, Additionally, `Zend_Acl_Role` is provided by `Zend_Acl` as a basic role implementation for developers to extend as needed.

In `Zend_Acl`, a role may inherit from one or more roles. This is to support inheritance of rules among roles. For example, a user role, such as "sally", may belong to one or more parent roles, such as "editor" and "administrator". The developer can assign rules to "editor" and "administrator" separately, and "sally" would inherit such rules from both, without having to assign rules directly to "sally".

Though the ability to inherit from multiple roles is very useful, multiple inheritance also introduces some degree of complexity. The following example illustrates the ambiguity condition and how Zend_Acl solves it.

Example 2.1. Multiple Inheritance among Roles

The following code defines three base roles - "guest", "member", and "admin" - from which other roles may inherit. Then, a role identified by "someUser" is established and inherits from the three other roles. The order in which these roles appear in the $parents array is important. When necessary, Zend_Acl searches for access rules defined not only for the queried role (herein, "someUser"), but also upon the roles from which the queried role inherits (herein, "guest", "member", and "admin"):

```
$acl = new Zend_Acl();

$acl->addRole(new Zend_Acl_Role('guest'))
    ->addRole(new Zend_Acl_Role('member'))
    ->addRole(new Zend_Acl_Role('admin'));

$parents = array('guest', 'member', 'admin');
$acl->addRole(new Zend_Acl_Role('someUser'), $parents);

$acl->add(new Zend_Acl_Resource('someResource'));

$acl->deny('guest', 'someResource');
$acl->allow('member', 'someResource');

echo $acl->isAllowed('someUser', 'someResource') ? 'allowed' : 'denied';
```

Since there is no rule specifically defined for the "someUser" role and "someResource", Zend_Acl must search for rules that may be defined for roles that "someUser" inherits. First, the "admin" role is visited, and there is no access rule defined for it. Next, the "member" role is visited, and Zend_Acl finds that there is a rule specifying that "member" is allowed access to "someResource".

If Zend_Acl were to continue examining the rules defined for other parent roles, however, it would find that "guest" is denied access to "someResource". This fact introduces an ambiguity because now "someUser" is both denied and allowed access to "someResource", by reason of having inherited conflicting rules from different parent roles.

Zend_Acl resolves this ambiguity by completing a query when it finds the first rule that is directly applicable to the query. In this case, since the "member" role is examined before the "guest" role, the example code would print "allowed".

Note

When specifying multiple parents for a role, keep in mind that the last parent listed is the first one searched for rules applicable to an authorization query.

Creating the Access Control List

An Access Control List (ACL) can represent any set of physical or virtual objects that you wish. For the purposes of demonstration, however, we will create a basic Content Management System (CMS) ACL that maintains several tiers of groups over a wide variety of areas. To create a new ACL object, we instantiate the ACL with no parameters:

```
$acl = new Zend_Acl();
```

Note

Until a developer specifies an "allow" rule, Zend_Acl denies access to every privilege upon every resource by every role.

Registering Roles

CMS's will nearly always require a hierarchy of permissions to determine the authoring capabilities of its users. There may be a 'Guest' group to allow limited access for demonstrations, a 'Staff' group for the majority of CMS users who perform most of the day-to-day operations, an 'Editor' group for those responsible for publishing, reviewing, archiving and deleting content, and finally an 'Administrator' group whose tasks may include all of those of the other groups as well as maintenance of sensitive information, user management, back-end configuration data and backup/export. This set of permissions can be represented in a role registry, allowing each group to inherit privileges from 'parent' groups, as well as providing distinct privileges for their unique group only. The permissions may be expressed as follows:

Table 2.1. Access Controls for an Example CMS

Name	Unique Permissions	Inherit Permissions From
Guest	View	N/A
Staff	Edit, Submit, Revise	Guest
Editor	Publish, Archive, Delete	Staff
Administrator	(Granted all access)	N/A

For this example, Zend_Acl_Role is used, but any object that implements Zend_Acl_Role_Interface is acceptable. These groups can be added to the role registry as follows:

```
$acl = new Zend_Acl();

// Add groups to the Role registry using Zend_Acl_Role
// Guest does not inherit access controls
$roleGuest = new Zend_Acl_Role('guest');
$acl->addRole($roleGuest);

// Staff inherits from guest
$acl->addRole(new Zend_Acl_Role('staff'), $roleGuest);

/*
Alternatively, the above could be written:
$acl->addRole(new Zend_Acl_Role('staff'), 'guest');
*/

// Editor inherits from staff
$acl->addRole(new Zend_Acl_Role('editor'), 'staff');

// Administrator does not inherit access controls
$acl->addRole(new Zend_Acl_Role('administrator'));
```

Defining Access Controls

Now that the ACL contains the relevant roles, rules can be established that define how resources may be accessed by roles. You may have noticed that we have not defined any particular resources for this example, which is simplified to illustrate that the rules apply to all resources. Zend_Acl provides an implementation whereby rules need only be assigned from general to specific, minimizing the number of rules needed, because resources and roles inherit rules that are defined upon their ancestors.

Note

In general, Zend_Acl obeys a given rule if and only if a more specific rule does not apply.

Consequently, we can define a reasonably complex set of rules with a minimum amount of code. To apply the base permissions as defined above:

```
$acl = new Zend_Acl();

$roleGuest = new Zend_Acl_Role('guest');
$acl->addRole($roleGuest);
$acl->addRole(new Zend_Acl_Role('staff'), $roleGuest);
$acl->addRole(new Zend_Acl_Role('editor'), 'staff');
$acl->addRole(new Zend_Acl_Role('administrator'));

// Guest may only view content
$acl->allow($roleGuest, null, 'view');

/*
Alternatively, the above could be written:
$acl->allow('guest', null, 'view');
//*/

// Staff inherits view privilege from guest, but also needs additional
// privileges
$acl->allow('staff', null, array('edit', 'submit', 'revise'));

// Editor inherits view, edit, submit, and revise privileges from
// staff, but also needs additional privileges
$acl->allow('editor', null, array('publish', 'archive', 'delete'));

// Administrator inherits nothing, but is allowed all privileges
$acl->allow('administrator');
```

The null values in the above allow() calls are used to indicate that the allow rules apply to all resources.

Querying an ACL

We now have a flexible ACL that can be used to determine whether requesters have permission to perform functions throughout the web application. Performing queries is quite simple using the isAllowed() method:

```
echo $acl->isAllowed('guest', null, 'view') ?
    "allowed" : "denied";
// allowed

echo $acl->isAllowed('staff', null, 'publish') ?
    "allowed" : "denied";
```

```
// denied

echo $acl->isAllowed('staff', null, 'revise') ?
     "allowed" : "denied";
// allowed

echo $acl->isAllowed('editor', null, 'view') ?
     "allowed" : "denied";
// allowed because of inheritance from guest

echo $acl->isAllowed('editor', null, 'update') ?
     "allowed" : "denied";
// denied because no allow rule for 'update'

echo $acl->isAllowed('administrator', null, 'view') ?
     "allowed" : "denied";
// allowed because administrator is allowed all privileges

echo $acl->isAllowed('administrator') ?
     "allowed" : "denied";
// allowed because administrator is allowed all privileges

echo $acl->isAllowed('administrator', null, 'update') ?
     "allowed" : "denied";
// allowed because administrator is allowed all privileges
```

Refining Access Controls

Precise Access Controls

The basic ACL as defined in the previous section shows how various privileges may be allowed upon the entire ACL (all resources). In practice, however, access controls tend to have exceptions and varying degrees of complexity. Zend_Acl allows to you accomplish these refinements in a straightforward and flexible manner.

For the example CMS, it has been determined that whilst the 'staff' group covers the needs of the vast majority of users, there is a need for a new 'marketing' group that requires access to the newsletter and latest news in the CMS. The group is fairly self-sufficient and will have the ability to publish and archive both newsletters and the latest news.

In addition, it has also been requested that the 'staff' group be allowed to view news stories but not to revise the latest news. Finally, it should be impossible for anyone (administrators included) to archive any 'announcement' news stories since they only have a lifespan of 1-2 days.

First we revise the role registry to reflect these changes. We have determined that the 'marketing' group has the same basic permissions as 'staff', so we define 'marketing' in such a way that it inherits permissions from 'staff':

```
// The new marketing group inherits permissions from staff
$acl->addRole(new Zend_Acl_Role('marketing'), 'staff');
```

Next, note that the above access controls refer to specific resources (e.g., "newsletter", "latest news", "announcement news"). Now we add these resources:

```
// Create Resources for the rules

// newsletter
$acl->add(new Zend_Acl_Resource('newsletter'));

// news
$acl->add(new Zend_Acl_Resource('news'));

// latest news
$acl->add(new Zend_Acl_Resource('latest'), 'news');

// announcement news
$acl->add(new Zend_Acl_Resource('announcement'), 'news');
```

Then it is simply a matter of defining these more specific rules on the target areas of the ACL:

```
// Marketing must be able to publish and archive newsletters and the
// latest news
$acl->allow('marketing',
            array('newsletter', 'latest'),
            array('publish', 'archive'));

// Staff (and marketing, by inheritance), are denied permission to
// revise the latest news
$acl->deny('staff', 'latest', 'revise');

// Everyone (including administrators) are denied permission to
// archive news announcements
$acl->deny(null, 'announcement', 'archive');
```

We can now query the ACL with respect to the latest changes:

```
echo $acl->isAllowed('staff', 'newsletter', 'publish') ?
    "allowed" : "denied";
// denied

echo $acl->isAllowed('marketing', 'newsletter', 'publish') ?
    "allowed" : "denied";
// allowed

echo $acl->isAllowed('staff', 'latest', 'publish') ?
    "allowed" : "denied";
// denied

echo $acl->isAllowed('marketing', 'latest', 'publish') ?
    "allowed" : "denied";
// allowed

echo $acl->isAllowed('marketing', 'latest', 'archive') ?
    "allowed" : "denied";
// allowed

echo $acl->isAllowed('marketing', 'latest', 'revise') ?
    "allowed" : "denied";
// denied

echo $acl->isAllowed('editor', 'announcement', 'archive') ?
    "allowed" : "denied";
// denied

echo $acl->isAllowed('administrator', 'announcement', 'archive') ?
    "allowed" : "denied";
// denied
```

Removing Access Controls

To remove one or more access rules from the ACL, simply use the available removeAllow() or removeDeny() methods. As with allow() and deny(), you may provide a null value to indicate application to all roles, resources, and/or privileges:

```
// Remove the denial of revising latest news to staff (and marketing,
// by inheritance)
$acl->removeDeny('staff', 'latest', 'revise');

echo $acl->isAllowed('marketing', 'latest', 'revise') ?
    "allowed" : "denied";
// allowed

// Remove the allowance of publishing and archiving newsletters to
// marketing
$acl->removeAllow('marketing',
                  'newsletter',
                  array('publish', 'archive'));

echo $acl->isAllowed('marketing', 'newsletter', 'publish') ?
    "allowed" : "denied";
// denied

echo $acl->isAllowed('marketing', 'newsletter', 'archive') ?
    "allowed" : "denied";
// denied
```

Privileges may be modified incrementally as indicated above, but a null value for the privileges overrides such incremental changes:

```
// Allow marketing all permissions upon the latest news
$acl->allow('marketing', 'latest');

echo $acl->isAllowed('marketing', 'latest', 'publish') ?
    "allowed" : "denied";
// allowed

echo $acl->isAllowed('marketing', 'latest', 'archive') ?
    "allowed" : "denied";
// allowed

echo $acl->isAllowed('marketing', 'latest', 'anything') ?
    "allowed" : "denied";
// allowed
```

Advanced Usage

Storing ACL Data for Persistence

Zend_Acl was designed in such a way that it does not require any particular backend technology such as a database or cache server for storage of the ACL data. Its complete PHP implementation enables customized administration tools to be built upon Zend_Acl with relative ease and flexibility. Many situations require some form of interactive maintenance of the ACL, and Zend_Acl provides methods for setting up, and querying against, the access controls of an application.

Storage of ACL data is therefore left as a task for the developer, since use cases are expected to vary widely for various situations. Because Zend_Acl is serializable, ACL objects may be serialized with PHP's serialize() [http://php.net/serialize] function, and the results may be stored anywhere the developer should desire, such as a file, database, or caching mechanism.

Writing Conditional ACL Rules with Assertions

Sometimes a rule for allowing or denying a role access to a resource should not be absolute but dependent upon various criteria. For example, suppose that certain access should be allowed, but only between the hours of 8:00am and 5:00pm. Another example would be denying access because a request comes from an IP address that has been flagged as a source of abuse. Zend_Acl has built-in support for implementing rules based on whatever conditions the developer needs.

Zend_Acl provides support for conditional rules with Zend_Acl_Assert_Interface. In order to use the rule assertion interface, a developer writes a class that implements the assert() method of the interface:

```
class CleanIPAssertion implements Zend_Acl_Assert_Interface
{
    public function assert(Zend_Acl $acl,
                           Zend_Acl_Role_Interface $role = null,
                           Zend_Acl_Resource_Interface $resource = null,
                           $privilege = null)
    {
        return $this->_isCleanIP($_SERVER['REMOTE_ADDR']);
    }

    protected function _isCleanIP($ip)
    {
        // ...
    }
}
```

Once an assertion class is available, the developer must supply an instance of the assertion class when assigning conditional rules. A rule that is created with an assertion only applies when the assertion method returns true.

```
$acl = new Zend_Acl();
$acl->allow(null, null, null, new CleanIPAssertion());
```

The above code creates a conditional allow rule that allows access to all privileges on everything by everyone, except when the requesting IP is "blacklisted." If a request comes in from an IP that is not considered "clean," then the allow rule does not apply. Since the rule applies to all roles, all resources, and all privileges, an "unclean" IP would result in a denial of access. This is a special case, however, and it should be understood that in all other cases (i.e., where a specific role, resource, or privilege is specified for the rule), a failed assertion results in the rule not applying, and other rules would be used to determine whether access is allowed or denied.

The assert() method of an assertion object is passed the ACL, role, resource, and privilege to which the authorization query (i.e., isAllowed()) applies, in order to provide a context for the assertion class to determine its conditions where needed.

Chapter 3. Zend_Amf

Introduction

Zend_Amf provides support for Adobe's Action Message Format [http://en.wikipedia.org/wiki/Action _Message_Format] (AMF), to allow communication between Adobe's Flash Player [http://en.wikipedia .org/wiki/Adobe_Flash_Player] and PHP. Specifically, it provides a gateway server implementation for handling requests sent from the Flash Player to the server and mapping these requests to object and class methods and arbitrary callbacks.

The AMF3 specification [http://download.macromedia.com/pub/labs/amf/amf3_spec_121207.pdf] is freely available, and serves as a reference for what types of messages may be sent between the Flash Player and server.

Zend_Amf_Server

Zend_Amf_Server provides an RPC-style server for handling requests made from the Adobe Flash Player using the AMF protocol. Like all Zend Framework server classes, it follows the SoapServer API, providing an easy to remember interface for creating servers.

Example 3.1. Basic AMF Server

Let's assume that you have created a class Foo with a variety of public methods. You may create an AMF server using the following code:

```
$server = new Zend_Amf_Server();
$server->setClass('Foo');
$response = $server->handle();
echo $response;
```

Alternately, you may choose to attach a simple function as a callback instead:

```
$server = new Zend_Amf_Server();
$server->addFunction('myUberCoolFunction');
$response = $server->handle();
echo $response;
```

You could also mix and match multiple classes and functions. When doing so, we suggest namespacing each to ensure that no method name collisions occur; this can be done by simply passing a second string argument to either addFunction() or setClass():

```
$server = new Zend_Amf_Server();
$server->addFunction('myUberCoolFunction', 'my')
       ->setClass('Foo', 'foo')
       ->setClass('Bar', 'bar');
$response = $server->handle();
echo $response;
```

The Zend Amf Server also allows services to be dynamically loaded based on a supplied directory path. You may add as many directories as you wish to the server. The order that you add the directories to the server will be the order that the LIFO search will be performed on the directories to match the class. Adding directories is completed with the addDirectory() method.

```
$server->addDirectory(dirname(__FILE__) .'/../services/');
$server->addDirectory(dirname(__FILE__) .'/../package/');
```

When calling remote services your source name can have underscore(_) and dot(.) directory delimiters. When an underscore is used PEAR and Zend Framework class naming conventions will be respected. This means that if you call the service com_Foo_Bar the server will look for the file Bar.php in the each of the included paths at com/Foo/Bar.php. If the dot notation is used for your remote service such as com.Foo.Bar each included path will have com/Foo/Bar.php append to the end to autoload Bar.php

All AMF requests sent to the script will then be handled by the server, and an AMF response will be returned.

All Attached Methods and Functions Need Docblocks

Like all other server components in Zend Framework, you must document your class methods using PHP docblocks. At the minimum, you need to provide annotations for each required argument as well as the return value. As examples:

```
// Function to attach:

/**
 * @param   string $name
 * @param   string $greeting
 * @return string
 */
function helloWorld($name, $greeting = 'Hello')
{
    return $greeting . ', ' . $name;
}


// Attached class

class World
{
    /**
     * @param   string $name
     * @param   string $greeting
     * @return string
     */
    public function hello($name, $greeting = 'Hello')
    {
        return $greeting . ', ' . $name;
    }
}
```

Other annotations may be used, but will be ignored.

Connecting to the Server from Flex

Connecting to your Zend_Amf_Server from your Flex project is quite simple; you simply need to point your endpoint URI to your Zend_Amf_Server script.

Say, for instance, you have created your server and placed it in the server.php file in your application root, and thus the URI is http://example.com/server.php. In this case, you would modify your services-config.xml file to set the channel endpoint uri attribute to this value.

If you have never created a service-config.xml file you can do so by opening your project in your Navigator window. Right click on the project name and select 'properties'. In the Project properties dialog go into 'Flex Build Path' menu, 'Library path' tab and be sure the 'rpc.swc' file is added to your projects path and Press Ok to close the window.

You will also need to tell the compiler to use the service-config.xml to find the RemoteObject endpoint. To do this open your project properties panel again by right clicking on the project folder from your Navigator and selecting properties. From the properties popup select 'Flex Compiler' and add the string: -services "services-config.xml". Press Apply then OK to return to update the option. What you have just done is told the Flex compiler to look to the services-config.xml file for runtime variables that will be used by the RemotingObject class.

We now need to tell Flex which services configuration file to use for connecting to our remote methods. For this reason create a new 'services-config.xml' file into your Flex project src folder. To do this right click on the project folder and select 'new' 'File' which will popup a new window. Select the project folder and then name the file 'services-config.xml' and press finish.

Flex has created the new services-config.xml and has it open. Use the following example text for your services-config.xml file. Make sure that you update your endpoint to match that of your testing server. Make sure you save the file.

```
<services-config>
    <services>
        <service id="zend-service"
            class="flex.messaging.services.RemotingService"
            messageTypes="flex.messaging.messages.RemotingMessage">
            <destination id="zend">
                <channels>
                    <channel ref="zend-endpoint"/>
                </channels>
                <properties>
                    <source>*</source>
                </properties>
            </destination>
        </service>
    </services>
    <channels>
        <channel-definition id="zend-endpoint"
            class="mx.messaging.channels.AMFChannel">
            <endpoint uri="http://example.com/server.php"
                class="flex.messaging.endpoints.AMFEndpoint"/>
        </channel-definition>
    </channels>
</services-config>
```

There are two key points in the example. First, but last in the listing, we create an AMF channel, and specify the endpoint as the URL to our Zend_Amf_Server:

```
<channel-definition id="zend-endpoint"
    <endpoint uri="http://example.com/server.php"
        class="flex.messaging.endpoints.AMFEndpoint"/>
</channel-definition>
```

Notice that we've given this channel an identifier, "zend-endpoint". The example create a service destination that refers to this channel, assigning it an ID as well -- in this case "zend".

Within our Flex MXML files, we need to bind a RemoteObject to the service. In MXML, this might be done as follows:

```
<mx:RemoteObject id="myservice"
    fault="faultHandler(event)"
    showBusyCursor="true"
    destination="zend">
```

Here, we've defined a new remote object identified by "myservice" bound to the service destination "zend" we defined in the `services-config.xml` file. We then call methods on it in in our ActionScript by simply calling "myservice.<method>". As an example:

```
myservice.hello("Wade");
```

When namespacing, you would use "myservice.<namespace>.<method>":

```
myservice.world.hello("Wade");
```

For more information on Flex RemoteObject invocation, visit the Adobe Flex 3 Help site [http://livedocs.adobe.com/flex/3/html/help.html?content=data_access_4.html].

Error Handling

By default, all exceptions thrown in your attached classes or functions will be caught and returned as AMF ErrorMessages. However, the content of these ErrorMessage objects will vary based on whether or not the server is in "production" mode (the default state).

When in production mode, only the exception code will be returned. If you disable production mode -- something that should be done for testing only -- most exception details will be returned: the exception message, line, and backtrace will all be attached.

To disable production mode, do the following:

```
$server->setProduction(false);
```

To re-enable it, pass a true boolean value instead:

```
$server->setProduction(true);
```

Disable production mode sparingly!

We recommend disabling production mode only when in development. Exception messages and backtraces can contain sensitive system information that you may not wish for outside parties to access. Even though AMF is a binary format, the specification is now open, meaning anybody can potentially deserialize the payload.

One area to be especially careful with is PHP errors themselves. When the `display_errors` INI directive is enabled, any PHP errors for the current error reporting level are rendered directly in the output -- potentially disrupting the AMF response payload. We suggest turning off the `display_errors` directive in production to prevent such problems

AMF Responses

Occasionally you may desire to manipulate the response object slightly, typically to return extra message headers. The `handle()` method of the server returns the response object, allowing you to do so.

Example 3.2. Adding Message Headers to the AMF Response

In this example, we add a 'foo' MessageHeader with the value 'bar' to the response prior to returning it.

```
$response = $server->handle();
$response->addAmfHeader(new Zend_Amf_Value_MessageHeader('foo', true,
    'bar'))
echo $response;
```

Typed Objects

Similar to SOAP, AMF allows passing objects between the client and server. This allows a great amount of flexibility and coherence between the two environments.

Zend_Amf provides three methods for mapping ActionScript and PHP objects.

- First, you may create explicit bindings at the server level, using the `setClassMap()` method. The first argument is the ActionScript class name, the second the PHP class name it maps to:

```
// Map the ActionScript class 'ContactVO' to the PHP class 'Contact':
$server->setClassMap('ContactVO', 'Contact');
```

- Second, you can set the public property `$_explicitType` in your PHP class, with the value representing the ActionScript class to map to:

```
class Contact
{
    public $_explicitType = 'ContactVO';
}
```

- Third, in a similar vein, you may define the public method `getASClassName()` in your PHP class; this method should return the appropriate ActionScript class:

```
class Contact
{
    public function getASClassName()
    {
        return 'ContactVO';
    }
}
```

Although we have created the ContactVO on the server we now need to make its corresponding class in AS3 for the server object to be mapped to.

Right click on the src folder of the Flex project and select New -> ActionScript File. Name the file ContactVO and press finish to see the new file. Copy the following code into the file to finish creating the class.

```
package
{
    [Bindable]
    [RemoteClass(alias="ContactVO")]
    public class ContactVO
    {
        public var id:int;
        public var firstname:String;
        public var lastname:String;
        public var email:String;
        public var mobile:String;
        public function ProductVO():void {
        }
    }
}
```

The class is syntactically equivalent to the PHP of the same name. The variable names are exactly the same and need to be in the same case to work properly. There are two unique AS3 meta tags in this class. The first is bindable which makes fire a change event when it is updated. The second tag is the RemoteClass tag which defines that this class can have a a remote object mapped with the alias name in this case ContactVO It is mandatory that this tag the value that was set is the PHP class are strictly equivalent.

```
[Bindable]
private var myContact:ContactVO;

private function getContactHandler(event:ResultEvent):void {
    myContact = ContactVO(event.result);
}
```

The following result event from the service call is cast instantly onto the Flex ContactVO. Anything that is bound to myContact will be updated with the returned ContactVO data.

Connecting to the Server from Flash

Connecting to your Zend_Amf_Server from your Flash project is slightly different than from Flex. However once the connection Flash functions with Zend_Amf_Server the same way is flex. The following example can also be used from a Flex AS3 file. We will reuse the same Zend_Amf_Server configuration along with the World class for our connection.

Open Flash CS and create and new Flash File (ActionScript 3). Name the document ZendExample.fla and save the document into a folder that you will use for this example. Create a new AS3 file in the same directory and call the file Main.as. Have both files open in your editor. We are now going to connect the two files via the document class. Select ZendExample and click on the stage. From the stage properties panel change the Document class to Main. This links the Main.as ActionScript file with the user interface in ZendExample.fla. When you run the Flash file ZendExample the Main.as class will now be run. Next we will add ActionScript to make the AMF call.

We now are going to make a Main class so that we can send the data to the server and display the result. Copy the following code into your Main.as file and then we will walk through the code to describe what each element's role is.

```
package {
  import flash.display.MovieClip;
  import flash.events.*;
  import flash.net.NetConnection;
  import flash.net.Responder;

  public class Main extends MovieClip {
    private var gateway:String = "http://example.com/server.php";
    private var connection:NetConnection;
    private var responder:Responder;

    public function Main() {
      responder = new Responder(onResult, onFault);
      connection = new NetConnection;
      connection.connect(gateway);
    }

    public function onComplete( e:Event ):void{
      var params = "Sent to Server";
      connection.call("World.hello", responder, params);
    }

    private function onResult(result:Object):void {
      // Display the returned data
      trace(String(result));
    }
    private function onFault(fault:Object):void {
      trace(String(fault.description));
    }
  }
}
```

We first need to import two ActionScript libraries that perform the bulk of the work. The first is NetConnection which acts like a by directional pipe between the client and the server. The second is a Responder object which handles the return values from the server related to the success or failure of the call.

```
import flash.net.NetConnection;
import flash.net.Responder;
```

In the class we need three variables to represent the NetConnection, Responder, and the gateway URL to our Zend_Amf_Server installation.

```
private var gateway:String = "http://example.com/server.php";
private var connection:NetConnection;
private var responder:Responder;
```

In the Main constructor we create a responder and a new connection to the `Zend_Amf_Server` endpoint. The responder defines two different methods for handling the response from the server. For simplicity I have called these onResult and onFault.

```
responder = new Responder(onResult, onFault);
connection = new NetConnection;
connection.connect(gateway);
```

In the onComplete function which is run as soon as the construct has completed we send the data to the server. We need to add one more line that makes a call to the `Zend_Amf_Server` World->hello function.

```
connection.call("World.hello", responder, params);
```

When we created the responder variable we defined an onResult and onFault function to handle the response from the server. We added this function for the successful result from the server. A successful event handler is run every time the connection is handled properly to the server.

```
private function onResult(result:Object):void {
    // Display the returned data
    trace(String(result));
}
```

The onFault function, is called if there was an invalid response from the server. This happens when there is an error on the server, the URL to the server is invalid, the remote service or method does not exist, and any other connection related issues.

```
private function onFault(fault:Object):void {
    trace(String(fault.description));
}
```

Adding in the ActionScript to make the remoting connection is now complete. Running the ZendExample file now makes a connection to Zend Amf. In review you have added the required variables to open a connection to the remote server, defined what methods should be used when your application receives a response from the server, and finally displayed the returned data to output via trace().

Chapter 4. Zend_Application

Introduction

Zend_Application provides a bootstrapping facility for applications which provides reusable resources, common- and module-based bootstrap classes and dependency checking. It also takes care of setting up the PHP environment and introduces autoloading by default.

Zend_Application Quick Start

There are two paths to getting started with Zend_Application, and they depend on how you start your project. In each case, you always start with creating a Bootstrap class, and a related configuration file.

If you plan on using Zend_Tool to create your project, continue reading below. If you will be adding Zend_Application to an existing project, you'll want to skip ahead.

Using Zend_Tool

The quickest way to start using Zend_Application is to use Zend_Tool to generate your project. This will also create your Bootstrap class and file.

To create a project, execute the zf command (on *nix systems):

```
% zf create project newproject
```

Or the Windows zf.bat command:

```
C:> zf.bat create project newproject
```

Both will create a project structure that looks like the following:

```
newproject
|-- application
|   |-- Bootstrap.php
|   |-- configs
|   |   `-- application.ini
|   |-- controllers
|   |   |-- ErrorController.php
|   |   `-- IndexController.php
|   |-- models
|   `-- views
|       |-- helpers
|       `-- scripts
|           |-- error
|           |   `-- error.phtml
|           `-- index
|               `-- index.phtml
|-- library
|-- public
|   `-- index.php
`-- tests
    |-- application
    |   `-- bootstrap.php
    |-- library
    |   `-- bootstrap.php
    `-- phpunit.xml
```

In the above diagram, your bootstrap is in `newproject/application/Bootstrap.php`, and looks like the following at first:

```
class Bootstrap extends Zend_Application_Bootstrap_Bootstrap
{

}
```

You'll also note that a configuration file, `newproject/application/configs/application.ini`, is created. It has the following contents:

```
[production]
phpSettings.display_startup_errors = 0
phpSettings.display_errors = 0
includePaths.library = APPLICATION_PATH "/../library"
bootstrap.path = APPLICATION_PATH "/Bootstrap.php"
bootstrap.class = "Bootstrap"
resources.frontController.controllerDirectory = APPLICATION_PATH
    "/controllers"

[staging : production]

[testing : production]
phpSettings.display_startup_errors = 1
phpSettings.display_errors = 1

[development : production]
phpSettings.display_startup_errors = 1
phpSettings.display_errors = 1
```

All settings in this configuration file are for use with `Zend_Application` and your bootstrap.

Another file of interest is the `newproject/public/index.php` file, which invokes `Zend_Application` and dispatches it.

```
// Define path to application directory
defined('APPLICATION_PATH')
    || define('APPLICATION_PATH',
            realpath(dirname(__FILE__) . '/../application'));

// Define application environment
defined('APPLICATION_ENV')
    || define('APPLICATION_ENV',
            (getenv('APPLICATION_ENV') ? getenv('APPLICATION_ENV')
                                       : 'production'));

/** Zend_Application */
require_once 'Zend/Application.php';

// Create application, bootstrap, and run
$application = new Zend_Application(
    APPLICATION_ENV,
    APPLICATION_PATH . '/configs/application.ini'
);
$application->bootstrap()
            ->run();
```

To continue the quick start, please skip to the Resources section.

Adding Zend_Application to your application

The basics of Zend_Application are fairly simple:

- Create an application/Bootstrap.php file, with the class Bootstrap.

- Create an application/configs/application.ini configuration file with the base configuration necessary for Zend_Application.

- Modify your public/index.php to utilize Zend_Application.

First, create your Bootstrap class. Create a file, application/Bootstrap.php, with the following contents:

```
class Bootstrap extends Zend_Application_Bootstrap_Bootstrap
{

}
```

Now, create your configuration. For this tutorial, we will use an INI style configuration; you may, of course, use an XML or PHP configuration file as well. Create the file application/configs/application.ini, and provide the following contents:

```
[production]
phpSettings.display_startup_errors = 0
phpSettings.display_errors = 0
includePaths.library = APPLICATION_PATH "/../library"
bootstrap.path = APPLICATION_PATH "/Bootstrap.php"
bootstrap.class = "Bootstrap"
resources.frontController.controllerDirectory = APPLICATION_PATH
    "/controllers"

[staging : production]

[testing : production]
phpSettings.display_startup_errors = 1
phpSettings.display_errors = 1

[development : production]
phpSettings.display_startup_errors = 1
phpSettings.display_errors = 1
```

Now, let's modify your gateway script, public/index.php. If the file does not exist, create it; otherwise, replace it with the following contents:

```
// Define path to application directory
defined('APPLICATION_PATH')
    || define('APPLICATION_PATH',
            realpath(dirname(__FILE__) . '/../application'));

// Define application environment
defined('APPLICATION_ENV')
    || define('APPLICATION_ENV',
            (getenv('APPLICATION_ENV') ? getenv('APPLICATION_ENV')
                                       : 'production'));
```

```
// Typically, you will also want to add your library/ directory
// to the include_path, particularly if it contains your ZF install
set_include_path(implode(PATH_SEPARATOR, array(
    dirname(dirname(__FILE__)) . '/library',
    get_include_path(),
)));

/** Zend_Application */
require_once 'Zend/Application.php';

// Create application, bootstrap, and run
$application = new Zend_Application(
    APPLICATION_ENV,
    APPLICATION_PATH . '/configs/application.ini'
);
$application->bootstrap()
            ->run();
```

You may note that the application environment constant value looks for an environment variable "APPLICATION_ENV". We recommend setting this in your web server environment. In Apache, you can set this either in your vhost definition, or in your .htaccess file. We recommend the following contents for your public/.htacces file:

```
SetEnv APPLICATION_ENV development

RewriteEngine On
RewriteCond %{REQUEST_FILENAME} -s [OR]
RewriteCond %{REQUEST_FILENAME} -l [OR]
RewriteCond %{REQUEST_FILENAME} -d
RewriteRule ^.*$ - [NC,L]
RewriteRule ^.*$ index.php [NC,L]
```

Learn about mod_rewrite

The above rewrite rules allow access to any file under your virtual host's document root. If there are files you do not want exposed in this way, you may want to be more restrictive in your rules. Go to the Apache website to learn more about mod_rewrite [http://httpd.apache.org /docs/ 2.0/mod/mod_rewrite.html].

At this point, you're all set to start taking advantage of Zend_Application.

Adding and creating resources

If you followed the directions above, then your bootstrap class will be utilizing a front controller, and when it is run, it will dispatch the front controller. However, in all liklihood, you'll need a little more configuration than this.

In this section, we'll look at adding two resources to your application. First, we'll setup your layouts, and then we'll customize your view object.

One of the standard resources provided with Zend_Application is the "layout" resource. This resource expects you to define configuration values which it will then use to configure your Zend_Layout instance.

To use it, all we need to do is update the configuration file.

```
[production]
phpSettings.display_startup_errors = 0
phpSettings.display_errors = 0
bootstrap.path = APPLICATION_PATH "/Bootstrap.php"
bootstrap.class = "Bootstrap"
resources.frontController.controllerDirectory = APPLICATION_PATH
    "/controllers"
; ADD THE FOLLOWING LINES
resources.layout.layout = "layout"
resources.layout.layoutPath = APPLICATION_PATH "/layouts/scripts"

[staging : production]

[testing : production]
phpSettings.display_startup_errors = 1
phpSettings.display_errors = 1

[development : production]
phpSettings.display_startup_errors = 1
phpSettings.display_errors = 1
```

If you haven't already, create the directory application/layouts/scripts/, and the file layout.phtml within that directory. A good starting layout is as follows (and ties in with the view resource covered next):

```
<?php echo $this->doctype() ?>
<html>
<head>
    <?php echo $this->headTitle() ?>
    <?php echo $this->headLink() ?>
    <?php echo $this->headStyle() ?>
    <?php echo $this->headScript() ?>
</head>
<body>
    <?php echo $this->layout()->content ?>
</body>
</html>
```

At this point, you will now have a working layout.

Now, we'll add a custom view resource. When initializing the view, we'll want to set the HTML DocType and a default value for the title to use in the HTML head. This can be accomplished by editing your Bootstrap class to add a method:

```
class Bootstrap extends Zend_Application_Bootstrap_Bootstrap
{
    protected function _initView()
    {
        // Initialize view
        $view = new Zend_View();
        $view->doctype('XHTML1_STRICT');
        $view->headTitle('My First Zend Framework Application');

        // Add it to the ViewRenderer
        $viewRenderer = Zend_Controller_Action_HelperBroker::getStaticHelper(
            'ViewRenderer'
        );
        $viewRenderer->setView($view);

        // Return it, so that it can be stored by the bootstrap
        return $view;
    }
}
```

This method will be automatically executed when you bootstrap the application, and will ensure your view is intialized according to your application needs.

Next steps with Zend_Application

The above should get you started with `Zend_Application` and creating your application bootstrap. From here, you should start creating resource methods, or, for maximum re-usability, resource plugin classes. Continue reading to learn more!

Theory of Operation

Getting an MVC application configured and ready to dispatch has required an increasing amount of code as more features become available: setting up the database, configuring your view and view helpers, configuring your layouts, registering plugins, registering action helpers, and more.

Additionally, you will often want to reuse the same code to bootstrap your tests, a cronjob, or a service script. While it's possible to simply include your bootstrap script, oftentimes there are initializations that are environment specific – you may not need the MVC for a cronjob, or just the DB layer for a service script.

`Zend_Application` aims to make this easier and to promote reuse by encapsulating bootstrapping into OOP paradigms.

`Zend_Application` is broken into three realms:

- `Zend_Application`: loads the PHP environment, including include_paths and autoloading, and instantiates the requested bootstrap class.

- `Zend_Application_Bootstrap`: provides interfaces for bootstrap classes. `Zend_Application_Bootstrap_Bootstrap` provides common functionality for most bootstrapping needs, including dependency checking algorithms and the ability to load bootstrap resources on demand.

- `Zend_Application_Resource` provides an interface for standard bootstrapping resources that can be loaded on demand by a bootstrap instance, as well as several default resource implementations.

Developers create a bootstrap class for their application, extending `Zend_Application _Bootstrap_Bootstrap` or implementing (minimally) `Zend_Application_Bootstrap _Bootstrapper`. The entry point (e.g., `public/index.php`) will load `Zend_Application`, and instantiate it by passing:

- The current environment

- Options for bootstrapping

The bootstrap options include the path to the file containing the bootstrap class and optionally:

- Any extra include_paths to set

- Any additional autoloader namespaces to register

- Any php.ini settings to initialize

- The class name for the bootstrap class (if not "Bootstrap")

- Resource prefix/path pairs to use

- Any resources to use (by class name or short name)

- Additional path to a configuration file to load

- Additional configuration options

Options may be an array, a `Zend_Config` object, or the path to a configuration file.

Bootstrapping

`Zend_Application`'s second area of responsibility is executing the application bootstrap. Bootstraps minimally need to implement `Zend_Application_Bootstrap_Bootstrapper`, which defines the following API:

```
interface Zend_Application_Bootstrap_Bootstrapper
{
    public function __construct($application);
    public function setOptions(array $options);
    public function getApplication();
    public function getEnvironment();
    public function getClassResources();
    public function getClassResourceNames();
    public function bootstrap($resource = null);
    public function run();
}
```

This API allows the bootstrap to accept the environment and configuration from the application object, report the resources its responsible for bootstrapping, and then bootstrap and run the application.

You can implement this interface on your own, extend `Zend_Application_Bootstrap_BootstrapAbstract`, or use `Zend_Application_Bootstrap_Bootstrap`.

Besides this functionality, there are a number of other areas of concern you should familiarize yourself with.

Resource Methods

The `Zend_Application_Bootstrap_BootstrapAbstract` implementation provides a simple convention for defining class resource methods. Any protected method beginning with a name prefixed with _init will be considered a resource method.

To bootstrap a single resource method, use the `bootstrap()` method, and pass it the name of the resource. The name will be the method name minus the _init prefix.

To bootstrap several resource methods, pass an array of names. Too bootstrap all resource methods, pass nothing.

Take the following bootstrap class:

```
class Bootstrap extends Zend_Application_Bootstrap_Bootstrap
{
    protected function _initFoo()
    {
        // ...
    }
```

```
    protected function _initBar()
    {
        // ...
    }

    protected function _initBaz()
    {
        // ...
    }
}
```

To bootstrap just the _initFoo() method, do the following:

```
$bootstrap->bootstrap('foo');
```

To bootstrap the _initFoo() and _initBar() methods, do the following:

```
$bootstrap->bootstrap(array('foo', 'bar'));
```

To bootstrap all resource methods, call bootstrap() with no arguments:

```
$bootstrap->bootstrap();
```

Bootstraps that use resource plugins

To make your bootstraps more re-usable, we have provided the ability to push your resources into resource plugin classes. This allows you to mix and match resources simply via configuration. We will cover how to create resources later; in this section we will show you how to utilize them only.

If your bootstrap should be capable of using resource plugins, you will need to implement an additional interface, Zend_Application_Bootstrap_ResourceBootstrapper. This interface defines an API for locating, registering, and loading resource plugins:

```
interface Zend_Application_Bootstrap_ResourceBootstrapper
{
    public function registerPluginResource($resource, $options = null);
    public function unregisterPluginResource($resource);
    public function hasPluginResource($resource);
    public function getPluginResource($resource);
    public function getPluginResources();
    public function getPluginResourceNames();
    public function setPluginLoader(Zend_Loader_PluginLoader_Interface
        $loader);
    public function getPluginLoader();
}
```

Resource plugins basically provide the ability to create resource intializers that can be re-used between applications. This allows you to keep your actual bootstrap relatively clean, and to introduce new resources without needing to touch your bootstrap itself.

Zend_Application_Bootstrap_BootstrapAbstract (and Zend_Application_Bootstrap_Bootstrap by extension) implement this interface as well, allowing you to utilize resource plugins.

To utilize resource plugins, you must specify them in the options passed to the application object and/or bootstrap. These options may come from a configuration file, or be passed in manually. Options will be of key/options pairs, with the key representing the resource name. The resource name will be the segment following the class prefix. For example, the resources shipped with Zend Framework have the class prefix "Zend_Application_Resource_"; anything following this would be the name of the resource. As an example,

```
$application = new Zend_Application(APPLICATION_ENV, array(
    'resources' => array(
        'FrontController' => array(
            'controllerDirectory' => APPLICATION_PATH . '/controllers',
        ),
    ),
));
```

This indicates that the "FrontController" resource should be used, with the options specified.

If you begin writing your own resource plugins, or utilize third-party resource plugins, you will need to tell your bootstrap where to look for them. Internally, the bootstrap utilizes Zend_Loader _PluginLoader, so you will only need to indicate the common class prefix an path pairs.

As an example, let's assume you have custom resource plugins in APPLICATION_PATH/ resources/ and that they share the common class prefix of My_Resource. You would then pass that information to the application object as follows:

```
$application = new Zend_Application(APPLICATION_ENV, array(
    'pluginPaths' => array(
        'My_Resource' => APPLICATION_PATH . '/resources/',
    ),
    'resources' => array(
        'FrontController' => array(
            'controllerDirectory' => APPLICATION_PATH . '/controllers',
        ),
    ),
));
```

You would now be able to use resources from that directory.

Just like resource methods, you use the bootstrap() method to execute resource plugins. Just like with resource methods, you can specify either a single resource plugin, multiple plugins (via an array), or all plugins. Additionally, you can mix and match to execute resource methods as well.

```
// Execute one:
$bootstrap->bootstrap('FrontController');

// Execute several:
$bootstrap->bootstrap(array('FrontController', 'Foo'));

// Execute all resource methods and plugins:
$bootstrap->bootstrap();
```

Resource Registry

Many, if not all, of your resource methods or plugins will initialize objects, and in many cases, these objects will be needed elsewhere in your application. How can you access them?

Zend_Application_Bootstrap_BootstrapAbstract provides a local registry for these objects. To store your objects in them, you simply return them from your resources.

For maximum flexibility, this registry is referred to as a "container" internally; its only requirements are that it is an object. Resources are then registered as properties named after the resource name. By default, an instance of Zend_Registry is used, but you may also specify any other object you wish. The methods setContainer() and getContainer() may be used to manipulate the container itself. getResource($resource) can be used to fetch a given resource from the container, and hasResource($resource) to check if the resource has actually been registered.

As an example, consider a basic view resource:

```
class Bootstrap extends Zend_Application_Bootstrap_Bootstrap
{
    protected function _initView()
    {
        $view = new Zend_View();
        // more initialization...

        return $view;
    }
}
```

You can then check for it and/or fetch it as follows:

```
// Using the has/getResource() pair:
if ($bootstrap->hasResource('view')) {
    $view = $bootstrap->getResource('view');
}

// Via the container:
$container = $bootstrap->getContainer();
if (isset($container->view)) {
    $view = $container->view;
}
```

Please note that the registry/container is not global. This means that you need access to the bootstrap in order to fetch resources. Zend_Application_Bootstrap_Bootstrap provides some convenience for this: during its run() execution, it registers itself as the front controller parameter "bootstrap", which allows you to fetch it from the router, dispatcher, plugins, and action controllers.

As an example, if you wanted access to the view resource from above within your action controller, you could do the following:

```
class FooController extends Zend_Controller_Action
{
    public function init()
    {
        $bootstrap = $this->getInvokeArg('bootstrap');
        $view = $bootstrap->getResource('view');
        // ...
    }
}
```

Dependency Tracking

In addition to executing resource methods and plugins, it's necessary to ensure that these are executed once and once only; these are meant to bootstrap an application, and executing multiple times can lead to resource overhead.

At the same time, some resources may depend on other resources being executed. To solve these two issues, Zend_Application_Bootstrap_BootstrapAbstract provides a simple, effective mechanism for dependency tracking.

As noted previously, all resources -- whether methods or plugins -- are bootstrapped by calling bootstrap($resource), where $resource is the name of a resource, an array of resources, or, left empty, indicates all resources should be run.

If a resource depends on another resource, it should call bootstrap() within its code to ensure that resource has been executed. Subsequent calls to it will then be ignored.

In a resource method, such a call would look like this:

```
class Bootstrap extends Zend_Application_Bootstrap_Bootstrap
{
    protected function _initRequest()
    {
        // Ensure the front controller is initialized
        $this->bootstrap('FrontController');

        // Retrieve the front controller from the bootstrap registry
        $front = $this->getResource('FrontController');

        $request = new Zend_Controller_Request_Http();
        $request->setBaseUrl('/foo');
        $front->setRequest($request);

        // Ensure the request is stored in the bootstrap registry
        return $request;
    }
}
```

Resource Plugins

As noted previously, a good way to create re-usable bootstrap resources and to offload much of your coding to discrete classes is to utilize resource plugins. While Zend Framework ships with a number of standard resource plugins, the intention is that developers should write their own to encapsulate their own initialization needs.

Resources need only implement Zend_Application_Resource_Resource, or, more simply still, extend Zend_Application_Resource_ResourceAbstract. The basic interface is simply this:

```
interface Zend_Application_Resource_Resource
{
    public function __construct($options = null);
    public function setBootstrap(
        Zend_Application_Bootstrap_Bootstrapper $bootstrap
    );
    public function getBootstrap();
    public function setOptions(array $options);
    public function getOptions();
    public function init();
}
```

The interface defines simply that a resource should accept options to the constructor, have mechanisms for setting and retrieving options, have mechanisms for setting and retrieving the bootstrap object, and an initialization method.

As an example, let's assume you have a common view intialization you use in your applications. You have a common doctype, CSS and JavaScript, and you want to be able to pass in a base document title via configuration. Such a resource might look like this:

```
class My_Resource_View extends Zend_Application_Resource_ResourceAbstract
{
    protected $_view;

    public function init()
    {
        // Return view so bootstrap will store it in the registry
        return $this->getView();
    }

    public function getView()
    {
        if (null === $this->_view) {
            $options = $this->getOptions();
            $title   = '';
            if (array_key_exists('title', $options)) {
                $title = $options['title'];
                unset($options['title']);
            }

            $view = new Zend_View($options);
            $view->doctype('XHTML1_STRICT');
            $view->headTitle($title);
            $view->headLink()->appendStylesheet('/css/site.css');
            $view->headScript()->appendfile('/js/analytics.js');

            $viewRenderer =
                Zend_Controller_Action_HelperBroker::getStaticHelper(
                    'ViewRenderer',
                );
            $viewRenderer->setView($view);

            $this->_view = $view;
        }
        return $this->_view;
    }
}
```

As long as you register the prefix path for this resource plugin, you can then use it in your application. Even better, because it uses the plugin loader, you are effectively overriding the shipped "View" resource plugin, ensuring that your own is used instead.

Examples

The Bootstrap class itself will typically be fairly minimal; often, it will simply be an empty stub extending the base bootstrap class:

```
class Bootstrap extends Zend_Application_Bootstrap_Bootstrap
{

}
```

With a corresponding configuration file:

```
; APPLICATION_PATH/configs/application.ini
[production]
bootstrap.path = APPLICATION_PATH "/Bootstrap.php"
bootstrap.class = "Bootstrap"
resources.frontController.controllerDirectory = APPLICATION_PATH
    "/controllers"

[development : testing]
[development : production]
```

However, should custom initialization be necessary, you have two choices. First, you can write methods prefixed with _init to specify discrete code to bootstrap. These methods will be called by bootstrap(), and can also be called as if they were public methods: bootstrap<resource>(). They should accept an optional array of options.

If your resource method returns a value, it will be stored in a container in the bootstrap. This can be useful when different resources need to interact (such as one resource injecting itself into another). The method getResource() can then be used to retrieve those values.

The example below shows a resource method for initializing the request object. It makes use of dependency tracking (it depends on the front controller resource), fetching a resource from the bootstrap, and returning a value to store in the bootstrap.

```
class Bootstrap extends Zend_Application_Bootstrap_Bootstrap
{
    protected function _initRequest(array $options = array())
    {
        // Ensure front controller instance is present, and fetch it
        $this->bootstrap('FrontController');
        $front = $this->getResource('FrontController');

        // Initialize the request object
        $request = new Zend_Controller_Request_Http();
        $request->setBaseUrl('/foo');

        // Add it to the front controller
        $front->setRequest($request);

        // Bootstrap will store this value in the 'request' key of its
            container
        return $request;
    }
}
```

Note in this example the call to bootstrap(); this ensures that the front controller has been initialized prior to calling this method. That call may trigger either a resource or another method in the class.

The other option is to use resource plugins. Resource plugins are objects that perform specific initializations, and may be specified:

• When instantiating the Zend_Application object

• During initialization of the bootstrap object

- By explicitly enabling them via method calls to the bootstrap object

Resource plugins implement Zend_Application_Bootstrap_Resource, which defines simply that they allow injection of the caller and options, and that they have an init() method. As an example, a custom "View" bootstrap resource might look like the following:

```
class My_Bootstrap_Resource_View
    extends Zend_Application_Resource_ResourceAbstract
{
    public function init()
    {
        $view = new Zend_View($this->getOptions());
        Zend_Dojo::enableView($view);

        $view->doctype('XHTML1_STRICT');
        $view->headTitle()->setSeparator(' - ')->append('My Site');
        $view->headMeta()->appendHttpEquiv('Content-Type',
                                          'text/html; charset=utf-8');

        $view->dojo()->setDjConfigOption('parseOnLoad', true)
                     ->setLocalPath('/js/dojo/dojo.js')
                     ->registerModulePath('../spindle', 'spindle')
                     ->addStylesheetModule('spindle.themes.spindle')
                     ->requireModule('spindle.main')
                     ->disable();

        $viewRenderer = Zend_Controller_Action_HelperBroker::getStaticHelper(
            'ViewRenderer'
        );
        $viewRenderer->setView($view);

        return $view;
    }
}
```

To tell the bootstrap to use this, you would need to provide either the class name of the resource, or a combination of a plugin loader prefix path and the short name of the resource (e.g, "view"):

```
$application = new Zend_Application(
    APPLICATION_ENV,
    array(
        'resources' => array(
            'My_Bootstrap_Resource_View' => array(), // full class name; OR
            'view' => array(),                        // short name

            'FrontController' => array(
                'controllerDirectory' => APPLICATION_PATH . '/controllers',
            ),
        ),

        // For short names, define plugin paths:
        'pluginPaths = array(
            'My_Bootstrap_Resource' => 'My/Bootstrap/Resource',
        )
    )
);
```

Resources can call on other resources and initializers by accessing the parent bootstrap:

```
class My_Bootstrap_Resource_Layout
    extends Zend_Application_Resource_ResourceAbstract
{
    public function init()
    {
        // ensure view is initialized...
        $this->getBootstrap()->bootstrap('view');

        // Get view object:
        $view = $this->getBootstrap()->getResource('view');

        // ...
    }
}
```

In normal usage, you would instantiate the application, bootstrap it, and run it:

```
$application = new Zend_Application(...);
$application->bootstrap()
            ->run();
```

For a custom script, you might need to simply initialize specific resources:

```
$application = new Zend_Application(...);
$application->getBootstrap()->bootstrap('db');

$service = new Zend_XmlRpc_Server();
$service->setClass('Foo');   // uses database...
echo $service->handle();
```

Instead of using the bootstrap() method to call the internal methods or resources, you may also use overloading:

```
$application = new Zend_Application(...);
$application->getBootstrap()->bootstrapDb();
```

Core Functionality

Here you'll find API-like documentation about all core components of Zend_Application.

Zend_Application

Zend_Application provides the base functionality of the component, and the entry point to your Zend Framework application. It's purpose is two-fold: to setup the PHP environment (including autoloading), and to execute your application bootstrap.

Typically, you will pass all configuration to the Zend_Application constructor, but you can also configure the object entirely using its own methods. This reference is intended to illustrate both use cases.

Table 4.1. Zend_Application options

Option	Description
phpSettings	Array of php.ini settings to use. Keys should be the php.ini keys.
includePaths	Additional paths to prepend to the include_path. Should be an array of paths.
autoloaderNamespaces	Array of additional namespaces to register with the Zend_Loader_Autoloader instance.
bootstrap	Either the string path to the bootstrap class, or an array with elements for the 'path' and 'class' for the application bootstrap.

Option names

Please note that option names are case insensitive.

Table 4.2. Zend_Application Methods

Method	Return Value	Parameters	Description

__construct ($environment, $options = null)	void	• $environment: required,. String representing the current application environment. Typical strings might include "development", "testing", "qa", or "production", but will be defined by your organizational requirements.
		
		• $options: optional. Argument may be one of the following values:
		
		  • String: path to a Zend_Config file to load as configuration for your application. $environment will be used to determine what section of the configuration to pull.
		
		  • Array: associative array of con-
			Constructor. Arguments are as described, and will be used to set initial object state. An instance of Zend_Loader_Autoloader is registered during instantiation. Options passed to the constructor are passed to setOptions().

Method	Return Value	Parameters	Description
		figuration data for your application. • *Zend_Config*: configuration object instance.	
`getEnvironment()`	`string`	N/A	Retrieve the environment string passed to the constructor.
`getAutoloader()`	`Zend_Loader_Auto loader`	N/A	Retrieve the `Zend_Loader _Autoloader` instance registered during instantiation.
`setOptions(array $options)`	`Zend_Application`	• `$options`: *required*. An array of application options.	All options are stored internally, and calling the method multiple times will merge options. Options matching the various setter methods will be passed to those methods. As an example, the option "phpSettings" will then be passed to `setPhpSettings()`. (Option names are case insensitive.)
`getOptions()`	`array`	N/A	Retrieve all options used to initialize the object; could be used to cache `Zend_Config` options to a serialized format between requests.
`hasOption($key)`	`boolean`	• `$key`: String option key to lookup	Determine whether or not an option with the specified key has been registered. Keys are case insensitive.
`getOption($key)`	`mixed`	• `$key`: String option key to lookup	Retrieve the option value of a given key. Returns null if the key does not exist.
`setPhpSettings (array $settings, $prefix = '')`	`Zend_Application`	• `$settings`: *required*. Associative array of PHP INI settings. • `$prefix`: *optional*. String prefix with which to prepend option keys. Used	Set run-time php.ini settings. Dot-separated settings may be nested hierarchically (which may occur with INI `Zend_Config` files) via an array-of-arrays, and will still resolve correctly.

Method	Return Value	Parameters	Description
		internally to allow mapping nested arrays to dot-separated php.ini keys. In normal usage, this argument should never be passed by a user.	
setAutoloaderName spaces(array $namespaces)	Zend_Application	• $namespaces: *required*. Array of strings representing the namespaces to register with the Zend_Loader_ Autoloader in-stance.	Register namespaces with the Zend_Loader _Autoloader instance.
setBootstrap ($path, $class = null)	Zend_Application	• $path: *required*. May be either a Zend_Applicati on_Bootstrap_B ootstrapper in-stance, a string path to the bootstrap class, an associative array of classname => filename, or an associative array with the keys 'class' and 'path'. • $class: *optional*. If $path is a string, $class may be specified, and should be a string class name of the class contained in the file represented by path.	
getBootstrap()	null | Zend_Application _Bootstrap_Boots trapper	N/A	Retrieve the registered bootstrap instance.
bootstrap()	void	N/A	Call the bootstrap's bootstrap() method to bootstrap the applica-tion.
run()	void	N/A	Call the bootstrap's run() method to dis-patch the application.

Zend_Application_Bootstrap_Bootstrapper

Zend_Application_Bootstrap_Bootstrapper is the base interface all bootstrap classes must implement. The base functionality is aimed at configuration, identifying resources, bootstrapping (either individual resources or the entire application), and dispatching the application.

The following methods make up the definition of the interface.

Table 4.3. Zend_Application_Bootstrap_Bootstrapper Interface

Method	Return Value	Parameters	Description
__construct($application)	void	• $application: *required*. Should accept a Zend_Application or a Zend_Application_Bootstrap_ Bootstrapper object as the sole argument.	Constructor. Accepts a single argument, which should be a Zend_Application object, or another bootstrap object.
setOptions(array $options)	Zend_Application_Bootstrap_Bootstrapper	• $options: *required*. Array of options to set.	Typically, any option that has a matching setter will invoke that setter; otherwise, the option will simply be stored for later retrieval.
getApplication()	Zend_Application | Zend_Application_Bootstrap_Bootstrapper	N/A	Retrieve the application/bootstrap object passed via the constructor.
getEnvironment()	string	N/A	Retrieve the environment string registered with the parent application/bootstrap object.
getClassResources()	array	N/A	Retrieve a list of available resource initializer names as defined in the class. This may be implementation specific.
bootstrap($resource = null)	mixed	• $resource: *optional*.	If $resource is empty, execute all bootstrap resources. If a string, execute that single resource; if an array, execute each resource in the array.
run()	void	N/A	Defines what application logic to run after bootstrapping.

Zend_Application_Bootstrap_ResourceBootstrapper

Zend_Application_Bootstrap_ResourceBootstrapper is an interface to use when a bootstrap class will be loading external resources -- i.e., one or more resources will not be defined directly in the class, but rather via plugins. It should be used in conjunction with Zend_Application_Bootstrap_Bootstrapper; Zend_Application_Bootstrap_BootstrapAbstract implements this functionality.

The following methods make up the definition of the interface.

Table 4.4. Zend_Application_Bootstrap_ResourceBootstrapper Interface

Method	Return Value	Parameters	Description
registerPlugin Resource ($resource, $options = null)	Zend_Application _Bootstrap_Resou rceBootstrapper	• $resource: *required*. A resource name or Zend_Applicati on_Resource_Re source object. • $options: *optional*. An array or Zend_Config object to pass to the resource on instantiation.	Register a resource with the class, providing optional configuration to pass to the resource.
unregisterPlugin Resource ($resource)	Zend_Application _Bootstrap_Resou rceBootstrapper	• $resource: *required*. Name of a resource to unregister from the class.	Remove a plugin resource from the class.
hasPluginResource ($resource)	boolean	• $resource: *required*. Name of the resource.	Determine if a specific resource has been registered with the class.
getPlugin Resource ($resource)	Zend_Application _Resource_Resour ce	• $resource: *required*. Name of a resource to retrieve (string).	Retrieve a plugin resource instance by name.
getPlugin ResourceNames()	array	N/A	Retrieve a list of all registered plugin resource names.
setPlugin Loader(Zend_ Loader_Plugin Loader_Interface $loader)	Zend_Application _Bootstrap_Resou rceBootstrapper	• $loader: *required*. Plugin loader instance to use when resolving plugin names to classes.	Register a plugin loader instance to use when resolving plugin class names.
getPluginLoader()	Zend_Loader_ PluginLoader_ Interface	N/A	Retrieve the registered plugin loader.

Zend_Application_Bootstrap_BootstrapAbstract

`Zend_Application_Bootstrap_BootstrapAbstract` is an abstract class which provides the base functionality of a common bootstrap. It implements both Zend_Application_Bootstrap_Bootstrapper and Zend_Application_Bootstrap_ResourceBootstrapper.

Table 4.5. Zend_Application_Bootstrap_BootstrapAbstract Methods

Method	Return Value	Parameters	Description
`__construct($app lication)`	`void`	• `$application:` *required.* Accepts either a `Zend_Applicati on` or a `Zend_Applicati on_Bootstrap_B ootstrapper` object as the sole argument.	Constructor. Accepts a single argument, which should be a `Zend_Application` object, or another bootstrap object.
`setOptions(array $options)`	`Zend_Application _Bootstrap_Boots trapper`	• `$options:` *required.* Array of options to set.	Any option that has a matching setter will invoke that setter; otherwise, the option will simply be stored for later retrieval. As an example, if your extending class defined a `setFoo()` method, the option 'foo' would pass the value to that method. Two additional, special options keys may also be used. `pluginPaths` may be used to specify prefix paths to plugin resources; it should be an array of class prefix/filesystem path pairs. `resources` may be used to specify plugin resources to use, and should consist of plugin resource/instantiation options pairs.
`getOption()`	`array`	N/A	Returns all options registered via `setOptions()`.
`hasOption($key)`	`boolean`	• `$key:` *required.* Option key to test.	Determine if an option key is present.
`getOption($key)`	`mixed`		Retrieve the value asso-

Method	Return Value	Parameters	Description
		• $key: *required*. Option key to retrieve.	ciated with an option key; returns null if no option is registered with that key.
setApplication (Zend_Application | Zend _Application _Bootstrap _Bootstrapper $application)	Zend_Application _Bootstrap_Boots trapAbstract	• $application: *required*.	Register the parent application/bootstrap object.
getApplication()	Zend_Application | Zend_Application _Bootstrap _Bootstrapper	N/A	Retrieve the application/ bootstrap object passed via the constructor.
getEnvironment()	string	N/A	Retrieve the environment string registered with the parent application/bootstrap object.
getClassResources()	array	N/A	Retrieve a list of available resource initializer names as defined in the class. This may be implementation specific.
getContainer()	object	N/A	Retrieves the container that stores resources. If no container is currently registered, it registers a Zend_Registry instance before returning it.
setContainer ($container)	Zend_Application _Bootstrap _BootstrapAbstract	• $container, *required*. An object in which to store resources.	Provide a container in which to store resources. When a resource method or plugin returns a value, it will be stored in this container for later retrieval.
hasResource ($name)	boolean	• $name, *required*. Name of a resource to check.	When a resource method or plugin returns a value, it will be stored in the resource container (see getContainer() and setContainer(). This method will indicate whether or not a value for that resource has been set.
getResource ($name)	mixed	• $name, *required*. Name of a resource to fetch.	When a resource method or plugin returns a value, it will be stored in the resource container (see getContainer() and setContainer().

Method	Return Value	Parameters	Description
			This method will retrieve a resources from the container.
bootstrap ($resource = null)	mixed	• $resource: *optional*.	If $resource is empty, execute all bootstrap resources. If a string, execute that single resource; if an array, execute each resource in the array.
			This method can be used to run individual bootstraps either defined in the class itself or via resource plugin classes. A resource defined in the class will be run in preference over a resource plugin in the case of naming conflicts.
run()	void	N/A	Defines what application logic to run after bootstrapping.
__call($method, $args)	mixed	• $method: *required*. The method name to call. • $args: *required*. Array of arguments to use in the method call.	Provides convenience to bootstrapping individual resources by allowing you to call 'bootstrap<ResourceName>()' instead of using the bootstrap() method.

Zend_Application_Bootstrap_Bootstrap

Zend_Application_Bootstrap_Bootstrap is a concrete implementation of Zend_Application_Bootstrap_BootstrapAbstract. It's primary feature are that it registers the Front Controller resource, and that the run() method first checks that a default module is defined and then dispatches the front controller.

In most cases, you will want to extend this class for your bootstrapping needs, or simply use this class and provide a list of resource plugins to utilize.

Zend_Application_Resource_Resource

Zend_Application_Resource_Resource is an interface for plugin resources used with bootstrap classes implementing Zend_Application_Bootstrap_ResourceBootstrapper. Resource plugins are expected to allow configuration, be bootstrap aware, and implement a strategy pattern for initializing the resource.

Table 4.6. Zend_Application_Resource_Resource Interface

Method	Return Value	Parameters	Description
`__construct ($options = null)`	`void`	• $options: *optional*. Options with which to set resource state.	The constructor should allow passing options with which to initialize state.
`setBootstrap (Zend_Application _Bootstrap _Bootstrapper $bootstrap)`	`Zend_Application _Resource_Resour ce`	• $bootstrap: *required*. Parent bootstrap initializing this resource.	Should allow registering the parent bootstrap object.
`getBootstrap()`	`Zend_Application _Bootstrap_Boots trapper`	N/A	Retrieve the registered bootstrap instance.
`setOptions(array $options)`	`Zend_Application _Resource_Resour ce`	• $options: *required*. Options with which to set state.	Set resource state.
`getOptions()`	`array`	N/A	Retrieve registered options.
`init()`	`mixed`	N/A	Strategy pattern: run initialization of the resource.

Zend_Application_Resource_ResourceAbstract

`Zend_Application_Resource_ResourceAbstract` is an abstract class implementing Zend_Application_Resource_Resource, and is a good starting point for creating your own custom plugin resources.

Note: this abstract class does not implement the `init()` method; this is left for definition in concrete extensions of the class.

Table 4.7. Zend_Application_Resource_ResourceAbstract Methods

Method	Return Value	Parameters	Description
`__construct ($options = null)`	`void`	• $options: *optional*. Options with which to set resource state.	The constructor should allow passing options with which to initialize state.
`setBootstrap (Zend_Application _Bootstrap _Bootstrapper $bootstrap)`	`Zend_Application _Resource_Resour ceAbstract`	• $bootstrap: *required*. Parent bootstrap initializing this resource.	Should allow registering the parent bootstrap object.
`getBootstrap()`	`Zend_Application _Bootstrap_Boots trapper`	N/A	Retrieve the registered bootstrap instance.

Method	Return Value	Parameters	Description
`setOptions(array $options)`	`Zend_Application _Resource_Resour ceAbstract`	• `$options:` *required.* Options with which to set state.	Set resource state.
`getOptions()`	`array`	N/A	Retrieve registered options.

Resource Names

When registering plugin resources, one issue that arises is how you should refer to them from the parent bootstrap class. There are three different mechanisms that may be used, depending on how you have configured the bootstrap and its plugin resources.

First, if your plugins are defined within a defined prefix path, you may refer to them simply by their "short name" -- i.e., the portion of the class name following the class prefix. As an example, the class "Zend_Application_Resource_View" may be referenced as simply "View", as the prefix path "ZenD_Application_Resource" is already registered. You may register them using the full class name or the short name:

```
$app = new Zend_Application(APPLICATION_ENV, array(
    'pluginPaths' => array(
        'My_Resource' => 'My/Resource/',
    ),
    'resources' => array(
        // if the following class exists:
        'My_Resource_View' => array(),

        // then this is equivalent:
        'View' => array(),
    ),
));
```

In each case, you can then bootstrap the resource and retrieve it later using the short name:

```
$bootstrap->bootstrap('view');
$view = $bootstrap->getResource('view');
```

Second, if no matching plugin path is defined, you may still pass a resource by the full class name. In this case, you can reference it using the resource's full class name:

```
$app = new Zend_Application(APPLICATION_ENV, array(
    'resources' => array(
        // This will load the standard 'View' resource:
        'View' => array(),

        // While this loads a resource with a specific class name:
        'My_Resource_View' => array(),
    ),
));
```

Obviously, this makes referencing the resource much more verbose:

```
$bootstrap->bootstrap('My_Resource_View');
$view = $bootstrap->getResource('My_Resource_View');
```

This brings us to the third option. You can specify an explicit name that a given resource class will register as. This can be done by adding a public $_explicitType property to the resource plugin class, with a string value; that value will then be used whenever you wish to reference the plugin resource via the bootstrap. As an example, let's define our own view class:

```
class My_Resource_View extends Zend_Application_Resource_ResourceAbstract
{
    public $_explicitType = 'My_View';

    public function init()
    {
        // do some initialization...
    }
}
```

We can then bootstrap that resource or retrieve it by the name "My_View":

```
$bootstrap->bootstrap('My_View');
$view = $bootstrap->getResource('My_View');
```

Using these various naming approaches, you can override existing resources, add your own, mix multiple resources to achieve complex initialization, and more.

Available Resource Plugins

Here you'll find API-like documentation about all resource plugins available by default in Zend_Application.

Zend_Application_Resource_Db

Zend_Application_Resource_Db will initialize a Zend_Db adapter based on the options passed to it. By default, it also sets the adapter as the default adapter for use with Zend_Db_Table.

The following configuration keys are recognized:

- adapter: Zend_Db adapter type.

- params: associative array of configuration parameters to use when retrieving the adapter instance.

- isDefaultTableAdapter: whether or not to establish this adapter as the default table adapter.

Example 4.1. Sample DB adapter resource configuration

Below is an example INI configuration that can be used to initialize the DB resource.

```
[production]
resources.db.adapter = "pdo_mysql"
```

```
resources.db.params.host = "localhost"
resources.db.params.username = "webuser"
resources.db.params.password = "XXXXXXX"
resources.db.params.dbname = "test"
resources.db.isDefaultTableAdapter = true
```

Retrieving the Adapter instance

If you choose not to make the adapter instantiated with this resource the default table adapter, how do you retrieve the adapter instance?

As with any resource plugin, you can fetch the DB resource plugin from your bootstrap:

```
$resource = $bootstrap->getPluginResource('db');
```

Once you have the resource object, you can fetch the DB adapter using the getDbAdapter() method:

```
$db = $resource->getDbAdapter();
```

Zend_Application_Resource_Frontcontroller

Probably the most common resource you will load with Zend_Application will be the Front Controller resource, which provides the ability to configure Zend_Controller_Front. This resource provides the ability to set arbitrary front controller parameters, specify plugins to initialize, and much more.

Once initialized, the resource assigns the frontController property of the bootstrap to the Zend_Controller_Front instance.

Available configuration keys include the following, and are case insensitive:

- controllerDirectory: either a string value specifying a single controller directory, or an array of module/controller directory pairs.

- moduleControllerDirectoryName: a string value indicating the subdirectory under a module that contains controllers.

- moduleDirectory: directory under which modules may be found.

- defaultControllerName: base name of the default controller (normally "index").

- defaultAction: base name of the default action (normally "index").

- defaultModule: base name of the default module (normally "default").

- baseUrl: explicit base URL to the application (normally auto-detected).

- plugins: array of front controller plugin class names. The resource will instantiate each class (with no constructor arguments) and then register the instance with the front controller.

- params: array of key/value pairs to register with the front controller.

If an unrecognized key is provided, it is registered as a front controller parameter by passing it to `setParam()`.

Example 4.2. Sample Front Controller resource configuration

Below is a sample INI snippet showing how to configure the front controller resource.

```
[production]
resources.frontController.controllerDirectory = APPLICATION_PATH
    "/controllers"
resources.frontController.moduleControllerDirectoryName = "actions"
resources.frontController.moduleDirectory = APPLICATION_PATH "/modules"
resources.frontController.defaultControllerName = "site"
resources.frontController.defaultAction = "home"
resources.frontController.defaultModule = "static"
resources.frontController.baseUrl = "/subdir"
resources.frontController.plugins.foo = "My_Plugin_Foo"
resources.frontController.plugins.bar = "My_Plugin_Bar"
resources.frontController.env = APPLICATION_ENV
```

Example 4.3. Retrieving the Front Controller in your bootstrap

Once your Front Controller resource has been initialized, you can fetch the Front Controller instance via the `frontController` property of your bootstrap.

```
$bootstrap->bootstrap('frontController');
$front = $bootstrap->frontController;
```

Zend_Application_Resource_Modules

`Zend_Application_Resource_Modules` is used to initialize your application modules. If your module has a `Bootstrap.php` file in its root, and it contains a class named `Module_Bootstrap` (where "Module" is the module name), then it will use that class to bootstrap the module.

By default, an instance of `Zend_Application_Module_Autoloader` will be created for the module, using the module name and directory to initialize it.

Front Controller resource dependency

The Modules resource has a dependency on the Front Controller resource. You can, of course, provide your own replacement for that resource via a custom Front Controller resource class or a class initializer method -- so long as the resource plugin class ends in "Frontcontroller" or the initializer method is named "_initFrontController" (case insensitive).

Example 4.4. Configuring Modules

You can specify module-specific configuration using the module name as a prefix/sub-section in your configuration file.

For example, let's assume that your application has a "news" module. The following are INI and XML examples showing configuration of resources in that module.

```
[production]
news.resources.db.adapter = "pdo_mysql"
news.resources.db.params.host = "localhost"
news.resources.db.params.username = "webuser"
news.resources.db.params.password = "XXXXXXX"
news.resources.db.params.dbname = "news"
news.resources.layout.layout = "news"
```

```xml
<?xml version="1.0"?>
<config>
    <production>
        <news>
            <resources>
                <db>
                    <adapter>pdo_mysql</adapter>
                    <params>
                        <host>localhost</host>
                        <username>webuser</username>
                        <password>XXXXXXX</password>
                        <dbname>news</dbname>
                    </params>
                    <isDefaultAdapter>true</isDefaultAdapter>
                </db>
            </resources>
        </news>
    </production>
</config>
```

Example 4.5. Retrieving a specific module bootstrap

On occasion, you may need to retrieve the bootstrap object for a specific module -- perhaps to run discrete bootstrap methods, or to fetch the autoloader in order to configure it. This can be done using the Modules resource's getExecutedBootstraps() method.

```
$resource = $bootstrap->getPluginResource('modules');
$moduleBootstraps = $resource->getExecutedBootstraps();
$newsBootstrap = $moduleBootstraps['news'];
```

Zend_Application_Resource_Session

Zend_Application_Resource_Session allows you to configure Zend_Session as well as optionally initialize a session SaveHandler.

To set a session save handler, simply pass the saveHandler (case insensitive) option key to the resource. The value of this option may be one of the following:

- string: A string indicating a class implementing Zend_Session_SaveHandler _Interface that should be instantiated.

- **array**: An array with the keys "class" and, optionally, "options", indicating a class implementing `Zend_Session_SaveHandler_Interface` that should be instantiated and an array of options to provide to its constructor.

- `Zend_Session_SaveHandler_Interface`: an object implementing this interface.

Any other option keys passed will be passed to `Zend_Session::setOptions()` to configure `Zend_Session`.

Example 4.6. Sample Session resource configuration

Below is a sample INI snippet showing how to configure the session resource. It sets several `Zend_Session` options, as well as configures a `Zend_Session_SaveHandler_DbTable` instance.

```
resources.session.save_path = APPLICATION_PATH "/../data/session"
resources.session.use_only_cookies = true
resources.session.remember_me_seconds = 864000
resources.session.saveHandler.class = "Zend_Session_SaveHandler_DbTable"
resources.session.saveHandler.options.name = "session"
resources.session.saveHandler.options.primary.session_id = "session_id"
resources.session.saveHandler.options.primary.save_path = "save_path"
resources.session.saveHandler.options.primary.name = "name"
resources.session.saveHandler.options.primaryAssignment.sessionId =
    "sessionId"
resources.session.saveHandler.options.primaryAssignment.sessionSavePath
    = "sessionSavePath"
resources.session.saveHandler.options.primaryAssignment.sessionName
    = "sessionName"
resources.session.saveHandler.options.modifiedColumn = "modified"
resources.session.saveHandler.options.dataColumn = "session_data"
resources.session.saveHandler.options.lifetimeColumn = "lifetime"
```

Bootstrap your database first!

If you are configuring the `Zend_Session_SaveHandler_DbTable` session save handler, you must first configure your database connection for it to work. Do this by either using the Db resource -- and make sure the "resources.db" key comes prior to the "resources.session" key -- or by writing your own resource that initializes the database, and specifically sets the default `Zend_Db_Table` adapter.

Zend_Application_Resource_View

`Zend_Application_Resource_View` can be used to configure a `Zend_View` instance. Configuration options are per the Zend_View options.

Once done configuring the view instance, it creates an instance of `Zend_Controller_Action_Helper_ViewRenderer` and registers the ViewRenderer with `Zend_Controller_Action_HelperBroker` -- from which you may retrieve it later.

Example 4.7. Sample View resource configuration

Below is a sample INI snippet showing how to configure the view resource.

```
resources.view.encoding = "UTF-8"
resources.view.basePath = APPLICATION_PATH "/views/scripts"
```

Chapter 5. Zend_Auth

Introduction

Zend_Auth provides an API for authentication and includes concrete authentication adapters for common use case scenarios.

Zend_Auth is concerned only with *authentication* and not with *authorization*. Authentication is loosely defined as determining whether an entity actually is what it purports to be (i.e., identification), based on some set of credentials. Authorization, the process of deciding whether to allow an entity access to, or to perform operations upon, other entities is outside the scope of Zend_Auth. For more information about authorization and access control with Zend Framework, please see Zend_Acl .

Note

The Zend_Auth class implements the Singleton pattern - only one instance of the class is available - through its static getInstance() method. This means that using the new operator and the clone keyword will not work with the Zend_Auth class; use Zend_Auth::getInstance() instead.

Adapters

A Zend_Auth adapter is used to authenticate against a particular type of authentication service, such as LDAP, RDBMS, or file-based storage. Different adapters are likely to have vastly different options and behaviors, but some basic things are common among authentication adapters. For example, accepting authentication credentials (including a purported identity), performing queries against the authentication service, and returning results are common to Zend_Auth adapters.

Each Zend_Auth adapter class implements Zend_Auth_Adapter_Interface. This interface defines one method, authenticate(), that an adapter class must implement for performing an authentication query. Each adapter class must be prepared prior to calling authenticate(). Such adapter preparation includes setting up credentials (e.g., username and password) and defining values for adapter- specific configuration options, such as database connection settings for a database table adapter.

The following is an example authentication adapter that requires a username and password to be set for authentication. Other details, such as how the authentication service is queried, have been omitted for brevity:

```
class MyAuthAdapter implements Zend_Auth_Adapter_Interface
{
    /**
     * Sets username and password for authentication
     *
     * @return void
     */
    public function __construct($username, $password)
    {
        // ...
    }

    /**
     * Performs an authentication attempt
     *
     * @throws Zend_Auth_Adapter_Exception If authentication cannot
     *                                      be performed
```

```
 * @return Zend_Auth_Result
 */
public function authenticate()
{
    // ...
}
}
```

As indicated in its docblock, `authenticate()` must return an instance of `Zend_Auth_Result` (or of a class derived from `Zend_Auth_Result`). If for some reason performing an authentication query is impossible, `authenticate()` should throw an exception that derives from `Zend_Auth_Adapter_Exception`.

Results

`Zend_Auth` adapters return an instance of `Zend_Auth_Result` with `authenticate()` in order to represent the results of an authentication attempt. Adapters populate the `Zend_Auth_Result` object upon construction, so that the following four methods provide a basic set of user-facing operations that are common to the results of `Zend_Auth` adapters:

- `isValid()` - returns true if and only if the result represents a successful authentication attempt

- `getCode()` - returns a `Zend_Auth_Result` constant identifier for determining the type of authentication failure or whether success has occurred. This may be used in situations where the developer wishes to distinguish among several authentication result types. This allows developers to maintain detailed authentication result statistics, for example. Another use of this feature is to provide specific, customized messages to users for usability reasons, though developers are encouraged to consider the risks of providing such detailed reasons to users, instead of a general authentication failure message. For more information, see the notes below.

- `getIdentity()` - returns the identity of the authentication attempt

- `getMessages()` - returns an array of messages regarding a failed authentication attempt

A developer may wish to branch based on the type of authentication result in order to perform more specific operations. Some operations developers might find useful are locking accounts after too many unsuccessful password attempts, flagging an IP address after too many nonexistent identities are attempted, and providing specific, customized authentication result messages to the user. The following result codes are available:

```
Zend_Auth_Result::SUCCESS
Zend_Auth_Result::FAILURE
Zend_Auth_Result::FAILURE_IDENTITY_NOT_FOUND
Zend_Auth_Result::FAILURE_IDENTITY_AMBIGUOUS
Zend_Auth_Result::FAILURE_CREDENTIAL_INVALID
Zend_Auth_Result::FAILURE_UNCATEGORIZED
```

The following example illustrates how a developer may branch on the result code:

```
// inside of AuthController / loginAction
$result = $this->_auth->authenticate($adapter);

switch ($result->getCode()) {

    case Zend_Auth_Result::FAILURE_IDENTITY_NOT_FOUND:
        /** do stuff for nonexistent identity **/
        break;
```

```
    case Zend_Auth_Result::FAILURE_CREDENTIAL_INVALID:
        /** do stuff for invalid credential **/
        break;

    case Zend_Auth_Result::SUCCESS:
        /** do stuff for successful authentication **/
        break;

    default:
        /** do stuff for other failure **/
        break;
}
```

Identity Persistence

Authenticating a request that includes authentication credentials is useful per se, but it is also important to support maintaining the authenticated identity without having to present the authentication credentials with each request.

HTTP is a stateless protocol, however, and techniques such as cookies and sessions have been developed in order to facilitate maintaining state across multiple requests in server-side web applications.

Default Persistence in the PHP Session

By default, Zend_Auth provides persistent storage of the identity from a successful authentication attempt using the PHP session. Upon a successful authentication attempt, Zend_Auth::authenticate() stores the identity from the authentication result into persistent storage. Unless configured otherwise, Zend_Auth uses a storage class named Zend_Auth_Storage_Session, which, in turn, uses Zend_Session . A custom class may instead be used by providing an object that implements Zend_Auth_Storage_Interface to Zend_Auth::setStorage().

Note

If automatic persistent storage of the identity is not appropriate for a particular use case, then developers may forgo using the Zend_Auth class altogether, instead using an adapter class directly.

Example 5.1. Modifying the Session Namespace

Zend_Auth_Storage_Session uses a session namespace of 'Zend_Auth'. This namespace may be overridden by passing a different value to the constructor of Zend_Auth_Storage_Session, and this value is internally passed along to the constructor of Zend_Session_Namespace. This should occur before authentication is attempted, since Zend_Auth::authenticate() performs the automatic storage of the identity.

```
// Save a reference to the Singleton instance of Zend_Auth
$auth = Zend_Auth::getInstance();

// Use 'someNamespace' instead of 'Zend_Auth'
$auth->setStorage(new Zend_Auth_Storage_Session('someNamespace'));
```

```
/**
 * @todo Set up the auth adapter, $authAdapter
 */

// Authenticate, saving the result, and persisting the identity on
// success
$result = $auth->authenticate($authAdapter);
```

Implementing Customized Storage

Sometimes developers may need to use a different identity storage mechanism than that provided by Zend_Auth_Storage_Session. For such cases developers may simply implement Zend_Auth_Storage_Interface and supply an instance of the class to Zend_Auth::setStorage().

Example 5.2. Using a Custom Storage Class

In order to use an identity persistence storage class other than Zend_Auth_Storage_Session, a developer implements Zend_Auth_Storage_Interface:

```
class MyStorage implements Zend_Auth_Storage_Interface
{
    /**
     * Returns true if and only if storage is empty
     *
     * @throws Zend_Auth_Storage_Exception If it is impossible to
     *                                     determine whether storage
     *                                     is empty
     * @return boolean
     */
    public function isEmpty()
    {
        /**
         * @todo implementation
         */
    }

    /**
     * Returns the contents of storage
     *
     * Behavior is undefined when storage is empty.
     *
     * @throws Zend_Auth_Storage_Exception If reading contents from
     *                                     storage is impossible
     * @return mixed
     */
    public function read()
    {
        /**
         * @todo implementation
         */
    }

    /**
     * Writes $contents to storage
     *
```

```
 * @param   mixed $contents
 * @throws Zend_Auth_Storage_Exception If writing $contents to
 *                                     storage is impossible
 * @return void
 */
public function write($contents)
{
    /**
     * @todo implementation
     */
}

/**
 * Clears contents from storage
 *
 * @throws Zend_Auth_Storage_Exception If clearing contents from
 *                                     storage is impossible
 * @return void
 */
public function clear()
{
    /**
     * @todo implementation
     */
}
}
```

In order to use this custom storage class, Zend_Auth::setStorage() is invoked before an authentication query is attempted:

```
// Instruct Zend_Auth to use the custom storage class
Zend_Auth::getInstance()->setStorage(new MyStorage());

/**
 * @todo Set up the auth adapter, $authAdapter
 */

// Authenticate, saving the result, and persisting the identity on
// success
$result = Zend_Auth::getInstance()->authenticate($authAdapter);
```

Usage

There are two provided ways to use Zend_Auth adapters:

1. indirectly, through Zend_Auth::authenticate()

2. directly, through the adapter's authenticate() method

The following example illustrates how to use a Zend_Auth adapter indirectly, through the use of the Zend_Auth class:

```
// Get a reference to the singleton instance of Zend_Auth
$auth = Zend_Auth::getInstance();

// Set up the authentication adapter
$authAdapter = new MyAuthAdapter($username, $password);
```

```
// Attempt authentication, saving the result
$result = $auth->authenticate($authAdapter);

if (!$result->isValid()) {
    // Authentication failed; print the reasons why
    foreach ($result->getMessages() as $message) {
        echo "$message\n";
    }
} else {
    // Authentication succeeded; the identity ($username) is stored
    // in the session
    // $result->getIdentity() === $auth->getIdentity()
    // $result->getIdentity() === $username
}
```

Once authentication has been attempted in a request, as in the above example, it is a simple matter to check whether a successfully authenticated identity exists:

```
$auth = Zend_Auth::getInstance();
if ($auth->hasIdentity()) {
    // Identity exists; get it
    $identity = $auth->getIdentity();
}
```

To remove an identity from persistent storage, simply use the clearIdentity() method. This typically would be used for implementing an application "logout" operation:

```
Zend_Auth::getInstance()->clearIdentity();
```

When the automatic use of persistent storage is inappropriate for a particular use case, a developer may simply bypass the use of the Zend_Auth class, using an adapter class directly. Direct use of an adapter class involves configuring and preparing an adapter object and then calling its authenticate() method. Adapter-specific details are discussed in the documentation for each adapter. The following example directly utilizes MyAuthAdapter:

```
// Set up the authentication adapter
$authAdapter = new MyAuthAdapter($username, $password);

// Attempt authentication, saving the result
$result = $authAdapter->authenticate();

if (!$result->isValid()) {
    // Authentication failed; print the reasons why
    foreach ($result->getMessages() as $message) {
        echo "$message\n";
    }
} else {
    // Authentication succeeded
    // $result->getIdentity() === $username
}
```

Database Table Authentication

Introduction

Zend_Auth_Adapter_DbTable provides the ability to authenticate against credentials stored in a database table. Because Zend_Auth_Adapter_DbTable requires an instance of Zend_Db_Adapter_Abstract to be passed to its constructor, each instance is bound to a particular database connection. Other configuration options may be set through the constructor and through instance methods, one for each option.

The available configuration options include:

- tableName: This is the name of the database table that contains the authentication credentials, and against which the database authentication query is performed.

- identityColumn: This is the name of the database table column used to represent the identity. The identity column must contain unique values, such as a username or e-mail address.

- credentialColumn: This is the name of the database table column used to represent the credential. Under a simple identity and password authentication scheme, the credential value corresponds to the password. See also the credentialTreatment option.

- credentialTreatment: In many cases, passwords and other sensitive data are encrypted, hashed, encoded, obscured, salted or otherwise treated through some function or algorithm. By specifying a parameterized treatment string with this method, such as 'MD5(?)' or 'PASSWORD(?)', a developer may apply such arbitrary SQL upon input credential data. Since these functions are specific to the underlying RDBMS, check the database manual for the availability of such functions for your database system.

Example 5.3. Basic Usage

As explained in the introduction, the Zend_Auth_Adapter_DbTable constructor requires an instance of Zend_Db_Adapter_Abstract that serves as the database connection to which the authentication adapter instance is bound. First, the database connection should be created.

The following code creates an adapter for an in-memory database, creates a simple table schema, and inserts a row against which we can perform an authentication query later. This example requires the PDO SQLite extension to be available:

```
// Create an in-memory SQLite database connection
$dbAdapter = new Zend_Db_Adapter_Pdo_Sqlite(array('dbname' =>
                                          ':memory:'));

// Build a simple table creation query
$sqlCreate = 'CREATE TABLE [users] ('
           . '[id] INTEGER  NOT NULL PRIMARY KEY, '
           . '[username] VARCHAR(50) UNIQUE NOT NULL, '
           . '[password] VARCHAR(32) NULL, '
           . '[real_name] VARCHAR(150) NULL)';

// Create the authentication credentials table
$dbAdapter->query($sqlCreate);

// Build a query to insert a row for which authentication may succeed
$sqlInsert = "INSERT INTO users (username, password, real_name) "
```

```
           . "VALUES ('my_username', 'my_password', 'My Real Name')";

// Insert the data
$dbAdapter->query($sqlInsert);
```

With the database connection and table data available, an instance of `Zend_Auth_Adapter_DbTable` may be created. Configuration option values may be passed to the constructor or deferred as parameters to setter methods after instantiation:

```
// Configure the instance with constructor parameters...
$authAdapter = new Zend_Auth_Adapter_DbTable(
    $dbAdapter,
    'users',
    'username',
    'password'
);

// ...or configure the instance with setter methods
$authAdapter = new Zend_Auth_Adapter_DbTable($dbAdapter);

$authAdapter
    ->setTableName('users')
    ->setIdentityColumn('username')
    ->setCredentialColumn('password')
;
```

At this point, the authentication adapter instance is ready to accept authentication queries. In order to formulate an authentication query, the input credential values are passed to the adapter prior to calling the `authenticate()` method:

```
// Set the input credential values (e.g., from a login form)
$authAdapter
    ->setIdentity('my_username')
    ->setCredential('my_password')
;

// Perform the authentication query, saving the result
```

In addition to the availability of the `getIdentity()` method upon the authentication result object, `Zend_Auth_Adapter_DbTable` also supports retrieving the table row upon authentication success:

```
// Print the identity
echo $result->getIdentity() . "\n\n";

// Print the result row
print_r($authAdapter->getResultRowObject());

/* Output:
my_username

Array
(
    [id] => 1
    [username] => my_username
    [password] => my_password
    [real_name] => My Real Name
)
```

Since the table row contains the credential value, it is important to secure the values against unintended access.

Advanced Usage: Persisting a DbTable Result Object

By default, `Zend_Auth_Adapter_DbTable` returns the identity supplied back to the auth object upon successful authentication. Another use case scenario, where developers want to store to the persistent storage mechanism of `Zend_Auth` an identity object containing other useful information, is solved by using the `getResultRowObject()` method to return a `stdClass` object. The following code snippet illustrates its use:

```
// authenticate with Zend_Auth_Adapter_DbTable
$result = $this->_auth->authenticate($adapter);

if ($result->isValid()) {
    // store the identity as an object where only the username and
    // real_name have been returned
    $storage = $this->_auth->getStorage();
    $storage->write($adapter->getResultRowObject(array(
        'username',
        'real_name',
    )));

    // store the identity as an object where the password column has
    // been omitted
    $storage->write($adapter->getResultRowObject(
        null,
        'password'
    ));

    /* ... */

} else {

    /* ... */

}
```

Advanced Usage By Example

While the primary purpose of `Zend_Auth` (and consequently `Zend_Auth_Adapter_DbTable`) is primarily *authentication* and not *authorization*, there are a few instances and problems that toe the line between which domain they fit within. Depending on how you've decided to explain your problem, it sometimes makes sense to solve what could look like an authorization problem within the authentication adapter.

With that disclaimer out of the way, `Zend_Auth_Adapter_DbTable` has some built in mechanisms that can be leveraged for additional checks at authentication time to solve some common user problems.

```
// The status field value of an account is not equal to "compromised"
$adapter = new Zend_Auth_Adapter_DbTable(
    $db,
    'users',
    'username',
    'password',
    'MD5(?) AND status != "compromised"'
);

// The active field value of an account is equal to "TRUE"
$adapter = new Zend_Auth_Adapter_DbTable(
```

```
    $db,
    'users',
    'username',
    'password',
    'MD5(?) AND active = "TRUE"'
```

Another scenario can be the implementation of a salting mechanism. Salting is a term referring to a technique which can highly improve your application's security. It's based on the idea that concatenating a random string to every password makes it impossible to accomplish a successful brute force attack on the database using pre-computed hash values from a dictionary.

Therefore, we need to modify our table to store our salt string:

```
$sqlAlter = "ALTER TABLE [users] "
          . "ADD COLUMN [password_salt] "
          . "AFTER [password]";
```

Here's a simple way to generate a salt string for every user at registration:

```
for ($i = 0; $i < 50; $i++) {
    $dynamicSalt .= chr(rand(33, 126));
```

And now let's build the adapter:

```
$adapter = new Zend_Auth_Adapter_DbTable(
    $db,
    'users',
    'username',
    'password',
    "MD5(CONCAT('"
    . Zend_Registry::get('staticSalt')
    . "', ?, password_salt))"
);
```

Note

You can improve security even more by using a static salt value hard coded into your application. In the case that your database is compromised (e. g. by an SQL injection attack) but your web server is intact your data is still unusable for the attacker.

Another alternative is to use the getDbSelect() method of the Zend_Auth_Adapter_DbTable after the adapter has been constructed. This method will return the Zend_Db_Select object instance it will use to complete the authenticate() routine. It is important to note that this method will always return the same object regardless if authenticate() has been called or not. This object *will not* have any of the identity or credential information in it as those values are placed into the select object at authenticate() time.

An example of a situation where one might want to use the getDbSelect() method would check the status of a user, in other words to see if that user's account is enabled.

```
// Continuing with the example from above
$adapter = new Zend_Auth_Adapter_DbTable(
    $db,
    'users',
```

```
    'username',
    'password',
    'MD5(?)'
);

// get select object (by reference)
$select = $adapter->getDbSelect();
$select->where('active = "TRUE"');

// authenticate, this ensures that users.active = TRUE
$adapter->authenticate();
```

Digest Authentication

Introduction

Digest authentication [http://en.wikipedia.org/wiki/Digest_access_authentication] is a method of HTTP authentication that improves upon Basic authentication [http://en.wikipedia.org/wiki/Basic _authentication_scheme] by providing a way to authenticate without having to transmit the password in clear text across the network.

This adapter allows authentication against text files containing lines having the basic elements of Digest authentication:

- username, such as "joe.user"

- realm, such as "Administrative Area"

- MD5 hash of the username, realm, and password, separated by colons
The above elements are separated by colons, as in the following example (in which the password is "somePassword"):

someUser:Some Realm:fde17b91c3a510ecbaf7dbd37f59d4f8

Specifics

The digest authentication adapter, Zend_Auth_Adapter_Digest, requires several input parameters:

- filename - Filename against which authentication queries are performed

- realm - Digest authentication realm

- username - Digest authentication user

- password - Password for the user of the realm
These parameters must be set prior to calling authenticate().

Identity

The digest authentication adapter returns a `Zend_Auth_Result` object, which has been populated with the identity as an array having keys of `realm` and `username`. The respective array values associated with these keys correspond to the values set before `authenticate()` is called.

```
$adapter = new Zend_Auth_Adapter_Digest($filename,
                                        $realm,
                                        $username,
                                        $password);

$result = $adapter->authenticate();

$identity = $result->getIdentity();

print_r($identity);

/*
Array
(
    [realm] => Some Realm
    [username] => someUser
)
*/
```

HTTP Authentication Adapter

Introduction

`Zend_Auth_Adapter_Http` provides a mostly-compliant implementation of RFC-2617 [http://tools.ietf.org/html/rfc2617], Basic [http://en.wikipedia.org/wiki/Basic_authentication_scheme] and Digest [http://en.wikipedia.org/wiki/Digest_access_authentication] HTTP Authentication. Digest authentication is a method of HTTP authentication that improves upon Basic authentication by providing a way to authenticate without having to transmit the password in clear text across the network.

Major Features:

• Supports both Basic and Digest authentication.

• Issues challenges in all supported schemes, so client can respond with any scheme it supports.

• Supports proxy authentication.

• Includes support for authenticating against text files and provides an interface for authenticating against other sources, such as databases.

There are a few notable features of RFC-2617 that are not implemented yet:

• Nonce tracking, which would allow for "stale" support, and increased replay attack protection.

• Authentication with integrity checking, or "auth-int".

• Authentication-Info HTTP header.

Design Overview

This adapter consists of two sub-components, the HTTP authentication class itself, and the so-called "Resolvers." The HTTP authentication class encapsulates the logic for carrying out both Basic and Digest authentication. It uses a Resolver to look up a client's identity in some data store (text file by default), and retrieve the credentials from the data store. The "resolved" credentials are then compared to the values submitted by the client to determine whether authentication is successful.

Configuration Options

The `Zend_Auth_Adapter_Http` class requires a configuration array passed to its constructor. There are several configuration options available, and some are required:

Table 5.1. Configuration Options

Option Name	Required	Description
accept_schemes	Yes	Determines which authentication schemes the adapter will accept from the client. Must be a space-separated list containing 'basic' and/or 'digest'.
realm	Yes	Sets the authentication realm; usernames should be unique within a given realm.
digest_domains	Yes, when 'accept _schemes' contains 'digest'	Space-separated list of URIs for which the same authentication information is valid. The URIs need not all point to the same server.
nonce_timeout	Yes, when 'accept _schemes' contains 'digest'	Sets the number of seconds for which the nonce is valid. See notes below.
proxy_auth	No	Disabled by default. Enable to perform Proxy authentication, instead of normal origin server authentication.

Note

The current implementation of the `nonce_timeout` has some interesting side effects. This setting is supposed to determine the valid lifetime of a given nonce, or effectively how long a client's authentication information is accepted. Currently, if it's set to 3600 (for example), it will cause the adapter to prompt the client for new credentials every hour, on the hour. This will be resolved in a future release, once nonce tracking and stale support are implemented.

Resolvers

The resolver's job is to take a username and realm, and return some kind of credential value. Basic authentication expects to receive the Base64 encoded version of the user's password. Digest authentication expects to receive a hash of the user's username, the realm, and their password (each separated by colons). Currently, the only supported hash algorithm is MD5.

Zend_Auth_Adapter_Http relies on objects implementing Zend_Auth_Adapter_Http _Resolver_Interface. A text file resolver class is included with this adapter, but any other kind of resolver can be created simply by implementing the resolver interface.

File Resolver

The file resolver is a very simple class. It has a single property specifying a filename, which can also be passed to the constructor. Its resolve() method walks through the text file, searching for a line with a matching username and realm. The text file format similar to Apache htpasswd files:

```
<username>:<realm>:<credentials>\n
```

Each line consists of three fields - username, realm, and credentials - each separated by a colon. The credentials field is opaque to the file resolver; it simply returns that value as-is to the caller. Therefore, this same file format serves both Basic and Digest authentication. In Basic authentication, the credentials field should be written in clear text. In Digest authentication, it should be the MD5 hash described above.

There are two equally easy ways to create a File resolver:

```
$path     = 'files/passwd.txt';
$resolver = new Zend_Auth_Adapter_Http_Resolver_File($path);
```

or

```
$path     = 'files/passwd.txt';
$resolver = new Zend_Auth_Adapter_Http_Resolver_File();
$resolver->setFile($path);
```

If the given path is empty or not readable, an exception is thrown.

Basic Usage

First, set up an array with the required configuration values:

```
$config = array(
    'accept_schemes' => 'basic digest',
    'realm'          => 'My Web Site',
    'digest_domains' => '/members_only /my_account',
    'nonce_timeout'  => 3600,
);
```

This array will cause the adapter to accept either Basic or Digest authentication, and will require authenticated access to all the areas of the site under /members_only and /my_account. The realm value is usually displayed by the browser in the password dialog box. The nonce_timeout, of course, behaves as described above.

Next, create the Zend_Auth_Adapter_Http object:

```
$adapter = new Zend_Auth_Adapter_Http($config);
```

Since we're supporting both Basic and Digest authentication, we need two different resolver objects. Note that this could just as easily be two different classes:

```
$basicResolver = new Zend_Auth_Adapter_Http_Resolver_File();
$basicResolver->setFile('files/basicPasswd.txt');

$digestResolver = new Zend_Auth_Adapter_Http_Resolver_File();
$digestResolver->setFile('files/digestPasswd.txt');

$adapter->setBasicResolver($basicResolver);
$adapter->setDigestResolver($digestResolver);
```

Finally, we perform the authentication. The adapter needs a reference to both the Request and Response objects in order to do its job:

```
assert($request instanceof Zend_Controller_Request_Http);
assert($response instanceof Zend_Controller_Response_Http);

$adapter->setRequest($request);
$adapter->setResponse($response);

$result = $adapter->authenticate();
if (!$result->isValid()) {
    // Bad userame/password, or canceled password prompt
}
```

LDAP Authentication

Introduction

Zend_Auth_Adapter_Ldap supports web application authentication with LDAP services. Its features include username and domain name canonicalization, multi-domain authentication, and failover capabilities. It has been tested to work with Microsoft Active Directory [http://www.microsoft.com/windowsserver2003/technologies/directory/activedirectory/] and OpenLDAP [http://www.openldap.org/], but it should also work with other LDAP service providers.

This documentation includes a guide on using Zend_Auth_Adapter_Ldap, an exploration of its API, an outline of the various available options, diagnostic information for troubleshooting authentication problems, and example options for both Active Directory and OpenLDAP servers.

Usage

To incorporate Zend_Auth_Adapter_Ldap authentication into your application quickly, even if you're not using Zend_Controller, the meat of your code should look something like the following:

```
$username = $this->_request->getParam('username');
$password = $this->_request->getParam('password');

$auth = Zend_Auth::getInstance();

$config = new Zend_Config_Ini('../application/config/config.ini',
                              'production');
$log_path = $config->ldap->log_path;
$options = $config->ldap->toArray();
unset($options['log_path']);

$adapter = new Zend_Auth_Adapter_Ldap($options, $username,
```

```
                                            $password);

$result = $auth->authenticate($adapter);

if ($log_path) {
    $messages = $result->getMessages();

    $logger = new Zend_Log();
    $logger->addWriter(new Zend_Log_Writer_Stream($log_path));
    $filter = new Zend_Log_Filter_Priority(Zend_Log::DEBUG);
    $logger->addFilter($filter);

    foreach ($messages as $i => $message) {
        if ($i-- > 1) { // $messages[2] and up are log messages
            $message = str_replace("\n", "\n    ", $message);
            $logger->log("Ldap: $i: $message", Zend_Log::DEBUG);
        }
    }
}
```

Of course, the logging code is optional, but it is highly recommended that you use a logger. Zend_Auth_Adapter_Ldap will record just about every bit of information anyone could want in $messages (more below), which is a nice feature in itself for something that has a history of being notoriously difficult to debug.

The Zend_Config_Ini code is used above to load the adapter options. It is also optional. A regular array would work equally well. The following is an example application/config/config.ini file that has options for two separate servers. With multiple sets of server options the adapter will try each, in order, until the credentials are successfully authenticated. The names of the servers (e.g., server1 and server2) are largely arbitrary. For details regarding the options array, see the *Server Options* section below. Note that Zend_Config_Ini requires that any values with "equals" characters (=) will need to be quoted (like the DNs shown below).

```
[production]

ldap.log_path = /tmp/ldap.log

; Typical options for OpenLDAP
ldap.server1.host = s0.foo.net
ldap.server1.accountDomainName = foo.net
ldap.server1.accountDomainNameShort = FOO
ldap.server1.accountCanonicalForm = 3
ldap.server1.username = "CN=user1,DC=foo,DC=net"
ldap.server1.password = pass1
ldap.server1.baseDn = "OU=Sales,DC=foo,DC=net"
ldap.server1.bindRequiresDn = true

; Typical options for Active Directory
ldap.server2.host = dc1.w.net
ldap.server2.useStartTls = true
ldap.server2.accountDomainName = w.net
ldap.server2.accountDomainNameShort = W
ldap.server2.accountCanonicalForm = 3
ldap.server2.baseDn = "CN=Users,DC=w,DC=net"
```

The above configuration will instruct Zend_Auth_Adapter_Ldap to attempt to authenticate users with the OpenLDAP server s0.foo.net first. If the authentication fails for any reason, the AD server dc1.w.net will be tried.

With servers in different domains, this configuration illustrates multi-domain authentication. You can also have multiple servers in the same domain to provide redundancy.

Note that in this case, even though OpenLDAP has no need for the short NetBIOS style domain name used by Windows, we provide it here for name canonicalization purposes (described in the *Username Canonicalization* section below).

The API

The Zend_Auth_Adapter_Ldap constructor accepts three parameters.

The $options parameter is required and must be an array containing one or more sets of options. Note that it is *an array of arrays* of Zend_Ldap options. Even if you will be using only one LDAP server, the options must still be within another array.

Below is print_r() [http://php.net/print_r] output of an example options parameter containing two sets of server options for LDAP servers s0.foo.net and dc1.w.net (the same options as the above INI representation):

```
Array
(
    [server2] => Array
        (
            [host] => dc1.w.net
            [useStartTls] => 1
            [accountDomainName] => w.net
            [accountDomainNameShort] => W
            [accountCanonicalForm] => 3
            [baseDn] => CN=Users,DC=w,DC=net
        )

    [server1] => Array
        (
            [host] => s0.foo.net
            [accountDomainName] => foo.net
            [accountDomainNameShort] => FOO
            [accountCanonicalForm] => 3
            [username] => CN=user1,DC=foo,DC=net
            [password] => pass1
            [baseDn] => OU=Sales,DC=foo,DC=net
            [bindRequiresDn] => 1
        )

)
```

The information provided in each set of options above is different mainly because AD does not require a username be in DN form when binding (see the bindRequiresDn option in the *Server Options* section below), which means we can omit a number of options associated with retrieving the DN for a username being authenticated.

What is a Distinguished Name?

A DN or "distinguished name" is a string that represents the path to an object within the LDAP directory. Each comma-separated component is an attribute and value representing a node. The components are evaluated in reverse. For example, the user account *CN=Bob Carter,CN=Users,DC=w,DC=net* is located directly within the *CN=Users,DC=w,DC=net container*. This structure is best explored with an LDAP browser like the ADSI Edit MMC snap-in for Active Directory or phpLDAPadmin.

The names of servers (e.g. 'server1' and 'server2' shown above) are largely arbitrary, but for the sake of using Zend_Config, the identifiers should be present (as opposed to being numeric indexes) and should not contain any special characters used by the associated file formats (e.g. the '.' INI property separator, '&' for XML entity references, etc).

With multiple sets of server options, the adapter can authenticate users in multiple domains and provide failover so that if one server is not available, another will be queried.

The Gory Details: What Happens in the Authenticate Method?

When the `authenticate()` method is called, the adapter iterates over each set of server options, sets them on the internal `Zend_Ldap` instance, and calls the `Zend_Ldap::bind()` method with the username and password being authenticated. The `Zend_Ldap` class checks to see if the username is qualified with a domain (e.g., has a domain component like *alice@foo.net* or *FOO\alice*). If a domain is present, but does not match either of the server's domain names (*foo.net* or *FOO*), a special exception is thrown and caught by `Zend_Auth_Adapter_Ldap` that causes that server to be ignored and the next set of server options is selected. If a domain *does* match, or if the user did not supply a qualified username, `Zend_Ldap` proceeds to try to bind with the supplied credentials. If the bind is not successful, `Zend_Ldap` throws a `Zend_Ldap_Exception` which is caught by `Zend_Auth_Adapter_Ldap` and the next set of server options is tried. If the bind is successful, the iteration stops, and the adapter's `authenticate()` method returns a successful result. If all server options have been tried without success, the authentication fails, and `authenticate()` returns a failure result with error messages from the last iteration.

The username and password parameters of the `Zend_Auth_Adapter_Ldap` constructor represent the credentials being authenticated (i.e., the credentials supplied by the user through your HTML login form). Alternatively, they may also be set with the `setUsername()` and `setPassword()` methods.

Server Options

Each set of server options *in the context of Zend_Auth_Adapter_Ldap* consists of the following options, which are passed, largely unmodified, to `Zend_Ldap::setOptions()`:

Table 5.2. Server Options

Name	Description
host	The hostname of LDAP server that these options represent. This option is required.
port	The port on which the LDAP server is listening. If *useSsl* is `true`, the default *port* value is 636. If *useSsl* is `false`, the default *port* value is 389.
useStartTls	Whether or not the LDAP client should use TLS (aka SSLv2) encrypted transport. A value of `true` is strongly favored in production environments to prevent passwords from be transmitted in clear text. The default value is `false`, as servers frequently require that a certificate be installed separately after installation. The `useSsl` and `useStartTls` options are mutually exclusive. The `useStartTls` option should be favored over `useSsl` but not all servers support this newer mechanism.
useSsl	Whether or not the LDAP client should use SSL encrypted transport. The `useSsl` and `useStartTls` options are mutually exclusive, but `useStartTls` should be favored if the server and LDAP client library support it. This value also changes the default *port* value (see *port* description

Name	Description
	above).
username	The DN of the account used to perform account DN lookups. LDAP servers that require the username to be in DN form when performing the "bind" require this option. Meaning, if *bindRequiresDn* is true, this option is required. This account does not need to be a privileged account; an account with read-only access to objects under the *baseDn* is all that is necessary (and preferred based on the *Principle of Least Privilege*).
password	The password of the account used to perform account DN lookups. If this option is not supplied, the LDAP client will attempt an "anonymous bind" when performing account DN lookups.
bindRequiresDn	Some LDAP servers require that the username used to bind be in DN form like *CN=Alice Baker,OU=Sales,DC=foo,DC=net* (basically all servers *except* AD). If this option is true, this instructs Zend_Ldap to automatically retrieve the DN corresponding to the username being authenticated, if it is not already in DN form, and then re-bind with the proper DN. The default value is false. Currently only Microsoft Active Directory Server (ADS) is known *not* to require usernames to be in DN form when binding, and therefore this option may be false with AD (and it should be, as retrieving the DN requires an extra round trip to the server). Otherwise, this option must be set to true (e.g. for OpenLDAP). This option also controls the default *acountFilterFormat* used when searching for accounts. See the *accountFilterFormat* option.
baseDn	The DN under which all accounts being authenticated are located. This option is required. If you are uncertain about the correct *baseDn* value, it should be sufficient to derive it from the user's DNS domain using *DC=* components. For example, if the user's principal name is *alice@foo.net*, a *baseDn* of *DC=foo,DC=net* should work. A more precise location (e.g., *OU=Sales,DC=foo,DC=net*) will be more efficient, however.
accountCanonicalForm	A value of 2, 3 or 4 indicating the form to which account names should be canonicalized after successful authentication. Values are as follows: 2 for traditional username style names (e.g., *alice*), 3 for backslash-style names (e.g., *FOO\alice*) or 4 for principal style usernames (e.g., *alice@foo.net*). The default value is 4 (e.g., *alice@foo.net*). For example, with a value of 3, the identity returned by Zend_Auth_Result::getIdentity() (and Zend_Auth::getIdentity(), if Zend_Auth was used) will always be *FOO\alice*, regardless of what form Alice supplied, whether it

Name	Description
	be *alice*, *alice@foo.net*, *FOO\alice*, *FoO\aLicE*, *foo.net\alice*, etc. See the *Account Name Canonicalization* section in the Zend_Ldap documentation for details. Note that when using multiple sets of server options it is recommended, but not required, that the same *accountCanonicalForm* be used with all server options so that the resulting usernames are always canonicalized to the same form (e.g., if you canonicalize to *EXAMPLE\username* with an AD server but to *username@example.com* with an OpenLDAP server, that may be awkward for the application's high-level logic).
accountDomainName	The FQDN domain name for which the target LDAP server is an authority (e.g., example.com). This option is used to canonicalize names so that the username supplied by the user can be converted as necessary for binding. It is also used to determine if the server is an authority for the supplied username (e.g., if *accountDomainName* is *foo.net* and the user supplies *bob@bar.net*, the server will not be queried, and a failure will result). This option is not required, but if it is not supplied, usernames in principal name form (e.g., *alice@foo.net*) are not supported. It is strongly recommended that you supply this option, as there are many use-cases that require generating the principal name form.
accountDomainNameShort	The 'short' domain for which the target LDAP server is an authority (e.g., *FOO*). Note that there is a 1:1 mapping between the *accountDomainName* and *accountDomainNameShort*. This option should be used to specify the NetBIOS domain name for Windows networks, but may also be used by non-AD servers (e.g., for consistency when multiple sets of server options with the backslash style *accountCanonicalForm*). This option is not required but if it is not supplied, usernames in backslash form (e.g., *FOO\alice*) are not supported.
accountFilterFormat	The LDAP search filter used to search for accounts. This string is a printf() [http://php.net/printf]-style expression that must contain one '%s' to accomodate the username. The default value is '(&(objectClass=user) (sAMAccountName=%s))', unless *bindRequiresDn* is set to true, in which case the default is '(&(objectClass=posix Account)(uid=%s))'. For example, if for some reason you wanted to use bindRequiresDn = true with AD you would need to set accountFilterFormat = '(&(objectClass=user)(sAMAccount Name=%s))'.
optReferrals	If set to true, this option indicates to the LDAP

Name	Description
	client that referrals should be followed. The default value is `false`.

Note

If you enable `useStartTls = true` or `useSsl = true` you may find that the LDAP client generates an error claiming that it cannot validate the server's certificate. Assuming the PHP LDAP extension is ultimately linked to the OpenLDAP client libraries, to resolve this issue you can set `"TLS_REQCERT never"` in the OpenLDAP client `ldap.conf` (and restart the web server) to indicate to the OpenLDAP client library that you trust the server. Alternatively, if you are concerned that the server could be spoofed, you can export the LDAP server's root certificate and put it on the web server so that the OpenLDAP client can validate the server's identity.

Collecting Debugging Messages

`Zend_Auth_Adapter_Ldap` collects debugging information within its `authenticate()` method. This information is stored in the `Zend_Auth_Result` object as messages. The array returned by `Zend_Auth_Result::getMessages()` is described as follows:

Table 5.3. Debugging Messages

Messages Array Index	Description
Index 0	A generic, user-friendly message that is suitable for displaying to users (e.g., "Invalid credentials"). If the authentication is successful, this string is empty.
Index 1	A more detailed error message that is not suitable to be displayed to users but should be logged for the benefit of server operators. If the authentication is successful, this string is empty.
Indexes 2 and higher	All log messages in order starting at index 2.

In practice, index 0 should be displayed to the user (e.g., using the FlashMessenger helper), index 1 should be logged and, if debugging information is being collected, indexes 2 and higher could be logged as well (although the final message always includes the string from index 1).

Common Options for Specific Servers

Options for Active Directory

For ADS, the following options are noteworthy:

Table 5.4. Options for Active Directory

Name	Additional Notes
host	As with all servers, this option is required.
useStartTls	For the sake of security, this should be `true` if the server has the necessary certificate installed.
useSsl	Possibly used as an alternative to `useStartTls`

Name	Additional Notes
	(see above).
baseDn	As with all servers, this option is required. By default AD places all user accounts under the *Users* container (e.g., *CN=Users,DC=foo,DC=net*), but the default is not common in larger organizations. Ask your AD administrator what the best DN for accounts for your application would be.
accountCanonicalForm	You almost certainly want this to be 3 for backslash style names (e.g., *FOO\alice*), which are most familiar to Windows users. You should *not* use the unqualified form 2 (e.g., *alice*), as this may grant access to your application to users with the same username in other trusted domains (e.g., *BAR\alice* and *FOO\alice* will be treated as the same user). (See also note below.)
accountDomainName	This is required with AD unless *accountCanonicalForm* 2 is used, which, again, is discouraged.
accountDomainNameShort	The NetBIOS name of the domain that users are in and for which the AD server is an authority. This is required if the backslash style *accountCanonicalForm* is used.

Note

Technically there should be no danger of accidental cross-domain authentication with the current `Zend_Auth_Adapter_Ldap` implementation, since server domains are explicitly checked, but this may not be true of a future implementation that discovers the domain at runtime, or if an alternative adapter is used (e.g., Kerberos). In general, account name ambiguity is known to be the source of security issues, so always try to use qualified account names.

Options for OpenLDAP

For OpenLDAP or a generic LDAP server using a typical posixAccount style schema, the following options are noteworthy:

Table 5.5. Options for OpenLDAP

Name	Additional Notes
host	As with all servers, this option is required.
useStartTls	For the sake of security, this should be `true` if the server has the necessary certificate installed.
useSsl	Possibly used as an alternative to `useStartTls` (see above).
username	Required and must be a DN, as OpenLDAP requires that usernames be in DN form when performing a bind. Try to use an unprivileged account.
password	The password corresponding to the username

Name	Additional Notes
	above, but this may be omitted if the LDAP server permits an anonymous binding to query user accounts.
bindRequiresDn	Required and must be `true`, as OpenLDAP requires that usernames be in DN form when performing a bind.
baseDn	As with all servers, this option is required and indicates the DN under which all accounts being authenticated are located.
accountCanonicalForm	Optional, but the default value is 4 (principal style names like *alice@foo.net*), which may not be ideal if your users are used to backslash style names (e.g., *FOO\alice*). For backslash style names use value 3.
accountDomainName	Required unless you're using *accountCanonical Form* 2, which is not recommended.
accountDomainNameShort	If AD is not also being used, this value is not required. Otherwise, if *accountCanonicalForm* 3 is used, this option is required and should be a short name that corresponds adequately to the *accountDomainName* (e.g., if your *accountDomainName* is *foo.net*, a good *accountDomainNameShort* value might be *FOO*).

Open ID Authentication

Introduction

The Zend_Auth_Adapter_OpenId adapter can be used to authenticate users using remote OpenID servers. This authentication method assumes that the user submits only their OpenID identity to the web application. They are then redirected to their OpenID provider to prove identity ownership using a password or some other method. This password is never provided to the web application.

The OpenID identity is just a URI that points to a web site with information about a user, along with special tags that describes which server to use and which identity to submit there. You can read more about OpenID at the OpenID official site [http://www.openid.net/].

The Zend_Auth_Adapter_OpenId class wraps the Zend_OpenId_Consumer component, which implements the OpenID authentication protocol itself.

Note

Zend_OpenId takes advantage of the GMP extension [http://php.net/gmp], where available. Consider enabling the GMP extension for better performance when using Zend_Auth_Adapter_OpenId.

Specifics

As is the case for all Zend_Auth adapters, the Zend_Auth_Adapter_OpenId class implements Zend_Auth_Adapter_Interface, which defines one method: authenticate(). This method performs the authentication itself, but the object must be prepared prior to calling it. Such adapter preparation includes setting up the OpenID identity and some other Zend_OpenId specific options.

However, as opposed to other Zend_Auth adapters, Zend_Auth_Adapter_OpenId performs authentication on an external server in two separate HTTP requests. So the Zend_Auth_Adapter_OpenId::authenticate() method must be called twice. On the first invocation the method won't return, but will redirect the user to their OpenID server. Then after the user is authenticated on the remote server, they will be redirected back and the script for this second request must call Zend_Auth_Adapter_OpenId::authenticate() again to verify the signature which comes with the redirected request from the server to complete the authentication process. On this second invocation, the method will return the Zend_Auth_Result object as expected.

The following example shows the usage of Zend_Auth_Adapter_OpenId. As previously mentioned, the Zend_Auth_Adapter_OpenId::authenticate() must be called two times. The first time is after the user submits the HTML form with the $_POST['openid_action'] set to "login", and the second time is after the HTTP redirection from OpenID server with $_GET['openid_mode'] or $_POST['openid_mode'] set.

```php
<?php
$status = "";
$auth = Zend_Auth::getInstance();
if ((isset($_POST['openid_action']) &&
     $_POST['openid_action'] == "login" &&
     !empty($_POST['openid_identifier'])) ||
    isset($_GET['openid_mode']) ||
    isset($_POST['openid_mode'])) {
    $result = $auth->authenticate(
        new Zend_Auth_Adapter_OpenId(@$_POST['openid_identifier']));
    if ($result->isValid()) {
        $status = "You are logged in as "
                . $auth->getIdentity()
                . "<br>\n";
    } else {
        $auth->clearIdentity();
        foreach ($result->getMessages() as $message) {
            $status .= "$message<br>\n";
        }
    }
} else if ($auth->hasIdentity()) {
    if (isset($_POST['openid_action']) &&
        $_POST['openid_action'] == "logout") {
        $auth->clearIdentity();
    } else {
        $status = "You are logged in as "
                . $auth->getIdentity()
                . "<br>\n";
    }
}
?>
<html><body>
<?php echo htmlspecialchars($status);?>
<form method="post"><fieldset>
<legend>OpenID Login</legend>
<input type="text" name="openid_identifier" value="">
<input type="submit" name="openid_action" value="login">
<input type="submit" name="openid_action" value="logout">
</fieldset></form></body></html>
*/
```

You may customize the OpenID authentication process in several way. You can, for example, receive the redirect from the OpenID server on a separate page, specifying the "root" of web site and using a custom `Zend_OpenId_Consumer_Storage` or a custom `Zend_Controller_Response`. You may also use the Simple Registration Extension to retrieve information about user from the OpenID server. All of these possibilities are described in more detail in the `Zend_OpenId_Consumer` chapter.

Chapter 6. Zend_Cache

Introduction

Zend_Cache provides a generic way to cache any data.

Caching in Zend Framework is operated by frontends while cache records are stored through backend adapters (File, Sqlite, Memcache...) through a flexible system of IDs and tags. Using those, it is easy to delete specific types of records afterwards (for example: "delete all cache records marked with a given tag").

The core of the module (Zend_Cache_Core) is generic, flexible and configurable. Yet, for your specific needs there are cache frontends that extend Zend_Cache_Core for convenience: Output, File, Function and Class.

Example 6.1. Getting a Frontend with Zend_Cache::factory()

Zend_Cache::factory() instantiates correct objects and ties them together. In this first example, we will use Core frontend together with File backend.

```
$frontendOptions = array(
    'lifetime' => 7200, // cache lifetime of 2 hours
    'automatic_serialization' => true
);

$backendOptions = array(
    'cache_dir' => './tmp/' // Directory where to put the cache files
);

// getting a Zend_Cache_Core object
$cache = Zend_Cache::factory('Core',
                             'File',
                             $frontendOptions,
                             $backendOptions);
```

Frontends and Backends Consisting of Multiple Words

Some frontends and backends are named using multiple words, such as 'ZendPlatform'. When specifying them to the factory, separate them using a word separator, such as a space (' '), hyphen ('-'), or period ('.').

Example 6.2. Caching a Database Query Result

Now that we have a frontend, we can cache any type of data (we turned on serialization). For example, we can cache a result from a very expensive database query. After it is cached, there is no need to even connect to the database; records are fetched from cache and unserialized.

```
// $cache initialized in previous example

// see if a cache already exists:
```

```
if(!$result = $cache->load('myresult')) {

    // cache miss; connect to the database

    $db = Zend_Db::factory( [...] );

    $result = $db->fetchAll('SELECT * FROM huge_table');

    $cache->save($result, 'myresult');

} else {

    // cache hit! shout so that we know
    echo "This one is from cache!\n\n";

}

print_r($result);
```

Example 6.3. Caching Output with Zend_Cache Output Frontend

We 'mark up' sections in which we want to cache output by adding some conditional logic, encapsulating the section within start() and end() methods (this resembles the first example and is the core strategy for caching).

Inside, output your data as usual - all output will be cached when execution hits the end() method. On the next run, the whole section will be skipped in favor of fetching data from cache (as long as the cache record is valid).

```
$frontendOptions = array(
    'lifetime' => 30,                        // cache lifetime of 30 seconds
    'automatic_serialization' => false   // this is the default anyways
);

$backendOptions = array('cache_dir' => './tmp/');

$cache = Zend_Cache::factory('Output',
                             'File',
                             $frontendOptions,
                             $backendOptions);

// we pass a unique identifier to the start() method
if(!$cache->start('mypage')) {
    // output as usual:

    echo 'Hello world! ';
    echo 'This is cached ('.time().') ';

    $cache->end(); // the output is saved and sent to the browser
}

echo 'This is never cached ('.time().').';
```

Notice that we output the result of time() twice; this is something dynamic for demonstration purposes. Try running this and then refreshing several times; you will notice that the first number doesn't change while second changes as time passes. That is because the first number was output in the cached section and is saved among other output. After half a minute (we've set lifetime to 30 seconds) the numbers should match again because the cache record expired -- only to be cached again. You should try this in your browser or console.

Note

When using Zend_Cache, pay attention to the important cache identifier (passed to save() and start()). It must be unique for every resource you cache, otherwise unrelated cache records may wipe each other or, even worse, be displayed in place of the other.

The Theory of Caching

There are three key concepts in Zend_Cache. One is the unique identifier (a string) that is used to identify cache records. The second one is the 'lifetime' directive as seen in the examples; it defines for how long the cached resource is considered 'fresh'. The third key concept is conditional execution so that parts of your code can be skipped entirely, boosting performance. The main frontend function (eg. Zend_Cache_Core::get()) is always designed to return false for a cache miss if that makes sense for the nature of a frontend. That enables end-users to wrap parts of the code they would like to cache (and skip) in if() { ... } statements where the condition is a Zend_Cache method itself. On the end if these blocks you must save what you've generated, however (eg. Zend_Cache_Core::save()).

Note

The conditional execution design of your generating code is not necessary in some frontends (Function, for an example) when the whole logic is implemented inside the frontend.

Note

'Cache hit' is a term for a condition when a cache record is found, is valid and is 'fresh' (in other words hasn't expired yet). 'Cache miss' is everything else. When a cache miss happens, you must generate your data (as you would normally do) and have it cached. When you have a cache hit, on the other hand, the backend automatically fetches the record from cache transparently.

The Zend_Cache Factory Method

A good way to build a usable instance of a Zend_Cache Frontend is given in the following example :

```
// We choose a backend (for example 'File' or 'Sqlite'...)
$backendName = '[...]';

// We choose a frontend (for example 'Core', 'Output', 'Page'...)
$frontendName = '[...]';

// We set an array of options for the choosen frontend
$frontendOptions = array([...]);

// We set an array of options for the choosen backend
$backendOptions = array([...]);

// We create an instance of Zend_Cache
// (of course, the two last arguments are optional)
$cache = Zend_Cache::factory($frontendName,
                             $backendName,
                             $frontendOptions,
                             $backendOptions);
```

In the following examples we will assume that the `$cache` variable holds a valid, instantiated frontend as shown and that you understand how to pass parameters to your chosen backends.

Note

Always use `Zend_Cache::factory()` to get frontend instances. Instantiating frontends and backends yourself will not work as expected.

Tagging Records

Tags are a way to categorize cache records. When you save a cache with the `save()` method, you can set an array of tags to apply for this record. Then you will be able to clean all cache records tagged with a given tag (or tags):

```
$cache->save($huge_data, 'myUniqueID', array('tagA', 'tagB', 'tagC'));
```

Note

note than the `save()` method accepts an optional fourth argument : `$specificLifetime` (if != false, it sets a specific lifetime for this particular cache record)

Cleaning the Cache

To remove/invalidate in particular cache id, you can use the `remove()` method :

```
$cache->remove('idToRemove');
```

To remove/invalidate several cache ids in one operation, you can use the `clean()` method. For example to remove all cache records :

```
// clean all records
$cache->clean(Zend_Cache::CLEANING_MODE_ALL);

// clean only outdated
$cache->clean(Zend_Cache::CLEANING_MODE_OLD);
```

If you want to remove cache entries matching the tags 'tagA' and 'tagC':

```
$cache->clean(
    Zend_Cache::CLEANING_MODE_MATCHING_TAG,
    array('tagA', 'tagC')
);
```

If you want to remove cache entries not matching the tags 'tagA' or 'tagC':

```
$cache->clean(
    Zend_Cache::CLEANING_MODE_NOT_MATCHING_TAG,
    array('tagA', 'tagC')
);
```

If you want to remove cache entries matching the tags 'tagA' or 'tagC':

```
$cache->clean(
    Zend_Cache::CLEANING_MODE_MATCHING_ANY_TAG,
    array('tagA', 'tagC')
);
```

Available cleaning modes are: CLEANING_MODE_ALL, CLEANING_MODE_OLD, CLEANING_MODE_MATCHING_TAG, CLEANING_MODE_NOT_MATCHING_TAG and CLEANING_MODE_MATCHING_ANY_TAG. The latter are, as their names suggest, combined with an array of tags in cleaning operations.

Zend_Cache Frontends

Zend_Cache_Core

Introduction

Zend_Cache_Core is a special frontend because it is the core of the module. It is a generic cache frontend and is extended by other classes.

Note

All frontends inherit from Zend_Cache_Core so that its methods and options (described below) would also be available in other frontends, therefore they won't be documented there.

Available options

These options are passed to the factory method as demonstrated in previous examples.

Table 6.1. Core Frontend Options

Option	Data Type	Default Value	Description
caching	boolean	true	enable / disable caching (can be very useful for the debug of cached scripts)
cache_id_prefix	string	null	A prefix for all cache ids, if set to null, no cache id prefix will be used. The cache id prefix essentially creates a namespace in the cache, allowing multiple applications or websites to use a shared cache. Each application or website can use a different cache id prefix so specific cache ids can be used more than once.
lifetime	int	3600	cache lifetime (in

Option	Data Type	Default Value	Description
			seconds), if set to `null`, the cache is valid forever.
logging	boolean	false	if set to true, logging through `Zend_Log` is activated (but the system is slower)
write_control	boolean	true	Enable / disable write control (the cache is read just after writing to detect corrupt entries), enabling write_control will lightly slow the cache writing but not the cache reading (it can detect some corrupt cache files but it's not a perfect control)
automatic_serialization	boolean	false	Enable / disable automatic serialization, it can be used to save directly datas which aren't strings (but it's slower)
automatic_cleaning_factor	int	10	Disable / Tune the automatic cleaning process (garbage collector): 0 means no automatic cache cleaning, 1 means systematic cache cleaning and x > 1 means automatic random cleaning 1 times in x write operations.
ignore_user_abort	boolean	false	if set to true, the core will set the ignore_user_abort PHP flag inside the save() method to avoid cache corruptions in some cases

Examples

An example is given in the manual at the very beginning.

If you store only strings into cache (because with "automatic_serialization" option, it's possible to store some booleans), you can use a more compact construction like:

```
// we assume you already have $cache

$id = 'myBigLoop'; // cache id of "what we want to cache"

if (!($data = $cache->load($id))) {
```

```
    // cache miss

    $data = '';
    for ($i = 0; $i < 10000; $i++) {
        $data = $data . $i;
    }

    $cache->save($data);

}

// [...] do something with $data (echo it, pass it on etc.)
```

If you want to cache multiple blocks or data instances, the idea is the same:

```
// make sure you use unique identifiers:
$id1 = 'foo';
$id2 = 'bar';

// block 1
if (!($data = $cache->load($id1))) {
    // cache missed

    $data = '';
    for ($i=0;$i<10000;$i++) {
        $data = $data . $i;
    }

    $cache->save($data);

}
echo($data);

// this isn't affected by caching
echo('NEVER CACHED! ');

// block 2
if (!($data = $cache->load($id2))) {
    // cache missed

    $data = '';
    for ($i=0;$i<10000;$i++) {
        $data = $data . '!';
    }

    $cache->save($data);

}
echo($data);
```

If you want to cache special values (boolean with "automatic_serialization" option) or empty strings you can't use the compact construction given above. You have to test formally the cache record.

```
// the compact construction
// (not good if you cache empty strings and/or booleans)
if (!($data = $cache->load($id))) {

    // cache missed

    // [...] we make $data
```

```
        $cache->save($data);

}

// we do something with $data

// [...]

// the complete construction (works in any case)
if (!($cache->test($id))) {

    // cache missed

    // [...] we make $data

    $cache->save($data);

} else {

    // cache hit

    $data = $cache->load($id);

}

// we do something with $data
```

Zend_Cache_Frontend_Output

Introduction

Zend_Cache_Frontend_Output is an output-capturing frontend. It utilizes output buffering in PHP to capture everything between its start() and end() methods.

Available Options

This frontend doesn't have any specific options other than those of Zend_Cache_Core.

Examples

An example is given in the manual at the very beginning. Here it is with minor changes:

```
// if it is a cache miss, output buffering is triggered
if (!($cache->start('mypage'))) {

    // output everything as usual
    echo 'Hello world! ';
    echo 'This is cached ('.time().') ';

    $cache->end(); // output buffering ends

}

echo 'This is never cached ('.time().').';
```

Using this form it is fairly easy to set up output caching in your already working project with little or no code refactoring.

Zend_Cache_Frontend_Function

Introduction

Zend_Cache_Frontend_Function caches the results of function calls. It has a single main method named call() which takes a function name and parameters for the call in an array.

Available Options

Table 6.2. Function Frontend Options

Option	Data Type	Default Value	Description
cache_by_default	boolean	true	if true, function calls will be cached by default
cached_functions	array		function names which will always be cached
non_cached_funct ions	array		function names which must never be cached

Examples

Using the call() function is the same as using call_user_func_array() in PHP:

```
$cache->call('veryExpensiveFunc', $params);

// $params is an array
// For example to call veryExpensiveFunc(1, 'foo', 'bar') with
// caching, you can use
// $cache->call('veryExpensiveFunc', array(1, 'foo', 'bar'))
```

Zend_Cache_Frontend_Function is smart enough to cache both the return value of the function and its internal output.

Note

You can pass any built in or user defined function with the exception of array(), echo(), empty(), eval(), exit(), isset(), list(), print() and unset().

Zend_Cache_Frontend_Class

Introduction

Zend_Cache_Frontend_Class is different from Zend_Cache_Frontend_Function because it allows caching of object and static method calls.

Available Options

Table 6.3. Class Frontend Options

Option	Data Type	Default Value	Description
cached_entity (required)	mixed		if set to a class name, we will cache an abstract class and will use only static calls; if set to an object, we will cache this object methods
cache_by_default	boolean	true	if true, calls will be cached by default
cached_methods	array		method names which will always be cached
non_cached_metho ds	array		method names which must never be cached

Examples

For example, to cache static calls :

```
class Test {

    // Static method
    public static function foobar($param1, $param2) {
        echo "foobar_output($param1, $param2)";
        return "foobar_return($param1, $param2)";
    }

}
// [...]
$frontendOptions = array(
    'cached_entity' => 'Test' // The name of the class
);
// [...]

// The cached call
$result = $cache->foobar('1', '2');
```

To cache classic method calls :

```
class Test {

    private $_string = 'hello !';

    public function foobar2($param1, $param2) {
        echo($this->_string);
        echo "foobar2_output($param1, $param2)";
        return "foobar2_return($param1, $param2)";
    }
```

```
}
// [...]
$frontendOptions = array(
    'cached_entity' => new Test() // An instance of the class
);
// [...]

// The cached call
$result = $cache->foobar2('1', '2');
```

Zend_Cache_Frontend_File

Introduction

Zend_Cache_Frontend_File is a frontend driven by the modification time of a "master file". It's really interesting for examples in configuration or templates issues. It's also possible to use multiple master files.

For instance, you have an XML configuration file which is parsed by a function which returns a "config object" (like with Zend_Config). With Zend_Cache_Frontend_File, you can store the "config object" into cache (to avoid the parsing of the XML config file at each time) but with a sort of strong dependency on the "master file". So, if the XML config file is modified, the cache is immediately invalidated.

Available Options

Table 6.4. File Frontend Options

Option	Data Type	Default Value	Description
master_file (deprecated)	string		the complete path and name of the master file
master_files	array		an array of complete path of master files
master_files_mode	string	Zend_Cache_Frontend_File::MODE_OR	Zend_Cache_Frontend_File::MODE_AND or Zend_Cache_Frontend_File::MODE_OR ; if MODE_AND, then all master files have to be touched to get a cache invalidation if MODE_OR, then a single touched master file is enough to get a cache invalidation
ignore_missing_master_files	boolean	false	if true, missing master files are ignored silently (an exception is raised else)

Examples

Use of this frontend is the same than of Zend_Cache_Core. There is no need of a specific example - the only thing to do is to define the master_file when using the factory.

Zend_Cache_Frontend_Page

Introduction

Zend_Cache_Frontend_Page is like Zend_Cache_Frontend_Output but designed for a complete page. It's impossible to use Zend_Cache_Frontend_Page for caching only a single block.

On the other hand, the "cache id" is calculated automatically with $_SERVER['REQUEST_URI'] and (depending on options) $_GET, $_POST, $_SESSION, $_COOKIE, $_FILES. More over, you have only one method to call (start()) because the end() call is fully automatic when the page is ended.

For the moment, it's not implemented but we plan to add a HTTP conditional system to save bandwidth (the system will send a HTTP 304 Not Modified if the cache is hit and if the browser has already the good version).

Available Options

Table 6.5. Page Frontend Options

Option	Data Type	Default Value	Description
http_conditional	boolean	false	use the http_conditional system (not implemented for the moment)
debug_header	boolean	false	if true, a debug text is added before each cached pages
default_options	array	array(...see below...)	an associative array of default options : • (boolean, true by default) cache : cache is on if true • (boolean, false by default) cache_with_get_variables : if true, cache is still on even if there are some variables in $_GET array • (boolean, false by default) cache_with_post_variables : if

Option	Data Type	Default Value	Description
			true, cache is still on even if there are some variables in $_POST array
			• (boolean, false by default) cache_with_session_variables : if true, cache is still on even if there are some variables in $_SESSION array
			• (boolean, false by default) cache_with_files_variables : if true, cache is still on even if there are some variables in $_FILES array
			• (boolean, false by default) cache_with_cookie_variables : if true, cache is still on even if there are some variables in $_COOKIE array
			• (boolean, true by default) make_id_with_get_variables : if true, the cache id will be dependent of the content of the $_GET array
			• (boolean, true by default) make_id_with_post_variables : if true, the cache id will be dependent of the content of the $_POST array
			• (boolean, true by default) make_id_with_ses-

Option	Data Type	Default Value	Description
			sion_variables : if true, the cache id will be dependent of the content of the $_SESSION array • (boolean, true by default) make_id_with_f iles_variables : if true, the cache id will be dependent of the content of the $_FILES array • (boolean, true by default) make_id_with_c ook- ie_variables : if true, the cache id will be dependent of the content of the $_COOKIE array • (int, false by default) specific_life time : if not false, the given lifetime will be used for the choosen regexp • (array, array() by default) tags : tags for the cache record • (int, null by default) priority : priority (if the backend supports it)
regexps	array	array()	an associative array to set options only for some REQUEST_URI, keys are (PCRE) regexps, values are associative arrays with specific options to set if the regexp matchs on $_SERVER['REQUEST _URI'] (see de- fault_options for the list of available options) ; if

Option	Data Type	Default Value	Description
			several regexps match the $_SERVER['REQUEST_URI'], only the last one will be used
memorize_headers	array	array()	an array of strings corresponding to some HTTP headers name. Listed headers will be stored with cache datas and "replayed" when the cache is hit

Examples

Use of Zend_Cache_Frontend_Page is really trivial:

```
// [...] // require, configuration and factory

$cache->start();
// if the cache is hit, the result is sent to the browser
// and the script stop here

// rest of the page ...
```

a more complex example which shows a way to get a centralized cache management in a bootstrap file (for using with Zend_Controller for example)

```
/*
 * You should avoid putting too many lines before the cache section.
 * For example, for optimal performances, "require_once" or
 * "Zend_Loader::loadClass" should be after the cache section.
 */

$frontendOptions = array(
    'lifetime' => 7200,
    'debug_header' => true, // for debugging
    'regexps' => array(
        // cache the whole IndexController
        '^/$' => array('cache' => true),

        // cache the whole IndexController
        '^/index/' => array('cache' => true),

        // we don't cache the ArticleController...
        '^/article/' => array('cache' => false),

        // ... but we cache the "view" action of this ArticleController
        '^/article/view/' => array(
            'cache' => true,

            // and we cache even there are some variables in $_POST
            'cache_with_post_variables' => true,

            // but the cache will be dependent on the $_POST array
            'make_id_with_post_variables' => true
```

```
            )
        )
);

$backendOptions = array(
    'cache_dir' => '/tmp/'
);

// getting a Zend_Cache_Frontend_Page object
$cache = Zend_Cache::factory('Page',
                             'File',
                             $frontendOptions,
                             $backendOptions);

$cache->start();
// if the cache is hit, the result is sent to the browser and the
// script stop here

// [...] the end of the bootstrap file
// these lines won't be executed if the cache is hit
```

The Specific Cancel Method

Because of design issues, in some cases (for example when using non HTTP/200 return codes), you could need to cancel the current cache process. So we introduce for this particular frontend, the cancel() method.

```
// [...] // require, configuration and factory

$cache->start();

// [...]

if ($someTest) {
    $cache->cancel();
    // [...]
}

// [...]
```

Zend_Cache Backends

There are two kinds of backends: standard ones and extended ones. Of course, extended backends offer more features.

Zend_Cache_Backend_File

This (extended) backends stores cache records into files (in a choosen directory).

Available options are :

Table 6.6. File Backend Options

Option	Data Type	Default Value	Description
cache_dir	string	'/tmp/'	Directory where to store cache files
file_locking	boolean	true	Enable / disable file_ locking : Can avoid cache corruption under bad circumstances but it doesn't help on multith-read webservers or on NFS filesystems...
read_control	boolean	true	Enable / disable read control : if enabled, a control key is embedded in the cache file and this key is compared with the one calculated after the reading.
read_control_type	string	'crc32'	Type of read control (only if read control is enabled). Available values are : 'md5' (best but slowest), 'crc32' (lightly less safe but faster, better choice), 'adler32' (new choice, faster than crc32), 'strlen' for a length only test (fastest).
hashed_directory _level	int	0	Hashed directory struc-ture level : 0 means "no hashed directory struc-ture", 1 means "one level of directory", 2 means "two levels"... This op-tion can speed up the cache only when you have many thousands of cache files. Only specif-ic benchs can help you to choose the perfect value for you. Maybe, 1 or 2 is a good start.
hashed_directory _umask	int	0700	Umask for the hashed directory structure
file_name_prefix	string	'zend_cache'	prefix for cache files ; be really careful with this option because a too generic value in a system cache dir (like /tmp) can cause disasters when cleaning the cache

Option	Data Type	Default Value	Description
`cache_file_umask`	`int`	`0700`	umask for cache files
`meta-tadatas_array_max_size`	`int`	`100`	internal max size for the metadatas array (don't change this value unless you know what you are doing)

Zend_Cache_Backend_Sqlite

This (extended) backends stores cache records into a SQLite database.

Available options are :

Table 6.7. Sqlite Backend Options

Option	Data Type	Default Value	Description
`cache_db_complete_path` (mandatory)	`string`	`null`	The complete path (filename included) of the SQLite database
`automatic_vacuum_factor`	`int`	`10`	Disable / Tune the automatic vacuum process. The automatic vacuum process defragment the database file (and make it smaller) when a clean() or delete() is called : 0 means no automatic vacuum ; 1 means systematic vacuum (when delete() or clean() methods are called) ; x (integer) > 1 => automatic vacuum randomly 1 times on x clean() or delete().

Zend_Cache_Backend_Memcached

This (extended) backends stores cache records into a memcached server. memcached [http://www.danga.com/memcached/] is a high-performance, distributed memory object caching system. To use this backend, you need a memcached daemon and the memcache PECL extension [http://pecl.php.net/package/memcache].

Be careful : with this backend, "tags" are not supported for the moment as the "doNotTestCacheValidity=true" argument.

Available options are :

Table 6.8. Memcached Backend Options

Option	Data Type	Default Value	Description
servers	array	`array(array('host => 'localhost', 'port' => 11211, 'persistent' => true, 'weight' => 1, 'timeout' => 5, 'retry_interval' => 15, 'status' => true, 'failure_callback => '' ))`	An array of memcached servers ; each memcached server is described by an associative array : 'host' => (string) : the name of the memcached server, 'port' => (int) : the port of the memcached server, 'persistent' => (bool) : use or not persistent connections to this memcached server 'weight' => (int) :the weight of the memcached server, 'timeout' => (int) :the time out of the memcached server, 'retry_interval' => (int) :the retry interval of the memcached server, 'status' => (bool) :the status of the memcached server, 'failure_callback' => (callback) : the failure_callback of the memcached server
compression	boolean	false	true if you want to use on-the-fly compression
compatibility	boolean	false	true if you want to use this compatibility mode with old memcache servers/extensions

Zend_Cache_Backend_Apc

This (extended) backends stores cache records in shared memory through the APC [http://pecl.php.net/package/APC] (Alternative PHP Cache) extension (which is of course need for using this backend).

Be careful : with this backend, "tags" are not supported for the moment as the "doNotTestCacheValidity=true" argument.

There is no option for this backend.

Zend_Cache_Backend_Xcache

This backends stores cache records in shared memory through the XCache [http://xcache.lighttpd.net/] extension (which is of course need for using this backend).

Be careful : with this backend, "tags" are not supported for the moment as the "doNotTestCacheValidity=true" argument.

Available options are :

Table 6.9. Xcache Backend Options

Option	Data Type	Default Value	Description
user	string	null	xcache.admin.user, necessary for the clean() method
password	string	null	xcache.admin.pass (in clear form, not MD5), necessary for the clean() method

Zend_Cache_Backend_ZendPlatform

This backend uses content caching API of the Zend Platform [http://www.zend.com/products/platform] product. Naturally, to use this backend you need to have Zend Platform installed.

This backend supports tags, but does not support CLEANING_MODE_NOT_MATCHING_TAG cleaning mode.

Specify this backend using a word separator -- '-', '.', ' ', or '_' -- between the words 'Zend' and 'Platform' when using the Zend_Cache::factory() method:

```
$cache = Zend_Cache::factory('Core', 'Zend Platform');
```

There are no options for this backend.

Zend_Cache_Backend_TwoLevels

This (extend) backend is an hybrid one. It stores cache records in two other backends : a fast one (but limited) like Apc, Memcache... and a "slow" one like File, Sqlite...

This backend will use the priority parameter (given at the frontend level when storing a record) and the remaining space in the fast backend to optimize the usage of these two backends. FIXME

Available options are :

Table 6.10. TwoLevels Backend Options

Option	Data Type	Default Value	Description
slow_backend	string	File	the "slow" backend name
fast_backend	string	Apc	the "fast" backend name
slow_backend_opt ions	array	array()	the "slow" backend options
fast_backend_opt ions	array	array()	the "fast" backend options
slow_backend_cus tom_naming	boolean	false	if true, the slow_backend argument is used as a complete class name ; if false, the frontend argument is used as the end of "Zend_Cache_Backend_ [...]" class name
fast_backend_cus tom_naming	boolean	false	if true, the fast_backend argument is used as a complete class name ; if false, the frontend argument is used as the end of "Zend_Cache_Backend_ [...]" class name
slow_backend_aut oload	boolean	false	if true, there will no require_once for the slow backend (useful only for custom backends)
fast_backend_aut oload	boolean	false	if true, there will no require_once for the fast backend (useful only for custom backends)
auto_refresh_fas t_cache	boolean	true	if true, auto refresh the fast cache when a cache record is hit
stats_update_fac tor	integer	10	disable / tune the computation of the fast backend filling percentage (when saving a record into cache, computation of the fast backend filling percentage randomly 1 times on x cache writes)

Zend_Cache_Backend_ZendServer_Disk and Zend_Cache_Backend_ZendServer_ShMem

These backends store cache records using Zend Server [http://www.zend.com/en/products/server/downloads-all?zfs=zf_download] caching functionality.

Be careful: with these backends, "tags" are not supported for the moment as the "doNotTestCacheValidity=true" argument.

These backend work only withing Zend Server environment for pages requested through HTTP(S) and don't work for command line script execution

There is no option for this backend.

Chapter 7. Zend_Captcha

Introduction

CAPTCHA [http://en.wikipedia.org/wiki/Captcha] stands for "Completely Automated Public Turing test to tell Computers and Humans Apart"; it is used as a challenge-response to ensure that the individual submitting information is a human and not an automated process. Typically, a captcha is used with form submissions where authenticated users are not necessary, but you want to prevent spam submissions.

Captchas can take a variety of forms, including asking logic questions, presenting skewed fonts, and presenting multiple images and asking how they relate. Zend_Captcha aims to provide a variety of back ends that may be utilized either standalone or in conjunction with Zend_Form.

Captcha Operation

All CAPTCHA adapter implement Zend_Captcha_Adapter, which looks like the following:

```
interface Zend_Captcha_Adapter extends Zend_Validate_Interface
{
    public function generate();

    public function render(Zend_View $view, $element = null);

    public function setName($name);

    public function getName();

    public function getDecorator();

    // Additionally, to satisfy Zend_Validate_Interface:
    public function isValid($value);

    public function getMessages();

    public function getErrors();
}
```

The name setter and getter are used to specify and retrieve the CAPTCHA identifier. getDecorator() can be used to specify a Zend_Form decorator either by name or returning an actual decorator object. The most interesting methods are generate() and render(). generate() is used to create the CAPTCHA token. This process typically will store the token in the session so that you may compare against it in subsequent requests. render() is used to render the information that represents the CAPTCHA- be it an image, a figlet, a logic problem, or some other CAPTCHA.

A typical use case might look like the following:

```
// Creating a Zend_View instance
$view = new Zend_View();

// Originating request:
$captcha = new Zend_Captcha_Figlet(array(
    'name' => 'foo',
    'wordLen' => 6,
    'timeout' => 300,
));
```

```
$id = $captcha->generate();
echo $captcha->render($view);

// On subsequent request:
// Assume captcha setup as before, and $value is the submitted value:
if ($captcha->isValid($_POST['foo'], $_POST)) {
    // Validated!
}
```

CAPTCHA Adapters

The following adapters are shipped with Zend Framework by default.

Zend_Captcha_Word

Zend_Captcha_Word is an abstract adapter that serves as the base class for most other CAPTCHA adapters. It provides mutators for specifying word length, session TTL, the session namespace object to use, and the session namespace class to use for persistence if you do not wish to use Zend_Session_Namespace. Zend_Captcha_Word encapsulates validation logic.

By default, the word length is 8 characters, the session timeout is 5 minutes, and Zend_Session_Namespace is used for persistence (using the namespace "Zend_Form _Captcha_<captcha ID>").

In addition to the methods required by the Zend_Captcha_Adapter interface, Zend_Captcha_Word exposes the following methods:

- setWordLen($length) and getWordLen() allow you to specify the length of the generated "word" in characters, and to retrieve the current value.

- setTimeout($ttl) and getTimeout() allow you to specify the time-to-live of the session token, and to retrieve the current value. $ttl should be specified in seconds.

- setSessionClass($class) and getSessionClass() allow you to specify an alternate Zend_Session_Namespace implementation to use to persist the CAPTCHA token and to retrieve the current value.

- getId() allows you to retrieve the current token identifier.

- getWord() allows you to retrieve the generated word to use with the CAPTCHA. It will generate the word for you if none has been generated yet.

- setSession(Zend_Session_Namespace $session) allows you to specify a session object to use for persisting the CAPTCHA token. getSession() allows you to retrieve the current session object.

All word CAPTCHAs allow you to pass an array of options to the constructor, or, alternately, pass them to setOptions(). You can also pass a Zend_Config object to setConfig(). By default, the wordLen, timeout, and sessionClass keys may all be used. Each concrete implementation may define additional keys or utilize the options in other ways.

Note

Zend_Captcha_Word is an abstract class and may not be instantiated directly.

Zend_Captcha_Dumb

The `Zend_Captch_Dumb` adapter is mostly self-descriptive. It provides a random string that must be typed in reverse to validate. As such, it's not a good CAPTCHA solution and should only be used for testing. It extends `Zend_Captcha_Word`.

Zend_Captcha_Figlet

The `Zend_Captcha_Figlet` adapter utilizes `Zend_Text_Figlet` to present a figlet to the user.

Options passed to the constructor will also be passed to the Zend_Text_Figlet object. See the Zend_Text_Figletdocumentation for details on what configuration options are available.

Zend_Captcha_Image

The Zend_Captcha_Image adapter takes the generated word and renders it as an image, performing various skewing permutations to make it difficult to automatically decipher. It requires the GD extension [http://php.net/gd] compiled with TrueType or Freetype support. Currently, the Zend_Captcha_Image adapter can only generate PNG images.

`Zend_Captcha_Image` extends `Zend_Captcha_Word`, and additionally exposes the following methods:

- `setExpiration($expiration)` and `getExpiration()` allow you to specify a maximum lifetime the CAPTCHA image may reside on the filesystem. This is typically a longer than the session lifetime. Garbage collection is run periodically each time the CAPTCHA object is invoked, deleting all images that have expired. Expiration values should be specified in seconds.

- `setGcFreq($gcFreq)` and `getGcFreg()` allow you to specify how frequently garbage collection should run. Garbage collection will run every 1/`$gcFreq` calls. The default is 100.

- `setFont($font)` and `getFont()` allow you to specify the font you will use. `$font` should be a fully qualified path to the font file. This value is required; the CAPTCHA will throw an exception during generation if the font file has not been specified.

- `setFontSize($fsize)` and `getFontSize()` allow you to specify the font size in pixels for generating the CAPTCHA. The default is 24px.

- `setHeight($height)` and `getHeight()` allow you to specify the height in pixels of the generated CAPTCHA image. The default is 50px.

- `setWidth($width)` and `getWidth()` allow you to specify the width in pixels of the generated CAPTCHA image. The default is 200px.

- `setImgDir($imgDir)` and `getImgDir()` allow you to specify the directory for storing CAPTCHA images. The default is "./images/captcha/", relative to the bootstrap script.

- `setImgUrl($imgUrl)` and `getImgUrl()` allow you to specify the relative path to a CAPTCHA image to use for HTML markup. The default is "/images/captcha/".

- `setSuffix($suffix)` and `getSuffix()` allow you to specify the filename suffix for the CAPTCHA image. The default is ".png". Note: changing this value will not change the type of the generated image.

All of the above options may be passed to the constructor by simply removing the 'set' method prefix and casting the initial letter to lowercase: "suffix", "height", "imgUrl", etc.

Zend_Captcha_ReCaptcha

The Zend_Captcha_ReCaptcha adapter uses Zend_Service_ReCaptcha to generate and validate CAPTCHAs. It exposes the following methods:

- setPrivKey($key) and getPrivKey() allow you to specify the private key to use for the ReCaptcha service. This must be specified during construction, although it may be overridden at any point.

- setPubKey($key) and getPubKey() allow you to specify the public key to use with the ReCaptcha service. This must be specified during construction, although it may be overridden at any point.

- setService(Zend_Service_ReCaptcha $service) and getService() allow you to set and get the ReCaptcha service object.

Chapter 8. Zend_CodeGenerator

Introduction

Zend_CodeGenerator provides facilities to generate arbitrary code using an object oriented interface, both to create new code as well as to update existing code. While the current implementation is limited to generating PHP code, you can easily extend the base class in order to provide code generation for other tasks: JavaScript, configuration files, apache vhosts, etc.

Theory of Operation

In the most typical use case, you will simply instantiate a code generator class and either pass it the appropriate configuration or configure it after instantiation. To generate the code, you will simply echo the object or call its generate() method.

```
// Passing configuration to the constructor:
$file = new Zend_CodeGenerator_Php_File(array(
    'classes' => array(
        new Zend_CodeGenerator_Php_Class(array(
            'name'    => 'World',
            'methods' => array(
                new Zend_CodeGenerator_Php_Method(array(
                    'name' => 'hello',
                    'body' => 'echo \'Hello world!\';',
                )),
            ),
        )),
    )
));

// Configuring after instantiation
$method = new Zend_CodeGenerator_Php_Method();
$method->setName('hello')
       ->setBody('echo \'Hello world!\';');

$class = new Zend_CodeGenerator_Php_Class();
$class->setName('World')
      ->setMethod($method);

$file = new Zend_CodeGenerator_Php_File();
$file->setClass($class);

// Render the generated file
echo $file;

// or write it to a file:
file_put_contents('World.php', $file->generate());
```

Both of the above samples will render the same result:

```
<?php

class World
{

    public function hello()
```

```
    {
        echo 'Hello world!';
    }

}
```

Another common use case is to update existing code -- for instance, to add a method to a class. In such a case, you must first inspect the existing code using reflection, and then add your new method. Zend_CodeGenerator makes this trivially simple, by leveraging Zend_Reflection.

As an example, let's say we've saved the above to the file "World.php", and have already included it. We could then do the following:

```
$class = Zend_CodeGenerator_Php_Class::fromReflection(
    new Zend_Reflection_Class('World')
);

$method = new Zend_CodeGenerator_Php_Method();
$method->setName('mrMcFeeley')
       ->setBody('echo \'Hello, Mr. McFeeley!\';');
$class->setMethod($method);

$file = new Zend_CodeGenerator_Php_File();
$file->setClass($class);

// Render the generated file
echo $file;

// Or, better yet, write it back to the original file:
file_put_contents('World.php', $file->generate());
```

The resulting class file will now look like this:

```
<?php

class World
{

    public function hello()
    {
        echo 'Hello world!';
    }

    public function mrMcFeeley()
    {
        echo 'Hellow Mr. McFeeley!';
    }

}
```

Zend_CodeGenerator Examples

Example 8.1. Generating PHP classes

The following example generates an empty class with a class-level DocBlock.

```
$foo       = new Zend_CodeGenerator_Php_Class();
$docblock = new Zend_CodeGenerator_Php_Docblock(array(
    'shortDescription' => 'Sample generated class',
    'longDescription'  => 'This is a class generated with Zend
        _CodeGenerator.',
    'tags'             => array(
        array(
            'name'        => 'version',
            'description' => '$Rev:$',
        ),
        array(
            'name'        => 'license',
            'description' => 'New BSD',
        ),
    ),
));
$foo->setName('Foo')
    ->setDocblock($docblock);
echo $foo->generate();
```

The above code will result in the following:

```
/**
 * Sample generated class
 *
 * This is a class generated with Zend_CodeGenerator.
 *
 * @version $Rev:$
 * @license New BSD
 *
 */
class Foo
{

}
```

Example 8.2. Generating PHP classes with class properties

Building on the previous example, we now add properties to our generated class.

```
$foo       = new Zend_CodeGenerator_Php_Class();
$docblock = new Zend_CodeGenerator_Php_Docblock(array(
    'shortDescription' => 'Sample generated class',
    'longDescription'  => 'This is a class generated with
        Zend_CodeGenerator.',
    'tags'             => array(
        array(
            'name'        => 'version',
            'description' => '$Rev:$',
        ),
        array(
            'name'        => 'license',
            'description' => 'New BSD',
        ),
    ),
));
```

```
$foo->setName('Foo')
    ->setDocblock($docblock)
    ->setProperties(array(
        array(
            'name'         => '_bar',
            'visibility'   => 'protected',
            'defaultValue' => 'baz',
        ),
        array(
            'name'         => 'baz',
            'visibility'    => 'public',
            'defaultValue' => 'bat',
        ),
        array(
            'name'         => 'bat',
            'const'        => true,
            'defaultValue' => 'foobarbazbat',
        ),
    ));
echo $foo->generate();
```

The above results in the following class definition:

```
/**
 * Sample generated class
 *
 * This is a class generated with Zend_CodeGenerator.
 *
 * @version $Rev:$
 * @license New BSD
 *
 */
class Foo
{

    protected $_bar = 'baz';

    public $baz = 'bat';

    const bat = 'foobarbazbat';

}
```

Example 8.3. Generating PHP classes with class methods

Zend_CodeGenerator_Php_Class allows you to attach methods with optional content to your classes. Methods may be attached as either arrays or concrete Zend_CodeGenerator _Php_Method instances.

```
$foo      = new Zend_CodeGenerator_Php_Class();
$docblock = new Zend_CodeGenerator_Php_Docblock(array(
    'shortDescription' => 'Sample generated class',
    'longDescription'  => 'This is a class generated with Zend
        _CodeGenerator.',
    'tags'             => array(
```

```
            array(
                'name'         => 'version',
                'description' => '$Rev:$',
            ),
            array(
                'name'         => 'license',
                'description' => 'New BSD',
            ),
        ),
    ));
$foo->setName('Foo')
    ->setDocblock($docblock)
    ->setProperties(array(
        array(
            'name'         => '_bar',
            'visibility'   => 'protected',
            'defaultValue' => 'baz',
        ),
        array(
            'name'         => 'baz',
            'visibility'   => 'public',
            'defaultValue' => 'bat',
        ),
        array(
            'name'         => 'bat',
            'const'        => true,
            'defaultValue' => 'foobarbazbat',
        ),
    ))
    ->setMethods(array(
        // Method passed as array
        array(
            'name'       => 'setBar',
            'parameters' => array(
                array('name' => 'bar'),
            ),
            'body'       => '$this->_bar = $bar;' . "\n" . 'return $this;',
            'docblock'   => new Zend_CodeGenerator_Php_Docblock(array(
                'shortDescription' => 'Set the bar property',
                'tags'             => array(
                    new Zend_CodeGenerator_Php_Docblock_Tag_Param(array(
                        'paramName' => 'bar',
                        'datatype'  => 'string'
                    )),
                    new Zend_CodeGenerator_Php_Docblock_Tag_Return(array(
                        'datatype'  => 'string',
                    )),
                ),
            )),
        ),
        // Method passed as concrete instance
        new Zend_CodeGenerator_Php_Method(array(
            'name' => 'getBar',
            'body'       => 'return $this->_bar;',
            'docblock'   => new Zend_CodeGenerator_Php_Docblock(array(
                'shortDescription' => 'Retrieve the bar property',
                'tags'             => array(
                    new Zend_CodeGenerator_Php_Docblock_Tag_Return(array(
                        'datatype'  => 'string|null',
                    )),
                ),
            )),
        )),
    ));
```

```
echo $foo->generate();
```

The above generates the following output:

```
/**
 * Sample generated class
 *
 * This is a class generated with Zend_CodeGenerator.
 *
 * @version $Rev:$
 * @license New BSD
 */
class Foo
{

    protected $_bar = 'baz';

    public $baz = 'bat';

    const bat = 'foobarbazbat';

    /**
     * Set the bar property
     *
     * @param string bar
     * @return string
     */
    public function setBar($bar)
    {
        $this->_bar = $bar;
        return $this;
    }

    /**
     * Retrieve the bar property
     *
     * @return string|null
     */


    public function getBar()
    {
        return $this->_bar;
    }
}
```

Example 8.4. Generating PHP files

Zend_CodeGenerator_Php_File can be used to generate the contents of a PHP file. You can include classes as well as arbitrary content body. When attaching classes, you should attach either concrete Zend_CodeGenerator_Php_Class instances or an array defining the class.

In the example below, we will assume you've defined $foo per one of the class definitions in a previous example.

```
$file = new Zend_CodeGenerator_Php_File(array(
    'classes'  => array($foo);
    'docblock' => new Zend_CodeGenerator_Php_Docblock(array(
        'shortDescription' => 'Foo class file',
        'tags'             => array(
            array(
                'name'        => 'license',
                'description' => 'New BSD',
            ),
        ),
    )),
    'body'     => 'define(\'APPLICATION_ENV\', \'testing\');',
));
```

Calling generate() will generate the code -- but not write it to a file. You will need to capture the contents and write them to a file yourself. As an example:

```
$code = $file->generate();
file_put_contents('Foo.php', $code);
```

The above will generate the following file:

```
<?php
/**
 * Foo class file
 *
 * @license New BSD
 */

/**
 * Sample generated class
 *
 * This is a class generated with Zend_CodeGenerator.
 *
 * @version $Rev:$
 * @license New BSD
 */
class Foo
{

    protected $_bar = 'baz';

    public $baz = 'bat';

    const bat = 'foobarbazbat';

    /**
     * Set the bar property
     *
     * @param string bar
     * @return string
     */
    public function setBar($bar)
    {
        $this->_bar = $bar;
        return $this;
    }

    /**
```

```
 * Retrieve the bar property
 *
 * @return string|null
 */
public function getBar()
{
    return $this->_bar;
}

}

define('APPLICATION_ENV', 'testing');
```

Example 8.5. Seeding PHP file code generation via reflection

You can add PHP code to an existing PHP file using the code generator. To do so, you need to first do reflection on it. The static method fromReflectedFileName() allows you to do this.

```
$generator = Zend_CodeGenerator_Php_File::fromReflectedFileName($path);
$body = $generator->getBody();
$body .= "\n\$foo->bar();";
file_put_contents($path, $generator->generate());
```

Example 8.6. Seeding PHP class generation via reflection

You may add code to an existing class. To do so, first use the static fromReflection() method to map the class into a generator object. From there, you may add additional properties or methods, and then regenerate the class.

```
$generator = Zend_CodeGenerator_Php_Class::fromReflection(
    new Zend_Reflection_Class($class)
);
$generator->setMethod(array(
    'name'       => 'setBaz',
    'parameters' => array(
        array('name' => 'baz'),
    ),
    'body'       => '$this->_baz = $baz;' . "\n" . 'return $this;',
    'docblock'   => new Zend_CodeGenerator_Php_Docblock(array(
        'shortDescription' => 'Set the baz property',
        'tags'             => array(
            new Zend_CodeGenerator_Php_Docblock_Tag_Param(array(
                'paramName' => 'baz',
                'datatype'  => 'string'
            )),
            new Zend_CodeGenerator_Php_Docblock_Tag_Return(array(
                'datatype'  => 'string',
            )),
        ),
    )),
));
$code = $generator->generate();
```

Zend_CodeGenerator Reference

Abstract Classes and Interfaces

Zend_CodeGenerator_Abstract

The base class from which all CodeGenerator classes inherit provides the minimal functionality necessary. It's API is as follows:

```
abstract class Zend_CodeGenerator_Abstract
{
    final public function __construct(Array $options = array())
    public function setOptions(Array $options)
    public function setSourceContent($sourceContent)
    public function getSourceContent()
    protected function _init()
    protected function _prepare()
    abstract public function generate();
    final public function __toString()
}
```

The constructor first calls _init() (which is left empty for the concrete extending class to implement), then passes the $options parameter to setOptions(), and finally calls _prepare() (again, to be implemented by an extending class).

Like most classes in Zend Framework, setOptions() compares an option key to existing setters in the class, and passes the value on to that method if found.

__toString() is marked as final, and proxies to generate().

setSourceContent() and getSourceContent() are intended to either set the default content for the code being generated, or to replace said content once all generation tasks are complete.

Zend_CodeGenerator_Php_Abstract

Zend_CodeGenerator_Php_Abstract extends Zend_CodeGenerator_Abstract, and adds some properties for tracking whether content has changed as well as the amount of indentation that should appear before generated content. Its API is as follows:

```
abstract class Zend_CodeGenerator_Php_Abstract
    extends Zend_CodeGenerator_Abstract
{
    public function setSourceDirty($isSourceDirty = true)
    public function isSourceDirty()
    public function setIndentation($indentation)
    public function getIndentation()
}
```

Zend_CodeGenerator_Php_Member_Abstract

Zend_CodeGenerator_Php_Member_Abstract is a base class for generating class members -- properties and methods -- and provides accessors and mutators for establishing visibility; whether or not the member is abstract, static, or final; and the name of the member. Its API is as follows:

```
abstract class Zend_CodeGenerator_Php_Member_Abstract
    extends Zend_CodeGenerator_Php_Abstract
{
    public function setAbstract($isAbstract)
    public function isAbstract()
    public function setStatic($isStatic)
    public function isStatic()
    public function setVisibility($visibility)
    public function getVisibility()
    public function setName($name)
    public function getName()
}
```

Concrete CodeGenerator Classes

Zend_CodeGenerator_Php_Body

Zend_CodeGenerator_Php_Body is intended for generating arbitrary procedural code to include within a file. As such, you simply set content for the object, and it will return that content when you invoke generate().

The API of the class is as follows:

```
class Zend_CodeGenerator_Php_Body extends Zend_CodeGenerator_Php
    _Abstract
{
    public function setContent($content)
    public function getContent()
    public function generate()
}
```

Zend_CodeGenerator_Php_Class

Zend_CodeGenerator_Php_Class is intended for generating PHP classes. The basic functionality just generates the PHP class itself, as well as optionally the related PHP DocBlock. Classes may implement or inherit from other classes, and may be marked as abstract. Utilizing other code generator classes, you can also attach class constants, properties, and methods.

The API is as follows:

```
class Zend_CodeGenerator_Php_Class extends Zend_CodeGenerator_Php_Abstract
{
    public static function fromReflection(
        Zend_Reflection_Class $reflectionClass
    )
    public function setDocblock(Zend_CodeGenerator_Php_Docblock $docblock)
    public function getDocblock()
    public function setName($name)
    public function getName()
    public function setAbstract($isAbstract)
    public function isAbstract()
    public function setExtendedClass($extendedClass)
    public function getExtendedClass()
    public function setImplementedInterfaces(Array $implementedInterfaces)
    public function getImplementedInterfaces()
    public function setProperties(Array $properties)
    public function setProperty($property)
    public function getProperties()
```

```
    public function getProperty($propertyName)
    public function setMethods(Array $methods)
    public function setMethod($method)
    public function getMethods()
    public function getMethod($methodName)
    public function hasMethod($methodName)
    public function isSourceDirty()
    public function generate()
}
```

The `setProperty()` method accepts an array of information that may be used to generate a `Zend_CodeGenerator_Php_Property` instance -- or simply an instance of `Zend_CodeGenerator_Php_Property`. Likewise, `setMethod()` accepts either an array of information for generating a `Zend_CodeGenerator_Php_Method` instance or a concrete instance of that class.

Note that `setDocBlock()` expects an instance of `Zend_CodeGenerator_Php_DocBlock`.

Zend_CodeGenerator_Php_Docblock

`Zend_CodeGenerator_Php_Docblock` can be used to generate arbitrary PHP docblocks, including all the standard docblock features: short and long descriptions and annotation tags.

Annotation tags may be set using the `setTag()` and `setTags()` methods; these each take either an array describing the tag that may be passed to the `Zend_CodeGenerator_Php_Docblock_Tag` constructor, or an instance of that class.

The API is as follows:

```
class Zend_CodeGenerator_Php_Docblock extends Zend_CodeGenerator_Php
    _Abstract
{
    public static function fromReflection(
        Zend_Reflection_Docblock $reflectionDocblock
    )
    public function setShortDescription($shortDescription)
    public function getShortDescription()
    public function setLongDescription($longDescription)
    public function getLongDescription()
    public function setTags(Array $tags)
    public function setTag($tag)
    public function getTags()
    public function generate()
}
```

Zend_CodeGenerator_Php_Docblock_Tag

`Zend_CodeGenerator_Php_Docblock_Tag` is intended for creating arbitrary annotation tags for inclusion in PHP docblocks. Tags are expected to contain a name (the portion immediately following the '@' symbol) and a description (everything following the tag name).

The class API is as follows:

```
class Zend_CodeGenerator_Php_Docblock_Tag
    extends Zend_CodeGenerator_Php_Abstract
{
    public static function fromReflection(
        Zend_Reflection_Docblock_Tag $reflectionTag
    )
    public function setName($name)
```

```
    public function getName()
    public function setDescription($description)
    public function getDescription()
    public function generate()
}
```

Zend_CodeGenerator_Php_DocBlock_Tag_Param

Zend_CodeGenerator_Php_DocBlock_Tag_Param is a specialized version of Zend _CodeGenerator_Php_DocBlock_Tag, and represents a method parameter. The tag name is therefor known ("param"), but due to the format of this annotation tag, additional information is required in order to generate it: the parameter name and data type it represents.

The class API is as follows:

```
class Zend_CodeGenerator_Php_Docblock_Tag_Param
    extends Zend_CodeGenerator_Php_Docblock_Tag
{
    public static function fromReflection(
        Zend_Reflection_Docblock_Tag $reflectionTagParam
    )
    public function setDatatype($datatype)
    public function getDatatype()
    public function setParamName($paramName)
    public function getParamName()
    public function generate()
}
```

Zend_CodeGenerator_Php_DocBlock_Tag_Return

Like the param docblock tag variant, Zend_CodeGenerator_Php_Docblock_Tab_Return is an annotation tag variant for representing a method return value. In this case, the annotation tag name is known ("return"), but requires a return type.

The class API is as follows:

```
class Zend_CodeGenerator_Php_Docblock_Tag_Param
    extends Zend_CodeGenerator_Php_Docblock_Tag
{
    public static function fromReflection(
        Zend_Reflection_Docblock_Tag $reflectionTagReturn
    )
    public function setDatatype($datatype)
    public function getDatatype()
    public function generate()
}
```

Zend_CodeGenerator_Php_File

Zend_CodeGenerator_Php_File is used to generate the full contents of a file that will contain PHP code. The file may contain classes or arbitrary PHP code, as well as a file-level docblock if desired.

When adding classes to the file, you will need to pass either an array of information to pass to the `Zend_CodeGenerator_Php_Class` constructor, or an instance of that class. Similarly, with docblocks, you will need to pass information for the `Zend_CodeGenerator_Php_Docblock` constructor to consume or an instance of the class.

The API of the class is as follows:

```
class Zend_CodeGenerator_Php_File extends Zend_CodeGenerator_Php
    _Abstract
{
    public static function fromReflectedFilePath(
        $filePath,
        $usePreviousCodeGeneratorIfItExists = true,
        $includeIfNotAlreadyIncluded = true)
    public static function fromReflection(Zend_Reflection_File
        $reflectionFile)
    public function setDocblock(Zend_CodeGenerator_Php_Docblock $docblock)
    public function getDocblock()
    public function setRequiredFiles($requiredFiles)
    public function getRequiredFiles()
    public function setClasses(Array $classes)
    public function getClass($name = null)
    public function setClass($class)
    public function setFilename($filename)
    public function getFilename()
    public function getClasses()
    public function setBody($body)
    public function getBody()
    public function isSourceDirty()
    public function generate()
}
```

Zend_CodeGenerator_Php_Member_Container

`Zend_CodeGenerator_Php_Member_Container` is used internally by `Zend_Code Generator_Php_Class` to keep track of class members -- properties and methods alike. These are indexed by name, using the concrete instances of the members as values.

The API of the class is as follows:

```
class Zend_CodeGenerator_Php_Member_Container extends ArrayObject
{
    public function __construct($type = self::TYPE_PROPERTY)
}
```

Zend_CodeGenerator_Php_Method

`Zend_CodeGenerator_Php_Method` describes a class method, and can generate both the code and the docblock for the method. The visibility and status as static, abstract, or final may be indicated, per its parent class, `Zend_CodeGenerator_Php_Member_Abstract`. Finally, the parameters and return value for the method may be specified.

Parameters may be set using `setParameter()` or `setParameters()`. In each case, a parameter should either be an array of information to pass to the `Zend_CodeGenerator_Php_Parameter` constructor or an instance of that class.

The API of the class is as follows:

```
class Zend_CodeGenerator_Php_Method
    extends Zend_CodeGenerator_Php_Member_Abstract
{
    public static function fromReflection(
```

```
        Zend_Reflection_Method $reflectionMethod
    )
    public function setDocblock(Zend_CodeGenerator_Php_Docblock
        $docblock)
    public function getDocblock()
    public function setFinal($isFinal)
    public function setParameters(Array $parameters)
    public function setParameter($parameter)
    public function getParameters()
    public function setBody($body)
    public function getBody()
    public function generate()
}
```

Zend_CodeGenerator_Php_Parameter

Zend_CodeGenerator_Php_Parameter may be used to specify method parameters. Each parameter may have a position (if unspecified, the order in which they are registered with the method will be used), a default value, and a data type; a parameter name is required.

The API of the class is as follows:

```
class Zend_CodeGenerator_Php_Parameter extends Zend_CodeGenerator_Php
    _Abstract
{
    public static function fromReflection(
        Zend_Reflection_Parameter $reflectionParameter
    )
    public function setType($type)
    public function getType()
    public function setName($name)
    public function getName()
    public function setDefaultValue($defaultValue)
    public function getDefaultValue()
    public function setPosition($position)
    public function getPosition()
    public function generate()
}
```

Zend_CodeGenerator_Php_Property

Zend_CodeGenerator_Php_Property describes a class property, which may be either a constant or a variable. In each case, the property may have an optional default value associated with it. Additionally, the visibility of variable properties may be set, per the parent class, Zend_CodeGenerator_Php_Member_Abstract.

The API of the class is as follows:

```
class Zend_CodeGenerator_Php_Property
    extends Zend_CodeGenerator_Php_Member_Abstract
{
    public static function fromReflection(
        Zend_Reflection_Property $reflectionProperty
    )
    public function setConst($const)
    public function isConst()
    public function setDefaultValue($defaultValue)
    public function getDefaultValue()
    public function generate()
}
```

Chapter 9. Zend_Config

Introduction

Zend_Config is designed to simplify the access to, and the use of, configuration data within applications. It provides a nested object property based user interface for accessing this configuration data within application code. The configuration data may come from a variety of media supporting hierarchical data storage. Currently Zend_Config provides adapters for configuration data that are stored in text files with Zend_Config_Ini and Zend_Config_Xml.

Example 9.1. Using Zend_Config

Normally it is expected that users would use one of the adapter classes such as Zend_Config_Ini or Zend_Config_Xml, but if configuration data are available in a PHP array, one may simply pass the data to the Zend_Config constructor in order to utilize a simple object-oriented interface:

```
// Given an array of configuration data
$configArray = array(
    'webhost'  => 'www.example.com',
    'database' => array(
        'adapter' => 'pdo_mysql',
        'params'  => array(
            'host'     => 'db.example.com',
            'username' => 'dbuser',
            'password' => 'secret',
            'dbname'   => 'mydatabase'
        )
    )
);

// Create the object-oriented wrapper upon the configuration data
$config = new Zend_Config($configArray);

// Print a configuration datum (results in 'www.example.com')
echo $config->webhost;

// Use the configuration data to connect to the database
$db = Zend_Db::factory($config->database->adapter,
                       $config->database->params->toArray());

// Alternative usage: simply pass the Zend_Config object.
// The Zend_Db factory knows how to interpret it.
$db = Zend_Db::factory($config->database);
```

As illustrated in the example above, Zend_Config provides nested object property syntax to access configuration data passed to its constructor.

Along with the object oriented access to the data values, Zend_Config also has get() which will return the supplied default value if the data element doesn't exist. For example:

```
$host = $config->database->get('host', 'localhost');
```

Example 9.2. Using Zend_Config with a PHP Configuration File

It is often desirable to use a pure PHP-based configuration file. The following code illustrates how easily this can be accomplished:

```
// config.php
return array(
    'webhost'  => 'www.example.com',
    'database' => array(
        'adapter' => 'pdo_mysql',
        'params'  => array(
            'host'     => 'db.example.com',
            'username' => 'dbuser',
            'password' => 'secret',
            'dbname'   => 'mydatabase'
        )
    )
);
```

```
// Configuration consumption
$config = new Zend_Config(require 'config.php');

// Print a configuration datum (results in 'www.example.com')
echo $config->webhost;
```

Theory of Operation

Configuration data are made accessible to the Zend_Config constructor through an associative array, which may be multi-dimensional, in order to support organizing the data from general to specific. Concrete adapter classes adapt configuration data from storage to produce the associative array for the Zend_Config constructor. User scripts may provide such arrays directly to the Zend_Config constructor, without using an adapter class, since it may be appropriate to do so in certain situations.

Each configuration data array value becomes a property of the Zend_Config object. The key is used as the property name. If a value is itself an array, then the resulting object property is created as a new Zend_Config object, loaded with the array data. This occurs recursively, such that a hierarchy of configuration data may be created with any number of levels.

Zend_Config implements the Countable and Iterator interfaces in order to facilitate simple access to configuration data. Thus, one may use the count() [http://php.net/count] function and PHP constructs such as foreach [http://php.net/foreach] with Zend_Config objects.

By default, configuration data made available through Zend_Config are read-only, and an assignment (e.g., $config->database->host = 'example.com') results in a thrown exception. This default behavior may be overridden through the constructor, however, to allow modification of data values. Also, when modifications are allowed, Zend_Config supports unsetting of values (i.e. unset($config->database->host);). The readOnly() method can be used to determine if modifications to a given Zend_Config object are allowed and the setReadOnly() method can be used to stop any further modifications to a Zend_Config object that was created allowing modifications.

Note

It is important not to confuse such in-memory modifications with saving configuration data out to specific storage media. Tools for creating and modifying configuration data for various storage media are out of scope with respect to Zend_Config. Third-party open source solutions are readily available for the purpose of creating and modifying configuration data for various storage media.

Adapter classes inherit from the Zend_Config class since they utilize its functionality.

The Zend_Config family of classes enables configuration data to be organized into sections. Zend_Config adapter objects may be loaded with a single specified section, multiple specified sections, or all sections (if none are specified).

Zend_Config adapter classes support a single inheritance model that enables configuration data to be inherited from one section of configuration data into another. This is provided in order to reduce or eliminate the need for duplicating configuration data for different purposes. An inheriting section may also override the values that it inherits through its parent section. Like PHP class inheritance, a section may inherit from a parent section, which may inherit from a grandparent section, and so on, but multiple inheritance (i.e., section C inheriting directly from parent sections A and B) is not supported.

If you have two Zend_Config objects, you can merge them into a single object using the merge() function. For example, given $config and $localConfig, you can merge data from $localConfig to $config using $config->merge($localConfig);. The items in $localConfig will override any items with the same name in $config.

Note

The Zend_Config object that is performing the merge must have been constructed to allow modifications, by passing true as the second parameter of the constructor. The setReadOnly() method can then be used to prevent any further modifications after the merge is complete.

Zend_Config_Ini

Zend_Config_Ini enables developers to store configuration data in a familiar INI format and read them in the application by using nested object property syntax. The INI format is specialized to provide both the ability to have a hierarchy of configuration data keys and inheritance between configuration data sections. Configuration data hierarchies are supported by separating the keys with the dot or period character (.). A section may extend or inherit from another section by following the section name with a colon character (:) and the name of the section from which data are to be inherited.

Parsing the INI File

Zend_Config_Ini utilizes the parse_ini_file() [http://php.net/parse_ini_file] PHP function. Please review this documentation to be aware of its specific behaviors, which propagate to Zend_Config_Ini, such as how the special values of true, false, yes, no, and null are handled.

Key Separator

By default, the key separator character is the period character (.). This can be changed, however, by changing the $options key 'nestSeparator' when constructing the Zend_Config_Ini object. For example:

```
$options['nestSeparator'] = ':';
$config = new Zend_Config_Ini('/path/to/config.ini',
                              'staging',
                              $options);
```

Example 9.3. Using Zend_Config_Ini

This example illustrates a basic use of Zend_Config_Ini for loading configuration data from an INI file. In this example there are configuration data for both a production system and for a staging system. Because the staging system configuration data are very similar to those for production, the staging section inherits from the production section. In this case, the decision is arbitrary and could have been written conversely, with the production section inheriting from the staging section, though this may not be the case for more complex situations. Suppose, then, that the following configuration data are contained in /path/to/config.ini:

```
; Production site configuration data
[production]
webhost                      = www.example.com
database.adapter             = pdo_mysql
database.params.host         = db.example.com
database.params.username     = dbuser
database.params.password     = secret
database.params.dbname       = dbname

; Staging site configuration data inherits from production and
; overrides values as necessary
[staging : production]
database.params.host         = dev.example.com
database.params.username     = devuser
database.params.password     = devsecret
```

Next, assume that the application developer needs the staging configuration data from the INI file. It is a simple matter to load these data by specifying the INI file and the staging section:

```
$config = new Zend_Config_Ini('/path/to/config.ini', 'staging');

echo $config->database->params->host;   // prints "dev.example.com"
echo $config->database->params->dbname; // prints "dbname"
```

Note

Table 9.1. Zend_Config_Ini Constructor Parameters

Parameter	Notes
$filename	The INI file to load.
$section	The [section] within the ini file that is to be loaded. Setting this parameter to null will load all sections. Alternatively, an array of section names may be supplied to load multiple sections.
$options = false	Options array. The following keys are supported:

Parameter	Notes
	• *allowModifications*: Set to true to allow subsequent modification of loaded file. Defaults to false
	• *nestSeparator*: Set to the character to be used as the nest separator. Defaults to "."

Zend_Config_Xml

Zend_Config_Xml enables developers to store configuration data in a simple XML format and read them via nested object property syntax. The root element of the XML file or string is irrelevant and may be named arbitrarily. The first level of XML elements correspond with configuration data sections. The XML format supports hierarchical organization through nesting of XML elements below the section-level elements. The content of a leaf-level XML element corresponds to the value of a configuration datum. Section inheritance is supported by a special XML attribute named extends, and the value of this attribute corresponds with the section from which data are to be inherited by the extending section.

Return Type

Configuration data read into Zend_Config_Xml are always returned as strings. Conversion of data from strings to other types is left to developers to suit their particular needs.

Example 9.4. Using Zend_Config_Xml

This example illustrates a basic use of Zend_Config_Xml for loading configuration data from an XML file. In this example there are configuration data for both a production system and for a staging system. Because the staging system configuration data are very similar to those for production, the staging section inherits from the production section. In this case, the decision is arbitrary and could have been written conversely, with the production section inheriting from the staging section, though this may not be the case for more complex situations. Suppose, then, that the following configuration data are contained in /path/to/config.xml:

```xml
<?xml version="1.0"?>
<configdata>
    <production>
        <webhost>www.example.com</webhost>
        <database>
            <adapter>pdo_mysql</adapter>
            <params>
                <host>db.example.com</host>
                <username>dbuser</username>
                <password>secret</password>
                <dbname>dbname</dbname>
            </params>
        </database>
    </production>
    <staging extends="production">
        <database>
            <params>
                <host>dev.example.com</host>
                <username>devuser</username>
                <password>devsecret</password>
```

```
            </params>
        </database>
    </staging>
</configdata>
```

Next, assume that the application developer needs the staging configuration data from the XML file. It is a simple matter to load these data by specifying the XML file and the staging section:

```
$config = new Zend_Config_Xml('/path/to/config.xml', 'staging');

echo $config->database->params->host;    // prints "dev.example.com"
echo $config->database->params->dbname;  // prints "dbname"
```

Example 9.5. Using Tag Attributes in Zend_Config_Xml

Zend_Config_Xml also supports two additional ways of defining nodes in the configuration. Both make use of attributes. Since the extends and the value attributes are reserved keywords (the latter one by the the second way of using attributes), they may not be used. The first way of making usage of attributes is to add attributes in a parent node, which then will be translated into children of that node:

```
<?xml version="1.0"?>
<configdata>
    <production webhost="www.example.com">
        <database adapter="pdo_mysql">
            <params host="db.example.com" username="dbuser" password
                ="secret" dbname="dbname"/>
        </database>
    </production>
    <staging extends="production">
        <database>
            <params host="dev.example.com" username="devuser" password
                ="devsecret"/>
        </database>
    </staging>
</configdata>
```

The other way does not really shorten the config, but keeps it easier to maintain since you don't have to write the tag name twice. You simply create an empty tag with the value in the value attribute:

```
<?xml version="1.0"?>
<configdata>
    <production>
        <webhost>www.example.com</webhost>
        <database>
            <adapter value="pdo_mysql"/>
            <params>
                <host value="db.example.com"/>
                <username value="dbuser"/>
                <password value="secret"/>
                <dbname value="dbname"/>
            </params>
        </database>
    </production>
    <staging extends="production">
```

```
    <database>
        <params>
            <host value="dev.example.com"/>
            <username value="devuser"/>
            <password value="devsecret"/>
        </params>
    </database>
  </staging>
</configdata>
```

XML strings

Zend_Config_Xml is able to load an XML string directly, such as that retrieved from a database. The string is passed as the first parameter to the constructor and must start with the characters '<?xml':

```
$string = <<<EOT
<?xml version="1.0"?>
<config>
    <production>
        <db>
            <adapter value="pdo_mysql"/>
            <params>
                <host value="db.example.com"/>
            </params>
        </db>
    </production>
    <staging extends="production">
        <db>
            <params>
                <host value="dev.example.com"/>
            </params>
        </db>
    </staging>
</config>
EOT;

$config = new Zend_Config_Xml($string, 'staging');
```

Chapter 10. Zend_Config_Writer

Zend_Config_Writer

Zend_Config_Writer gives you the ability to write config files out of Zend_Config objects. It works with an adapter-less system and thus is very easy to use. By default Zend_Config_Writer ships with three adapters, which all work the same. You instantiate a writer with specific options, which can be filename and config. Then you call the write() method of the writer and the config file is created. You can also give $filename and $config directly to the write() method. Currently the following writers are shipped with Zend_Config_Writer:

- Zend_Config_Writer_Array

- Zend_Config_Writer_Ini

- Zend_Config_Writer_Xml

As an exception, Zend_Config_Writer_Ini has an additional option parameter nestSeparator, which defines with which character the single nodes are separated. The default is a single dot, like it is accepted by Zend_Config_Ini by default.

When modifying or creating a Zend_Config object, there are some things to know. To create or modify a value, you simply say set the parameter of the Zend_Config object via the parameter accessor (->). To create a section in the root or to create a branch, you just create a new array ($config->branch = array();). To define which section extends another one, you call the setExtend() method on the root Zend_Config object.

Example 10.1. Using Zend_Config_Writer

This example illustrates the basic use of Zend_Config_Writer_Xml to create a new config file:

```
// Create the config object
$config = new Zend_Config(array(), true);
$config->production = array();
$config->staging    = array();

$config->setExtend('staging', 'production');

$config->production->db = array();
$config->production->db->hostname = 'localhost';
$config->production->db->username = 'production';

$config->staging->db = array();
$config->staging->db->username = 'staging';

// Write the config file in one of the following ways:
// a)
$writer = new Zend_Config_Writer_Xml(array('config'   => $config,
                                           'filename' => 'config.xml'));
$writer->write();

// b)
$writer = new Zend_Config_Writer_Xml();
$writer->setConfig($config)
       ->setFilename('config.xml')
```

```
            ->write();

// c)
$writer = new Zend_Config_Writer_Xml();
$writer->write('config.xml', $config);
```

This will create an XML config file with the sections production and staging, where staging extends production.

Example 10.2. Modifying an Existing Config

This example demonstrates how to edit an existing config file.

```
// Load all sections from an existing config file, while skipping
    the extends.
$config = new Zend_Config_Ini('config.ini',
                              null,
                              array('skipExtends'        => true,
                                    'allowModifications' => true));

// Modify a value
$config->production->hostname = 'foobar';

// Write the config file
$writer = new Zend_Config_Writer_Ini(array('config'   => $config,
                                           'filename' => 'config.ini'));
$writer->write();
```

Loading a Config File

When loading an existing config file for modifications it is very important to load all sections and to skip the extends, so that no values are merged. This is done by giving the skipExtends as option to the constructor.

Chapter 11. Zend_Console_Getopt

Introduction

The `Zend_Console_Getopt` class helps command-line applications to parse their options and arguments.

Users may specify command-line arguments when they execute your application. These arguments have meaning to the application, to change the behavior in some way, or choose resources, or specify parameters. Many options have developed customary meaning, for example `"--verbose"` enables extra output from many applications. Other options may have a meaning that is different for each application. For example, `"-c"` enables different features in **grep**, **ls**, and **tar**.

Below are a few definitions of terms. Common usage of the terms varies, but this documentation will use the definitions below.

- "argument": a string that occurs on the command-line following the name of the command. Arguments may be options or else may appear without an option, to name resources on which the command operates.

- "option": an argument that signifies that the command should change its default behavior in some way.

- "flag": the first part of an option, identifies the purpose of the option. A flag is preceded conventionally by one or two dashes (`"-"` or `"--"`). A single dash precedes a single-character flag or a cluster of single-character flags. A double-dash precedes a multi-character flag. Long flags cannot be clustered.

- "parameter": the secondary part of an option; a data value that may accompany a flag, if it is applicable to the given option. For example, many commands accept a `"--verbose"` option, but typically this option has no parameter. However, an option like `"--user"` almost always requires a following parameter.

  A parameter may be given as a separate argument following a flag argument, or as part of the same argument string, separated from the flag by an equals symbol (`"="`). The latter form is supported only by long flags. For example, `-u username`, `--user username`, and `--user=username` are forms supported by `Zend_Console_Getopt`.

- "cluster": multiple single-character flags combined in a single string argument and preceded by a single dash. For example, **"ls -1str"** uses a cluster of four short flags. This command is equivalent to **"ls -1 -s -t -r"**. Only single-character flags can be clustered. You cannot make a cluster of long flags.

For example, in `"mysql --user=root mydatabase"`, `"mysql"` is a *command*, `"--user=root"` is an *option*, `"--user"` is a *flag*, `"root"` is a *parameter* to the option, and `"mydatabase"` is an argument but not an option by our definition.

`Zend_Console_Getopt` provides an interface to declare which flags are valid for your application, output an error and usage message if they use an invalid flag, and report to your application code which flags the user specified.

Getopt is not an Application Framework

`Zend_Console_Getopt` does *not* interpret the meaning of flags and parameters, nor does this class implement application workflow or invoke application code. You must implement those actions in your own application code. You can use the `Zend_Console_Getopt` class to parse the command-line and provide object-oriented methods for querying which options were given by a user, but code to use this information to invoke parts of your application should be in another PHP class.

The following sections describe usage of `Zend_Console_Getopt`.

Declaring Getopt Rules

The constructor for the `Zend_Console_Getopt` class takes from one to three arguments. The first argument declares which options are supported by your application. This class supports alternative syntax forms for declaring the options. See the sections below for the format and usage of these syntax forms.

The constructor takes two more arguments, both of which are optional. The second argument may contain the command-line arguments. This defaults to `$_SERVER['argv']`.

The third argument of the constructor may contain an configuration options to customize the behavior of `Zend_Console_Getopt`. See Adding Configuration for reference on the options available.

Declaring Options with the Short Syntax

`Zend_Console_Getopt` supports a compact syntax similar to that used by GNU Getopt (see http://www.gnu.org/software/libc/manual/html_node/Getopt.html. This syntax supports only single-character flags. In a single string, you type each of the letters that correspond to flags supported by your application. A letter followed by a colon character (":") indicates a flag that requires a parameter.

Example 11.1. Using the Short Syntax

```
$opts = new Zend_Console_Getopt('abp:');
```

The example above shows using `Zend_Console_Getopt` to declare that options may be given as "-a", "-b", or "-p". The latter flag requires a parameter.

The short syntax is limited to flags of a single character. Aliases, parameter types, and help strings are not supported in the short syntax.

Declaring Options with the Long Syntax

A different syntax with more features is also available. This syntax allows you to specify aliases for flags, types of option parameters, and also help strings to describe usage to the user. Instead of the single string used in the short syntax to declare the options, the long syntax uses an associative array as the first argument to the constructor.

The key of each element of the associative array is a string with a format that names the flag, with any aliases, separated by the pipe symbol ("|"). Following this series of flag aliases, if the option requires a parameter, is an equals symbol ("=") with a letter that stands for the *type* of the parameter:

- "=s" for a string parameter

- "=w" for a word parameter (a string containing no whitespace)

- "=i" for an integer parameter

If the parameter is optional, use a dash ("-") instead of the equals symbol.

The value of each element in the associative array is a help string to describe to a user how to use your program.

Example 11.2. Using the Long Syntax

```
$opts = new Zend_Console_Getopt(
  array(
    'apple|a'    => 'apple option, with no parameter',
    'banana|b=i' => 'banana option, with required integer parameter',
    'pear|p-s'   => 'pear option, with optional string parameter'
  )
);
```

In the example declaration above, there are three options. "--apple" and "-a" are aliases for each other, and the option takes no parameter. "--banana" and "-b" are aliases for each other, and the option takes a mandatory integer parameter. Finally, "--pear" and "-p" are aliases for each other, and the option may take an optional string parameter.

Fetching Options and Arguments

After you have declared the options that the Zend_Console_Getopt object should recognize, and supply arguments from the command-line or an array, you can query the object to find out which options were specified by a user in a given command-line invocation of your program. The class implements magic methods so you can query for options by name.

The parsing of the data is deferred until the first query you make against the Zend_Console_Getopt object to find out if an option was given, the object performs its parsing. This allows you to use several method calls to configure the options, arguments, help strings, and configuration options before parsing takes place.

Handling Getopt Exceptions

If the user gave any invalid options on the command-line, the parsing function throws a Zend_Console_Getopt_Exception. You should catch this exception in your application code. You can use the parse() method to force the object to parse the arguments. This is useful because you can invoke parse() in a try block. If it passes, you can be sure that the parsing won't throw an exception again. The exception thrown has a custom method getUsageMessage(), which returns as a string the formatted set of usage messages for all declared options.

Example 11.3. Catching Getopt Exceptions

```
try {
    $opts = new Zend_Console_Getopt('abp:');
    $opts->parse();
} catch (Zend_Console_Getopt_Exception $e) {
    echo $e->getUsageMessage();
    exit;
}
```

Cases where parsing throws an exception include:

- Option given is not recognized.

- Option requires a parameter but none was given.

- Option parameter is of the wrong type. E.g. a non-numeric string when an integer was required.

Fetching Options by Name

You can use the getOption() method to query the value of an option. If the option had a parameter, this method returns the value of the parameter. If the option had no parameter but the user did specify it on the command-line, the method returns true. Otherwise the method returns null.

Example 11.4. Using getOption()

```
$opts = new Zend_Console_Getopt('abp:');
$b = $opts->getOption('b');
$p_parameter = $opts->getOption('p');
```

Alternatively, you can use the magic __get() function to retrieve the value of an option as if it were a class member variable. The __isset() magic method is also implemented.

Example 11.5. Using __get() and __isset() Magic Methods

```
$opts = new Zend_Console_Getopt('abp:');
if (isset($opts->b)) {
    echo "I got the b option.\n";
}
$p_parameter = $opts->p; // null if not set
```

If your options are declared with aliases, you may use any of the aliases for an option in the methods above.

Reporting Options

There are several methods to report the full set of options given by the user on the current command-line.

- As a string: use the toString() method. The options are returned as a space-separated string of "flag=value" pairs. The value of an option that does not have a parameter is the literal string "true".

- As an array: use the toArray() method. The options are returned in a simple integer-indexed array of strings, the flag strings followed by parameter strings, if any.

- As a string containing JSON data: use the toJson() method.

- As a string containing XML data: use the `toXml()` method.

In all of the above dumping methods, the flag string is the first string in the corresponding list of aliases. For example, if the option aliases were declared like "`verbose|v`", then the first string, "`verbose`", is used as the canonical name of the option. The name of the option flag does not include any preceding dashes.

Fetching Non-option Arguments

After option arguments and their parameters have been parsed from the command-line, there may be additional arguments remaining. You can query these arguments using the `getRemainingArgs()` method. This method returns an array of the strings that were not part of any options.

Example 11.6. Using getRemainingArgs()

```
$opts = new Zend_Console_Getopt('abp:');
$opts->setArguments(array('-p', 'p_parameter', 'filename'));
$args = $opts->getRemainingArgs(); // returns array('filename')
```

`Zend_Console_Getopt` supports the GNU convention that an argument consisting of a double-dash signifies the end of options. Any arguments following this signifier must be treated as non-option arguments. This is useful if you might have a non-option argument that begins with a dash. For example: **"rm -- -filename-with-dash"**.

Configuring Zend_Console_Getopt

Adding Option Rules

You can add more option rules in addition to those you specified in the `Zend_Console_Getopt` constructor, using the `addRules()` method. The argument to `addRules()` is the same as the first argument to the class constructor. It is either a string in the format of the short syntax options specification, or else an associative array in the format of a long syntax options specification. See Declaring Getopt Rules for details on the syntax for specifying options.

Example 11.7. Using addRules()

```
$opts = new Zend_Console_Getopt('abp:');
$opts->addRules(
  array(
    'verbose|v' => 'Print verbose output'
  )
);
```

The example above shows adding the "`--verbose`" option with an alias of "`-v`" to a set of options defined in the call to the constructor. Notice that you can mix short format options and long format options in the same instance of `Zend_Console_Getopt`.

Adding Help Messages

In addition to specifying the help strings when declaring option rules in the long format, you can associate help strings with option rules using the setHelp() method. The argument to the setHelp() method is an associative array, in which the key is a flag, and the value is a corresponding help string.

Example 11.8. Using setHelp()

```
$opts = new Zend_Console_Getopt('abp:');
$opts->setHelp(
    array(
        'a' => 'apple option, with no parameter',
        'b' => 'banana option, with required integer parameter',
        'p' => 'pear option, with optional string parameter'
    )
);
```

If you declared options with aliases, you can use any of the aliases as the key of the associative array.

The setHelp() method is the only way to define help strings if you declared the options using the short syntax.

Adding Option Aliases

You can declare aliases for options using the setAliases method. The argument is an associative array, whose key is a flag string declared previously, and whose value is a new alias for that flag. These aliases are merged with any existing aliases. In other words, aliases you declared earlier are still in effect.

An alias may be declared only once. If you try to redefine an alias, a Zend_Console _Getopt_Exception is thrown.

Example 11.9. Using setAliases()

```
$opts = new Zend_Console_Getopt('abp:');
$opts->setAliases(
    array(
        'a' => 'apple',
        'a' => 'apfel',
        'p' => 'pear'
    )
);
```

In the example above, after declaring these aliases, "-a", "--apple" and "--apfel" are aliases for each other. Also "-p" and "--pear" are aliases for each other.

The setAliases() method is the only way to define aliases if you declared the options using the short syntax.

Adding Argument Lists

By default, Zend_Console_Getopt uses $_SERVER['argv'] for the array of command-line arguments to parse. You can alternatively specify the array of arguments as the second constructor argument. Finally, you can append more arguments to those already used using the addArguments() method, or you can replace the current array of arguments using the setArguments() method. In both cases, the parameter to these methods is a simple array of strings. The former method appends the array to the current arguments, and the latter method substitutes the array for the current arguments.

Example 11.10. Using addArguments() and setArguments()

```
// By default, the constructor uses $_SERVER['argv']
$opts = new Zend_Console_Getopt('abp:⊤');

// Append an array to the existing arguments
$opts->addArguments(array('-a', '-p', 'p_parameter', 'non_option_arg'));

// Substitute a new array for the existing arguments
$opts->setArguments(array('-a', '-p', 'p_parameter', 'non_option_arg'));
```

Adding Configuration

The third parameter to the Zend_Console_Getopt constructor is an array of configuration options that affect the behavior of the object instance returned. You can also specify configuration options using the setOptions() method, or you can set an individual option using the setOption() method.

Clarifying the Term "option"

The term "option" is used for configuration of the Zend_Console_Getopt class to match terminology used elsewhere in Zend Framework. These are not the same things as the command-line options that are parsed by the Zend_Console_Getopt class.

The currently supported options have const definitions in the class. The options, their const identifiers (with literal values in parentheses) are listed below:

• Zend_Console_Getopt::CONFIG_DASHDASH ("dashDash"), if true, enables the special flag "--" to signify the end of flags. Command-line arguments following the double-dash signifier are not interpreted as options, even if the arguments start with a dash. This configuration option is true by default.

• Zend_Console_Getopt::CONFIG_IGNORECASE ("ignoreCase"), if true, makes flags aliases of each other if they differ only in their case. That is, "-a" and "-A" will be considered to be synonymous flags. This configuration option is false by default.

• Zend_Console_Getopt::CONFIG_RULEMODE ("ruleMode") may have values Zend_Console_Getopt::MODE_ZEND ("zend") and Zend_Console_Getopt::MODE_GNU ("gnu"). It should not be necessary to use this option unless you extend the class with additional syntax forms. The two modes supported in the base Zend_Console_Getopt class are unambiguous. If the specifier is a string, the class assumes MODE_GNU, otherwise it assumes MODE_ZEND. But if you extend the class and add more syntax forms, you may need to specify the mode using this option.

More configuration options may be added as future enhancements of this class.

The two arguments to the setOption() method are a configuration option name and an option value.

Example 11.11. Using setOption()

```
$opts = new Zend_Console_Getopt('abp:');
$opts->setOption('ignoreCase', true);
```

The argument to the setOptions() method is an associative array. The keys of this array are the configuration option names, and the values are configuration values. This is also the array format used in the class constructor. The configuration values you specify are merged with the current configuration; you don't have to list all options.

Example 11.12. Using setOptions()

```
$opts = new Zend_Console_Getopt('abp:');
$opts->setOptions(
    array(
        'ignoreCase' => true,
        'dashDash'   => false
    )
);
```

Chapter 12. Zend_Controller

Zend_Controller Quick Start

Introduction

`Zend_Controller` is the heart of Zend Framework's MVC system. MVC stands for Model-View-Controller [http://en.wikipedia.org/wiki/Model-view-controller] and is a design pattern targeted at separating application logic from display logic. `Zend_Controller_Front` implements a Front Controller [http://www.martinfowler.com/eaaCatalog/frontController.html] pattern, in which all requests are intercepted by the front controller and dispatched to individual Action Controllers based on the URL requested.

The `Zend_Controller` system was built with extensibility in mind, either by subclassing the existing classes, writing new classes that implement the various interfaces and abstract classes that form the foundation of the controller family of classes, or writing plugins or action helpers to augment or manipulate the functionality of the system.

Quick Start

If you need more in-depth information, see the following sections. If you just want to get up and running quickly, read on.

Create the Filesystem Layout

The first step is to create your file system layout. The typical layout is as follows:

```
application/
    controllers/
        IndexController.php
    models/
    views/
        scripts/
            index/
                index.phtml
        helpers/
        filters/
html/
    .htaccess
    index.php
```

Set the Document Root

In your web server, point your document root to the `html` directory of the above file system layout.

Create the Rewrite Rules

Edit the `html/.htaccess` file above to read as follows:

```
RewriteEngine On
RewriteCond %{REQUEST_FILENAME} -s [OR]
RewriteCond %{REQUEST_FILENAME} -l [OR]
```

```
RewriteCond %{REQUEST_FILENAME} -d
RewriteRule ^.*$ - [NC,L]
RewriteRule ^.*$ index.php [NC,L]
```

Learn about mod_rewrite

The above rewrite rules allow access to any file under your virtual host's document root. If there are files you do not want exposed in this way, you may want to be more restrictive in your rules. Go to the Apache website to learn more about mod_rewrite [http://httpd.apache.org /docs/2.0/mod/mod_rewrite.html].

If using IIS 7.0, use the following as your rewrite configuration:

```
<configuration>
    <system.webServer>
        <rewrite>
            <rules>
                <rule name="Imported Rule 1" stopProcessing="true">
                    <match url="^.*$" />
                    <conditions logicalGrouping="MatchAny">
                        <add input="{REQUEST_FILENAME}"
                            matchType="IsFile" pattern=""
                            ignoreCase="false" />
                        <add input="{REQUEST_FILENAME}"
                            matchType="IsDirectory"
                            pattern="" ignoreCase="false" />
                    </conditions>
                    <action type="None" />
                </rule>
                <rule name="Imported Rule 2" stopProcessing="true">
                    <match url="^.*$" />
                    <action type="Rewrite" url="index.php" />
                </rule>
            </rules>
        </rewrite>
    </system.webServer>
</configuration>
```

The above rules will route requests to existing resources (existing symlinks, non-empty files, or non-empty directories) accordingly, and all other requests to the front controller.

Note

The above rewrite rules are for Apache; for examples of rewrite rules for other web servers, see the router documentation.

Create the Bootstrap File

The bootstrap file is the page all requests are routed through -- `html/index.php` in this case. Open up `html/index.php` in the editor of your choice and add the following:

```
Zend_Controller_Front::run('/path/to/app/controllers');
```

This will instantiate and dispatch the front controller, which will route requests to action controllers.

Create the Default Action Controller

Before discussing action controllers, you should first understand how requests are routed in Zend Framework. By default, the first segment of a URL path maps to a controller, and the second to an action. For example, given the URL `http://framework.zend.com/roadmap/components`, the path is `/roadmap/components`, which will map to the controller `roadmap` and the action `components`. If no action is provided, the action `index` is assumed, and if no controller is provided, the controller `index` is assumed (following the Apache convention that maps a `DirectoryIndex` automatically).

`Zend_Controller`'s dispatcher then takes the controller value and maps it to a class. By default, it Title-cases the controller name and appends the word `Controller`. Thus, in our example above, the controller `roadmap` is mapped to the class `RoadmapController`.

Similarly, the action value is mapped to a method of the controller class. By default, the value is lower-cased, and the word `Action` is appended. Thus, in our example above, the action `components` becomes `componentsAction`, and the final method called is `RoadmapController::componentsAction()`.

So, moving on, let's now create a default action controller and action method. As noted earlier, the default controller and action called are both `index`. Open the file `application/controllers/IndexController.php`, and enter the following:

```
/** Zend_Controller_Action */
class IndexController extends Zend_Controller_Action
{
    public function indexAction()
    {

    }
}
```

By default, the ViewRenderer action helper is enabled. What this means is that by simply defining an action method and a corresponding view script, you will immediately get content rendered. By default, `Zend_View` is used as the View layer in the MVC. The `ViewRenderer` does some magic, and uses the controller name (e.g., `index`) and the current action name (e.g., `index`) to determine what template to pull. By default, templates end in the `.phtml` extension, so this means that, in the above example, the template `index/index.phtml` will be rendered. Additionally, the `ViewRenderer` automatically assumes that the directory `views` at the same level as the controller directory will be the base view directory, and that the actual view scripts will be in the `views/scripts/` subdirectory. Thus, the template rendered will be found in `application/views/scripts/index/index.phtml`.

Create the View Script

As mentioned in the previous section, view scripts are found in `application/views/scripts/`; the view script for the default controller and action is in `application/views/scripts/index/index.phtml`. Create this file, and type in some HTML:

```
<!DOCTYPE html
PUBLIC "-//W3C//DTD XHTML 1.0 Strict//EN"
"http://www.w3.org/TR/xhtml1/DTD/xhtml1-strict.dtd">
<html>
<head>
  <meta http-equiv="Content-Type" content="text/html; charset=utf-8" />
  <title>My first Zend Framework App</title>
</head>
```

```
<body>
    <h1>Hello, World!</h1>
</body>
</html>
```

Create the Error Controller

By default, the error handler plugin is registered. This plugin expects that a controller exists to handle errors. By default, it assumes an `ErrorController` in the default module with an `errorAction` method:

```
class ErrorController extends Zend_Controller_Action
{
    public function errorAction()
    {

    }
}
```

Assuming the already discussed directory layout, this file will go in `application/controllers/ErrorController.php`. You will also need to create a view script in `application/views/scripts/error/error.phtml`; sample content might look like:

```
<!DOCTYPE html
PUBLIC "-//W3C//DTD XHTML 1.0 Strict//EN"
"http://www.w3.org/TR/xhtml1/DTD/xhtml1-strict.dtd">
<html>
<head>
  <meta http-equiv="Content-Type" content="text/html; charset=utf-8" />
  <title>Error</title>
</head>
<body>
    <h1>An error occurred</h1>
    <p>An error occurred; please try again later.</p>
</body>
</html>
```

View the Site!

With your first controller and view under your belt, you can now fire up your browser and browse to the site. Assuming `example.com` is your domain, any of the following URLs will get to the page we've just created:

* `http://example.com/`

* `http://example.com/index`

* `http://example.com/index/index`

You're now ready to start creating more controllers and action methods. Congratulations!

Zend_Controller Basics

The Zend_Controller system is designed to be lightweight, modular, and extensible. It is a minimalist design to permit flexibility and some freedom to users while providing enough structure so that systems built around Zend_Controller share some common conventions and similar code layout.

The following diagram depicts the workflow, and the narrative following describes in detail the interactions:

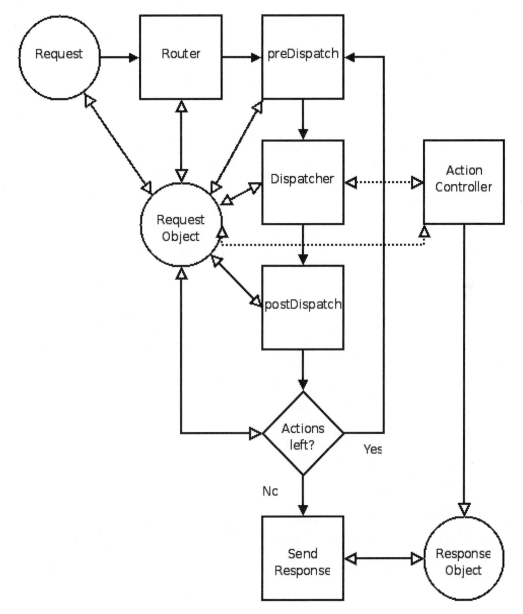

The Zend_Controller workflow is implemented by several components. While it is not necessary to completely understand the underpinnings of all of these components to use the system, having a working knowledge of the process is helpful.

- Zend_Controller_Front orchestrates the entire workflow of the Zend_Controller system. It is an interpretation of the FrontController pattern. Zend_Controller_Front processes all requests received by the server and is ultimately responsible for delegating requests to ActionControllers (Zend_Controller_Action).

- Zend_Controller_Request_Abstract (often referred to as the Request Object) represents the request environment and provides methods for setting and retrieving the controller and action names and any request parameters. Additionally it keeps track of whether or not the action it contains has been dispatched by Zend_Controller_Dispatcher. Extensions to the abstract request object can be used to encapsulate the entire request environment, allowing routers to pull information from the request environment in order to set the controller and action names.

    By default, Zend_Controller_Request_Http is used, which provides access to the entire HTTP request environment.

- Zend_Controller_Router_Interface is used to define routers. Routing is the process of examining the request environment to determine which controller, and action of that controller, should receive the request. This controller, action, and optional parameters are then set in the request object to be processed by Zend_Controller_Dispatcher_Standard. Routing occurs only once: when the request is initially received and before the first controller is dispatched.

    The default router, Zend_Controller_Router_Rewrite, takes a URI endpoint as specified in Zend_Controller_Request_Http and decomposes it into a controller, action, and parameters based on the path information in the url. As an example, the URL http://localhost/foo/bar/key/value would be decoded to use the foo controller, bar action, and specify a parameter key with a value of value.

    Zend_Controller_Router_Rewrite can also be used to match arbitrary paths; see the router documentation for more information.

- Zend_Controller_Dispatcher_Interface is used to define dispatchers. Dispatching is the process of pulling the controller and action from the request object and mapping them to a controller file/class and action method in the controller class. If the controller or action do not exist, it handles determining default controllers and actions to dispatch.

    The actual dispatching process consists of instantiating the controller class and calling the action method in that class. Unlike routing, which occurs only once, dispatching occurs in a loop. If the request object's dispatched status is reset at any point, the loop will be repeated, calling whatever action is currently set in the request object. The first time the loop finishes with the request object's dispatched status set (boolean true), it will finish processing.

    The default dispatcher is Zend_Controller_Dispatcher_Standard. It defines controllers as MixedCasedClasses ending in the word Controller, and action methods as camelCasedMethods ending in the word Action: FooController::barAction(). In this case, the controller would be referred to as foo and the action as bar.

Case Naming Conventions

Since humans are notoriously inconsistent at maintaining case sensitivity when typing links, Zend Framework actually normalizes path information to lowercase. This, of course, will affect how you name your controller and actions... or refer to them in links.

If you wish to have your controller class or action method name have multiple MixedCasedWords or camelCasedWords, you will need to separate those words on the url with either a '-' or '.' (though you can configure the character used).

As an example, if you were going to the action in `FooBarController::bazBatAction()`, you'd refer to it on the url as `/foo-bar/ baz-bat` or `/foo.bar/baz.bat`.

- `Zend_Controller_Action` is the base action controller component. Each controller is a single class that extends the `Zend_Controller_Action class` and should contain one or more action methods.

- `Zend_Controller_Response_Abstract` defines a base response class used to collect and return responses from the action controllers. It collects both headers and body content.

  The default response class is `Zend_Controller_Response_Http`, which is suitable for use in an HTTP environment.

The workflow of `Zend_Controller` is relatively simple. A request is received by `Zend_Controller_Front`, which in turn calls `Zend_Controller_Router_Rewrite` to determine which controller (and action in that controller) to dispatch. `Zend_Controller_Router_Rewrite` decomposes the URI in order to set the controller and action names in the request. `Zend_Controller_Front` then enters a dispatch loop. It calls `Zend_Controller_Dispatcher_Standard`, passing it the request, to dispatch to the controller and action specified in the request (or use defaults). After the controller has finished, control returns to `Zend_Controller_Front`. If the controller has indicated that another controller should be dispatched by resetting the dispatched status of the request, the loop continues and another dispatch is performed. Otherwise, the process ends.

The Front Controller

Overview

`Zend_Controller_Front` implements a Front Controller pattern [http://www.martinfowler.com/eaaCatalog/frontController.html] used in Model-View-Controller (MVC) [http://en.wikipedia.org/wiki/Model-view-controller] applications. Its purpose is to initialize the request environment, route the incoming request, and then dispatch any discovered actions; it aggregates any responses and returns them when the process is complete.

`Zend_Controller_Front` also implements the Singleton pattern [http://en.wikipedia.org/wiki/Singleton_pattern], meaning only a single instance of it may be available at any given time. This allows it to also act as a registry on which the other objects in the dispatch process may draw.

`Zend_Controller_Front` registers a plugin broker with itself, allowing various events it triggers to be observed by plugins. In most cases, this gives the developer the opportunity to tailor the dispatch process to the site without the need to extend the front controller to add functionality.

At a bare minimum, the front controller needs one or more paths to directories containing action controllers in order to do its work. A variety of methods may also be invoked to further tailor the front controller environment and that of its helper classes.

Default Behaviour

By default, the front controller loads the ErrorHandler plugin, as well as the ViewRenderer action helper plugin. These are to simplify error handling and view renderering in your controllers, respectively.

To disable the `ErrorHandler`, perform the following at any point prior to calling `dispatch()`:

```
// Disable the ErrorHandler plugin:
$front->setParam('noErrorHandler', true);
```

To disable the ViewRenderer, do the following prior to calling dispatch():

```
// Disable the ViewRenderer helper:
$front->setParam('noViewRenderer', true);
```

Primary Methods

The front controller has several accessors for setting up its environment. However, there are three primary methods key to the front controller's functionality:

getInstance()

getInstance() is used to retrieve a front controller instance. As the front controller implements a Singleton pattern, this is also the only means possible for instantiating a front controller object.

```
$front = Zend_Controller_Front::getInstance();
```

setControllerDirectory() and addControllerDirectory

setControllerDirectory() is used to tell the dispatcher where to look for action controller class files. It accepts either a single path or an associative array of module/path pairs.

As some examples:

```
// Set the default controller directory:
$front->setControllerDirectory('../application/controllers');

// Set several module directories at once:
$front->setControllerDirectory(array(
    'default' => '../application/controllers',
    'blog'    => '../modules/blog/controllers',
    'news'    => '../modules/news/controllers',
));

// Add a 'foo' module directory:
$front->addControllerDirectory('../modules/foo/controllers', 'foo');
```

Note

If you use addControllerDirectory() without a module name, it will set the directory for the default module -- overwriting it if it already exists.

You can get the current settings for the controller directory using getControllerDirectory(); this will return an array of module/directory pairs.

addModuleDirectory() and getModuleDirectory()

One aspect of the front controller is that you may define a modular directory structure for creating standalone components; these are called "modules".

Each module should be in its own directory and mirror the directory structure of the default module -- i.e., it should have a "controllers" subdirectory at the minimum, and typically a "views" subdirectory and other application subdirectories.

addModuleDirectory() allows you to pass the name of a directory containing one or more module directories. It then scans it and adds them as controller directories to the front controller.

Later, if you want to determine the path to a particular module or the current module, you can call getModuleDirectory(), optionally passing a module name to get that specific module directory.

dispatch()

dispatch(Zend_Controller_Request_Abstract $request = null, Zend_Controller _Response_Abstract $response = null) does the heavy work of the front controller. It may optionally take a request object and/or a response object, allowing the developer to pass in custom objects for each.

If no request or response object are passed in, dispatch() will check for previously registered objects and use those or instantiate default versions to use in its process (in both cases, the HTTP flavor will be used as the default).

Similarly, dispatch() checks for registered router and dispatcher objects, instantiating the default versions of each if none is found.

The dispatch process has three distinct events:

- Routing

- Dispatching

- Response

Routing takes place exactly once, using the values in the request object when dispatch() is called. Dispatching takes place in a loop; a request may either indicate multiple actions to dispatch, or the controller or a plugin may reset the request object to force additional actions to dispatch. When all is done, the front controller returns a response.

run()

Zend_Controller_Front::run($path) is a static method taking simply a path to a directory containing controllers. It fetches a front controller instance (via getInstance(), registers the path provided via setControllerDirectory(), and finally dispatches.

Basically, run() is a convenience method that can be used for site setups that do not require customization of the front controller environment.

```
// Instantiate front controller, set controller directory, and dispatch
    in one
// easy step:
Zend_Controller_Front::run('../application/controllers');
```

Environmental Accessor Methods

In addition to the methods listed above, there are a number of accessor methods that can be used to affect the front controller environment -- and thus the environment of the classes to which the front controller delegates.

- resetInstance() can be used to clear all current settings. Its primary purpose is for testing, but it can also be used for instances where you wish to chain together multiple front controllers.

- (set|get)DefaultControllerName() let you specify a different name to use for the default controller ('index' is used otherwise) and retrieve the current value. They proxy to the dispatcher.

- (set|get)DefaultAction() let you specify a different name to use for the default action ('index' is used otherwise) and retrieve the current value. They proxy to the dispatcher.

- (set|get)Request() let you specify the request class or object to use during the dispatch process and to retrieve the current object. When setting the request object, you may pass in a request class name, in which case the method will load the class file and instantiate it.

- (set|get)Router() let you specify the router class or object to use during the dispatch process and to retrieve the current object. When setting the router object, you may pass in a router class name, in which case the method will load the class file and instantiate it.

  When retrieving the router object, it first checks to see if one is present, and if not, instantiates the default router (rewrite router).

- (set|get)BaseUrl() let you specify the base URL to strip when routing requests and to retrieve the current value. The value is provided to the request object just prior to routing.

- (set|get)Dispatcher() let you specify the dispatcher class or object to use during the dispatch process and retrieve the current object. When setting the dispatcher object, you may pass in a dispatcher class name, in which case the method will load the class file and instantiate it.

  When retrieving the dispatcher object, it first checks to see if one is present, and if not, instantiates the default dispatcher.

- (set|get)Response() let you specify the response class or object to use during the dispatch process and to retrieve the current object. When setting the response object, you may pass in a response class name, in which case the method will load the class file and instantiate it.

- registerPlugin(Zend_Controller_Plugin_Abstract $plugin, $stackIndex = null) allows you to register plugin objects. By setting the optional $stackIndex, you can control the order in which plugins will execute.

- unregisterPlugin($plugin) let you unregister plugin objects. $plugin may be either a plugin object or a string denoting the class of plugin to unregister.

- throwExceptions($flag) is used to turn on/off the ability to throw exceptions during the dispatch process. By default, exceptions are caught and placed in the response object; turning on throwExceptions() will override this behaviour.

  For more information, read the section called "MVC Exceptions".

- returnResponse($flag) is used to tell the front controller whether to return the response (true) from dispatch(), or if the response should be automatically emitted (false). By default, the response is automatically emitted (by calling Zend_Controller_Response _Abstract::sendResponse()); turning on returnResponse() will override this behaviour.

  Reasons to return the response include a desire to check for exceptions prior to emitting the response, needing to log various aspects of the response (such as headers), etc.

Front Controller Parameters

In the introduction, we indicated that the front controller also acts as a registry for the various controller components. It does so through a family of "param" methods. These methods allow you to register arbitrary data -- objects and variables -- with the front controller to be retrieved at any time in the dispatch chain. These values are passed on to the router, dispatcher, and action controllers. The methods include:

- `setParam($name, $value)` allows you to set a single parameter of $name with value $value.

- `setParams(array $params)` allows you to set multiple parameters at once using an associative array.

- `getParam($name)` allows you to retrieve a single parameter at a time, using $name as the identifier.

- `getParams()` allows you to retrieve the entire list of parameters at once.

- `clearParams()` allows you to clear a single parameter (by passing a string identifier), multiple named parameters (by passing an array of string identifiers), or the entire parameter stack (by passing nothing).

There are several pre-defined parameters that may be set that have specific uses in the dispatch chain:

- `useDefaultControllerAlways` is used to hint to the dispatcher to use the default controller in the default module for any request that is not dispatchable (i.e., the module, controller, and/or action do not exist). By default, this is off.

  See the section called "MVC Exceptions You May Encounter" for more detailed information on using this setting.

- `disableOutputBuffering` is used to hint to the dispatcher that it should not use output buffering to capture output generated by action controllers. By default, the dispatcher captures any output and appends it to the response object body content.

- `noViewRenderer` is used to disable the ViewRenderer. Set this parameter to true to disable it.

- `noErrorHandler` is used to disable the Error Handler plugin. Set this parameter to true to disable it.

Extending the Front Controller

To extend the Front Controller, at the very minimum you will need to override the `getInstance()` method:

```
class My_Controller_Front extends Zend_Controller_Front
{
    public static function getInstance()
    {
        if (null === self::$_instance) {
            self::$_instance = new self();
        }

        return self::$_instance;
    }
}
```

Overriding the `getInstance()` method ensures that subsequent calls to `Zend_Controller_Front::getInstance()` will return an instance of your new subclass instead of a `Zend_Controller_Front` instance -- this is particularly useful for some of the alternate routers and view helpers.

Typically, you will not need to subclass the front controller unless you need to add new functionality (for instance, a plugin autoloader, or a way to specify action helper paths). Some points where you may want to alter behaviour may include modifying how controller directories are stored, or what default router or dispatcher are used.

The Request Object

Introduction

The request object is a simple value object that is passed between `Zend_Controller_Front` and the router, dispatcher, and controller classes. It packages the names of the requested module, controller, action, and optional parameters, as well as the rest of the request environment, be it HTTP, the CLI, or PHP-GTK.

- The module name is accessed by `getModuleName()` and `setModuleName()`.

- The controller name is accessed by `getControllerName()` and `setControllerName()`.

- The name of the action to call within that controller is accessed by `getActionName()` and `setActionName()`.

- Parameters to be accessible by the action are an associative array of key/value pairs that are retrieved by `getParams()` and set with `setParams()`, or individually by `getParam()` and `setParam()`.

Based on the type of request, there may be more methods available. The default request used, `Zend_Controller_Request_Http`, for instance, has methods for retrieving the request URI, path information, `$_GET` and `$_POST` parameters, etc.

The request object is passed to the front controller, or if none is provided, it is instantiated at the beginning of the dispatch process, before routing occurs. It is passed through to every object in the dispatch chain.

Additionally, the request object is particularly useful in testing. The developer may craft the request environment, including module, controller, action, parameters, URI, etc, and pass the request object to the front controller to test application flow. When paired with the response object, elaborate and precise unit testing of MVC applications becomes possible.

HTTP Requests

Accessing Request Data

`Zend_Controller_Request_Http` encapsulates access to relevant values such as the key name and value for the controller and action router variables, and all additional parameters parsed from the URI. It additionally allows access to values contained in the superglobals as public members, and manages the current Base URL and Request URI. Superglobal values cannot be set on a request object, instead use the setParam/getParam methods to set or retrieve user parameters.

Superglobal Data

When accessing superglobal data through `Zend_Controller_Request_Http` as public member properties, it is necessary to keep in mind that the property name (superglobal array key) is matched to a superglobal in a specific order of precedence: 1. GET, 2. POST, 3. COOKIE, 4. SERVER, 5. ENV.

Specific superglobals can be accessed using a public method as an alternative. For example, the raw value of `$_POST['user']` can be accessed by calling `getPost('user')` on the request object. These include `getQuery()` for retrieving `$_GET` elements, and `getHeader()` for retrieving request headers.

GET and POST Data

Be cautious when accessing data from the request object as it is not filtered in any way. The router and dispatcher validate and filter data for use with their tasks, but leave the data untouched in the request object.

Retrieving the Raw POST Data

As of 1.5.0, you can also retrieve the raw post data via the `getRawBody()` method. This method returns false if no data was submitted in that fashion, but the full body of the post otherwise.

This is primarily useful for accepting content when developing a RESTful MVC application.

You may also set user parameters in the request object using `setParam()` and retrieve these later using `getParam()`. The router makes use of this functionality to set parameters matched in the request URI into the request object.

getParam() Retrieves More than User Parameters

In order to do some of its work, `getParam()` actually retrieves from several sources. In order of priority, these include: user parameters set via `setParam()`, GET parameters, and finally POST parameters. Be aware of this when pulling data via this method.

If you wish to pull only from parameters you set via `setParam()`, use the `getUserParam()`.

Additionally, as of 1.5.0, you can lock down which parameter sources will be searched. `setParamSources()` allows you to specify an empty array or an array with one or more of the values '_GET' or '_POST' indicating which parameter sources are allowed (by default, both are allowed); if you wish to restrict access to only '_GET' specify `setParamSources(array('_GET'))`.

Apache Quirks

If you are using Apache's 404 handler to pass incoming requests to the front controller, or using a PT flag with rewrite rules, `$_SERVER['REDIRECT_URL']` contains the URI you need, not `$_SERVER['REQUEST_URI']`. If you are using such a setup and getting invalid routing, you should use the `Zend_Controller_Request_Apache404` class instead of the default Http class for your request object:

```
$request = new Zend_Controller_Request_Apache404();
$front->setRequest($request);
```

This class extends the `Zend_Controller_Request_Http` class and simply modifies the autodiscovery of the request URI. It can be used as a drop-in replacement.

Base Url and Subdirectories

`Zend_Controller_Request_Http` allows `Zend_Controller_Router_Rewrite` to be used in subdirectories. Zend_Controller_Request_Http will attempt to automatically detect your base URL and set it accordingly.

For example, if you keep your index.php in a webserver subdirectory named /projects/myapp/index.php, base URL (rewrite base) should be set to /projects/myapp. This string will then be stripped from the beginning of the path before calculating any route matches. This frees one from the necessity of prepending it to any of your routes. A route of 'user/:username' will match URIs like http://localhost/projects/myapp/user/martel and http://example.com/user/martel.

URL Detection is Case Sensitive

Automatic base URL detection is case sensitive, so make sure your URL will match a subdirectory name in a filesystem (even on Windows machines). If it doesn't, an exception will be raised.

Should base URL be detected incorrectly you can override it with your own base path with the help of the setBaseUrl() method of either the Zend_Controller_Request_Http class, or the Zend_Controller_Front class. The easiest method is to set it in Zend_Controller_Front, which will proxy it into the request object. Example usage to set a custom base URL:

```
/**
 * Dispatch Request with custom base URL with Zend_Controller_Front.
 */
$router     = new Zend_Controller_Router_Rewrite();
$controller = Zend_Controller_Front::getInstance();
$controller->setControllerDirectory('./application/controllers')
           ->setRouter($router)
           ->setBaseUrl('/projects/myapp'); // set the base url!
$response   = $controller->dispatch();
```

Determining the Request Method

getMethod() allows you to determine the HTTP request method used to request the current resource. Additionally, a variety of methods exist that allow you to get boolean responses when asking if a specific type of request has been made:

* isGet()

* isPost()

* isPut()

* isDelete()

* isHead()

* isOptions()

The primary use case for these is for creating RESTful MVC architectures.

Detecting AJAX Requests

Zend_Controller_Request_Http has a rudimentary method for detecting AJAX requests: isXmlHttpRequest(). This method looks for an HTTP request header X-Requested-With with the value 'XMLHttpRequest'; if found, it returns true.

Currently, this header is known to be passed by default with the following JS libraries:

- Prototype/Scriptaculous (and libraries derived from Prototype)

- Yahoo! UI Library

- jQuery

- MochiKit

Most AJAX libraries allow you to send custom HTTP request headers; if your library does not send this header, simply add it as a request header to ensure the isXmlHttpRequest() method works for you.

Subclassing the Request Object

The base request class used for all request objects is the abstract class Zend_Controller _Request_Abstract. At its most basic, it defines the following methods:

```
abstract class Zend_Controller_Request_Abstract
{
    /**
     * @return string
     */
    public function getControllerName();

    /**
     * @param string $value
     * @return self
     */
    public function setControllerName($value);

    /**
     * @return string
     */
    public function getActionName();

    /**
     * @param string $value
     * @return self
     */
    public function setActionName($value);

    /**
     * @return string
     */
    public function getControllerKey();

    /**
     * @param string $key
     * @return self
     */
    public function setControllerKey($key);

    /**
     * @return string
     */
    public function getActionKey();

    /**
     * @param string $key
     * @return self
     */
    public function setActionKey($key);
```

```
    /**
     * @param string $key
     * @return mixed
     */
    public function getParam($key);

    /**
     * @param string $key
     * @param mixed $value
     * @return self
     */
    public function setParam($key, $value);

    /**
     * @return array
     */
     public function getParams();

    /**
     * @param array $array
     * @return self
     */
    public function setParams(array $array);

    /**
     * @param boolean $flag
     * @return self
     */
    public function setDispatched($flag = true);

    /**
     * @return boolean
     */
    public function isDispatched();
}
```

The request object is a container for the request environment. The controller chain really only needs to know how to set and retrieve the controller, action, optional parameters, and dispatched status. By default, the request will search its own parameters using the controller or action keys in order to determine the controller and action.

Extend this class, or one of its derivatives, when you need the request class to interact with a specific environment in order to retrieve data for use in the above tasks. Examples include the HTTP environment, a CLI environment, or a PHP-GTK environment.

The Standard Router

Introduction

Zend_Controller_Router_Rewrite is the standard framework router. Routing is the process of taking a URI endpoint (that part of the URI which comes after the base URL) and decomposing it into parameters to determine which module, controller, and action of that controller should receive the request. This values of the module, controller, action and other parameters are packaged into a Zend_Controller_Request_Http object which is then processed by Zend_Controller _Dispatcher_Standard. Routing occurs only once: when the request is initially received and before the first controller is dispatched.

Zend_Controller_Router_Rewrite is designed to allow for mod_rewrite-like functionality using pure PHP structures. It is very loosely based on Ruby on Rails routing and does not require any prior knowledge of webserver URL rewriting. It is designed to work with a single Apache mod_rewrite rule (one of):

```
RewriteEngine on
RewriteRule !\.(js|ico|gif|jpg|png|css|html)$ index.php
```

or (preferred):

```
RewriteEngine On
RewriteCond %{REQUEST_FILENAME} -s [OR]
RewriteCond %{REQUEST_FILENAME} -l [OR]
RewriteCond %{REQUEST_FILENAME} -d
RewriteRule ^.*$ - [NC,L]
RewriteRule ^.*$ index.php [NC,L]
```

The rewrite router can also be used with the IIS webserver (versions <= 7.0) if Isapi_Rewrite [http://www.isapirewrite.com] has been installed as an Isapi extension with the following rewrite rule:

```
RewriteRule ^[\w/\%]*(?:\.(?!(?:js|ico|gif|jpg|png|css|html)$)[\w\%]*$)?
    /index.php [I]
```

IIS Isapi_Rewrite

When using IIS, $_SERVER['REQUEST_URI'] will either not exist, or be set as an empty string. In this case, Zend_Controller_Request_Http will attempt to use the $_SERVER['HTTP_X_REWRITE_URL'] value set by the Isapi_Rewrite extension.

IIS 7.0 introduces a native URL rewriting module, and it can be configured as follows:

```
<configuration>
    <system.webServer>
        <rewrite>
            <rules>
                <rule name="Imported Rule 1" stopProcessing="true">
                    <match url="^.*$" />
                    <conditions logicalGrouping="MatchAny">
                        <add input="{REQUEST_FILENAME}"
                            matchType="IsFile" pattern=""
                            ignoreCase="false" />
                        <add input="{REQUEST_FILENAME}"
                            matchType="IsDirectory"
                            pattern="" ignoreCase="false" />
                    </conditions>
                    <action type="None" />
                </rule>
                <rule name="Imported Rule 2" stopProcessing="true">
                    <match url="^.*$" />
                    <action type="Rewrite" url="index.php" />
                </rule>
            </rules>
        </rewrite>
    </system.webServer>
</configuration>
```

If using Lighttpd, the following rewrite rule is valid:

```
url.rewrite-once = (
    ".*\?(.*)$" => "/index.php?$1",
    ".*\.(js|ico|gif|jpg|png|css|html)$" => "$0",
    "" => "/index.php"
)
```

Using a Router

To properly use the rewrite router you have to instantiate it, add some user defined routes and inject it into the controller. The following code illustrates the procedure:

```
// Create a router

$router = $ctrl->getRouter(); // returns a rewrite router by default
$router->addRoute(
    'user',
    new Zend_Controller_Router_Route('user/:username',
                                     array('controller' => 'user',
                                           'action' => 'info'))
);
```

Basic Rewrite Router Operation

The heart of the RewriteRouter is the definition of user defined routes. Routes are added by calling the addRoute method of RewriteRouter and passing in a new instance of a class implementing Zend_Controller_Router_Route_Interface. Eg.:

```
$router->addRoute('user',
                  new Zend_Controller_Router_Route('user/:username'));
```

Rewrite Router comes with six basic types of routes (one of which is special):

- the section called "Zend_Controller_Router_Route"

- the section called "Zend_Controller_Router_Route_Static"

- the section called "Zend_Controller_Router_Route_Regex"

- the section called "Zend_Controller_Router_Route_Hostname"

- the section called "Zend_Controller_Router_Route_Chain"

- the section called "Default Routes" *

Routes may be used numerous times to create a chain or user defined application routing schema. You may use any number of routes in any configuration, with the exception of the Module route, which should rather be used once and probably as the most generic route (i.e., as a default). Each route will be described in greater detail later on.

The first parameter to addRoute is the name of the route. It is used as a handle for getting the routes out of the router (e.g., for URL generation purposes). The second parameter being the route itself.

Note

The most common use of the route name is through the means of Zend_View url helper:

```
<a href=
"<?php echo $this->url(array('username' => 'martel'), 'user') ?>">
    Martel</a>
```

Which would result in the href: user/martel.

Routing is a simple process of iterating through all provided routes and matching its definitions to current request URI. When a positive match is found, variable values are returned from the Route instance and are injected into the Zend_Controller_Request object for later use in the dispatcher as well as in user created controllers. On a negative match result, the next route in the chain is checked.

If you need to determine which route was matched, you can use the getCurrentRouteName() method, which will return the identifier used when registering the route with the router. If you want the actual route object, you can use getCurrentRoute().

Reverse Matching

Routes are matched in reverse order so make sure your most generic routes are defined first.

Returned Values

Values returned from routing come from URL parameters or user defined route defaults. These variables are later accessible through the Zend_Controller_Request::getParam() or Zend_Controller_Action::_getParam() methods.

There are three special variables which can be used in your routes - 'module', 'controller' and 'action'. These special variables are used by Zend_Controller_Dispatcher to find a controller and action to dispatch to.

Special Variables

The names of these special variables may be different if you choose to alter the defaults in Zend_Controller_Request_Http by means of the setControllerKey and setActionKey methods.

Default Routes

Zend_Controller_Router_Rewrite comes preconfigured with a default route, which will match URIs in the shape of controller/action. Additionally, a module name may be specified as the first path element, allowing URIs of the form module/controller/action. Finally, it will also match any additional parameters appended to the URI by default - controller/action/var1/value1/var2/value2.

Some examples of how such routes are matched:

```
// Assuming the following:
$ctrl->setControllerDirectory(
    array(
        'default' => '/path/to/default/controllers',
        'news'    => '/path/to/news/controllers',
        'blog'    => '/path/to/blog/controllers'
    )
);

Module only:
```

```
http://example/news
    module == news

Invalid module maps to controller name:
http://example/foo
    controller == foo

Module + controller:
http://example/blog/archive
    module     == blog
    controller == archive

Module + controller + action:
http://example/blog/archive/list
    module     == blog
    controller == archive
    action     == list

Module + controller + action + params:
http://example/blog/archive/list/sort/alpha/date/desc
    module     == blog
    controller == archive
    action     == list
    sort       == alpha
    date       == desc
```

The default route is simply a Zend_Controller_Router_Route_Module object stored under the name (index) of 'default' in RewriteRouter. It's created more-or-less like below:

```
$compat = new Zend_Controller_Router_Route_Module(array(),
                                                   $dispatcher,
                                                   $request);
$this->addRoute('default', $compat);
```

If you do not want this particular default route in your routing schema, you may override it by creating your own 'default' route (i.e., storing it under the name of 'default') or removing it altogether by using removeDefaultRoutes():

```
// Remove any default routes
$router->removeDefaultRoutes();
```

Base URL and Subdirectories

The rewrite router can be used in subdirectories (e.g., http://domain.com/~user/application-root/) in which case the base URL of the application (/~user/application-root) should be automatically detected by Zend_Controller_Request_Http and used accordingly.

Should the base URL be detected incorrectly you can override it with your own base path by using Zend_Controller_Request_Http and calling the setBaseUrl() method (see the section called "Base Url and Subdirectories"):

```
$request->setBaseUrl('/~user/application-root/');
```

Global Parameters

You can set global parameters in a router which are automatically supplied to a route when assembling through the setGlobalParam. If a global parameter is set but also given to the assemble method directly, the user parameter overrides the global parameter. You can set a global parameter this way:

```
$router->setGlobalParam('lang', 'en');
```

Route Types

Zend_Controller_Router_Route

Zend_Controller_Router_Route is the standard framework route. It combines ease of use with flexible route definition. Each route consists primarily of URL mapping (of static and dynamic parts (variables)) and may be initialized with defaults as well as with variable requirements.

Let's imagine our fictional application will need some informational page about the content authors. We want to be able to point our web browsers to http://domain.com/author/martel to see the information about this "martel" guy. And the route for such functionality could look like:

```
$route = new Zend_Controller_Router_Route(
    'author/:username',
    array(
        'controller' => 'profile',
        'action'     => 'userinfo'
    )
);

$router->addRoute('user', $route);
```

The first parameter in the Zend_Controller_Router_Route constructor is a route definition that will be matched to a URL. Route definitions consist of static and dynamic parts separated by the slash ('/') character. Static parts are just simple text: author. Dynamic parts, called variables, are marked by prepending a colon to the variable name: :username.

Character Usage

The current implementation allows you to use any character (except a slash) as a variable identifier, but it is strongly recommended that one uses only characters that are valid for PHP variable identifiers. Future implementations may alter this behaviour, which could result in hidden bugs in your code.

This example route should be matched when you point your browser to http://domain.com/author/martel, in which case all its variables will be injected to the Zend_Controller_Request object and will be accessible in your ProfileController. Variables returned by this example may be represented as an array of the following key and value pairs:

```
$values = array(
    'username'   => 'martel',
    'controller' => 'profile',
    'action'     => 'userinfo'
);
```

Later on, Zend_Controller_Dispatcher_Standard should invoke the userin foAction() method of your ProfileController class (in the default module) based on these values. There you will be able to access all variables by means of the Zend_Controller_Action::_getParam() or Zend_Controller_Request ::getParam() methods:

```
public function userinfoAction()
{
    $request = $this->getRequest();
    $username = $request->getParam('username');

    $username = $this->_getParam('username');
}
```

Route definition can contain one more special character - a wildcard - represented by '*' symbol. It is used to gather parameters similarly to the default Module route (var => value pairs defined in the URI). The following route more-or-less mimics the Module route behavior:

```
$route = new Zend_Controller_Router_Route(
    ':module/:controller/:action/*',
    array('module' => 'default')
);
$router->addRoute('default', $route);
```

Variable Defaults

Every variable in the route can have a default and this is what the second parameter of the Zend_Controller_Router_Route constructor is used for. This parameter is an array with keys representing variable names and with values as desired defaults:

```
$route = new Zend_Controller_Router_Route(
    'archive/:year',
    array('year' => 2006)
);
$router->addRoute('archive', $route);
```

The above route will match URLs like http://domain.com/archive/2005 and http://example.com/archive. In the latter case the variable year will have an initial default value of 2006.

This example will result in injecting a year variable to the request object. Since no routing information is present (no controller and action parameters are defined), the application will be dispatched to the default controller and action method (which are both defined in Zend_Controller _Dispatcher_Abstract). To make it more usable, you have to provide a valid controller and a valid action as the route's defaults:

```
$route = new Zend_Controller_Router_Route(
    'archive/:year',
    array(
        'year'       => 2006,
        'controller' => 'archive',
        'action'     => 'show'
    )
);
$router->addRoute('archive', $route);
```

This route will then result in dispatching to the method showAction() of the class ArchiveController.

Variable Requirements

One can add a third parameter to the Zend_Controller_Router_Route constructor where variable requirements may be set. These are defined as parts of a regular expression:

```
$route = new Zend_Controller_Router_Route(
    'archive/:year',
    array(
        'year'       => 2006,
        'controller' => 'archive',
        'action'     => 'show'
    ),
    array('year' => '\d+')
);
$router->addRoute('archive', $route);
```

With a route defined like above, the router will match it only when the year variable will contain numeric data, eg. http://domain.com/archive/2345. A URL like http://example.com/archive/test will not be matched and control will be passed to the next route in the chain instead.

Translated segments

The standard route supports translated segments. To use this feature, you have to define at least a translator (an instance of Zend_Translate) via one of the following ways:

- Put it into the registry with the key Zend_Translate.

- Set it via the static method Zend_Controller_Router_Route::setDefault Translator().

- Pass it as fourth parameter to the constructor.

By default, the locale specified in the Zend_Translate instance will be used. To override it, you set it (an instance of Zend_Locale or a locale string) in one of the following ways:

- Put it into the registry with the key Zend_Locale.

- Set it via the static method Zend_Controller_Router_Route::setDefaultLocale().

- Pass it as fifth parameter to the constructor.

- Pass it as @locale parameter to the assemble method.

Translated segments are separated into two parts. Fixed segments are prefixed by a single @-sign, and will be translated to the current locale when assembling and reverted to the message ID when matching again. Dynamic segments are prefixed by :@. When assembling, the given parameter will be translated and inserted into the parameter position. When matching, the translated parameter from the URL will be reverted to the message ID again.

Message IDs and separate language file

Occasionally a message ID which you want to use in one of your routes is already used in a view script or somewhere else. To have full control over safe URLs, you should use a separate language file for the messages used in the route.

The following is the simplest way to prepare the standard route for translated segment usage:

```
// Prepare the translator
$translator = new Zend_Translate('array', array(), 'en');
$translator->addTranslation(array('archive' => 'archiv',
                                  'year'    => 'jahr',
                                  'month'   => 'monat',
                                  'index'   => 'uebersicht'),
                            'de');

// Set the current locale for the translator
$translator->setLocale('en');

// Set it as default translator for routes
Zend_Controller_Router_Route::setDefaultTranslator($translator);
```

This example demonstrates the usage of static segments:

```
// Create the route
$route = new Zend_Controller_Router_Route(
    '@archive',
    array(
        'controller' => 'archive',
        'action'     => 'index'
    )
);
$router->addRoute('archive', $route);

// Assemble the URL in default locale: archive
$route->assemble(array());

// Assemble the URL in german: archiv
$route->assemble(array());
```

You can use the dynamic segments to create a module-route like translated version:

```
// Create the route
$route = new Zend_Controller_Router_Route(
    ':@controller/:@action/*',
    array(
        'controller' => 'index',
        'action'     => 'index'
    )
);
$router->addRoute('archive', $route);

// Assemble the URL in default locale: archive/index/foo/bar
$route->assemble(array('controller' => 'archive', 'foo' => 'bar'));

// Assemble the URL in german: archiv/uebersicht/foo/bar
$route->assemble(array('controller' => 'archive', 'foo' => 'bar'));
```

You can also mix static and dynamic segments:

```
// Create the route
$route = new Zend_Controller_Router_Route(
    '@archive/:@mode/:value',
    array(
        'mode'       => 'year'
        'value'      => 2005,
        'controller' => 'archive',
        'action'     => 'show'
    ),
    array('mode'  => '(month|year)'
          'value' => '\d+')
);
$router->addRoute('archive', $route);

// Assemble the URL in default locale: archive/month/5
$route->assemble(array('mode' => 'month', 'value' => '5'));

// Assemble the URL in german: archiv/monat/5
$route->assemble(array('mode' => 'month', 'value' => '5',
    '@locale' => 'de'));
```

Zend_Controller_Router_Route_Static

The examples above all use dynamic routes -- routes that contain patterns to match against. Sometimes, however, a particular route is set in stone, and firing up the regular expression engine would be an overkill. The answer to this situation is to use static routes:

```
$route = new Zend_Controller_Router_Route_Static(
    'login',
    array('controller' => 'auth', 'action' => 'login')
);
$router->addRoute('login', $route);
```

Above route will match a URL of `http://domain.com/login`, and dispatch to `AuthController::loginAction()`.

Warning: Static Routes must Contain Sane Defaults

Since a static route does not pass any part of the URL to the request object as parameters, you *must* pass all parameters necessary for dispatching a request as defaults to the route. Omitting the "controller" or "action" default values will have unexpected results, and will likely result in the request being undispatchable.

As a rule of thumb, always provide each of the following default values:

- controller

- action

- module (if not default)

Optionally, you can also pass the "useDefaultControllerAlways" parameter to the front controller during bootstrapping:

```
$front->setParam('useDefaultControllerAlways', true);
```

However, this is considered a workaround; it is always better to explicitly define sane defaults.

Zend_Controller_Router_Route_Regex

In addition to the default and static route types, a Regular Expression route type is available. This route offers more power and flexibility over the others, but at a slight cost of complexity. At the same time, it should be faster than the standard Route.

Like the standard route, this route has to be initialized with a route definition and some defaults. Let's create an archive route as an example, similar to the previously defined one, only using the Regex route this time:

```
$route = new Zend_Controller_Router_Route_Regex(
    'archive/(\d+)',
    array(
        'controller' => 'archive',
        'action'     => 'show'
    )
);
$router->addRoute('archive', $route);
```

Every defined regex subpattern will be injected to the request object. With our above example, after successful matching `http://domain.com/archive/2006`, the resulting value array may look like:

```
$values = array(
    1           => '2006',
    'controller' => 'archive',
    'action'     => 'show'
);
```

Note

Leading and trailing slashes are trimmed from the URL in the Router prior to a match. As a result, matching the URL `http://domain.com/foo/bar/`, would involve a regex of `foo/bar`, and not `/foo/bar`.

Note

Line start and line end anchors ('^' and '$', respectively) are automatically pre- and appended to all expressions. Thus, you should not use these in your regular expressions, and you should match the entire string.

Note

This route class uses the # character for a delimiter. This means that you will need to escape hash characters ('#') but not forward slashes ('/') in your route definitions. Since the '#' character (named anchor) is rarely passed to the webserver, you will rarely need to use that character in your regex.

You can get the contents of the defined subpatterns the usual way:

```
public function showAction()
{
    $request = $this->getRequest();
    $year    = $request->getParam(1); // $year = '2006';
```

}

Note

Notice the key is an integer (1) instead of a string ('1').

This route will not yet work exactly the same as its standard route counterpart since the default for 'year' is not yet set. And what may not yet be evident is that we will have a problem with a trailing slash even if we declare a default for the year and make the subpattern optional. The solution is to make the whole year part optional along with the slash but catch only the numeric part:

```
$route = new Zend_Controller_Router_Route_Regex(
    'archive(?:/(\d+))?',
    array(
        1           => '2006',
        'controller' => 'archive',
        'action'     => 'show'
    )
);
$router->addRoute('archive', $route);
```

Now let's get to the problem you have probably noticed on your own by now. Using integer based keys for parameters is not an easily manageable solution and may be potentially problematic in the long run. And that's where the third parameter comes in. This parameter is an associative array that represents a map of regex subpatterns to parameter named keys. Let's work on our easier example:

```
$route = new Zend_Controller_Router_Route_Regex(
    'archive/(\d+)',
    array(
        'controller' => 'archive',
        'action' => 'show'
    ),
    array(
        1 => 'year'
    )
);
$router->addRoute('archive', $route);
```

This will result in following values injected into Request:

```
$values = array(
    'year'       => '2006',
    'controller' => 'archive',
    'action'     => 'show'
);
```

The map may be defined in either direction to make it work in any environment. Keys may contain variable names or subpattern indexes:

```
$route = new Zend_Controller_Router_Route_Regex(
    'archive/(\d+)',
    array( ... ),
    array(1 => 'year')
);
```

```
// OR

$route = new Zend_Controller_Router_Route_Regex(
    'archive/(\d+)',
    array( ... ),
    array('year' => 1)
);
```

Note

Subpattern keys have to be represented by integers.

Notice that the numeric index in Request values is now gone and a named variable is shown in its place. Of course you can mix numeric and named variables if you wish:

```
$route = new Zend_Controller_Router_Route_Regex(
    'archive/(\d+)/page/(\d+)',
    array( ... ),
    array('year' => 1)
);
```

Which will result in mixed values available in the Request. As an example, the URL `http://domain.com/archive/2006/page/10` will result in following values:

```
$values = array(
    'year'       => '2006',
    2            => 10,
    'controller' => 'archive',
    'action'     => 'show'
);
```

Since regex patterns are not easily reversed, you will need to prepare a reverse URL if you wish to use a URL helper or even an assemble method of this class. This reversed path is represented by a string parsable by sprintf() and is defined as a fourth construct parameter:

```
$route = new Zend_Controller_Router_Route_Regex(
    'archive/(\d+)',
    array( ... ),
    array('year' => 1),
    'archive/%s'
);
```

All of this is something which was already possible by the means of a standard route object, so where's the benefit in using the Regex route, you ask? Primarily, it allows you to describe any type of URL without any restrictions. Imagine you have a blog and wish to create URLs like: `http://domain.com/blog/archive/01-Using_the_Regex_Router.html`, and have it decompose the last path element, `01-Using_the_Regex_Router.html`, into an article ID and article title/description; this is not possible with the standard route. With the Regex route, you can do something like the following solution:

```
$route = new Zend_Controller_Router_Route_Regex(
    'blog/archive/(\d+)-(.+)\.html',
    array(
        'controller' => 'blog',
        'action'     => 'view'
```

```
    ),
    array(
        1 => 'id',
        2 => 'description'
    ),
    'blog/archive/%d-%s.html'
);
$router->addRoute('blogArchive', $route);
```

As you can see, this adds a tremendous amount of flexibility over the standard route.

Zend_Controller_Router_Route_Hostname

Zend_Controller_Router_Route_Hostname is the hostname route of the framework. It works similar to the standard route, but it works on the with the hostname of the called URL instead with the path.

Let's use the example from the standard route and see how it would look like in a hostname based way. Instead of calling the user via a path, we'd want to have a user to be able to call http://martel.users.example.com to see the information about the user "martel":

```
$hostnameRoute = new Zend_Controller_Router_Route_Hostname(
    ':username.users.example.com',
    array(
        'controller' => 'profile',
        'action'     => 'userinfo'
    )
);

$plainPathRoute = new Zend_Controller_Router_Route_Static('');

$router->addRoute('user', $hostnameRoute->chain($plainPathRoute);
```

The first parameter in the Zend_Controller_Router_Route_Hostname constructor is a route definition that will be matched to a hostname. Route definitions consist of static and dynamic parts separated by the dot ('.') character. Dynamic parts, called variables, are marked by prepending a colon to the variable name: :username. Static parts are just simple text: user.

Hostname routes can, but never should be used as is. The reason behind that is, that a hostname route alone would match any path. So what you have to do is to chain a path route to the hostname route. This is done like in the example by calling $hostnameRoute->chain($pathRoute);. By doing this, $hostnameRoute isn't modified, but a new route (Zend_Controller_Router_Route _Chain) is returned, which can then be given to the router.

Zend_Controller_Router_Route_Chain

Zend_Controller_Router_Route_Chain is a route which allows to chain multiple routes together. This allows you to chain hostname-routes and path routes, or multiple path routes for example. Chaining can be done either programatically or within a configuration file.

Parameter Priority

When chaining routes together, the parameters of the outer route have a higher priority than the parameters of the inner route. Thus if you define a controller in the outer and in the inner route, the controller of the outer route will be selected.

When chaining programatically, there are two ways to archive this. The first one is to create a new

Zend_Controller_Router_Route_Chain instance and then calling the chain method multiple times with all routes which should be chained together. The other way is to take the first route, e.g. a hostname route, and calling the chain method on it with the route which should be appended to it. This will not modify the hostname route, but return a new instance of Zend_Controller_Router_Route_Chain, which then has both routes chained together:

```
// Create two routes
$hostnameRoute = new Zend_Controller_Router_Route_Hostname(...);
$pathRoute     = new Zend_Controller_Router_Route(...);

// First way, chain them via the chain route
$chainedRoute = new Zend_Controller_Router_Route_Chain();
$chainedRoute->chain($hostnameRoute)
             ->chain($pathRoute);

// Second way, chain them directly
$chainedRoute = $hostnameRoute->chain($pathRoute);
```

When chaining routes together, their default separator is a slash by default. There may be cases when you want to have a different separator:

```
// Create two routes
$firstRoute  = new Zend_Controller_Router_Route('foo');
$secondRoute = new Zend_Controller_Router_Route('bar');

// Chain them together with a different separator
$chainedRoute = $firstRoute->chain($secondRoute, '-');

// Assemble the route: "foo-bar"
echo $chainedRoute->assemble();
```

Chain Routes via Zend_Config

To chain routes together in a config file, there are additional parameters for the configuration of those. The simpler approach is to use the chains parameters. This one is simply a list of routes, which will be chained with the parent route. Neither the parent- nor the child-route will be added directly to the router but only the resulting chained route. The name of the chained route in the router will be the parent route name and the child route name concatenated with a dash (-). A simple config in XML would look like this:

```
<routes>
    <www type="Zend_Controller_Router_Route_Hostname">
        <route>www.example.com</route>
        <chains>
            <language type="Zend_Controller_Router_Route">
                <route>:language</route>
                <reqs language="[a-z]{2}">
                <chains>
                    <index type="Zend_Controller_Router_Route_Static">
                        <route></route>
                        <defaults module="default" controller="index"
                            action="index" />
                    </index>
                    <imprint type="Zend_Controller_Router_Route_Static">
                        <route>imprint</route>
                        <defaults module="default" controller="index"
                            action="index" />
                    </imprint>
                </chains>
```

```
                </language>
            </chains>
        </www>
        <users type="Zend_Controller_Router_Route_Hostname">
            <route>users.example.com</route>
            <chains>
                <profile type="Zend_Controller_Router_Route">
                    <route>:username</route>
                    <defaults module="users" controller="profile"
                        action="index" />
                </profile>
            </chains>
        </users>
        <misc type="Zend_Controller_Router_Route_Static">
            <route>misc</route>
        </misc>
    </routes>
```

This will result in the three routes www-language-index, www-language-imprint and users-language-profile which will only match based on the hostname and the route misc, which will match with any hostname.

The alternative way of creating a chained route is via the chain parameter, which can only be used with the chain-route type directly, and also just works in the root level:

```
<routes>
    <www type="Zend_Controller_Router_Route_Chain">
        <route>www.example.com</route>
    </www>
    <language type="Zend_Controller_Router_Route">
        <route>:language</route>
        <reqs language="[a-z]{2}">
    </language>
    <index type="Zend_Controller_Router_Route_Static">
        <route></route>
        <defaults module="default" controller="index" action="index" />
    </index>
    <imprint type="Zend_Controller_Router_Route_Static">
        <route>imprint</route>
        <defaults module="default" controller="index" action="index" />
    </imprint>

    <www-index type="Zend_Controller_Router_Route_Chain">
        <chain>www, language, index</chain>
    </www-index>
    <www-imprint type="Zend_Controller_Router_Route_Chain">
        <chain>www, language, imprint</chain>
    </www-imprint>
</routes>
```

You can also give the chain parameter as array instead of separating the routes with a comma:

```
<routes>
    <www-index type="Zend_Controller_Router_Route_Chain">
        <chain>www</chain>
        <chain>language</chain>
        <chain>index</chain>
    </www-index>
    <www-imprint type="Zend_Controller_Router_Route_Chain">
        <chain>www</chain>
```

```
            <chain>language</chain>
            <chain>imprint</chain>
        </www-imprint>
    </routes>
```

Using Zend_Config with the RewriteRouter

Sometimes it is more convenient to update a configuration file with new routes than to change the code. This is possible via the `addConfig()` method. Basically, you create a `Zend_Config`-compatible configuration, and in your code read it in and pass it to the RewriteRouter.

As an example, consider the following INI file:

```
[production]
routes.archive.route = "archive/:year/*"
routes.archive.defaults.controller = archive
routes.archive.defaults.action = show
routes.archive.defaults.year = 2000
routes.archive.reqs.year = "\d+"

routes.news.type = "Zend_Controller_Router_Route_Static"
routes.news.route = "news"
routes.news.defaults.controller = "news"
routes.news.defaults.action = "list"

routes.archive.type = "Zend_Controller_Router_Route_Regex"
routes.archive.route = "archive/(\d+)"
routes.archive.defaults.controller = "archive"
routes.archive.defaults.action = "show"
routes.archive.map.1 = "year"
; OR: routes.archive.map.year = 1
```

The above INI file can then be read into a `Zend_Config` object as follows:

```
$config = new Zend_Config_Ini('/path/to/config.ini', 'production');
$router = new Zend_Controller_Router_Rewrite();
$router->addConfig($config, 'routes');
```

In the above example, we tell the router to use the 'routes' section of the INI file to use for its routes. Each first-level key under that section will be used to define a route name; the above example defines the routes 'archive' and 'news'. Each route then requires, at minimum, a 'route' entry and one or more 'defaults' entries; optionally one or more 'reqs' (short for 'required') may be provided. All told, these correspond to the three arguments provided to a `Zend_Controller_Router_Route _Interface` object. An option key, 'type', can be used to specify the route class type to use for that particular route; by default, it uses `Zend_Controller_Router_Route`. In the example above, the 'news' route is defined to use `Zend_Controller_Router_Route_Static`.

Subclassing the Router

The standard rewrite router should provide most functionality you may need; most often, you will only need to create a new route type in order to provide new or modified functionality over the provided routes.

That said, you may at some point find yourself wanting to use a different routing paradigm. The interface `Zend_Controller_Router_Interface` provides the minimal information required to create a router, and consists of a single method.

```
interface Zend_Controller_Router_Interface
{
  /**
   * @param  Zend_Controller_Request_Abstract $request
   * @throws Zend_Controller_Router_Exception
   * @return Zend_Controller_Request_Abstract
   */
  public function route(Zend_Controller_Request_Abstract $request);
}
```

Routing only occurs once: when the request is first received into the system. The purpose of the router is to determine the controller, action, and optional parameters based on the request environment, and then set them in the request. The request object is then passed to the dispatcher. If it is not possible to map a route to a dispatch token, the router should do nothing to the request object.

The Dispatcher

Overview

Dispatching is the process of taking the request object, `Zend_Controller_Request_Abstract`, extracting the module name, controller name, action name, and optional parameters contained in it, and then instantiating a controller and calling an action of that controller. If any of the module, controller, or action are not found, it will use default values for them. `Zend_Controller_Dispatcher_Standard` specifies `index` for each of the controller and action defaults and `default` for the module default value, but allows the developer to change the default values for each using the `setDefaultController()`, `setDefaultAction()`, and `setDefaultModule()` methods, respectively.

Default Module

When creating modular applications, you may find that you want your default module namespaced as well (the default configuration is that the default module is *not* namespaced). As of 1.5.0, you can now do so by specifying the `prefixDefaultModule` as true in either the front controller or your dispatcher:

```
// In your front controller:
$front->setParam('prefixDefaultModule', true);

// In your dispatcher:
$dispatcher->setParam('prefixDefaultModule', true);
```

This allows you to re-purpose an existing module to be the default module for an application.

Dispatching happens in a loop in the front controller. Before dispatching occurs, the front controller routes the request to find user specified values for the module, controller, action, and optional parameters. It then enters a dispatch loop, dispatching the request.

At the beginning of each iteration, it sets a flag in the request object indicating that the action has been dispatched. If an action or pre/postDispatch plugin resets that flag, the dispatch loop will continue and attempt to dispatch the new request. By changing the controller and/or action in the request and resetting the dispatched flag, the developer may define a chain of requests to perform.

The action controller method that controls such dispatching is `_forward()`; call this method from any of the pre/postDispatch() or action methods, providing an action, controller, module, and optionally any additional parameters you may wish to send to the new action:

```
public function fooAction()
{
    // forward to another action in the current controller and module:
    $this->_forward('bar', null, null, array('baz' => 'bogus'));
}

public function barAction()
{
    // forward to an action in another controller:
    // FooController::bazAction(),
    // in the current module:
    $this->_forward('baz', 'foo', null, array('baz' => 'bogus'));
}

public function bazAction()
{
    // forward to an action in another controller in another module,
    // Foo_BarController::bazAction():
    $this->_forward('baz', 'bar', 'foo', array('baz' => 'bogus'));
}
```

Subclassing the Dispatcher

Zend_Controller_Front will first call the router to determine the first action in the request. It then enters a dispatch loop, which calls on the dispatcher to dispatch the action.

The dispatcher needs a variety of data in order to do its work - it needs to know how to format controller and action names, where to look for controller class files, whether or not a provided module name is valid, and an API for determining if a given request is even dispatchable based on the other information available.

Zend_Controller_Dispatcher_Interface defines the following methods as required for any dispatcher implementation:

```
interface Zend_Controller_Dispatcher_Interface
{
    /**
     * Format a string into a controller class name.
     *
     * @param string $unformatted
     * @return string
     */
    public function formatControllerName($unformatted);

    /**
     * Format a string into an action method name.
     *
     * @param string $unformatted
     * @return string
     */
    public function formatActionName($unformatted);

    /**
     * Determine if a request is dispatchable
     *
     * @param  Zend_Controller_Request_Abstract $request
     * @return boolean
     */
```

```
public function isDispatchable(
    Zend_Controller_Request_Abstract $request
);

/**
 * Set a user parameter (via front controller, or for local use)
 *
 * @param string $name
 * @param mixed $value
 * @return Zend_Controller_Dispatcher_Interface
 */
public function setParam($name, $value);

/**
 * Set an array of user parameters
 *
 * @param array $params
 * @return Zend_Controller_Dispatcher_Interface
 */
public function setParams(array $params);

/**
 * Retrieve a single user parameter
 *
 * @param string $name
 * @return mixed
 */
public function getParam($name);

/**
 * Retrieve all user parameters
 *
 * @return array
 */
public function getParams();

/**
 * Clear the user parameter stack, or a single user parameter
 *
 * @param null|string|array single key or array of keys for
 *         params to clear
 * @return Zend_Controller_Dispatcher_Interface
 */
public function clearParams($name = null);

/**
 * Set the response object to use, if any
 *
 * @param Zend_Controller_Response_Abstract|null $response
 * @return void
 */
public function setResponse(
    Zend_Controller_Response_Abstract $response = null
);

/**
 * Retrieve the response object, if any
 *
 * @return Zend_Controller_Response_Abstract|null
 */
```

```php
public function getResponse();

/**
 * Add a controller directory to the controller directory stack
 *
 * @param string $path
 * @param string $args
 * @return Zend_Controller_Dispatcher_Interface
 */
public function addControllerDirectory($path, $args = null);

/**
 * Set the directory (or directories) where controller files are
 * stored
 *
 * @param string|array $dir
 * @return Zend_Controller_Dispatcher_Interface
 */
public function setControllerDirectory($path);

/**
 * Return the currently set directory(ies) for controller file
 * lookup
 *
 * @return array
 */
public function getControllerDirectory();

/**
 * Dispatch a request to a (module/)controller/action.
 *
 * @param   Zend_Controller_Request_Abstract $request
 * @param   Zend_Controller_Response_Abstract $response
 * @return Zend_Controller_Request_Abstract|boolean
 */
public function dispatch(
    Zend_Controller_Request_Abstract $request,
    Zend_Controller_Response_Abstract $response
);

/**
 * Whether or not a given module is valid
 *
 * @param string $module
 * @return boolean
 */
public function isValidModule($module);

/**
 * Retrieve the default module name
 *
 * @return string
 */
public function getDefaultModule();

/**
 * Retrieve the default controller name
 *
 * @return string
 */
```

```
    public function getDefaultControllerName();

    /**
     * Retrieve the default action
     *
     * @return string
     */
    public function getDefaultAction();
}
```

In most cases, however, you should simply extend the abstract class Zend_Controller_Dispatcher_Abstract, in which each of these have already been defined, or Zend_Controller_Dispatcher_Standard to modify functionality of the standard dispatcher.

Possible reasons to subclass the dispatcher include a desire to use a different class or method naming schema in your action controllers, or a desire to use a different dispatching paradigm such as dispatching to action files under controller directories (instead of dispatching to class methods).

Action Controllers

Introduction

Zend_Controller_Action is an abstract class you may use for implementing Action Controllers for use with the Front Controller when building a website based on the Model-View-Controller (MVC) pattern.

To use Zend_Controller_Action, you will need to subclass it in your actual action controller classes (or subclass it to create your own base class for action controllers). The most basic operation is to subclass it, and create action methods that correspond to the various actions you wish the controller to handle for your site. Zend_Controller's routing and dispatch handling will autodiscover any methods ending in 'Action' in your class as potential controller actions.

For example, let's say your class is defined as follows:

```
class FooController extends Zend_Controller_Action
{
    public function barAction()
    {
        // do something
    }

    public function bazAction()
    {
        // do something
    }
}
```

The above FooController class (controller foo) defines two actions, bar and baz.

There's much more that can be accomplished than this, such as custom initialization actions, default actions to call should no action (or an invalid action) be specified, pre- and post-dispatch hooks, and a variety of helper methods. This chapter serves as an overview of the action controller functionality

Default Behaviour

By default, the front controller enables the ViewRenderer action helper. This helper takes care of injecting the view object into the controller, as well as automatically rendering views. You may disable it within your action controller via one of the following methods:

```
class FooController extends Zend_Controller_Action
{
    public function init()
    {
        // Local to this controller only; affects all actions,
        // as loaded in init:
        $this->_helper->viewRenderer->setNoRender(true);

        // Globally:
        $this->_helper->removeHelper('viewRenderer');

        // Also globally, but would need to be in conjunction with the
        // local version in order to propagate for this controller:
        Zend_Controller_Front::getInstance()
            ->setParam('noViewRenderer', true);
    }
}
```

initView(), getViewScript(), render(), and renderScript() each proxy to the ViewRenderer unless the helper is not in the helper broker or the noViewRenderer flag has been set.

You can also simply disable rendering for an individual view by setting the ViewRenderer's noRender flag:

```
class FooController extends Zend_Controller_Action
{
    public function barAction()
    {
        // disable autorendering for this action only:
        $this->_helper->viewRenderer->setNoRender();
    }
}
```

The primary reasons to disable the ViewRenderer are if you simply do not need a view object or if you are not rendering via view scripts (for instance, when using an action controller to serve web service protocols such as SOAP, XML-RPC, or REST). In most cases, you will never need to globally disable the ViewRenderer, only selectively within individual controllers or actions.

Object Initialization

While you can always override the action controller's constructor, we do not recommend this. Zend_Controller_Action::__construct() performs some important tasks, such as registering the request and response objects, as well as any custom invocation arguments passed in from the front controller. If you must override the constructor, be sure to call parent::__construct($request, $response, $invokeArgs).

The more appropriate way to customize instantiation is to use the init() method, which is called as the last task of __construct(). For example, if you want to connect to a database at instantiation:

```
class FooController extends Zend_Controller_Action
{
    public function init()
    {
        $this->db = Zend_Db::factory('Pdo_Mysql', array(
            'host'     => 'myhost',
            'username' => 'user',
            'password' => 'XXXXXXX',
            'dbname'   => 'website'
        ));
    }
}
```

Pre- and Post-Dispatch Hooks

Zend_Controller_Action specifies two methods that may be called to bookend a requested action, preDispatch() and postDispatch(). These can be useful in a variety of ways: verifying authentication and ACLs prior to running an action (by calling _forward() in preDispatch(), the action will be skipped), for instance, or placing generated content in a sitewide template (postDispatch()).

Accessors

A number of objects and variables are registered with the object, and each has accessor methods.

- *Request Object*: getRequest() may be used to retrieve the request object used to call the action.

- *Response Object*: getResponse() may be used to retrieve the response object aggregating the final response. Some typical calls might look like:

```
$this->getResponse()->setHeader('Content-Type', 'text/xml');
$this->getResponse()->appendBody($content);
```

- *Invocation Arguments*: the front controller may push parameters into the router, dispatcher, and action controller. To retrieve these, use getInvokeArg($key); alternatively, fetch the entire list using getInvokeArgs().

- *Request parameters*: The request object aggregates request parameters, such as any _GET or _POST parameters, or user parameters specified in the URL's path information. To retrieve these, use _getParam($key) or _getAllParams(). You may also set request parameters using _setParam(); this is useful when forwarding to additional actions.

To test whether or not a parameter exists (useful for logical branching), use _hasParam($key).

Note

_getParam() may take an optional second argument containing a default value to use if the parameter is not set or is empty. Using it eliminates the need to call _hasParam() prior to retrieving a value:

```
// Use default value of 1 if id is not set
$id = $this->_getParam('id', 1);
```

```
// Instead of:
if ($this->_hasParam('id') {
    $id = $this->_getParam('id');
} else {
    $id = 1;
}
```

View Integration

Default View Integration is Via the ViewRenderer

The content in this section is only valid when you have explicitly disabled the ViewRenderer. Otherwise, you can safely skip over this section.

Zend_Controller_Action provides a rudimentary and flexible mechanism for view integration. Two methods accomplish this, initView() and render(); the former method lazy-loads the $view public property, and the latter renders a view based on the current requested action, using the directory hierarchy to determine the script path.

View Initialization

initView() initializes the view object. render() calls initView() in order to retrieve the view object, but it may be initialized at any time; by default it populates the $view property with a Zend_View object, but any class implementing Zend_View_Interface may be used. If $view is already initialized, it simply returns that property.

The default implementation makes the following assumption of the directory structure:

```
applicationOrModule/
    controllers/
        IndexController.php
    views/
        scripts/
            index/
                index.phtml
        helpers/
        filters/
```

In other words, view scripts are assumed to be in the views/scripts/ subdirectory, and the views subdirectory is assumed to contain sibling functionality (helpers, filters). When determining the view script name and path, the views/scripts/ directory will be used as the base path, with directories named after the individual controllers providing a hierarchy of view scripts.

Rendering Views

render() has the following signature:

```
string render(string $action = null,
              string $name = null,
              bool $noController = false);
```

render() renders a view script. If no arguments are passed, it assumes that the script requested is [controller]/[action].phtml (where .phtml is the value of the $viewSuffix property). Passing a value for $action will render that template in the [controller] subdirectory. To override using the [controller] subdirectory, pass a true value for $noController. Finally, templates are rendered into the response object; if you wish to render to a specific named segment in the response object, pass a value to $name.

Note

Since controller and action names may contain word delimiter characters such as '_', '.', and '-', render() normalizes these to '-' when determining the script name. Internally, it uses the dispatcher's word and path delimiters to do this normalization. Thus, a request to /foo.bar/baz-bat will render the script foo-bar/baz-bat.phtml. If your action method contains camelCasing, please remember that this will result in '-' separated words when determining the view script file name.

Some examples:

```
class MyController extends Zend_Controller_Action
{
    public function fooAction()
    {
        // Renders my/foo.phtml
        $this->render();

        // Renders my/bar.phtml
        $this->render('bar');

        // Renders baz.phtml
        $this->render('baz', null, true);

        // Renders my/login.phtml to the 'form' segment of the
        // response object
        $this->render('login', 'form');

        // Renders site.phtml to the 'page' segment of the response
        // object; does not use the 'my/' subirectory
        $this->render('site', 'page', true);
    }

    public function bazBatAction()
    {
        // Renders my/baz-bat.phtml
        $this->render();
    }
}
```

Utility Methods

Besides the accessors and view integration methods, Zend_Controller_Action has several utility methods for performing common tasks from within your action methods (or from pre-/post-dispatch).

- _forward($action, $controller = null, $module = null, array $params = null): perform another action. If called in preDispatch(), the currently requested action will be skipped in favor of the new one. Otherwise, after the current action is processed, the action requested in _forward() will be executed.

- _redirect($url, array $options = array()): redirect to another location. This method takes a URL and an optional set of options. By default, it performs an HTTP 302 redirect.

  The options may include one or more of the following:

  - *exit:* whether or not to exit immediately. If requested, it will cleanly close any open sessions and perform the redirect.

You may set this option globally within the controller using the `setRedirectExit()` accessor.

- *prependBase:* whether or not to prepend the base URL registered with the request object to the URL provided.

  You may set this option globally within the controller using the `setRedirectPrependBase()` accessor.

- *code:* what HTTP code to utilize in the redirect. By default, an HTTP 302 is utilized; any code between 301 and 306 may be used.

  You may set this option globally within the controller using the `setRedirectCode()` accessor.

Subclassing the Action Controller

By design, `Zend_Controller_Action` must be subclassed in order to create an action controller. At the minimum, you will need to define action methods that the controller may call.

Besides creating useful functionality for your web applications, you may also find that you're repeating much of the same setup or utility methods in your various controllers; if so, creating a common base controller class that extends `Zend_Controller_Action` could solve such redundancy.

Example 12.1. Handling Non-Existent Actions

If a request to a controller is made that includes an undefined action method, `Zend_Controller_Action::__call()` will be invoked. `__call()` is, of course, PHP's magic method for method overloading.

By default, this method throws a `Zend_Controller_Action_Exception` indicating the requested method was not found in the controller. If the method requested ends in 'Action', the assumption is that an action was requested and does not exist; such errors result in an exception with a code of 404. All other methods result in an exception with a code of 500. This allows you to easily differentiate between page not found and application errors in your error handler.

You should override this functionality if you wish to perform other operations. For instance, if you wish to display an error message, you might write something like this:

```
class MyController extends Zend_Controller_Action
{
    public function __call($method, $args)
    {
        if ('Action' == substr($method, -6)) {
            // If the action method was not found, render the error
            // template
            return $this->render('error');
        }

        // all other methods throw an exception
        throw new Exception('Invalid method "'
                            . $method
                            . '" called',
                            500);
    }
}
```

Another possibility is that you may want to forward on to a default controller page:

```
class MyController extends Zend_Controller_Action
{
    public function indexAction()
    {
        $this->render();
    }

    public function __call($method, $args)
    {
        if ('Action' == substr($method, -6)) {
            // If the action method was not found, forward to the
            // index action
            return $this->_forward('index');
        }

        // all other methods throw an exception
        throw new Exception('Invalid method "'
                            . $method
                            . '" called',
                            500);
    }
}
```

Besides overriding __call(), each of the initialization, utility, accessor, view, and dispatch hook methods mentioned previously in this chapter may be overridden in order to customize your controllers. As an example, if you are storing your view object in a registry, you may want to modify your initView() method with code resembling the following:

```
abstract class My_Base_Controller extends Zend_Controller_Action
{
    public function initView()
    {
        if (null === $this->view) {
            if (Zend_Registry::isRegistered('view')) {
                $this->view = Zend_Registry::get('view');
            } else {
                $this->view = new Zend_View();
                $this->view->setBasePath(dirname(__FILE__) . '/../views');
            }
        }

        return $this->view;
    }
}
```

Hopefully, from the information in this chapter, you can see the flexibility of this particular component and how you can shape it to your application's or site's needs.

Action Helpers

Introduction

Action Helpers allow developers to inject runtime and/or on-demand functionality into any Action Controllers that extend Zend_Controller_Action. Action Helpers aim to minimize the necessity to extend the abstract Action Controller in order to inject common Action Controller functionality.

There are a number of ways to use Action Helpers. Action Helpers employ the use of a brokerage system, similar to the types of brokerage you see in Zend_View_Helper, and that of Zend_Controller_Plugin. Action Helpers (like `Zend_View_Helper`) may be loaded and called on demand, or they may be instantiated at request time (bootstrap) or action controller creation time (init()). To understand this more fully, please see the usage section below.

Helper Initialization

A helper can be initialized in several different ways, based on your needs as well as the functionality of that helper.

The helper broker is stored as the `$_helper` member of `Zend_Controller_Action`; use the broker to retrieve or call on helpers. Some methods for doing so include:

- Explicitly using `getHelper()`. Simply pass it a name, and a helper object is returned:

```
$flashMessenger = $this->_helper->getHelper('FlashMessenger');
$flashMessenger->addMessage('We did something in the last request');
```

- Use the helper broker's `__get()` functionality and retrieve the helper as if it were a member property of the broker:

```
$flashMessenger = $this->_helper->FlashMessenger;
$flashMessenger->addMessage('We did something in the last request');
```

- Finally, most action helpers implement the method `direct()` which will call a specific, default method in the helper. In the example of the `FlashMessenger`, it calls `addMessage()`:

```
$this->_helper->FlashMessenger('We did something in the last request');
```

Note

All of the above examples are functionally equivalent.

You may also instantiate helpers explicitly. You may wish to do this if using the helper outside of an action controller, or if you wish to pass a helper to the helper broker for use by any action. Instantiation is as per any other PHP class.

The Helper Broker

`Zend_Controller_Action_HelperBroker` handles the details of registering helper objects and helper paths, as well as retrieving helpers on-demand.

To register a helper with the broker, use `addHelper`:

```
Zend_Controller_Action_HelperBroker::addHelper($helper);
```

Of course, instantiating and passing helpers to the broker is a bit time and resource intensive, so two methods exists to automate things slightly: `addPrefix()` and `addPath()`.

- `addPrefix()` takes a class prefix and uses it to determine a path where helper classes have been defined. It assumes the prefix follows Zend Framework class naming conventions.

```
// Add helpers prefixed with My_Action_Helpers in My/Action/Helpers/
Zend_Controller_Action_HelperBroker::addPrefix('My_Action_Helpers');
```

- addPath() takes a directory as its first argument and a class prefix as the second argument (defaulting to 'Zend_Controller_Action_Helper'). This allows you to map your own class prefixes to specific directories.

```
// Add helpers prefixed with Helper in Plugins/Helpers/
Zend_Controller_Action_HelperBroker::addPath('./Plugins/Helpers',
                                             'Helper');
```

Since these methods are static, they may be called at any point in the controller chain in order to dynamically add helpers as needed.

Internally, the helper broker uses a PluginLoader instance to maintain paths. You can retrieve the PluginLoader using the static method getPluginLoader(), or, alternately, inject a custom PluginLoader instance using setPluginLoader().

To determine if a helper exists in the helper broker, use hasHelper($name), where $name is the short name of the helper (minus the prefix):

```
// Check if 'redirector' helper is registered with the broker:
if (Zend_Controller_Action_HelperBroker::hasHelper('redirector')) {
    echo 'Redirector helper registered';
}
```

There are also two static methods for retrieving helpers from the helper broker: getExistingHelper() and getStaticHelper(). getExistingHelper() will retrieve a helper only if it has previously been invoked by or explicitly registered with the helper broker; it will throw an exception if not. getStaticHelper() does the same as getExistingHelper(), but will attempt to instantiate the helper if has not yet been registered with the helper stack. getStaticHelper() is a good choice for retrieving helpers which you wish to configure.

Both methods take a single argument, $name, which is the short name of the helper (minus the prefix).

```
// Check if 'redirector' helper is registered with the broker, and fetch:
if (Zend_Controller_Action_HelperBroker::hasHelper('redirector')) {
    $redirector =
        Zend_Controller_Action_HelperBroker::getExistingHelper('redirector');
}

// Or, simply retrieve it, not worrying about whether or not it was
// previously registered:
$redirector =
    Zend_Controller_Action_HelperBroker::getStaticHelper('redirector');
}
```

Finally, to delete a registered helper from the broker, use removeHelper($name), where $name is the short name of the helper (minus the prefix):

```
// Conditionally remove the 'redirector' helper from the broker:
if (Zend_Controller_Action_HelperBroker::hasHelper('redirector')) {
    Zend_Controller_Action_HelperBroker::removeHelper('redirector')
}
```

Built-in Action Helpers

Zend Framework includes several action helpers by default: `AutoComplete` for automating responses for AJAX autocompletion; `ContextSwitch` and `AjaxContext` for serving alternate response formats for your actions; a `FlashMessenger` for handling session flash messages; `Json` for encoding and sending JSON responses; a `Redirector`, to provide different implementations for redirecting to internal and external pages from your application; and a `ViewRenderer` to automate the process of setting up the view object in your controllers and rendering views.

ActionStack

The `ActionStack` helper allows you to push requests to the ActionStack front controller plugin, effectively helping you create a queue of actions to execute during the request. The helper allows you to add actions either by specifying new request objects or action/controller/module sets.

Invoking ActionStack Helper Initializes the ActionStack Plugin

Invoking the `ActionStack` helper implicitly registers the `ActionStack` plugin -- which means you do not need to explicitly register the `ActionStack` plugin to use this functionality.

Example 12.2. Adding a Task Using Action, Controller and Module Names

Often, it's simplest to simply specify the action, controller, and module (and optional request parameters), much as you would when calling `Zend_Controller_Action::_forward()`:

```
class FooController extends Zend_Controller_Action
{
    public function barAction()
    {
        // Add two actions to the stack
        // Add call to /foo/baz/bar/baz
        // (FooController::bazAction() with request var bar == baz)
        $this->_helper->actionStack('baz',
                                    'foo',
                                    'default',
                                    array('bar' => 'baz'));

        // Add call to /bar/bat
        // (BarController::batAction())
        $this->_helper->actionStack('bat', 'bar');
    }
}
```

Example 12.3. Adding a Task Using a Request Object

Sometimes the OOP nature of a request object makes most sense; you can pass such an object to the `ActionStack` helper as well.

```
class FooController extends Zend_Controller_Action
{
    public function barAction()
```

```
    {
        // Add two actions to the stack
        // Add call to /foo/baz/bar/baz
        // (FooController::bazAction() with request var bar == baz)
        $request = clone $this->getRequest();
        // Don't set controller or module; use current values
        $request->setActionName('baz')
                ->setParams(array('bar' => 'baz'));
        $this->_helper->actionStack($request);

        // Add call to /bar/bat
        // (BarController::batAction())
        $request = clone $this->getRequest();
        // don't set module; use current value
        $request->setActionName('bat')
                ->setControllerName('bar');
        $this->_helper->actionStack($request);
    }
}
```

AutoComplete

Many AJAX javascript libraries offer functionality for providing autocompletion whereby a selectlist of potentially matching results is displayed as the user types. The AutoComplete helper aims to simplify returning acceptable responses to such methods.

Since not all JS libraries implement autocompletion in the same way, the AutoComplete helper provides some abstract base functionality necessary to many libraries, and concrete implementations for individual libraries. Return types are generally either JSON arrays of strings, JSON arrays of arrays (with each member array being an associative array of metadata used to create the selectlist), or HTML.

Basic usage for each implementation is the same:

```
class FooController extends Zend_Controller_Action
{
    public function barAction()
    {
        // Perform some logic...

        // Encode and send response;
        $this->_helper->autoCompleteDojo($data);

        // Or explicitly:
        $response = $this->_helper->autoCompleteDojo
                                  ->sendAutoCompletion($data);

        // Or simply prepare autocompletion response:
        $response = $this->_helper->autoCompleteDojo
                                  ->prepareAutoCompletion($data);
    }
}
```

By default, autocompletion does the following:

*   Disables layouts and ViewRenderer.

*   Sets appropriate response headers.

*   Sets response body with encoded/formatted autocompletion data.

*   Sends response.

Available methods of the helper include:

- `disableLayouts()` can be used to disable layouts and the ViewRenderer. Typically, this is called within `prepareAutoCompletion()`.

- `encodeJson($data, $keepLayouts = false)` will encode data to JSON, optionally enabling or disabling layouts. Typically, this is called within `prepareAutoCompletion()`.

- `prepareAutoCompletion($data, $keepLayouts = false)` is used to prepare data in the response format necessary for the concrete implementation, optionally enabling or disabling layouts. The return value will vary based on the implementation.

- `sendAutoCompletion($data, $keepLayouts = false)` is used to send data in the response format necessary for the concrete implementation. It calls `prepareAutoCompletion()`, and then sends the response.

- `direct($data, $sendNow = true, $keepLayouts = false)` is used when calling the helper as a method of the helper broker. The `$sendNow` flag is used to determine whether to call `sendAutoCompletion()` or `prepareAutoCompletion()`, respectively.

Currently, `AutoComplete` supports the Dojo and Scriptaculous AJAX libraries.

AutoCompletion with Dojo

Dojo does not have an AutoCompletion widget per se, but has two widgets that can perform AutoCompletion: ComboBox and FilteringSelect. In both cases, they require a data store that implements the QueryReadStore; for more information on these topics, see the dojo.data [http://dojotoolkit.org/book/dojo-book-0-9/part-3-programmatic-dijit-and-dojo/data-retrieval-dojo-data-0] documentation.

In Zend Framework, you can pass a simple indexed array to the AutoCompleteDojo helper, and it will return a JSON response suitable for use with such a store:

```
// within a controller action:
$this->_helper->autoCompleteDojo($data);
```

Example 12.4. AutoCompletion with Dojo Using Zend MVC

AutoCompletion with Dojo via the Zend MVC requires several things: generating a form object for the ComboBox on which you want AutoCompletion, a controller action for serving the AutoCompletion results, creating a custom QueryReadStore to connect to the AutoCompletion action, and generation of the javascript to use to initialize AutoCompletion on the server side.

First, let's look at the javascript necessary. Dojo offers a complete framework for creating OOP javascript, much as Zend Framework does for PHP. Part of that is the ability to create pseudo-namespaces using the directory hierarchy. We'll create a 'custom' directory at the same level as the Dojo directory that's part of the Dojo distribution. Inside that directory, we'll create a javascript file, TestNameReadStore.js, with the following contents:

```
dojo.provide("custom.TestNameReadStore");
dojo.declare("custom.TestNameReadStore", dojox.data.QueryReadStore, {
    fetch:function (request) {
        request.serverQuery = { test:request.query.name };
        return this.inherited("fetch", arguments);
    }
});
```

This class is simply an extension of Dojo's own QueryReadStore, which is itself an abstract class. We simply define a method by which to request, and assigning it to the 'test' element.

Next, let's create the form element for which we want AutoCompletion:

```
class TestController extends Zend_Controller_Action
{
    protected $_form;

    public function getForm()
    {
        if (null === $this->_form) {
            $this->_form = new Zend_Form();
            $this->_form->setMethod('get')
                ->setAction(
                    $this->getRequest()->getBaseUrl() . '/test/process'
                )
                ->addElements(array(
                    'test' => array('type' => 'text', 'options' => array(
                        'filters'          => array('StringTrim'),
                        'dojoType'         => array('dijit.form.ComboBox'),
                        'store'            => 'testStore',
                        'autoComplete'     => 'false',
                        'hasDownArrow'     => 'true',
                        'label' => 'Your input:',
                    )),
                    'go' => array('type' => 'submit',
                                  'options' => array('label' => 'Go!'))
                ));
        }
        return $this->_form;
    }
}
```

Here, we simply create a form with 'test' and 'go' methods. The 'test' method adds several special, Dojo-specific attributes: dojoType, store, autoComplete, and hasDownArrow. The dojoType is used to indicate that we are creating a ComboBox, and we will link it to a data store (key 'store') of 'testStore' -- more on that later. Specifying 'autoComplete' as false tells Dojo not to automatically select the first match, but instead show a list of matches. Finally, 'hasDownArrow' creates a down arrow similar to a select box so we can show and hide the matches.

Let's add a method to display the form, as well as an end point for processing AutoCompletion:

```
class TestController extends Zend_Controller_Action
{
    // ...

    /**
     * Landing page
     */
    public function indexAction()
    {
        $this->view->form = $this->getForm();
    }

    public function autocompleteAction()
    {
        if ('ajax' != $this->_getParam('format', false)) {
            return $this->_helper->redirector('index');
        }
        if ($this->getRequest()->isPost()) {
            return $this->_helper->redirector('index');
        }

        $match = trim($this->getRequest()->getQuery('test', ''));
```

```
            $matches = array();
            foreach ($this->getData() as $datum) {
                if (0 === strpos($datum, $match)) {
                    $matches[] = $datum;
                }
            }
            $this->_helper->autoCompleteDojo($matches);
        }
    }
```

In our `autocompleteAction()` we do a number of things. First, we look to make sure we have a post request, and that there is a 'format' parameter set to the value 'ajax'; these are simply to help reduce spurious queries to the action. Next, we check for a 'test' parameter, and compare it against our data. (I purposely leave out the implementation of `getData()` here -- it could be any sort of data source.) Finally, we send our matches to our AutoCompletion helper.

Now that we have all the pieces on the backend, let's look at what we need to deliver in our view script for the landing page. First, we need to setup our data store, then render our form, and finally ensure that the appropriate Dojo libraries -- including our custom data store -- get loaded. Let's look at the view script, which comments the steps:

```
<?php // setup our data store: ?>
<div dojoType="custom.TestNameReadStore" jsId="testStore"
    url="<?php echo $this->baseUrl() ?>/unit-test/autocomplete/format/ajax"
    requestMethod="get"></div>

<?php // render our form: ?>
<?php echo $this->form ?>

<?php // setup Dojo-related CSS to load in HTML head: ?>
<?php $this->headStyle()->captureStart() ?>
@import "<?php echo $this->baseUrl()
?>/javascript/dijit/themes/tundra/tundra.css";
@import "<?php echo $this->baseUrl() ?>/javascript/dojo/resources/dojo.css";
<?php $this->headStyle()->captureEnd() ?>

<?php // setup javascript to load in HTML head, including all required
    // Dojo libraries: ?>
<?php $this->headScript()
        ->setAllowArbitraryAttributes(true)
        ->appendFile($this->baseUrl() . '/javascript/dojo/dojo.js',
            'text/javascript',
            array('djConfig' => 'parseOnLoad: true'))
        ->captureStart() ?>
djConfig.usePlainJson=true;
dojo.registerModulePath("custom","../custom");
dojo.require("dojo.parser");
dojo.require("dojox.data.QueryReadStore");
dojo.require("dijit.form.ComboBox");
dojo.require("custom.TestNameReadStore");
<?php $this->headScript()->captureEnd() ?>
```

Note the calls to view helpers such as headStyle and headScript; these are placeholders, which we can then render in the HTML head section of our layout view script.

We now have all the pieces to get Dojo AutoCompletion working.

AutoCompletion with Scriptaculous

Scriptaculous [http://wiki.script.aculo.us/scriptaculous/show/Ajax.Autocompleter] expects an HTML response in a specific format.

The helper to use with this library is 'AutoCompleteScriptaculous'. Simply provide it an array of data, and the helper will create an HTML response compatible with Ajax.Autocompleter.

ContextSwitch and AjaxContext

The ContextSwitch action helper is intended for facilitating returning different response formats on request. The AjaxContext helper is a specialized version of ContextSwitch that facilitates returning responses to XmlHttpRequests.

To enable either one, you must provide hinting in your controller as to what actions can respond to which contexts. If an incoming request indicates a valid context for the given action, the helper will then:

- Disable layouts, if enabled.
- Set an alternate view suffix, effectively requiring a separate view script for the context.
- Send appropriate response headers for the context desired.
- Optionally, call specified callbacks to setup the context and/or perform post-processing.

As an example, let's consider the following controller:

```
class NewsController extends Zend_Controller_Action
{
    /**
     * Landing page; forwards to listAction()
     */
    public function indexAction()
    {
        $this->_forward('list');
    }

    /**
     * List news items
     */
    public function listAction()
    {

    }

    /**
     * View a news item
     */
    public function viewAction()
    {

    }
}
```

Let's say that we want the listAction() to also be available in an XML format. Instead of creating a different action, we can hint that it can return an XML response:

```
class NewsController extends Zend_Controller_Action
{
    public function init()
    {
        $contextSwitch = $this->_helper->getHelper('contextSwitch');
```

```
        $contextSwitch->addActionContext('list', 'xml')
                      ->initContext();
    }

    // ...
}
```

What this will do is:

- Set the 'Content-Type' response header to 'text/xml'.

- Change the view suffix to 'xml.phtml' (or, if you use an alternate view suffix, 'xml.[your suffix]').

Now, you'll need to create a new view script, 'news/list.xml.phtml', which will create and render the XML.

To determine if a request should initiate a context switch, the helper checks for a token in the request object. By default, it looks for the 'format' parameter, though this may be configured. This means that, in most cases, to trigger a context switch, you can add a 'format' parameter to your request:

- Via URL parameter: /news/list/format/xml (recall, the default routing schema allows for arbitrary key/value pairs following the action)

- Via GET parameter: /news/list?format=xml

ContextSwitch allows you to specify arbitrary contexts, including what suffix change will occur (if any), any response headers that should be sent, and arbitrary callbacks for initialization and post processing.

Default Contexts Available

By default, two contexts are available to the ContextSwitch helper: json and xml.

- *JSON*. The JSON context sets the 'Content-Type' response header to 'application/json', and the view script suffix to 'json.phtml'.

  By default, however, no view script is required. It will simply serialize all view variables, and emit the JSON response immediately.

  This behaviour can be disabled by turning off auto-JSON serialization:

  ```
  $this->_helper->contextSwitch()->setAutoJsonSerialization(false);
  ```

- *XML*. The XML context sets the 'Content-Type' response header to 'text/xml', and the view script suffix to 'xml.phtml'. You will need to create a new view script for the context.

Creating Custom Contexts

Sometimes, the default contexts are not enough. For instance, you may wish to return YAML, or serialized PHP, an RSS or ATOM feed, etc. ContextSwitch allows you to do so.

The easiest way to add a new context is via the addContext() method. This method takes two arguments, the name of the context, and an array specification. The specification should include one or more of the following:

- *suffix*: the suffix to prepend to the default view suffix as registered in the ViewRenderer.

- *headers*: an array of header/value pairs you wish sent as part of the response.

- *callbacks*: an array containing one or more of the keys 'init' or 'post', pointing to valid PHP callbacks that can be used for context initialization and post processing.

Initialization callbacks occur when the context is detected by `ContextSwitch`. You can use it to perform arbitrary logic that should occur. As an example, the JSON context uses a callback to disable the ViewRenderer when auto-JSON serialization is on.

Post processing occurs during the action's `postDispatch()` routine, and can be used to perform arbitrary logic. As an example, the JSON context uses a callback to determine if auto-JSON serialization is on; if so, it serializes the view variables to JSON and sends the response, but if not, it re-enables the ViewRenderer.

There are a variety of methods for interacting with contexts:

- `addContext($context, array $spec)`: add a new context. Throws an exception if the context already exists.

- `setContext($context, array $spec)`: add a new context or overwrite an existing context. Uses the same specification as `addContext()`.

- `addContexts(array $contexts)`: add many contexts at once. The `$contexts` array should be an array of context/specification pairs. If any of the contexts already exists, it will throw an exception.

- `setContexts(array $contexts)`: add new contexts and overwrite existing ones. Uses the same specification as `addContexts()`.

- `hasContext($context)`: returns true if the context exists, false otherwise.

- `getContext($context)`: retrieve a single context by name. Returns an array following the specification used in `addContext()`.

- `getContexts()`: retrieve all contexts. Returns an array of context/specification pairs.

- `removeContext($context)`: remove a single context by name. Returns true if successful, false if the context was not found.

- `clearContexts()`: remove all contexts.

Setting Contexts Per Action

There are two mechanisms for setting available contexts. You can either manually create arrays in your controller, or use several methods in `ContextSwitch` to assemble them.

The principle method for adding action/context relations is `addActionContext()`. It expects two arguments, the action to which the context is being added, and either the name of a context or an array of contexts. As an example, consider the following controller class:

```
class FooController extends Zend_Controller_Action
{
    public function listAction()
    {

    }

    public function viewAction()
    {

    }

    public function commentsAction()
    {

    }
```

```
    public function updateAction()
    {

    }
}
```

Let's say we wanted to add an XML context to the 'list' action, and XML and JSON contexts to the 'comments' action. We could do so in the `init()` method:

```
class FooController extends Zend_Controller_Action
{
    public function init()
    {
        $this->_helper->contextSwitch()
            ->addActionContext('list', 'xml')
            ->addActionContext('comments', array('xml', 'json'))
            ->initContext();
    }
}
```

Alternately, you could simply define the array property `$contexts`:

```
class FooController extends Zend_Controller_Action
{
    public $contexts = array(
        'list'     => array('xml'),
        'comments' => array('xml', 'json')
    );

    public function init()
    {
        $this->_helper->contextSwitch()->initContext();
    }
}
```

The above is less overhead, but also prone to potential errors.

The following methods can be used to build the context mappings:

- `addActionContext($action, $context)`: marks one or more contexts as available to an action. If mappings already exists, simply appends to those mappings. `$context` may be a single context, or an array of contexts.

  A value of `true` for the context will mark all available contexts as available for the action.

  An empty value for $context will disable all contexts for the given action.

- `setActionContext($action, $context)`: marks one or more contexts as available to an action. If mappings already exists, it replaces them with those specified. `$context` may be a single context, or an array of contexts.

- `addActionContexts(array $contexts)`: add several action/context pairings at once. `$contexts` should be an associative array of action/context pairs. It proxies to `addActionContext()`, meaning that if pairings already exist, it appends to them.

- `setActionContexts(array $contexts)`: acts like `addActionContexts()`, but overwrites existing action/context pairs.

- `hasActionContext($action, $context)`: determine if a particular action has a given context.

- `getActionContexts($action = null)`: returns either all contexts for a given action, or all action/context pairs.

- `removeActionContext($action, $context)`: remove one or more contexts from a given action. `$context` may be a single context or an array of contexts.

- `clearActionContexts($action = null)`: remove all contexts from a given action, or from all actions with contexts.

Initializing Context Switching

To initialize context switching, you need to call `initContext()` in your action controller:

```
class NewsController extends Zend_Controller_Action
{
    public function init()
    {
        $this->_helper->contextSwitch()->initContext();
    }
}
```

In some cases, you may want to force the context used; for instance, you may only want to allow the XML context if context switching is activated. You can do so by passing the context to `initContext()`:

```
$contextSwitch->initContext('xml');
```

Additional Functionality

A variety of methods can be used to alter the behaviour of the `ContextSwitch` helper. These include:

- `setAutoJsonSerialization($flag)`: By default, JSON contexts will serialize any view variables to JSON notation and return this as a response. If you wish to create your own response, you should turn this off; this needs to be done prior to the call to `initContext()`.

  ```
  $contextSwitch->setAutoJsonSerialization(false);
  $contextSwitch->initContext();
  ```

  You can retrieve the value of the flag with `getAutoJsonSerialization()`.

- `setSuffix($context, $suffix, $prependViewRendererSuffix)`: With this method, you can specify a different suffix to use for a given context. The third argument is used to indicate whether or not to prepend the current ViewRenderer suffix with the new suffix; this flag is enabled by default.

  Passing an empty value to the suffix will cause only the ViewRenderer suffix to be used.

- `addHeader($context, $header, $content)`: Add a response header for a given context. `$header` is the header name, and `$content` is the value to pass for that header.

  Each context can have multiple headers; `addHeader()` adds additional headers to the context's header stack.

  If the `$header` specified already exists for the context, an exception will be thrown.

- `setHeader($context, $header, $content)`: `setHeader()` acts just like `addHeader ()`, except it allows you to overwrite existing context headers.

- addHeaders($context, array $headers): Add multiple headers at once to a given context. Proxies to addHeader(), so if the header already exists, an exception will be thrown. $headers is an array of header/context pairs.

- setHeaders($context, array $headers.): like addHeaders(), except it proxies to setHeader(), allowing you to overwrite existing headers.

- getHeader($context, $header): retrieve the value of a header for a given context. Returns null if not found.

- removeHeader($context, $header): remove a single header for a given context.

- clearHeaders($context, $header): remove all headers for a given context.

- setCallback($context, $trigger, $callback): set a callback at a given trigger for a given context. Triggers may be either 'init' or 'post' (indicating callback will be called at either context initialization or postDispatch). $callback should be a valid PHP callback.

- setCallbacks($context, array $callbacks): set multiple callbacks for a given context. $callbacks should be trigger/callback pairs. In actuality, the most callbacks that can be registered are two, one for initialization and one for post processing.

- getCallback($context, $trigger): retrieve a callback for a given trigger in a given context.

- getCallbacks($context): retrieve all callbacks for a given context. Returns an array of trigger/callback pairs.

- removeCallback($context, $trigger): remove a callback for a given trigger and context.

- clearCallbacks($context): remove all callbacks for a given context.

- setContextParam($name): set the request parameter to check when determining if a context switch has been requested. The value defaults to 'format', but this accessor can be used to set an alternate value.

  getContextParam() can be used to retrieve the current value.

- setAutoDisableLayout($flag): By default, layouts are disabled when a context switch occurs; this is because typically layouts will only be used for returning normal responses, and have no meaning in alternate contexts. However, if you wish to use layouts (perhaps you may have a layout for the new context), you can change this behaviour by passing a false value to setAutoDisableLayout(). You should do this *before* calling initContext().

  To get the value of this flag, use the accessor getAutoDisableLayout().

- getCurrentContext() can be used to determine what context was detected, if any. This returns null if no context switch occurred, or if called before initContext() has been invoked.

AjaxContext Functionality

The AjaxContext helper extends ContextSwitch, so all of the functionality listed for ContextSwitch is available to it. There are a few key differences, however.

First, it uses a different action controller property for determining contexts, $ajaxable. This is so you can have different contexts used for AJAX versus normal HTTP requests. The various *ActionContext*() methods of AjaxContext will write to this property.

Second, it will only trigger if an XmlHttpRequest has occurred, as determined by the request object's isXmlHttpRequest() method. Thus, if the context parameter ('format') is passed in the request, but the request was not made as an XmlHttpRequest, no context switch will trigger.

Third, AjaxContext adds an additional context, HTML. In this context, it sets the suffix to 'ajax.phtml' in order to differentiate the context from a normal request. No additional headers are returned.

Example 12.5. Allowing Actions to Respond To Ajax Requests

In this following example, we're allowing requests to the actions 'view', 'form', and 'process' to respond to AJAX requests. In the first two cases, 'view' and 'form', we'll return HTML snippets with which to update the page; in the latter, we'll return JSON.

```
class CommentController extends Zend_Controller_Action
{
    public function init()
    {
        $ajaxContext = $this->_helper->getHelper('AjaxContext');
        $ajaxContext->addActionContext('view', 'html')
                    ->addActionContext('form', 'html')
                    ->addActionContext('process', 'json')
                    ->initContext();
    }

    public function viewAction()
    {
        // Pull a single comment to view.
        // When AjaxContext detected, uses the comment/view.ajax.phtml
        // view script.
    }

    public function formAction()
    {
        // Render the "add new comment" form.
        // When AjaxContext detected, uses the comment/form.ajax.phtml
        // view script.
    }

    public function processAction()
    {
        // Process a new comment
        // Return the results as JSON; simply assign the results as
        // view variables, and JSON will be returned.
    }
}
```

On the client end, your AJAX library will simply request the endpoints '/comment/view', '/comment/form', and '/comment/process', and pass the 'format' parameter: '/comment/view/format/html', '/comment/form/format/html', '/comment/process/format/json'. (Or you can pass the parameter via query string: e.g., "?format=json".)

Assuming your library passes the 'X-Requested-With: XmlHttpRequest' header, these actions will then return the appropriate response format.

FlashMessenger

Introduction

The FlashMessenger helper allows you to pass messages that the user may need to see on the next request. To accomplish this, FlashMessenger uses Zend_Session_Namespace to store messages for future or next request retrieval. It is generally a good idea that if you plan on using Zend_Session or Zend_Session_Namespace, that you initialize with Zend_Session ::start() in your bootstrap file. (See the Zend_Session documentation for more details on its usage.)

Basic Usage Example

The usage example below shows the use of the flash messenger at its most basic. When the action /some/my is called, it adds the flash message "Record Saved!" A subsequent request to the action /some/my-next-request will retrieve it (and thus delete it as well).

```
class SomeController extends Zend_Controller_Action
{
    /**
     * FlashMessenger
     *
     * @var Zend_Controller_Action_Helper_FlashMessenger
     */
    protected $_flashMessenger = null;

    public function init()
    {
        $this->_flashMessenger =
            $this->_helper->getHelper('FlashMessenger');
        $this->initView();
    }

    public function myAction()
    {
        /**
         * default method of getting
         * Zend_Controller_Action_Helper_FlashMessenger instance
         * on-demand
         */
        $this->_flashMessenger->addMessage('Record Saved!');
    }

    public function myNextRequestAction()
    {
        $this->view->messages = $this->_flashMessenger->getMessages();
        $this->render();
    }
}
```

JSON

JSON responses are rapidly becoming the response of choice when dealing with AJAX requests that expect dataset responses; JSON can be immediately parsed on the client-side, leading to quick execution.

The JSON action helper does several things:

- Disables layouts if currently enabled.

- Optionally, an array of options to pass as the second argument to Zend_Json::encode(). This array of options allows enabling layouts and encoding using Zend_Json_Expr.

  ```
  $this->_helper->json($data, array('enableJsonExprFinder' => true));
  ```

- Disables the ViewRenderer if currently enabled.

- Sets the 'Content-Type' response header to 'application/json'.

- By default, immediately returns the response, without waiting for the action to finish execution.

Usage is simple: either call it as a method of the helper broker, or call one of the methods encodeJson() or sendJson():

```
class FooController extends Zend_Controller_Action
{
    public function barAction()
    {
        // do some processing...
        // Send the JSON response:
        $this->_helper->json($data);

        // or...
        $this->_helper->json->sendJson($data);

        // or retrieve the json:
        $json = $this->_helper->json->encodeJson($data);
    }
}
```

Keeping Layouts

If you have a separate layout for JSON responses -- perhaps to wrap the JSON response in some sort of context -- each method in the JSON helper accepts a second, optional argument: a flag to enable or disable layouts. Passing a boolean true value will keep layouts enabled:

```
$this->_helper->json($data, true);
```

Optionally, you can pass an array as the second parameter. This array may contain a variety of options, including the keepLayouts option:

```
$this->_helper->json($data, array('keepLayouts' => true);
```

Enabling encoding using Zend_Json_Expr

Zend_Json::encode() allows the encoding of native JSON expressions using Zend_Json_Expr objects. This option is disabled by default. To enable this option, pass a boolean true value to the enableJsonExprFinder option:

```
$this->_helper->json($data, array('enableJsonExprFinder' => true);
```

If you desire to do this, you *must* pass an array as the second argument. This also allows you to combine other options, such as the keepLayouts option. All such options are then passed to Zend_Json::encode().

```
$this->_helper->json($data, array(
    'enableJsonExprFinder' => true,
    'keepLayouts'          => true,
));
```

Redirector

Introduction

The `Redirector` helper allows you to use a redirector object to fulfill your application's needs for redirecting to a new URL. It provides numerous benefits over the `_redirect()` method, such as being able to preconfigure sitewide behavior into the redirector object or using the built in `gotoSimple($action, $controller, $module, $params)` interface similar to that of `Zend_Controller_Action::_forward()`.

The `Redirector` has a number of methods that can be used to affect the behaviour at redirect:

- `setCode()` can be used to set the HTTP response code to use during the redirect.

- `setExit()` can be used to force an `exit()` following a redirect. By default this is true.

- `setGotoSimple()` can be used to set a default URL to use if none is passed to `gotoSimple()`. Uses the API of `Zend_Controller_Action::_forward()`: setGotoSimple($action, $controller = null, $module = null, array $params = array());

- `setGotoRoute()` can be used to set a URL based on a registered route. Pass in an array of key/value pairs and a route name, and it will assemble the URL according to the route type and definition.

- `setGotoUrl()` can be used to set a default URL to use if none is passed to `gotoUrl()`. Accepts a single URL string.

- `setPrependBase()` can be used to prepend the request object's base URL to a URL specified with `setGotoUrl()`, `gotoUrl()`, or `gotoUrlAndExit()`.

- `setUseAbsoluteUri()` can be used to force the `Redirector` to use absolute URIs when redirecting. When this option is set, it uses the value of `$_SERVER['HTTP_HOST']`, `$_SERVER['SERVER_PORT']`, and `$_SERVER['HTTPS']` to form a full URI to the URL specified by one of the redirect methods. This option is off by default, but may be enabled by default in later releases.

Additionally, there are a variety of methods in the redirector for performing the actual redirects:

- `gotoSimple()` uses `setGotoSimple()` (`_forward()-like` API) to build a URL and perform a redirect.

- `gotoRoute()` uses `setGotoRoute()` (route-assembly) to build a URL and perform a redirect.

- `gotoUrl()` uses `setGotoUrl()` (URL string) to build a URL and perform a redirect.

Finally, you can determine the current redirect URL at any time using `getRedirectUrl()`.

Basic Usage Examples

Example 12.6. Setting Options

This example overrides several options, including setting the HTTP status code to use in the redirect ('303'), not defaulting to exit on redirect, and defining a default URL to use when redirecting.

```
class SomeController extends Zend_Controller_Action
{
    /**
     * Redirector - defined for code completion
```

```
 *
 * @var Zend_Controller_Action_Helper_Redirector
 */
protected $_redirector = null;

public function init()
{
    $this->_redirector = $this->_helper->getHelper('Redirector');

    // Set the default options for the redirector
    // Since the object is registered in the helper broker, these
    // become relevant for all actions from this point forward
    $this->_redirector->setCode(303)
                      ->setExit(false)
                      ->setGotoSimple("this-action",
                                       "some-controller");
}

public function myAction()
{
    /* do some stuff */

    // Redirect to a previously registered URL, and force an exit
    // to occur when done:
    $this->_redirector->redirectAndExit();
    return; // never reached
}
}
```

Example 12.7. Using Defaults

This example assumes that the defaults are used, which means that any redirect will result in an immediate exit().

```
// ALTERNATIVE EXAMPLE
class AlternativeController extends Zend_Controller_Action
{
    /**
     * Redirector - defined for code completion
     *
     * @var Zend_Controller_Action_Helper_Redirector
     */
    protected $_redirector = null;

    public function init()
    {
        $this->_redirector = $this->_helper->getHelper('Redirector');
    }

    public function myAction()
    {
        /* do some stuff */

        $this->_redirector
            ->gotoUrl('/my-controller/my-action/param1/test/param2/test2');
        return; // never reached since default is to goto and exit
    }
}
```

Example 12.8. Using goto()'s _forward() API

gotoSimple()'s API mimics that of Zend_Controller_Action::_forward(). The primary difference is that it builds a URL from the parameters passed, and using the default :module/:controller/:action/* format of the default router. It then redirects instead of chaining the action.

```
class ForwardController extends Zend_Controller_Action
{
    /**
     * Redirector - defined for code completion
     *
     * @var Zend_Controller_Action_Helper_Redirector
     */
    protected $_redirector = null;

    public function init()
    {
        $this->_redirector = $this->_helper->getHelper('Redirector');
    }

    public function myAction()
    {
        /* do some stuff */

        // Redirect to 'my-action' of 'my-controller' in the current
        // module, using the params param1 => test and param2 => test2
        $this->_redirector->gotoSimple('my-action',
                                       'my-controller',
                                       null,
                                       array('param1' => 'test',
                                             'param2' => 'test2'
                                       )
                                    );
    }
}
```

Example 12.9. Using Route Assembly with gotoRoute()

The following example uses the router's assemble() method to create a URL based on an associative array of parameters passed. It assumes the following route has been registered:

```
$route = new Zend_Controller_Router_Route(
    'blog/:year/:month/:day/:id',
    array('controller' => 'archive',
          'module' => 'blog',
          'action' => 'view')
);
$router->addRoute('blogArchive', $route);
```

Given an array with year set to 2006, month to 4, day to 24, and id to 42, it would then build the URL /blog/2006/4/24/42.

```
class BlogAdminController extends Zend_Controller_Action
{
    /**
     * Redirector - defined for code completion
     *
     * @var Zend_Controller_Action_Helper_Redirector
     */
    protected $_redirector = null;

    public function init()
    {
        $this->_redirector = $this->_helper->getHelper('Redirector');
    }

    public function returnAction()
    {
        /* do some stuff */

        // Redirect to blog archive. Builds the following URL:
        // /blog/2006/4/24/42
        $this->_redirector->gotoRoute(
            array('year' => 2006,
                  'month' => 4,
                  'day' => 24,
                  'id' => 42),
            'blogArchive'
        );
    }
}
```

ViewRenderer

Introduction

The ViewRenderer helper is designed to satisfy the following goals:

- Eliminate the need to instantiate view objects within controllers; view objects will be automatically registered with the controller.

- Automatically set view script, helper, and filter paths based on the current module, and automatically associate the current module name as a class prefix for helper and filter classes.

- Create a globally available view object for all dispatched controllers and actions.

- Allow the developer to set default view rendering options for all controllers.

- Add the ability to automatically render a view script with no intervention.

- Allow the developer to create her own specifications for the view base path and for view script paths.

Note

If you perform a _forward(), redirect, or render manually, autorendering will not occur, as by performing any of these actions you are telling the ViewRenderer that you are determining your own output.

Note

The `ViewRenderer` is enabled by default. You may disable it via the front controller `noViewRenderer` param (`$front->setParam('noViewRenderer', true)`) or removing the helper from the helper broker stack (`Zend_Controller_Action _HelperBroker::removeHelper('viewRenderer')`).

If you wish to modify settings of the `ViewRenderer` prior to dispatching the front controller, you may do so in one of two ways:

- Instantiate and register your own `ViewRenderer` object and pass it to the helper broker:

```
$viewRenderer = new Zend_Controller_Action_Helper_ViewRenderer();
$viewRenderer->setView($view)
             ->setViewSuffix('php');
Zend_Controller_Action_HelperBroker::addHelper($viewRenderer);
```

- Initialize and/or retrieve a `ViewRenderer` object on demand via the helper broker:

```
$viewRenderer =
    Zend_Controller_Action_HelperBroker::getStaticHelper
        ('viewRenderer');
$viewRenderer->setView($view)
             ->setViewSuffix('php');
```

API

At its most basic usage, you simply instantiate the `ViewRenderer` and pass it to the action helper broker. The easiest way to instantiate it and register in one go is to use the helper broker's `getStaticHelper()` method:

```
Zend_Controller_Action_HelperBroker::getStaticHelper('viewRenderer');
```

The first time an action controller is instantiated, it will trigger the `ViewRenderer` to instantiate a view object. Each time a controller is instantiated, the `ViewRenderer`'s `init()` method is called, which will cause it to set the view property of the action controller, and call `addScriptPath()` with a path relative to the current module; this will be called with a class prefix named after the current module, effectively namespacing all helper and filter classes you define for the module.

Each time `postDispatch()` is called, it will call `render()` for the current action.

As an example, consider the following class:

```
// A controller class, foo module:
class Foo_BarController extends Zend_Controller_Action
{
    // Render bar/index.phtml by default; no action required
    public function indexAction()
    {

    }

    // Render bar/populate.phtml with variable 'foo' set to 'bar'.
    // Since view object defined at preDispatch(), it's already available.
    public function populateAction()
    {
        $this->view->foo = 'bar';
    }
```

```
}

...

// in one of your view scripts:
$this->foo(); // call Foo_View_Helper_Foo::foo()
```

The ViewRenderer also defines a number of accessors to allow setting and retrieving view options:

- setView($view) allows you to set the view object for the ViewRenderer. It gets set as the public class property $view.

- setNeverRender($flag = true) can be used to disable or enable autorendering globally, i.e., for all controllers. If set to true, postDispatch() will not automatically call render() in the current controller. getNeverRender() retrieves the current value.

- setNoRender($flag = true) can be used to disable or enable autorendering. If set to true, postDispatch() will not automatically call render() in the current controller. This setting is reset each time preDispatch() is called (i.e., you need to set this flag for each controller for which you don't want autorenderering to occur). getNoRender() retrieves the current value.

- setNoController($flag = true) can be used to tell render() not to look for the action script in a subdirectory named after the controller (which is the default behaviour). getNoController() retrieves the current value.

- setNeverController($flag = true) is analogous to setNoController(), but works on a global level -- i.e., it will not be reset for each dispatched action. getNeverController() retrieves the current value.

- setScriptAction($name) can be used to specify the action script to render. $name should be the name of the script minus the file suffix (and without the controller subdirectory, unless noController has been turned on). If not specified, it looks for a view script named after the action in the request object. getScriptAction() retrieves the current value.

- setResponseSegment($name) can be used to specify which response object named segment to render into. If not specified, it renders into the default segment. getResponseSegment() retrieves the current value.

- initView($path, $prefix, $options) may be called to specify the base view path, class prefix for helper and filter scripts, and ViewRenderer options. You may pass any of the following flags: neverRender, noRender, noController, scriptAction, and responseSegment.

- setRender($action = null, $name = null, $noController = false) allows you to set any of scriptAction, responseSegment, and noController in one pass. direct() is an alias to this method, allowing you to call this method easily from your controller:

```
// Render 'foo' instead of current action script
$this->_helper->viewRenderer('foo');

// render form.phtml to the 'html' response segment, without using a
// controller view script subdirectory:
$this->_helper->viewRenderer('form', 'html', true);
```

Note

setRender() and direct() don't actually render the view script, but instead set hints that postDispatch() and render() will use to render the view.

The constructor allows you to optionally pass the view object and ViewRenderer options; it accepts the same flags as initView():

```
$view     = new Zend_View(array('encoding' => 'UTF-8'));
$options = array('noController' => true, 'neverRender' => true);
$viewRenderer =
    new Zend_Controller_Action_Helper_ViewRenderer($view, $options);
```

There are several additional methods for customizing path specifications used for determining the view base path to add to the view object, and the view script path to use when autodetermining the view script to render. These methods each take one or more of the following placeholders:

- :moduleDir refers to the current module's base directory (by convention, the parent directory of the module's controller directory).

- :module refers to the current module name.

- :controller refers to the current controller name.

- :action refers to the current action name.

- :suffix refers to the view script suffix (which may be set via setViewSuffix()).

The methods for controlling path specifications are:

- setViewBasePathSpec($spec) allows you to change the path specification used to determine the base path to add to the view object. The default specification is :moduleDir/views. You may retrieve the current specification at any time using getViewBasePathSpec().

- setViewScriptPathSpec($spec) allows you to change the path specification used to determine the path to an individual view script (minus the base view script path). The default specification is :controller/:action.:suffix. You may retrieve the current specification at any time using getViewScriptPathSpec().

- setViewScriptPathNoControllerSpec($spec) allows you to change the path specification used to determine the path to an individual view script when noController is in effect (minus the base view script path). The default specification is :action.:suffix. You may retrieve the current specification at any time using getViewScriptPathNoControllerSpec().

For fine-grained control over path specifications, you may use Zend_Filter_Inflector. Under the hood, the ViewRenderer uses an inflector to perform path mappings already. To interact with the inflector -- either to set your own for use, or to modify the default inflector, the following methods may be used:

- getInflector() will retrieve the inflector. If none exists yet in the ViewRenderer, it creates one using the default rules.

  By default, it uses static rule references for the suffix and module directory, as well as a static target; this allows various ViewRenderer properties the ability to dynamically modify the inflector.

- setInflector($inflector, $reference) allows you to set a custom inflector for use with the ViewRenderer. If $reference is true, it will set the suffix and module directory as static references to ViewRenderer properties, as well as the target.

Default Lookup Conventions

The ViewRenderer does some path normalization to make view script lookups easier. The default rules are as follows:

- :module: MixedCase and camelCasedWords are separated by dashes, and the entire string cast to lowercase. E.g.: "FooBarBaz" becomes "foo-bar-baz".

  Internally, the inflector uses the filters Zend_Filter_Word_CamelCaseToDash and

`Zend_Filter_StringToLower`.

- `:controller`: MixedCase and camelCasedWords are separated by dashes; underscores are converted to directory separators, and the entire string cast to lower case. Examples: "FooBar" becomes "foo-bar"; "FooBar_Admin" becomes "foo-bar/admin".

  Internally, the inflector uses the filters `Zend_Filter_Word_CamelCaseToDash`, `Zend_Filter_Word_UnderscoreToSeparator`, and `Zend_Filter_StringToLower`.

- `:action`: MixedCase and camelCasedWords are separated by dashes; non-alphanumeric characters are translated to dashes, and the entire string cast to lower case. Examples: "fooBar" becomes "foo-bar"; "foo-barBaz" becomes "foo-bar-baz".

  Internally, the inflector uses the filters `Zend_Filter_Word_CamelCaseToDash`, `Zend_Filter_PregReplace`, and `Zend_Filter_StringToLower`.

The final items in the `ViewRenderer` API are the methods for actually determining view script paths and rendering views. These include:

- `renderScript($script, $name)` allows you to render a script with a path you specify, optionally to a named path segment. When using this method, the `ViewRenderer` does no autodetermination of the script name, but instead directly passes the `$script` argument directly to the view object's `render()` method.

Note

Once the view has been rendered to the response object, it sets the `noRender` to prevent accidentally rendering the same view script multiple times.

Note

By default, `Zend_Controller_Action::renderScript()` proxies to the `ViewRenderer`'s `renderScript()` method.

- `getViewScript($action, $vars)` creates the path to a view script based on the action passed and/or any variables passed in `$vars`. Keys for this array may include any of the path specification keys ('moduleDir', 'module', 'controller', 'action', and 'suffix'). Any variables passed will be used; otherwise, values based on the current request will be utlized.

  `getViewScript()` will use either the `viewScriptPathSpec` or `viewScriptPathNoControllerSpec` based on the setting of the `noController` flag.

  Word delimiters occurring in module, controller, or action names will be replaced with dashes ('-'). Thus, if you have the controller name 'foo.bar' and the action 'baz:bat', using the default path specification will result in a view script path of 'foo-bar/baz-bat.phtml'.

Note

By default, `Zend_Controller_Action::getViewScript()` proxies to the `ViewRenderer`'s `getViewScript()` method.

- `render($action, $name, $noController)` checks first to see if either `$name` or `$noController` have been passed, and if so, sets the appropriate flags (responseSegment and noController, respectively) in the ViewRenderer. It then passes the `$action` argument, if any, on to `getViewScript()`. Finally, it passes the calculated view script path to `renderScript()`.

Note

Be aware of the side-effects of using render(): the values you pass for the response segment name and for the noController flag will persist in the object. Additionally, noRender will be set after rendering is completed.

Note

By default, Zend_Controller_Action::render() proxies to the ViewRenderer's render() method.

- renderBySpec($action, $vars, $name) allows you to pass path specification variables in order to determine the view script path to create. It passes $action and $vars to getScriptPath(), and then passes the resulting script path and $name on to renderScript().

Basic Usage Examples

Example 12.10. Basic Usage

At its most basic, you simply initialize and register the ViewRenderer helper with the helper broker in your bootstrap, and then set variables in your action methods.

```
// In your bootstrap:
Zend_Controller_Action_HelperBroker::getStaticHelper('viewRenderer');

...

// 'foo' module, 'bar' controller:
class Foo_BarController extends Zend_Controller_Action
{
    // Render bar/index.phtml by default; no action required
    public function indexAction()
    {

    }

    // Render bar/populate.phtml with variable 'foo' set to 'bar'.
    // Since view object defined at preDispatch(), it's already available.
    public function populateAction()
    {
        $this->view->foo = 'bar';
    }

    // Renders nothing as it forwards to another action; the new action
    // will perform any rendering
    public function bazAction()
    {
        $this->_forward('index');
    }

    // Renders nothing as it redirects to another location
    public function batAction()
    {
        $this->_redirect('/index');
    }
}
```

Naming Conventions: Word Delimiters in Controller and Action Names

If your controller or action name is composed of several words, the dispatcher requires that these are separated on the URL by specific path and word delimiter characters. The ViewRenderer replaces any path delimiter found in the controller name with an actual path delimiter ('/'), and any word delimiter found with a dash ('-') when creating paths. Thus, a call to the action `/foo.bar/baz.bat` would dispatch to `FooBarController::baz BatAction()` in FooBarController.php, which would render `foo-bar/baz-bat .phtml`; a call to the action `/bar_baz/baz-bat` would dispatch to `Bar_BazController ::bazBatAction()` in `Bar/BazController.php` (note the path separation) and render `bar/baz/baz-bat.phtml`.

Note that the in the second example, the module is still the default module, but that, because of the existence of a path separator, the controller receives the name `Bar_BazController`, in `Bar/BazController.php`. The ViewRenderer mimics the controller directory hierarchy.

Example 12.11. Disabling Autorender

For some actions or controllers, you may want to turn off the autorendering -- for instance, if you're wanting to emit a different type of output (XML, JSON, etc), or if you simply want to emit nothing. You have two options: turn off all cases of autorendering (`setNeverRender()`), or simply turn it off for the current action (`setNoRender()`).

```
// Baz controller class, bar module:
class Bar_BazController extends Zend_Controller_Action
{
    public function fooAction()
    {
        // Don't auto render this action
        $this->_helper->viewRenderer->setNoRender();
    }
}

// Bat controller class, bar module:
class Bar_BatController extends Zend_Controller_Action
{
    public function preDispatch()
    {
        // Never auto render this controller's actions
        $this->_helper->viewRenderer->setNoRender();
    }
}
```

Note

In most cases, it makes no sense to turn off autorendering globally (ala `setNeverRender()`), as the only thing you then gain from ViewRenderer is the autosetup of the view object.

Example 12.12. Choosing a Different View Script

Some situations require that you render a different script than one named after the action. For instance, if you have a controller that has both add and edit actions, they may both display the same 'form' view, albeit with different values set. You can easily change the script name used with either `setScriptAction()`, `setRender()`, or calling the helper as a method, which will invoke `setRender()`.

```
// Bar controller class, foo module:
class Foo_BarController extends Zend_Controller_Action
{
```

```
public function addAction()
{
    // Render 'bar/form.phtml' instead of 'bar/add.phtml'
    $this->_helper->viewRenderer('form');
}

public function editAction()
{
    // Render 'bar/form.phtml' instead of 'bar/edit.phtml'
    $this->_helper->viewRenderer->setScriptAction('form');
}

public function processAction()
{
    // do some validation...
    if (!$valid) {
        // Render 'bar/form.phtml' instead of 'bar/process.phtml'
        $this->_helper->viewRenderer->setRender('form');
        return;
    }

    // otherwise continue processing...
}
}
```

Example 12.13. Modifying the Registered View

What if you need to modify the view object -- for instance, change the helper paths, or the encoding?
You can do so either by modifying the view object set in your controller, or by grabbing the view object
out of the ViewRenderer; both are references to the same object.

```
// Bar controller class, foo module:
class Foo_BarController extends Zend_Controller_Action
{
    public function preDispatch()
    {
        // change view encoding
        $this->view->setEncoding('UTF-8');
    }

    public function bazAction()
    {
        // Get view object and set escape callback to 'htmlspecialchars'
        $view = $this->_helper->viewRenderer->view;
        $view->setEscape('htmlspecialchars');
    }
}
```

Advanced Usage Examples

Example 12.14. Changing the Path Specifications

In some circumstances, you may decide that the default path specifications do not fit your site's needs.
For instance, you may want to have a single template tree to which you may then give access to your

designers (this is very typical when using Smarty [http://smarty.php.net/], for instance). In such a case, you may want to hardcode the view base path specification, and create an alternate specification for the action view script paths themselves.

For purposes of this example, let's assume that the base path to views should be '/opt/vendor/templates', and that you wish for view scripts to be referenced by ':moduleDir/:controller/:action.:suffix'; if the noController flag has been set, you want to render out of the top level instead of in a subdirectory (':action.:suffix'). Finally, you want to use 'tpl' as the view script filename suffix.

```
/**
 * In your bootstrap:
 */

// Different view implementation
$view = new ZF_Smarty();

$viewRenderer = new Zend_Controller_Action_Helper_ViewRenderer($view);
$viewRenderer->setViewBasePathSpec('/opt/vendor/templates')
             ->setViewScriptPathSpec(':module/:controller/:action.:suffix')
             ->setViewScriptPathNoControllerSpec(':action.:suffix')
             ->setViewSuffix('tpl');
Zend_Controller_Action_HelperBroker::addHelper($viewRenderer);
```

Example 12.15. Rendering Multiple View Scripts from a Single Action

At times, you may need to render multiple view scripts from a single action. This is very straightforward -- simply make multiple calls to render():

```
class SearchController extends Zend_Controller_Action
{
    public function resultsAction()
    {
        // Assume $this->model is the current model
        $this->view->results =
            $this->model->find($this->_getParam('query', ''));

        // render() by default proxies to the ViewRenderer
        // Render first the search form and then the results
        $this->render('form');
        $this->render('results');
    }

    public function formAction()
    {
        // do nothing; ViewRenderer autorenders the view script
    }
}
```

Writing Your Own Helpers

Action helpers extend Zend_Controller_Action_Helper_Abstract, an abstract class that provides the basic interface and functionality required by the helper broker. These include the following methods:

- `setActionController()` is used to set the current action controller.

- `init()`, triggered by the helper broker at instantiation, can be used to trigger initialization in the helper; this can be useful for resetting state when multiple controllers use the same helper in chained actions.

- `preDispatch()`, is triggered prior to a dispatched action.

- `postDispatch()` is triggered when a dispatched action is done -- even if a `preDispatch()` plugin has skipped the action. Mainly useful for cleanup.

- `getRequest()` retrieves the current request object.

- `getResponse()` retrieves the current response object.

- `getName()` retrieves the helper name. It retrieves the portion of the class name following the last underscore character, or the full class name otherwise. As an example, if the class is named `Zend_Controller_Action_Helper_Redirector`, it will return `Redirector`; a class named `FooMessage` will simply return itself.

You may optionally include a `direct()` method in your helper class. If defined, it allows you to treat the helper as a method of the helper broker, in order to allow easy, one-off usage of the helper. As an example, the redirector defines `direct()` as an alias of `goto()`, allowing use of the helper like this:

```
// Redirect to /blog/view/item/id/42
$this->_helper->redirector('item', 'view', 'blog', array('id' => 42));
```

Internally, the helper broker's `__call()` method looks for a helper named `redirector`, then checks to see if that helper has a defined `direct` class, and calls it with the arguments provided.

Once you have created your own helper class, you may provide access to it as described in the sections above.

The Response Object

Usage

The response object is the logical counterpart to the request object. Its purpose is to collate content and/or headers so that they may be returned en masse. Additionally, the front controller will pass any caught exceptions to the response object, allowing the developer to gracefully handle exceptions. This functionality may be overridden by setting `Zend_Controller_Front::throwExceptions (true)`:

```
$front->throwExceptions(true);
```

To send the response output, including headers, use `sendResponse()`.

```
$response->sendResponse();
```

Note

By default, the front controller calls `sendResponse()` when it has finished dispatching the request; typically you will never need to call it. However, if you wish to manipulate the response or use it in testing, you can override this behaviour by setting the `returnResponse` flag with `Zend_Controller_Front::returnResponse(true)`:

```
$front->returnResponse(true);
$response = $front->dispatch();

// do some more processing, such as logging...
// and then send the output:
$response->sendResponse();
```

Developers should make use of the response object in their action controllers. Instead of directly rendering output and sending headers, push them to the response object:

```
// Within an action controller action:
// Set a header
$this->getResponse()
    ->setHeader('Content-Type', 'text/html')
    ->appendBody($content);
```

By doing this, all headers get sent at once, just prior to displaying the content.

Note

If using the action controller view integration, you do not need to set the rendered view script content in the response object, as Zend_Controller_Action::render() does this by default.

Should an exception occur in an application, check the response object's isException() flag, and retrieve the exception using getException(). Additionally, one may create custom response objects that redirect to error pages, log exception messages, do pretty formatting of exception messages (for development environments), etc.

You may retrieve the response object following the front controller dispatch(), or request the front controller to return the response object instead of rendering output.

```
// retrieve post-dispatch:
$front->dispatch();
$response = $front->getResponse();
if ($response->isException()) {
    // log, mail, etc...
}

// Or, have the front controller dispatch() process return it
$front->returnResponse(true);
$response = $front->dispatch();

// do some processing...

// finally, echo the response
$response->sendResponse();
```

By default, exception messages are not displayed. This behaviour may be overridden by calling renderExceptions(), or enabling the front controller to throwExceptions(), as shown above:

```
$response->renderExceptions(true);
$front->dispatch($request, $response);

// or:
$front->returnResponse(true);
```

```
$response = $front->dispatch();
$response->renderExceptions();
$response->sendResponse();

// or:
$front->throwExceptions(true);
$front->dispatch();
```

Manipulating Headers

As stated previously, one aspect of the response object's duties is to collect and emit HTTP response headers. A variety of methods exist for this:

- canSendHeaders() is used to determine if headers have already been sent. It takes an optional flag indicating whether or not to throw an exception if headers have already been sent. This can be overridden by setting the property headersSentThrowsException to false.

- setHeader($name, $value, $replace = false) is used to set an individual header. By default, it does not replace existing headers of the same name in the object; however, setting $replace to true will force it to do so.

  Before setting the header, it checks with canSendHeaders() to see if this operation is allowed at this point, and requests that an exception be thrown.

- setRedirect($url, $code = 302) sets an HTTP Location header for a redirect. If an HTTP status code has been provided, it will use that status code.

  Internally, it calls setHeader() with the $replace flag on to ensure only one such header is ever sent.

- getHeaders() returns an array of all headers. Each array element is an array with the keys 'name' and 'value'.

- clearHeaders() clears all registered headers.

- setRawHeader() can be used to set headers that are not key/value pairs, such as an HTTP status header.

- getRawHeaders() returns any registered raw headers.

- clearRawHeaders() clears any registered raw headers.

- clearAllHeaders() clears both regular key/value headers as well as raw headers.

In addition to the above methods, there are accessors for setting and retrieving the HTTP response code for the current request, setHttpResponseCode() and getHttpResponseCode().

Named Segments

The response object has support for "named segments". This allows you to segregate body content into different segments and order those segments so output is returned in a specific order. Internally, body content is saved as an array, and the various accessor methods can be used to indicate placement and names within that array.

As an example, you could use a preDispatch() hook to add a header to the response object, then have the action controller add body content, and a postDispatch() hook add a footer:

```
// Assume that this plugin class is registered with the front controller
class MyPlugin extends Zend_Controller_Plugin_Abstract
{
```

```
    public function preDispatch(Zend_Controller_Request_Abstract $request)
    {
        $response = $this->getResponse();
        $view = new Zend_View();
        $view->setBasePath('../views/scripts');

        $response->prepend('header', $view->render('header.phtml'));
    }

    public function postDispatch(Zend_Controller_Request_Abstract $request)
    {
        $response = $this->getResponse();
        $view = new Zend_View();
        $view->setBasePath('../views/scripts');

        $response->append('footer', $view->render('footer.phtml'));
    }
}

// a sample action controller
class MyController extends Zend_Controller_Action
{
    public function fooAction()
    {
        $this->render();
    }
}
```

In the above example, a call to /my/foo will cause the final body content of the response object to have the following structure:

```
array(
    'header'  => ..., // header content
    'default' => ..., // body content from MyController::fooAction()
    'footer'  => ...  // footer content
);
```

When this is rendered, it will render in the order in which elements are arranged in the array.

A variety of methods can be used to manipulate the named segments:

- setBody() and appendBody() both allow you to pass a second value, $name, indicating a named segment. In each case, if you provide this, it will overwrite that specific named segment or create it if it does not exist (appending to the array by default). If no named segment is passed to setBody(), it resets the entire body content array. If no named segment is passed to appendBody(), the content is appended to the value in the 'default' name segment.

- prepend($name, $content) will create a segment named $name and place it at the beginning of the array. If the segment exists already, it will be removed prior to the operation (i.e., overwritten and replaced).

- append($name, $content) will create a segment named $name and place it at the end of the array. If the segment exists already, it will be removed prior to the operation (i.e., overwritten and replaced).

- insert($name, $content, $parent = null, $before = false) will create a segment named $name. If provided with a $parent segment, the new segment will be placed either before or after that segment (based on the value of $before) in the array. If the segment exists already, it will be removed prior to the operation (i.e., overwritten and replaced).

- clearBody($name = null) will remove a single named segment if a $name is provided (and the entire array otherwise).

- getBody($spec = false) can be used to retrieve a single array segment if $spec is the name of a named segment. If $spec is false, it returns a string formed by concatenating all named segments in order. If $spec is true, it returns the body content array.

Testing for Exceptions in the Response Object

As mentioned earlier, by default, exceptions caught during dispatch are registered with the response object. Exceptions are registered in a stack, which allows you to keep all exceptions thrown -- application exceptions, dispatch exceptions, plugin exceptions, etc. Should you wish to check for particular exceptions or to log exceptions, you'll want to use the response object's exception API:

- setException(Exception $e) allows you to register an exception.

- isException() will tell you if an exception has been registered.

- getException() returns the entire exception stack.

- hasExceptionOfType($type) allows you to determine if an exception of a particular class is in the stack.

- hasExceptionOfMessage($message) allows you to determine if an exception with a specific message is in the stack.

- hasExceptionOfCode($code) allows you to determine if an exception with a specific code is in the stack.

- getExceptionByType($type) allows you to retrieve all exceptions of a specific class from the stack. It will return false if none are found, and an array of exceptions otherwise.

- getExceptionByMessage($message) allows you to retrieve all exceptions with a specific message from the stack. It will return false if none are found, and an array of exceptions otherwise.

- getExceptionByCode($code) allows you to retrieve all exceptions with a specific code from the stack. It will return false if none are found, and an array of exceptions otherwise.

- renderExceptions($flag) allows you to set a flag indicating whether or not exceptions should be emitted when the response is sent.

Subclassing the Response Object

The purpose of the response object is to collect headers and content from the various actions and plugins and return them to the client; secondarily, it also collects any errors (exceptions) that occur in order to process them, return them, or hide them from the end user.

The base response class is Zend_Controller_Response_Abstract, and any subclass you create should extend that class or one of its derivatives. The various methods available have been listed in the previous sections.

Reasons to subclass the response object include modifying how output is returned based on the request environment (e.g., not sending headers for CLI or PHP-GTK requests), adding functionality to return a final view based on content stored in named segments, etc.

Plugins

Introduction

The controller architecture includes a plugin system that allows user code to be called when certain events occur in the controller process lifetime. The front controller uses a plugin broker as a registry for user plugins, and the plugin broker ensures that event methods are called on each plugin registered with the front controller.

The event methods are defined in the abstract class Zend_Controller_Plugin_Abstract, from which user plugin classes inherit:

- routeStartup() is called before Zend_Controller_Front calls on the router to evaluate the request against the registered routes.

- routeShutdown() is called after the router finishes routing the request.

- dispatchLoopStartup() is called before Zend_Controller_Front enters its dispatch loop.

- preDispatch() is called before an action is dispatched by the dispatcher. This callback allows for proxy or filter behavior. By altering the request and resetting its dispatched flag (via Zend_Controller_Request_Abstract::setDispatched(false)), the current action may be skipped and/or replaced.

- postDispatch() is called after an action is dispatched by the dispatcher. This callback allows for proxy or filter behavior. By altering the request and resetting its dispatched flag (via Zend_Controller_Request_Abstract::setDispatched(false)), a new action may be specified for dispatching.

- dispatchLoopShutdown() is called after Zend_Controller_Front exits its dispatch loop.

Writing Plugins

In order to write a plugin class, simply include and extend the abstract class Zend_Controller_Plugin_Abstract:

```
class MyPlugin extends Zend_Controller_Plugin_Abstract
{
    // ...
}
```

None of the methods of Zend_Controller_Plugin_Abstract are abstract, and this means that plugin classes are not forced to implement any of the available event methods listed above. Plugin writers may implement only those methods required by their particular needs.

Zend_Controller_Plugin_Abstract also makes the request and response objects available to controller plugins via the getRequest() and getResponse() methods, respectively.

Using Plugins

Plugin classes are registered with Zend_Controller_Front::registerPlugin(), and may be registered at any time. The following snippet illustrates how a plugin may be used in the controller chain:

```
class MyPlugin extends Zend_Controller_Plugin_Abstract
{
    public function routeStartup(Zend_Controller_Request_Abstract $request)
    {
        $this->getResponse()
            ->appendBody("<p>routeStartup() called</p>\n");
    }

    public function routeShutdown(Zend_Controller_Request_Abstract $request)
```

```
    {
        $this->getResponse()
            ->appendBody("<p>routeShutdown() called</p>\n");
    }

    public function dispatchLoopStartup(
        Zend_Controller_Request_Abstract $request)
    {
        $this->getResponse()
            ->appendBody("<p>dispatchLoopStartup() called</p>\n");
    }

    public function preDispatch(Zend_Controller_Request_Abstract $request)
    {
        $this->getResponse()
            ->appendBody("<p>preDispatch() called</p>\n");
    }

    public function postDispatch(Zend_Controller_Request_Abstract $request)
    {
        $this->getResponse()
            ->appendBody("<p>postDispatch() called</p>\n");
    }

    public function dispatchLoopShutdown()
    {
        $this->getResponse()
            ->appendBody("<p>dispatchLoopShutdown() called</p>\n");
    }
}

$front = Zend_Controller_Front::getInstance();
$front->setControllerDirectory('/path/to/controllers')
      ->setRouter(new Zend_Controller_Router_Rewrite())
      ->registerPlugin(new MyPlugin());
$front->dispatch();
```

Assuming that no actions called emit any output, and only one action is called, the functionality of the above plugin would still create the following output:

```
<p>routeStartup() called</p>
<p>routeShutdown() called</p>
<p>dispatchLoopStartup() called</p>
<p>preDispatch() called</p>
<p>postDispatch() called</p>
<p>dispatchLoopShutdown() called</p>
```

Note

Plugins may be registered at any time during the front controller execution. However, if an event has passed for which the plugin has a registered event method, that method will not be triggered.

Retrieving and Manipulating Plugins

On occasion, you may need to unregister or retrieve a plugin. The following methods of the front controller allow you to do so:

- getPlugin($class) allows you to retrieve a plugin by class name. If no plugins match, it returns false. If more than one plugin of that class is registered, it returns an array.

- `getPlugins()` retrieves the entire plugin stack.

- `unregisterPlugin($plugin)` allows you to remove a plugin from the stack. You may pass a plugin object, or the class name of the plugin you wish to unregister. If you pass the class name, any plugins of that class will be removed.

Plugins Included in the Standard Distribution

Zend Framework includes a plugin for error handling in its standard distribution.

ActionStack

The `ActionStack` plugin allows you to manage a stack of requests, and operates as a `postDispatch` plugin. If a forward (i.e., a call to another action) is already detected in the current request object, it does nothing. However, if not, it checks its stack and pulls the topmost item off it and forwards to the action specified in that request. The stack is processed in LIFO order.

You can retrieve the plugin from the front controller at any time using `Zend_Controller_Front::getPlugin('Zend_Controller_Plugin_ActionStack')`. Once you have the plugin object, there are a variety of mechanisms you can use to manipulate it.

- `getRegistry()` and `setRegistry()`. Internally, `ActionStack` uses a `Zend_Registry` instance to store the stack. You can substitute a different registry instance or retrieve it with these accessors.

- `getRegistryKey()` and `setRegistryKey()`. These can be used to indicate which registry key to use when pulling the stack. Default value is 'Zend_Controller_Plugin_ActionStack'.

- `getStack()` allows you to retrieve the stack of actions in its entirety.

- `pushStack()` and `popStack()` allow you to add to and pull from the stack, respectively. `pushStack()` accepts a request object.

An additional method, `forward()`, expects a request object, and sets the state of the current request object in the front controller to the state of the provided request object, and markes it as undispatched (forcing another iteration of the dispatch loop).

Zend_Controller_Plugin_ErrorHandler

`Zend_Controller_Plugin_ErrorHandler` provides a drop-in plugin for handling exceptions thrown by your application, including those resulting from missing controllers or actions; it is an alternative to the methods listed in the MVC Exceptions section.

The primary targets of the plugin are:

- Intercept exceptions raised due to missing controllers or action methods

- Intercept exceptions raised within action controllers

In other words, the `ErrorHandler` plugin is designed to handle HTTP 404-type errors (page missing) and 500-type errors (internal error). It is not intended to catch exceptions raised in other plugins or routing.

By default, `Zend_Controller_Plugin_ErrorHandler` will forward to `ErrorController::errorAction()` in the default module. You may set alternate values for these by using the various accessors available to the plugin:

- `setErrorHandlerModule()` sets the controller module to use.

- `setErrorHandlerController()` sets the controller to use.

- `setErrorHandlerAction()` sets the controller action to use.

- `setErrorHandler()` takes an associative array, which may contain any of the keys 'module', 'controller', or 'action', with which it will set the appropriate values.

Additionally, you may pass an optional associative array to the constructor, which will then proxy to `setErrorHandler()`.

`Zend_Controller_Plugin_ErrorHandler` registers a `postDispatch()` hook and checks for exceptions registered in the response object. If any are found, it attempts to forward to the registered error handler action.

If an exception occurs dispatching the error handler, the plugin will tell the front controller to throw exceptions, and rethrow the last exception registered with the response object.

Using the ErrorHandler as a 404 Handler

Since the `ErrorHandler` plugin captures not only application errors, but also errors in the controller chain arising from missing controller classes and/or action methods, it can be used as a 404 handler. To do so, you will need to have your error controller check the exception type.

Exceptions captured are logged in an object registered in the request. To retrieve it, use `Zend_Controller_Action::_getParam('error_handler')`:

```
class ErrorController extends Zend_Controller_Action
{
    public function errorAction()
    {
        $errors = $this->_getParam('error_handler');
    }
}
```

Once you have the error object, you can get the type via `$errors->type`. It will be one of the following:

- `Zend_Controller_Plugin_ErrorHandler::EXCEPTION_NO_CONTROLLER`, indicating the controller was not found.

- `Zend_Controller_Plugin_ErrorHandler::EXCEPTION_NO_ACTION`, indicating the requested action was not found.

- `Zend_Controller_Plugin_ErrorHandler::EXCEPTION_OTHER`, indicating other exceptions.

You can then test for either of the first two types, and, if so, indicate a 404 page:

```
class ErrorController extends Zend_Controller_Action
{
    public function errorAction()
    {
        $errors = $this->_getParam('error_handler');

        switch ($errors->type) {
            case Zend_Controller_Plugin_ErrorHandler::EXCEPTION_NO
                _CONTROLLER:
            case Zend_Controller_Plugin_ErrorHandler::EXCEPTION_NO_ACTION:
                // 404 error -- controller or action not found
                $this->getResponse()
                    ->setRawHeader('HTTP/1.1 404 Not Found');

                // ... get some output to display...
```

```
                 break;
             default:
                 // application error; display error page, but don't
                 // change status code
                 break;
         }
     }
}
```

Finally, you can retrieve the exception that triggered the error handler by grabbing the `exception` property of the `error_handler` object:

```
public function errorAction()
{
        $errors = $this->_getParam('error_handler');

        switch ($errors->type) {
            case Zend_Controller_Plugin_ErrorHandler::EXCEPTION_NO
                _CONTROLLER:
            case Zend_Controller_Plugin_ErrorHandler::EXCEPTION_NO_ACTION:
                // 404 error -- controller or action not found
                $this->getResponse()
                    ->setRawHeader('HTTP/1.1 404 Not Found');

                // ... get some output to display...
                break;
            default:
                // application error; display error page, but don't change
                // status code

                // ...

                // Log the exception:
                $exception = $errors->exception;
                $log = new Zend_Log(
                    new Zend_Log_Writer_Stream(
                        '/tmp/applicationException.log'
                    )
                );
                $log->debug($exception->getMessage() . "\n" .
                        $exception->getTraceAsString());
                break;
        }
}
```

Handling Previously Rendered Output

If you dispatch multiple actions in a request, or if your action makes multiple calls to `render()`, it's possible that the response object already has content stored within it. This can lead to rendering a mixture of expected content and error content.

If you wish to render errors inline in such pages, no changes will be necessary. If you do not wish to render such content, you should clear the response body prior to rendering any views:

```
$this->getResponse()->clearBody();
```

Plugin Usage Examples

Example 12.16. Standard Usage

```
$front = Zend_Controller_Front::getInstance();
$front->registerPlugin(new Zend_Controller_Plugin_ErrorHandler());
```

Example 12.17. Setting a Different Error Handler

```
$front = Zend_Controller_Front::getInstance();
$front->registerPlugin(new Zend_Controller_Plugin_ErrorHandler(array(
    'module'     => 'mystuff',
    'controller' => 'static',
    'action'     => 'error'
)));
```

Example 12.18. Using Accessors

```
$plugin = new Zend_Controller_Plugin_ErrorHandler();
$plugin->setErrorHandlerModule('mystuff')
       ->setErrorHandlerController('static')
       ->setErrorHandlerAction('error');

$front = Zend_Controller_Front::getInstance();
$front->registerPlugin($plugin);
```

Error Controller Example

In order to use the Error Handler plugin, you need an error controller. Below is a simple example.

```
class ErrorController extends Zend_Controller_Action
{
    public function errorAction()
    {
        $errors = $this->_getParam('error_handler');

        switch ($errors->type) {
            case Zend_Controller_Plugin_ErrorHandler::EXCEPTION_NO
                _CONTROLLER:
            case Zend_Controller_Plugin_ErrorHandler::EXCEPTION_NO_ACTION:
                // 404 error -- controller or action not found
                $this->getResponse()->setRawHeader('HTTP/1.1 404 Not Found')

                $content =<<<EOH
<h1>Error!</h1>
<p>The page you requested was not found.</p>
```

```
EOH;
                break;
            default:
                // application error
                $content =<<<EOH
<h1>Error!</h1>
<p>An unexpected error occurred. Please try again later.</p>
EOH;
                break;
        }

        // Clear previous content
        $this->getResponse()->clearBody();

        $this->view->content = $content;
    }
}
```

Using a Conventional Modular Directory Structure

Introduction

The Conventional Modular directory structure allows you to separate different MVC applications into self-contained units, and re-use them with different front controllers. To illustrate such a directory structure:

```
docroot/
    index.php
application/
    default/
        controllers/
            IndexController.php
            FooController.php
        models/
        views/
            scripts/
                index/
                foo/
            helpers/
            filters/
    blog/
        controllers/
            IndexController.php
        models/
        views/
            scripts/
                index/
            helpers/
            filters/
    news/
        controllers/
            IndexController.php
            ListController.php
        models/
        views/
            scripts/
                index/
```

```
list/
helpers/
filters/
```

In this paradigm, the module name serves as a prefix to the controllers it contains. The above example contains three module controllers, 'Blog_IndexController', 'News_IndexController', and 'News_ListController'. Two global controllers, 'IndexController' and 'FooController' are also defined; neither of these will be namespaced. This directory structure will be used for examples in this chapter.

No Namespacing in the Default Module

Note that in the default module, controllers do not need a namespace prefix. Thus, in the example above, the controllers in the default module do not need a prefix of 'Default_' -- they are simply dispatched according to their base controller name: 'IndexController' and 'FooController'. A namespace prefix is used in all other modules, however.

So, how do you implement such a directory layout using the Zend Framework MVC components?

Specifying Module Controller Directories

The first step to making use of modules is to modify how you specify the controller directory list in the front controller. In the basic MVC series, you pass either an array or a string to setControllerDirectory(), or a path to addControllerDirectory(). When using modules, you need to alter your calls to these methods slightly.

With setControllerDirectory(), you will need to pass an associative array and specify key/value pairs of module name/directory paths. The special key default will be used for global controllers (those not needing a module namespace). All entries should contain a string key pointing to a single path, and the default key must be present. As an example:

```
$front->setControllerDirectory(array(
    'default' => '/path/to/application/controllers',
    'blog'    => '/path/to/application/blog/controllers'
));
```

addControllerDirectory() will take an optional second argument. When using modules, pass the module name as the second argument; if not specified, the path will be added to the default namespace. As an example:

```
$front->addControllerDirectory('/path/to/application/news/controllers',
                                'news');
```

Saving the best for last, the easiest way to specify module directories is to do so en masse, with all modules under a common directory and sharing the same structure. This can be done with addModuleDirectory():

```
/**
 * Assuming the following directory structure:
 * application/
 *     modules/
 *         default/
 *             controllers/
 *         foo/
 *             controllers/
 *         bar/
 *             controllers/
```

```
 */
$front->addModuleDirectory('/path/to/application/modules');
```

The above example will define the default, foo, and bar modules, each pointing to the controllers subdirectory of their respective module.

You may customize the controller subdirectory to use within your modules by using setModuleControllerDirectoryName():

```
/**
 * Change the controllers subdirectory to be 'con'
 * application/
 *     modules/
 *         default/
 *             con/
 *         foo/
 *             con/
 *         bar/
 *             con/
 */
$front->setModuleControllerDirectoryName('con');
$front->addModuleDirectory('/path/to/application/modules');
```

Note

You can indicate that no controller subdirectory be used for your modules by passing an empty value to setModuleControllerDirectoryName().

Routing to Modules

The default route in Zend_Controller_Router_Rewrite is an object of type Zend_Controller_Router_Route_Module. This route expects one of the following routing schemas:

- :module/:controller/:action/*

- :controller/:action/*

In other words, it will match a controller and action by themselves or with a preceding module. The rules for matching specify that a module will only be matched if a key of the same name exists in the controller directory array passed to the front controller and dispatcher.

Module or Global Default Controller

In the default router, if a controller was not specified in the URL, a default controller is used (IndexController, unless otherwise requested). With modular controllers, if a module has been specified but no controller, the dispatcher first looks for this default controller in the module path, and then falls back on the default controller found in the 'default', global, namespace.

If you wish to always default to the global namespace, set the useDefaultControllerAlways parameter in the front controller:

```
$front->setParam('useDefaultControllerAlways', true);
```

MVC Exceptions

Introduction

The MVC components in Zend Framework utilize a Front Controller, which means that all requests to a given site will go through a single entry point. As a result, all exceptions bubble up to the Front Controller eventually, allowing the developer to handle them in a single location.

However, exception messages and backtrace information often contain sensitive system information, such as SQL statements, file locations, and more. To help protect your site, by default Zend_Controller_Front catches all exceptions and registers them with the response object; in turn, by default, the response object does not display exception messages.

Handling Exceptions

Several mechanisms are built in to the MVC components already to allow you to handle exceptions.

- By default, the error handler plugin is registered and active. This plugin was designed to handle:

  - Errors due to missing controllers or actions

  - Errors occurring within action controllers

  It operates as a postDispatch() plugin, and checks to see if a dispatcher, action controller, or other exception has occurred. If so, it forwards to an error handler controller.

  This handler will cover most exceptional situations, and handle missing controllers and actions gracefully.

- Zend_Controller_Front::throwExceptions()

  By passing a boolean true value to this method, you can tell the front controller that instead of aggregating exceptions in the response object or using the error handler plugin, you'd rather handle them yourself. As an example:

  ```
  $front->throwExceptions(true);
  try {
      $front->dispatch();
  } catch (Exception $e) {
      // handle exceptions yourself
  }
  ```

  This method is probably the easiest way to add custom exception handling covering the full range of possible exceptions to your front controller application.

- Zend_Controller_Response_Abstract::renderExceptions()

  By passing a boolean true value to this method, you tell the response object that it should render an exception message and backtrace when rendering itself. In this scenario, any exception raised by your application will be displayed. This is only recommended for non-production environments.

- Zend_Controller_Front::returnResponse() and Zend_Controller_Response _Abstract::isException().

  By passing a boolean true to Zend_Controller_Front::returnResponse(), Zend_Controller_Front::dispatch() will not render the response, but instead return it. Once you have the response, you may then test to see if any exceptions were trapped using its isException() method, and retrieving the exceptions via the getException() method. As an example:

```
$front->returnResponse(true);
$response = $front->dispatch();
if ($response->isException()) {
    $exceptions = $response->getException();
    // handle exceptions ...
} else {
    $response->sendHeaders();
    $response->outputBody();
}
```

The primary advantage this method offers over Zend_Controller_Front::throw Excep-
tions() is to allow you to conditionally render the response after handling the exception. This will
catch any exception in the controller chain, unlike the error handler plugin.

MVC Exceptions You May Encounter

The various MVC components -- request, router, dispatcher, action controller, and response objects --
may each throw exceptions on occasion. Some exceptions may be conditionally overridden, and others
are used to indicate the developer may need to consider their application structure.

As some examples:

- Zend_Controller_Dispatcher::dispatch() will, by default, throw an exception if an
  invalid controller is requested. There are two recommended ways to deal with this.

  - Set the useDefaultControllerAlways parameter.

    In your front controller, or your dispatcher, add the following directive:

    ```
    $front->setParam('useDefaultControllerAlways', true);

    // or

    $dispatcher->setParam('useDefaultControllerAlways', true);
    ```

    When this flag is set, the dispatcher will use the default controller and action instead of throwing
    an exception. The disadvantage to this method is that any typos a user makes when accessing
    your site will still resolve and display your home page, which can wreak havoc with search
    engine optimization.

  - The exception thrown by dispatch() is a Zend_Controller_Dispatcher
    _Exception containing the text 'Invalid controller specified'. Use one of the methods outlined
    in the previous section to catch the exception, and then redirect to a generic error page or the
    home page.

- Zend_Controller_Action::__call() will throw a Zend_Controller_Action
  _Exception if it cannot dispatch a non-existent action to a method. Most likely, you will want to
  use some default action in the controller in cases like this. Ways to achieve this include:

  - Subclass Zend_Controller_Action and override the __call() method. As an example:

    ```
    class My_Controller_Action extends Zend_Controller_Action
    {
        public function __call($method, $args)
        {
            if ('Action' == substr($method, -6)) {
                $controller = $this->getRequest()->getControllerName();
    ```

```
            $url = '/' . $controller . '/index';
            return $this->_redirect($url);
        }

        throw new Exception('Invalid method');
    }
}
```

The example above intercepts any undefined action method called and redirects it to the default action in the controller.

- Subclass `Zend_Controller_Dispatcher` and override the `getAction()` method to verify the action exists. As an example:

```
class My_Controller_Dispatcher extends Zend_Controller_Dispatcher
{
    public function getAction($request)
    {
        $action = $request->getActionName();
        if (empty($action)) {
            $action = $this->getDefaultAction();
            $request->setActionName($action);
            $action = $this->formatActionName($action);
        } else {
            $controller = $this->getController();
            $action      = $this->formatActionName($action);
            if (!method_exists($controller, $action)) {
                $action = $this->getDefaultAction();
                $request->setActionName($action);
                $action = $this->formatActionName($action);
            }
        }

        return $action;
    }
}
```

The above code checks to see that the requested action exists in the controller class; if not, it resets the action to the default action.

This method is nice because you can transparently alter the action prior to final dispatch. However, it also means that typos in the URL may still dispatch correctly, which is not great for search engine optimization.

- Use `Zend_Controller_Action::preDispatch()` or `Zend_Controller_Plugin _Abstract::preDispatch()` to identify invalid actions.

By subclassing `Zend_Controller_Action` and modifying `preDispatch()`, you can modify all of your controllers to forward to another action or redirect prior to actually dispatching the action. The code for this will look similar to the code for overriding `__call()`, above.

Alternatively, you can check this information in a global plugin. This has the advantage of being action controller independent; if your application consists of a variety of action controllers, and not all of them inherit from the same class, this method can add consistency in handling your various classes.

As an example:

```
class My_Controller_PreDispatchPlugin extends Zend_Controller_Plugin
    _Abstract
{
    public function preDispatch(Zend_Controller_Request_Abstract
        $request)
    {
        $front       = Zend_Controller_Front::getInstance();
        $dispatcher = $front->getDispatcher();
        $class       = $dispatcher->getControllerClass($request);
        if (!$controller) {
            $class = $dispatcher->getDefaultControllerClass($request);
        }

        $r       = new ReflectionClass($class);
        $action = $dispatcher->getActionMethod($request);

        if (!$r->hasMethod($action)) {
            $defaultAction  = $dispatcher->getDefaultAction();
            $controllerName = $request->getControllerName();
            $response        = $front->getResponse();
            $response->setRedirect('/' . $controllerName
                                     . '/' . $defaultAction);
            $response->sendHeaders();
            exit;
        }
    }
}
```

In this example, we check to see if the action requested is available in the controller. If not, we redirect to the default action in the controller, and exit script execution immediately.

Migrating from Previous Versions

The API of the MVC components has changed over time. If you started using Zend Framework in an early version, follow the guidelines below to migrate your scripts to use the new architecture.

Migrating from 1.7.x to 1.8.0 or newer

Standard Route Changes

As translated segments were introduced into the new standard route, the @ character is now a special character in the beginning of a route segment. To be able to use it in a static segment, you must escape it by prefixing it with second @ character. The same rule now applies for the : character.

Migrating from 1.6.x to 1.7.0 or newer

Dispatcher Interface Changes

Users brought to our attention the fact that Zend_Controller_Action _Helper_ViewRenderer were using a method of the dispatcher abstract class that was not in the dispatcher interface. We have now added the following method to ensure that custom dispatchers will continue to work with the shipped implementations:

- formatModuleName(): should be used to take a raw controller name, such as one that would be packaged inside a request object, and reformat it to a proper class name that a class extending Zend_Controller_Action would use

Migrating from 1.5.x to 1.6.0 or Newer

Dispatcher Interface Changes

Users brought to our attention the fact that `Zend_Controller_Front` and `Zend_Controller_Router_Route_Module` were each using methods of the dispatcher that were not in the dispatcher interface. We have now added the following three methods to ensure that custom dispatchers will continue to work with the shipped implementations:

- `getDefaultModule()`: should return the name of the default module.

- `getDefaultControllerName()`: should return the name of the default controller.

- `getDefaultAction()`: should return the name of the default action.

Migrating from 1.0.x to 1.5.0 or Newer

Though most basic functionality remains the same, and all documented functionality remains the same, there is one particular *undocumented* "feature" that has changed.

When writing URLs, the documented way to write camelCased action names is to use a word separator; these are '.' or '-' by default, but may be configured in the dispatcher. The dispatcher internally lowercases the action name, and uses these word separators to re-assemble the action method using camelCasing. However, because PHP functions are not case sensitive, you *could* still write URLs using camelCasing, and the dispatcher would resolve these to the same location. For example, 'camel-cased' would become 'camelCasedAction' by the dispatcher, whereas 'camelCased' would become 'camelcasedAction'; however, due to the case insensitivity of PHP, both will execute the same method.

This causes issues with the ViewRenderer when resolving view scripts. The canonical, documented way is that all word separators are converted to dashes, and the words lowercased. This creates a semantic tie between the actions and view scripts, and the normalization ensures that the scripts can be found. However, if the action 'camelCased' is called and actually resolves, the word separator is no longer present, and the ViewRenderer attempts to resolve to a different location -- 'camelcased.phtml' instead of 'camel-cased.phtml'.

Some developers relied on this "feature", which was never intended. Several changes in the 1.5.0 tree, however, made it so that the ViewRenderer no longer resolves these paths; the semantic tie is now enforced. First among these, the dispatcher now enforces case sensitivity in action names. What this means is that referring to your actions on the url using camelCasing will no longer resolve to the same method as using word separators (i.e., 'camel-casing'). This leads to the ViewRenderer now only honoring the word-separated actions when resolving view scripts.

If you find that you were relying on this "feature", you have several options:

- Best option: rename your view scripts. Pros: forward compatibility. Cons: if you have many view scripts that relied on the former, unintended behavior, you will have a lot of renaming to do.

- Second best option: The ViewRenderer now delegates view script resolution to `Zend_Filter_Inflector`; you can modify the rules of the inflector to no longer separate the words of an action with a dash:

```
$viewRenderer =
    Zend_Controller_Action_HelperBroker::getStaticHelper('viewRenderer');
$inflector = $viewRenderer->getInflector();
$inflector->setFilterRule(':action', array(
    new Zend_Filter_PregReplace(
        '#[^a-z0-9' . preg_quote(DIRECTORY_SEPARATOR, '#') . ']+#i',
        ''
    ),
    'StringToLower'
));
```

The above code will modify the inflector to no longer separate the words with dash; you may also want to remove the 'StringToLower' filter if you *do* want the actual view script names camelCased as well.

If renaming your view scripts would be too tedious or time consuming, this is your best option until you can find the time to do so.

- Least desirable option: You can force the dispatcher to dispatch camelCased action names with a new front controller flag, 'useCaseSensitiveActions':

```
$front->setParam('useCaseSensitiveActions', true);
```

This will allow you to use camelCasing on the url and still have it resolve to the same action as when you use word separators. However, this will mean that the original issues will cascade on through; you will likely need to use the second option above in addition to this for things to work at all reliably.

Note, also, that usage of this flag will raise a notice that this usage is deprecated.

Migrating from 0.9.3 to 1.0.0RC1 or Newer

The principal changes introduced in 1.0.0RC1 are the introduction of and default enabling of the ErrorHandler plugin and the ViewRenderer action helper. Please read the documentation to each thoroughly to see how they work and what effect they may have on your applications.

The `ErrorHandler` plugin runs during `postDispatch()` checking for exceptions, and forwarding to a specified error handler controller. You should include such a controller in your application. You may disable it by setting the front controller parameter `noErrorHandler`:

```
$front->setParam('noErrorHandler', true);
```

The `ViewRenderer` action helper automates view injection into action controllers as well as autorendering of view scripts based on the current action. The primary issue you may encounter is if you have actions that do not render view scripts and neither forward or redirect, as the `ViewRenderer` will attempt to render a view script based on the action name.

There are several strategies you can take to update your code. In the short term, you can globally disable the `ViewRenderer` in your front controller bootstrap prior to dispatching:

```
// Assuming $front is an instance of Zend_Controller_Front
$front->setParam('noViewRenderer', true);
```

However, this is not a good long term strategy, as it means most likely you'll be writing more code.

When you're ready to start using the `ViewRenderer` functionality, there are several things to look for in your controller code. First, look at your action methods (the methods ending in 'Action'), and determine what each is doing. If none of the following is happening, you'll need to make changes:

- Calls to $this->render()

- Calls to $this->_forward()

- Calls to $this->_redirect()

- Calls to the Redirector action helper

The easiest change is to disable auto-rendering for that method:

```
$this->_helper->viewRenderer->setNoRender();
```

If you find that none of your action methods are rendering, forwarding, or redirecting, you will likely want to put the above line in your preDispatch() or init() methods:

```
public function preDispatch()
{
    // disable view script autorendering
    $this->_helper->viewRenderer->setNoRender()
    // .. do other things...
}
```

If you are calling render(), and you're using the Conventional Modular directory structure, you'll want to change your code to make use of autorendering:

- If you're rendering multiple view scripts in a single action, you don't need to change a thing.

- If you're simply calling render() with no arguments, you can remove such lines.

- If you're calling render() with arguments, and not doing any processing afterwards or rendering multiple view scripts, you can change these calls to read $this->_helper->viewRenderer().

If you're not using the conventional modular directory structure, there are a variety of methods for setting the view base path and script path specifications so that you can make use of the ViewRenderer. Please read the ViewRenderer documentation for information on these methods.

If you're using a view object from the registry, or customizing your view object, or using a different view implementation, you'll want to inject the ViewRenderer with this object. This can be done easily at any time.

- Prior to dispatching a front controller instance:

```
// Assuming $view has already been defined
$viewRenderer = new Zend_Controller_Action_Helper_ViewRenderer($view);
Zend_Controller_Action_HelperBroker::addHelper($viewRenderer);
```

- Any time during the bootstrap process:

```
$viewRenderer =
    Zend_Controller_Action_HelperBroker::getStaticHelper('viewRenderer');
$viewRenderer->setView($view);
```

There are many ways to modify the ViewRenderer, including setting a different view script to render, specifying replacements for all replaceable elements of a view script path (including the suffix), choosing a response named segment to utilize, and more. If you aren't using the conventional modular directory structure, you can even associate different path specifications with the ViewRenderer.

We encourage you to adapt your code to use the ErrorHandler and ViewRenderer as they are now core functionality.

Migrating from 0.9.2 to 0.9.3 or Newer

0.9.3 introduces action helpers. As part of this change, the following methods have been removed as they are now encapsulated in the redirector action helper:

- setRedirectCode(); use Zend_Controller_Action_Helper_Redirector ::setCode().

- setRedirectPrependBase(); use Zend_Controller_Action_Helper_Redirector ::setPrependBase().

- setRedirectExit(); use Zend_Controller_Action_Helper_Redirector ::setExit().

Read the action helpers documentation for more information on how to retrieve and manipulate helper objects, and the redirector helper documentation for more information on setting redirect options (as well as alternate methods for redirecting).

Migrating from 0.6.0 to 0.8.0 or Newer

Per previous changes, the most basic usage of the MVC components remains the same:

```
Zend_Controller_Front::run('/path/to/controllers');
```

However, the directory structure underwent an overhaul, several components were removed, and several others either renamed or added. Changes include:

- Zend_Controller_Router was removed in favor of the rewrite router.

- Zend_Controller_RewriteRouter was renamed to Zend_Controller _Router_Rewrite, and promoted to the standard router shipped with the framework; Zend_Controller_Front will use it by default if no other router is supplied.

- A new route class for use with the rewrite router was introduced, Zend_Controller _Router_Route_Module; it covers the default route used by the MVC, and has support for controller modules.

- Zend_Controller_Router_StaticRoute was renamed to Zend_Controller _Router_Route_Static.

- Zend_Controller_Dispatcher was renamed Zend_Controller _Dispatcher_Standard.

- Zend_Controller_Action::_forward()'s arguments have changed. The signature is now:

```
final protected function _forward($action,
                                  $controller = null,
                                  $module = null,
                                  array $params = null);
```

$action is always required; if no controller is specified, an action in the current controller is assumed. $module is always ignored unless $controller is specified. Finally, any $params provided will be appended to the request object. If you do not require the controller or module, but still need to pass parameters, simply specify null for those values.

Migrating from 0.2.0 or before to 0.6.0

The most basic usage of the MVC components has not changed; you can still do each of the following:

```
Zend_Controller_Front::run('/path/to/controllers');


/* -- create a router -- */
$router = new Zend_Controller_RewriteRouter();
$router->addRoute('user',
                  'user/:username',
                  array('controller' => 'user', 'action' => 'info')
);

/* -- set it in a controller -- */
$ctrl = Zend_Controller_Front::getInstance();
$ctrl->setRouter($router);

/* -- set controller directory and dispatch -- */
$ctrl->setControllerDirectory('/path/to/controllers');
$ctrl->dispatch();
```

We encourage use of the Response object to aggregate content and headers. This will allow for more flexible output format switching (for instance, JSON or XML instead of XHTML) in your applications. By default, dispatch() will render the response, sending both headers and rendering any content. You may also have the front controller return the response using returnResponse(), and then render the response using your own logic. A future version of the front controller may enforce use of the response object via output buffering.

There are many additional features that extend the existing API, and these are noted in the documentation.

The main changes you will need to be aware of will be found when subclassing the various components. Key amongst these are:

- Zend_Controller_Front::dispatch() by default traps exceptions in the response object, and does not render them, in order to prevent sensitive system information from being rendered. You can override this in several ways:

  - Set throwExceptions() in the front controller:

    ```
    $front->throwExceptions(true);
    ```

  - Set renderExceptions() in the response object:

    ```
    $response->renderExceptions(true);
    $front->setResponse($response);
    $front->dispatch();

    // or:
    $front->returnResponse(true);
    $response = $front->dispatch();
    $response->renderExceptions(true);
    echo $response;
    ```

- Zend_Controller_Dispatcher_Interface::dispatch() now accepts and returns a the section called "The Request Object" object instead of a dispatcher token.

- Zend_Controller_Router_Interface::route() now accepts and returns a the section called "The Request Object" object instead of a dispatcher token.

- `Zend_Controller_Action` changes include:

  - The constructor now accepts exactly three arguments, `Zend_Controller_Request_Abstract $request`, `Zend_Controller_Response_Abstract $response`, and `array $params` (optional). `Zend_Controller_Action::__construct()` uses these to set the request, response, and invokeArgs properties of the object, and if overriding the constructor, you should do so as well. Better yet, use the `init()` method to do any instance configuration, as this method is called as the final action of the constructor.

  - `run()` is no longer defined as final, but is also no longer used by the front controller; its sole purpose is for using the class as a page controller. It now takes two optional arguments, a `Zend_Controller_Request_Abstract $request` and a `Zend_Controller_Response_Abstract $response`.

  - `indexAction()` no longer needs to be defined, but is encouraged as the default action. This allows using the RewriteRouter and action controllers to specify different default action methods.

  - `__call()` should be overridden to handle any undefined actions automatically.

  - `_redirect()` now takes an optional second argument, the HTTP code to return with the redirect, and an optional third argument, `$prependBase`, that can indicate that the base URL registered with the request object should be prepended to the url specified.

  - The `_action` property is no longer set. This property was a `Zend_Controller_Dispatcher_Token`, which no longer exists in the current incarnation. The sole purpose of the token was to provide information about the requested controller, action, and URL parameters. This information is now available in the request object, and can be accessed as follows:

```
// Retrieve the requested controller name
// Access used to be via: $this->_action->getControllerName().
// The example below uses getRequest(), though you may also directly
// access the $_request property; using getRequest() is recommended as
// a parent class may override access to the request object.
$controller = $this->getRequest()->getControllerName();

// Retrieve the requested action name
// Access used to be via: $this->_action->getActionName().
$action = $this->getRequest()->getActionName();

// Retrieve the request parameters
// This hasn't changed; the _getParams() and _getParam() methods simply
// proxy to the request object now.
$params = $this->_getParams();
// request 'foo' parameter, using 'default' as default value if not found
$foo = $this->_getParam('foo', 'default');
```

  - `noRouteAction()` has been removed. The appropriate way to handle non-existent action methods should you wish to route them to a default action is using `__call()`:

```
public function __call($method, $args)
{
    // If an unmatched 'Action' method was requested, pass on to the
    // default action method:
    if ('Action' == substr($method, -6)) {
        return $this->defaultAction();
    }

    throw new Zend_Controller_Exception('Invalid method called');
}
```

- `Zend_Controller_RewriteRouter::setRewriteBase()` has been removed. Use `Zend_Controller_Front::setBaseUrl()` instead (or `Zend_Controller_Request_Http::setBaseUrl()`, if using that request class).

- `Zend_Controller_Plugin_Interface` was replaced by `Zend_Controller_Plugin_Abstract`. All methods now accept and return a the section called "The Request Object" object instead of a dispatcher token.

Chapter 13. Zend_Currency

Introduction to Zend_Currency

Zend_Currency is part of the strong support for i18n in Zend Framework. It handles all issues related to currency, money representation and formatting. It also provides additional methods which provide localized information on currencies, such as which currency is used in which region.

Why use Zend_Currency?

Zend_Currency offers the following functions for handling currency manipulations.

- *Complete Locale support*

  Zend_Currency works with all available locales and therefore knows about over 100 different localized currencies. This includes currency names, abbreviations, money signs and more.

- *Reusable Currency Definitions*

  Zend_Currency does not include the value of the currency. This is the reason why its functionality is not included in Zend_Locale_Format. Zend_Currency has the advantage that already defined currency representations can be reused.

- *Fluent Interface*

  Zend_Currency includes fluent interfaces where possible.

- *Additional Methods*

  Zend_Currency includes additional methods that offer information about which regions a currency is used in or which currency is used in a specified region.

How to Work with Currencies

To use Zend_Currency within your application, create an instance of it without any parameters. This will create an instance of Zend_Currency with your locale set and defines the currency which should be used for this locale.

Example 13.1. Creating an Instance of Zend_Currency from the Locale

Assume you have 'en_US' set as the set locale by the user or your environment. By passing no parameters while creating the instance you tell Zend_Currency to use the currency from the locale 'en_US'. This leads to an instance with US Dollar set as the currency with formatting rules from 'en_US'.

```
$currency = new Zend_Currency();
```

Zend_Currency also supports the usage of an application-wide locale. You can set a Zend_Locale instance in the registry as shown below. With this notation you can avoid setting the locale manually for each instance when you want to use the same locale throughout the application.

```
// in your bootstrap file
$locale = new Zend_Locale('de_AT');
Zend_Registry::set('Zend_Locale', $locale);
```

```
// somewhere in your application
$currency = new Zend_Currency();
```

Note

If your system has no default locale, or if the locale of your system can not be detected automatically, `Zend_Currency` will throw an exception. If see this exception, you should consider setting the locale manually.

Depending on your needs, several parameters can be speicified at instantiation. Each of these parameters is optional and can be omitted. Even the order of the parameters can be switched. The meaning of each parameter is described in this list:

- *currency*:

  A locale can include several currencies. Therefore the first parameter *'currency'* can define which currency should be used by giving the short name or full name of that currency. If that currency in not recognized in any locale an exception will be thrown. Currency short names are always made up of 3 letters, written in uppercase. Well known currency shortnames include USD or EUR.

- *locale*:

  The *'locale'* parameter defines which locale should be used for formatting the currency. The specified locale will also be used to get the script and symbol for this currency if these parameters are not given.

Note

Note that Zend_Currency only accepts locales which include a region. This means that all locales that only include a language will result in an exception. For example the locale *en* will cause an exception to be thrown whereas the locale *en_US* will return *USD* as currency.

Example 13.2. Other Ways to Create Instances of Zend_Currency

```
// expect standard locale 'de_AT'

// creates an instance from 'en_US' using 'USD' which is default
// currency for 'en_US'
$currency = new Zend_Currency('en_US');

// creates an instance from the set locale ('de_AT') using 'EUR' as
// currency
$currency = new Zend_Currency();

// creates an instance using 'EUR' as currency, 'en_US' for number
// formating
$currency = new Zend_Currency('en_US', 'EUR');
```

You can omit any of the parameters to `Zend_Currency`'s constructor if you want to use the default values. This has no negative effect on handling the currencies. It can be useful if, for example, you don't know the default currency for a region.

Note

For many countries there are several known currencies. Typically, one currency will currently be in use, with one or more ancient currencies. If the *'currency'* parameter is suppressed the contemporary currency will be used. The region '*de*' for example knows the currencies '*EUR*' and '*DEM*'... '*EUR*' is the contemporary currency and will be used if the currency parameter is omitted.

Creating and Output String from a Currency

To get a numeric value converted to an output string formatted for the currency at hand, use the method *toCurrency()*. It takes the value which should be converted. The value itself can be any normalized number.

If you have a localized number you will have to convert it first to an normalized number with Zend_Locale_Format::getNumber(). It may then be used with `toCurrency()` to create a currency output string.

`toCurrency(array $options)` accepts an array with options which can be used to temporarily set another format or currency representation. For details about which options can be used see Changing the Format of a Currency.

Example 13.3. Creating an Output String for a Currency

```
// creates an instance with 'en_US' using 'USD', which is the default
// values for 'en_US'
$currency = new Zend_Currency('en_US');

// prints '$ 1,000.00'
echo $currency->toCurrency(1000);

// prints '$ 1.000,00'
echo $currency->toCurrency(1000, array('format' => 'de_AT'));

// prints '$ ########'
echo $currency->toCurrency(1000, array('script' => 'Arab'));
```

Changing the Format of a Currency

The format which is used by creation of a `Zend_Currency` instance is, of course, the standard format. But occasionally it is necessary to change this format.

The format of an currency output includes the following parts:

- *Currency symbol, shortname or name*:

  The symbol of the currency is normally displayed within the currency output string. It can be suppressed when needed or even overwritten.

- *Currency position*:

  The position of the currency symbol is normally automatically defined by the locale. It can be changed if necessary.

- *Script*:

  The script which shall be used to display digits. Detailed information about scripts and their usage can be found in the documentation of `Zend_Locale` in supported number scripts.

- *Number formatting*:

  The amount of currency (formally known as value of money) is formatted by the usage of formatting rules within the locale. For example is in English the ',' sign used as separator for thousands, and in German the '.' sign.

So if you need to change the format, you should the *setFormat()* method. It takes an array which should include every option you want to change. The `options` array supports the following settings:

- *position*: Defines the position at which the currency description should be displayed. The supported positions can be found in this table.

- *script*: Defined which script should be used for displaying digits. The default script for most locales is *'Latn'*, which includes the digits 0 to 9. Other scripts such as 'Arab' (Arabian) can be used. All supported scripts can be found in this table.

- *format*: Defines the format which should be used for displaying numbers. This number-format includes for example the thousand separator. You can eighter use a default format by giving a locale identifier, or define the number-format manually. If no format is set the locale from the Zend_Currency object will be used.

- *display*: Defines which part of the currency should be used for displaying the currency representation. There are 4 representations which can be used and which are all described in this table.

- *precision*: Defines the precision which should be used for the currency representation. The default value is *2*.

- *name*: Defines the full currency name which should be displayed. This option overwrites any currency name which is set through the creation of Zend_Currency.

- *currency*: Defines the international abbreviation which should be displayed. This option overwrites any abbreviation which is set through the creation of Zend_Currency.

- *symbol*: Defines the currency symbol which should be displayed. This option overwrites any symbol which is set through the creation of Zend_Currency.

Table 13.1. Constants for the selecting the currency description

constant	description
NO_SYMBOL	Do not display any currency representation
USE_SYMBOL	Display the currency symbol
USE_SHORTNAME	Display the 3 lettered international currency abbreviation
USE_NAME	Display the full currency name

Table 13.2. Constants for the selecting the position of the currency description

constant	description
STANDARD	Set the standard position as defined within the locale
RIGHT	Display the currency representation at the right side of the value
LEFT	Display the currency representation at the left side of the value

Example 13.4. Changing the displayed format of a currency

```
// creates an instance with 'en_US' using 'USD', 'Latin' and 'en_US' as
// these are the default values from 'en_US'
$currency = new Zend_Currency('en_US');
```

```
// prints 'US$ 1,000.00'
echo $currency->toCurrency(1000);

$currency->setFormat(array('display' => Zend_Currency::USE_NAME,
                           'position' => Zend_Currency::RIGHT));

// prints '1.000,00 US Dollar'
echo $currency->toCurrency(1000);

$currency->setFormat(array('name' => 'American Dollar'));
// prints '1.000,00 American Dollar'
echo $currency->toCurrency(1000);

$currency->setFormat(array('format' => '##0.00'));
// prints '1000,00 American Dollar'
echo $currency->toCurrency(1000);
```

Reference Methods for Zend_Currency

Of course, Zend_Currency supports also methods to get information about any existing and many ancient currencies from Zend_Locale. The supported methods are:

- *getSymbol()*:

  Returns the known symbol of the set currency or a given currency. For example *$* for the US Dollar within the locale *'en_US*.

- *getShortName()*:

  Returns the abbreviation of the set currency or a given currency. For example *USD* for the US Dollar within the locale *'en_US*.

- *getName()*:

  Returns the full name of the set currency of a given currency. For example *US Dollar* for the US Dollar within the locale *'en_US*.

- *getRegionList()*:

  Returns a list of regions where the set currency or a given one is known to be used. It is possible that a currency is used within several regions, so the return value is always an array.

- *getCurrencyList()*:

  Returns a list of currencies which are used in the given region.

The function getSymbol(), getShortName() and getName() accept two optional parameters. If no parameter is given the expected data will be returned from the set currency. The first parameter takes the shortname of a currency. Short names are always three lettered, for example EUR for euro or USD for US Dollar. The second parameter defines from which locale the data should be read. If no locale is given, the set locale is used.

Example 13.5. Getting Information about Currencies

```
// creates an instance with 'en_US' using 'USD', 'Latin' and 'en_US'
// as these are the default values from 'en_US'
$currency = new Zend_Currency('en_US');

// prints '$'
echo $currency->getSymbol();
```

```
// prints 'EUR'
echo $currency->getShortName('EUR');

// prints 'Österreichische Schilling'
echo $currency->getName('ATS', 'de_AT');

// returns an array with all regions where USD is used
print_r($currency->getRegionList());

// returns an array with all currencies which were ever used in this
// region
print_r($currency->getCurrencyList('de_AT'));
```

Settings new default values

The method setLocale allows to set a new locale for Zend_Currency. All default values for the currency will be overwritten when this method is invoked. This includes currency name, abbreviation and symbol.

Example 13.6. Setting a New Locale

```
// get the currency for US
$currency = new Zend_Currency('en_US');
print $currency->toCurrency(1000);

// get the currency for AT
$currency->setLocale('de_AT');
print $currency->toCurrency(1000);
```

Zend_Currency Performance Optimization

Zend_Currency's performance can be optimized using Zend_Cache. The static method Zend_Currency::setCache($cache) accepts one option: a Zend_Cache adapter. If the cache adapter is set, the localization data that Zend_Currency uses are cached. There are some static methods for manipulating the cache: getCache(), hasCache(), clearCache() and removeCache().

Example 13.7. Caching currencies

```
// creating a cache object
$cache = Zend_Cache::factory('Core',
                             'File',
                             array('lifetime' => 120,
                                   'automatic_serialization' => true),
                             array('cache_dir'
                                        => dirname(__FILE__) . '/_files/'));
Zend_Currency::setCache($cache);
```

Migrating from Previous Versions

The API of Zend_Currency has changed in the past to enhance usability. If you started using Zend_Currency with a version which is mentioned in this chapter follow the guidelines below to migrate your scripts to the new API.

Migrating from 1.0.2 to 1.0.3 or Newer

Creating an object of Zend_Currency has become simpler. You no longer have to give a script or set it to null. The optional script parameter is now an option which can be set through the setFormat() method.

```
$currency = new Zend_Currency($currency, $locale);
```

The setFormat() method takes now an array of options. These options are set permanently and override all previously set values. Also a new option 'precision' has been added. The following options have been refactored:

- *position*: Replacement for the old 'rules' parameter.

- *script*: Replacement for the old 'script' parameter.

- *format*: Replacement for the old 'locale' parameter which does not set new currencies but only the number format.

- *display*: Replacement for the old 'rules' parameter.

- *precision*: New parameter.

- *name*: Replacement for the ole 'rules' parameter. Sets the full currencies name.

- *currency*: New parameter.

- *symbol*: New parameter.

```
$currency->setFormat(array $options);
```

The toCurrency() method no longer supports the optional 'script' and 'locale' parameters. Instead it takes an options array which can contain the same keys as for the setFormat method.

```
$currency->toCurrency($value, array $options);
```

The methods getSymbol(), getShortName(), getName(), getRegionList() and getCurrencyList() are no longer static and can be called from within the object. They return the set values of the object if no parameter has been set.

Chapter 14. Zend_Date

Introduction

The `Zend_Date` component offers a detailed, but simple API for manipulating dates and times. Its methods accept a wide variety of types of information, including date parts, in numerous combinations yielding many features and possibilities above and beyond the existing PHP date related functions. For the very latest manual updates, please see our online manual (frequently synced to Subversion) [http://framework.zend.com/wiki/display/ZFDOCDEV/Home] .

Although simplicity remains the goal, working with localized dates and times while modifying, combining, and comparing parts involves some unavoidable complexity. Dates, as well as times, are often written differently in different locales. For example, some place the month first, while other write the year first when expressing calendar dates. For more information about handling localization and normalization, please refer to `Zend_Locale` .

`Zend_Date` also supports abbreviated names of months in many languages. `Zend_Locale` facilitates the normalization of localized month and weekday names to timestamps, which may, in turn, be shown localized to other regions.

Always Set a Default Timezone

Before using any date related functions in PHP or Zend Framework, first make certain your application has a correct default timezone, by either setting the TZ environment variable, using the `date.timezone` php.ini setting, or using `date_default_timezone_set()` [http://php.net /date_default_timezone_set] . In PHP, we can adjust all date and time related functions to work for a particular user by setting a default timezone according to the user's expectations. For a complete list of timezone settings, see the CLDR Timezone Identifier List [http://unicode.org/cldr/data /diff/supplemental/territory_containment_un_m_49.html] .

Example 14.1. Setting a Default Timezone

```
// timezone for an American in California
date_default_timezone_set('America/Los_Angeles');
// timezone for a German in Germany
date_default_timezone_set('Europe/Berlin');
```

When creating Zend_Date instances, their timezone will automatically become the current default timezone! Thus, the timezone setting will account for any Daylight Savings Time (DST) in effect, eliminating the need to explicitly specify DST.

Keep in mind that the timezones *UTC* and *GMT* do not include Daylight Saving Time. This means that even if you define per hand that `Zend_Date` should work with DST, it would automatically be switched back for the instances of `Zend_Date` which have been set to UTC or GMT.

Why Use Zend_Date?

`Zend_Date` offers the following features, which extend the scope of PHP date functions:

- Simple API

  `Zend_Date` offers a very simple API, which combines the best of date/time functionality from four programming languages. It is possible, for example, to add or compare two times within a single row.

- Completely internationalized

  All full and abbreviated names of months and weekdays are supported for more than 130 languages. Methods support both input and the output of dates using the localized names of months and weekdays, in the conventional format associated with each locale.

- Unlimited timestamps

  Although PHP 5.2 docs state, "The valid range of a timestamp is typically from Fri, 13 Dec 1901 20:45:54 GMT to Tue, 19 Jan 2038 03:14:07 GMT," Zend_Date supports a nearly unlimited range, with the help of the BCMath extension. If BCMath is not available, then Zend_Date will have reduced support only for timestamps within the range of the float type supported by your server. "The size of a float is platform-dependent, although a maximum of ~1.8e308 with a precision of roughly 14 decimal digits is a common value (that's 64 bit IEEE format)." [http://www.php.net/float]. Additionally, inherent limitations of float data types, and rounding error of float numbers may introduce errors into calculations. To avoid these problems, the ZF I18n components use BCMath extension, if available.

- Support for ISO_8601 date specifications

  ISO_8601 date specifications are supported. Even partially compliant ISO_8601 date specifications will be identified. These date formats are particularly useful when working with databases. For example, even though MsSQL and MySQL [http://dev.mysql.com/doc /refman/5.0/en/date-and-time-functions.html] differ a little from each other, both are supported by Zend_Date using the Zend_Date::ISO_8601 format specification constant. When date strings conform to "Y/m/d" or "Y-m-d H:i:s", according to PHP date() format tokens, use Zend_Date's built-in support for ISO 8601 formatted dates.

- Calculate sunrise and sunset

  For any place and day, the times for sunrise and sunset can be displayed, so that you won't miss a single daylight second for working on your favorite PHP project :)

Theory of Operation

Why is there only one class Zend_Date for handling dates and times in the Zend Framework?

Many languages split the handling of times and calendar dates into two classes. However, Zend Framework strives for extreme simplicity, and forcing the developer to manage different objects with different methods for times and dates becomes a burden in many situations. Since Zend_Date methods support working with ambiguous dates that might not include all parts (era, year, month, day, hour, minute, second, timezone), developers enjoy the flexibility and ease of using the same class and the same methods to perform the same manipulations (e.g. addition, subtraction, comparison, merging of date parts, etc.). Splitting the handling of these date fragments into multiple classes would create complications when smooth interoperation is desired with a small learning curve. A single class reduces code duplication for similar operations, without the need for a complex inheritance hierarchy.

Internals

- UNIX Timestamp

  All dates and times, even ambiguous ones (e.g. no year), are represented internally as absolute moments in time, represented as a UNIX timestamp expressing the difference between the desired time and January 1st, 1970 00:00:00 GMT/UTC. This was only possible, because Zend_Date is not limited to UNIX timestamps nor integer values. The BCMath extension is required to support extremely large dates outside of the range Fri, 13 Dec 1901 20:45:54 GMT to Tue, 19 Jan 2038 03:14:07 GMT. Additional, tiny math errors may arise due to the inherent limitations of float data types and rounding, unless using the BCMath extension.

- Date parts as timestamp offsets

  Thus, an instance object representing three hours would be expressed as three hours after January 1st, 1970 00:00:00 GMT/UTC -i.e. 0 + 3 * 60 * 60 = 10800.

- PHP functions

  Where possible, Zend_Date usually uses PHP functions to improve performance.

Basic Methods

The following sections show basic usage of Zend_Date primarily by example. For this manual, "dates" always imply a calendar date with a time, even when not explicitly mentioned, and vice-versa. The part not specified defaults to an internal representation of "zero". Thus, adding a date having no calendar date and a time value of 12 hours to another date consisting only of a calendar date would result in a date having that calendar date and a time of "noon".

Setting only a specific date, with no time part, implies a time set to 00:00:00. Conversely, setting only a specific time implies a date internally set to 01.01.1970 plus the number of seconds equal to the elapsed hours, minutes, and seconds identified by the time. Normally, people measure things from a starting point, such as the year 0 A.D. However, many software systems use the first second of the year 1970 as the starting point, and denote times as a timestamp offset counting the number of seconds elapsed from this starting point.

Current Date

Without any arguments, constructing an instance returns an object in the default locale with the current, local date using PHP's time() function to obtain the UNIX timestamp [http://en.wikipedia.org/wiki/Unix_Time] for the object. Make sure your PHP environment has the correct default timezone .

Example 14.2. Creating the Current Date

```
$date = new Zend_Date();

// Output of the current timestamp
print $date;
```

Zend_Date by Example

Reviewing basic methods of Zend_Date is a good place to start for those unfamiliar with date objects in other languages or frameworks. A small example will be provided for each method below.

Output a Date

The date in a Zend_Date object may be obtained as a localized integer or string using the get() method. There are many available options, which will be explained in later sections.

Example 14.3. get() - Output a Date

```
$date = new Zend_Date();

// Output of the desired date
print $date->get();
```

Setting a Date

The set() method alters the date stored in the object, and returns the final date value as a timestamp (not an object). Again, there are many options which will be explored in later sections.

Example 14.4. set() - Set a Date

```
$date = new Zend_Date();

// Setting of a new time
$date->set('13:00:00',Zend_Date::TIMES);
print $date->get(Zend_Date::W3C);
```

Adding and Subtracting Dates

Adding two dates with add() usually involves adding a real date in time with an artificial timestamp representing a date part, such as 12 hours, as shown in the example below. Both add() and sub() use the same set of options as set(), which will be explained later.

Example 14.5. add() - Adding Dates

```
$date = new Zend_Date();

// changes $date by adding 12 hours
$date->add('12:00:00', Zend_Date::TIMES);

echo "Date via get() = ", $date->get(Zend_Date::W3C), "\n";

// use magic __toString() method to call Zend_Date's toString()
echo "Date via toString() = ", $date, "\n";
```

Comparison of Dates

All basic Zend_Date methods can operate on entire dates contained in the objects, or can operate on date parts, such as comparing the minutes value in a date to an absolute value. For example, the current minutes in the current time may be compared with a specific number of minutes using compare(), as in the example below.

Example 14.6. compare() - Compare Dates

```
$date = new Zend_Date();

// Comparation of both times
if ($date->compare(10, Zend_Date::MINUTE) == -1) {
    print "This hour is less than 10 minutes old";
} else {
    print "This hour is at least 10 minutes old";
}
```

For simple equality comparisons, use `equals()`, which returns a boolean.

Example 14.7. equals() - Identify a Date or Date Part

```
$date = new Zend_Date();

// Comparison of the two dates
if ($date->equals(10, Zend_Date::HOUR)) {
    print "It's 10 o'clock. Time to get to work.";
} else {
    print "It is not 10 o'clock. You can keep sleeping.";
}
```

Zend_Date API Overview

While the `Zend_Date` API remains simplistic and unitary, its design remains flexible and powerful through the rich permutations of operations and operands.

Zend_Date Options

Selecting the Date Format Type

Several methods use date format strings, in a way similar to PHP's `date()`. If you are more comfortable with PHP's date format specifier than with ISO format specifiers, then you can use `Zend_Date::setOptions(array('format_type' => 'php'))`. Afterward, use PHP's date format specifiers for all functions which accept a `$format` parameter. Use `Zend_Date::setOptions(array('format_type' => 'iso'))` to switch back to the default mode of supporting only ISO date format tokens. For a list of supported format codes, see the section called "Self-Defined OUTPUT Formats Using PHP's date() Format Specifiers"

DST and Date Math

When dates are manipulated, sometimes they cross over a DST change, normally resulting in the date losing or gaining an hour. For exmaple, when adding months to a date before a DST change, if the resulting date is after the DST change, then the resulting date will appear to lose or gain an hour, resulting in the time value of the date changing. For boundary dates, such as midnight of the first or last day of a month, adding enough months to cross a date boundary results in the date losing an hour and becoming the last hour of the preceding month, giving the appearance of an "off by 1" error. To avoid this situation, the DST change ignored by using the `fix_dst` option. When crossing the Summer/Winter DST boundary, normally an hour is substracted or added depending on the date. For example, date math crossing the Spring DST leads to a date having a day value one less than expected, if the time part of the date was originally 00:00:00. Since Zend_Date is based on timestamps, and not calendar dates with a time component, the timestamp loses an hour, resulting in the date having a calendar day value one less than expected. To prevent such problems use the option `fix_dst`, which defaults to true, causing DST to have no effect on date "math" (`addMonth()`, `subMonth()`). Use `Zend_Date::setOptions(array('fix_dst' => false))` to enable the subtraction or addition of the DST adjustment when performing date "math".

If your actual timezone within the instance of `Zend_Date` is set to UTC or GMT the option `'fix_dst'` will not be used because these two timezones do not work with DST. When you change the timezone for this instance again to a timezone which is not UTC or GMT the previous set 'fix_dst' option will be used again for date "math".

Month Calculations

When adding or substracting months from an existing date, the resulting value for the day of the month might be unexpected, if the original date fell on a day close to the end of the month. For example, when adding one month to January 31st, people familiar with SQL will expect February 28th as the result. On the other side, people familiar with Excel and OpenOffice will expect March 3rd as the result. The problem only occurs, if the resulting month does not have the day, which is set in the original date. For ZF developers, the desired behavior is selectable using the extend_month option to choose either the SQL behaviour, if set to false, or the spreadsheet behaviour when set to true. The default behaviour for extend_month is false, providing behavior compatible to SQL. By default, Zend_Date computes month calculations by truncating dates to the end of the month (if necessary), without wrapping into the next month when the original date designates a day of the month exceeding the number of days in the resulting month. Use Zend_Date::setOptions(array('extend_month' => true)); to make month calculations work like popular spreadsheet programs.

Speed up Date Localization and Normalization with Zend_Cache

You can speed up Zend_Date by using an Zend_Cache adapter. This speeds up all methods of Zend_Date when you are using localized data. For example all methods which accept Zend_Date::DATE and Zend_Date::TIME constants would benefit from this. To set an Zend_Cache adapter to Zend_Date just use Zend_Date::setOptions(array('cache' => $adapter));.

Receiving Syncronised Timestamps with Zend_TimeSync

Normally the clocks from servers and computers differ from each other. Zend_Date is able to handle such problems with the help of Zend_TimeSync. You can set a timeserver with Zend_Date::setOptions(array('timesync' => $timeserver)); which will set the offset between the own actual timestamp and the real actual timestamp for all instances of Zend_Date. Using this option does not change the timestamp of existing instances. So best usage is to set it within the bootstrap file.

Working with Date Values

Once input has been normalized via the creation of a Zend_Date object, it will have an associated timezone, but an internal representation using standard UNIX timestamps [http://en.wikipedia.org/wiki/Unix_Time] . In order for a date to be rendered in a localized manner, a timezone must be known first. The default timezone is always GMT/UTC. To examine an object's timezone use getTimeZone(). To change an object's timezone, use setTimeZone(). All manipulations of these objects are assumed to be relative to this timezone.

Beware of mixing and matching operations with date parts between date objects for different timezones, which generally produce undesireable results, unless the manipulations are only related to the timestamp. Operating on Zend_Date objects having different timezones generally works, except as just noted, since dates are normalized to UNIX timestamps on instantiation of Zend_Date.

Most methods expect a constant selecting the desired $part of a date, such as Zend_Date::HOUR. These constants are valid for all of the functions below. A list of all available constants is provided in the section called "List of All Constants" . If no $part is specified, then Zend_Date::TIMESTAMP is assumed. Alternatively, a user-specified format may be used for $part, using the same underlying mechanism and format codes as Zend_Locale_Format::getDate() . If a date object is constructed using an obviously invalid date (e.g. a month number greater than 12), then Zend_Date will throw an exception, unless no specific date format has been selected -i.e. $part is either null or Zend_Date::DATES (a "loose" format).

Example 14.8. User-Specified Input Date Format

```
$date1 = new Zend_Date('Feb 31, 2007', null, 'en_US');
echo $date1, "\n"; // outputs "Mar 3, 2007 12:00:00 AM"

$date2 = new Zend_Date('Feb 31, 2007', Zend_Date::DATES, 'en_US');
echo $date2, "\n"; // outputs "Mar 3, 2007 12:00:00 AM"

// strictly restricts interpretation to specified format
$date3 = new Zend_Date('Feb 31, 2007', 'MM.dd.yyyy');
echo $date3, "\n"; // outputs "Mar 3, 2007 12:00:00 AM"
```

If the optional $locale parameter is provided, then the $locale disambiguates the $date operand by replacing month and weekday names for string $date operands, and even parsing date strings expressed according to the conventions of that locale (see Zend_Locale_Format::getDate()). The automatic normalization of localized $date operands of a string type occurs when $part is one of the Zend_Date::DATE* or Zend_Date::TIME* constants. The locale identifies which language should be used to parse month names and weekday names, if the $date is a string containing a date. If there is no $date input parameter, then the $locale parameter specifies the locale to use for localizing output (e.g. the date format for a string representation). Note that the $date input parameter might actually have a type name instead (e.g. $hour for addHour()), although that does not prevent the use of Zend_Date objects as arguments for that parameter. If no $locale was specified, then the locale of the current object is used to interpret $date, or select the localized format for output.

Since Zend Framework 1.7.0 Zend_Date does also support the usage of an application wide locale. You can simply set a Zend_Locale instance to the registry like shown below. With this notation you can forget about setting the locale manually with each instance when you want to use the same locale multiple times.

```
// in your bootstrap file
$locale = new Zend_Locale('de_AT');
Zend_Registry::set('Zend_Locale', $locale);

// somewhere in your application
$date = new Zend_Date('31.Feb.2007');
```

Basic Zend_Date Operations Common to Many Date Parts

The methods add(), sub(), compare(), get(), and set() operate generically on dates. In each case, the operation is performed on the date held in the instance object. The $date operand is required for all of these methods, except get(), and may be a Zend_Date instance object, a numeric string, or an integer. These methods assume $date is a timestamp, if it is not an object. However, the $part operand controls which logical part of the two dates are operated on, allowing operations on parts of the object's date, such as year or minute, even when $date contains a long form date string, such as, "December 31, 2007 23:59:59". The result of the operation changes the date in the object, except for compare(), and get().

Example 14.9. Operating on Parts of Dates

```
$date = new Zend_Date(); // $date's timestamp === time()

// changes $date by adding 12 hours
```

```
$date->add('12', Zend_Date::HOUR);
print $date;
```

Convenience methods exist for each combination of the basic operations and several common date parts as shown in the tables below. These convenience methods help us lazy programmers avoid having to type out the date part constants when using the general methods above. Conveniently, they are named by combining a prefix (name of a basic operation) with a suffix (type of date part), such as addYear(). In the list below, all combinations of "Date Parts" and "Basic Operations" exist. For example, the operation "add" exists for each of these date parts, including addDay(), addYear(), etc.

These convenience methods have the same equivalent functionality as the basic operation methods, but expect string and integer $date operands containing only the values representing the type indicated by the suffix of the convenience method. Thus, the names of these methods (e.g. "Year" or "Minute") identify the units of the $date operand, when $date is a string or integer.

List of Date Parts

Table 14.1. Date Parts

Date Part	Explanation
Timestamp [http://en.wikipedia.org/wiki/Unix_Time]	UNIX timestamp, expressed in seconds elapsed since January 1st, 1970 00:00:00 GMT/UTC.
Year [http://en.wikipedia.org/wiki/Gregorian_calendar]	Gregorian calendar year (e.g. 2006)
Month [http://en.wikipedia.org/wiki/Month#Julian_and_Gregorian_calendars]	Gregorian calendar month (1-12, localized names supported)
24 hour clock [http://en.wikipedia.org/wiki/24-hour_clock]	Hours of the day (0-23) denote the hours elapsed, since the start of the day.
minute [http://en.wikipedia.org/wiki/Minute]	Minutes of the hour (0-59) denote minutes elapsed, since the start of the hour.
Second [http://en.wikipedia.org/wiki/Second]	Seconds of the minute (0-59) denote the elapsed seconds, since the start of the minute.
millisecond [http://en.wikipedia.org/wiki/Millisecond]	Milliseconds denote thousandths of a second (0-999). Zend_Date supports two additional methods for working with time units smaller than seconds. By default, Zend_Date instances use a precision defaulting to milliseconds, as seen using getFractionalPrecision(). To change the precision use setFractionalPrecision ($precision). However, precision is limited practically to microseconds, since Zend_Date uses microtime() [http://php.net/microtime] .
Day [http://en.wikipedia.org/wiki/Day]	Zend_Date::DAY_SHORT is extracted from $date if the $date operand is an instance of Zend_Date or a numeric string. Otherwise, an attempt is made to extract the day according to the conventions documented for these constants: Zend_Date::WEEKDAY_NARROW, Zend_Date::WEEKDAY_NAME, Zend_Date::WEEKDAY_SHORT, Zend_Date::WEEKDAY (Gregorian calendar assumed)

Date Part	Explanation
Week [http://en.wikipedia.org/wiki/Week]	Zend_Date::WEEK is extracted from $date if the $date operand is an instance of Zend_Date or a numeric string. Otherwise an exception is raised. (Gregorian calendar assumed)
Date	Zend_Date::DAY_MEDIUM is extracted from $date if the $date operand is an instance of Zend_Date. Otherwise, an attempt is made to normalize the $date string into a Zend_Date::DATE_MEDIUM formatted date. The format of Zend_Date::DAY_MEDIUM depends on the object's locale.
Weekday	Weekdays are represented numerically as 0 (for Sunday) through 6 (for Saturday). Zend_Date::WEEKDAY_DIGIT is extracted from $date, if the $date operand is an instance of Zend_Date or a numeric string. Otherwise, an attempt is made to extract the day according to the conventions documented for these constants: Zend_Date::WEEKDAY_NARROW, Zend_Date::WEEKDAY_NAME, Zend_Date::WEEKDAY_SHORT, Zend_Date::WEEKDAY (Gregorian calendar assumed)
DayOfYear	In Zend_Date, the day of the year represents the number of calendar days elapsed since the start of the year (0-365). As with other units above, fractions are rounded down to the nearest whole number. (Gregorian calendar assumed)
Arpa [http://www.faqs.org/rfcs/rfc822.html]	Arpa dates (i.e. RFC 822 formatted dates) are supported. Output uses either a "GMT" or "Local differential hours+min" format (see section 5 of RFC 822). Before PHP 5.2.2, using the DATE_RFC822 constant with PHP date functions sometimes produces incorrect results [http://bugs.php.net/bug.php?id=40308]. Zend_Date's results are correct. Example: Mon, 31 Dec 06 23:59:59 GMT
Iso [http://en.wikipedia.org/wiki/ISO_8601]	Only complete ISO 8601 dates are supported for output. Example: 2009-02-14T00:31:30 +01:00

List of Date Operations

The basic operations below can be used instead of the convenience operations for specific date parts, if the appropriate constant is used for the $part parameter.

Table 14.2. Basic Operations

Basic Operation	Explanation
get()	*get($part = null, $locale = null)* Use get($part) to retrieve the date $part of this object's date localized to $locale as a

Basic Operation	Explanation
	formatted string or integer. When using the BCMath extension, numeric strings might be returned instead of integers for large values. *NOTE:* Unlike `get()`, the other `get*()` convenience methods only return instances of `Zend_Date` containing a date representing the selected or computed date/time.
set()	*set($date, $part = null, $locale = null)* Sets the `$part` of the current object to the corresponding value for that part found in the input `$date` having a locale `$locale`.
add()	*add($date, $part = null, $locale = null)* Adds the `$part` of `$date` having a locale `$locale` to the current object's date.
sub()	*sub($date, $part = null, $locale = null)* Subtracts the `$part` of `$date` having a locale `$locale` from the current object's date.
copyPart()	*copyPart($part, $locale = null)* Returns a cloned object, with only `$part` of the object's date copied to the clone, with the clone have its locale arbitrarily set to `$locale` (if specified).
compare()	*compare($date, $part = null, $locale = null)* compares `$part` of `$date` to this object's timestamp, returning 0 if they are equal, 1 if this object's part was more recent than $date's part, otherwise -1.

Comparing Dates

The following basic operations do not have corresponding convenience methods for the date parts listed in the section called "Zend_Date API Overview" .

Table 14.3. Date Comparison Methods

Method	Explanation
equals()	*equals($date, $part = null, $locale = null)* returns true, if `$part` of `$date` having locale `$locale` is the same as this object's date `$part`, otherwise false
isEarlier()	*isEarlier($date, $part = null, $locale = null)* returns true, if `$part` of this object's date is earlier than `$part` of `$date` having a locale

Method	Explanation
	$locale
isLater()	*isLater($date, $part = null, $locale = null)*
	returns true, if $part of this object's date is later than $part of $date having a locale $locale
isToday()	*isToday()*
	Tests if today's year, month, and day match this object's date value, using this object's timezone.
isTomorrow()	*isTomorrow()*
	Tests if tomorrow's year, month, and day match this object's date value, using this object's timezone.
isYesterday()	*isYesterday()*
	Tests if yesterday's year, month, and day match this object's date value, using this object's timezone.
isLeapYear()	*isLeapYear()*
	Use isLeapYear() to determine if the current object is a leap year, or use Zend_Date::checkLeapYear($year) to check $year, which can be a string, integer, or instance of Zend_Date. Is the year a leap year?
isDate()	*isDate($date, $format = null, $locale = null)*
	This method checks if a given date is a real date and returns true if all checks are ok. It works like PHP's checkdate() function but can also check for localized month names and for dates extending the range of checkdate() false

Getting Dates and Date Parts

Several methods support retrieving values related to a Zend_Date instance.

Table 14.4. Date Output Methods

Method	Explanation
toString()	*toString($format = null, $locale = null)*
	Invoke directly or via the magic method __toString(). The toString() method automatically formats the date object's value according to the conventions of the object's locale, or an optionally specified $locale. For a list of supported format codes, see the section called "Self-Defined OUTPUT Formats with ISO".

Method	Explanation
toArray()	*toArray()* Returns an array representation of the selected date according to the conventions of the object's locale. The returned array is equivalent to PHP's getdate() [http://php.net/getdate] function and includes: • Number of day as *'day'* (Zend_Date::DAY_SHORT) • Number of month as *'month'* (Zend_Date::MONTH_SHORT) • Year as *'year'* (Zend_Date::YEAR) • Hour as *'hour'* (Zend_Date::HOUR_SHORT) • Minute as *'minute'* (Zend_Date::MINUTE_SHORT) • Second as *'second'* (Zend_Date::SECOND_SHORT) • Abbreviated timezone as *'timezone'* (Zend_Date::TIMEZONE) • Unix timestamp as *'timestamp'* (Zend_Date::TIMESTAMP) • Number of weekday as *'weekday'* (Zend_Date::WEEKDAY_DIGIT) • Day of year as *'dayofyear'* (Zend_Date::DAY_OF_YEAR) • Week as *'week'* (Zend_Date::WEEK) • Delay of timezone to GMT as *'gmtsecs'* (Zend_Date::GMT_SECS)
toValue()	*toValue($part = null)* Returns an integer representation of the selected date $part according to the conventions of the object's locale. Returns false when $part selects a non-numeric value, such as Zend_Date::MONTH_NAME_SHORT. *NOTE:* This method calls get() and casts the result to a PHP integer, which will give unpredictable results, if get() returns a numeric string containing a number too large for a PHP integer on your system. Use get() instead.
get()	*get($part = null, $locale = null)* This method returns the $part of object's date localized to $locale as a formatted string or integer. See the section called "List of Date Operations" for more information.

Method	Explanation
now()	*now($locale = null)* This convenience function is equivalent to `new Zend_Date()`. It returns the current date as a `Zend_Date` object, having `$locale`

Working with Fractions of Seconds

Several methods support retrieving values related to a `Zend_Date` instance.

Table 14.5. Date Output Methods

Method	Explanation
getFractionalPrecision()	Return the precision of the part seconds
setFractionalPrecision()	Set the precision of the part seconds

Sunrise / Sunset

Three methods provide access to geographically localized information about the Sun, including the time of sunrise and sunset.

Table 14.6. Miscellaneous Methods

Method	Explanation
getSunrise($location)	Return the date's time of sunrise
getSunset($location)	Return the date's time of sunset
getSunInfo($location)	Return an array with the date's sun dates

Creation of Dates

`Zend_Date` provides several different ways to create a new instance of itself. As there are different needs the most convenient ways will be shown in this chapter.

Create the Actual Date

The simplest way of creating a date object is to create the actual date. You can either create a new instance with *new Zend_Date()* or use the convenient static method *Zend_Date::now()* which both will return the actual date as new instance of `Zend_Date`. The actual date always include the actual date and time for the actual set timezone.

Example 14.10. Date Creation by Instance

Date creation by creating a new instance means that you do not need to give an parameter. Of course there are several parameters which will be described later but normally this is the simplest and most used way to get the actual date as Zend_Date instance.

```
$date = new Zend_Date();
```

Example 14.11. Static Date Creation

Sometimes it is easier to use a static method for date creation. Therefor you can use the *now ()* method. It returns a new instance of Zend_Date the same way as if you would use new Zend_Date(). But it will always return the actual date and can not be changed by giving optional parameters.

```
$date = Zend_Date::now();
```

Create a Date from Database

Databases are often used to store date values. But the problem is, that every database outputs its date values in a different way. MsSQL databases use a quite different standard date output than MySQL databases. But for simplification Zend_Date makes it very easy to create a date from database date values.

Of course each database can be said to convert the output of a defined column to a special value. For example you could convert a datetime value to output a minute value. But this is time expensive and often you are in need of handling dates in an other way than expected when creating the database query.

So we have one quick and one convenient way of creating dates from database values.

Example 14.12. Quick Creation of Dates from Database Date Values

All databases are known to handle queries as fast as possible. They are built to act and respond quick. The quickest way for handling dates is to get unix timestamps from the database. All databases store date values internal as timestamp (not unix timestamp). This means that the time for creating a timestamp through a query is much smaller than converting it to a specified format.

```
// SELECT UNIX_TIMESTAMP(my_datetime_column) FROM my_table
$date = new Zend_Date($unixtimestamp, Zend_Date::TIMESTAMP);
```

Example 14.13. Convenient Creation of Dates from Database Date Values

The standard output of all databases is quite different even if it looks the same on the first eyecatch. But all are part of the ISO Standard and explained through it. So the easiest way of date creation is the usage of Zend_Date::ISO_8601. Databases which are known to be recognised by Zend_Date::ISO_8601 are MySQL, MsSQL for example. But all databases are also able to return a ISO 8601 representation of a date column. ISO 8601 has the big advantage that it is human readable. The disadvantage is that ISO 8601 needs more time for computation than a simple unix timestamp. But it should also be mentioned that unix timestamps are only supported for dates after 1 January 1970.

```
// SELECT datecolumn FROM my_table
$date = new Zend_Date($datecolumn, Zend_Date::ISO_8601);
```

Create Dates from an Array

Dates can also be created by the usage of an array. This is a simple and easy way. The used array keys are:

- *day*: day of the date as number

- *month*: month of the date as number

- *year*: full year of the date

- *hour*: hour of the date

- *minute*: minute of the date

- *second*: second of the date

Example 14.14. Date Creation by Array

Normally you will give a complete date array for creation of a new date instance. But when you do not give all values, the not given array values are zeroed. This means that if f.e. no hour is given the hour *0* is used.

```
$datearray = array('year' => 2006,
                   'month' => 4,
                   'day' => 18,
                   'hour' => 12,
                   'minute' => 3,
                   'second' => 10);
$date = new Zend_Date($datearray);


$datearray = array('year' => 2006, 'month' => 4, 'day' => 18);
$date = new Zend_Date($datearray);
```

Constants for General Date Functions

Whenever a Zend_Date method has a $parts parameter, one of the constants below can be used as the argument for that parameter, in order to select a specific part of a date or indicate the date format used or desired (e.g. RFC 822).

Using Constants

For example, the constant Zend_Date::HOUR can be used in the ways shown below. When working with days of the week, calendar dates, hours, minutes, seconds, and any other date parts that are expressed differently when in different parts of the world, the object's timezone will automatically be used to compute the correct value, even though the internal timestamp is the same for the same moment in time, regardless of the user's physical location in the world. Regardless of the units involved, output must be expressed either as GMT/UTC or localized to a locale. The example output below reflects localization to Europe/GMT+1 hour (e.g. Germany, Austria, France).

Table 14.7. Operations Involving Zend_Date::HOUR

Function/input	Description	Original date	Effect/output
get(Zend_Date::HOUR)	Output of the hour	2009-02-13T14:53:27 +01:00	14
set(12, Zend_Date::HOUR)	Set new hour	2009-02-13T14:53:27 +01:00	2009-02-13T12:53:27 +01:00
add(12, Zend_Date::HOUR)	Add hours	2009-02-13T14:53:27 +01:00	2009-02-14T02:53:27 +01:00
sub(12, Zend_Date::HOUR)	Subtract hours	2009-02-13T14:53:27 +01:00	2009-02-13T02:53:27 +01:00
compare(12, Zend_Date::HOUR)	Compare hour, returns 0, 1 or -1	2009-02-13T14:53:27 +01:00	1 (if object > argument)
copy(Zend_Date ::HOUR)	Copies only the hour part	2009-02-13T14:53:27 +01:00	1970-01-01T14:00:00 +01:00
equals(14, Zend_Date::HOUR)	Compares the hour, returns TRUE or FALSE	2009-02-13T14:53:27 +01:00	TRUE
isEarlier(12, Zend_Date::HOUR)	Compares the hour, returns TRUE or FALSE	2009-02-13T14:53:27 +01:00	TRUE
isLater(12, Zend_Date::HOUR)	Compares the hour, returns TRUE or FALSE	2009-02-13T14:53:27 +01:00	FALSE

List of All Constants

Each part of a date/time has a unique constant in Zend_Date. All constants supported by Zend_Date are listed below.

Table 14.8. Day Constants

Constant	Description	Date	Affected part/example
Zend_Date::DAY	Day (as a number, two digit)	2009-02-06T14:53:27 +01:00	2009-02-06T14:53:27 +01:00 (06)
Zend_Date::DAY_SHORT	Day (as a number, one or two digit)	2009-02-06T14:53:27 +01:00	2009-02-06T14:53:27 +01:00 (6)
Zend_Date::WEEKDAY	Weekday (Name of the day, localized, complete)	2009-02-06T14:53:27 +01:00	*Friday*
Zend_Date::WEEKDAY _SHORT	Weekday (Name of the day, localized, abbreviated, the first three digits)	2009-02-06T14:53:27 +01:00	*Fri* for Friday
Zend_Date::WEEKDAY _NAME	Weekday (Name of the day, localized, abbreviated, the first two digits)	2009-02-06T14:53:27 +01:00	*Fr* for Friday
Zend_Date::WEEKDAY	Weekday (Name of the	2009-02-06T14:53:27	*F* for Friday

Constant	Description	Date	Affected part/example
_NARROW	day, localized, abbreviated, only the first digit)	+01:00	
Zend_Date::WEEKDAY _DIGIT	Weekday (0 = Sunday, 6 = Saturday)	2009-02-06T14:53:27 +01:00	5 for Friday
Zend_Date::WEEKDAY _8601	Weekday according to ISO 8601 (1 = Monday, 7 = Sunday)	2009-02-06T14:53:27 +01:00	5 for Friday
Zend_Date::DAY_OF _YEAR	Day (as a number, one or two digit)	2009-02-06T14:53:27 +01:00	43
Zend_Date::DAY _SUFFIX	English addendum for the day (st, nd, rd, th)	2009-02-06T14:53:27 +01:00	th

Table 14.9. Week Constants

Constant	Description	Date	Affected part/example
Zend_Date::WEEK	Week (as a number, 1-53)	2009-02-06T14:53:27 +01:00	7

Table 14.10. Month Constants

Constant	Description	Date	Affected part/example
Zend_Date::MONTH _NAME	Month (Name of the month, localized, complete)	2009-02-06T14:53:27 +01:00	February
Zend_Date::MONTH _NAME_SHORT	Month (Name of the month, localized, abbreviated, three digit)	2009-02-06T14:53:27 +01:00	Feb
Zend_Date::MONTH _NAME_NARROW	Month (Name of the month, localized, abbreviated, one digit)	2009-02-06T14:53:27 +01:00	F
Zend_Date::MONTH	Month (Number of the month, two digit)	2009-02-06T14:53:27 +01:00	2009-02-06T14:53:27 +01:00 (02)
Zend_Date::MONTH _SHORT	Month (Number of the month, one or two digit)	2009-02-06T14:53:27 +01:00	2009-02-06T14:53:27 +01:00 (2)
Zend_Date::MONTH _DAYS	Number of days for this month (number)	2009-02-06T14:53:27 +01:00	28

Table 14.11. Year Constants

Constant	Description	Date	Affected part/example
Zend_Date::YEAR	Year (number)	2009-02-06T14:53:27 +01:00	2009-02-06T14:53:27 +01:00
Zend_Date::YEAR_8601	Year according to ISO 8601 (number)	2009-02-06T14:53:27 +01:00	2009

Constant	Description	Date	Affected part/example
Zend_Date::YEAR _SHORT	Year (number, two digit)	2009-02-06T14:53:27 +01:00	20*09*-02-06T14:53:27 +01:00
Zend_Date::YEAR _SHORT_8601	Year according to ISO 8601 (number, two digit)	2009-02-06T14:53:27 +01:00	*09*
Zend_Date::LEAPYEAR	Is the year a leap year? (TRUE or FALSE)	2009-02-06T14:53:27 +01:00	*FALSE*

Table 14.12. Time Constants

Constant	Description	Date	Affected part/example
Zend_Date::HOUR	Hour (00-23, two digit)	2009-02-06T14:53:27 +01:00	*14*
Zend_Date::HOUR _SHORT	Hour (0-23, one or two digit)	2009-02-06T14:53:27 +01:00	*14*
Zend_Date::HOUR _SHORT_AM	Hour (1-12, one or two digit)	2009-02-06T14:53:27 +01:00	*2*
Zend_Date::HOUR_AM	Hour (01-12, two digit)	2009-02-06T14:53:27 +01:00	*02*
Zend_Date::MINUTE	Minute (00-59, two digit)	2009-02-06T14:53:27 +01:00	2009-02-06T14:*53*:27 +01:00
Zend_Date::MINUTE _SHORT	Minute (0-59, one or two digit)	2009-02-06T14:03:27 +01:00	2009-02-06T14:*03*:27 +01:00
Zend_Date::SECOND	Second (00-59, two digit)	2009-02-06T14:53:27 +01:00	2009-02-06T14:53:*27* +01:00
Zend_Date::SECOND _SHORT	Second (0-59, one or two digit)	2009-02-06T14:53:07 +01:00	2009-02-06T14:53:*07* +01:00
Zend_Date:: MILLISECOND	Millisecond (theoretically infinite)	2009-02-06T14:53: 27.20546	2009-02-06T14:53:27. *20546*
Zend_Date::MERIDIEM	Time of day (forenoon/afternoon)	2009-02-06T14:53:27 +01:00	*afternoon*
Zend_Date::SWATCH	Swatch Internet Time	2009-02-06T14:53:27 +01:00	*620*

Table 14.13. Timezone Constants

Constant	Description	Date	Affected part/example
Zend_Date::TIMEZONE	Name der time zone (string, abbreviated)	2009-02-06T14:53:27 +01:00	*CET*
Zend_Date::TIMEZONE _NAME	Name of the time zone (string, complete)	2009-02-06T14:53:27 +01:00	*Europe/Paris*
Zend_Date::TIMEZONE _SECS	Difference of the time zone to GMT in seconds (integer)	2009-02-06T14:53:27 +01:00	*3600* seconds to GMT
Zend_Date::GMT_DIFF	Difference to GMT in seconds (string)	2009-02-06T14:53:27 +01:00	*+0100*
Zend_Date::GMT_DIFF	Difference to GMT in	2009-02-06T14:53:27	*+01:00*

Constant	Description	Date	Affected part/example
_SEP	seconds (string, separated)	+01:00	
Zend_Date::DAYLIGHT	Summer time or Winter time? (TRUE or FALSE)	2009-02-06T14:53:27 +01:00	*FALSE*

Table 14.14. Date Format Constants (formats include timezone)

Constant	Description	Date	Affected part/example
Zend_Date::ISO_8601	Date according to ISO 8601 (string, complete)	2009-02-13T14:53:27 +01:00	*2009-02-13T14:53:27 +01:00*
Zend_Date::RFC_2822	Date according to RFC 2822 (string)	2009-02-13T14:53:27 +01:00	*Fri, 13 Feb 2009 14:53:27 +0100*
Zend_Date::TIMESTAMP	Unix time [http://en.wikipedia.org/wiki/Unix_Time] (seconds since 1.1.1970, mixed)	2009-02-13T14:53:27 +01:00	*1234533207*
Zend_Date::ATOM	Date according to ATOM (string)	2009-02-13T14:53:27 +01:00	*2009-02-13T14:53:27 +01:00*
Zend_Date::COOKIE	Date for Cookies (string, for Cookies)	2009-02-13T14:53:27 +01:00	*Friday, 13-Feb-09 14:53:27 Europe/Paris*
Zend_Date::RFC_822	Date according to RFC 822 (string)	2009-02-13T14:53:27 +01:00	*Fri, 13 Feb 09 14:53:27 +0100*
Zend_Date::RFC_850	Date according to RFC 850 (string)	2009-02-13T14:53:27 +01:00	*Friday, 13-Feb-09 14:53:27 Europe/Paris*
Zend_Date::RFC_1036	Date according to RFC 1036 (string)	2009-02-13T14:53:27 +01:00	*Fri, 13 Feb 09 14:53:27 +0100*
Zend_Date::RFC_1123	Date according to RFC 1123 (string)	2009-02-13T14:53:27 +01:00	*Fri, 13 Feb 2009 14:53:27 +0100*
Zend_Date::RSS	Date for RSS Feeds (string)	2009-02-13T14:53:27 +01:00	*Fri, 13 Feb 2009 14:53:27 +0100*
Zend_Date::W3C	Date for HTML/HTTP according to W3C (string)	2009-02-13T14:53:27 +01:00	*2009-02-13T14:53:27 +01:00*

Especially note Zend_Date::DATES, since this format specifier has a unique property within Zend_Date as an *input* format specifier. When used as an input format for $part, this constant provides the most flexible acceptance of a variety of similar date formats. Heuristics are used to automatically extract dates from an input string and then "fix" simple errors in dates (if any), such as swapping of years, months, and days, when possible.

Table 14.15. Date and Time Formats (format varies by locale)

Constant	Description	Date	Affected part/example
Zend_Date::ERA	Epoch (string, localized, abbreviated)	2009-02-06T14:53:27 +01:00	*AD (anno Domini)*
Zend_Date::ERA	Epoch (string, localized,	2009-02-06T14:53:27	*anno domini (anno*

Constant	Description	Date	Affected part/example
_NAME	complete)	+01:00	Domini)
Zend_Date::DATES	Standard date (string, localized, default value).	2009-02-13T14:53:27 +01:00	*13.02.2009*
Zend_Date::DATE _FULL	Complete date (string, localized, complete)	2009-02-13T14:53:27 +01:00	*Friday, 13. February 2009*
Zend_Date::DATE _LONG	Long date (string, localized, long)	2009-02-13T14:53:27 +01:00	*13. February 2009*
Zend_Date::DATE _MEDIUM	Normal date (string, localized, normal)	2009-02-13T14:53:27 +01:00	*13.02.2009*
Zend_Date::DATE _SHORT	Abbreviated Date (string, localized, abbreviated)	2009-02-13T14:53:27 +01:00	*13.02.09*
Zend_Date::TIMES	Standard time (string, localized, default value)	2009-02-13T14:53:27 +01:00	*14:53:27*
Zend_Date::TIME _FULL	Complete time (string, localized, complete)	2009-02-13T14:53:27 +01:00	*14:53 Uhr CET*
Zend_Date::TIME _LONG	Long time (string, localized, Long)	2009-02-13T14:53:27 +01:00	*14:53:27 CET*
Zend_Date::TIME _MEDIUM	Normal time (string, localized, normal)	2009-02-13T14:53:27 +01:00	*14:53:27*
Zend_Date::TIME _SHORT	Abbreviated time (string, localized, abbreviated)	2009-02-13T14:53:27 +01:00	*14:53*

Self-Defined OUTPUT Formats with ISO

If you need a date format not shown above, then use a self-defined format composed from the ISO format token specifiers below. The following examples illustrate the usage of constants from the table below to create self-defined ISO formats. The format length is unlimited. Also, multiple usage of format constants is allowed.

The accepted format specifiers can be changed from ISO Format to PHP's date format if you are more comfortable with it. However, not all formats defined in the ISO norm are supported with PHP's date format specifiers. Use the Zend_Date::setOptions(array('format_type' => 'php')) method to switch Zend_Date methods from supporting ISO format specifiers to PHP date() type specifiers (see the section called "Self-Defined OUTPUT Formats Using PHP's date() Format Specifiers" below).

Example 14.15. Self-Defined ISO Formats

```
$locale = new Zend_Locale('de_AT');
$date = new Zend_Date(1234567890, false, $locale);
print $date->toString("'Era:GGGG='GGGG, ' Date:yy.MMMM.dd'yy.MMMM.dd");
```

Table 14.16. Constants for ISO 8601 Date Output

Constant	Description	Corresponds best to	Affected part/example
G	Epoch, localized, abbreviated	Zend_Date::ERA	*AD*
GG	Epoch, localized, abbreviated	Zend_Date::ERA	*AD*
GGG	Epoch, localized, abbreviated	Zend_Date::ERA	*AD*
GGGG	Epoch, localized, complete	Zend_Date::ERA_NAME	*anno domini*
GGGGG	Epoch, localized, abbreviated	Zend_Date::ERA	*a*
y	Year, at least one digit	Zend_Date::YEAR	*9*
yy	Year, at least two digit	Zend_Date::YEAR _SHORT	*09*
yyy	Year, at least three digit	Zend_Date::YEAR	*2009*
yyyy	Year, at least four digit	Zend_Date::YEAR	*2009*
yyyyy	Year, at least five digit	Zend_Date::YEAR	*02009*
Y	Year according to ISO 8601, at least one digit	Zend_Date::YEAR_8601	*9*
YY	Year according to ISO 8601, at least two digit	Zend_Date::YEAR _SHORT_8601	*09*
YYY	Year according to ISO 8601, at least three digit	Zend_Date::YEAR_8601	*2009*
YYYY	Year according to ISO 8601, at least four digit	Zend_Date::YEAR_8601	*2009*
YYYYY	Year according to ISO 8601, at least five digit	Zend_Date::YEAR_8601	*02009*
M	Month, one or two digit	Zend_Date::MONTH _SHORT	*2*
MM	Month, two digit	Zend_Date::MONTH	*02*
MMM	Month, localized, abbreviated	Zend_Date::MONTH _NAME_SHORT	*Feb*
MMMM	Month, localized, complete	Zend_Date::MONTH _NAME	*February*
MMMMM	Month, localized, abbreviated, one digit	Zend_Date::MONTH _NAME_NARROW	*F*
w	Week, one or two digit	Zend_Date::WEEK	*5*
ww	Week, two digit	Zend_Date::WEEK	*05*
d	Day of the month, one or two digit	Zend_Date::DAY _SHORT	*9*
dd	Day of the month, two digit	Zend_Date::DAY	*09*
D	Day of the year, one, two or three digit	Zend_Date::DAY_OF _YEAR	*7*

Constant	Description	Corresponds best to	Affected part/example
DD	Day of the year, two or three digit	Zend_Date::DAY_OF_YEAR	*07*
DDD	Day of the year, three digit	Zend_Date::DAY_OF_YEAR	*007*
E	Day of the week, localized, abbreviated, one char	Zend_Date::WEEKDAY_NARROW	*M*
EE	Day of the week, localized, abbreviated, two or more chars	Zend_Date::WEEKDAY_NAME	*Mo*
EEE	Day of the week, localized, abbreviated, three chars	Zend_Date::WEEKDAY_SHORT	*Mon*
EEEE	Day of the week, localized, complete	Zend_Date::WEEKDAY	*Monday*
EEEEE	Day of the week, localized, abbreviated, one digit	Zend_Date::WEEKDAY_NARROW	*M*
e	Number of the day, one digit	Zend_Date::WEEKDAY_NARROW	*4*
ee	Number of the day, two digit	Zend_Date::WEEKDAY_NARROW	*04*
a	Time of day, localized	Zend_Date::MERIDIEM	*vorm.*
h	Hour, (1-12), one or two digit	Zend_Date::HOUR_SHORT_AM	*2*
hh	Hour, (01-12), two digit	Zend_Date::HOUR_AM	*02*
H	Hour, (0-23), one or two digit	Zend_Date::HOUR_SHORT	*2*
HH	Hour, (00-23), two digit	Zend_Date::HOUR	*02*
m	Minute, (0-59), one or two digit	Zend_Date::MINUTE_SHORT	*2*
mm	Minute, (00-59), two digit	Zend_Date::MINUTE	*02*
s	Second, (0-59), one or two digit	Zend_Date::SECOND_SHORT	*2*
ss	Second, (00-59), two digit	Zend_Date::SECOND	*02*
S	Millisecond	Zend_Date::MILLISECOND	*20536*
z	Time zone, localized, abbreviated	Zend_Date::TIMEZONE	*CET*
zz	Time zone, localized, abbreviated	Zend_Date::TIMEZONE	*CET*
zzz	Time zone, localized, abbreviated	Zend_Date::TIMEZONE	*CET*
zzzz	Time zone, localized, complete	Zend_Date::TIMEZONE_NAME	*Europe/Paris*
Z	Difference of time zone	Zend_Date::GMT_DIFF	*+0100*

Constant	Description	Corresponds best to	Affected part/example
ZZ	Difference of time zone	Zend_Date::GMT_DIFF	+0100
ZZZ	Difference of time zone	Zend_Date::GMT_DIFF	+0100
ZZZZ	Difference of time zone, separated	Zend_Date::GMT_DIFF _SEP	+01:00
A	Millisecond	Zend_Date:: MILLISECOND	20563

Note

Note that the default ISO format differs from PHP's format which can be irritating if you have not used in previous. Especially the format specifiers for *Year and Minute* are often not used in the intended way.

For *year* there are two specifiers available which are often mistaken. The *Y* specifier for the ISO year and the *y* specifier for the real year. The difference is small but significant. *Y* calculates the ISO year, which is often used for calendar formats. See for example the 31. December 2007. The real year is 2007, but it is the first day of the first week in the week 1 of the year 2008. So, if you are using 'dd.MM.yyyy' you will get '31.December.2007' but if you use 'dd.MM.YYYY' you will get '31.December.2008'. As you see this is no bug but a expected behaviour depending on the used specifiers.

For *minute* the difference is not so big. ISO uses the specifier *m* for the minute, unlike PHP which uses *i*. So if you are getting no minute in your format check if you have used the right specifier.

Self-Defined OUTPUT Formats Using PHP's date() Format Specifiers

If you are more comfortable with PHP's date format specifier than with ISO format specifiers, then you can use the Zend_Date::setOptions(array('format_type' => 'php')) method to switch Zend_Date methods from supporting ISO format specifiers to PHP date() type specifiers. Afterwards, all format parameters must be given with PHP's date() format specifiers [http://php.net/date] . The PHP date format lacks some of the formats supported by the ISO Format, and vice-versa. If you are not already comfortable with it, then use the standard ISO format instead. Also, if you have legacy code using PHP's date format, then either manually convert it to the ISO format using Zend_Locale_Format::convertPhpToIsoFormat() , or use setOptions() . The following examples illustrate the usage of constants from the table below to create self-defined formats.

Example 14.16. Self-Defined Formats with PHP Specifier

```
$locale = new Zend_Locale('de_AT');
Zend_Date::setOptions(array('format_type' => 'php'));
$date = new Zend_Date(1234567890, false, $locale);

// outputs something like 'February 16, 2007, 3:36 am'
print $date->toString('F j, Y, g:i a');

print $date->toString("'Format:D M j G:i:s T Y='D M j G:i:s T Y");
```

The following table shows the list of PHP date format specifiers with their equivalent Zend_Date constants and CLDR/ISO equivalent format specifiers. In most cases, when the CLDR/ISO format does

not have an equivalent format specifier, the PHP format specifier is not altered by
`Zend_Locale_Format::convertPhpToIsoFormat()`, and the Zend_Date methods then
recognize these "peculiar" PHP format specifiers, even when in the default "ISO" format mode.

Table 14.17. Constants for PHP Date Output

Constant	Description	Corresponds best to	closest CLDR equivalent	Affected part/example
d	Day of the month, two digit	Zend_Date::DAY	dd	09
D	Day of the week, localized, abbreviated, three digit	Zend_Date::WEEK DAY_SHORT	EEE	Mon
j	Day of the month, one or two digit	Zend_Date::DAY _SHORT	d	9
l (lowercase L)	Day of the week, localized, complete	Zend_Date:: WEEKDAY	EEEE	Monday
N	Number of the weekday, one digit	Zend_Date:: WEEKDAY_8601	e	4
S	English suffixes for day of month, two chars	no equivalent	no equivalent	st
w	Number of the weekday, 0=sunday, 6=saturday	Zend_Date:: WEEKDAY_DIGIT	no equivalent	4
z	Day of the year, one, two or three digit	Zend_Date::DAY_OF _YEAR	D	7
W	Week, one or two digit	Zend_Date::WEEK	w	5
F	Month, localized, complete	Zend_Date:: MONTH_NAME	MMMM	February
m	Month, two digit	Zend_Date::MONTH	MM	02
M	Month, localized, abbreviated	Zend_Date:: MONTH_NAME _SHORT	MMM	Feb
n	Month, one or two digit	Zend_Date:: MONTH_SHORT	M	2
t	Number of days per month, one or two digits	Zend_Date:: MONTH_DAYS	no equivalent	30
L	Leapyear, boolean	Zend_Date:: LEAPYEAR	no equivalent	true
o	Year according to ISO 8601, at least four digit	Zend_Date:: YEAR_8601	YYYY	2009
Y	Year, at least four digit	Zend_Date::YEAR	yyyy	2009

Constant	Description	Corresponds best to	closest CLDR equivalent	Affected part/example
y	Year, at least two digit	Zend_Date:: YEAR_SHORT	yy	*09*
a	Time of day, localized	Zend_Date:: MERIDIEM	a (sort of, but likely to be uppercase)	*vorm.*
A	Time of day, localized	Zend_Date:: MERIDIEM	a (sort of, but no guarantee that the format is uppercase)	*VORM.*
B	Swatch internet time	Zend_Date:: SWATCH	no equivalent	*1463*
g	Hour, (1-12), one or two digit	Zend_Date:: HOUR_SHORT _AM	h	*2*
G	Hour, (0-23), one or two digit	Zend_Date:: HOUR_SHORT	H	*2*
h	Hour, (01-12), two digit	Zend_Date:: HOUR_AM	hh	*02*
H	Hour, (00-23), two digit	Zend_Date::HOUR	HH	*02*
i	Minute, (00-59), two digit	Zend_Date:: MINUTE	mm	*02*
s	Second, (00-59), two digit	Zend_Date:: SECOND	ss	*02*
e	Time zone, localized, complete	Zend_Date:: TIMEZONE _NAME	zzzz	*Europe/Paris*
I	Daylight	Zend_Date:: DAYLIGHT	no equivalent	*1*
O	Difference of time zone	Zend_Date:: GMT_DIFF	Z or ZZ or ZZZ	*+0100*
P	Difference of time zone, separated	Zend_Date:: GMT_DIFF_SEP	ZZZZ	*+01:00*
T	Time zone, localized, abbreviated	Zend_Date:: TIMEZONE	z or zz or zzz	*CET*
Z	Time zone offset in seconds	Zend_Date:: TIMEZONE_SECS	no equivalent	*3600*
c	Standard Iso format output	Zend_Date:: ISO_8601	no equivalent	*2004-02-12 T15:19:21+00:00*
r	Standard Rfc 2822 format output	Zend_Date:: RFC_2822	no equivalent	*Thu, 21 Dec 2000 16:01:07 +0200*
U	Unix timestamp	Zend_Date:: TIMESTAMP	no equivalent	*15275422364*

Working Examples

Within this chapter, we will describe several additional functions which are also available through Zend_Date. Of course all described functions have additional examples to show the expected working and the simple API for the proper using of them.

Checking Dates

Probably most dates you will get as input are strings. But the problem with strings is that you can not be sure if the string is a real date. Therefor Zend_Date has spent an own static function to check date strings. Zend_Locale has an own function getDate($date, $locale); which parses a date and returns the proper and normalized date parts. A monthname for example will be recognised and returned just a month number. But as Zend_Locale does not know anything about dates because it is a normalizing and localizing class we have integrated an own function isDate($date); which checks this.

isDate($date, $format, $locale); can take up to 3 parameters and needs minimum one parameter. So what we need to verify a date is, of course, the date itself as string. The second parameter can be the format which the date is expected to have. If no format is given the standard date format from your locale is used. For details about how formats should look like see the chapter about self defined formats .

The third parameter is also optional as the second parameter and can be used to give a locale. We need the locale to normalize monthnames and daynames. So with the third parameter we are able to recognise dates like '01.Jänner.2000' or '01.January.2000' depending on the given locale.

isDate(); of course checks if a date does exist. Zend_Date itself does not check a date. So it is possible to create a date like '31.February.2000' with Zend_Date because Zend_Date will automatically correct the date and return the proper date. In our case '03.March.2000'. isDate() on the other side does this check and will return false on '31.February.2000' because it knows that this date is impossible.

Example 14.17. Checking Dates

```
// Checking dates
$date = '01.03.2000';
if (Zend_Date::isDate($date)) {
    print "String $date is a date";
} else {
    print "String $date is NO date";
}

// Checking localized dates
$date = '01 February 2000';
if (Zend_Date::isDate($date,'dd MMMM yyyy', 'en')) {
    print "String $date is a date";
} else {
    print "String $date is NO date";
}

// Checking impossible dates
$date = '30 February 2000';
if (Zend_Date::isDate($date,'dd MMMM yyyy', 'en')) {
    print "String $date is a date";
} else {
    print "String $date is NO date";
}
```

Sunrise and Sunset

Zend_Date has also functions integrated for getting informations from the sun. Often it is necessary to get the time for sunrise or sunset within a particularly day. This is quite easy with Zend_Date as just the expected day has to be given and additionally location for which the sunrise or sunset has to be calculated.

As most people do not know the location of their city we have also spent a helper class which provides the location data for about 250 capital and other big cities around the whole world. Most people could use cities near themself as the difference for locations situated to each other can only be measured within some seconds.

For creating a listbox and choosing a special city the function Zend_Date_Cities ::getCityList can be used. It returns the names of all available predefined cities for the helper class.

Example 14.18. Getting all Available Cities

```
// Output the complete list of available cities
print_r (Zend_Date_Cities::getCityList());
```

The location itself can be received with the Zend_Date_Cities::City() function. It accepts the name of the city as returned by the Zend_Date_Cities::getCityList() function and optional as second parameter the horizon to set.

There are 4 defined horizons which can be used with locations to receive the exact time of sunset and sunrise. The 'horizon' parameter is always optional in all functions. If it is not set, the 'effective' horizon is used.

Table 14.18. Types of Supported Horizons for Sunset and Sunrise

Horizon	Description	Usage
effective	Standard horizon	Expects the world to be a ball. This horizon is always used if non is defined.
civil	Common horizon	Often used in common medias like TV or radio
nautic	Nautic horizon	Often used in sea navigation
astronomic	Astronomic horizon	Often used for calculation with stars

Of course also a self-defined location can be given and calculated with. Therefor a 'latitude' and a 'longitude' has to be given and optional the 'horizon'.

Example 14.19. Getting the Location for a City

```
// Get the location for a defined city
```

```
// uses the effective horizon as no horizon is defined
print_r (Zend_Date_Cities::City('Vienna'));

// use the nautic horizon
print_r (Zend_Date_Cities::City('Vienna', 'nautic'));

// self definition of a location
$mylocation = array('latitude' => 41.5, 'longitude' => 13.2446);
```

As now all needed data can be set the next is to create a Zend_Date object with the day where sunset or sunrise should be calculated. For the calculation there are 3 functions available. It is possible to calculate sunset with 'getSunset()', sunrise with 'getSunrise()' and all available informations related to the sun with 'getSunInfo()'. After the calculation the Zend_Date object will be returned with the calculated time.

Example 14.20. Calculating Sun Information

```
// Get the location for a defined city
$city = Zend_Date_Cities::City('Vienna');

// create a date object for the day for which the sun has to be calculated
$date = new Zend_Date('10.03.2007', Zend_Date::ISO_8601, 'de');

// calculate sunset
$sunset = $date->getSunset($city);
print $sunset->get(Zend_Date::ISO_8601);

// calculate all sun informations
$info = $date->getSunInfo($city);
foreach ($info as $sun) {
    print "\n" . $sun->get(Zend_Date::ISO_8601);
}
```

Time Zones

Time zones are as important as dates themselves. There are several time zones depending on where in the world a user lives. So working with dates also means to set the proper timezone. This may sound complicated but it's easier as expected. As already mentioned in the first chapter of Zend_Date the default timezone has to be set. Either by php.ini or by definition within the bootstrap file.

A Zend_Date object of course also stores the actual timezone. Even if the timezone is changed after the creation of the object it remembers the original timezone and works with it. It is also not necessary to change the timezone within the code with PHP functions. Zend_Date has two built-in functions which makes it possible to handle this.

getTimezone() returns the actual set timezone of within the Zend_Date object. Remember that Zend_Date is not coupled with PHP internals. So the returned timezone is not the timezone of the PHP script but the timezone of the object. setTimezone($zone) is the second function and makes it possible to set new timezone for Zend_Date. A given timezone is always checked. If it does not exist an exception will be thrown. Additionally the actual scripts or systems timezone can be set to the date object by calling setTimezone() without the zone parameter. This is also done automatically when the date object is created.

Example 14.21. Working with Time Zones

```
// Set a default timezone... this has to be done within the bootstrap
// file or php.ini.
// We do this here just for having a complete example.
date_default_timezone_set('Europe/Vienna');

// create a date object
$date = new Zend_Date('10.03.2007', Zend_Date::DATES, 'de');

// view our date object
print $date->getIso();

// what timezone do we have ?
print $date->getTimezone();

// set another timezone
$date->setTimezone('America/Chicago');

// what timezone do we now have ?
print $date->getTimezone();

// see the changed date object
print $date->getIso();
```

Zend_Date always takes the actual timezone for object creation as shown in the first lines of the example. Changing the timezone within the created object also has an effect to the date itself. Dates are always related to a timezone. Changing the timezone for a Zend_Date object does not change the time of Zend_Date. Remember that internally dates are always stored as timestamps and in GMT. So the timezone means how much hours should be substracted or added to get the actual global time for the own timezone and region.

Having the timezone coupled within Zend_Date has another positive effect. It is possible to have several dates with different timezones.

Example 14.22. Multiple Time Zones

```
// Set a default timezone... this has to be done within the bootstrap
// file or php.ini.
// We do this here just for having a complete example.
date_default_timezone_set('Europe/Vienna');

// create a date object
$date = new Zend_Date('10.03.2007 00:00:00', Zend_Date::ISO_8601, 'de');

// view our date object
print $date->getIso();

// the date stays unchanged even after changeing the timezone
date_default_timezone_set('America/Chicago');
print $date->getIso();

$otherdate = clone $date;
$otherdate->setTimezone('Brazil/Acre');

// view our date object
```

```
print $otherdate->getIso();

// set the object to the actual systems timezone
$lastdate = clone $date;
$lastdate->setTimezone();

// view our date object
print $lastdate->getIso();
```

Chapter 15. Zend_Db

Zend_Db_Adapter

Zend_Db and its related classes provide a simple SQL database interface for Zend Framework. The Zend_Db_Adapter is the basic class you use to connect your PHP application to an RDBMS. There is a different Adapter class for each brand of RDBMS.

The Zend_Db adapters create a bridge from the vendor-specific PHP extensions to a common interface to help you write PHP applications once and deploy with multiple brands of RDBMS with very little effort.

The interface of the adapter class is similar to the interface of the PHP Data Objects [http://www.php.net/pdo] extension. Zend_Db provides Adapter classes to PDO drivers for the following RDBMS brands:

- IBM DB2 and Informix Dynamic Server (IDS), using the pdo_ibm [http://www.php.net/pdo-ibm] PHP extension

- MySQL, using the pdo_mysql [http://www.php.net/pdo-mysql] PHP extension

- Microsoft SQL Server, using the pdo_mssql [http://www.php.net/pdo-mssql] PHP extension

- Oracle, using the pdo_oci [http://www.php.net/pdo-oci] PHP extension

- PostgreSQL, using the pdo_pgsql [http://www.php.net/pdo-pgsql] PHP extension

- SQLite, using the pdo_sqlite [http://www.php.net/pdo-sqlite] PHP extension

In addition, Zend_Db provides Adapter classes that utilize PHP database extensions for the following RDBMS brands:

- MySQL, using the mysqli [http://www.php.net/mysqli] PHP extension

- Oracle, using the oci8 [http://www.php.net/oci8] PHP extension

- IBM DB2 and DB2/i5, using the ibm_db2 [http://www.php.net/ibm_db2] PHP extension

- Firebird/Interbase, using the php_interbase [http://www.php.net/ibase] PHP extension

Note

Each Zend_Db Adapter uses a PHP extension. You must have the respective PHP extension enabled in your PHP environment to use a Zend_Db Adapter. For example, if you use any of the PDO Zend_Db Adapters, you need to enable both the PDO extension and the PDO driver for the brand of RDBMS you use.

Connecting to a Database Using an Adapter

This section describes how to create an instance of a database Adapter. This corresponds to making a connection to your RDBMS server from your PHP application.

Using a Zend_Db Adapter Constructor

You can create an instance of an adapter using its constructor. An adapter constructor takes one argument, which is an array of parameters used to declare the connection.

Example 15.1. Using an Adapter Constructor

```
$db = new Zend_Db_Adapter_Pdo_Mysql(array(
    'host'     => '127.0.0.1',
    'username' => 'webuser',
    'password' => 'xxxxxxxx',
    'dbname'   => 'test'
));
```

Using the Zend_Db Factory

As an alternative to using an adapter constructor directly, you can create an instance of an adapter using the static method Zend_Db::factory(). This method dynamically loads the adapter class file on demand using Zend_Loader::loadClass().

The first argument is a string that names the base name of the adapter class. For example the string 'Pdo_Mysql' corresponds to the class Zend_Db_Adapter_Pdo_Mysql. The second argument is the same array of parameters you would have given to the adapter constructor.

Example 15.2. Using the Adapter Factory Method

```
// We don't need the following statement because the
// Zend_Db_Adapter_Pdo_Mysql file will be loaded for us by the Zend_Db
// factory method.

// require_once 'Zend/Db/Adapter/Pdo/Mysql.php';

// Automatically load class Zend_Db_Adapter_Pdo_Mysql
// and create an instance of it.
$db = Zend_Db::factory('Pdo_Mysql', array(
    'host'     => '127.0.0.1',
    'username' => 'webuser',
    'password' => 'xxxxxxxx',
    'dbname'   => 'test'
));
```

If you create your own class that extends Zend_Db_Adapter_Abstract_Adapter, but you do not name your class with the "Zend_Db_Adapter" package prefix, you can use the factory() method to load your adapter if you specify the leading portion of the adapter class with the 'adapterNamespace' key in the parameters array.

Example 15.3. Using the Adapter Factory Method for a Custom Adapter Class

```
// We don't need to load the adapter class file
// because it will be loaded for us by the Zend_Db factory method.

// Automatically load class MyProject_Db_Adapter_Pdo_Mysql and create
// an instance of it.
$db = Zend_Db::factory('Pdo_Mysql', array(
    'host'             => '127.0.0.1',
    'username'         => 'webuser',
```

```
    'password'          => 'xxxxxxxx',
    'dbname'            => 'test',
    'adapterNamespace' => 'MyProject_Db_Adapter'
));
```

Using Zend_Config with the Zend_Db Factory

Optionally, you may specify either argument of the factory() method as an object of type Zend_Config.

If the first argument is a config object, it is expected to contain a property named adapter, containing the string naming the adapter class name base. Optionally, the object may contain a property named params, with subproperties corresponding to adapter parameter names. This is used only if the second argument of the factory() method is absent.

Example 15.4. Using the Adapter Factory Method with a Zend_Config Object

In the example below, a Zend_Config object is created from an array. You can also load data from an external file using classes such as Zend_Config_Ini and Zend_Config_Xml.

```
$config = new Zend_Config(
    array(
        'database' => array(
            'adapter' => 'Mysqli',
            'params'  => array(
                'host'     => '127.0.0.1',
                'dbname'   => 'test',
                'username' => 'webuser',
                'password' => 'secret',
            )
        )
    )
);

$db = Zend_Db::factory($config->database);
```

The second argument of the factory() method may be an associative array containing entries corresponding to adapter parameters. This argument is optional. If the first argument is of type Zend_Config, it is assumed to contain all parameters, and the second argument is ignored.

Adapter Parameters

The following list explains common parameters recognized by Zend_Db Adapter classes.

- *host*: a string containing a hostname or IP address of the database server. If the database is running on the same host as the PHP application, you may use 'localhost' or '127.0.0.1'.

- *username*: account identifier for authenticating a connection to the RDBMS server.

- *password*: account password credential for authenticating a connection to the RDBMS server.

- *dbname*: database instance name on the RDBMS server.

- *port*: some RDBMS servers can accept network connections on a administrator-specified port number. The port parameter allow you to specify the port to which your PHP application connects, to match the port configured on the RDBMS server.

- *options*: this parameter is an associative array of options that are generic to all `Zend_Db_Adapter` classes.

- *driver_options*: this parameter is an associative array of additional options that are specific to a given database extension. One typical use of this parameter is to set attributes of a PDO driver.

- *adapterNamespace*: names the initial part of the class name for the adapter, instead of 'Zend_Db_Adapter'. Use this if you need to use the `factory()` method to load a non-Zend database adapter class.

Example 15.5. Passing the Case-Folding Option to the Factory

You can specify this option by the constant `Zend_Db::CASE_FOLDING`. This corresponds to the `ATTR_CASE` attribute in PDO and IBM DB2 database drivers, adjusting the case of string keys in query result sets. The option takes values `Zend_Db::CASE_NATURAL` (the default), `Zend_Db::CASE_UPPER`, and `Zend_Db::CASE_LOWER`.

```
$options = array(
    Zend_Db::CASE_FOLDING => Zend_Db::CASE_UPPER
);

$params = array(
    'host'          => '127.0.0.1',
    'username'      => 'webuser',
    'password'      => 'xxxxxxxx',
    'dbname'        => 'test',
    'options'       => $options
);

$db = Zend_Db::factory('Db2', $params);
```

Example 15.6. Passing the Auto-Quoting Option to the Factory

You can specify this option by the constant `Zend_Db::AUTO_QUOTE_IDENTIFIERS`. If the value is `true` (the default), identifiers like table names, column names, and even aliases are delimited in all SQL syntax generated by the Adapter object. This makes it simple to use identifiers that contain SQL keywords, or special characters. If the value is `false`, identifiers are not delimited automatically. If you need to delimit identifiers, you must do so yourself using the `quoteIdentifier()` method.

```
$options = array(
    Zend_Db::AUTO_QUOTE_IDENTIFIERS => false
);

$params = array(
    'host'          => '127.0.0.1',
    'username'      => 'webuser',
    'password'      => 'xxxxxxxx',
    'dbname'        => 'test',
    'options'       => $options
);

$db = Zend_Db::factory('Pdo_Mysql', $params);
```

Example 15.7. Passing PDO Driver Options to the Factory

```
$pdoParams = array(
    PDO::MYSQL_ATTR_USE_BUFFERED_QUERY => true
);

$params = array(
    'host'            => '127.0.0.1',
    'username'        => 'webuser',
    'password'        => 'xxxxxxxx',
    'dbname'          => 'test',
    'driver_options'  => $pdoParams
);

$db = Zend_Db::factory('Pdo_Mysql', $params);

echo $db->getConnection()
        ->getAttribute(PDO::MYSQL_ATTR_USE_BUFFERED_QUERY);
```

Example 15.8. Passing Serialization Options to the Factory

```
$options = array(
    Zend_Db::ALLOW_SERIALIZATION => false
);

$params = array(
    'host'       => '127.0.0.1',
    'username'   => 'webuser',
    'password'   => 'xxxxxxxx',
    'dbname'     => 'test',
    'options'    => $options
);

$db = Zend_Db::factory('Pdo_Mysql', $params);
```

Managing Lazy Connections

Creating an instance of an Adapter class does not immediately connect to the RDBMS server. The Adapter saves the connection parameters, and makes the actual connection on demand, the first time you need to execute a query. This ensures that creating an Adapter object is quick and inexpensive. You can create an instance of an Adapter even if you are not certain that you need to run any database queries during the current request your application is serving.

If you need to force the Adapter to connect to the RDBMS, use the getConnection() method. This method returns an object for the connection as represented by the respective PHP database extension. For example, if you use any of the Adapter classes for PDO drivers, then getConnection() returns the PDO object, after initiating it as a live connection to the specific database.

It can be useful to force the connection if you want to catch any exceptions it throws as a result of invalid account credentials, or other failure to connect to the RDBMS server. These exceptions are not thrown until the connection is made, so it can help simplify your application code if you handle the exceptions in one place, instead of at the time of the first query against the database.

Additionally, an adapter can get serialized to store it, for example, in a session variable. This can be very useful not only for the adapter itself, but for other objects that aggregate it, like a Zend_Db_Select object. By default, adapters are allowed to be serialized, if you don't want it, you should consider passing the Zend_Db::ALLOW_SERIALIZATION=false option, see the example above. To respect lazy connections principle, the adapter won't reconnect itself after being unserialized. You must then call getConnection() yourself. You can make the adapter auto-reconnect by passing the Zend_Db::AUTO_RECONNECT_ON_UNSERIALIZE=true as an adapter option.

Example 15.9. Handling Connection Exceptions

```
try {
    $db = Zend_Db::factory('Pdo_Mysql', $parameters);
    $db->getConnection();
} catch (Zend_Db_Adapter_Exception $e) {
    // perhaps a failed login credential, or perhaps the RDBMS
        is not running
} catch (Zend_Exception $e) {
    // perhaps factory() failed to load the specified Adapter class
}
```

Example Database

In the documentation for Zend_Db classes, we use a set of simple tables to illustrate usage of the classes and methods. These example tables could store information for tracking bugs in a software development project. The database contains four tables:

- *accounts* stores information about each user of the bug-tracking database.

- *products* stores information about each product for which a bug can be logged.

- *bugs* stores information about bugs, including that current state of the bug, the person who reported the bug, the person who is assigned to fix the bug, and the person who is assigned to verify the fix.

- *bugs_products* stores a relationship between bugs and products. This implements a many-to-many relationship, because a given bug may be relevant to multiple products, and of course a given product can have multiple bugs.

The following SQL data definition language pseudocode describes the tables in this example database. These example tables are used extensively by the automated unit tests for Zend_Db.

```
CREATE TABLE accounts (
  account_name      VARCHAR(100) NOT NULL PRIMARY KEY
);

CREATE TABLE products (
  product_id        INTEGER NOT NULL PRIMARY KEY,
  product_name      VARCHAR(100)
);

CREATE TABLE bugs (
  bug_id            INTEGER NOT NULL PRIMARY KEY,
  bug_description   VARCHAR(100),
  bug_status        VARCHAR(20),
  reported_by       VARCHAR(100) REFERENCES accounts(account_name),
  assigned_to       VARCHAR(100) REFERENCES accounts(account_name),
  verified_by       VARCHAR(100) REFERENCES accounts(account_name)
);
```

```
CREATE TABLE bugs_products (
  bug_id              INTEGER NOT NULL REFERENCES bugs,
  product_id          INTEGER NOT NULL REFERENCES products,
  PRIMARY KEY         (bug_id, product_id)
);
```

Also notice that the bugs table contains multiple foreign key references to the accounts table. Each of these foreign keys may reference a different row in the accounts table for a given bug.

The diagram below illustrates the physical data model of the example database.

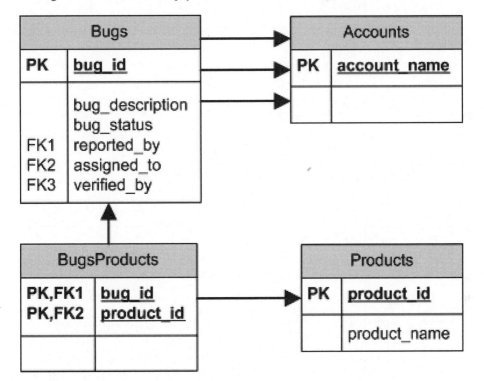

Reading Query Results

This section describes methods of the Adapter class with which you can run SELECT queries and retrieve the query results.

Fetching a Complete Result Set

You can run a SQL SELECT query and retrieve its results in one step using the fetchAll() method.

The first argument to this method is a string containing a SELECT statement. Alternatively, the first argument can be an object of class Zend_Db_Select. The Adapter automatically converts this object to a string representation of the SELECT statement.

The second argument to fetchAll() is an array of values to substitute for parameter placeholders in the SQL statement.

Example 15.10. Using fetchAll()

```
$sql = 'SELECT * FROM bugs WHERE bug_id = ?';

$result = $db->fetchAll($sql, 2);
```

Changing the Fetch Mode

By default, `fetchAll()` returns an array of rows, each of which is an associative array. The keys of the associative array are the columns or column aliases named in the select query.

You can specify a different style of fetching results using the `setFetchMode()` method. The modes supported are identified by constants:

- *Zend_Db::FETCH_ASSOC*: return data in an array of associative arrays. The array keys are column names, as strings. This is the default fetch mode for `Zend_Db_Adapter` classes.

  Note that if your select-list contains more than one column with the same name, for example if they are from two different tables in a JOIN, there can be only one entry in the associative array for a given name. If you use the FETCH_ASSOC mode, you should specify column aliases in your SELECT query to ensure that the names result in unique array keys.

  By default, these strings are returned as they are returned by the database driver. This is typically the spelling of the column in the RDBMS server. You can specify the case for these strings, using the `Zend_Db::CASE_FOLDING` option. Specify this when instantiating the Adapter. See Example 15.5, "Passing the Case-Folding Option to the Factory".

- *Zend_Db::FETCH_NUM*: return data in an array of arrays. The arrays are indexed by integers, corresponding to the position of the respective field in the select-list of the query.

- *Zend_Db::FETCH_BOTH*: return data in an array of arrays. The array keys are both strings as used in the FETCH_ASSOC mode, and integers as used in the FETCH_NUM mode. Note that the number of elements in the array is double that which would be in the array if you used either FETCH_ASSOC or FETCH_NUM.

- *Zend_Db::FETCH_COLUMN*: return data in an array of values. The value in each array is the value returned by one column of the result set. By default, this is the first column, indexed by 0.

- *Zend_Db::FETCH_OBJ*: return data in an array of objects. The default class is the PHP built-in class stdClass. Columns of the result set are available as public properties of the object.

Example 15.11. Using setFetchMode()

```
$db->setFetchMode(Zend_Db::FETCH_OBJ);

$result = $db->fetchAll('SELECT * FROM bugs WHERE bug_id = ?', 2);

// $result is an array of objects
echo $result[0]->bug_description;
```

Fetching a Result Set as an Associative Array

The `fetchAssoc()` method returns data in an array of associative arrays, regardless of what value you have set for the fetch mode.

Example 15.12. Using fetchAssoc()

```
$db->setFetchMode(Zend_Db::FETCH_OBJ);

$result = $db->fetchAssoc('SELECT * FROM bugs WHERE bug_id = ?', 2);

// $result is an array of associative arrays, in spite of the fetch mode
echo $result[0]['bug_description'];
```

Fetching a Single Column from a Result Set

The fetchCol() method returns data in an array of values, regardless of the value you have set for the fetch mode. This only returns the first column returned by the query. Any other columns returned by the query are discarded. If you need to return a column other than the first, see the section called "Fetching a Single Column from a Result Set".

Example 15.13. Using fetchCol()

```
$db->setFetchMode(Zend_Db::FETCH_OBJ);

$result = $db->fetchCol(
    'SELECT bug_description, bug_id FROM bugs WHERE bug_id = ?', 2);

// contains bug_description; bug_id is not returned
echo $result[0];
```

Fetching Key-Value Pairs from a Result Set

The fetchPairs() method returns data in an array of key-value pairs, as an associative array with a single entry per row. The key of this associative array is taken from the first column returned by the SELECT query. The value is taken from the second column returned by the SELECT query. Any other columns returned by the query are discarded.

You should design the SELECT query so that the first column returned has unique values. If there are duplicates values in the first column, entries in the associative array will be overwritten.

Example 15.14. Using fetchPairs()

```
$db->setFetchMode(Zend_Db::FETCH_OBJ);

$result = $db->fetchPairs('SELECT bug_id, bug_status FROM bugs');

echo $result[2];
```

Fetching a Single Row from a Result Set

The fetchRow() method returns data using the current fetch mode, but it returns only the first row fetched from the result set.

Example 15.15. Using fetchRow()

```
$db->setFetchMode(Zend_Db::FETCH_OBJ);

$result = $db->fetchRow('SELECT * FROM bugs WHERE bug_id = 2');

// note that $result is a single object, not an array of objects
echo $result->bug_description;
```

Fetching a Single Scalar from a Result Set

The fetchOne() method is like a combination of fetchRow() with fetchCol(), in that it returns data only for the first row fetched from the result set, and it returns only the value of the first column in that row. Therefore it returns only a single scalar value, not an array or an object.

Example 15.16. Using fetchOne()

```
$result = $db->fetchOne('SELECT bug_status FROM bugs WHERE bug_id = 2');

// this is a single string value
echo $result;
```

Writing Changes to the Database

You can use the Adapter class to write new data or change existing data in your database. This section describes methods to do these operations.

Inserting Data

You can add new rows to a table in your database using the insert() method. The first argument is a string that names the table, and the second argument is an associative array, mapping column names to data values.

Example 15.17. Inserting in a Table

```
$data = array(
    'created_on'      => '2007-03-22',
    'bug_description' => 'Something wrong',
    'bug_status'      => 'NEW'
);

$db->insert('bugs', $data);
```

Columns you exclude from the array of data are not specified to the database. Therefore, they follow the same rules that an SQL INSERT statement follows: if the column has a DEFAULT clause, the column takes that value in the row created, otherwise the column is left in a NULL state.

By default, the values in your data array are inserted using parameters. This reduces risk of some types of security issues. You don't need to apply escaping or quoting to values in the data array.

You might need values in the data array to be treated as SQL expressions, in which case they should not be quoted. By default, all data values passed as strings are treated as string literals. To specify that the value is an SQL expression and therefore should not be quoted, pass the value in the data array as an object of type Zend_Db_Expr instead of a plain string.

Example 15.18. Inserting Expressions in a Table

```
$data = array(
    'created_on'      => new Zend_Db_Expr('CURDATE()'),
    'bug_description' => 'Something wrong',
    'bug_status'      => 'NEW'
);

$db->insert('bugs', $data);
```

Retrieving a Generated Value

Some RDBMS brands support auto-incrementing primary keys. A table defined this way generates a primary key value automatically during an INSERT of a new row. The return value of the insert() method is *not* the last inserted ID, because the table might not have an auto-incremented column. Instead, the return value is the number of rows affected (usually 1).

If your table is defined with an auto-incrementing primary key, you can call the lastInsertId() method after the insert. This method returns the last value generated in the scope of the current database connection.

Example 15.19. Using lastInsertId() for an Auto-Increment Key

```
$db->insert('bugs', $data);

// return the last value generated by an auto-increment column
$id = $db->lastInsertId();
```

Some RDBMS brands support a sequence object, which generates unique values to serve as primary key values. To support sequences, the lastInsertId() method accepts two optional string arguments. These arguments name the table and the column, assuming you have followed the convention that a sequence is named using the table and column names for which the sequence generates values, and a suffix "_seq". This is based on the convention used by PostgreSQL when naming sequences for SERIAL columns. For example, a table "bugs" with primary key column "bug_id" would use a sequence named "bugs_bug_id_seq".

Example 15.20. Using lastInsertId() for a Sequence

```
$db->insert('bugs', $data);

// return the last value generated by sequence 'bugs_bug_id_seq'.
$id = $db->lastInsertId('bugs', 'bug_id');

// alternatively, return the last value generated by sequence 'bugs_seq'.
$id = $db->lastInsertId('bugs');
```

If the name of your sequence object does not follow this naming convention, use the `lastSequenceId()` method instead. This method takes a single string argument, naming the sequence literally.

Example 15.21. Using lastSequenceId()

```
$db->insert('bugs', $data);

// return the last value generated by sequence 'bugs_id_gen'.
$id = $db->lastSequenceId('bugs_id_gen');
```

For RDBMS brands that don't support sequences, including MySQL, Microsoft SQL Server, and SQLite, the arguments to the lastInsertId() method are ignored, and the value returned is the most recent value generated for any table by INSERT operations during the current connection. For these RDBMS brands, the lastSequenceId() method always returns `null`.

Why Not Use "SELECT MAX(id) FROM table"?

Sometimes this query returns the most recent primary key value inserted into the table. However, this technique is not safe to use in an environment where multiple clients are inserting records to the database. It is possible, and therefore is bound to happen eventually, that another client inserts another row in the instant between the insert performed by your client application and your query for the MAX(id) value. Thus the value returned does not identify the row you inserted, it identifies the row inserted by some other client. There is no way to know when this has happened.

Using a strong transaction isolation mode such as "repeatable read" can mitigate this risk, but some RDBMS brands don't support the transaction isolation required for this, or else your application may use a lower transaction isolation mode by design.

Furthermore, using an expression like "MAX(id)+1" to generate a new value for a primary key is not safe, because two clients could do this query simultaneously, and then both use the same calculated value for their next INSERT operation.

All RDBMS brands provide mechanisms to generate unique values, and to return the last value generated. These mechanisms necessarily work outside of the scope of transaction isolation, so there is no chance of two clients generating the same value, and there is no chance that the value generated by another client could be reported to your client's connection as the last value generated.

Updating Data

You can update rows in a database table using the `update()` method of an Adapter. This method takes three arguments: the first is the name of the table; the second is an associative array mapping columns to change to new values to assign to these columns.

The values in the data array are treated as string literals. See the section called "Inserting Data" for information on using SQL expressions in the data array.

The third argument is a string containing an SQL expression that is used as criteria for the rows to change. The values and identifiers in this argument are not quoted or escaped. You are responsible for ensuring that any dynamic content is interpolated into this string safely. See the section called "Quoting Values and Identifiers" for methods to help you do this.

The return value is the number of rows affected by the update operation.

Example 15.22. Updating Rows

```
$data = array(
    'updated_on'        => '2007-03-23',
    'bug_status'        => 'FIXED'
);

$n = $db->update('bugs', $data, 'bug_id = 2');
```

If you omit the third argument, then all rows in the database table are updated with the values specified in the data array.

If you provide an array of strings as the third argument, these strings are joined together as terms in an expression separated by AND operators.

Example 15.23. Updating Rows Using an Array of Expressions

```
$data = array(
    'updated_on'        => '2007-03-23',
    'bug_status'        => 'FIXED'
);

$where[] = "reported_by = 'goofy'";
$where[] = "bug_status = 'OPEN'";

$n = $db->update('bugs', $data, $where);

// Resulting SQL is:
//   UPDATE "bugs" SET "update_on" = '2007-03-23', "bug_status" = 'FIXED'
//   WHERE ("reported_by" = 'goofy') AND ("bug_status" = 'OPEN')
```

Deleting Data

You can delete rows from a database table using the delete() method. This method takes two arguments: the first is a string naming the table.

The second argument is a string containing an SQL expression that is used as criteria for the rows to delete. The values and identifiers in this argument are not quoted or escaped. You are responsible for ensuring that any dynamic content is interpolated into this string safely. See the section called "Quoting Values and Identifiers" for methods to help you do this.

The return value is the number of rows affected by the delete operation.

Example 15.24. Deleting Rows

```
$n = $db->delete('bugs', 'bug_id = 3');
```

If you omit the second argument, the result is that all rows in the database table are deleted.

If you provide an array of strings as the second argument, these strings are joined together as terms in an expression separated by AND operators.

Quoting Values and Identifiers

When you form SQL queries, often it is the case that you need to include the values of PHP variables in SQL expressions. This is risky, because if the value in a PHP string contains certain symbols, such as the quote symbol, it could result in invalid SQL. For example, notice the imbalanced quote characters in the following query:

```
$name = "O'Reilly";
$sql = "SELECT * FROM bugs WHERE reported_by = '$name'";

echo $sql;
// SELECT * FROM bugs WHERE reported_by = 'O'Reilly'
```

Even worse is the risk that such code mistakes might be exploited deliberately by a person who is trying to manipulate the function of your web application. If they can specify the value of a PHP variable through the use of an HTTP parameter or other mechanism, they might be able to make your SQL queries do things that you didn't intend them to do, such as return data to which the person should not have privilege to read. This is a serious and widespread technique for violating application security, known as "SQL Injection" (see http://en.wikipedia.org/wiki/SQL_Injection).

The Zend_Db Adapter class provides convenient functions to help you reduce vulnerabilities to SQL Injection attacks in your PHP code. The solution is to escape special characters such as quotes in PHP values before they are interpolated into your SQL strings. This protects against both accidental and deliberate manipulation of SQL strings by PHP variables that contain special characters.

Using quote()

The quote() method accepts a single argument, a scalar string value. It returns the value with special characters escaped in a manner appropriate for the RDBMS you are using, and surrounded by string value delimiters. The standard SQL string value delimiter is the single-quote (').

Example 15.25. Using quote()

```
$name = $db->quote("O'Reilly");
echo $name;
// 'O\'Reilly'

$sql = "SELECT * FROM bugs WHERE reported_by = $name";

echo $sql;
// SELECT * FROM bugs WHERE reported_by = 'O\'Reilly'
```

Note that the return value of quote() includes the quote delimiters around the string. This is different from some functions that escape special characters but do not add the quote delimiters, for example mysql_real_escape_string() [http://www.php.net/mysqli_real_escape_string].

Values may need to be quoted or not quoted according to the SQL datatype context in which they are used. For instance, in some RDBMS brands, an integer value must not be quoted as a string if it is compared to an integer-type column or expression. In other words, the following is an error in some SQL implementations, assuming intColumn has a SQL datatype of INTEGER

```
SELECT * FROM atable WHERE intColumn = '123'
```

You can use the optional second argument to the quote() method to apply quoting selectively for the SQL datatype you specify.

Example 15.26. Using quote() with a SQL Type

```
$value = '1234';
$sql = 'SELECT * FROM atable WHERE intColumn = '
    . $db->quote($value, 'INTEGER');
```

Each Zend_Db_Adapter class has encoded the names of numeric SQL datatypes for the respective brand of RDBMS. You can also use the constants Zend_Db::INT_TYPE, Zend_Db ::BIGINT_TYPE, and Zend_Db::FLOAT_TYPE to write code in a more RDBMS-independent way.

Zend_Db_Table specifies SQL types to quote() automatically when generating SQL queries that reference a table's key columns.

Using quoteInto()

The most typical usage of quoting is to interpolate a PHP variable into a SQL expression or statement. You can use the quoteInto() method to do this in one step. This method takes two arguments: the first argument is a string containing a placeholder symbol (?), and the second argument is a value or PHP variable that should be substituted for that placeholder.

The placeholder symbol is the same symbol used by many RDBMS brands for positional parameters, but the quoteInto() method only emulates query parameters. The method simply interpolates the value into the string, escapes special characters, and applies quotes around it. True query parameters maintain the separation between the SQL string and the parameters as the statement is parsed in the RDBMS server.

Example 15.27. Using quoteInto()

```
$sql = $db->quoteInto("SELECT * FROM bugs WHERE reported_by = ?",
    "O'Reilly");

echo $sql;
// SELECT * FROM bugs WHERE reported_by = 'O\'Reilly'
```

You can use the optional third parameter of quoteInto() to specify the SQL datatype. Numeric datatypes are not quoted, and other types are quoted.

Example 15.28. Using quoteInto() with a SQL Type

```
$sql = $db
    ->quoteInto("SELECT * FROM bugs WHERE bug_id = ?", '1234',
        'INTEGER');

echo $sql;
// SELECT * FROM bugs WHERE reported_by = 1234
```

Using quoteIdentifier()

Values are not the only part of SQL syntax that might need to be variable. If you use PHP variables to name tables, columns, or other identifiers in your SQL statements, you might need to quote these strings too. By default, SQL identifiers have syntax rules like PHP and most other programming languages. For example, identifiers should not contain spaces, certain punctuation or special characters, or international characters. Also certain words are reserved for SQL syntax, and should not be used as identifiers.

However, SQL has a feature called *delimited identifiers*, which allows broader choices for the spelling of identifiers. If you enclose a SQL identifier in the proper types of quotes, you can use identifiers with spellings that would be invalid without the quotes. Delimited identifiers can contain spaces, punctuation, or international characters. You can also use SQL reserved words if you enclose them in identifier delimiters.

The quoteIdentifier() method works like quote(), but it applies the identifier delimiter characters to the string according to the type of Adapter you use. For example, standard SQL uses double-quotes (") for identifier delimiters, and most RDBMS brands use that symbol. MySQL uses back-quotes (`) by default. The quoteIdentifier() method also escapes special characters within the string argument.

Example 15.29. Using quoteIdentifier()

```
// we might have a table name that is an SQL reserved word
$tableName = $db->quoteIdentifier("order");

$sql = "SELECT * FROM $tableName";

echo $sql
// SELECT * FROM "order"
```

SQL delimited identifiers are case-sensitive, unlike unquoted identifiers. Therefore, if you use delimited identifiers, you must use the spelling of the identifier exactly as it is stored in your schema, including the case of the letters.

In most cases where SQL is generated within Zend_Db classes, the default is that all identifiers are delimited automatically. You can change this behavior with the option Zend_Db ::AUTO_QUOTE_IDENTIFIERS. Specify this when instantiating the Adapter. See Example 15.6, "Passing the Auto-Quoting Option to the Factory".

Controlling Database Transactions

Databases define transactions as logical units of work that can be committed or rolled back as a single change, even if they operate on multiple tables. All queries to a database are executed within the context of a transaction, even if the database driver manages them implicitly. This is called *auto-commit* mode, in which the database driver creates a transaction for every statement you execute, and commits that transaction after your SQL statement has been executed. By default, all Zend_Db Adapter classes operate in auto-commit mode.

Alternatively, you can specify the beginning and resolution of a transaction, and thus control how many SQL queries are included in a single group that is committed (or rolled back) as a single operation. Use the beginTransaction() method to initiate a transaction. Subsequent SQL statements are executed in the context of the same transaction until you resolve it explicitly.

To resolve the transaction, use either the commit() or rollBack() methods. The commit() method marks changes made during your transaction as committed, which means the effects of these changes are shown in queries run in other transactions.

The rollBack() method does the opposite: it discards the changes made during your transaction. The changes are effectively undone, and the state of the data returns to how it was before you began your transaction. However, rolling back your transaction has no effect on changes made by other transactions running concurrently.

After you resolve this transaction, Zend_Db_Adapter returns to auto-commit mode until you call beginTransaction() again.

Example 15.30. Managing a Transaction to Ensure Consistency

```
// Start a transaction explicitly.
$db->beginTransaction();

try {
    // Attempt to execute one or more queries:
    $db->query(...);
    $db->query(...);
    $db->query(...);

    // If all succeed, commit the transaction and all changes
    // are committed at once.
    $db->commit();

} catch (Exception $e) {
    // If any of the queries failed and threw an exception,
    // we want to roll back the whole transaction, reversing
    // changes made in the transaction, even those that succeeded.
    // Thus all changes are committed together, or none are.
    $db->rollBack();
    echo $e->getMessage();
}
```

Listing and Describing Tables

The listTables() method returns an array of strings, naming all tables in the current database.

The describeTable() method returns an associative array of metadata about a table. Specify the name of the table as a string in the first argument to this method. The second argument is optional, and names the schema in which the table exists.

The keys of the associative array returned are the column names of the table. The value corresponding to each column is also an associative array, with the following keys and values:

Table 15.1. Metadata Fields Returned by describeTable()

Key	Type	Description
SCHEMA_NAME	(string)	Name of the database schema in which this table exists.
TABLE_NAME	(string)	Name of the table to which this column belongs.
COLUMN_NAME	(string)	Name of the column.
COLUMN_POSITION	(integer)	Ordinal position of the column in the table.
DATA_TYPE	(string)	RDBMS name of the datatype of

Key	Type	Description
		the column.
DEFAULT	(string)	Default value for the column, if any.
NULLABLE	(boolean)	True if the column accepts SQL NULLs, false if the column has a NOT NULL constraint.
LENGTH	(integer)	Length or size of the column as reported by the RDBMS.
SCALE	(integer)	Scale of SQL NUMERIC or DECIMAL type.
PRECISION	(integer)	Precision of SQL NUMERIC or DECIMAL type.
UNSIGNED	(boolean)	True if an integer-based type is reported as UNSIGNED.
PRIMARY	(boolean)	True if the column is part of the primary key of this table.
PRIMARY_POSITION	(integer)	Ordinal position (1-based) of the column in the primary key.
IDENTITY	(boolean)	True if the column uses an auto-generated value.

How the IDENTITY Metadata Field Relates to Specific RDBMSs

The IDENTITY metadata field was chosen as an 'idiomatic' term to represent a relation to surrogate keys. This field can be commonly known by the following values:-

* IDENTITY - DB2, MSSQL

* AUTO_INCREMENT - MySQL

* SERIAL - PostgreSQL

* SEQUENCE - Oracle

If no table exists matching the table name and optional schema name specified, then describeTable() returns an empty array.

Closing a Connection

Normally it is not necessary to close a database connection. PHP automatically cleans up all resources and the end of a request. Database extensions are designed to close the connection as the reference to the resource object is cleaned up.

However, if you have a long-duration PHP script that initiates many database connections, you might need to close the connection, to avoid exhausting the capacity of your RDBMS server. You can use the Adapter's closeConnection() method to explicitly close the underlying database connection.

Since release 1.7.2, you could check you are currently connected to the RDBMS server with the method isConnected(). This means that a connection resource has been initiated and wasn't closed. This function is not currently able to test for example a server side closing of the connection. This is internally use to close the connection. It allow you to close the connection multiple times without errors. It was already the case before 1.7.2 for PDO adapters but not for the others.

Example 15.31. Closing a Database Connection

```
$db->closeConnection();
```

Does Zend_Db Support Persistent Connections?

The usage of persistent connections is not supported or encouraged in Zend_Db.

Using persistent connections can cause an excess of idle connections on the RDBMS server, which causes more problems than any performance gain you might achieve by reducing the overhead of making connections.

Database connections have state. That is, some objects in the RDBMS server exist in session scope. Examples are locks, user variables, temporary tables, and information about the most recently executed query, such as rows affected, and last generated id value. If you use persistent connections, your application could access invalid or privileged data that were created in a previous PHP request.

Running Other Database Statements

There might be cases in which you need to access the connection object directly, as provided by the PHP database extension. Some of these extensions may offer features that are not surfaced by methods of Zend_Db_Adapter_Abstract.

For example, all SQL statements run by Zend_Db are prepared, then executed. However, some database features are incompatible with prepared statements. DDL statements like CREATE and ALTER cannot be prepared in MySQL. Also, SQL statements don't benefit from the MySQL Query Cache [http://dev.mysql.com/doc/refman/5.1/en/query-cache-how.html], prior to MySQL 5.1.17.

Most PHP database extensions provide a method to execute SQL statements without preparing them. For example, in PDO, this method is exec(). You can access the connection object in the PHP extension directly using getConnection().

Example 15.32. Running a Non-Prepared Statement in a PDO Adapter

```
$result = $db->getConnection()->exec('DROP TABLE bugs');
```

Similarly, you can access other methods or properties that are specific to PHP database extensions. Be aware, though, that by doing this you might constrain your application to the interface provided by the extension for a specific brand of RDBMS.

In future versions of Zend_Db, there will be opportunities to add method entry points for functionality that is common to the supported PHP database extensions. This will not affect backward compatibility.

Retrieving Server Version

Since release 1.7.2, you could retrieve the server version in PHP syntax style to be able to use version_compare(). If the information isn't available, you will receive null.

Example 15.33. Verifying server version before running a query

```
$version = $db->getServerVersion();
if (!is_null($version)) {
    if (version_compare($version, '5.0.0', '>=')) {
        // do something
    } else {
        // do something else
    }
} else {
    // impossible to read server version
}
```

Notes on Specific Adapters

This section lists differences between the Adapter classes of which you should be aware.

IBM DB2

- Specify this Adapter to the factory() method with the name 'Db2'.

- This Adapter uses the PHP extension ibm_db2.

- IBM DB2 supports both sequences and auto-incrementing keys. Therefore the arguments to lastInsertId() are optional. If you give no arguments, the Adapter returns the last value generated for an auto-increment key. If you give arguments, the Adapter returns the last value generated by the sequence named according to the convention '*table_column*_seq'.

MySQLi

- Specify this Adapter to the factory() method with the name 'Mysqli'.

- This Adapter utilizes the PHP extension mysqli.

- MySQL does not support sequences, so lastInsertId() ignores its arguments and always returns the last value generated for an auto-increment key. The lastSequenceId() method returns null.

Oracle

- Specify this Adapter to the factory() method with the name 'Oracle'.

- This Adapter uses the PHP extension oci8.

- Oracle does not support auto-incrementing keys, so you should specify the name of a sequence to lastInsertId() or lastSequenceId().

- The Oracle extension does not support positional parameters. You must use named parameters.

- Currently the Zend_Db::CASE_FOLDING option is not supported by the Oracle adapter. To use this option with Oracle, you must use the PDO OCI adapter.

- By default, LOB fields are returned as OCI-Lob objects. You could retrieve them as string for all requests by using driver options 'lob_as_string' or for particular request by using setLobAsString(boolean) on adapter or on statement.

PDO for IBM DB2 and Informix Dynamic Server (IDS)

- Specify this Adapter to the `factory()` method with the name 'Pdo_Ibm'.

- This Adapter uses the PHP extensions pdo and pdo_ibm.

- You must use at least PDO_IBM extension version 1.2.2. If you have an earlier version of this extension, you must upgrade the PDO_IBM extension from PECL.

PDO Microsoft SQL Server

- Specify this Adapter to the `factory()` method with the name 'Pdo_Mssql'.

- This Adapter uses the PHP extensions pdo and pdo_mssql.

- Microsoft SQL Server does not support sequences, so `lastInsertId()` ignores its arguments and always returns the last value generated for an auto-increment key. The `lastSequenceId()` method returns `null`.

- If you are working with unicode strings in an encoding other than UCS-2 (such as UTF-8), you may have to perform a conversion in your application code or store the data in a binary column. Please refer to Microsoft's Knowledge Base [http://support.microsoft.com/kb/232580] for more information.

- `Zend_Db_Adapter_Pdo_Mssql` sets `QUOTED_IDENTIFIER` `ON` immediately after connecting to a SQL Server database. This makes the driver use the standard SQL identifier delimiter symbol (") instead of the proprietary square-brackets syntax SQL Server uses for delimiting identifiers.

- You can specify `pdoType` as a key in the options array. The value can be "mssql" (the default), "dblib", "freetds", or "sybase". This option affects the DSN prefix the adapter uses when constructing the DSN string. Both "freetds" and "sybase" imply a prefix of "sybase:", which is used for the FreeTDS [http://www.freetds.org/] set of libraries. See also http://www.php.net /manual/en/ref.pdo-dblib.connection.php [http://www.php.net/manual/en/ref.pdo-dblib.connection .php] for more information on the DSN prefixes used in this driver.

PDO MySQL

- Specify this Adapter to the `factory()` method with the name 'Pdo_Mysql'.

- This Adapter uses the PHP extensions pdo and pdo_mysql.

- MySQL does not support sequences, so `lastInsertId()` ignores its arguments and always returns the last value generated for an auto-increment key. The `lastSequenceId()` method returns `null`.

PDO Oracle

- Specify this Adapter to the `factory()` method with the name 'Pdo_Oci'.

- This Adapter uses the PHP extensions pdo and pdo_oci.

- Oracle does not support auto-incrementing keys, so you should specify the name of a sequence to `lastInsertId()` or `lastSequenceId()`.

PDO PostgreSQL

- Specify this Adapter to the `factory()` method with the name 'Pdo_Pgsql'.

- This Adapter uses the PHP extensions pdo and pdo_pgsql.

- PostgreSQL supports both sequences and auto-incrementing keys. Therefore the arguments to `lastInsertId()` are optional. If you give no arguments, the Adapter returns the last value generated for an auto-increment key. If you give arguments, the Adapter returns the last value generated by the sequence named according to the convention '*table_column*_seq'.

PDO SQLite

- Specify this Adapter to the `factory()` method with the name 'Pdo_Sqlite'.

- This Adapter uses the PHP extensions pdo and pdo_sqlite.

- SQLite does not support sequences, so `lastInsertId()` ignores its arguments and always returns the last value generated for an auto-increment key. The `lastSequenceId()` method returns `null`.

- To connect to an SQLite2 database, specify `'sqlite2'=>true` in the array of parameters when creating an instance of the Pdo_Sqlite Adapter.

- To connect to an in-memory SQLite database, specify `'dbname'=>':memory:'` in the array of parameters when creating an instance of the Pdo_Sqlite Adapter.

- Older versions of the SQLite driver for PHP do not seem to support the PRAGMA commands necessary to ensure that short column names are used in result sets. If you have problems that your result sets are returned with keys of the form "tablename.columnname" when you do a join query, then you should upgrade to the current version of PHP.

Firebird/Interbase

- This Adapter uses the PHP extension php_interbase.

- Firebird/interbase does not support auto-incrementing keys, so you should specify the name of a sequence to `lastInsertId()` or `lastSequenceId()`.

- Currently the `Zend_Db::CASE_FOLDING` option is not supported by the Firebird/interbase adapter. Unquoted identifiers are automatically returned in upper case.

- Adapter name is ZendX_Db_Adapter_Firebird.

  Remember to use the param adapterNamespace with value ZendX_Db_Adapter.

  We recommend to update the gds32.dll (or linux equivalent) bundled with php, to the same version of the server. For Firebird the equivalent gds32.dll is fbclient.dll.

  By default all identifiers (tables names, fields) are returned in upper case.

Zend_Db_Statement

In addition to convenient methods such as `fetchAll()` and `insert()` documented in the section called "Zend_Db_Adapter", you can use a statement object to gain more options for running queries and fetching result sets. This section describes how to get an instance of a statement object, and how to use its methods.

`Zend_Db_Statement` is based on the PDOStatement object in the PHP Data Objects [http://www.php.net/pdo] extension.

Creating a Statement

Typically, a statement object is returned by the `query()` method of the database Adapter class. This method is a general way to prepare any SQL statement. The first argument is a string containing an SQL statement. The optional second argument is an array of values to bind to parameter placeholders in the SQL string.

Example 15.34. Creating a SQL statement object with query()

```
$stmt = $db->query(
        'SELECT * FROM bugs WHERE reported_by = ? AND bug_status = ?',
        array('goofy', 'FIXED')
    );
```

The statement object corresponds to a SQL statement that has been prepared, and executed once with the bind-values specified. If the statement was a SELECT query or other type of statement that returns a result set, it is now ready to fetch results.

You can create a statement with its constructor, but this is less typical usage. There is no factory method to create this object, so you need to load the specific statement class and call its constructor. Pass the Adapter object as the first argument, and a string containing an SQL statement as the second argument. The statement is prepared, but not executed.

Example 15.35. Using a SQL statement constructor

```
$sql = 'SELECT * FROM bugs WHERE reported_by = ? AND bug_status = ?';

$stmt = new Zend_Db_Statement_Mysqli($db, $sql);
```

Executing a Statement

You need to execute a statement object if you create it using its constructor, or if you want to execute the same statement multiple times. Use the execute() method of the statement object. The single argument is an array of value to bind to parameter placeholders in the statement.

If you use *positional parameters*, or those that are marked with a question mark symbol (?), pass the bind values in a plain array.

Example 15.36. Executing a statement with positional parameters

```
$sql = 'SELECT * FROM bugs WHERE reported_by = ? AND bug_status = ?';

$stmt = new Zend_Db_Statement_Mysqli($db, $sql);

$stmt->execute(array('goofy', 'FIXED'));
```

If you use *named parameters*, or those that are indicated by a string identifier preceded by a colon character (:), pass the bind values in an associative array. The keys of this array should match the parameter names.

Example 15.37. Executing a statement with named parameters

```
$sql = 'SELECT * FROM bugs WHERE ' .
       'reported_by = :reporter AND bug_status = :status';

$stmt = new Zend_Db_Statement_Mysqli($db, $sql);

$stmt->execute(array(':reporter' => 'goofy', ':status' => 'FIXED'));
```

PDO statements support both positional parameters and named parameters, but not both types in a single SQL statement. Some of the Zend_Db_Statement classes for non-PDO extensions may support only one type of parameter or the other.

Fetching Results from a SELECT Statement

You can call methods on the statement object to retrieve rows from SQL statements that produce result set. SELECT, SHOW, DESCRIBE and EXPLAIN are examples of statements that produce a result set. INSERT, UPDATE, and DELETE are examples of statements that don't produce a result set. You can execute the latter SQL statements using Zend_Db_Statement, but you cannot call methods to fetch rows of results from them.

Fetching a Single Row from a Result Set

To retrieve one row from the result set, use the fetch() method of the statement object. All three arguments of this method are optional:

- *Fetch style* is the first argument. This controls the structure in which the row is returned. See the section called "Changing the Fetch Mode" for a description of the valid values and the corresponding data formats.

- *Cursor orientation* is the second argument. The default is Zend_Db::FETCH_ORI_NEXT, which simply means that each call to fetch() returns the next row in the result set, in the order returned by the RDBMS.

- *Offset* is the third argument. If the cursor orientation is Zend_Db::FETCH_ORI_ABS, then the offset number is the ordinal number of the row to return. If the cursor orientation is Zend_Db::FETCH_ORI_REL, then the offset number is relative to the cursor position before fetch() was called.

fetch() returns false if all rows of the result set have been fetched.

Example 15.38. Using fetch() in a loop

```
$stmt = $db->query('SELECT * FROM bugs');

while ($row = $stmt->fetch()) {
    echo $row['bug_description'];
}
```

See also PDOStatement::fetch() [http://www.php.net/PDOStatement-fetch].

Fetching a Complete Result Set

To retrieve all the rows of the result set in one step, use the `fetchAll()` method. This is equivalent to calling the `fetch()` method in a loop and returning all the rows in an array. The `fetchAll()` method accepts two arguments. The first is the fetch style, as described above, and the second indicates the number of the column to return, when the fetch style is Zend_Db::FETCH_COLUMN.

Example 15.39. Using fetchAll()

```
$stmt = $db->query('SELECT * FROM bugs');

$rows = $stmt->fetchAll();

echo $rows[0]['bug_description'];
```

See also PDOStatement::fetchAll() [http://www.php.net/PDOStatement-fetchAll].

Changing the Fetch Mode

By default, the statement object returns rows of the result set as associative arrays, mapping column names to column values. You can specify a different format for the statement class to return rows, just as you can in the Adapter class. You can use the `setFetchMode()` method of the statement object to specify the fetch mode. Specify the fetch mode using Zend_Db class constants FETCH_ASSOC, FETCH_NUM, FETCH_BOTH, FETCH_COLUMN, and FETCH_OBJ. See the section called "Changing the Fetch Mode" for more information on these modes. Subsequent calls to the statement methods `fetch()` or `fetchAll()` use the fetch mode that you specify.

Example 15.40. Setting the fetch mode

```
$stmt = $db->query('SELECT * FROM bugs');

$stmt->setFetchMode(Zend_Db::FETCH_NUM);

$rows = $stmt->fetchAll();

echo $rows[0][0];
```

See also PDOStatement::setFetchMode() [http://www.php.net/PDOStatement-setFetchMode].

Fetching a Single Column from a Result Set

To return a single column from the next row of the result set, use `fetchColumn()`. The optional argument is the integer index of the column, and it defaults to 0. This method returns a scalar value, or `false` if all rows of the result set have been fetched.

Note this method operates differently than the `fetchCol()` method of the Adapter class. The `fetchColumn()` method of a statement returns a single value from one row. The `fetchCol()` method of an adapter returns an array of values, taken from the first column of all rows of the result set.

Example 15.41. Using fetchColumn()

```
$stmt = $db->query('SELECT bug_id, bug_description, bug_status FROM bugs');

$bug_status = $stmt->fetchColumn(2);
```

See also PDOStatement::fetchColumn() [http://www.php.net/PDOStatement-fetchColumn].

Fetching a Row as an Object

To retrieve a row from the result set structured as an object, use the fetchObject(). This method takes two optional arguments. The first argument is a string that names the class name of the object to return; the default is 'stdClass'. The second argument is an array of values that will be passed to the constructor of that class.

Example 15.42. Using fetchObject()

```
$stmt = $db->query('SELECT bug_id, bug_description, bug_status FROM bugs');

$obj = $stmt->fetchObject();

echo $obj->bug_description;
```

See also PDOStatement::fetchObject() [http://www.php.net/PDOStatement-fetchObject].

Zend_Db_Profiler

Introduction

Zend_Db_Profiler can be enabled to allow profiling of queries. Profiles include the queries processed by the adapter as well as elapsed time to run the queries, allowing inspection of the queries that have been performed without needing to add extra debugging code to classes. Advanced usage also allows the developer to filter which queries are profiled.

Enable the profiler by either passing a directive to the adapter constructor, or by asking the adapter to enable it later.

```
$params = array(
    'host'     => '127.0.0.1',
    'username' => 'webuser',
    'password' => 'xxxxxxxx',
    'dbname'   => 'test'
    'profiler' => true  // turn on profiler
                        // set to false to disable (disabled by default)
);

$db = Zend_Db::factory('PDO_MYSQL', $params);

// turn off profiler:
$db->getProfiler()->setEnabled(false);

// turn on profiler:
$db->getProfiler()->setEnabled(true);
```

The value of the 'profiler' option is flexible. It is interpreted differently depending on its type. Most often, you should use a simple boolean value, but other types enable you to customize the profiler behavior.

A boolean argument sets the profiler to enabled if it is a true value, or disabled if false. The profiler class is the adapter's default profiler class, Zend_Db_Profiler.

```
$params['profiler'] = true;
```

```
$db = Zend_Db::factory('PDO_MYSQL', $params);
```

An instance of a profiler object makes the adapter use that object. The object type must be Zend_Db_Profiler or a subclass thereof. Enabling the profiler is done separately.

```
$profiler = MyProject_Db_Profiler();
$profiler->setEnabled(true);
$params['profiler'] = $profiler;
$db = Zend_Db::factory('PDO_MYSQL', $params);
```

The argument can be an associative array containing any or all of the keys 'enabled', 'instance', and 'class'. The 'enabled' and 'instance' keys correspond to the boolean and instance types documented above. The 'class' key is used to name a class to use for a custom profiler. The class must be Zend_Db_Profiler or a subclass. The class is instantiated with no constructor arguments. The 'class' option is ignored when the 'instance' option is supplied.

```
$params['profiler'] = array(
    'enabled' => true,
    'class'   => 'MyProject_Db_Profiler'
);
$db = Zend_Db::factory('PDO_MYSQL', $params);
```

Finally, the argument can be an object of type Zend_Config containing properties, which are treated as the array keys described above. For example, a file "config.ini" might contain the following data:

```
[main]
db.profiler.class   = "MyProject_Db_Profiler"
db.profiler.enabled = true
```

This configuration can be applied by the following PHP code:

```
$config = new Zend_Config_Ini('config.ini', 'main');
$params['profiler'] = $config->db->profiler;
$db = Zend_Db::factory('PDO_MYSQL', $params);
```

The 'instance' property may be used as in the following:

```
$profiler = new MyProject_Db_Profiler();
$profiler->setEnabled(true);
$configData = array(
    'instance' => $profiler
    );
$config = new Zend_Config($configData);
$params['profiler'] = $config;
$db = Zend_Db::factory('PDO_MYSQL', $params);
```

Using the Profiler

At any point, grab the profiler using the adapter's getProfiler() method:

```
$profiler = $db->getProfiler();
```

This returns a Zend_Db_Profiler object instance. With that instance, the developer can examine your queries using a variety of methods:

- getTotalNumQueries() returns the total number of queries that have been profiled.

- `getTotalElapsedSecs()` returns the total number of seconds elapsed for all profiled queries.

- `getQueryProfiles()` returns an array of all query profiles.

- `getLastQueryProfile()` returns the last (most recent) query profile, regardless of whether or not the query has finished (if it hasn't, the end time will be null)

- `clear()` clears any past query profiles from the stack.

The return value of `getLastQueryProfile()` and the individual elements of `getQueryProfiles()` are `Zend_Db_Profiler_Query` objects, which provide the ability to inspect the individual queries themselves:

- `getQuery()` returns the SQL text of the query. The SQL text of a prepared statement with parameters is the text at the time the query was prepared, so it contains parameter placeholders, not the values used when the statement is executed.

- `getQueryParams()` returns an array of parameter values used when executing a prepared query. This includes both bound parameters and arguments to the statement's `execute()` method. The keys of the array are the positional (1-based) or named (string) parameter indices.

- `getElapsedSecs()` returns the number of seconds the query ran.

The information `Zend_Db_Profiler` provides is useful for profiling bottlenecks in applications, and for debugging queries that have been run. For instance, to see the exact query that was last run:

```
$query = $profiler->getLastQueryProfile();

echo $query->getQuery();
```

Perhaps a page is generating slowly; use the profiler to determine first the total number of seconds of all queries, and then step through the queries to find the one that ran longest:

```
$totalTime   = $profiler->getTotalElapsedSecs();
$queryCount  = $profiler->getTotalNumQueries();
$longestTime = 0;
$longestQuery = null;

foreach ($profiler->getQueryProfiles() as $query) {
    if ($query->getElapsedSecs() > $longestTime) {
        $longestTime  = $query->getElapsedSecs();
        $longestQuery = $query->getQuery();
    }
}

echo 'Executed ' . $queryCount . ' queries in ' . $totalTime .
    ' seconds' . "\n";
echo 'Average query length: ' . $totalTime / $queryCount .
    ' seconds' . "\n";
echo 'Queries per second: ' . $queryCount / $totalTime . "\n";
echo 'Longest query length: ' . $longestTime . "\n";
echo "Longest query: \n" . $longestQuery . "\n";
```

Advanced Profiler Usage

In addition to query inspection, the profiler also allows the developer to filter which queries get profiled. The following methods operate on a `Zend_Db_Profiler` instance:

Filter by query elapsed time

setFilterElapsedSecs() allows the developer to set a minimum query time before a query is profiled. To remove the filter, pass the method a null value.

```
// Only profile queries that take at least 5 seconds:
$profiler->setFilterElapsedSecs(5);

// Profile all queries regardless of length:
$profiler->setFilterElapsedSecs(null);
```

Filter by query type

setFilterQueryType() allows the developer to set which types of queries should be profiled; to profile multiple types, logical OR them. Query types are defined as the following Zend_Db_Profiler constants:

- Zend_Db_Profiler::CONNECT: connection operations, or selecting a database.

- Zend_Db_Profiler::QUERY: general database queries that do not match other types.

- Zend_Db_Profiler::INSERT: any query that adds new data to the database, generally SQL INSERT.

- Zend_Db_Profiler::UPDATE: any query that updates existing data, usually SQL UPDATE.

- Zend_Db_Profiler::DELETE: any query that deletes existing data, usually SQL DELETE.

- Zend_Db_Profiler::SELECT: any query that retrieves existing data, usually SQL SELECT.

- Zend_Db_Profiler::TRANSACTION: any transactional operation, such as start transaction, commit, or rollback.

As with setFilterElapsedSecs(), you can remove any existing filters by passing null as the sole argument.

```
// profile only SELECT queries
$profiler->setFilterQueryType(Zend_Db_Profiler::SELECT);

// profile SELECT, INSERT, and UPDATE queries
$profiler->setFilterQueryType(Zend_Db_Profiler::SELECT |
                              Zend_Db_Profiler::INSERT |
                              Zend_Db_Profiler::UPDATE);

// profile DELETE queries
$profiler->setFilterQueryType(Zend_Db_Profiler::DELETE);

// Remove all filters
$profiler->setFilterQueryType(null);
```

Retrieve profiles by query type

Using setFilterQueryType() can cut down on the profiles generated. However, sometimes it can be more useful to keep all profiles, but view only those you need at a given moment. Another feature of getQueryProfiles() is that it can do this filtering on-the-fly, by passing a query type (or logical combination of query types) as its first argument; see the section called "Filter by query type" for a list of the query type constants.

```
// Retrieve only SELECT query profiles
$profiles = $profiler->getQueryProfiles(Zend_Db_Profiler::SELECT);
```

```
// Retrieve only SELECT, INSERT, and UPDATE query profiles
$profiles = $profiler->getQueryProfiles(Zend_Db_Profiler::SELECT |
                                         Zend_Db_Profiler::INSERT |
                                         Zend_Db_Profiler::UPDATE);

// Retrieve DELETE query profiles
$profiles = $profiler->getQueryProfiles(Zend_Db_Profiler::DELETE);
```

Specialized Profilers

A Specialized Profiler is an object that inherits from Zend_Db_Profiler. Specialized Profilers treat profiling information in specific ways.

Profiling with Firebug

Zend_Db_Profiler_Firebug sends profiling infomation to the Firebug [http://www.getfirebug.com/] Console [http://getfirebug.com/logging.html].

All data is sent via the Zend_Wildfire_Channel_HttpHeaders component which uses HTTP headers to ensure the page content is not disturbed. Debugging AJAX requests that require clean JSON and XML responses is possible with this approach.

Requirements:

*   Firefox Browser ideally version 3 but version 2 is also supported.

*   Firebug Firefox Extension which you can download from https://addons.mozilla.org /en-US/firefox/addon/1843.

*   FirePHP Firefox Extension which you can download from https://addons.mozilla.org /en-US/firefox/addon/6149.

Example 15.43. DB Profiling with Zend_Controller_Front

```
// In your bootstrap file

$profiler = new Zend_Db_Profiler_Firebug('All DB Queries');
$profiler->setEnabled(true);

// Attach the profiler to your db adapter
$db->setProfiler($profiler)

// Dispatch your front controller

// All DB queries in your model, view and controller
// files will now be profiled and sent to Firebug
```

Example 15.44. DB Profiling without Zend_Controller_Front

```
$profiler = new Zend_Db_Profiler_Firebug('All DB Queries');
$profiler->setEnabled(true);

// Attach the profiler to your db adapter
$db->setProfiler($profiler)
```

```
$request  = new Zend_Controller_Request_Http();
$response = new Zend_Controller_Response_Http();
$channel  = Zend_Wildfire_Channel_HttpHeaders::getInstance();
$channel->setRequest($request);
$channel->setResponse($response);

// Start output buffering
ob_start();

// Now you can run your DB queries to be profiled

// Flush profiling data to browser
$channel->flush();
$response->sendHeaders();
```

Zend_Db_Select

Introduction

The Zend_Db_Select object represents a SQL SELECT query statement. The class has methods for adding individual parts to the query. You can specify some parts of the query using PHP methods and data structures, and the class forms the correct SQL syntax for you. After you build a query, you can execute the query as if you had written it as a string.

The value offered by Zend_Db_Select includes:

- Object-oriented methods for specifying SQL queries in a piece-by-piece manner;

- Database-independent abstraction of some parts of the SQL query;

- Automatic quoting of metadata identifiers in most cases, to support identifiers containing SQL reserved words and special characters;

- Quoting identifiers and values, to help reduce risk of SQL injection attacks.

Using Zend_Db_Select is not mandatory. For very simple SELECT queries, it is usually simpler to specify the entire SQL query as a string and execute it using Adapter methods like query() or fetchAll(). Using Zend_Db_Select is helpful if you need to assemble a SELECT query procedurally, or based on conditional logic in your application.

Creating a Select Object

You can create an instance of a Zend_Db_Select object using the select() method of a Zend_Db_Adapter_Abstract object.

Example 15.45. Example of the database adapter's select() method

```
$db = Zend_Db::factory( ...options... );
$select = $db->select();
```

Another way to create a Zend_Db_Select object is with its constructor, specifying the database adapter as an argument.

Example 15.46. Example of creating a new Select object

```
$db = Zend_Db::factory( ...options... );
$select = new Zend_Db_Select($db);
```

Building Select queries

When building the query, you can add clauses of the query one by one. There is a separate method to add each clause to the Zend_Db_Select object.

Example 15.47. Example of the using methods to add clauses

```
// Create the Zend_Db_Select object
$select = $db->select();

// Add a FROM clause
$select->from( ...specify table and columns... )

// Add a WHERE clause
$select->where( ...specify search criteria... )

// Add an ORDER BY clause
$select->order( ...specify sorting criteria... );
```

You also can use most methods of the Zend_Db_Select object with a convenient fluent interface. A fluent interface means that each method returns a reference to the object on which it was called, so you can immediately call another method.

Example 15.48. Example of the using the fluent interface

```
$select = $db->select()
    ->from( ...specify table and columns... )
    ->where( ...specify search criteria... )
    ->order( ...specify sorting criteria... );
```

The examples in this section show usage of the fluent interface, but you can use the non-fluent interface in all cases. It is often necessary to use the non-fluent interface, for example, if your application needs to perform some logic before adding a clause to a query.

Adding a FROM clause

Specify the table for this query using the from() method. You can specify the table name as a simple string. Zend_Db_Select applies identifier quoting around the table name, so you can use special characters.

Example 15.49. Example of the from() method

```
// Build this query:
//    SELECT *
//    FROM "products"

$select = $db->select()
            ->from( 'products' );
```

You can also specify the correlation name (sometimes called the "table alias") for a table. Instead of a simple string, use an associative array mapping the correlation name to the table name. In other clauses of the SQL query, use this correlation name. If your query joins more than one table, Zend_Db_Select generates unique correlation names based on the table names, for any tables for which you don't specify the correlation name.

Example 15.50. Example of specifying a table correlation name

```
// Build this query:
//    SELECT p.*
//    FROM "products" AS p

$select = $db->select()
            ->from( array('p' => 'products') );
```

Some RDBMS brands support a leading schema specifier for a table. You can specify the table name as "schemaName.tableName", where Zend_Db_Select quotes each part individually, or you may specify the schema name separately. A schema name specified in the table name takes precedence over a schema provided separately in the event that both are provided.

Example 15.51. Example of specifying a schema name

```
// Build this query:
//    SELECT *
//    FROM "myschema"."products"

$select = $db->select()
            ->from( 'myschema.products' );

// or

$select = $db->select()
            ->from('products', '*', 'myschema');
```

Adding Columns

In the second argument of the from() method, you can specify the columns to select from the respective table. If you specify no columns, the default is "*", the SQL wildcard for "all columns".

You can list the columns in a simple array of strings, or as an associative mapping of column alias to column name. If you only have one column to query, and you don't need to specify a column alias, you can list it as a plain string instead of an array.

If you give an empty array as the columns argument, no columns from the respective table are included in the result set. See a code example under the section on the join() method.

You can specify the column name as "correlationName.columnName". Zend_Db_Select quotes each part individually. If you don't specify a correlation name for a column, it uses the correlation name for the table named in the current from() method.

Example 15.52. Examples of specifying columns

```
// Build this query:
//    SELECT p."product_id", p."product_name"
//    FROM "products" AS p

$select = $db->select()
            ->from(array('p' => 'products'),
                array('product_id', 'product_name'));

// Build the same query, specifying correlation names:
//    SELECT p."product_id", p."product_name"
//    FROM "products" AS p

$select = $db->select()
            ->from(array('p' => 'products'),
                array('p.product_id', 'p.product_name'));

// Build this query with an alias for one column:
//    SELECT p."product_id" AS prodno, p."product_name"
//    FROM "products" AS p

$select = $db->select()
            ->from(array('p' => 'products'),
                array('prodno' => 'product_id', 'product_name'));
```

Adding Expression Columns

Columns in SQL queries are sometimes expressions, not simply column names from a table. Expressions should not have correlation names or quoting applied. If your column string contains parentheses, Zend_Db_Select recognizes it as an expression.

You also can create an object of type Zend_Db_Expr explicitly, to prevent a string from being treated as a column name. Zend_Db_Expr is a minimal class that contains a single string. Zend_Db_Select recognizes objects of type Zend_Db_Expr and converts them back to string, but does not apply any alterations, such as quoting or correlation names.

Note

Using Zend_Db_Expr for column names is not necessary if your column expression contains parentheses; Zend_Db_Select recognizes parentheses and treats the string as an expression, skipping quoting and correlation names.

Example 15.53. Examples of specifying columns containing expressions

```
// Build this query:
//   SELECT p."product_id", LOWER(product_name)
//   FROM "products" AS p
// An expression with parentheses implicitly becomes
// a Zend_Db_Expr.

$select = $db->select()
             ->from(array('p' => 'products'),
                    array('product_id', 'LOWER(product_name)'));

// Build this query:
//   SELECT p."product_id", (p.cost * 1.08) AS cost_plus_tax
//   FROM "products" AS p

$select = $db->select()
             ->from(array('p' => 'products'),
                    array('product_id',
                          'cost_plus_tax' => '(p.cost * 1.08)')
                    );

// Build this query using Zend_Db_Expr explicitly:
//   SELECT p."product_id", p.cost * 1.08 AS cost_plus_tax
//   FROM "products" AS p

$select = $db->select()
             ->from(array('p' => 'products'),
                    array('product_id',
                          'cost_plus_tax' =>
                              new Zend_Db_Expr('p.cost * 1.08'))
                    );
```

In the cases above, Zend_Db_Select does not alter the string to apply correlation names or identifier quoting. If those changes are necessary to resolve ambiguity, you must make the changes manually in the string.

If your column names are SQL keywords or contain special characters, you should use the Adapter's quoteIdentifier() method and interpolate the result into the string. The quoteIdentifier() method uses SQL quoting to delimit the identifier, which makes it clear that it is an identifier for a table or a column, and not any other part of SQL syntax.

Your code is more database-independent if you use the quoteIdentifier() method instead of typing quotes literally in your string, because some RDBMS brands use nonstandard symbols for quoting identifiers. The quoteIdentifier() method is designed to use the appropriate quoting symbols based on the adapter type. The quoteIdentifier() method also escapes any quote characters that appear within the identifier name itself.

Example 15.54. Examples of quoting columns in an expression

```
// Build this query,
// quoting the special column name "from" in the expression:
//   SELECT p."from" + 10 AS origin
//   FROM "products" AS p

$select = $db->select()
```

```
            ->from(array('p' => 'products'),
                  array('origin' =>
                              '(p.' . $db->quoteIdentifier('from') . '
                                 + 10)')
              );
```

Adding columns to an existing FROM or JOIN table

There may be cases where you wish to add columns to an existing FROM or JOIN table after those methods have been called. The columns() method allows you to add specific columns at any point before the query is executed. You can supply the columns as either a string or Zend_Db_Expr or as an array of these elements. The second argument to this method can be omitted, implying that the columns are to be added to the FROM table, otherwise an existing correlation name must be used.

Example 15.55. Examples of adding columns with the columns() method

```
// Build this query:
//   SELECT p."product_id", p."product_name"
//   FROM "products" AS p

$select = $db->select()
             ->from(array('p' => 'products'), 'product_id')
             ->columns('product_name');

// Build the same query, specifying correlation names:
//   SELECT p."product_id", p."product_name"
//   FROM "products" AS p

$select = $db->select()
             ->from(array('p' => 'products'), 'p.product_id')
             ->columns('product_name', 'p');
             // Alternatively use columns('p.product_name')
```

Adding Another Table to the Query with JOIN

Many useful queries involve using a JOIN to combine rows from multiple tables. You can add tables to a Zend_Db_Select query using the join() method. Using this method is similar to the from() method, except you can also specify a join condition in most cases.

Example 15.56. Example of the join() method

```
// Build this query:
//   SELECT p."product_id", p."product_name", l.*
//   FROM "products" AS p JOIN "line_items" AS l
//       ON p.product_id = l.product_id

$select = $db->select()
             ->from(array('p' => 'products'),
                    array('product_id', 'product_name'))
             ->join(array('l' => 'line_items'),
                    'p.product_id = l.product_id');
```

The second argument to join() is a string that is the join condition. This is an expression that declares the criteria by which rows in one table match rows in the the other table. You can use correlation names in this expression.

Note

No quoting is applied to the expression you specify for the join condition; if you have column names that need to be quoted, you must use `quoteIdentifier()` as you form the string for the join condition.

The third argument to `join()` is an array of column names, like that used in the `from()` method. It defaults to `"*"`, supports correlation names, expressions, and `Zend_Db_Expr` in the same way as the array of column names in the `from()` method.

To select no columns from a table, use an empty array for the list of columns. This usage works in the `from()` method too, but typically you want some columns from the primary table in your queries, whereas you might want no columns from a joined table.

Example 15.57. Example of specifying no columns

```
// Build this query:
//    SELECT p."product_id", p."product_name"
//    FROM "products" AS p JOIN "line_items" AS l
//      ON p.product_id = l.product_id

$select = $db->select()
            ->from(array('p' => 'products'),
                   array('product_id', 'product_name'))
            ->join(array('l' => 'line_items'),
                   'p.product_id = l.product_id',
                   array() ); // empty list of columns
```

Note the empty `array()` in the above example in place of a list of columns from the joined table.

SQL has several types of joins. See the list below for the methods to support different join types in `Zend_Db_Select`.

- **INNER JOIN** with the `join(table, join, [columns])` or `joinInner(table, join, [columns])` methods.

  This may be the most common type of join. Rows from each table are compared using the join condition you specify. The result set includes only the rows that satisfy the join condition. The result set can be empty if no rows satisfy this condition.

  All RDBMS brands support this join type.

- **LEFT JOIN** with the `joinLeft(table, condition, [columns])` method.

  All rows from the left operand table are included, matching rows from the right operand table included, and the columns from the right operand table are filled with NULLs if no row exists matching the left table.

  All RDBMS brands support this join type.

- **RIGHT JOIN** with the `joinRight(table, condition, [columns])` method.

  Right outer join is the complement of left outer join. All rows from the right operand table are included, matching rows from the left operand table included, and the columns from the left operand table are filled with NULLs if no row exists matching the right table.

  Some RDBMS brands don't support this join type, but in general any right join can be represented as a left join by reversing the order of the tables.

- **FULL JOIN** with the `joinFull(table, condition, [columns])` method.

A full outer join is like combining a left outer join and a right outer join. All rows from both tables are included, paired with each other on the same row of the result set if they satisfy the join condition, and otherwise paired with NULLs in place of columns from the other table.

Some RDBMS brands don't support this join type.

- **CROSS JOIN** with the `joinCross(table, [columns])` method.

A cross join is a Cartesian product. Every row in the first table is matched to every row in the second table. Therefore the number of rows in the result set is equal to the product of the number of rows in each table. You can filter the result set using conditions in a WHERE clause; in this way a cross join is similar to the old SQL-89 join syntax.

The `joinCross()` method has no parameter to specify the join condition. Some RDBMS brands don't support this join type.

- **NATURAL JOIN** with the `joinNatural(table, [columns])` method.

A natural join compares any column(s) that appear with the same name in both tables. The comparison is equality of all the column(s); comparing the columns using inequality is not a natural join. Only natural inner joins are supported by this API, even though SQL permits natural outer joins as well.

The `joinNatural()` method has no parameter to specify the join condition.

In addition to these join methods, you can simplify your queries by using the JoinUsing methods. Instead of supplying a full condition to your join, you simply pass the column name on which to join and the `Zend_Db_Select` object completes the condition for you.

Example 15.58. Example of the joinUsing() method

```
// Build this query:
//    SELECT *
//    FROM "table1"
//    JOIN "table2"
//    ON "table1".column1 = "table2".column1
//    WHERE column2 = 'foo'

$select = $db->select()
            ->from('table1')
            ->joinUsing('table2', 'column1')
            ->where('column2 = ?', 'foo');
```

Each of the applicable join methods in the `Zend_Db_Select` component has a corresponding 'using' method.

- `joinUsing(table, join, [columns])` and `joinInnerUsing(table, join, [columns])`

- `joinLeftUsing(table, join, [columns])`

- `joinRightUsing(table, join, [columns])`

- `joinFullUsing(table, join, [columns])`

Adding a WHERE Clause

You can specify criteria for restricting rows of the result set using the where() method. The first argument of this method is a SQL expression, and this expression is used in a SQL WHERE clause in the query.

Example 15.59. Example of the where() method

```
// Build this query:
//   SELECT product_id, product_name, price
//   FROM "products"
//   WHERE price > 100.00

$select = $db->select()
             ->from('products',
                 array('product_id', 'product_name', 'price'))
             ->where('price > 100.00');
```

> ## Note
>
> No quoting is applied to expressions given to the where() or orWhere() methods. If you have column names that need to be quoted, you must use quoteIdentifier() as you form the string for the condition.

The second argument to the where() method is optional. It is a value to substitute into the expression. Zend_Db_Select quotes the value and substitutes it for a question-mark ("?") symbol in the expression.

This method accepts only one parameter. If you have an expression into which you need to substitute multiple variables, you must format the string manually, interpolating variables and performing quoting yourself.

Example 15.60. Example of a parameter in the where() method

```
// Build this query:
//   SELECT product_id, product_name, price
//   FROM "products"
//   WHERE (price > 100.00)

$minimumPrice = 100;

$select = $db->select()
             ->from('products',
                 array('product_id', 'product_name', 'price'))
             ->where('price > ?', $minimumPrice);
```

You can invoke the where() method multiple times on the same Zend_Db_Select object. The resulting query combines the multiple terms together using AND between them.

Example 15.61. Example of multiple where() methods

```
// Build this query:
//    SELECT product_id, product_name, price
//    FROM "products"
//    WHERE (price > 100.00)
//      AND (price < 500.00)

$minimumPrice = 100;
$maximumPrice = 500;

$select = $db->select()
             ->from('products',
                    array('product_id', 'product_name', 'price'))
             ->where('price > ?', $minimumPrice)
             ->where('price < ?', $maximumPrice);
```

If you need to combine terms together using OR, use the orWhere() method. This method is used in the same way as the where() method, except that the term specified is preceded by OR, instead of AND.

Example 15.62. Example of the orWhere() method

```
// Build this query:
//    SELECT product_id, product_name, price
//    FROM "products"
//    WHERE (price < 100.00)
//      OR (price > 500.00)

$minimumPrice = 100;
$maximumPrice = 500;

$select = $db->select()
             ->from('products',
                    array('product_id', 'product_name', 'price'))
             ->where('price < ?', $minimumPrice)
             ->orWhere('price > ?', $maximumPrice);
```

Zend_Db_Select automatically puts parentheses around each expression you specify using the where() or orWhere() methods. This helps to ensure that Boolean operator precedence does not cause unexpected results.

Example 15.63. Example of parenthesizing Boolean expressions

```
// Build this query:
//    SELECT product_id, product_name, price
//    FROM "products"
//    WHERE (price < 100.00 OR price > 500.00)
//      AND (product_name = 'Apple')

$minimumPrice = 100;
```

```
$maximumPrice = 500;
$prod = 'Apple';

$select = $db->select()
            ->from('products',
                array('product_id', 'product_name', 'price'))
            ->where("price < $minimumPrice OR price > $maximumPrice")
            ->where('product_name = ?', $prod);
```

In the example above, the results would be quite different without the parentheses, because AND has higher precedence than OR. Zend_Db_Select applies the parentheses so the effect is that each expression in successive calls to the where() bind more tightly than the AND that combines the expressions.

Adding a GROUP BY Clause

In SQL, the GROUP BY clause allows you to reduce the rows of a query result set to one row per unique value found in the column(s) named in the GROUP BY clause.

In Zend_Db_Select, you can specify the column(s) to use for calculating the groups of rows using the group() method. The argument to this method is a column or an array of columns to use in the GROUP BY clause.

Example 15.64. Example of the group() method

```
// Build this query:
//   SELECT p."product_id", COUNT(*) AS line_items_per_product
//   FROM "products" AS p JOIN "line_items" AS l
//     ON p.product_id = l.product_id
//   GROUP BY p.product_id

$select = $db->select()
            ->from(array('p' => 'products'),
                array('product_id'))
            ->join(array('l' => 'line_items'),
                'p.product_id = l.product_id',
                array('line_items_per_product' => 'COUNT(*)'))
            ->group('p.product_id');
```

Like the columns array in the from() method, you can use correlation names in the column name strings, and the column is quoted as an identifier unless the string contains parentheses or is an object of type Zend_Db_Expr.

Adding a HAVING Clause

In SQL, the HAVING clause applies a restriction condition on groups of rows. This is similar to how a WHERE clause applies a restriction condition on rows. But the two clauses are different because WHERE conditions are applied before groups are defined, whereas HAVING conditions are applied after groups are defined.

In Zend_Db_Select, you can specify conditions for restricting groups using the having() method. Its usage is similar to that of the where() method. The first argument is a string containing a SQL expression. The optional second argument is a value that is used to replace a positional parameter placeholder in the SQL expression. Expressions given in multiple invocations of the having() method are combined using the Boolean AND operator, or the OR operator if you use the orHaving() method.

Example 15.65. Example of the having() method

```
// Build this query:
//    SELECT p."product_id", COUNT(*) AS line_items_per_product
//    FROM "products" AS p JOIN "line_items" AS l
//      ON p.product_id = l.product_id
//    GROUP BY p.product_id
//    HAVING line_items_per_product > 10

$select = $db->select()
            ->from(array('p' => 'products'),
                   array('product_id'))
            ->join(array('l' => 'line_items'),
                   'p.product_id = l.product_id',
                   array('line_items_per_product' => 'COUNT(*)'))
            ->group('p.product_id')
            ->having('line_items_per_product > 10');
```

Note

No quoting is applied to expressions given to the having() or orHaving() methods. If you have column names that need to be quoted, you must use quoteIdentifier() as you form the string for the condition.

Adding an ORDER BY Clause

In SQL, the ORDER BY clause specifies one or more columns or expressions by which the result set of a query is sorted. If multiple columns are listed, the secondary columns are used to resolve ties; the sort order is determined by the secondary columns if the preceding columns contain identical values. The default sorting is from least value to greatest value. You can also sort by greatest value to least value for a given column in the list by specifying the keyword DESC after that column.

In Zend_Db_Select, you can use the order() method to specify a column or an array of columns by which to sort. Each element of the array is a string naming a column. Optionally with the ASC DESC keyword following it, separated by a space.

Like in the from() and group() methods, column names are quoted as identifiers, unless they contain contain parentheses or are an object of type Zend_Db_Expr.

Example 15.66. Example of the order() method

```
// Build this query:
//    SELECT p."product_id", COUNT(*) AS line_items_per_product
//    FROM "products" AS p JOIN "line_items" AS l
//      ON p.product_id = l.product_id
//    GROUP BY p.product_id
//    ORDER BY "line_items_per_product" DESC, "product_id"

$select = $db->select()
            ->from(array('p' => 'products'),
                   array('product_id'))
            ->join(array('l' => 'line_items'),
                   'p.product_id = l.product_id',
                   array('line_items_per_product' => 'COUNT(*)'))
            ->group('p.product_id')
```

```
            ->order(array('line_items_per_product DESC',
                          'product_id'));
```

Adding a LIMIT Clause

Some RDBMS brands extend SQL with a query clause known as the LIMIT clause. This clause reduces the number of rows in the result set to at most a number you specify. You can also specify to skip a number of rows before starting to output. This feature makes it easy to take a subset of a result set, for example when displaying query results on progressive pages of output.

In Zend_Db_Select, you can use the limit() method to specify the count of rows and the number of rows to skip. The first argument to this method is the desired count of rows. The second argument is the number of rows to skip.

Example 15.67. Example of the limit() method

```
// Build this query:
//   SELECT p."product_id", p."product_name"
//   FROM "products" AS p
//   LIMIT 10, 20

$select = $db->select()
             ->from(array('p' => 'products'),
                 array('product_id', 'product_name'))
             ->limit(10, 20);
```

Note

The LIMIT syntax is not supported by all RDBMS brands. Some RDBMS require different syntax to support similar functionality. Each Zend_Db_Adapter_Abstract class includes a method to produce SQL appropriate for that RDBMS.

Use the limitPage() method for an alternative way to specify row count and offset. This method allows you to limit the result set to one of a series of fixed-length subsets of rows from the query's total result set. In other words, you specify the length of a "page" of results, and the ordinal number of the single page of results you want the query to return. The page number is the first argument of the limitPage() method, and the page length is the second argument. Both arguments are required; they have no default values.

Example 15.68. Example of the limitPage() method

```
// Build this query:
//   SELECT p."product_id", p."product_name"
//   FROM "products" AS p
//   LIMIT 10, 20

$select = $db->select()
             ->from(array('p' => 'products'),
                 array('product_id', 'product_name'))
             ->limitPage(2, 10);
```

Adding the DISTINCT Query Modifier

The distinct() method enables you to add the DISTINCT keyword to your SQL query.

Example 15.69. Example of the distinct() method

```
// Build this query:
//     SELECT DISTINCT p."product_name"
//     FROM "products" AS p

$select = $db->select()
            ->distinct()
            ->from(array('p' => 'products'), 'product_name');
```

Adding the FOR UPDATE Query Modifier

The forUpdate() method enables you to add the FOR UPDATE modifier to your SQL query.

Example 15.70. Example of forUpdate() method

```
// Build this query:
//     SELECT FOR UPDATE p.*
//     FROM "products" AS p

$select = $db->select()
            ->forUpdate()
            ->from(array('p' => 'products'));
```

Executing Select Queries

This section describes how to execute the query represented by a Zend_Db_Select object.

Executing Select Queries from the Db Adapter

You can execute the query represented by the Zend_Db_Select object by passing it as the first argument to the query() method of a Zend_Db_Adapter_Abstract object. Use the Zend_Db_Select objects instead of a string query.

The query() method returns an object of type Zend_Db_Statement or PDOStatement, depending on the adapter type.

Example 15.71. Example using the Db adapter's query() method

```
$select = $db->select()
            ->from('products');

$stmt = $db->query($select);
$result = $stmt->fetchAll();
```

Executing Select Queries from the Object

As an alternative to using the query() method of the adapter object, you can use the query() method of the Zend_Db_Select object. Both methods return an object of type Zend_Db_Statement or PDOStatement, depending on the adapter type.

Example 15.72. Example using the Select object's query method

```
$select = $db->select()
            ->from('products');

$stmt = $select->query();
$result = $stmt->fetchAll();
```

Converting a Select Object to a SQL String

If you need access to a string representation of the SQL query corresponding to the Zend_Db_Select object, use the __toString() method.

Example 15.73. Example of the __toString() method

```
$select = $db->select()
            ->from('products');

$sql = $select->__toString();
echo "$sql\n";

// The output is the string:
//   SELECT * FROM "products"
```

Other methods

This section describes other methods of the Zend_Db_Select class that are not covered above: getPart() and reset().

Retrieving Parts of the Select Object

The getPart() method returns a representation of one part of your SQL query. For example, you can use this method to return the array of expressions for the WHERE clause, or the array of columns (or column expressions) that are in the SELECT list, or the values of the count and offset for the LIMIT clause.

The return value is not a string containing a fragment of SQL syntax. The return value is an internal representation, which is typically an array structure containing values and expressions. Each part of the query has a different structure.

The single argument to the getPart() method is a string that identifies which part of the Select query to return. For example, the string 'from' identifies the part of the Select object that stores information about the tables in the FROM clause, including joined tables.

The `Zend_Db_Select` class defines constants you can use for parts of the SQL query. You can use these constant definitions, or you can the literal strings.

Table 15.2. Constants used by getPart() and reset()

Constant	String value
Zend_Db_Select::DISTINCT	'distinct'
Zend_Db_Select::FOR_UPDATE	'forupdate'
Zend_Db_Select::COLUMNS	'columns'
Zend_Db_Select::FROM	'from'
Zend_Db_Select::WHERE	'where'
Zend_Db_Select::GROUP	'group'
Zend_Db_Select::HAVING	'having'
Zend_Db_Select::ORDER	'order'
Zend_Db_Select::LIMIT_COUNT	'limitcount'
Zend_Db_Select::LIMIT_OFFSET	'limitoffset'

Example 15.74. Example of the getPart() method

```
$select = $db->select()
            ->from('products')
            ->order('product_id');

// You can use a string literal to specify the part
$orderData = $select->getPart( 'order' );

// You can use a constant to specify the same part
$orderData = $select->getPart( Zend_Db_Select::ORDER );

// The return value may be an array structure, not a string.
// Each part has a different structure.
print_r( $orderData );
```

Resetting Parts of the Select Object

The `reset()` method enables you to clear one specified part of the SQL query, or else clear all parts of the SQL query if you omit the argument.

The single argument is optional. You can specify the part of the query to clear, using the same strings you used in the argument to the `getPart()` method. The part of the query you specify is reset to a default state.

If you omit the parameter, `reset()` changes all parts of the query to their default state. This makes the `Zend_Db_Select` object equivalent to a new object, as though you had just instantiated it.

Example 15.75. Example of the reset() method

```
// Build this query:
//    SELECT p.*
//    FROM "products" AS p
//    ORDER BY "product_name"

$select = $db->select()
             ->from(array('p' => 'products'))
             ->order('product_name');

// Changed requirement, instead order by a different columns:
//    SELECT p.*
//    FROM "products" AS p
//    ORDER BY "product_id"

// Clear one part so we can redefine it
$select->reset( Zend_Db_Select::ORDER );

// And specify a different column
$select->order('product_id');

// Clear all parts of the query
$select->reset();
```

Zend_Db_Table

Introduction

The `Zend_Db_Table` class is an object-oriented interface to database tables. It provides methods for many common operations on tables. The base class is extensible, so you can add custom logic.

The `Zend_Db_Table` solution is an implementation of the Table Data Gateway [http://www.martinfowler.com /eaaCatalog/tableDataGateway.html] pattern. The solution also includes a class that implements the Row Data Gateway [http://www.martinfowler.com/eaaCatalog/row DataGateway.html] pattern.

Defining a Table Class

For each table in your database that you want to access, define a class that extends `Zend_Db_Table_Abstract`.

Defining the Table Name and Schema

Declare the database table for which this class is defined, using the protected variable $_name. This is a string, and must contain the name of the table spelled as it appears in the database.

Example 15.76. Declaring a table class with explicit table name

```
class Bugs extends Zend_Db_Table_Abstract
{
    protected $_name = 'bugs';
}
```

If you don't specify the table name, it defaults to the name of the class. If you rely on this default, the class name must match the spelling of the table name as it appears in the database.

Example 15.77. Declaring a table class with implicit table name

```
class bugs extends Zend_Db_Table_Abstract
{
    // table name matches class name
}
```

You can also declare the schema for the table, either with the protected variable $_schema, or with the schema prepended to the table name in the $_name property. Any schema specified with the $_name property takes precedence over a schema specified with the $_schema property. In some RDBMS brands, the term for schema is "database" or "tablespace," but it is used similarly.

Example 15.78. Declaring a table class with schema

```
// First alternative:
class Bugs extends Zend_Db_Table_Abstract
{
    protected $_schema = 'bug_db';
    protected $_name   = 'bugs';
}

// Second alternative:
class Bugs extends Zend_Db_Table_Abstract
{
    protected $_name = 'bug_db.bugs';
}

// If schemas are specified in both $_name and $_schema, the one
// specified in $_name takes precedence:

class Bugs extends Zend_Db_Table_Abstract
{
    protected $_name   = 'bug_db.bugs';
    protected $_schema = 'ignored';
}
```

The schema and table names may also be specified via constructor configuration directives, which override any default values specified with the $_name and $_schema properties. A schema specification given with the name directive overrides any value provided with the schema option.

Example 15.79. Declaring table and schema names upon instantiation

```
class Bugs extends Zend_Db_Table_Abstract
{

}
```

```
// First alternative:

$tableBugs = new Bugs(array('name' => 'bugs', 'schema' => 'bug_db'));

// Second alternative:

$tableBugs = new Bugs(array('name' => 'bug_db.bugs'));

// If schemas are specified in both 'name' and 'schema', the one
// specified in 'name' takes precedence:

$tableBugs = new Bugs(array('name' => 'bug_db.bugs',
                            'schema' => 'ignored'));
```

If you don't specify the schema name, it defaults to the schema to which your database adapter instance is connected.

Defining the Table Primary Key

Every table must have a primary key. You can declare the column for the primary key using the protected variable $_primary. This is either a string that names the single column for the primary key, or else it is an array of column names if your primary key is a compound key.

Example 15.80. Example of specifying the primary key

```
class Bugs extends Zend_Db_Table_Abstract
{
    protected $_name = 'bugs';
    protected $_primary = 'bug_id';
}
```

If you don't specify the primary key, Zend_Db_Table_Abstract tries to discover the primary key based on the information provided by the describeTable()´ method.

Note

Every table class must know which column(s) can be used to address rows uniquely. If no primary key column(s) are specified in the table class definition or the table constructor arguments, or discovered in the table metadata provided by describeTable(), then the table cannot be used with Zend_Db_Table.

Overriding Table Setup Methods

When you create an instance of a Table class, the constructor calls a set of protected methods that initialize metadata for the table. You can extend any of these methods to define metadata explicitly. Remember to call the method of the same name in the parent class at the end of your method.

Example 15.81. Example of overriding the _setupTableName() method

```
class Bugs extends Zend_Db_Table_Abstract
{
    protected function _setupTableName()
```

```
        {
            $this->_name = 'bugs';
            parent::_setupTableName();
        }
    }
```

The setup methods you can override are the following:

- _setupDatabaseAdapter() checks that an adapter has been provided; gets a default adapter from the registry if needed. By overriding this method, you can set a database adapter from some other source.

- _setupTableName() defaults the table name to the name of the class. By overriding this method, you can set the table name before this default behavior runs.

- _setupMetadata() sets the schema if the table name contains the pattern "schema.table"; calls describeTable() to get metadata information; defaults the $_cols array to the columns reported by describeTable(). By overriding this method, you can specify the columns.

- _setupPrimaryKey() defaults the primary key columns to those reported by describeTable(); checks that the primary key columns are included in the $_cols array. By overriding this method, you can specify the primary key columns.

Table initialization

If application-specific logic needs to be initialized when a Table class is constructed, you can select to move your tasks to the init() method, which is called after all Table metadata has been processed. This is recommended over the __construct method if you do not need to alter the metadata in any programmatic way.

Example 15.82. Example usage of init() method

```
class Bugs extends Zend_Db_Table_Abstract
{
    protected $_observer;
    public function init()
    {
        $this->_observer = new MyObserverClass();
    }
}
```

Creating an Instance of a Table

Before you use a Table class, create an instance using its constructor. The constructor's argument is an array of options. The most important option to a Table constructor is the database adapter instance, representing a live connection to an RDBMS. There are three ways of specifying the database adapter to a Table class, and these three ways are described below:

Specifying a Database Adapter

The first way to provide a database adapter to a Table class is by passing it as an object of type Zend_Db_Adapter_Abstract in the options array, identified by the key 'db'.

Example 15.83. Example of constructing a Table using an Adapter object

```
$db = Zend_Db::factory('PDO_MYSQL', $options);
$table = new Bugs(array('db' => $db));
```

Setting a Default Database Adapter

The second way to provide a database adapter to a Table class is by declaring an object of type Zend_Db_Adapter_Abstract to be a default database adapter for all subsequent instances of Tables in your application. You can do this with the static method Zend_Db_Table_Abstract::setDefaultAdapter(). The argument is an object of type Zend_Db_Adapter_Abstract.

Example 15.84. Example of constructing a Table using a the Default Adapter

```
$db = Zend_Db::factory('PDO_MYSQL', $options);
Zend_Db_Table_Abstract::setDefaultAdapter($db);
// Later...
$table = new Bugs();
```

It can be convenient to create the database adapter object in a central place of your application, such as the bootstrap, and then store it as the default adapter. This gives you a means to ensure that the adapter instance is the same throughout your application. However, setting a default adapter is limited to a single adapter instance.

Storing a Database Adapter in the Registry

The third way to provide a database adapter to a Table class is by passing a string in the options array, also identified by the 'db' key. The string is used as a key to the static Zend_Registry instance, where the entry at that key is an object of type Zend_Db_Adapter_Abstract.

Example 15.85. Example of constructing a Table using a Registry key

```
$db = Zend_Db::factory('PDO_MYSQL', $options);
Zend_Registry::set('my_db', $db);
// Later...
$table = new Bugs(array('db' => 'my_db'));
```

Like setting the default adapter, this gives you the means to ensure that the same adapter instance is used throughout your application. Using the registry is more flexible, because you can store more than one adapter instance. A given adapter instance is specific to a certain RDBMS brand and database instance. If your application needs access to multiple databases or even multiple database brands, then you need to use multiple adapters.

Inserting Rows to a Table

You can use the Table object to insert rows into the database table on which the Table object is based. Use the insert() method of your Table object. The argument is an associative array, mapping column names to values.

Example 15.86. Example of inserting to a Table

```
$table = new Bugs();
$data = array(
    'created_on'      => '2007-03-22',
    'bug_description' => 'Something wrong',
    'bug_status'      => 'NEW'
);
$table->insert($data);
```

By default, the values in your data array are inserted as literal values, using parameters. If you need them to be treated as SQL expressions, you must make sure they are distinct from plain strings. Use an object of type Zend_Db_Expr to do this.

Example 15.87. Example of inserting expressions to a Table

```
$table = new Bugs();
$data = array(
    'created_on'      => new Zend_Db_Expr('CURDATE()'),
    'bug_description' => 'Something wrong',
    'bug_status'      => 'NEW'
);
```

In the examples of inserting rows above, it is assumed that the table has an auto-incrementing primary key. This is the default behavior of Zend_Db_Table_Abstract, but there are other types of primary keys as well. The following sections describe how to support different types of primary keys.

Using a Table with an Auto-incrementing Key

An auto-incrementing primary key generates a unique integer value for you if you omit the primary key column from your SQL INSERT statement.

In Zend_Db_Table_Abstract, if you define the protected variable $_sequence to be the Boolean value true, then the class assumes that the table has an auto-incrementing primary key.

Example 15.88. Example of declaring a Table with auto-incrementing primary key

```
class Bugs extends Zend_Db_Table_Abstract
{
    protected $_name = 'bugs';
    // This is the default in the Zend_Db_Table_Abstract class;
    // you do not need to define this.
    protected $_sequence = true;
}
```

MySQL, Microsoft SQL Server, and SQLite are examples of RDBMS brands that support auto-incrementing primary keys.

PostgreSQL has a SERIAL notation that implicitly defines a sequence based on the table and column name, and uses the sequence to generate key values for new rows. IBM DB2 has an IDENTITY notation that works similarly. If you use either of these notations, treat your Zend_Db_Table class as having an auto-incrementing column with respect to declaring the $_sequence member as true.

Using a Table with a Sequence

A sequence is a database object that generates a unique value, which can be used as a primary key value in one or more tables of the database.

If you define $_sequence to be a string, then Zend_Db_Table_Abstract assumes the string to name a sequence object in the database. The sequence is invoked to generate a new value, and this value is used in the INSERT operation.

Example 15.89. Example of declaring a Table with a sequence

```
class Bugs extends Zend_Db_Table_Abstract
{
    protected $_name = 'bugs';
    protected $_sequence = 'bug_sequence';
}
```

Oracle, PostgreSQL, and IBM DB2 are examples of RDBMS brands that support sequence objects in the database.

PostgreSQL and IBM DB2 also have syntax that defines sequences implicitly and associated with columns. If you use this notation, treat the table as having an auto-incrementing key column. Define the sequence name as a string only in cases where you would invoke the sequence explicitly to get the next key value.

Using a Table with a Natural Key

Some tables have a natural key. This means that the key is not automatically generated by the table or by a sequence. You must specify the value for the primary key in this case.

If you define the $_sequence to be the Boolean value false, then Zend_Db_Table_Abstract assumes that the table has a natural primary key. You must provide values for the primary key columns in the array of data to the insert() method, or else this method throws a Zend_Db_Table_Exception.

Example 15.90. Example of declaring a Table with a natural key

```
class BugStatus extends Zend_Db_Table_Abstract
{
    protected $_name = 'bug_status';
    protected $_sequence = false;
}
```

Note

All RDBMS brands support tables with natural keys. Examples of tables that are often declared as having natural keys are lookup tables, intersection tables in many-to-many relationships, or most tables with compound primary keys.

Updating Rows in a Table

You can update rows in a database table using the `update` method of a Table class. This method takes two arguments: an associative array of columns to change and new values to assign to these columns; and an SQL expression that is used in a WHERE clause, as criteria for the rows to change in the UPDATE operation.

Example 15.91. Example of updating rows in a Table

```
$table = new Bugs();
$data = array(
    'updated_on'        => '2007-03-23',
    'bug_status'        => 'FIXED'
);
$where = $table->getAdapter()->quoteInto('bug_id = ?', 1234);
$table->update($data, $where);
```

Since the table update() method proxies to the database adapter update() method, the second argument can be an array of SQL expressions. The expressions are combined as Boolean terms using an AND operator.

Note

The values and identifiers in the SQL expression are not quoted for you. If you have values or identifiers that require quoting, you are responsible for doing this. Use the quote(), quoteInto(), and quoteIdentifier() methods of the database adapter.

Deleting Rows from a Table

You can delete rows from a database table using the delete() method. This method takes one argument, which is an SQL expression that is used in a WHERE clause, as criteria for the rows to delete.

Example 15.92. Example of deleting rows from a Table

```
$table = new Bugs();
$where = $table->getAdapter()->quoteInto('bug_id = ?', 1235);
$table->delete($where);
```

Since the table delete() method proxies to the database adapter delete() method, the argument can also be an array of SQL expressions. The expressions are combined as Boolean terms using an AND operator.

Note

The values and identifiers in the SQL expression are not quoted for you. If you have values or identifiers that require quoting, you are responsible for doing this. Use the quote(), quoteInto(), and quoteIdentifier() methods of the database adapter.

Finding Rows by Primary Key

You can query the database table for rows matching specific values in the primary key, using the find() method. The first argument of this method is either a single value or an array of values to match against the primary key of the table.

Example 15.93. Example of finding rows by primary key values

```
$table = new Bugs();
// Find a single row
// Returns a Rowset
$rows = $table->find(1234);
// Find multiple rows
// Also returns a Rowset
$rows = $table->find(array(1234, 5678));
```

If you specify a single value, the method returns at most one row, because a primary key cannot have duplicate values and there is at most one row in the database table matching the value you specify. If you specify multiple values in an array, the method returns at most as many rows as the number of distinct values you specify.

The find() method might return fewer rows than the number of values you specify for the primary key, if some of the values don't match any rows in the database table. The method even may return zero rows. Because the number of rows returned is variable, the find() method returns an object of type Zend_Db_Table_Rowset_Abstract.

If the primary key is a compound key, that is, it consists of multiple columns, you can specify the additional columns as additional arguments to the find() method. You must provide as many arguments as the number of columns in the table's primary key.

To find multiple rows from a table with a compound primary key, provide an array for each of the arguments. All of these arrays must have the same number of elements. The values in each array are formed into tuples in order; for example, the first element in all the array arguments define the first compound primary key value, then the second elements of all the arrays define the second compound primary key value, and so on.

Example 15.94. Example of finding rows by compound primary key values

The call to find() below to match multiple rows can match two rows in the database. The first row must have primary key value (1234, 'ABC'), and the second row must have primary key value (5678, 'DEF').

```
class BugsProducts extends Zend_Db_Table_Abstract
{
    protected $_name = 'bugs_products';
    protected $_primary = array('bug_id', 'product_id');
}
$table = new BugsProducts();
// Find a single row with a compound primary key
// Returns a Rowset
$rows = $table->find(1234, 'ABC');
// Find multiple rows with compound primary keys
// Also returns a Rowset
$rows = $table->find(array(1234, 5678), array('ABC', 'DEF'));
```

Querying for a Set of Rows

Select API

Warning

The API for fetch operations has been superseded to allow a Zend_Db_Table_Select object to modify the query. However, the deprecated usage of the fetchRow() and fetchAll() methods will continue to work without modification.

The following statements are all legal and functionally identical, however it is recommended to update your code to take advantage of the new usage where possible.

```
// Fetching a rowset
$rows = $table->fetchAll('bug_status = "NEW"', 'bug_id ASC', 10, 0);
$rows = $table->fetchAll($table->select()->where('bug_status = ?', 'NEW')
                                 ->order('bug_id ASC')
                                 ->limit(10, 0));
// Fetching a single row
$row = $table->fetchRow('bug_status = "NEW"', 'bug_id ASC');
$row = $table->fetchRow($table->select()->where('bug_status = ?', 'NEW')
                                 ->order('bug_id ASC'));
```

The Zend_Db_Table_Select object is an extension of the Zend_Db_Select object that applies specific restrictions to a query. The enhancements and restrictions are:

- You *can* elect to return a subset of columns within a fetchRow or fetchAll query. This can provide optimization benefits where returning a large set of results for all columns is not desirable.

- You *can* specify columns that evaluate expressions from within the selected table. However this will mean that the returned row or rowset will be readOnly and cannot be used for save() operations. A Zend_Db_Table_Row with readOnly status will throw an exception if a save() operation is attempted.

- You *can* allow JOIN clauses on a select to allow multi-table lookups.

- You *can not* specify columns from a JOINed tabled to be returned in a row/rowset. Doing so will trigger a PHP error. This was done to ensure the integrity of the Zend_Db_Table is retained. i.e. A Zend_Db_Table_Row should only reference columns derived from its parent table.

Example 15.95. Simple usage

```
$table = new Bugs();
$select = $table->select();
$select->where('bug_status = ?', 'NEW');
$rows = $table->fetchAll($select);
```

Fluent interfaces are implemented across the component, so this can be rewritten this in a more abbreviated form.

Example 15.96. Example of fluent interface

```
$table = new Bugs();
$rows =
    $table->fetchAll($table->select()->where('bug_status = ?', 'NEW'));
```

Fetching a rowset

You can query for a set of rows using any criteria other than the primary key values, using the fetchAll() method of the Table class. This method returns an object of type Zend_Db_Table_Rowset_Abstract.

Example 15.97. Example of finding rows by an expression

```
$table = new Bugs();
$select = $table->select()->where('bug_status = ?', 'NEW');
$rows = $table->fetchAll($select);
```

You may also pass sorting criteria in an ORDER BY clause, as well as count and offset integer values, used to make the query return a specific subset of rows. These values are used in a LIMIT clause, or in equivalent logic for RDBMS brands that do not support the LIMIT syntax.

Example 15.98. Example of finding rows by an expression

```
$table = new Bugs();
$order  = 'bug_id';
// Return the 21st through 30th rows
$count  = 10;
$offset = 20;
$select = $table->select()->where(array('bug_status = ?' => 'NEW'))
                          ->order($order)
                          ->limit($count, $offset);
$rows = $table->fetchAll($select);
```

All of the arguments above are optional. If you omit the ORDER clause, the result set includes rows from the table in an unpredictable order. If no LIMIT clause is set, you retrieve every row in the table that matches the WHERE clause.

Advanced usage

For more specific and optimized requests, you may wish to limit the number of columns returned in a row/rowset. This can be achieved by passing a FROM clause to the select object. The first argument in the FROM clause is identical to that of a Zend_Db_Select object with the addition of being able to pass an instance of Zend_Db_Table_Abstract and have it automatically determine the table name.

Example 15.99. Retrieving specific columns

```
$table = new Bugs();
$select = $table->select();
$select->from($table, array('bug_id', 'bug_description'))
       ->where('bug_status = ?', 'NEW');
$rows = $table->fetchAll($select);
```

Important

The rowset contains rows that are still 'valid' - they simply contain a subset of the columns of a table. If a save() method is called on a partial row then only the fields available will be modified.

You can also specify expressions within a FROM clause and have these returned as a readOnly row/rowset. In this example we will return a rows from the bugs table that show an aggregate of the number of new bugs reported by individuals. Note the GROUP clause. The 'count' column will be made available to the row for evaluation and can be accessed as if it were part of the schema.

Example 15.100. Retrieving expressions as columns

```
$table = new Bugs();
$select = $table->select();
$select->from($table,
              array('COUNT(reported_by) as `count`', 'reported_by'))
       ->where('bug_status = ?', 'NEW')
       ->group('reported_by');
$rows = $table->fetchAll($select);
```

You can also use a lookup as part of your query to further refine your fetch operations. In this example the accounts table is queried as part of a search for all new bugs reported by 'Bob'.

Example 15.101. Using a lookup table to refine the results of fetchAll()

```
$table = new Bugs();
$select = $table->select();
$select->where('bug_status = ?', 'NEW')
       ->join('accounts', 'accounts.account_name = bugs.reported_by')
       ->where('accounts.account_name = ?', 'Bob');
$rows = $table->fetchAll($select);
```

The Zend_Db_Table_Select is primarily used to constrain and validate so that it may enforce the criteria for a legal SELECT query. However there may be certain cases where you require the flexibility of the Zend_Db_Table_Row component and do not require a writable or deletable row. For this specific user case, it is possible to retrieve a row/rowset by passing a false value to setIntegrityCheck. The resulting row/rowset will be returned as a 'locked' row (meaning the save(), delete() and any field-setting methods will throw an exception).

Example 15.102. Removing the integrity check on Zend_Db_Table_Select to allow JOINed rows

```
$table = new Bugs();
$select = $table->select()->setIntegrityCheck(false);
$select->where('bug_status = ?', 'NEW')
        ->join('accounts',
                'accounts.account_name = bugs.reported_by',
                'account_name')
        ->where('accounts.account_name = ?', 'Bob');
$rows = $table->fetchAll($select);
```

Querying for a Single Row

You can query for a single row using criteria similar to that of the fetchAll() method.

Example 15.103. Example of finding a single row by an expression

```
$table = new Bugs();
$select  = $table->select()->where('bug_status = ?', 'NEW')
                            ->order('bug_id');
$row = $table->fetchRow($select);
```

This method returns an object of type Zend_Db_Table_Row_Abstract. If the search criteria you specified match no rows in the database table, then fetchRow() returns PHP's null value.

Retrieving Table Metadata Information

The Zend_Db_Table_Abstract class provides some information about its metadata. The info() method returns an array structure with information about the table, its columns and primary key, and other metadata.

Example 15.104. Example of getting the table name

```
$table = new Bugs();
$info = $table->info();
echo "The table name is " . $info['name'] . "\n";
```

The keys of the array returned by the info() method are described below:

- *name* => the name of the table.

- *cols* => an array, naming the column(s) of the table.

- *primary* => an array, naming the column(s) in the primary key.

- *metadata* => an associative array, mapping column names to information about the columns. This is the information returned by the describeTable() method.

- *rowClass* => the name of the concrete class used for Row objects returned by methods of this table instance. This defaults to `Zend_Db_Table_Row`.

- *rowsetClass* => the name of the concrete class used for Rowset objects returned by methods of this table instance. This defaults to `Zend_Db_Table_Rowset`.

- *referenceMap* => an associative array, with information about references from this table to any parent tables. See the section called "Defining Relationships".

- *dependentTables* => an array of class names of tables that reference this table. See the section called "Defining Relationships".

- *schema* => the name of the schema (or database or tablespace) for this table.

Caching Table Metadata

By default, `Zend_Db_Table_Abstract` queries the underlying database for table metadata whenever that data is needed to perform table operations. The table object fetches the table metadata from the database using the adapter's `describeTable()` method. Operations requiring this introspection include:

- `insert()`

- `find()`

- `info()`

In some circumstances, particularly when many table objects are instantiated against the same database table, querying the database for the table metadata for each instance may be undesirable from a performance standpoint. In such cases, users may benefit by caching the table metadata retrieved from the database.

There are two primary ways in which a user may take advantage of table metadata caching:

- *Call `Zend_Db_Table_Abstract::setDefaultMetadataCache()`* - This allows a developer to once set the default cache object to be used for all table classes.

- *Configure `Zend_Db_Table_Abstract::__construct()`* - This allows a developer to set the cache object to be used for a particular table class instance.

In both cases, the cache specification must be either null (i.e., no cache used) or an instance of `Zend_Cache_Core` . The methods may be used in conjunction when it is desirable to have both a default metadata cache and the ability to change the cache for individual table objects.

Example 15.105. Using a Default Metadata Cache for all Table Objects

The following code demonstrates how to set a default metadata cache to be used for all table objects:

```
<
// First, set up the Cache
$frontendOptions = array(
    'automatic_serialization' => true
    );
$backendOptions   = array(
    'cache_dir'                => 'cacheDir'
    );
$cache = Zend_Cache::factory('Core',
                    'File',
                    $frontendOptions,
                    $backendOptions);
// Next, set the cache to be used with all table objects
Zend_Db_Table_Abstract::setDefaultMetadataCache($cache);
```

```
// A table class is also needed
class Bugs extends Zend_Db_Table_Abstract
{
    // ...
}
// Each instance of Bugs now uses the default metadata cache
$bugs = new Bugs();
```

Example 15.106. Using a Metadata Cache for a Specific Table Object

The following code demonstrates how to set a metadata cache for a specific table object instance:

```
// First, set up the Cache
$frontendOptions = array(
    'automatic_serialization' => true
    );
$backendOptions  = array(
    'cache_dir'                 => 'cacheDir'
    );
$cache = Zend_Cache::factory('Core',
                             'File',
                             $frontendOptions,
                             $backendOptions);
// A table class is also needed
class Bugs extends Zend_Db_Table_Abstract
{
    // ...
}
// Configure an instance upon instantiation
$bugs = new Bugs(array('metadataCache' => $cache));
```

Automatic Serialization with the Cache Frontend

Since the information returned from the adapter's describeTable() method is an array, ensure that the `automatic_serialization` option is set to `true` for the Zend_Cache_Core frontend.

Though the above examples use Zend_Cache_Backend_File, developers may use whatever cache backend is appropriate for the situation. Please see Zend_Cache for more information.

Hardcoding Table Metadata

To take metadata caching a step further, you can also choose to hardcode metadata. In this particular case, however, any changes to the table schema will require a change in your code. As such, it is only recommended for those who are optimizing for production usage.

The metadata structure is as follows:

```
protected $_metadata = array(
    '<column_name>' => array(
        'SCHEMA_NAME'      => <string>,
        'TABLE_NAME'       => <string>,
        'COLUMN_NAME'      => <string>,
        'COLUMN_POSITION'  => <int>,
        'DATA_TYPE'        => <string>,
        'DEFAULT'          => NULL|<value>,
```

```
        'NULLABLE'           => <bool>,
        'LENGTH'             => <string - length>,
        'SCALE'              => NULL|<value>,
        'PRECISION'          => NULL|<value>,
        'UNSIGNED'           => NULL|<bool>,
        'PRIMARY'            => <bool>,
        'PRIMARY_POSITION'   => <int>,
        'IDENTITY'           => <bool>,
    ),
    // additional columns...
);
```

An easy way to get the appropriate values is to use the metadata cache, and then to deserialize values stored in the cache.

You can disable this optimization by turning of the `metadataCacheInClass` flag:

```
// At instantiation:
$bugs = new Bugs(array('metadataCacheInClass' => false));
// Or later:
$bugs->setMetadataCacheInClass(false);
```

The flag is enabled by default, which ensures that the $_metadata array is only populated once per instance.

Customizing and Extending a Table Class

Using Custom Row or Rowset Classes

By default, methods of the Table class return a Rowset in instances of the concrete class Zend_Db_Table_Rowset, and Rowsets contain a collection of instances of the concrete class Zend_Db_Table_Row You can specify an alternative class to use for either of these, but they must be classes that extend Zend_Db_Table_Rowset_Abstract and Zend_Db_Table_Row _Abstract, respectively.

You can specify Row and Rowset classes using the Table constructor's options array, in keys 'rowClass' and 'rowsetClass' respectively. Specify the names of the classes using strings.

Example 15.107. Example of specifying the Row and Rowset classes

```
class My_Row extends Zend_Db_Table_Row_Abstract
{
    ...
}
class My_Rowset extends Zend_Db_Table_Rowset_Abstract
{
    ...
}
$table = new Bugs(
    array(
        'rowClass'    => 'My_Row',
        'rowsetClass' => 'My_Rowset'
    )
);
$where = $table->getAdapter()->quoteInto('bug_status = ?', 'NEW')
// Returns an object of type My_Rowset,
// containing an array of objects of type My_Row.
$rows = $table->fetchAll($where);
```

You can change the classes by specifying them with the setRowClass() and setRowsetClass() methods. This applies to rows and rowsets created subsequently; it does not change the class of any row or rowset objects you have created previously.

Example 15.108. Example of changing the Row and Rowset classes

```
$table = new Bugs();
$where = $table->getAdapter()->quoteInto('bug_status = ?', 'NEW')
// Returns an object of type Zend_Db_Table_Rowset
// containing an array of objects of type Zend_Db_Table_Row.
$rowsStandard = $table->fetchAll($where);
$table->setRowClass('My_Row');
$table->setRowsetClass('My_Rowset');
// Returns an object of type My_Rowset,
// containing an array of objects of type My_Row.
$rowsCustom = $table->fetchAll($where);
// The $rowsStandard object still exists, and it is unchanged.
```

For more information on the Row and Rowset classes, see the section called "Zend_Db_Table_Row" and the section called "Zend_Db_Table_Rowset".

Defining Custom Logic for Insert, Update, and Delete

You can override the insert() and update() methods in your Table class. This gives you the opportunity to implement custom code that is executed before performing the database operation. Be sure to call the parent class method when you are done.

Example 15.109. Custom logic to manage timestamps

```
class Bugs extends Zend_Db_Table_Abstract
{
    protected $_name = 'bugs';
    public function insert(array $data)
    {
        // add a timestamp
        if (empty($data['created_on'])) {
            $data['created_on'] = time();
        }
        return parent::insert($data);
    }
    public function update(array $data, $where)
    {
        // add a timestamp
        if (empty($data['updated_on'])) {
            $data['updated_on'] = time();
        }
        return parent::update($data, $where);
    }
}
```

You can also override the delete() method.

Define Custom Search Methods in Zend_Db_Table

You can implement custom query methods in your Table class, if you have frequent need to do queries against this table with specific criteria. Most queries can be written using fetchAll(), but this requires that you duplicate code to form the query conditions if you need to run the query in several places in your application. Therefore it can be convenient to implement a method in the Table class to perform frequently-used queries against this table.

Example 15.110. Custom method to find bugs by status

```
class Bugs extends Zend_Db_Table_Abstract
{
    protected $_name = 'bugs';
    public function findByStatus($status)
    {
        $where = $this->getAdapter()->quoteInto('bug_status = ?', $status);
        return $this->fetchAll($where, 'bug_id');
    }
}
```

Define Inflection in Zend_Db_Table

Some people prefer that the table class name match a table name in the RDBMS by using a string transformation called *inflection*.

For example, if your table class name is "BugsProducts", it would match the physical table in the database called "bugs_products," if you omit the explicit declaration of the $_name class property. In this inflection mapping, the class name spelled in "CamelCase" format would be transformed to lower case, and words are separated with an underscore.

You can specify the database table name independently from the class name by declaring the table name with the $_name class property in each of your table classes.

Zend_Db_Table_Abstract performs no inflection to map the class name to the table name. If you omit the declaration of $_name in your table class, the class maps to a database table that matches the spelling of the class name exactly.

It is inappropriate to transform identifiers from the database, because this can lead to ambiguity or make some identifiers inaccessible. Using the SQL identifiers exactly as they appear in the database makes Zend_Db_Table_Abstract both simpler and more flexible.

If you prefer to use inflection, then you must implement the transformation yourself, by overriding the _setupTableName() method in your Table classes. One way to do this is to define an abstract class that extends Zend_Db_Table_Abstract, and then the rest of your tables extend your new abstract class.

Example 15.111. Example of an abstract table class that implements inflection

```
abstract class MyAbstractTable extends Zend_Db_Table_Abstract
{
    protected function _setupTableName()
    {
        if (!$this->_name) {
            $this->_name = myCustomInflector(get_class($this));
        }
        parent::_setupTableName();
```

```
    }
}
class BugsProducts extends MyAbstractTable
{
}
```

You are responsible for writing the functions to perform inflection transformation. Zend Framework does not provide such a function.

Zend_Db_Table_Row

Introduction

Zend_Db_Table_Row is a class that contains an individual row of a Zend_Db_Table object. When you run a query against a Table class, the result is returned in a set of Zend_Db_Table_Row objects. You can also use this object to create new rows and add them to the database table.

Zend_Db_Table_Row is an implementation of the Row Data Gateway [http://www.martinfowler.com/eaaCatalog/rowDataGateway.html] pattern.

Fetching a Row

Zend_Db_Table_Abstract provides methods find() and fetchAll(), which each return an object of type Zend_Db_Table_Rowset, and the method fetchRow(), which returns an object of type Zend_Db_Table_Row.

Example 15.112. Example of fetching a row

```
$bugs = new Bugs();
$row = $bugs->fetchRow($bugs->select()->where('bug_id = ?', 1));
```

A Zend_Db_Table_Rowset object contains a collection of Zend_Db_Table_Row objects. See the section called "Zend_Db_Table_Rowset".

Example 15.113. Example of reading a row in a rowset

```
$bugs = new Bugs();
$rowset = $bugs->fetchAll($bugs->select()->where('bug_status = ?', 1));
$row = $rowset->current();
```

Reading column values from a row

Zend_Db_Table_Row_Abstract provides accessor methods so you can reference columns in the row as object properties.

Example 15.114. Example of reading a column in a row

```
$bugs = new Bugs();
$row = $bugs->fetchRow($bugs->select()->where('bug_id = ?', 1));
// Echo the value of the bug_description column
echo $row->bug_description;
```

Note

Earlier versions of `Zend_Db_Table_Row` mapped these column accessors to the database column names using a string transformation called *inflection*.

Currently, `Zend_Db_Table_Row` does not implement inflection. Accessed property names need to match the spelling of the column names as they appear in your database.

Retrieving Row Data as an Array

You can access the row's data as an array using the `toArray()` method of the Row object. This returns an associative array of the column names to the column values.

Example 15.115. Example of using the toArray() method

```
$bugs = new Bugs();
$row = $bugs->fetchRow($bugs->select()->where('bug_id = ?', 1));
// Get the column/value associative array from the Row object
$rowArray = $row->toArray();
// Now use it as a normal array
foreach ($rowArray as $column => $value) {
    echo "Column: $column\n";
    echo "Value:  $value\n";
}
```

The array returned from `toArray()` is not updateable. You can modify values in the array as you can with any array, but you cannot save changes to this array to the database directly.

Fetching data from related tables

The `Zend_Db_Table_Row_Abstract` class provides methods for fetching rows and rowsets from related tables. See the section called "Zend_Db_Table Relationships" for more information on table relationships.

Writing rows to the database

Changing column values in a row

You can set individual column values using column accessors, similar to how the columns are read as object properties in the example above.

Using a column accessor to set a value changes the column value of the row object in your application, but it does not commit the change to the database yet. You can do that with the `save()` method.

Example 15.116. Example of changing a column in a row

```
$bugs = new Bugs();
$row = $bugs->fetchRow($bugs->select()->where('bug_id = ?', 1));
// Change the value of one or more columns
$row->bug_status = 'FIXED';
// UPDATE the row in the database with new values
$row->save();
```

Inserting a new row

You can create a new row for a given table with the `createRow()` method of the table class. You can access fields of this row with the object-oriented interface, but the row is not stored in the database until you call the `save()` method.

Example 15.117. Example of creating a new row for a table

```
$bugs = new Bugs();
$newRow = $bugs->createRow();
// Set column values as appropriate for your application
$newRow->bug_description = '...description...';
$newRow->bug_status = 'NEW';
// INSERT the new row to the database
$newRow->save();
```

The optional argument to the createRow() method is an associative array, with which you can populate fields of the new row.

Example 15.118. Example of populating a new row for a table

```
$data = array(
    'bug_description' => '...description...',
    'bug_status'      => 'NEW'
);
$bugs = new Bugs();
$newRow = $bugs->createRow($data);
// INSERT the new row to the database
$newRow->save();
```

> ## Note
>
> The `createRow()` method was called `fetchNew()` in earlier releases of Zend_Db_Table. You are encouraged to use the new method name, even though the old name continues to work for the sake of backward compatibility.

Changing values in multiple columns

Zend_Db_Table_Row_Abstract provides the `setFromArray()` method to enable you to set several columns in a single row at once, specified in an associative array that maps the column names to values. You may find this method convenient for setting values both for new rows and for rows you need to update.

Example 15.119. Example of using setFromArray() to set values in a new Row

```
$bugs = new Bugs();
$newRow = $bugs->createRow();
// Data are arranged in an associative array
$data = array(
    'bug_description' => '...description...',
```

```
    'bug_status'        => 'NEW'
);
// Set all the column values at once
$newRow->setFromArray($data);
// INSERT the new row to the database
$newRow->save();
```

Deleting a row

You can call the `delete()` method on a Row object. This deletes rows in the database matching the primary key in the Row object.

Example 15.120. Example of deleting a row

```
$bugs = new Bugs();
$row = $bugs->fetchRow('bug_id = 1');
// DELETE this row
$row->delete();
```

You do not have to call `save()` to apply the delete; it is executed against the database immediately.

Serializing and unserializing rows

It is often convenient to save the contents of a database row to be used later. *Serialization* is the name for the operation that converts an object into a form that is easy to save in offline storage (for example, a file). Objects of type `Zend_Db_Table_Row_Abstract` are serializable.

Serializing a Row

Simply use PHP's `serialize()` function to create a string containing a byte-stream representation of the Row object argument.

Example 15.121. Example of serializing a row

```
$bugs = new Bugs();
$row = $bugs->fetchRow('bug_id = 1');
// Convert object to serialized form
$serializedRow = serialize($row);
// Now you can write $serializedRow to a file, etc.
```

Unserializing Row Data

Use PHP's `unserialize()` function to restore a string containing a byte-stream representation of an object. The function returns the original object.

Note that the Row object returned is in a *disconnected* state. You can read the Row object and its properties, but you cannot change values in the Row or execute other methods that require a database connection (for example, queries against related tables).

Example 15.122. Example of unserializing a serialized row

```
$rowClone = unserialize($serializedRow);
// Now you can use object properties, but read-only
echo $rowClone->bug_description;
```

Why do Rows unserialize in a disconnected state?

A serialized object is a string that is readable to anyone who possesses it. It could be a security risk to store parameters such as database account and password in plain, unencrypted text in the serialized string. You would not want to store such data to a text file that is not protected, or send it in an email or other medium that is easily read by potential attackers. The reader of the serialized object should not be able to use it to gain access to your database without knowing valid credentials.

Reactivating a Row as Live Data

You can reactivate a disconnected Row, using the setTable() method. The argument to this method is a valid object of type Zend_Db_Table_Abstract, which you create. Creating a Table object requires a live connection to the database, so by reassociating the Table with the Row, the Row gains access to the database. Subsequently, you can change values in the Row object and save the changes to the database.

Example 15.123. Example of reactivating a row

```
$rowClone = unserialize($serializedRow);
$bugs = new Bugs();
// Reconnect the row to a table, and
// thus to a live database connection
$rowClone->setTable($bugs);
// Now you can make changes to the row and save them
$rowClone->bug_status = 'FIXED';
$rowClone->save();
```

Extending the Row class

Zend_Db_Table_Row is the default concrete class that extends Zend_Db_Table_Row_Abstract. You can define your own concrete class for instances of Row by extending Zend_Db_Table_Row_Abstract. To use your new Row class to store results of Table queries, specify the custom Row class by name either in the $_rowClass protected member of a Table class, or in the array argument of the constructor of a Table object.

Example 15.124. Specifying a custom Row class

```
class MyRow extends Zend_Db_Table_Row_Abstract
{
    // ...customizations
}
```

```
// Specify a custom Row to be used by default
// in all instances of a Table class.
class Products extends Zend_Db_Table_Abstract
{
    protected $_name = 'products';
    protected $_rowClass = 'MyRow';
}
// Or specify a custom Row to be used in one
// instance of a Table class.
$bugs = new Bugs(array('rowClass' => 'MyRow'));
```

Row initialization

If application-specific logic needs to be initialized when a row is constructed, you can select to move your tasks to the init() method, which is called after all row metadata has been processed. This is recommended over the __construct method if you do not need to alter the metadata in any programmatic way.

Example 15.125. Example usage of init() method

```
class MyApplicationRow extends Zend_Db_Table_Row_Abstract
{
    protected $_role;
    public function init()
    {
        $this->_role = new MyRoleClass();
    }
}
```

Defining Custom Logic for Insert, Update, and Delete in Zend_Db_Table_Row

The Row class calls protected methods _insert(), _update(), and _delete() before performing the corresponding operations INSERT, UPDATE, and DELETE. You can add logic to these methods in your custom Row subclass.

If you need to do custom logic in a specific table, and the custom logic must occur for every operation on that table, it may make more sense to implement your custom code in the insert(), update() and delete() methods of your Table class. However, sometimes it may be necessary to do custom logic in the Row class.

Below are some example cases where it might make sense to implement custom logic in a Row class instead of in the Table class:

Example 15.126. Example of custom logic in a Row class

The custom logic may not apply in all cases of operations on the respective Table. You can provide custom logic on demand by implementing it in a Row class and creating an instance of the Table class with that custom Row class specified. Otherwise, the Table uses the default Row class.

You need data operations on this table to record the operation to a Zend_Log object, but only if the application configuration has enabled this behavior.

```
class MyLoggingRow extends Zend_Db_Table_Row_Abstract
{
    protected function _insert()
    {
        $log = Zend_Registry::get('database_log');
        $log->info(Zend_Debug::dump($this->_data,
                                    "INSERT: $this->_tableClass",
                                    false)
                  );
    }
}
// $loggingEnabled is an example property that depends
// on your application configuration
if ($loggingEnabled) {
    $bugs = new Bugs(array('rowClass' => 'MyLoggingRow'));
} else {
    $bugs = new Bugs();
}
```

Example 15.127. Example of a Row class that logs insert data for multiple tables

The custom logic may be common to multiple tables. Instead of implementing the same custom logic in every one of your Table classes, you can implement the code for such actions in the definition of a Row class, and use this Row in each of your Table classes.

In this example, the logging code is identical in all table classes.

```
class MyLoggingRow extends Zend_Db_Table_Row_Abstract
{
    protected function _insert()
    {
        $log = Zend_Registry::get('database_log');
        $log->info(Zend_Debug::dump($this->_data,
                                    "INSERT: $this->_tableClass",
                                    false)
                  );
    }
}
class Bugs extends Zend_Db_Table_Abstract
{
    protected $_name = 'bugs';
    protected $_rowClass = 'MyLoggingRow';
}
class Products extends Zend_Db_Table_Abstract
{
    protected $_name = 'products';
    protected $_rowClass = 'MyLoggingRow';
}
```

Define Inflection in Zend_Db_Table_Row

Some people prefer that the table class name match a table name in the RDBMS by using a string transformation called *inflection*.

Zend_Db classes do not implement inflection by default. See the section called "Define Inflection in Zend_Db_Table" for an explanation of this policy.

If you prefer to use inflection, then you must implement the transformation yourself, by overriding the _transformColumn() method in a custom Row class, and using that custom Row class when you perform queries against your Table class.

Example 15.128. Example of defining an inflection transformation

This allows you to use an inflected version of the column name in the accessors. The Row class uses the _transformColumn() method to change the name you use to the native column name in the database table.

```
class MyInflectedRow extends Zend_Db_Table_Row_Abstract
{
    protected function _transformColumn($columnName)
    {
        $nativeColumnName = myCustomInflector($columnName);
        return $nativeColumnName;
    }
}
class Bugs extends Zend_Db_Table_Abstract
{
    protected $_name = 'bugs';
    protected $_rowClass = 'MyInflectedRow';
}
$bugs = new Bugs();
$row = $bugs->fetchNew();
// Use camelcase column names, and rely on the
// transformation function to change it into the
// native representation.
$row->bugDescription = 'New description';
```

You are responsible for writing the functions to perform inflection transformation. Zend Framework does not provide such a function.

Zend_Db_Table_Rowset

Introduction

When you run a query against a Table class using the find() or fetchAll() methods, the result is returned in an object of type Zend_Db_Table_Rowset_Abstract. A Rowset contains a collection of objects descending from Zend_Db_Table_Row_Abstract. You can iterate through the Rowset and access individual Row objects, reading or modifying data in the Rows.

Fetching a Rowset

Zend_Db_Table_Abstract provides methods find() and fetchAll(), each of which returns an object of type Zend_Db_Table_Rowset_Abstract.

Example 15.129. Example of fetching a rowset

```
$bugs    = new Bugs();
$rowset = $bugs->fetchAll("bug_status = 'NEW'");
```

Retrieving Rows from a Rowset

The Rowset itself is usually less interesting than the Rows that it contains. This section illustrates how to get the Rows that comprise the Rowset.

A legitimate query returns zero rows when no rows in the database match the query conditions. Therefore, a Rowset object might contain zero Row objects. Since Zend_Db_Table _Rowset_Abstract implements the Countable interface, you can use count() to determine the number of Rows in the Rowset.

Example 15.130. Counting the Rows in a Rowset

```
$rowset    = $bugs->fetchAll("bug_status = 'FIXED'");
$rowCount = count($rowset);
if ($rowCount > 0) {
    echo "found $rowCount rows";
} else {
    echo 'no rows matched the query';
}
```

Example 15.131. Reading a Single Row from a Rowset

The simplest way to access a Row from a Rowset is to use the current() method. This is particularly appropriate when the Rowset contains exactly one Row.

```
$bugs    = new Bugs();
$rowset = $bugs->fetchAll("bug_id = 1");
$row     = $rowset->current();
```

If the Rowset contains zero rows, current() returns PHP's null value.

Example 15.132. Iterating through a Rowset

Objects descending from Zend_Db_Table_Rowset_Abstract implement the Seekable Iterator interface, which means you can loop through them using the foreach construct. Each value you retrieve this way is a Zend_Db_Table_Row_Abstract object that corresponds to one record from the table.

```
$bugs = new Bugs();
// fetch all records from the table
$rowset = $bugs->fetchAll();
foreach ($rowset as $row) {
    // output 'Zend_Db_Table_Row' or similar
    echo get_class($row) . "\n";
    // read a column in the row
    $status = $row->bug_status;
    // modify a column in the current row
    $row->assigned_to = 'mmouse';
    // write the change to the database
    $row->save();
}
```

Example 15.133. Seeking to a known position into a Rowset

SeekableIterator allows you to seek to a position that you would like the iterator to jump to. Simply use the seek() method for that. Pass it an integer representing the number of the Row you would like your Rowset to point to next, don't forget that it starts with index 0. If the index is wrong, ie doesn't exist, an exception will be thrown. You should use count() to check the number of results before seeking to a position.

```
$bugs = new Bugs();
// fetch all records from the table
$rowset = $bugs->fetchAll();
// takes the iterator to the 9th element (zero is one element) :
$rowset->seek(8);
// retrieve it
$row9 = $rowset->current();
// and use it
$row9->assigned_to = 'mmouse';
$row9->save();
```

getRow() allows you to get a specific row in the Rowset, knowing its position; don't forget however that positions start with index zero. The first parameter for getRow() is an integer for the position asked. The second optional parameter is a boolean; it tells the Rowset iterator if it must seek to that position in the same time, or not (default is false). This method returns a Zend_Db_Table_Row object by default. If the position requested does not exist, an exception will be thrown. Here is an example :

```
$bugs = new Bugs();
// fetch all records from the table
$rowset = $bugs->fetchAll();
// retrieve the 9th element immediately:
$row9->getRow(8);
// and use it:
$row9->assigned_to = 'mmouse';
$row9->save();
```

After you have access to an individual Row object, you can manipulate the Row using methods described in the section called "Zend_Db_Table_Row".

Retrieving a Rowset as an Array

You can access all the data in the Rowset as an array using the toArray() method of the Rowset object. This returns an array containing one entry per Row. Each entry is an associative array having keys that correspond to column names and elements that correspond to the respective column values.

Example 15.134. Using toArray()

```
$bugs    = new Bugs();
$rowset = $bugs->fetchAll();
$rowsetArray = $rowset->toArray();
$rowCount = 1;
foreach ($rowsetArray as $rowArray) {
```

```
        echo "row #$rowCount:\n";
        foreach ($rowArray as $column => $value) {
            echo "\t$column => $value\n";
        }
        ++$rowCount;
        echo "\n";
}
```

The array returned from `toArray()` is not updateable. That is, you can modify values in the array as you can with any array, but changes to the array data are not propagated to the database.

Serializing and Unserializing a Rowset

Objects of type `Zend_Db_Table_Rowset_Abstract` are serializable. In a similar fashion to serializing an individual Row object, you can serialize a Rowset and unserialize it later.

Example 15.135. Serializing a Rowset

Simply use PHP's `serialize()` function to create a string containing a byte-stream representation of the Rowset object argument.

```
$bugs    = new Bugs();
$rowset = $bugs->fetchAll();
// Convert object to serialized form
$serializedRowset = serialize($rowset);
// Now you can write $serializedRowset to a file, etc.
```

Example 15.136. Unserializing a Serialized Rowset

Use PHP's `unserialize()` function to restore a string containing a byte-stream representation of an object. The function returns the original object.

Note that the Rowset object returned is in a *disconnected* state. You can iterate through the Rowset and read the Row objects and their properties, but you cannot change values in the Rows or execute other methods that require a database connection (for example, queries against related tables).

```
$rowsetDisconnected = unserialize($serializedRowset);
// Now you can use object methods and properties, but read-only
$row = $rowsetDisconnected->current();
echo $row->bug_description;
```

Why do Rowsets unserialize in a disconnected state?

A serialized object is a string that is readable to anyone who possesses it. It could be a security risk to store parameters such as database account and password in plain, unencrypted text in the serialized string. You would not want to store such data to a text file that is not protected, or send it in an email or other medium that is easily read by potential attackers. The reader of the serialized object should not be able to use it to gain access to your database without knowing valid credentials.

You can reactivate a disconnected Rowset using the `setTable()` method. The argument to this method is a valid object of type `Zend_Db_Table_Abstract`, which you create. Creating a Table object requires a live connection to the database, so by reassociating the Table with the Rowset, the Rowset gains access to the database. Subsequently, you can change values in the Row objects contained in the Rowset and save the changes to the database.

Example 15.137. Reactivating a Rowset as Live Data

```
$rowset = unserialize($serializedRowset);
$bugs = new Bugs();
// Reconnect the rowset to a table, and
// thus to a live database connection
$rowset->setTable($bugs);
$row = $rowset->current();
// Now you can make changes to the row and save them
$row->bug_status = 'FIXED';
$row->save();
```

Reactivating a Rowset with setTable() also reactivates all the Row objects contained in that Rowset.

Extending the Rowset class

You can use an alternative concrete class for instances of Rowsets by extending Zend_Db_Table_Rowset_Abstract. Specify the custom Rowset class by name either in the $_rowsetClass protected member of a Table class, or in the array argument of the constructor of a Table object.

Example 15.138. Specifying a custom Rowset class

```
class MyRowset extends Zend_Db_Table_Rowset_Abstract
{
    // ...customizations
}
// Specify a custom Rowset to be used by default
// in all instances of a Table class.
class Products extends Zend_Db_Table_Abstract
{
    protected $_name = 'products';
    protected $_rowsetClass = 'MyRowset';
}
// Or specify a custom Rowset to be used in one
// instance of a Table class.
$bugs = new Bugs(array('rowsetClass' => 'MyRowset'));
```

Typically, the standard Zend_Db_Rowset concrete class is sufficient for most usage. However, you might find it useful to add new logic to a Rowset, specific to a given Table. For example, a new method could calculate an aggregate over all the Rows in the Rowset.

Example 15.139. Example of Rowset class with a new method

```
class MyBugsRowset extends Zend_Db_Table_Rowset_Abstract
{
    /**
     * Find the Row in the current Rowset with the
     * greatest value in its 'updated_at' column.
     */
    public function getLatestUpdatedRow()
    {
        $max_updated_at = 0;
        $latestRow = null;
        foreach ($this as $row) {
            if ($row->updated_at > $max_updated_at) {
                $latestRow = $row;
            }
        }
        return $latestRow;
    }
}
class Bugs extends Zend_Db_Table_Abstract
{
    protected $_name = 'bugs';
    protected $_rowsetClass = 'MyBugsRowset';
}
```

Zend_Db_Table Relationships

Introduction

Tables have relationships to each other in a relational database. An entity in one table can be linked to one or more entities in another table by using referential integrity constraints defined in the database schema.

The Zend_Db_Table_Row class has methods for querying related rows in other tables.

Defining Relationships

Define classes for each of your tables, extending the abstract class Zend_Db_Table_Abstract, as described in the section called "Defining a Table Class". Also see the section called "Example Database" for a description of the example database for which the following example code is designed.

Below are the PHP class definitions for these tables:

```
class Accounts extends Zend_Db_Table_Abstract
{
    protected $_name            = 'accounts';
    protected $_dependentTables = array('Bugs');
}
class Products extends Zend_Db_Table_Abstract
{
    protected $_name            = 'products';
    protected $_dependentTables = array('BugsProducts');
}
class Bugs extends Zend_Db_Table_Abstract
```

```
{
    protected $_name            = 'bugs';
    protected $_dependentTables = array('BugsProducts');
    protected $_referenceMap    = array(
        'Reporter' => array(
            'columns'           => 'reported_by',
            'refTableClass'     => 'Accounts',
            'refColumns'        => 'account_name'
        ),
        'Engineer' => array(
            'columns'           => 'assigned_to',
            'refTableClass'     => 'Accounts',
            'refColumns'        => 'account_name'
        ),
        'Verifier' => array(
            'columns'           => array('verified_by'),
            'refTableClass'     => 'Accounts',
            'refColumns'        => array('account_name')
        )
    );
}
class BugsProducts extends Zend_Db_Table_Abstract
{
    protected $_name = 'bugs_products';
    protected $_referenceMap    = array(
        'Bug' => array(
            'columns'           => array('bug_id'),
            'refTableClass'     => 'Bugs',
            'refColumns'        => array('bug_id')
        ),
        'Product' => array(
            'columns'           => array('product_id'),
            'refTableClass'     => 'Products',
            'refColumns'        => array('product_id')
        )
    );
}
```

If you use Zend_Db_Table to emulate cascading UPDATE and DELETE operations, declare the $_dependentTables array in the class for the parent table. List the class name for each dependent table. Use the class name, not the physical name of the SQL table.

Note

Skip declaration of $_dependentTables if you use referential integrity constraints in the RDBMS server to implement cascading operations. See the section called "Cascading Write Operations" for more information.

Declare the $_referenceMap array in the class for each dependent table. This is an associative array of reference "rules". A reference rule identifies which table is the parent table in the relationship, and also lists which columns in the dependent table reference which columns in the parent table.

The rule key is a string used as an index to the $_referenceMap array. This rule key is used to identify each reference relationship. Choose a descriptive name for this rule key. It's best to use a string that can be part of a PHP method name, as you will see later.

In the example PHP code above, the rule keys in the Bugs table class are: 'Reporter', 'Engineer', 'Verifier', and 'Product'.

The value of each rule entry in the $_referenceMap array is also an associative array. The elements of this rule entry are described below:

- *columns* => A string or an array of strings naming the foreign key column name(s) in the dependent table.

  It's common for this to be a single column, but some tables have multi-column keys.

- *refTableClass* => The class name of the parent table. Use the class name, not the physical name of the SQL table.

  It's common for a dependent table to have only one reference to its parent table, but some tables have multiple references to the same parent table. In the example database, there is one reference from the bugs table to the products table, but three references from the bugs table to the accounts table. Put each reference in a separate entry in the $_referenceMap array.

- *refColumns* => A string or an array of strings naming the primary key column name(s) in the parent table.

  It's common for this to be a single column, but some tables have multi-column keys. If the reference uses a multi-column key, the order of columns in the 'columns' entry must match the order of columns in the 'refColumns' entry.

  It is optional to specify this element. If you don't specify the refColumns, the column(s) reported as the primary key columns of the parent table are used by default.

- *onDelete* => The rule for an action to execute if a row is deleted in the parent table. See the section called "Cascading Write Operations" for more information.

- *onUpdate* => The rule for an action to execute if values in primary key columns are updated in the parent table. See the section called "Cascading Write Operations" for more information.

Fetching a Dependent Rowset

If you have a Row object as the result of a query on a parent table, you can fetch rows from dependent tables that reference the current row. Use the method:

```
$row->findDependentRowset($table, [$rule]);
```

This method returns a Zend_Db_Table_Rowset_Abstract object, containing a set of rows from the dependent table $table that refer to the row identified by the $row object.

The first argument $table can be a string that specifies the dependent table by its class name. You can also specify the dependent table by using an object of that table class.

Example 15.140. Fetching a Dependent Rowset

This example shows getting a Row object from the table Accounts, and finding the Bugs reported by that account.

```
$accountsTable = new Accounts();
$accountsRowset = $accountsTable->find(1234);
$user1234 = $accountsRowset->current();
$bugsReportedByUser = $user1234->findDependentRowset('Bugs');
```

The second argument $rule is optional. It is a string that names the rule key in the $_referenceMap array of the dependent table class. If you don't specify a rule, the first rule in the array that references the parent table is used. If you need to use a rule other than the first, you need to specify the key.

In the example code above, the rule key is not specified, so the rule used by default is the first one that matches the parent table. This is the rule `'Reporter'`.

Example 15.141. Fetching a Dependent Rowset By a Specific Rule

This example shows getting a Row object from the table `Accounts`, and finding the `Bugs` assigned to be fixed by the user of that account. The rule key string that corresponds to this reference relationship in this example is `'Engineer'`.

```
$accountsTable = new Accounts();
$accountsRowset = $accountsTable->find(1234);
$user1234 = $accountsRowset->current();
$bugsAssignedToUser = $user1234->findDependentRowset('Bugs', 'Engineer');
```

You can also add criteria, ordering and limits to your relationships using the parent row's select object.

Example 15.142. Fetching a Dependent Rowset using a Zend_Db_Table_Select

This example shows getting a Row object from the table `Accounts`, and finding the `Bugs` assigned to be fixed by the user of that account, limited only to 3 rows and ordered by name.

```
$accountsTable = new Accounts();
$accountsRowset = $accountsTable->find(1234);
$user1234 = $accountsRowset->current();
$select = $accountsTable->select()->order('name ASC')
                                  ->limit(3);
$bugsAssignedToUser = $user1234->findDependentRowset('Bugs',
                                                     'Engineer',
                                                     $select);
```

Alternatively, you can query rows from a dependent table using a special mechanism called a "magic method". `Zend_Db_Table_Row_Abstract` invokes the method: `findDependentRowset('<TableClass>', '<Rule>')` if you invoke a method on the Row object matching either of the following patterns:

- `$row->find<TableClass>()`

- `$row->find<TableClass>By<Rule>()`

In the patterns above, `<TableClass>` and `<Rule>` are strings that correspond to the class name of the dependent table, and the dependent table's rule key that references the parent table.

Note

Some application frameworks, such as Ruby on Rails, use a mechanism called "inflection" to allow the spelling of identifiers to change depending on usage. For simplicity, `Zend_Db_Table_Row` does not provide any inflection mechanism. The table identity and the rule key named in the method call must match the spelling of the class and rule key exactly.

Example 15.143. Fetching Dependent Rowsets using the Magic Method

This example shows finding dependent Rowsets equivalent to those in the previous examples. In this case, the application uses the magic method invocation instead of specifying the table and rule as strings.

```
$accountsTable = new Accounts();
$accountsRowset = $accountsTable->find(1234);
$user1234 = $accountsRowset->current();
// Use the default reference rule
$bugsReportedBy = $user1234->findBugs();
// Specify the reference rule
$bugsAssignedTo = $user1234->findBugsByEngineer();
```

Fetching a Parent Row

If you have a Row object as the result of a query on a dependent table, you can fetch the row in the parent to which the dependent row refers. Use the method:

```
$row->findParentRow($table, [$rule]);
```

There always should be exactly one row in the parent table referenced by a dependent row, therefore this method returns a Row object, not a Rowset object.

The first argument $table can be a string that specifies the parent table by its class name. You can also specify the parent table by using an object of that table class.

Example 15.144. Fetching the Parent Row

This example shows getting a Row object from the table Bugs (for example one of those bugs with status 'NEW'), and finding the row in the Accounts table for the user who reported the bug.

```
$bugsTable = new Bugs();
$bugsRowset = $bugsTable->fetchAll(array('bug_status = ?' => 'NEW'));
$bug1 = $bugsRowset->current();
$reporter = $bug1->findParentRow('Accounts');
```

The second argument $rule is optional. It is a string that names the rule key in the $_referenceMap array of the dependent table class. If you don't specify a rule, the first rule in the array that references the parent table is used. If you need to use a rule other than the first, you need to specify the key.

In the example above, the rule key is not specified, so the rule used by default is the first one that matches the parent table. This is the rule 'Reporter'.

Example 15.145. Fetching a Parent Row By a Specific Rule

This example shows getting a Row object from the table Bugs, and finding the account for the engineer assigned to fix that bug. The rule key string that corresponds to this reference relationship in this example is 'Engineer'.

```
$bugsTable = new Bugs();
```

```
$bugsRowset = $bugsTable->fetchAll(array('bug_status = ?', 'NEW'));
$bug1 = $bugsRowset->current();
$engineer = $bug1->findParentRow('Accounts', 'Engineer');
```

Alternatively, you can query rows from a parent table using a "magic method". Zend_Db_Table_Row_Abstract invokes the method: findParentRow('<TableClass>', '<Rule>') if you invoke a method on the Row object matching either of the following patterns:

- $row->findParent<TableClass>([Zend_Db_Table_Select $select])

- $row->findParent<TableClass>By<Rule>([Zend_Db_Table_Select $select])

In the patterns above, <TableClass> and <Rule> are strings that correspond to the class name of the parent table, and the dependent table's rule key that references the parent table.

Note

The table identity and the rule key named in the method call must match the spelling of the class and rule key exactly.

Example 15.146. Fetching the Parent Row using the Magic Method

This example shows finding parent Rows equivalent to those in the previous examples. In this case, the application uses the magic method invocation instead of specifying the table and rule as strings.

```
$bugsTable = new Bugs();
$bugsRowset = $bugsTable->fetchAll(array('bug_status = ?', 'NEW'));
$bug1 = $bugsRowset->current();
// Use the default reference rule
$reporter = $bug1->findParentAccounts();
// Specify the reference rule
$engineer = $bug1->findParentAccountsByEngineer();
```

Fetching a Rowset via a Many-to-many Relationship

If you have a Row object as the result of a query on one table in a many-to-many relationship (for purposes of the example, call this the "origin" table), you can fetch corresponding rows in the other table (call this the "destination" table) via an intersection table. Use the method:

```
$row->findManyToManyRowset($table,
                           $intersectionTable,
                           [$rule1,
                               [$rule2,
                                   [Zend_Db_Table_Select $select]
                               ]
                           ]);
```

This method returns a Zend_Db_Table_Rowset_Abstract containing rows from the table $table, satisfying the many-to-many relationship. The current Row object $row from the origin table is used to find rows in the intersection table, and that is joined to the destination table.

The first argument $table can be a string that specifies the destination table in the many-to-many relationship by its class name. You can also specify the destination table by using an object of that table class.

The second argument $intersectionTable can be a string that specifies the intersection table between the two tables in the the many-to-many relationship by its class name. You can also specify the intersection table by using an object of that table class.

Example 15.147. Fetching a Rowset with the Many-to-many Method

This example shows getting a Row object from from the origin table Bugs, and finding rows from the destination table Products, representing products related to that bug.

```
$bugsTable = new Bugs();
$bugsRowset = $bugsTable->find(1234);
$bug1234 = $bugsRowset->current();
$productsRowset = $bug1234->findManyToManyRowset('Products',
                                                 'BugsProducts');
```

The third and fourth arguments $rule1 and $rule2 are optional. These are strings that name the rule keys in the $_referenceMap array of the intersection table.

The $rule1 key names the rule for the relationship from the intersection table to the origin table. In this example, this is the relationship from BugsProducts to Bugs.

The $rule2 key names the rule for the relationship from the intersection table to the destination table. In this example, this is the relationship from Bugs to Products.

Similarly to the methods for finding parent and dependent rows, if you don't specify a rule, the method uses the first rule in the $_referenceMap array that matches the tables in the relationship. If you need to use a rule other than the first, you need to specify the key.

In the example code above, the rule key is not specified, so the rules used by default are the first ones that match. In this case, $rule1 is 'Reporter' and $rule2 is 'Product'.

Example 15.148. Fetching a Rowset with the Many-to-many Method By a Specific Rule

This example shows geting a Row object from from the origin table Bugs, and finding rows from the destination table Products, representing products related to that bug.

```
$bugsTable = new Bugs();
$bugsRowset = $bugsTable->find(1234);
$bug1234 = $bugsRowset->current();
$productsRowset = $bug1234->findManyToManyRowset('Products',
                                                 'BugsProducts',
                                                 'Bug');
```

Alternatively, you can query rows from the destination table in a many-to-many relationship using a "magic method." Zend_Db_Table_Row_Abstract invokes the method: findManyToMany Rowset('<TableClass>', '<IntersectionTableClass>', '<Rule1>', '<Rule2>') if you invoke a method matching any of the following patterns:

- $row->find<TableClass>Via<IntersectionTableClass>
  ([Zend_Db_Table_Select $select])

- $row->find<TableClass>Via<IntersectionTableClass>By<Rule1>
  ([Zend_Db_Table_Select $select])

- `$row->find<TableClass>Via<IntersectionTableClass>By<Rule1>And<Rule2>
  ([Zend_Db_Table_Select $select])`

In the patterns above, `<TableClass>` and `<IntersectionTableClass>` are strings that correspond to the class names of the destination table and the intersection table, respectively. `<Rule1>` and `<Rule2>` are strings that correspond to the rule keys in the intersection table that reference the origin table and the destination table, respectively.

Note

The table identities and the rule keys named in the method call must match the spelling of the class and rule key exactly.

Example 15.149. Fetching Rowsets using the Magic Many-to-many Method

This example shows finding rows in the destination table of a many-to-many relationship representing products related to a given bug.

```
$bugsTable = new Bugs();
$bugsRowset = $bugsTable->find(1234);
$bug1234 = $bugsRowset->current();
// Use the default reference rule
$products = $bug1234->findProductsViaBugsProducts();
// Specify the reference rule
$products = $bug1234->findProductsViaBugsProductsByBug();
```

Cascading Write Operations

Declare DRI in the database:

Declaring cascading operations in Zend_Db_Table is intended *only* for RDBMS brands that do not support declarative referential integrity (DRI).

For example, if you use MySQL's MyISAM storage engine, or SQLite, these solutions do not support DRI. You may find it helpful to declare the cascading operations with Zend_Db_Table.

If your RDBMS implements DRI and the ON DELETE and ON UPDATE clauses, you should declare these clauses in your database schema, instead of using the cascading feature in Zend_Db_Table. Declaring cascading DRI rules in the RDBMS is better for database performance, consistency, and integrity.

Most importantly, do not declare cascading operations both in the RDBMS and in your Zend_Db_Table class.

You can declare cascading operations to execute against a dependent table when you apply an UPDATE or a DELETE to a row in a parent table.

Example 15.150. Example of a Cascading Delete

This example shows deleting a row in the Products table, which is configured to automatically delete dependent rows in the Bugs table.

```
$productsTable = new Products();
```

```
$productsRowset = $productsTable->find(1234);
$product1234 = $productsRowset->current();
$product1234->delete();
// Automatically cascades to Bugs table
// and deletes dependent rows.
```

Similarly, if you use UPDATE to change the value of a primary key in a parent table, you may want the value in foreign keys of dependent tables to be updated automatically to match the new value, so that such references are kept up to date.

It's usually not necessary to update the value of a primary key that was generated by a sequence or other mechanism. But if you use a *natural key* that may change value occasionally, it is more likely that you need to apply cascading updates to dependent tables.

To declare a cascading relationship in the Zend_Db_Table, edit the rules in the $_referenceMap. Set the associative array keys 'onDelete' and 'onUpdate' to the string 'cascade' (or the constant self::CASCADE). Before a row is deleted from the parent table, or its primary key values updated, any rows in the dependent table that refer to the parent's row are deleted or updated first.

Example 15.151. Example Declaration of Cascading Operations

In the example below, rows in the Bugs table are automatically deleted if the row in the Products table to which they refer is deleted. The 'onDelete' element of the reference map entry is set to self::CASCADE.

No cascading update is done in the example below if the primary key value in the parent class is changed. The 'onUpdate' element of the reference map entry is self::RESTRICT. You can get the same result by omitting the 'onUpdate' entry.

```
class BugsProducts extends Zend_Db_Table_Abstract
{
    ...
    protected $_referenceMap = array(
        'Product' => array(
            'columns'           => array('product_id'),
            'refTableClass'     => 'Products',
            'refColumns'        => array('product_id'),
            'onDelete'          => self::CASCADE,
            'onUpdate'          => self::RESTRICT
        ),
        ...
    );
}
```

Notes Regarding Cascading Operations

Cascading operations invoked by Zend_Db_Table are not atomic.

This means that if your database implements and enforces referential integrity constraints, a cascading UPDATE executed by a Zend_Db_Table class conflicts with the constraint, and results in a referential integrity violation. You can use cascading UPDATE in Zend_Db_Table *only* if your database does not enforce that referential integrity constraint.

Cascading DELETE suffers less from the problem of referential integrity violations. You can delete dependent rows as a non-atomic action before deleting the parent row that they reference.

However, for both UPDATE and DELETE, changing the database in a non-atomic way also creates the risk that another database user can see the data in an inconsistent state. For example, if you delete a row and all its dependent rows, there is a small chance that another database client program can query the database after you have deleted the dependent rows, but before you delete the parent row. That client program may see the parent row with no dependent rows, and assume this is the intended state of the data. There is no way for that client to know that its query read the database in the middle of a change.

The issue of non-atomic change can be mitigated by using transactions to isolate your change. But some RDBMS brands don't support transactions, or allow clients to read "dirty" changes that have not been committed yet.

Cascading operations in Zend_Db_Table *are invoked only by* Zend_Db_Table.

Cascading deletes and updates defined in your Zend_Db_Table classes are applied if you execute the save() or delete() methods on the Row class. However, if you update or delete data using another interface, such as a query tool or another application, the cascading operations are not applied. Even when using update() and delete() methods in the Zend_Db_Adapter class, cascading operations defined in your Zend_Db_Table classes are not executed.

No Cascading INSERT.

There is no support for a cascading INSERT. You must insert a row to a parent table in one operation, and insert row(s) to a dependent table in a separate operation.

Chapter 16. Zend_Debug

Dumping Variables

The static method `Zend_Debug::dump()` prints or returns information about an expression. This simple technique of debugging is common, because it is easy to use in an ad hoc fashion, and requires no initialization, special tools, or debugging environment.

Example 16.1. Example of dump() method

```
Zend_Debug::dump($var, $label=null, $echo=true);
```

The `$var` argument specifies the expression or variable about which the `Zend_Debug::dump()` method outputs information.

The `$label` argument is a string to be prepended to the output of `Zend_Debug::dump()`. It may be useful, for example, to use labels if you are dumping information about multiple variables on a given screen.

The boolean `$echo` argument specifies whether the output of `Zend_Debug::dump()` is echoed or not. If `true`, the output is echoed. Regardless of the value of the `$echo` argument, the return value of this method contains the output.

It may be helpful to understand that internally, `Zend_Debug::dump()` method wraps the PHP function `var_dump()` [http://php.net/var_dump]. If the output stream is detected as a web presentation, the output of `var_dump()` is escaped using `htmlspecialchars()` [http://php.net/htmlspecialchars] and wrapped with (X)HTML `<pre>` tags.

Debugging with Zend_Log

Using `Zend_Debug::dump()` is best for ad hoc debugging during software development. You can add code to dump a variable and then remove the code very quickly.

Also consider the Zend_Log component when writing more permanent debugging code. For example, you can use the DEBUG log level and the Stream log writer, to output the string returned by `Zend_Debug::dump()`.

Chapter 17. Zend_Dojo

Introduction

Zend Framework ships Dojo Toolkit [http://dojotoolkit.org] to support out-of-the-box rich internet application development. Integration points with Dojo include:

- JSON-RPC support

- dojo.data compatibility

- View helper to help setup the Dojo environment

- Dijit-specific `Zend_View` helpers

- Dijit-specific `Zend_Form` elements and decorators

The Dojo distribution itself may be found in the `externals/dojo/` directory of the Zend Framework distribution. This is a source distribution, which includes Dojo's full javascript source, unit tests, and build tools. You can symlink this into your javascript directory, copy it, or use the build tool to create your own custom build to include in your project. Alternatively, you can use one of the Content Delivery Networks that offer Dojo (ZF supports both the official AOL CDN as well as the Google CDN).

Zend_Dojo_Data: dojo.data Envelopes

Dojo provides data abstraction for data-enabled widgets via its dojo.data component. This component provides the ability to attach a data store, provide some metadata regarding the identity field and optionally a label field, and an API for querying, sorting, and retrieving records and sets of records from the datastore.

dojo.data is often used with XmlHttpRequest to pull dynamic data from the server. The primary mechanism for this is to extend the QueryReadStore to point at a URL and specify the query information. The server side then returns data in the following JSON format:

```
{
    identifier: '<name>',
    <label: '<label>',>
    items: [
        { name: '...', label: '...', someKey: '...' },
        ...
    ]
}
```

`Zend_Dojo_Data` provides a simple interface for building such structures programmatically, interacting with them, and serializing them to an array or JSON.

Zend_Dojo_Data Usage

At its simplest, dojo.data requires that you provide the name of the identifier field in each item, and a set of items (data). You can either pass these in via the constructor, or via mutators:

Example 17.1. Zend_Dojo_Data initialization via constructor

```
$data = new Zend_Dojo_Data('id', $items);
```

Example 17.2. Zend_Dojo_Data initialization via mutators

```
$data = new Zend_Dojo_Data();
$data->setIdentifier('id')
    ->addItems($items);
```

You can also add a single item at a time, or append items, using addItem() and addItems().

Example 17.3. Appending data to Zend_Dojo_Data

```
$data = new Zend_Dojo_Data($identifier, $items);
$data->addItem($someItem);
$data->addItems($someMoreItems);
```

Always use an identifier!

Every dojo.data data store requires that the identifier column be provided as metadata, including Zend_Dojo_Data. In fact, if you attempt to add items without an identifier, it will raise an exception.

Individual items may be one of the following:

• Associative arrays

• Objects implementing a toArray() method

• Any other objects (will serialize via get_object_vars())

You can attach collections of the above items via addItems() or setItems() (overwrites all previously set items); when doing so, you may pass a single argument:

• Arrays

• Objects implementing the Traversable interface ,which includes the interfaces Iterator and ArrayAccess.

If you want to specify a field that will act as a label for the item, call setLabel():

Example 17.4. Specifying a label field in Zend_Dojo_Data

```
$data->setLabel('name');
```

Finally, you can also load a Zend_Dojo_Data item from a dojo.data JSON array, using the fromJson() method.

Example 17.5. Populating Zend_Dojo_Data from JSON

```
$data->fromJson($json);
```

Adding metadata to your containers

Some Dojo components require additional metadata along with the dojo.data payload. As an example, dojox.grid.Grid can pull data dynamically from a dojox.data.QueryReadStore. For pagination to work correctly, each return payload should contain a numRows key with the total number of rows that could be returned by the query. With this data, the grid knows when to continue making small requests to the server for subsets of data and when to stop making more requests (i.e., it has reached the last page of data). This technique is useful for serving large sets of data in your grids without loading the entire set at once.

Zend_Dojo_Data allows assigning metadata properties as to the object. The following illustrates usage:

```
// Set the "numRows" to 100
$data->setMetadata('numRows', 100);
// Set several items at once:
$data->setMetadata(array(
    'numRows' => 100,
    'sort'    => 'name',
));
// Inspect a single metadata value:
$numRows = $data->getMetadata('numRows');
// Inspect all metadata:
$metadata = $data->getMetadata();
// Remove a metadata item:
$data->clearMetadata('numRows');
// Remove all metadata:
$data->clearMetadata();
```

Advanced Use Cases

Besides acting as a serializable data container, Zend_Dojo_Data also provides the ability to manipulate and traverse the data in a variety of ways.

Zend_Dojo_Data implements the interfaces ArrayAccess, Iterator, and Countable. You can therefore use the data collection almost as if it were an array.

All items are referenced by the identifier field. Since identifiers must be unique, you can use the values of this field to pull individual records. There are two ways to do this: with the getItem() method, or via array notation.

```
// Using getItem():
$item = $data->getItem('foo');
// Or use array notation:
$item = $data['foo'];
```

If you know the identifier, you can use it to retrieve an item, update it, delete it, create it, or test for it:

```
// Update or create an item:
$data['foo'] = array('title' => 'Foo', 'email' => 'foo@foo.com');
```

```
// Delete an item:
unset($data['foo']);
// Test for an item:
if (isset($data[foo])) {
}
```

You can loop over all items as well. Internally, all items are stored as arrays.

```
foreach ($data as $item) {
    echo $item['title'] . ': ' . $item['description'] . "\n";
}
```

Or even count to see how many items you have:

```
echo count($data), " items found!";
```

Finally, as the class implements __toString(), you can also cast it to JSON simply by echoing it or casting to string:

```
echo $data; // echo as JSON string
$json = (string) $data; // cast to string == cast to JSON
```

Available Methods

Besides the methods necessary for implementing the interfaces listed above, the following methods are available.

- setItems($items): set multiple items at once, overwriting any items that were previously set in the object. $items should be an array or a Traversable object.

- setItem($item, $id = null): set an individual item, optionally passing an explicit identifier. Overwrites the item if it is already in the collection. Valid items include associative arrays, objects implementing toArray(), or any object with public properties.

- addItem($item, $id = null): add an individual item, optionally passing an explicit identifier. Will raise an exception if the item already exists in the collection. Valid items include associative arrays, objects implementing toArray(), or any object with public properties.

- addItems($items): add multiple items at once, appending them to any current items. Will raise an exception if any of the new items have an identifier matching an identifier already in the collection. $items should be an array or a Traversable object.

- getItems(): retrieve all items as an array of arrays.

- hasItem($id): determine whether an item with the given identifier exists in the collection.

- getItem($id): retrieve an item with the given identifier from the collection; the item returned will be an associative array. If no item matches, a null value is returned.

- removeItem($id): remove an item with the given identifier from the collection.

- clearItems(): remove all items from the collection.

- setIdentifier($identifier): set the name of the field that represents the unique identifier for each item in the collection.

- getIdentifier(): retrieve the name of the identifier field.

- setLabel($label): set the name of a field to be used as a display label for an item.

- `getLabel()`: retrieve the label field name.

- `toArray()`: cast the object to an array. At a minimum, the array will contain the keys 'identifier', 'items', and 'label' if a label field has been set in the object.

- `toJson()`: cast the object to a JSON representation.

Dojo View Helpers

Zend Framework provides the following Dojo-specific view helpers:

- *dojo():* setup the Dojo environment for your page, including dojo configuration values, custom module paths, module require statements, theme stylesheets, CDN usage, and more.

Example 17.6. Using Dojo View Helpers

To use Dojo view helpers, you will need to tell your view object where to find them. You can do this by calling `addHelperPath()`:

```
$view->addHelperPath('Zend/Dojo/View/Helper/', 'Zend_Dojo_View_Helper');
```

Alternately, you can use `Zend_Dojo`'s `enableView()` method to do the work for you:

```
Zend_Dojo::enableView($view);
```

dojo() View Helper

The `dojo()` view helper is intended to simplify setting up the Dojo environment, including the following responsibilities:

- Specifying either a CDN or a local path to a Dojo install.

- Specifying paths to custom Dojo modules.

- Specifying dojo.require statements.

- Specifying dijit stylesheet themes to use.

- Specifying dojo.addOnLoad() events.

The `dojo()` view helper implementation is an example of a placeholder implementation. The data set in it persists between view objects and may be directly echoed from your layout script.

Example 17.7. dojo() View Helper Usage Example

For this example, let's assume the developer will be using Dojo from a local path, will require several dijits, and will be utilizing the Tundra dijit theme.

On many pages, the developer may not utilize Dojo at all. So, we will first focus on a view script where Dojo is needed and then on the layout script, where we will setup some of the Dojo environment and then render it.

First, we need to tell our view object to use the Dojo view helper paths. This can be done in your bootstrap or an early-running plugin; simply grab your view object and execute the following:

```
$view->addHelperPath('Zend/Dojo/View/Helper/', 'Zend_Dojo_View_Helper');
```

Next, the view script. In this case, we're going to specify that we will be using a FilteringSelect -- which will consume a custom store based on QueryReadStore, which we'll call 'PairedStore' and store in our 'custom' module.

```
<?php // setup data store for FilteringSelect ?>
<div dojoType="custom.PairedStore" jsId="stateStore"
    url="/data/autocomplete/type/state/format/ajax"
    requestMethod="get"></div>
<?php // Input element: ?>
State: <input id="state" dojoType="dijit.form.FilteringSelect"
    store="stateStore" pageSize="5" />
<?php // setup required dojo elements:
$this->dojo()->enable()
            ->setDjConfigOption('parseOnLoad', true)
            ->registerModulePath('custom', '../custom/')
            ->requireModule('dijit.form.FilteringSelect')
            ->requireModule('custom.PairedStore'); ?>
```

In our layout script, we'll then check to see if Dojo is enabled, and, if so, we'll do some more general configuration and assemble it:

```
<?php echo $this->doctype() ?>
<html>
<head>
    <?php echo $this->headTitle() ?>
    <?php echo $this->headMeta() ?>
    <?php echo $this->headLink() ?>
    <?php echo $this->headStyle() ?>
<?php if ($this->dojo()->isEnabled()){
    $this->dojo()->setLocalPath('/js/dojo/dojo.js')
                ->addStyleSheetModule('dijit.themes.tundra');
    echo $this->dojo();
    }
?>
    <?php echo $this->headScript() ?>
</head>
<body class="tundra">
    <?php echo $this->layout()->content ?>
    <?php echo $this->inlineScript() ?>
</body>
</html>
```

At this point, you only need to ensure that your files are in the correct locations and that you've created the end point action for your FilteringSelect!

Programmatic and Declarative Usage of Dojo

Dojo allows both *declarative* and *programmatic* usage of many of its features. *Declarative* usage uses standard HTML elements with non-standard attributes that are parsed when the page is loaded. While this is a powerful and simple syntax to utilize, for many developers this can cause issues with page validation.

Programmatic usage allows the developer to decorate existing elements by pulling them by ID or CSS selectors and passing them to the appropriate object constructors in Dojo. Because no non-standard HTML attributes are used, pages continue to validate.

In practice, both use cases allow for graceful degradation when javascript is disabled or the various Dojo script resources are unreachable. To promote standards and document validation, Zend Framework uses programmatic usage by default; the various view helpers will generate javascript and push it to the dojo() view helper for inclusion when rendered.

Developers using this technique may also wish to explore the option of writing their own programmatic decoration of the page. One benefit would be the ability to specify handlers for dijit events.

To allow this, as well as the ability to use declarative syntax, there are a number of static methods available to set this behavior globally.

Example 17.8. Specifying Declarative and Programmatic Dojo Usage

To specify declarative usage, simply call the static setUseDeclarative() method:

```
Zend_Dojo_View_Helper_Dojo::setUseDeclarative();
```

If you decide instead to use programmatic usage, call the static setUseProgrammatic() method:

```
Zend_Dojo_View_Helper_Dojo::setUseProgrammatic();
```

Finally, if you want to create your own programmatic rules, you should specify programmatic usage, but pass in the value '-1'; in this situation, no javascript for decorating any dijits used will be created.

```
Zend_Dojo_View_Helper_Dojo::setUseProgrammatic(-1);
```

Themes

Dojo allows the creation of themes for its dijits (widgets). You may select one by passing in a module path:

```
$view->dojo()->addStylesheetModule('dijit.themes.tundra');
```

The module path is discovered by using the character '.' as a directory separator and using the last value in the list as the name of the CSS file in that theme directory to use; in the example above, Dojo will look for the theme in 'dijit/themes/tundra/tundra.css'.

When using a theme, it is important to remember to pass the theme class to, at the least, a container surrounding any dijits you are using; the most common use case is to pass it in the body:

```
<body class="tundra">
```

Using Layers (Custom Builds)

By default, when you use a dojo.require statement, dojo will make a request back to the server to grab the appropriate javascript file. If you have many dijits in place, this results in many requests to the server -- which is not optimal.

Dojo's answer to this is to provide the ability to create *custom builds*. Builds do several things:

- Groups required files into *layers*; a layer lumps all required files into a single JS file. (Hence the name of this section.)

- "Interns" non-javascript files used by dijits (typically, template files). These are also grouped in the same JS file as the layer.

- Passes the file through ShrinkSafe, which strips whitespace and comments, as well as shortens variable names.

Some files can not be layered, but the build process will create a special release directory with the layer file and all other files. This allows you to have a slimmed-down distribution customized for your site or application needs.

To use a layer, the `dojo()` view helper has a `addLayer()` method for adding paths to required layers:

```
$view->dojo()->addLayer('/js/foo/foo.js');
```

For more information on creating custom builds, please refer to the Dojo build documentation [http://dojotoolkit.org/book/dojo-book-0-9/part-4-meta-dojo/package-system-and-custom-builds].

Methods Available

The `dojo()` view helper always returns an instance of the dojo placeholder container. That container object has the following methods available:

- `setView(Zend_View_Interface $view)`: set a view instance in the container.

- `enable()`: explicitly enable Dojo integration.

- `disable()`: disable Dojo integration.

- `isEnabled()`: determine whether or not Dojo integration is enabled.

- `requireModule($module)`: setup a `dojo.require` statement.

- `getModules()`: determine what modules have been required.

- `registerModulePath($module, $path)`: register a custom Dojo module path.

- `getModulePaths()`: get list of registered module paths.

- `addLayer($path)`: add a layer (custom build) path to use.

- `getLayers()`: get a list of all registered layer paths (custom builds).

- `removeLayer($path)`: remove the layer that matches $path from the list of registered layers (custom builds).

- `setCdnBase($url)`: set the base URL for a CDN; typically, one of the `Zend_Dojo::CDN_BASE_AOL` or `Zend_Dojo::CDN_BASE_GOOGLE`, but it only needs to be the URL string prior to the version number.

- `getCdnBase()`: retrieve the base CDN url to utilize.

- `setCdnVersion($version = null)`: set which version of Dojo to utilize from the CDN.

- `getCdnVersion()`: retrieve what version of Dojo from the CDN will be used.

- `setCdnDojoPath($path)`: set the relative path to the dojo.js or dojo.xd.js file on a CDN; typically, one of the `Zend_Dojo::CDN_DOJO_PATH_AOL` or `Zend_Dojo::CDN_DOJO_PATH_GOOGLE`, but it only needs to be the path string following the version number.

- `getCdnDojoPath()`: retrieve the last path segment of the CDN url pointing to the dojo.js file.

- `useCdn()`: tell the container to utilize the CDN; implicitly enables integration.

- `setLocalPath($path)`: tell the container the path to a local Dojo install (should be a path relative to the server, and contain the dojo.js file itself); implicitly enables integration.

- `getLocalPath()`: determine what local path to Dojo is being used.

- `useLocalPath()`: is the integration utilizing a Dojo local path?

- `setDjConfig(array $config)`: set dojo/dijit configuration values (expects assoc array).

- `setDjConfigOption($option, $value)`: set a single dojo/dijit configuration value.

- `getDjConfig()`: get all dojo/dijit configuration values.

- `getDjConfigOption($option, $default = null)`: get a single dojo/dijit configuration value.

- `addStylesheetModule($module)`: add a stylesheet based on a module theme.

- `getStylesheetModules()`: get stylesheets registered as module themes.

- `addStylesheet($path)`: add a local stylesheet for use with Dojo.

- `getStylesheets()`: get local Dojo stylesheets.

- `addOnLoad($spec, $function = null)`: add a lambda for dojo.onLoad to call. If one argument is passed, it is assumed to be either a function name or a javascript closure. If two arguments are passed, the first is assumed to be the name of an object instance variable and the second either a method name in that object or a closure to utilize with that object.

- `prependOnLoad($spec, $function = null)`: exactly like `addOnLoad()`, excepts prepends to beginning of onLoad stack.

- `getOnLoadActions()`: retrieve all dojo.onLoad actions registered with the container. This will be an array of arrays.

- `onLoadCaptureStart($obj = null)`: capture data to be used as a lambda for dojo.onLoad(). If $obj is provided, the captured JS code will be considered a closure to use with that Javascript object.

- `onLoadCaptureEnd($obj = null)`: finish capturing data for use with dojo.onLoad().

- `javascriptCaptureStart()`: capture arbitrary javascript to be included with Dojo JS (onLoad, require, etc. statements).

- `javascriptCaptureEnd()`: finish capturing javascript.

- `__toString()`: cast the container to a string; renders all HTML style and script elements.

Dijit-Specific View Helpers

From the Dojo manual: "Dijit is a widget system layered on top of dojo." Dijit includes a variety of layout and form widgets designed to provide accessibility features, localization, and standardized (and themeable) look-and-feel.

Zend Framework ships a variety of view helpers that allow you to render and utilize dijits within your view scripts. There are three basic types:

- *Layout Containers*: these are designed to be used within your view scripts or consumed by form decorators for forms, sub forms, and display groups. They wrap the various classes offerred in dijit.layout. Each dijit layout view helper expects the following arguments:

  - `$id`: the container name or DOM ID.

  - `$content`: the content to wrap in the layout container.

- $params (optional): dijit-specific parameters. Basically, any non-HTML attribute that can be used to configure the dijit layout container.

- $attribs (optional): any additional HTML attributes that should be used to render the container div. If the key 'id' is passed in this array, it will be used for the form element DOM id, and $id will be used for its name.

If you pass no arguments to a dijit layout view helper, the helper itself will be returned. This allows you to capture content, which is often an easier way to pass content to the layout container. Examples of this functionality will be shown later in this section.

- *Form Dijit*: the dijit.form.Form dijit, while not completely necessary for use with dijit form elements, will ensure that if an attempt is made to submit a form that does not validate against client-side validations, submission will be halted and validation error messages raised. The form dijit view helper expects the following arguments:

  - $id: the container name or DOM ID.

  - $attribs (optional): any additional HTML attributes that should be used to render the container div.

  - $content (optional): the content to wrap in the form. If none is passed, an empty string will be used.

  The argument order varies from the other dijits in order to keep compatibility with the standard form() view helper.

- *Form Elements*: these are designed to be consumed with Zend_Form, but can be used standalone within view scripts as well. Each dijit element view helper expects the following arguments:

  - $id: the element name or DOM ID.

  - $value (optional): the current value of the element.

  - $params (optional): dijit-specific parameters. Basically, any non-HTML attribute that can be used to configure a dijit.

  - $attribs (optional): any additional HTML attributes that should be used to render the dijit. If the key 'id' is passed in this array, it will be used for the form element DOM id, and $id will be used for its name.

  Some elements require more arguments; these will be noted with the individual element helper descriptions.

In order to utilize these view helpers, you need to register the path to the dojo view helpers with your view object.

Example 17.9. Registering the Dojo View Helper Prefix Path

```
$view->addHelperPath('Zend/Dojo/View/Helper', 'Zend_Dojo_View_Helper');
```

Dijit Layout Elements

The dijit.layout family of elements are for creating custom, predictable layouts for your site. For any questions on general usage, read more about them in the Dojo manual [http://dojotoolkit.org/book/dojo-book-0-9/part-2-dijit/layout].

All dijit layout elements have the signature string ($id = null, $content = '', array

$params = array(), array $attribs = array()). In all caess, if you pass no arguments, the helper object itself will be returned. This gives you access to the captureStart() and captureEnd() methods, which allow you to capture content instead of passing it to the layout container.

- *AccordionContainer*: dijit.layout.AccordionContainer. Stack all panes together vertically; clicking on a pane titlebar will expand and display that particular pane.

```php
<?php echo $view->accordionContainer(
    'foo',
    $content,
    array(
        'duration' => 200,
    ),
    array(
        'style' => 'width: 200px; height: 300px;',
    ),
); ?>
```

- *AccordionPane*: dijit.layout.AccordionPane. For use within AccordionContainer.

```php
<?php echo $view->accordionPane(
    'foo',
    $content,
    array(
        'title' => 'Pane Title',
    ),
    array(
        'style' => 'background-color: lightgray;',
    ),
); ?>
```

- *BorderContainer*: dijit.layout.BorderContainer. Achieve layouts with optionally resizable panes such as you might see in a traditional application.

```php
<?php echo $view->borderContainer(
    'foo',
    $content,
    array(
        'design' => 'headline',
    ),
    array(
        'style' => 'width: 100%; height: 100%',
    ),
); ?>
```

- *ContentPane*: dijit.layout.ContentPane. Use inside any container except AccordionContainer.

```php
<?php echo $view->contentPane(
    'foo',
    $content,
    array(
        'title'  => 'Pane Title',
        'region' => 'left',
    ),
    array(
        'style' => 'width: 120px; background-color: lightgray;',
    ),
); ?>
```

- *SplitContainer*: dijit.layout.SplitContainer. Allows resizable content panes; deprecated in Dojo in favor of BorderContainer.

```php
<?php echo $view->splitContainer(
    'foo',
    $content,
    array(
        'orientation'  => 'horizontal',
        'sizerWidth'   => 7,
        'activeSizing' => true,
    ),
    array(
        'style' => 'width: 400px; height: 500px;',
    ),
); ?>
```

- *StackContainer*: dijit.layout.StackContainer. All panes within a StackContainer are placed in a stack; build buttons or functionality to reveal one at a time.

```php
<?php echo $view->stackContainer(
    'foo',
    $content,
    array(),
    array(
        'style' => 'width: 400px; height: 500px; border: 1px;',
    ),
); ?>
```

- *TabContainer*: dijit.layout.TabContainer. All panes within a TabContainer are placed in a stack, with tabs positioned on one side for switching between them.

```php
<?php echo $view->tabContainer(
    'foo',
    $content,
    array(),
    array(
        'style' => 'width: 400px; height: 500px; border: 1px;',
    ),
); ?>
```

The following capture methods are available for all layout containers:

- `captureStart($id, array $params = array(), array $attribs = array())`: begin capturing content to include in a container. `$params` refers to the dijit params to use with the container, while `$attribs` refer to any general HTML attributes to use.

  Containers may be nested when capturing, *so long as no ids are duplicated*.

- `captureEnd($id)`: finish capturing content to include in a container. `$id` should refer to an id previously used with a `captureStart()` call. Returns a string representing the container and its contents, just as if you'd simply passed content to the helper itself.

Example 17.10. BorderContainer layout dijit example

BorderContainers, particularly when coupled with the ability to capture content, are especially useful for achieving complex layout effects.

```
$view->borderContainer()->captureStart('masterLayout',
                                        array('design' => 'headline'));
echo $view->contentPane(
    'menuPane',
    'This is the menu pane',
    array('region' => 'top'),
    array('style' => 'background-color: darkblue;')
);
echo  $view->contentPane(
    'navPane',
    'This is the navigation pane',
    array('region' => 'left'),
    array('style' => 'width: 200px; background-color: lightblue;')
);
echo $view->contentPane(
    'mainPane',
    'This is the main content pane area',
    array('region' => 'center'),
    array('style' => 'background-color: white;')
);
echo $view->contentPane(
    'statusPane',
    'Status area',
    array('region' => 'bottom'),
    array('style' => 'background-color: lightgray;')
);
echo $view->borderContainer()->captureEnd('masterLayout');
```

Dijit Form Elements

Dojo's form validation and input dijits are in the dijit.form tree. For more information on general usage of these elements, as well as accepted parameters, please visit the dijit.form documentation [http://dojotoolkit.org/book/dojo-book-0-9/part-2-dijit/form-validation-specialized-input].

The following dijit form elements are available in Zend Framework. Except where noted, all have the signature string ($id, $value = '', array $params = array(), array $attribs = array()).

- *Button*: dijit.form.Button. Display a form button.

    ```
    <?php echo $view->button(
        'foo',
        'Show Me!',
        array('iconClass' => 'myButtons'),
    ); ?>
    ```

- *CheckBox*: dijit.form.CheckBox. Display a checkbox. Accepts an optional fifth argument, the array $checkedOptions, which may contain either:

    - an indexed array with two values, a checked value and unchecked value, in that order; or

    - an associative array with the keys 'checkedValue' and 'unCheckedValue'.

    If $checkedOptions is not provided, 1 and 0 are assumed.

    ```
    <?php echo $view->checkBox(
        'foo',
        'bar',
        array(),
    ```

```
      array(),
      array('checkedValue' => 'foo', 'unCheckedValue' => 'bar')
); ?>
```

- *ComboBox*: dijit.layout.ComboBox. ComboBoxes are a hybrid between a select and a text box with autocompletion. The key difference is that you may type an option that is not in the list of available options, and it will still consider it valid input. It accepts an optional fifth argument, an associative array `$options`; if provided, ComboBox will be rendered as a `select`. Note also that the *label values* of the `$options` array will be returned in the form -- not the values themselves.

  Alternately, you may pass information regarding a dojo.data datastore to use with the element. If provided, the ComboBox will be rendered as a text `input`, and will pull its options via that datastore.

  To specify a datastore, provide one of the following `$params` key combinations:

  - The key 'store', with an array value; the array should contain the keys:

    - *store*: the name of the javascript variable representing the datastore (this could be the name you would like for it to use).

    - *type*: the datastore type to use; e.g., 'dojo.data.ItemFileReadStore'.

    - *params* (optional): an associative array of key/value pairs to use to configure the datastore. The 'url' param is a typical example.

  - The keys:

    - *store*: a string indicating the datastore name to use.

    - *storeType*: a string indicating the datastore dojo.data type to use (e.g., 'dojo.data.ItemFileReadStore').

    - *storeParams*: an associative array of key/value pairs with which to configure the datastore.

```
// As a select element:
echo $view->comboBox(
    'foo',
    'bar',
    array(
        'autocomplete' => false,
    ),
    array(),
    array(
        'foo' => 'Foo',
        'bar' => 'Bar',
        'baz' => 'Baz',
    )
);
// As a dojo.data-enabled element:
echo $view->comboBox(
    'foo',
    'bar',
    array(
        'autocomplete' => false,
        'store'        => 'stateStore',
        'storeType'    => 'dojo.data.ItemFileReadStore',
        'storeParams'  => array('url' => '/js/states.json'),
    ),
);
```

- *CurrencyTextBox*: dijit.form.CurrencyTextBox. Inherits from ValidationTextBox, and provides client-side validation of currency. It expects that the dijit parameter 'currency' will be provided with an appropriate 3-character currency code. You may also specify any dijit parameters valid for ValidationTextBox and TextBox.

```
echo $view->currencyTextBox(
    'foo',
    '$25.00',
    array('currency' => 'USD'),
    array('maxlength' => 20)
);
```

Issues with Builds

There are currently known issues with using CurrencyTextBox with build layers [http://trac.dojotoolkit.org/ticket/7183]. A known work-around is to ensure that your document's Content-Type http-equiv meta tag sets the character set to utf-8, which you can do by calling:

```
$view->headMeta()->appendHttpEquiv('Content-Type',
                                   'text/html; charset=utf-8');
```

This will mean, of course, that you will need to ensure that the headMeta() placeholder is echoed in your layout script.

- *DateTextBox*: dijit.form.DateTextBox. Inherits from ValidationTextBox, and provides both client-side validation of dates, as well as a dropdown calendar from which to select a date. You may specify any dijit parameters available to ValidationTextBox or TextBox.

```
echo $view->dateTextBox(
    'foo',
    '2008-07-11',
    array('required' => true)
);
```

- *Editor*: dijit.Editor. Provides a WYSIWYG editor via which users may create or edit content. dijit.Editor is a pluggable, extensible editor with a variety of parameters you can utilize for customization; see the dijit.Editor documentation [http://dojotoolkit.org/book /dojo-book-0-9/part-2-dijit/advanced-editing-and-display/editor-rich-text] for more details.

```
echo $view->editor('foo');
```

- *FilteringSelect*: dijit.form.FilteringSelect. Similar to ComboBox, this is a select/text hybrid that can either render a provided list of options or those fetched via a dojo.data datastore. Unlike ComboBox, however, FilteringSelect does not allow typing in an option not in its list. Additionally, it operates like a standard select in that the option values, not the labels, are returned when the form is submitted.

Please see the information above on ComboBox for examples and available options for defining datastores.

- *HorizontalSlider* and *VerticalSlider*: dijit.form.HorizontalSlider and dijit.form.VerticalSlider. Sliders allow are UI widgets for selecting numbers in a given range; these are horizontal and vertical variants.

At their most basic, they require the dijit parameters 'minimum', 'maximum', and 'discreteValues'. These define the range of values. Other common options are:

- 'intermediateChanges' can be set to indicate whether or not to fire onChange events while the handle is being dragged.

- 'clickSelect' can be set to allow clicking a location on the slider to set the value.

- 'pageIncrement' can specify the value by which to increase/decrease when pageUp and pageDown are used.

- 'showButtons' can be set to allow displaying buttons on either end of the slider for manipulating the value.

The Zend Framework implementation creates a hidden element to store the value of the slider.

You may optionally desire to show a rule or labels for the slider. To do so, you will assign one or more of the dijit params 'topDecoration' and/or 'bottomDecoration' (HorizontalSlider) or 'leftDecoration' and/or 'rightDecoration' (VerticalSlider). Each of these expects the following options:

- *container*: name of the container.

- *labels* (optional): an array of labels to utilize. Use empty strings on either end to provide labels for inner values only. Required when specifying one of the 'Labels' dijit variants.

- *dijit* (optional): one of HorizontalRule, HorizontalRuleLabels, VerticalRule, or VerticalRuleLabels, Defaults to one of the Rule dijits.

- *params* (optional): dijit params for configuring the Rule dijit in use. Parameters specific to these dijits include:

  - *container* (optional): array of parameters and attributes for the rule container.

  - *labels* (optional): array of parameters and attributes for the labels list container.

- *attribs* (optional): HTML attributes to use with the rules/labels. This should follow the `params` option format and be an associative array with the keys 'container' and 'labels'.

```
echo $view->horizontalSlider(
    'foo',
    1,
    array(
        'minimum'              => -10,
        'maximum'              => 10,
        'discreteValues'       => 11,
        'intermediateChanges'  => true,
        'showButtons'          => true,
        'topDecoration'        => array(
            'container' => 'topContainer'
            'dijit'     => 'HorizontalRuleLabels',
            'labels'    => array(
                ' ',
                '20%',
                '40%',
                '60%',
                '80%',
                ' ',
            ),
            'params' => array(
                'container' => array(
                    'style' => 'height:1.2em; font-size=75%;color:gray;',
                ),
```

```
                'labels' => array(
                    'style' => 'height:1em; font-size=75%;color:gray;',
                ),
            ),
        ),
        'bottomDecoration'    => array(
            'container' => 'bottomContainer'
            'labels'    => array(
                '0%',
                '50%',
                '100%',
            ),
            'params' => array(
                'container' => array(
                    'style' => 'height:1.2em; font-size=75%;color:gray;',
                ),
                'labels' => array(
                    'style' => 'height:1em; font-size=75%;color:gray;',
                ),
            ),
        ),
    )
);
```

- *NumberSpinner*: dijit.form.NumberSpinner. Text box for numeric entry, with buttons for incrementing and decrementing.

  Expects either an associative array for the dijit parameter 'constraints', or simply the keys 'min', 'max', and 'places' (these would be the expected entries of the constraints parameter as well). 'places' can be used to indicate how much the number spinner will increment and decrement.

```
echo $view->numberSpinner(
    'foo',
    5,
    array(
        'min'    => -10,
        'max'    => 10,
        'places' => 2,
    ),
    array(
        'maxlenth' => 3,
    )
);
```

- *NumberTextBox*: dijit.form.NumberTextBox. NumberTextBox provides the ability to format and display number entries in a localized fashion, as well as validate numerical entries, optionally against given constraints.

```
echo $view->numberTextBox(
    'foo',
    5,
    array(
        'places' => 4,
        'type'   => 'percent',
    ),
    array(
        'maxlength' => 20,
    )
);
```

- *PasswordTextBox*: dijit.form.ValidationTextBox tied to a password input. PasswordTextBox provides the ability to create password input that adheres to the current dijit theme, as well as allow for client-side validation.

```
echo $view->passwordTextBox(
    'foo',
    '',
    array(
        'required' => true,
    ),
    array(
        'maxlength' => 20,
    )
);
```

- *RadioButton*: dijit.form.RadioButton. A set of options from which only one may be selected. This behaves in every way like a regular radio, but has a look-and-feel consistent with other dijits.

  RadioButton accepts an option fourth argument, $options, an associative array of value/label pairs used as the radio options. You may also pass these as the $attribs key options.

```
echo $view->radioButton(
    'foo',
    'bar',
    array(),
    array(),
    array(
        'foo' => 'Foo',
        'bar' => 'Bar',
        'baz' => 'Baz',
    )
);
```

- *SimpleTextarea*: dijit.form.SimpleTextarea. These act like normal textareas, but are styled using the current dijit theme. You do not need to specify either the rows or columns attributes; use ems or percentages for the width and height, instead.

```
echo $view->simpleTextarea(
    'foo',
    'Start writing here...',
    array(),
    array('style' => 'width: 90%; height: 5ems;')
);
```

- *SubmitButton*: a dijit.form.Button tied to a submit input element. See the Button view helper for more details; the key difference is that this button can submit a form.

- *Textarea*: dijit.form.Textarea. These act like normal textareas, except that instead of having a set number of rows, they expand as the user types. The width should be specified via a style setting.

```
echo $view->textarea(
    'foo',
    'Start writing here...',
    array(),
    array('style' => 'width: 300px;')
);
```

- *TextBox*: dijit.form.TextBox. This element is primarily present to provide a common look-and-feel between various dijit elements, and to provide base functionality for the other TextBox-derived classes (ValidationTextBox, NumberTextBox, CurrencyTextBox, DateTextBox, and TimeTextBox).

  Common dijit parameter flags include 'lowercase' (cast to lowercase), 'uppercase' (cast to UPPERCASE), 'propercase' (cast to Proper Case), and trim (trim leading and trailing whitespace); all accept boolean values. Additionally, you may specifiy the parameters 'size' and 'maxLength'.

  ```
  echo $view->textBox(
      'foo',
      'some text',
      array(
          'trim'       => true,
          'propercase' => true,
          'maxLength'  => 20,
      ),
      array(
          'size' => 20,
      )
  );
  ```

- *TimeTextBox*: dijit.form.TimeTextBox. Also in the TextBox family, TimeTextBox provides a scrollable drop down selection of times from which a user may select. Dijit parameters allow you to specify the time increments available in the select as well as the visible range of times available.

  ```
  echo $view->timeTextBox(
      'foo',
      '',
      array(
          'am.pm'            => true,
          'visibleIncrement' => 'T00:05:00', // 5-minute increments
          'visibleRange'     => 'T02:00:00', // show 2 hours of increments
      ),
      array(
          'size' => 20,
      )
  );
  ```

- *ValidationTextBox*: dijit.form.ValidateTextBox. Provide client-side validations for a text element. Inherits from TextBox.

  Common dijit parameters include:

  - *invalidMessage*: a message to display when an invalid entry is detected.

  - *promptMessage*: a tooltip help message to use.

  - *regExp*: a regular expression to use to validate the text. Regular expression does not require boundary markers.

  - *required*: whether or not the element is required. If so, and the element is embedded in a dijit.form.Form, it will be flagged as invalid and prevent submission.

  ```
  echo $view->validationTextBox(
      'foo',
      '',
      array(
          'required' => true,
          'regExp'   => '[\w]+',
  ```

```
            'invalidMessage' => 'No spaces or non-word characters allowed',
            'promptMessage'  => 'Single word consisting of alphanumeric ' .
                                'characters and underscores only',
        ),
        array(
            'maxlength' => 20,
        )
    );
```

Custom Dijits

If you delve into Dojo much at all, you'll find yourself writing custom dijits, or using experimental dijits from Dojox. While Zend Framework cannot support every dijit directly, it does provide some rudimentary support for arbitrary dijit types via the CustomDijit view helper.

The CustomDijit view helper's API is exactly that of any other dijit, with one major difference: the third "params" argument *must* contain the attribute "dojotype". The value of this attribute should be the Dijit class you plan to use.

CustomDijit extends the base DijitContainer view helper, which also allows it to capture content (using the captureStart()/captureEnd() pair of methods). captureStart() also expects that you pass the "dojoType" attribute to its "params" argument.

Example 17.11. Using CustomDijit to render a dojox.layout.ContentPane

dojox.layout.ContentPane is a next-generation iteration of dijit.layout.ContentPane, and provides a superset of that class's capabilities. Until it's functionality stabilizes, it will continue to live in Dojox. However, if you want to use it in Zend Framework today, you can, using the CustomDijit view helper.

At its most basic, you can do the following:

```
<?php echo $this->customDijit(
    'foo',
    $content,
    array(
        'dojoType' => 'dojox.layout.ContentPane',
        'title'    => 'Custom pane',
        'region'   => 'center'
    )
); ?>
```

If you wanted to capture content instead, simply use the captureStart() method, and pass the "dojoType" to the "params" argument:

```
<?php $this->customDijit()->captureStart(
    'foo',
    array(
        'dojoType' => 'dojox.layout.ContentPane',
        'title'    => 'Custom pane',
        'region'   => 'center'
    )
); ?>
This is the content of the pane
<?php echo $this->customDijit()->captureEnd('foo'); ?>
```

You can also extend `CustomDijit` easily to create support for your own custom dijits. As an example, if you extended `dijit.layout.ContentPane` to create your own `foo.ContentPane` class, you could create the following helper to support it:

```
class My_View_Helper_FooContentPane
    extends Zend_Dojo_View_Helper_CustomDijit
{
    protected $_defaultDojoType = 'foo.ContentPane';
    public function fooContentPane(
        $id = null, $value = null,
        array $params = array(), array $attribs = array()
    ) {
        return $this->customDijit($id, $value, $params, $attribs);
    }
}
```

As long as your custom dijit follows the same basic API as official dijits, using or extending `CustomDijit` should work correctly.

Dojo Form Elements and Decorators

Building on the dijit view helpers, the `Zend_Dojo_Form` family of classes provides the ability to utilize Dijits natively within your forms.

There are three options for utilizing the Dojo form elements with your forms:

- Use `Zend_Dojo::enableForm()`. This will add plugin paths for decorators and elements to all attached form items, recursively. Additionally, it will dojo-enable the view object. Note, however, that any sub forms you attach *after* this call will also need to be passed through `Zend_Dojo::enableForm()`.

- Use the Dojo-specific form and subform implementations, `Zend_Dojo_Form` and `Zend_Dojo_Form_SubForm` respectively. These can be used as drop-in replacements for `Zend_Form` and `Zend_Form_SubForm`, contain all the appropriate decorator and element paths, set a Dojo-specific default DisplayGroup class, and dojo-enable the view.

- Last, and most tedious, you can set the appropriate decorator and element paths yourself, set the default DisplayGroup class, and dojo-enable the view. Since `Zend_Dojo::enableForm()` does this already, there's little reason to go this route.

Example 17.12. Enabling Dojo in your existing forms

"But wait," you say; "I'm already extending `Zend_Form` with my own custom form class! How can I Dojo-enable it?"'

First, and easiest, simply change from extending `Zend_Form` to extending `Zend_Dojo_Form`, and update any places where you instantiate `Zend_Form_SubForm` to instantiate `Zend_Dojo_Form_SubForm`.

A second approach is to call `Zend_Dojo::enableForm()` within your custom form's `init()` method; when the form definition is complete, loop through all SubForms to dojo-enable them:

```
class My_Form_Custom extends Zend_Form
{
    public function init()
    {
        // Dojo-enable the form:
```

```
Zend_Dojo::enableForm($this);
// ... continue form definition from here
// Dojo-enable all sub forms:
foreach ($this->getSubForms() as $subForm) {
    Zend_Dojo::enableForm($subForm);
}
    }
}
```

Usage of the dijit-specific form decorators and elements is just like using any other form decorator or element.

Dijit-Specific Form Decorators

Most form elements can use the DijitElement decorator, which will grab the dijit parameters from the elements, and pass these and other metadata to the view helper specified by the element. For decorating forms, sub forms, and display groups, however, there are a set of decorators corresponding to the various layout dijits.

All dijit decorators look for the dijitParams property of the given element being decorated, and push them as the $params array to the dijit view helper being used; these are then separated from any other properties so that no duplication of information occurs.

DijitElement Decorator

Just like the ViewHelper decorator, DijitElement expects a helper property in the element which it will then use as the view helper when rendering. Dijit parameters will typically be pulled directly from the element, but may also be passed in as options via the dijitParams key (the value of that key should be an associative array of options).

It is important that each element have a unique ID (as fetched from the element's getId() method). If duplicates are detected within the dojo() view helper, the decorator will trigger a notice, but then create a unique ID by appending the return of uniqid() to the identifier.

Standard usage is to simply associate this decorator as the first in your decorator chain, with no additional options.

Example 17.13. DijitElement Decorator Usage

```
$element->setDecorators(array(
    'DijitElement',
    'Errors',
    'Label',
    'ContentPane',
));
```

DijitForm Decorator

The DijitForm decorator is very similar to the Form decorator; in fact, it can be used basically interchangeably with it, as it utilizes the same view helper name ('form').

Since dijit.form.Form does not require any dijit parameters for configuration, the main difference is that the dijit form view helper require that a DOM ID is passed to ensure that programmatic dijit creation can work. The decorator ensures this, by passing the form name as the identifier.

DijitContainer-based Decorators

The `DijitContainer` decorator is actually an abstract class from which a variety of other decorators derive. It offers the same functionality of DijitElement, with the addition of title support. Many layout dijits require or can utilize a title; DijitContainer will utilize the element's legend property, if available, and can also utilize either the 'legend' or 'title' decorator option, if passed. The title will be translated if a translation adapter with a corresponding translation is present.

The following is a list of decorators that inherit from `DijitContainer`:

- AccordionContainer

- AccordionPane

- BorderContainer

- ContentPane

- SplitContainer

- StackContainer

- TabContainer

Example 17.14. DijitContainer Decorator Usage

```
// Use a TabContainer for your form:
$form->setDecorators(array(
    'FormElements',
    array('TabContainer', array(
        'id'          => 'tabContainer',
        'style'       => 'width: 600px; height: 500px;',
        'dijitParams' => array(
            'tabPosition' => 'top'
        ),
    )),
    'DijitForm',
));
// Use a ContentPane in your sub form (which can be used with all but
// AccordionContainer):
$subForm->setDecorators(array(
    'FormElements',
    array('HtmlTag', array('tag' => 'dl')),
    'ContentPane',
));
```

Dijit-Specific Form Elements

Each form dijit for which a view helper is provided has a corresponding `Zend_Form` element. All of them have the following methods available for manipulating dijit parameters:

- `setDijitParam($key, $value)`: set a single dijit parameter. If the dijit parameter already exists, it will be overwritten.

- `setDijitParams(array $params)`: set several dijit parameters at once. Any passed parameters matching those already present will overwrite.

- `hasDijitParam($key)`: If a given dijit parameter is defined and present, return TRUE, otherwise return FALSE.

- `getDijitParam($key)`: retrieve the given dijit parameter. If not available, a null value is returned.

- `getDijitParams()`: retrieve all dijit parameters.

- `removeDijitParam($key)`: remove the given dijit parameter.

- `clearDijitParams()`: clear all currently defined dijit parameters.

Dijit parameters are stored in the `dijitParams` public property. Thus, you can dijit-enable an existing form element simply by setting this property on the element; you simply will not have the above accessors to facilitate manipulating the parameters.

Additionally, dijit-specific elements implement a different list of decorators, corresponding to the following:

```
$element->addDecorator('DijitElement')
        ->addDecorator('Errors')
        ->addDecorator('HtmlTag', array('tag' => 'dd'))
        ->addDecorator('Label', array('tag' => 'dt'));
```

In effect, the DijitElement decorator is used in place of the standard ViewHelper decorator.

Finally, the base Dijit element ensures that the Dojo view helper path is set on the view.

A variant on DijitElement, DijitMulti, provides the functionality of the `Multi` abstract form element, allowing the developer to specify 'multiOptions' -- typically select options or radio options.

The following dijit elements are shipped in the standard Zend Framework distribution.

Button

While not deriving from the standard Button element, it does implement the same functionality, and can be used as a drop-in replacement for it. The following functionality is exposed:

- `getLabel()` will utilize the element name as the button label if no name is provided. Additionally, it will translate the name if a translation adapter with a matching translation message is available.

- `isChecked()` determines if the value submitted matches the label; if so, it returns true. This is useful for determining which button was used when a form was submitted.

Additionally, only the decorators `DijitElement` and `DtDdWrapper` are utilized for Button elements.

Example 17.15. Example Button dijit element usage

```
$form->addElement(
    'Button',
    'foo',
    array(
        'label' => 'Button Label',
    )
);
```

CheckBox

While not deriving from the standard Checkbox element, it does implement the same functionality. This means that the following methods are exposed:

- `setCheckedValue($value)`: set the value to use when the element is checked.

- `getCheckedValue()`: get the value of the item to use when checked.

- `setUncheckedValue($value)`: set the value of the item to use when it is unchecked.

- `getUncheckedValue()`: get the value of the item to use when it is unchecked.

- `setChecked($flag)`: mark the element as checked or unchecked.

- `isChecked()`: determine if the element is currently checked.

Example 17.16. Example CheckBox dijit element usage

```
$form->addElement(
    'CheckBox',
    'foo',
    array(
        'label'           => 'A check box',
        'checkedValue'    => 'foo',
        'uncheckedValue'  => 'bar',
        'checked'         => true,
    )
);
```

ComboBox and FilteringSelect

As noted in the ComboBox dijit view helper documentation, ComboBoxes are a hybrid between select and text input, allowing for autocompletion and the ability to specify an alternate to the options provided. FilteringSelects are the same, but do not allow arbitrary input.

ComboBoxes return the label values

ComboBoxes return the label values, and not the option values, which can lead to a disconnect in expectations. For this reason, ComboBoxes do not auto-register an `InArray` validator (though FilteringSelects do).

The ComboBox and FilteringSelect form elements provide accessors and mutators for examining and setting the select options as well as specifying a dojo.data datastore (if used). They extend from DijitMulti, which allows you to specify select options via the `setMultiOptions()` and `setMultiOption()` methods. In addition, the following methods are available:

- `getStoreInfo()`: get all datastore information currently set. Returns an empty array if no data is currently set.

- `setStoreId($identifier)`: set the store identifier variable (usually referred to by the attribute 'jsId' in Dojo). This should be a valid javascript variable name.

- `getStoreId()`: retrieve the store identifier variable name.

- `setStoreType($dojoType)`: set the datastore class to use; e.g., "dojo.data.ItemFileReadStore".

- `getStoreType()`: get the dojo datastore class to use.

- `setStoreParams(array $params)`: set any parameters used to configure the datastore object. As an example, dojo.data.ItemFileReadStore datastore would expect a 'url' parameter pointing to a location that would return the dojo.data object.

- `getStoreParams()`: get any datastore parameters currently set; if none, an empty array is returned.

- `setAutocomplete($flag)`: indicate whether or not the selected item will be used when the user leaves the element.

- `getAutocomplete()`: get the value of the autocomplete flag.

By default, if no dojo.data store is registered with the element, this element registers an `InArray` validator which validates against the array keys of registered options. You can disable this behavior by either calling `setRegisterInArrayValidator(false)`, or by passing a false value to the `registerInArrayValidator` configuration key.

Example 17.17. ComboBox dijit element usage as select input

```
$form->addElement(
    'ComboBox',
    'foo',
    array(
        'label'        => 'ComboBox (select)',
        'value'        => 'blue',
        'autocomplete' => false,
        'multiOptions' => array(
            'red'    => 'Rouge',
            'blue'   => 'Bleu',
            'white'  => 'Blanc',
            'orange' => 'Orange',
            'black'  => 'Noir',
            'green'  => 'Vert',
        ),
    )
);
```

Example 17.18. ComboBox dijit element usage with datastore

```
$form->addElement(
    'ComboBox',
    'foo',
    array(
        'label'       => 'ComboBox (datastore)',
        'storeId'     => 'stateStore',
        'storeType'   => 'dojo.data.ItemFileReadStore',
        'storeParams' => array(
            'url' => '/js/states.txt',
        ),
        'dijitParams' => array(
            'searchAttr' => 'name',
        ),
    )
);
```

The above examples could also utilize `FilteringSelect` instead of `ComboBox`.

CurrencyTextBox

The CurrencyTextBox is primarily for supporting currency input. The currency may be localized, and can support both fractional and non-fractional values.

Internally, CurrencyTextBox derives from NumberTextBox, ValidationTextBox, and TextBox; all methods available to those classes are available. In addition, the following constraint methods can be used:

- `setCurrency($currency)`: set the currency type to use; should follow the ISO-4217 [http://en.wikipedia.org/wiki/ISO_4217] specification.

- `getCurrency()`: retrieve the current currency type.

- `setSymbol($symbol)`: set the 3-letter ISO-4217 [http://en.wikipedia.org/wiki/ISO_4217] currency symbol to use.

- `getSymbol()`: get the current currency symbol.

- `setFractional($flag)`: set whether or not the currency should allow for fractional values.

- `getFractional()`: retrieve the status of the fractional flag.

Example 17.19. Example CurrencyTextBox dijit element usage

```
$form->addElement(
    'CurrencyTextBox',
    'foo',
    array(
        'label'          => 'Currency:',
        'required'       => true,
        'currency'       => 'USD',
        'invalidMessage' => 'Invalid amount. ' .
                            'Include dollar sign, commas, and cents.',
        'fractional'     => false,
    )
);
```

DateTextBox

DateTextBox provides a calendar drop-down for selecting a date, as well as client-side date validation and formatting.

Internally, DateTextBox derives from ValidationTextBox and TextBox; all methods available to those classes are available. In addition, the following methods can be used to set individual constraints:

- `setAmPm($flag)` and `getAmPm()`: Whether or not to use AM/PM strings in times.

- `setStrict($flag)` and `getStrict()`: whether or not to use strict regular expression matching when validating input. If false, which is the default, it will be lenient about whitespace and some abbreviations.

- `setLocale($locale)` and `getLocale()`: Set and retrieve the locale to use with this specific element.

- `setDatePattern($pattern)` and `getDatePattern()`: provide and retrieve the unicode date format pattern [http://www.unicode.org/reports/tr35/#Date_Format_Patterns] for formatting the date.

- `setFormatLength($formatLength)` and `getFormatLength()`: provide and retrieve the format length type to use; should be one of "long", "short", "medium" or "full".

- `setSelector($selector)` and `getSelector()`: provide and retrieve the style of selector; should be either "date" or "time".

Example 17.20. Example DateTextBox dijit element usage

```
$form->addElement(
    'DateTextBox',
    'foo',
    array(
        'label'          => 'Date:',
        'required'       => true,
        'invalidMessage' => 'Invalid date specified.',
        'formatLength'   => 'long',
    )
);
```

Editor

Editor provides a WYSIWYG editor that can be used to both create and edit rich HTML content. dijit.Editor is pluggable and may be extended with custom plugins if desired; see the dijit.Editor documentation [http://dojotoolkit.org/book/dojo-book-0-9/part-2-dijit/advanced-editing-and-display/editor-rich-text] for more details.

The Editor form element provides a number of accessors and mutators for manipulating various dijit parameters, as follows:

- *captureEvents* are events that connect to the editing area itself. The following accessors and mutators are available for manipulating capture events:

  - `addCaptureEvent($event)`

  - `addCaptureEvents(array $events)`

  - `setCaptureEvents(array $events)`

  - `getCaptureEvents()`

  - `hasCaptureEvent($event)`

  - `removeCaptureEvent($event)`

  - `clearCaptureEvents()`

- *events* are standard DOM events, such as onClick, onKeyUp, etc. The following accessors and mutators are available for manipulating events:

  - `addEvent($event)`

  - `addEvents(array $events)`

  - `setEvents(array $events)`

  - `getEvents()`

- hasEvent($event)

- removeEvent($event)

- clearEvents()

- *plugins* add functionality to the Editor -- additional tools for the toolbar, additional styles to allow, etc. The following accessors and mutators are available for manipulating plugins:

  - addPlugin($plugin)

  - addPlugins(array $plugins)

  - setPlugins(array $plugins)

  - getPlugins()

  - hasPlugin($plugin)

  - removePlugin($plugin)

  - clearPlugins()

- *editActionInterval* is used to group events for undo operations. By default, this value is 3 seconds. The method setEditActionInterval($interval) may be used to set the value, while getEditActionInterval() will retrieve it.

- *focusOnLoad* is used to determine whether this particular editor will receive focus when the page has loaded. By default, this is false. The method setFocusOnLoad($flag) may be used to set the value, while getFocusOnLoad() will retrieve it.

- *height* specifies the height of the editor; by default, this is 300px. The method setHeight($height) may be used to set the value, while getHeight() will retrieve it.

- *inheritWidth* is used to determine whether the editor will use the parent container's width or simply default to 100% width. By default, this is false (i.e., it will fill the width of the window). The method setInheritWidth($flag) may be used to set the value, while getInheritWidth() will retrieve it.

- *minHeight* indicates the minimum height of the editor; by default, this is 1em. The method setMinHeight($height) may be used to set the value, while getMinHeight() will retrieve it.

- *styleSheets* indicate what additional CSS stylesheets should be used to affect the display of the Editor. By default, none are registered, and it inherits the page styles. The following accessors and mutators are available for manipulating editor stylesheets:

  - addStyleSheet($styleSheet)

  - addStyleSheets(array $styleSheets)

  - setStyleSheets(array $styleSheets)

  - getStyleSheets()

  - hasStyleSheet($styleSheet)

  - removeStyleSheet($styleSheet)

  - clearStyleSheets()

Example 17.21. Example Editor dijit element usage

```
$form->addElement('editor', 'content', array(
    'plugins'           => array('undo', '|', 'bold', 'italic'),
    'editActionInterval' => 2,
    'focusOnLoad'       => true,
    'height'            => '250px',
    'inheritWidth'      => true,
    'styleSheets'       => array('/js/custom/editor.css'),
));
```

HorizontalSlider

HorizontalSlider provides a slider UI widget for selecting a numeric value in a range. Internally, it sets the value of a hidden element which is submitted by the form.

HorizontalSlider derives from the abstract Slider dijit element. Additionally, it has a variety of methods for setting and configuring slider rules and rule labels.

- `setTopDecorationDijit($dijit)` and `setBottomDecorationDijit($dijit)`: set the name of the dijit to use for either the top or bottom of the slider. This should not include the "dijit.form." prefix, but rather only the final name -- one of "HorizontalRule" or "HorizontalRule Labels".

- `setTopDecorationContainer($container)` and `setBottomDecoration Container($container)`: specify the name to use for the container element of the rules; e.g. 'topRule', 'topContainer', etc.

- `setTopDecorationLabels(array $labels)` and `setBottomDecorationLabels (array $labels)`: set the labels to use for one of the RuleLabels dijit types. These should be an indexed array; specify a single empty space to skip a given label position (such as the beginning or end).

- `setTopDecorationParams(array $params)` and `setBottomDecorationParams (array $params)`: dijit parameters to use when configuring the given Rule or RuleLabels dijit.

- `setTopDecorationAttribs(array $attribs)` and `setBottomDecorationAttribs(array $attribs)`: HTML attributes to specify for the given Rule or RuleLabels HTML element container.

- `getTopDecoration()` and `getBottomDecoration()`: retrieve all metadata for a given Rule or RuleLabels definition, as provided by the above mutators.

Example 17.22. Example HorizontalSlider dijit element usage

The following will create a horizontal slider selection with integer values ranging from -10 to 10. The top will have labels at the 20%, 40%, 60%, and 80% marks. The botton will have rules at 0, 50%, and 100%. Each time the value is changed, the hidden element storing the value will be updated.

```
$form->addElement(
    'HorizontalSlider',
    'horizontal',
    array(
        'label'                 => 'HorizontalSlider',
        'value'                 => 5,
```

```
'minimum'                     => -10,
'maximum'                     => 10,
'discreteValues'              => 11,
'intermediateChanges'         => true,
'showButtons'                 => true,
'topDecorationDijit'          => 'HorizontalRuleLabels',
'topDecorationContainer'      => 'topContainer',
'topDecorationLabels'         => array(
        ' ',
        '20%',
        '40%',
        '60%',
        '80%',
        ' ',
),
'topDecorationParams'         => array(
    'container' => array(
        'style' => 'height:1.2em; font-size=75%;color:gray;',
    ),
    'list' => array(
        'style' => 'height:1em; font-size=75%;color:gray;',
    ),
),
'bottomDecorationDijit'       => 'HorizontalRule',
'bottomDecorationContainer'   => 'bottomContainer',
'bottomDecorationLabels'      => array(
        '0%',
        '50%',
        '100%',
),
'bottomDecorationParams'      => array(
    'list' => array(
        'style' => 'height:1em; font-size=75%;color:gray;',
    ),
),
    )
);
```

NumberSpinner

A number spinner is a text element for entering numeric values; it also includes elements for incrementing and decrementing the value by a set amount.

The following methods are available:

- `setDefaultTimeout($timeout)` and `getDefaultTimeout()`: set and retrieve the default timeout, in milliseconds, between when the button is held pressed and the value is changed.

- `setTimeoutChangeRate($rate)` and `getTimeoutChangeRate()`: set and retrieve the rate, in milliseconds, at which changes will be made when a button is held pressed.

- `setLargeDelta($delta)` and `getLargeDelta()`: set and retrieve the amount by which the numeric value should change when a button is held pressed.

- `setSmallDelta($delta)` and `getSmallDelta()`: set and retrieve the delta by which the number should change when a button is pressed once.

- `setIntermediateChanges($flag)` and `getIntermediateChanges()`: set and retrieve the flag indicating whether or not each value change should be shown when a button is held pressed.

- `setRangeMessage($message)` and `getRangeMessage()`: set and retrieve the message indicating the range of values available.

- `setMin($value)` and `getMin()`: set and retrieve the minimum value possible.

- `setMax($value)` and `getMax()`: set and retrieve the maximum value possible.

Example 17.23. Example NumberSpinner dijit element usage

```
$form->addElement(
    'NumberSpinner',
    'foo',
    array(
        'value'              => '7',
        'label'              => 'NumberSpinner',
        'smallDelta'         => 5,
        'largeDelta'         => 25,
        'defaultTimeout'     => 500,
        'timeoutChangeRate'  => 100,
        'min'                => 9,
        'max'                => 1550,
        'places'             => 0,
        'maxlength'          => 20,
    )
);
```

NumberTextBox

A number text box is a text element for entering numeric values; unlike NumberSpinner, numbers are entered manually. Validations and constraints can be provided to ensure the number stays in a particular range or format.

Internally, NumberTextBox derives from ValidationTextBox and TextBox; all methods available to those classes are available. In addition, the following methods can be used to set individual constraints:

- `setLocale($locale)` and `getLocale()`: specify and retrieve a specific or alternate locale to use with this dijit.

- `setPattern($pattern)` and `getPattern()`: set and retrieve a number pattern format [http://www.unicode.org/reports/tr35/#Number_Format_Patterns] to use to format the number.

- `setType($type)` and `getType()`: set and retrieve the numeric format type to use (should be one of 'decimal', 'percent', or 'currency').

- `setPlaces($places)` and `getPlaces()`: set and retrieve the number of decimal places to support.

- `setStrict($flag)` and `getStrict()`: set and retrieve the value of the strict flag, which indicates how much leniency is allowed in relation to whitespace and non-numeric characters.

Example 17.24. Example NumberTextBox dijit element usage

```
$form->addElement(
    'NumberTextBox',
    'elevation',
    array(
        'label'           => 'NumberTextBox',
        'required'        => true,
        'invalidMessage'  => 'Invalid elevation.',
        'places'          => 0,
        'constraints'     => array(
```

```
              'min'    => -20000,
              'max'    => 20000,
        ),
    )
);
```

PasswordTextBox

PasswordTextBox is simply a ValidationTextBox that is tied to a password input; its sole purpose is to allow for a dijit-themed text entry for passwords that also provides client-side validation.

Internally, NumberTextBox derives from ValidationTextBox and TextBox; all methods available to those classes are available.

Example 17.25. Example PasswordTextBox dijit element usage

```
$form->addElement(
    'PasswordTextBox',
    'password',
    array(
        'label'           => 'Password',
        'required'        => true,
        'trim'            => true,
        'lowercase'       => true,
        'regExp'          => '^[a-z0-9]{6,}$',
        'invalidMessage'  => 'Invalid password; ' .
                            'must be at least 6 alphanumeric characters',
    )
);
```

RadioButton

RadioButton wraps standard radio input elements to provide a consistent look and feel with other dojo dijits.

RadioButton extends from DijitMulti, which allows you to specify select options via the setMultiOptions() and setMultiOption() methods.

By default, this element registers an InArray validator which validates against the array keys of registered options. You can disable this behavior by either calling setRegisterIn ArrayValidator(false), or by passing a false value to the registerInArrayValidator configuration key.

Example 17.26. Example RadioButton dijit element usage

```
$form->addElement(
    'RadioButton',
    'foo',
    array(
        'label' => 'RadioButton',
        'multiOptions'   => array(
            'foo' => 'Foo',
            'bar' => 'Bar',
            'baz' => 'Baz',
        ),
```

```
                'value' => 'bar',
        )
);
```

SimpleTextarea

SimpleTextarea acts primarily like a standard HTML textarea. However, it does not support either the rows or cols settings. Instead, the textarea width should be specified using standard CSS measurements. Unlike Textarea, it will not grow automatically

Example 17.27. Example SimpleTextarea dijit element usage

```
$form->addElement(
    'SimpleTextarea',
    'simpletextarea',
    array(
        'label'    => 'SimpleTextarea',
        'required' => true,
        'style'    => 'width: 80em; height: 25em;',
    )
);
```

Slider abstract element

Slider is an abstract element from which HorizontalSlider and VerticalSlider both derive. It exposes a number of common methods for configuring your sliders, including:

- setClickSelect($flag) and getClickSelect(): set and retrieve the flag indicating whether or not clicking the slider changes the value.

- setIntermediateChanges($flag) and getIntermediateChanges(): set and retrieve the flag indicating whether or not the dijit will send a notification on each slider change event.

- setShowButtons($flag) and getShowButtons(): set and retrieve the flag indicating whether or not buttons on either end will be displayed; if so, the user can click on these to change the value of the slider.

- setDiscreteValues($value) and getDiscreteValues(): set and retrieve the number of discrete values represented by the slider.

- setMaximum($value) and getMaximum(): set the maximum value of the slider.

- setMinimum($value) and getMinimum(): set the minimum value of the slider.

- setPageIncrement($value) and getPageIncrement(): set the amount by which the slider will change on keyboard events.

Example usage is provided with each concrete extending class.

SubmitButton

While there is no Dijit named SubmitButton, we include one here to provide a button dijit capable of submitting a form without requiring any additional javascript bindings. It works exactly like the Button dijit.

Example 17.28. Example SubmitButton dijit element usage

```
$form->addElement(
    'SubmitButton',
    'foo',
    array(
        'required'    => false,
        'ignore'      => true,
        'label'       => 'Submit Button!',
    )
);
```

TextBox

TextBox is included primarily to provide a text input with consistent look-and-feel to the other dijits. However, it also includes some minor filtering and validation capabilities, represented in the following methods:

- `setLowercase($flag)` and `getLowercase()`: set and retrieve the flag indicating whether or not input should be cast to lowercase.

- `setPropercase($flag)` and `getPropercase()`: set and retrieve the flag indicating whether or not the input should be cast to Proper Case.

- `setUppercase($flag)` and `getUppercase()`: set and retrieve the flag indicating whether or not the input should be cast to UPPERCASE.

- `setTrim($flag)` and `getTrim()`: set and retrieve the flag indicating whether or not leading or trailing whitespace should be stripped.

- `setMaxLength($length)` and `getMaxLength()`: set and retrieve the maximum length of input.

Example 17.29. Example TextBox dijit element usage

```
$form->addElement(
    'TextBox',
    'foo',
    array(
        'value'       => 'some text',
        'label'       => 'TextBox',
        'trim'        => true,
        'propercase' => true,
    )
);
```

Textarea

Textarea acts primarily like a standard HTML textarea. However, it does not support either the rows or cols settings. Instead, the textarea width should be specified using standard CSS measurements; rows should be omitted entirely. The textarea will then grow vertically as text is added to it.

Example 17.30. Example Textarea dijit element usage

```
$form->addElement(
    'Textarea',
    'textarea',
    array(
        'label'    => 'Textarea',
        'required' => true,
        'style'    => 'width: 200px;',
    )
);
```

TimeTextBox

TimeTextBox is a text input that provides a drop-down for selecting a time. The drop-down may be configured to show a certain window of time, with specified increments.

Internally, TimeTextBox derives from DateTextBox, ValidationTextBox and TextBox; all methods available to those classes are available. In addition, the following methods can be used to set individual constraints:

- `setTimePattern($pattern)` and `getTimePattern()`: set and retrieve the unicode time format pattern [http://www.unicode.org/reports/tr35/#Date_Format_Patterns] for formatting the time.

- `setClickableIncrement($format)` and `getClickableIncrement()`: set the ISO-8601 [http://en.wikipedia.org/wiki/ISO_8601] string representing the amount by which every clickable element in the time picker increases.

- `setVisibleIncrement($format)` and `getVisibleIncrement()`: set the increment visible in the time chooser; must follow ISO-8601 formats.

- `setVisibleRange($format)` and `getVisibleRange()`: set and retrieve the range of time visible in the time chooser at any given moment; must follow ISO-8601 formats.

Example 17.31. Example TimeTextBox dijit element usage

The following will create a TimeTextBox that displays 2 hours at a time, with increments of 10 minutes.

```
$form->addElement(
    'TimeTextBox',
    'foo',
    array(
        'label'              => 'TimeTextBox',
        'required'           => true,
        'visibleRange'       => 'T04:00:00',
        'visibleIncrement'   => 'T00:10:00',
        'clickableIncrement' => 'T00:10:00',
    )
);
```

ValidationTextBox

ValidationTextBox provides the ability to add validations and constraints to a text input. Internally, it derives from TextBox, and adds the following accessors and mutators for manipulating dijit parameters:

- `setInvalidMessage($message)` and `getInvalidMessage()`: set and retrieve the tooltip message to display when the value does not validate.

- `setPromptMessage($message)` and `getPromptMessage()`: set and retrieve the tooltip message to display for element usage.

- `setRegExp($regexp)` and `getRegExp()`: set and retrieve the regular expression to use for validating the element. The regular expression does not need boundaries (unlike PHP's preg* family of functions).

- `setConstraint($key, $value)` and `getConstraint($key)`: set and retrieve additional constraints to use when validating the element; used primarily with subclasses. Constraints are stored in the 'constraints' key of the dijit parameters.

- `setConstraints(array $constraints)` and `getConstraints()`: set and retrieve individual constraints to use when validating the element; used primarily with subclasses.

- `hasConstraint($key)`: test whether a given constraint exists.

- `removeConstraint($key)` and `clearConstraints()`: remove an individual or all constraints for the element.

Example 17.32. Example ValidationTextBox dijit element usage

The following will create a ValidationTextBox that requires a single string consisting solely of word characters (i.e., no spaces, most punctuation is invalid).

```
$form->addElement(
    'ValidationTextBox',
    'foo',
    array(
        'label'          => 'ValidationTextBox',
        'required'       => true,
        'regExp'         => '[\w]+',
        'invalidMessage' => 'Invalid non-space text.',
    )
);
```

VerticalSlider

VerticalSlider is the sibling of HorizontalSlider, and operates in every way like that element. The only real difference is that the 'top*' and 'bottom*' methods are replaced by 'left*' and 'right*', and instead of using HorizontalRule and HorizontalRuleLabels, VerticalRule and VerticalRuleLabels should be used.

Example 17.33. Example VerticalSlider dijit element usage

The following will create a vertical slider selection with integer values ranging from -10 to 10. The left will have labels at the 20%, 40%, 60%, and 80% marks. The right will have rules at 0, 50%, and 100%. Each time the value is changed, the hidden element storing the value will be updated.

```
$form->addElement(
    'VerticalSlider',
    'foo',
    array(
        'label'                    => 'VerticalSlider',
        'value'                    => 5,
```

```
        'style'                    => 'height: 200px; width: 3em;',
        'minimum'                  => -10,
        'maximum'                  => 10,
        'discreteValues'           => 11,
        'intermediateChanges'      => true,
        'showButtons'              => true,
        'leftDecorationDijit'      => 'VerticalRuleLabels',
        'leftDecorationContainer'  => 'leftContainer',
        'leftDecorationLabels'     => array(
                ' ',
                '20%',
                '40%',
                '60%',
                '80%',
                ' ',
        ),
        'rightDecorationDijit' => 'VerticalRule',
        'rightDecorationContainer' => 'rightContainer',
        'rightDecorationLabels' => array(
                '0%',
                '50%',
                '100%',
        ),
    )
);
```

Dojo Form Examples

Example 17.34. Using Zend_Dojo_Form

The easiest way to utilize Dojo with Zend_Form is to utilize Zend_Dojo_Form, either through direct usage or by extending it. This example shows extending Zend_Dojo_Form, and shows usage of all dijit elements. It creates four sub forms, and decorates the form to utilize a TabContainer, showing each sub form in its own tab.

```
class My_Form_Test extends Zend_Dojo_Form
{
    /**
     * Options to use with select elements
     */
    protected $_selectOptions = array(
        'red'    => 'Rouge',
        'blue'   => 'Bleu',
        'white'  => 'Blanc',
        'orange' => 'Orange',
        'black'  => 'Noir',
        'green'  => 'Vert',
    );
    /**
     * Form initialization
     *
     * @return void
     */
    public function init()
    {
        $this->setMethod('post');
        $this->setAttribs(array(
            'name'   => 'masterForm',
```

```
));
$this->setDecorators(array(
    'FormElements',
    array('TabContainer', array(
        'id' => 'tabContainer',
        'style' => 'width: 600px; height: 500px;',
        'dijitParams' => array(
            'tabPosition' => 'top'
        ),
    )),
    'DijitForm',
));
$textForm = new Zend_Dojo_Form_SubForm();
$textForm->setAttribs(array(
    'name'   => 'textboxtab',
    'legend' => 'Text Elements',
    'dijitParams' => array(
        'title' => 'Text Elements',
    ),
));
$textForm->addElement(
        'TextBox',
        'textbox',
        array(
            'value'      => 'some text',
            'label'      => 'TextBox',
            'trim'       => true,
            'propercase' => true,
        )
    )
    ->addElement(
        'DateTextBox',
        'datebox',
        array(
            'value' => '2008-07-05',
            'label' => 'DateTextBox',
            'required'  => true,
        )
    )
    ->addElement(
        'TimeTextBox',
        'timebox',
        array(
            'label' => 'TimeTextBox',
            'required'  => true,
        )
    )
    ->addElement(
        'CurrencyTextBox',
        'currencybox',
        array(
            'label' => 'CurrencyTextBox',
            'required'  => true,
            // 'currency' => 'USD',
            'invalidMessage' => 'Invalid amount. ' .
                                'Include dollar sign, commas, ' .
                                'and cents.',
            // 'fractional' => true,
            // 'symbol' => 'USD',
            // 'type' => 'currency',
        )
    )
    ->addElement(
        'NumberTextBox',
```

```
            'numberbox',
            array(
                'label' => 'NumberTextBox',
                'required'  => true,
                'invalidMessage' => 'Invalid elevation.',
                'constraints' => array(
                    'min' => -20000,
                    'max' => 20000,
                    'places' => 0,
                )
            )
        )
    ->addElement(
        'ValidationTextBox',
        'validationbox',
        array(
            'label' => 'ValidationTextBox',
            'required'  => true,
            'regExp' => '[\w]+',
            'invalidMessage' => 'Invalid non-space text.',
        )
    )
    ->addElement(
        'Textarea',
        'textarea',
        array(
            'label'    => 'Textarea',
            'required' => true,
            'style'    => 'width: 200px;',
        )
    );
$editorForm = new Zend_Dojo_Form_SubForm();
$editorForm->setAttribs(array(
    'name'   => 'editortab',
    'legend' => 'Editor',
    'dijitParams' => array(
        'title' => 'Editor'
    ),
))
$editorForm->addElement(
    'Editor',
    'wysiwyg',
    array(
        'label'        => 'Editor',
        'inheritWidth' => 'true',
    )
);
$toggleForm = new Zend_Dojo_Form_SubForm();
$toggleForm->setAttribs(array(
    'name'   => 'toggletab',
    'legend' => 'Toggle Elements',
));
$toggleForm->addElement(
        'NumberSpinner',
        'ns',
        array(
            'value'             => '7',
            'label'             => 'NumberSpinner',
            'smallDelta'        => 5,
            'largeDelta'        => 25,
            'defaultTimeout'    => 1000,
            'timeoutChangeRate' => 100,
            'min'               => 9,
            'max'               => 1550,
```

```
                             'places'                => 0,
                             'maxlength'             => 20,
                    )
           )
      ->addElement(
           'Button',
           'dijitButton',
           array(
                 'label' => 'Button',
           )
      )
      ->addElement(
           'CheckBox',
           'checkbox',
           array(
                 'label' => 'CheckBox',
                 'checkedValue'  => 'foo',
                 'uncheckedValue'  => 'bar',
                 'checked' => true,
           )
      )
      ->addElement(
           'RadioButton',
           'radiobutton',
           array(
                 'label' => 'RadioButton',
                 'multiOptions'  => array(
                     'foo' => 'Foo',
                     'bar' => 'Bar',
                     'baz' => 'Baz',
                 ),
                 'value' => 'bar',
           )
      );
$selectForm = new Zend_Dojo_Form_SubForm();
$selectForm->setAttribs(array(
      'name'  => 'selecttab',
      'legend' => 'Select Elements',
));
$selectForm->addElement(
           'ComboBox',
           'comboboxselect',
           array(
                 'label' => 'ComboBox (select)',
                 'value' => 'blue',
                 'autocomplete' => false,
                 'multiOptions' => $this->_selectOptions,
           )
      )
      ->addElement(
           'ComboBox',
           'comboboxremote',
           array(
                 'label' => 'ComboBox (remoter)',
                 'storeId' => 'stateStore',
                 'storeType' => 'dojo.data.ItemFileReadStore',
                 'storeParams' => array(
                     'url' => '/js/states.txt',
                 ),
                 'dijitParams' => array(
                     'searchAttr' => 'name',
                 ),
           )
      )
```

```
        ->addElement(
            'FilteringSelect',
            'filterselect',
            array(
                'label' => 'FilteringSelect (select)',
                'value' => 'blue',
                'autocomplete' => false,
                'multiOptions' => $this->_selectOptions,
            )
        )
        ->addElement(
            'FilteringSelect',
            'filterselectremote',
            array(
                'label' => 'FilteringSelect (remoter)',
                'storeId' => 'stateStore',
                'storeType' => 'dojo.data.ItemFileReadStore',
                'storeParams' => array(
                    'url' => '/js/states.txt',
                ),
                'dijitParams' => array(
                    'searchAttr' => 'name',
                ),
            )
        );
$sliderForm = new Zend_Dojo_Form_SubForm();
$sliderForm->setAttribs(array(
    'name'   => 'slidertab',
    'legend' => 'Slider Elements',
));
$sliderForm->addElement(
        'HorizontalSlider',
        'horizontal',
        array(
            'label' => 'HorizontalSlider',
            'value' => 5,
            'minimum' => -10,
            'maximum' => 10,
            'discreteValues' => 11,
            'intermediateChanges' => true,
            'showButtons' => true,
            'topDecorationDijit' => 'HorizontalRuleLabels',
            'topDecorationContainer' => 'topContainer',
            'topDecorationLabels' => array(
                    ' ',
                    '20%',
                    '40%',
                    '60%',
                    '80%',
                    ' ',
            ),
            'topDecorationParams' => array(
                'container' => array(
                    'style' => 'height:1.2em; ' .
                               'font-size=75%;color:gray;',
                ),
                'list' => array(
                    'style' => 'height:1em; ' .
                               'font-size=75%;color:gray;',
                ),
            ),
            'bottomDecorationDijit' => 'HorizontalRule',
            'bottomDecorationContainer' => 'bottomContainer',
            'bottomDecorationLabels' => array(
```

```
                                '0%',
                                '50%',
                                '100%',
                    ),
                    'bottomDecorationParams' => array(
                        'list' => array(
                            'style' => 'height:1em; ' .
                                        'font-size=75%;color:gray;',
                        ),
                    ),
                )
            )
            ->addElement(
                'VerticalSlider',
                'vertical',
                array(
                    'label' => 'VerticalSlider',
                    'value' => 5,
                    'style' => 'height: 200px; width: 3em;',
                    'minimum' => -10,
                    'maximum' => 10,
                    'discreteValues' => 11,
                    'intermediateChanges' => true,
                    'showButtons' => true,
                    'leftDecorationDijit' => 'VerticalRuleLabels',
                    'leftDecorationContainer' => 'leftContainer',
                    'leftDecorationLabels' => array(
                            ' ',
                            '20%',
                            '40%',
                            '60%',
                            '80%',
                            ' ',
                    ),
                    'rightDecorationDijit' => 'VerticalRule',
                    'rightDecorationContainer' => 'rightContainer',
                    'rightDecorationLabels' => array(
                            '0%',
                            '50%',
                            '100%',
                    ),
                )
            );
        $this->addSubForm($textForm, 'textboxtab')
            ->addSubForm($editorForm, 'editortab')
            ->addSubForm($toggleForm, 'toggletab')
            ->addSubForm($selectForm, 'selecttab')
            ->addSubForm($sliderForm, 'slidertab');
    }
}
```

Example 17.35. Modifying an existing form to utilize Dojo

Existing forms can be modified to utilize Dojo as well, by use of the Zend_Dojo::enableForm() static method.

This first example shows decorating an existing form instance:

```
$form = new My_Custom_Form();
Zend_Dojo::enableForm($form);
```

```
$form->addElement(
'ComboBox',
'query',
array(
    'label'        => 'Color:',
    'value'        => 'blue',
    'autocomplete' => false,
    'multiOptions' => array(
        'red'    => 'Rouge',
        'blue'   => 'Bleu',
        'white'  => 'Blanc',
        'orange' => 'Orange',
        'black'  => 'Noir',
        'green'  => 'Vert',
    ),
)
);
```

Alternately, you can make a slight tweak to your form initialization:

```
class My_Custom_Form extends Zend_Form
{
    public function init()
    {
        Zend_Dojo::enableForm($this);
        // ...
    }
}
```

Of course, if you can do that... you could and should simply alter the class to inherit from Zend_Dojo_Form, which is a drop-in replacement of Zend_Form that's already Dojo-enabled...

Chapter 18. Zend_Dom

Introduction

Zend_Dom provides tools for working with DOM documents and structures. Currently, we offer Zend_Dom_Query, which provides a unified interface for querying DOM documents utilizing both XPath and CSS selectors.

Zend_Dom_Query

Zend_Dom_Query provides mechanisms for querying XML and (X)HTML documents utilizing either XPath or CSS selectors. It was developed to aid with functional testing of MVC applications, but could also be used for rapid development of screen scrapers.

CSS selector notation is provided as a simpler and more familiar notation for web developers to utilize when querying documents with XML structures. The notation should be familiar to anybody who has developed Cascading Style Sheets or who utilizes Javascript toolkits that provide functionality for selecting nodes utilizing CSS selectors (Prototype's $$() [http://prototypejs.org/api/utility/dollar-dollar] and Dojo's dojo.query [http://api.dojotoolkit.org/jsdoc/dojo/HEAD/dojo.query] were both inspirations for the component).

Theory of Operation

To use Zend_Dom_Query, you instantiate a Zend_Dom_Query object, optionally passing a document to query (a string). Once you have a document, you can use either the query() or queryXpath() methods; each method will return a Zend_Dom_Query_Result object with any matching nodes.

The primary difference between Zend_Dom_Query and using DOMDocument + DOMXPath is the ability to select against CSS selectors. You can utilize any of the following, in any combination:

- *element types*: provide an element type to match: 'div', 'a', 'span', 'h2', etc.

- *style attributes*: CSS style attributes to match: '.error', 'div.error', 'label.required', etc. If an element defines more than one style, this will match as long as the named style is present anywhere in the style declaration.

- *id attributes*: element ID attributes to match: '#content', 'div#nav', etc.

- *arbitrary attributes*: arbitrary element attributes to match. Three different types of matching are provided:

  - *exact match*: the attribute exactly matches the string: 'div[bar="baz"]' would match a div element with a "bar" attribute that exactly matches the value "baz".

  - *word match*: the attribute contains a word matching the string: 'div[bar~="baz"]' would match a div element with a "bar" attribute that contains the word "baz". '<div bar="foo baz">' would match, but '<div bar="foo bazbat">' would not.

  - *substring match*: the attribute contains the string: 'div[bar*="baz"]' would match a div element with a "bar" attribute that contains the string "baz" anywhere within it.

- *direct descendents*: utilize '>' between selectors to denote direct descendents. 'div > span' would select only 'span' elements that are direct descendents of a 'div'. Can also be used with any of the selectors above.

- *descendents*: string together multiple selectors to indicate a hierarchy along which to search. 'div .foo span #one' would select an element of id 'one' that is a descendent of arbitrary depth beneath a 'span' element, which is in turn a descendent of arbitrary depth beneath an element with a class of 'foo', that is an descendent of arbitrary depth beneath a 'div' element. For example, it would match the link to the word 'One' in the listing below:

```
<div>
<table>
    <tr>
        <td class="foo">
            <div>
                Lorem ipsum <span class="bar">
                    <a href="/foo/bar" id="one">One</a>
                    <a href="/foo/baz" id="two">Two</a>
                    <a href="/foo/bat" id="three">Three</a>
                    <a href="/foo/bla" id="four">Four</a>
                </span>
            </div>
        </td>
    </tr>
</table>
</div>
```

Once you've performed your query, you can then work with the result object to determine information about the nodes, as well as to pull them and/or their content directly for examination and manipulation. Zend_Dom_Query_Result implements Countable and Iterator, and store the results internally as DOMNodes/DOMElements. As an example, consider the following call, that selects against the HTML above:

```
$dom = new Zend_Dom_Query($html);
$results = $dom->query('.foo .bar a');
$count = count($results); // get number of matches: 4
foreach ($results as $result) {
    // $result is a DOMElement
}
```

Zend_Dom_Query also allows straight XPath queries utilizing the queryXpath() method; you can pass any valid XPath query to this method, and it will return a Zend_Dom_Query_Result object.

Methods Available

The Zend_Dom_Query family of classes have the following methods available.

Zend_Dom_Query

The following methods are available to Zend_Dom_Query:

- setDocumentXml($document): specify an XML string to query against.

- setDocumentXhtml($document): specify an XHTML string to query against.

- setDocumentHtml($document): specify an HTML string to query against.

- setDocument($document): specify a string to query against; Zend_Dom_Query will then attempt to autodetect the document type.

- getDocument(): retrieve the original document string provided to the object.

- getDocumentType(): retrieve the document type of the document provided to the object; will be one of the DOC_XML, DOC_XHTML, or DOC_HTML class constants.

- `query($query)`: query the document using CSS selector notation.

- `queryXpath($xPathQuery)`: query the document using XPath notation.

Zend_Dom_Query_Result

As mentioned previously, `Zend_Dom_Query_Result` implements both `Iterator` and `Countable`, and as such can be used in a `foreach` loop as well as with the `count()` function. Additionally, it exposes the following methods:

- `getCssQuery()`: return the CSS selector query used to produce the result (if any).

- `getXpathQuery()`: return the XPath query used to produce the result. Internally, `Zend_Dom_Query` converts CSS selector queries to XPath, so this value will always be populated.

- `getDocument()`: retrieve the DOMDocument the selection was made against.

Chapter 19. Zend_Exception

Using Exceptions

Zend_Exception is simply the base class for all exceptions thrown within Zend Framework.

Example 19.1. Catching an Exception

The following code listing demonstrates how to catch an exception thrown in a Zend Framework class:

```
try {
    // Calling Zend_Loader::loadClass() with a non-existant class will cause
    // an exception to be thrown in Zend_Loader
    Zend_Loader::loadClass('nonexistantclass');
} catch (Zend_Exception $e) {
    echo "Caught exception: " . get_class($e) . "\n";
    echo "Message: " . $e->getMessage() . "\n";
    // Other code to recover from the error
}
```

Zend_Exception can be used as a catch-all exception class in a catch block to trap all exceptions thrown by Zend Framework classes. This can be useful when the program can not recover by catching a specific exception type.

The documentation for each Zend Framework component and class will contain specific information on which methods throw exceptions, the circumstances that cause an exception to be thrown, and the class of all exceptions that may be thrown.

Chapter 20. Zend_Feed

Introduction

Zend_Feed provides functionality for consuming RSS and Atom feeds. It provides a natural syntax for accessing elements of feeds, feed attributes, and entry attributes. Zend_Feed also has extensive support for modifying feed and entry structure with the same natural syntax, and turning the result back into XML. In the future, this modification support could provide support for the Atom Publishing Protocol.

Programmatically, Zend_Feed consists of a base Zend_Feed class, abstract Zend_Feed_Abstract and Zend_Feed_Entry_Abstract base classes for representing Feeds and Entries, specific implementations of feeds and entries for RSS and Atom, and a behind-the-scenes helper for making the natural syntax magic work.

In the example below, we demonstrate a simple use case of retrieving an RSS feed and saving relevant portions of the feed data to a simple PHP array, which could then be used for printing the data, storing to a database, etc.

Be aware

Many RSS feeds have different channel and item properties available. The RSS specification provides for many optional properties, so be aware of this when writing code to work with RSS data.

Example 20.1. Putting Zend_Feed to Work on RSS Feed Data

```
// Fetch the latest Slashdot headlines
try {
    $slashdotRss =
        Zend_Feed::import('http://rss.slashdot.org/Slashdot/slashdot');
} catch (Zend_Feed_Exception $e) {
    // feed import failed
    echo "Exception caught importing feed: {$e->getMessage()}\n";
    exit;
}
// Initialize the channel data array
$channel = array(
    'title'       => $slashdotRss->title(),
    'link'        => $slashdotRss->link(),
    'description' => $slashdotRss->description(),
    'items'       => array()
    );
// Loop over each channel item and store relevant data
foreach ($slashdotRss as $item) {
    $channel['items'][] = array(
        'title'       => $item->title(),
        'link'        => $item->link(),
        'description' => $item->description()
        );
}
```

Importing Feeds

Zend_Feed enables developers to retrieve feeds very easily. If you know the URI of a feed, simply use the Zend_Feed::import() method:

```
$feed = Zend_Feed::import('http://feeds.example.com/feedName');
```

You can also use Zend_Feed to fetch the contents of a feed from a file or the contents of a PHP string variable:

```
// importing a feed from a text file
$feedFromFile = Zend_Feed::importFile('feed.xml');
// importing a feed from a PHP string variable
$feedFromPHP = Zend_Feed::importString($feedString);
```

In each of the examples above, an object of a class that extends Zend_Feed_Abstract is returned upon success, depending on the type of the feed. If an RSS feed were retrieved via one of the import methods above, then a Zend_Feed_Rss object would be returned. On the other hand, if an Atom feed were imported, then a Zend_Feed_Atom object is returned. The import methods will also throw a Zend_Feed_Exception object upon failure, such as an unreadable or malformed feed.

Custom feeds

Zend_Feed enables developers to create custom feeds very easily. You just have to create an array and to import it with Zend_Feed. This array can be imported with Zend_Feed::importArray() or with Zend_Feed::importBuilder(). In this last case the array will be computed on the fly by a custom data source implementing Zend_Feed_Builder_Interface.

Importing a custom array

```
// importing a feed from an array
$atomFeedFromArray = Zend_Feed::importArray($array);
// the following line is equivalent to the above;
// by default a Zend_Feed_Atom instance is returned
$atomFeedFromArray = Zend_Feed::importArray($array, 'atom');
// importing a rss feed from an array
$rssFeedFromArray = Zend_Feed::importArray($array, 'rss');
```

The format of the array must conform to this structure:

```
array(
    //required
    'title' => 'title of the feed',
    'link'  => 'canonical url to the feed',
    // optional
    'lastUpdate' => 'timestamp of the update date',
    'published'  => 'timestamp of the publication date',
    // required
    'charset' => 'charset of the textual data',
    // optional
    'description' => 'short description of the feed',
    'author'      => 'author/publisher of the feed',
    'email'       => 'email of the author',
    // optional, ignored if atom is used
    'webmaster' => 'email address for person responsible '
                .  'for technical issues',
```

```
// optional
'copyright' => 'copyright notice',
'image'     => 'url to image',
'generator' => 'generator',
'language'  => 'language the feed is written in',
// optional, ignored if atom is used
'ttl'     => 'how long in minutes a feed can be cached '
      .   'before refreshing',
'rating' => 'The PICS rating for the channel.',
// optional, ignored if atom is used
// a cloud to be notified of updates
'cloud'       => array(
    // required
    'domain' => 'domain of the cloud, e.g. rpc.sys.com',
    // optional, defaults to 80
    'port' => 'port to connect to',
    // required
    'path'               => 'path of the cloud, e.g. /RPC2',
    'registerProcedure' => 'procedure to call, e.g. myCloud
        .rssPlsNotify',
    'protocol'           => 'protocol to use, e.g. soap or xml-rpc'
),
// optional, ignored if atom is used
// a text input box that can be displayed with the feed
'textInput'    => array(
    // required
    'title'        => 'label of the Submit button in the text
                        input area',
    'description' => 'explains the text input area',
    'name'         => 'the name of the text object in the text
                        input area',
    'link'         => 'URL of the CGI script processing text
                        input requests'
),
// optional, ignored if atom is used
// Hint telling aggregators which hours they can skip
'skipHours' => array(
    // up to 24 rows whose value is a number between 0 and 23
    // e.g 13 (1pm)
    'hour in 24 format'
),
// optional, ignored if atom is used
// Hint telling aggregators which days they can skip
'skipDays ' => array(
    // up to 7 rows whose value is
    // Monday, Tuesday, Wednesday, Thursday, Friday, Saturday or Sunday
    // e.g Monday
    'a day to skip'
),
// optional, ignored if atom is used
// Itunes extension data
'itunes' => array(
    // optional, default to the main author value
    'author' => 'Artist column',
    // optional, default to the main author value
    // Owner of the podcast
    'owner' => array(
        'name'  => 'name of the owner',
        'email' => 'email of the owner'
    ),
    // optional, default to the main image value
    'image' => 'album/podcast art',
    // optional, default to the main description value
    'subtitle' => 'short description',
```

```
    'summary'  => 'longer description',
    // optional
    'block' => 'Prevent an episode from appearing (yes|no)',
    // required, Category column and in iTunes Music Store Browse
    'category' => array(
        // up to 3 rows
        array(
            // required
            'main' => 'main category',
            // optional
            'sub'  => 'sub category'
        )
    ),
    // optional
    'explicit'     => 'parental advisory graphic (yes|no|clean)',
    'keywords'     => 'a comma separated list of 12 keywords maximum',
    'new-feed-url' => 'used to inform iTunes of new feed URL location'
),
'entries' => array(
    array(
        //required
        'title' => 'title of the feed entry',
        'link'  => 'url to a feed entry',
        // required, only text, no html
        'description' => 'short version of a feed entry',
        // optional
        'guid' => 'id of the article, '
              . 'if not given link value will used',
        // optional, can contain html
        'content' => 'long version',
        // optional
        'lastUpdate' => 'timestamp of the publication date',
        'comments'   => 'comments page of the feed entry',
        'commentRss' => 'the feed url of the associated comments',
        // optional, original source of the feed entry
        'source' => array(
            // required
            'title' => 'title of the original source',
            'url'   => 'url of the original source'
        ),
        // optional, list of the attached categories
        'category' => array(
            array(
                // required
                'term' => 'first category label',
                // optional
                'scheme' => 'url that identifies a categorization scheme'
            ),
            array(
                // data for the second category and so on
            )
        ),
        // optional, list of the enclosures of the feed entry
        'enclosure'    => array(
            array(
                // required
                'url' => 'url of the linked enclosure',
                // optional
                'type' => 'mime type of the enclosure',
                'length' => 'length of the linked content in octets'
            ),
            array(
                //data for the second enclosure and so on
            )
```

```
        )
    ),
    array(
        //data for the second entry and so on
    )
  )
);
```

References:

- RSS 2.0 specification: RSS 2.0 [http://blogs.law.harvard.edu/tech/rss]

- Atom specification: RFC 4287 [http://tools.ietf.org/html/rfc4287]

- WFW specification: Well Formed Web [http://wellformedweb.org/news/wfw_namespace_elements]

- iTunes specification: iTunes Technical Specifications [http://www.apple.com/itunes/store/podcaststechspecs.html]

Importing a custom data source

You can create a Zeed_Feed instance from any data source implementing Zend_Feed_Builder_Interface. You just have to implement the getHeader() and getEntries() methods to be able to use your object with Zend_Feed::importBuilder(). As a simple reference implementation, you can use Zend_Feed_Builder, which takes an array in its constructor, performs some minor validation, and then can be used in the importBuilder() method. The getHeader() method must return an instance of Zend_Feed_Builder_Header, and getEntries() must return an array of Zend_Feed_Builder_Entry instances.

Note

Zend_Feed_Builder serves as a concrete implementation to demonstrate the usage. Users are encouraged to make their own classes to implement Zend_Feed_Builder_Interface.

Here is an example of Zend_Feed::importBuilder() usage:

```
// importing a feed from a custom builder source
$atomFeedFromArray =
    Zend_Feed::importBuilder(new Zend_Feed_Builder($array));
// the following line is equivalent to the above;
// by default a Zend_Feed_Atom instance is returned
$atomFeedFromArray =
    Zend_Feed::importArray(new Zend_Feed_Builder($array), 'atom');
// importing a rss feed from a custom builder array
$rssFeedFromArray =
    Zend_Feed::importArray(new Zend_Feed_Builder($array), 'rss');
```

Dumping the contents of a feed

To dump the contents of a Zend_Feed_Abstract instance, you may use send() or saveXml() methods.

```
assert($feed instanceof Zend_Feed_Abstract);
// dump the feed to standard output
print $feed->saveXML();
// send http headers and dump the feed
$feed->send();
```

Retrieving Feeds from Web Pages

Web pages often contain <link> tags that refer to feeds with content relevant to the particular page. Zend_Feed enables you to retrieve all feeds referenced by a web page with one simple method call:

```
$feedArray = Zend_Feed::findFeeds('http://www.example.com/news.html');
```

Here the findFeeds() method returns an array of Zend_Feed_Abstract objects that are referenced by <link> tags on the news.html web page. Depending on the type of each feed, each respective entry in the $feedArray array may be a Zend_Feed_Rss or Zend_Feed_Atom instance. Zend_Feed will throw a Zend_Feed_Exception upon failure, such as an HTTP 404 response code or a malformed feed.

Consuming an RSS Feed

Reading an RSS feed is as simple as instantiating a Zend_Feed_Rss object with the URL of the feed:

```
$channel = new Zend_Feed_Rss('http://rss.example.com/channelName');
```

If any errors occur fetching the feed, a Zend_Feed_Exception will be thrown.

Once you have a feed object, you can access any of the standard RSS "channel" properties directly on the object:

```
echo $channel->title();
```

Note the function syntax. Zend_Feed uses a convention of treating properties as XML object if they are requested with variable "getter" syntax ($obj->property) and as strings if they are access with method syntax ($obj->property()). This enables access to the full text of any individual node while still allowing full access to all children.

If channel properties have attributes, they are accessible using PHP's array syntax:

```
echo $channel->category['domain'];
```

Since XML attributes cannot have children, method syntax is not necessary for accessing attribute values.

Most commonly you'll want to loop through the feed and do something with its entries. Zend_Feed_Abstract implements PHP's Iterator interface, so printing all titles of articles in a channel is just a matter of:

```
foreach ($channel as $item) {
    echo $item->title() . "\n";
}
```

If you are not familiar with RSS, here are the standard elements you can expect to be available in an RSS channel and in individual RSS items (entries).

Required channel elements:

- title - The name of the channel

- link - The URL of the web site corresponding to the channel

- `description` - A sentence or several describing the channel

Common optional channel elements:

- `pubDate` - The publication date of this set of content, in RFC 822 date format

- `language` - The language the channel is written in

- `category` - One or more (specified by multiple tags) categories the channel belongs to

RSS `<item>` elements do not have any strictly required elements. However, either `title` or `description` must be present.

Common item elements:

- `title` - The title of the item

- `link` - The URL of the item

- `description` - A synopsis of the item

- `author` - The author's email address

- `category` - One more more categories that the item belongs to

- `comments` - URL of comments relating to this item

- `pubDate` - The date the item was published, in RFC 822 date format

In your code you can always test to see if an element is non-empty with:

```
if ($item->propname()) {
    // ... proceed.
}
```

If you use `$item->propname` instead, you will always get an empty object which will evaluate to TRUE, so your check will fail.

For further information, the official RSS 2.0 specification is available at: http://blogs.law.harvard.edu/tech/rss

Consuming an Atom Feed

`Zend_Feed_Atom` is used in much the same way as `Zend_Feed_Rss`. It provides the same access to feed-level properties and iteration over entries in the feed. The main difference is in the structure of the Atom protocol itself. Atom is a successor to RSS; it is more generalized protocol and it is designed to deal more easily with feeds that provide their full content inside the feed, splitting RSS' `description` tag into two elements, `summary` and `content`, for that purpose.

Example 20.2. Basic Use of an Atom Feed

Read an Atom feed and print the `title` and `summary` of each entry:

```
$feed = new Zend_Feed_Atom('http://atom.example.com/feed/');
echo 'The feed contains ' . $feed->count() . ' entries.' . "\n\n";
foreach ($feed as $entry) {
    echo 'Title: ' . $entry->title() . "\n";
```

```
        echo 'Summary: ' . $entry->summary() . "\n\n";
}
```

In an Atom feed you can expect to find the following feed properties:

- `title` - The feed's title, same as RSS's channel title

- `id` - Every feed and entry in Atom has a unique identifier

- `link` - Feeds can have multiple links, which are distinguished by a `type` attribute

  The equivalent to RSS's channel link would be `type="text/html"`. If the link is to an alternate version of the same content that's in the feed, it would have a `rel="alternate"` attribute.

- `subtitle` - The feed's description, equivalent to RSS' channel description

  `author->name()` - The feed author's name

  `author->email()` - The feed author's email address

Atom entries commonly have the following properties:

- `id` - The entry's unique identifier

- `title` - The entry's title, same as RSS item titles

- `link` - A link to another format or an alternate view of this entry

- `summary` - A summary of this entry's content

- `content` - The full content of the entry; can be skipped if the feed just contains summaries

- `author` - with `name` and `email` sub-tags like feeds have

- `published` - the date the entry was published, in RFC 3339 format

- `updated` - the date the entry was last updated, in RFC 3339 format

For more information on Atom and plenty of resources, see http://www.atomenabled.org/.

Consuming a Single Atom Entry

Single Atom `<entry>` elements are also valid by themselves. Usually the URL for an entry is the feed's URL followed by `/<entryId>`, such as `http://atom.example.com/feed/1`, using the example URL we used above.

If you read a single entry, you will still have a `Zend_Feed_Atom` object, but it will automatically create an "anonymous" feed to contain the entry.

Example 20.3. Reading a Single-Entry Atom Feed

```
$feed = new Zend_Feed_Atom('http://atom.example.com/feed/1');
echo 'The feed has: ' . $feed->count() . ' entry.';
$entry = $feed->current();
```

Alternatively, you could instantiate the entry object directly if you know you are accessing an `<entry>`-only document:

Example 20.4. Using the Entry Object Directly for a Single-Entry Atom Feed

```
$entry = new Zend_Feed_Entry_Atom('http://atom.example.com/feed/1');
echo $entry->title();
```

Modifying Feed and Entry structures

Zend_Feed's natural syntax extends to constructing and modifying feeds and entries as well as reading them. You can easily turn your new or modified objects back into well-formed XML for saving to a file or sending to a server.

Example 20.5. Modifying an Existing Feed Entry

```
$feed = new Zend_Feed_Atom('http://atom.example.com/feed/1');
$entry = $feed->current();
$entry->title = 'This is a new title';
$entry->author->email = 'my_email@example.com';
echo $entry->saveXML();
```

This will output a full (includes <?xml ... > prologue) XML representation of the new entry, including any necessary XML namespaces.

Note that the above will work even if the existing entry does not already have an author tag. You can use as many levels of -> access as you like before getting to an assignment; all of the intervening levels will be created for you automatically if necessary.

If you want to use a namespace other than atom:, rss:, or osrss: in your entry, you need to register the namespace with Zend_Feed using Zend_Feed::registerNamespace(). When you are modifying an existing element, it will always maintain its original namespace. When adding a new element, it will go into the default namespace if you do not explicitly specify another namespace.

Example 20.6. Creating an Atom Entry with Elements of Custom Namespaces

```
$entry = new Zend_Feed_Entry_Atom();
// id is always assigned by the server in Atom
$entry->title = 'my custom entry';
$entry->author->name = 'Example Author';
$entry->author->email = 'me@example.com';
// Now do the custom part.
Zend_Feed::registerNamespace('myns', 'http://www.example.com/myns/1.0');
$entry->{'myns:myelement_one'} = 'my first custom value';
$entry->{'myns:container_elt'}->part1 = 'first nested custom part';
$entry->{'myns:container_elt'}->part2 = 'second nested custom part';
echo $entry->saveXML();
```

Custom Feed and Entry Classes

Finally, you can extend the Zend_Feed classes if you'd like to provide your own format or niceties like automatic handling of elements that should go into a custom namespace.

Here is an example of a custom Atom entry class that handles its own myns: namespace entries. Note that it also makes the registerNamespace() call for you, so the end user doesn't need to worry about namespaces at all.

Example 20.7. Extending the Atom Entry Class with Custom Namespaces

```
/**
 * The custom entry class automatically knows the feed URI (optional) and
 * can automatically add extra namespaces.
 */
class MyEntry extends Zend_Feed_Entry_Atom
{
    public function __construct($uri = 'http://www.example.com/myfeed/',
                               $xml = null)
    {
        parent::__construct($uri, $xml);
        Zend_Feed::registerNamespace('myns',
                                     'http://www.example.com/myns/1.0');
    }
    public function __get($var)
    {
        switch ($var) {
            case 'myUpdated':
                // Translate myUpdated to myns:updated.
                return parent::__get('myns:updated');
            default:
                return parent::__get($var);
        }
    }
    public function __set($var, $value)
    {
        switch ($var) {
            case 'myUpdated':
                // Translate myUpdated to myns:updated.
                parent::__set('myns:updated', $value);
                break;
            default:
                parent::__set($var, $value);
        }
    }
    public function __call($var, $unused)
    {
        switch ($var) {
            case 'myUpdated':
                // Translate myUpdated to myns:updated.
                return parent::__call('myns:updated', $unused);
            default:
                return parent::__call($var, $unused);
        }
    }
}
```

Then to use this class, you'd just instantiate it directly and set the myUpdated property:

```
$entry = new MyEntry();
$entry->myUpdated = '2005-04-19T15:30';
// method-style call is handled by __call function
$entry->myUpdated();
// property-style call is handled by __get function
$entry->myUpdated;
```

Chapter 21. Zend_File

Zend_File_Transfer

Zend_File_Transfer provides extensive support for file uploads and downloads. It comes with built-in validators for files plus functionality to change files with filters. Protocol adapters allow Zend_File_Transfer to expose the same API for transport protocols like HTTP, FTP, WEBDAV and more.

Limitation

The current implementation of Zend_File_Transfer is limited to HTTP Post Uploads. Other adapters supporting downloads and other protocols will be added in future releases. Unimplemented methods will throw an exception. For now, you should use Zend_File_Transfer_Adapter_Http directly. As soon as there are multiple adapters available you can use a common interface.

Forms

When you are using Zend_Form you should use the APIs provided by Zend_Form and not Zend_File_Transfer directly. The file transfer support in Zend_Form is implemented with Zend_File_Transfer, so the information in this chapter may be useful for advanced users of Zend_Form.

The usage of Zend_File_Transfer is relatively simple. It consists of two parts. The HTTP form does the upload, while the Zend_File_Transfer handles the uploaded files. See the following example:

Example 21.1. Simple Form for Uploading Files

This example illustrates basic file uploading. The first part is the file form. In our example there is one file to upload.

```
<form enctype="multipart/form-data" action="/file/upload" method="POST">
    <input type="hidden" name="MAX_FILE_SIZE" value="100000" />
        Choose a file to upload: <input name="uploadedfile" type="file" />
    <br />
    <input type="submit" value="Upload File" />
</form>
```

For convenience, you can use Zend_Form_Element_File instead of building the HTML manually.

The next step is to create the receiver of the upload. In our example the receiver is located at /file/upload. So next we will create the file controller and the upload action.

```
$adapter = new Zend_File_Transfer_Adapter_Http();
$adapter->setDestination('C:\temp');
if (!$adapter->receive()) {
    $messages = $adapter->getMessages();
    echo implode("\n", $messages);
}
```

This code listing demonstrates the simplest usage of Zend_File_Transfer. A local destination is set with the setDestination method, then the receive() method is called. If there are any upload errors, an error will be returned.

Attention

This example is suitable only for demonstrating the basic API of Zend_File_Transfer. You should *never* use this code listing in a production environment, because severe security issues may be introduced. You should always use validators to increase security.

Supported Adapters for Zend_File_Transfer

Zend_File_Transfer is designed to support a variety of adapters and transfer directions. With Zend_File_Transfer you can upload, download and even forward (upload one adapter and download with another adapter at the same time) files.

Options for Zend_File_Transfer

Zend_File_Transfer and its adapters support different options. You can set all options either by passing them to the constructor or by calling setOptions($options). getOptions() will return the options that are currently set. The following is a list of all supported options.

• *ignoreNoFile*: If this option is set to true, all validators will ignore files that have not been uploaded by the form. The default value is false which results in an error if no files were specified.

Checking Files

Zend_File_Transfer has several methods that check for various states of the specified file. These are useful if you must process files after they have been uploaded. These methods include:

• *isValid($files = null)*: This method will check if the given files are valid, based on the validators that are attached to the files. If no files are specified, all files will be checked. You can call isValid() before calling receive(); in this case, receive() will not call isValid internally again when receiving the file.

• *isUploaded($files = null)*: This method will check if the specified files have been uploaded by the user. This is useful when you have defined one or more optional files. When no files are specified, all files will be checked.

• *isReceived($files = null)*: This method will check if the given files have already been received. When no files are specified, all files will be checked.

Example 21.2. Checking Files

```
$upload = new Zend_File_Transfer();
// Returns all known internal file information
$files = $upload->getFileInfo();
foreach ($files as $file => $info) {
    // file uploaded ?
    if (!$upload->isUploaded($file)) {
        print "Why havn't you uploaded the file ?";
        continue;
    }
    // validators are ok ?
    if (!$upload->isValid($file)) {
        print "Sorry but $file is not what we wanted";
        continue;
    }
}
$upload->receive();
```

Additional File Informations

Zend_File_Transfer can return additional information on files. The following methods are available:

- *getFileName($file = null, $path = true)*: This method will return the real file name of a transferred file.

- *getFileInfo($file = null)*: This method will return all internal information for the given file.

- *getFileSize($file = null)*: This method will return the real filesize for the given file.

- *getHash($hash = 'crc32', $files = null)*: This method returns a hash of the content of a given transferred file.

- *getMimeType($files = null)*: This method returns the mimetype of a given transferred file.

getFileName() accepts the name of the element as first parameter. If no name is given, all known filenames will be returned in an array. If the file is a multifile, you will also get an array. If there is only a single file a string will be returned.

By default file names will be returned with the complete path. If you only need the file name without path, you can set the second parameter, $path, which will truncate the file path when set to false.

Example 21.3. Getting the Filename

```
$upload = new Zend_File_Transfer();
$upload->receive();
// Returns the file names from all files
$names = $upload->getFileName();
// Returns the file names from the 'foo' form element
$names = $upload->getFileName('foo');
```

Note

Note that the file name can change after you receive the file, because all filters will be applied once the file is received. So you should always call getFileName() after the files have been received.

getFileSize() returns per default the real filesize in SI notation which means you will get 2kB instead of 2048. If you need only the plain size set the useByteString option to false.

Example 21.4. Getting the size of a file

```
$upload = new Zend_File_Transfer();
$upload->receive();
// Returns the sizes from all files as array if more than one file
    was uploaded
$size = $upload->getFileSize();
// Switches of the SI notation to return plain numbers
$upload->setOption(array('useByteString' => false));
$size = $upload->getFileSize();
```

getHash() accepts the name of a hash algorithm as first parameter. For a list of known algorithms refer to PHP's hash_algos method [http://php.net/hash_algos]. If you don't specify an algorithm, the crc32 algorithm will be used by default.

Example 21.5. Getting the hash of a file

```
$upload = new Zend_File_Transfer();
$upload->receive();
// Returns the hashes from all files as array if more than one file
    was uploaded
$hash = $upload->getHash('md5');
// Returns the hash for the 'foo' form element
$names = $upload->getHash('crc32', 'foo');
```

Note

Note that if the given file or form name contains more than one file, the returned value will be an array.

getMimeType() returns the mimetype of a file. If more than one file was uploaded it returns an array, otherwise a string.

Example 21.6. Getting the mimetype of a file

```
$upload = new Zend_File_Transfer();
$upload->receive();
$mime = $upload->getMimeType();
// Returns the mimetype for the 'foo' form element
$names = $upload->getMimeType('foo');
```

Note

Note that this method uses the fileinfo extension if it is available. If this extension can not be found, it uses the mimemagic extension. When no extension was found it uses the mimetype given by the fileserver when the file was uploaded.

Progress for file uploads

Zend_File_Transfer can give you the actual state of a fileupload in progress. To use this feature you need either the APC extension which is provided with most default PHP installations, or the uploadprogress extension. Both extensions are detected and used automatically. To be able to get the progress you need to meet some prerequisites.

First, you need to have either APC or uploadprogress to be enabled. Note that you can disable this feature of APC within your php.ini.

Second, you need to have the proper hidden fields added in the form which sends the files. When you use Zend_Form_Element_File this hidden fields are automatically added by Zend_Form.

When the above two points are provided then you are able to get the actual progress of the file upload by using the getProgress method. Actually there are 2 official ways to handle this.

Using a progressbar adapter

You can use the convinient *Zend_ProgressBar* to get the actual progress and can display it in a simple manner to your user.

To archive this, you have to add the wished *Zend_ProgressBar_Adapter* to `getProgress()` when you are calling it the first time. For details about the right adapter to use, look into the chapter Zend_ProgressBar Standard Adapters.

Example 21.7. Using the progressbar adapter to retrieve the actual state

```
$adapter = new Zend_ProgressBar_Adapter_Console();
$upload  = Zend_File_Transfer_Adapter_Http::getProgress($adapter);
$upload = null;
while (!$upload['done']) {
    $upload = Zend_File_Transfer_Adapter_Http:getProgress($upload);
}
```

The complete handling is done by `getProgress()` for you in the background.

Using getProgress() manually

You can also work manually with `getProgress()` without the usage of `Zend_ProgressBar`.

Call `getProgress()` without settings. It will return you an array with several keys. They differ according to the used PHP extension. But the following keys are given independently of the extension:

- *id*: The ID of this upload. This ID identifies the upload within the extension. It is filled automatically. You should never change or give this value yourself.

- *total*: The total filesize of the uploaded files in bytes as integer.

- *current*: The current uploaded filesize in bytes as integer.

- *rate*: The average upload speed in bytes per second as integer.

- *done*: Returns true when the upload is finished and false otherwise.

- *message*: The actual message. Eighter the progress as text in the form *10kB / 200kB*, or a helpful message in the case of a problem. Problems could be, that there is no upload in progress, that there was a failure while retrieving the data for the progress, or that the upload has been canceled.

- *progress*: This optional key takes a instance of Zend_ProgressBar_Adapter or Zend_ProgressBar and allows to get the actual upload state within a progressbar.

- *session*: This optional key takes the name of a session namespace which will be used within Zend_ProgressBar. When this key is not given it defaults to `Zend_File_Transfer_Adapter_Http_ProgressBar`.

All other returned keys are provided directly from the extensions and will not be checked.

The following example shows a possible manual usage:

Example 21.8. Manual usage of the file progress

```
$upload  = Zend_File_Transfer_Adapter_Http::getProgress();
while (!$upload['done']) {
    $upload = Zend_File_Transfer_Adapter_Http:getProgress($upload);
    print "\nActual progress:".$upload['message'];
    // do whatever you need
}
```

Validators for Zend_File_Transfer

Zend_File_Transfer is delivered with several file-related validators which can be used to increase security and prevent possible attacks. Note that these validators are only as effective as how effectively you apply them. All validators provided with Zend_File_Transfer can be found in the Zend_Validator component and are named Zend_Validate_File_*. The following validators are available:

- Count: This validator checks for the number of files. A minimum and maximum range can be specified. An error will be thrown if either limit is crossed.

- Crc32: This validator checks for the crc32 hash value of the content from a file. It is based on the Hash validator and provides a convenient and simple validator that only supports Crc32.

- ExcludeExtension: This validator checks the extension of files. It will throw an error when an given file has a defined extension. With this validator, you can exclude defined extensions from being validated.

- ExcludeMimeType: This validator validates the MIME type of files. It can also validate MIME types and will throw an error if the MIME type of specified file matches.

- Exists: This validator checks for the existence of files. It will throw an error when a specified file does not exist.

- Extension: This validator checks the extension of files. It will throw an error when a specified file has an undefined extension.

- FilesSize: This validator checks the size of validated files. It remembers internally the size of all checked files and throws an error when the sum of all specified files exceed the defined size. It also provides minimum and maximum values.

- ImageSize: This validator checks the size of image. It validates the width and height and enforces minimum and maximum dimensions.

- IsCompressed: This validator checks whether the file is compressed. It is based on the MimeType validator and validates for compression archives like zip or arc. You can also limit it to other archives.

- IsImage: This validator checks whether the file is an image. It is based on the MimeType validator and validates for image files like jpg or gif. You can also limit it to other image types.

- Hash: This validator checks the hash value of the content from a file. It supports multiple algorithms.

- Md5: This validator checks for the md5 hash value of the content from a file. It is based on the Hash validator and provides a convenient and simple validator that only supports Md5.

- `MimeType`: This validator validates the MIME type of files. It can also validate MIME types and will throw an error if the MIME type of a specified file does not match.

- `NotExists`: This validator checks for the existence of files. It will throw an error when an given file does exist.

- `Sha1`: This validator checks for the sha1 hash value of the content from a file. It is based on the `Hash` validator and provides a convenient and simple validator that only supports sha1.

- `Size`: This validator is able to check files for its file size. It provides a minimum and maximum size range and will throw an error when either of these thesholds are crossed.

- `Upload`: This validator is internal. It checks if an upload has resulted in an error. You must not set it, as it's automatically set by `Zend_File_Transfer` itself. So you do not use this validator directly. You should only know that it exists.

- `WordCount`: This validator is able to check the number of words within files. It provides a minimum and maximum count and will throw an error when either of these thresholds are crossed.

Using Validators with Zend_File_Transfer

Putting validators to work is quite simple. There are several methods for adding and manipulating validators:

- `isValid($files = null)`: Checks the specified files using all validators. `$files` may be either a real filename, the element's name or the name of the temporary file.

- `addValidator($validator, $breakChainOnFailure, $options = null, $files = null)`: Adds the specified validator to the validator stack (optionally only to the file(s) specified). `$validator` may be either an actual validator instance or a short name specifying the validator type (e.g., 'Count').

- `addValidators(array $validators, $files = null)`: Adds the specified validators to the stack of validators. Each entry may be either a validator type/options pair or an array with the key 'validator' specifying the validator. All other options will be considered validator options for instantiation.

- `setValidators(array $validators, $files = null)`: Overwrites any existing validators with the validators specified. The validators should follow the syntax for `addValidators()`.

- `hasValidator($name)`: Indicates whether a validator has been registered.

- `getValidator($name)`: Returns a previously registered validator.

- `getValidators($files = null)`: Returns registered validators. If `$files` is specified, returns validators for that particular file or set of files.

- `removeValidator($name)`: Removes a previously registered validator.

- `clearValidators()`: Clears all registered validators.

Example 21.9. Add Validators to a File Transfer Object

```
$upload = new Zend_File_Transfer();
// Set a file size with 20000 bytes
$upload->addValidator('Size', false, 20000);
// Set a file size with 20 bytes minimum and 20000 bytes maximum
```

```
$upload->addValidator('Size', false, array('min' => 20, 'max' => 20000));
// Set a file size with 20 bytes minimum and 20000 bytes maximum and
// a file count in one step
$upload->setValidators(array(
    'Size'  => array('min' => 20, 'max' => 20000),
    'Count' => array('min' => 1, 'max' => 3),
));
```

Example 21.10. Limit Validators to Single Files

addValidator(), addValidators(), and setValidators() each accept a final $files argument. This argument can be used to specify a particular file or array of files on which to set the given validator.

```
$upload = new Zend_File_Transfer();
// Set a file size with 20000 bytes and limits it only to 'file2'
$upload->addValidator('Size', false, 20000, 'file2');
```

Normally, you should use the addValidators() method, which can be called multiple times.

Example 21.11. Add Multiple Validators

Often it's simpler just to call addValidator() multiple times with one call for each validator. This also increases readability and makes your code more maintainable. All methods provide a fluent interface, so you can couple the calls as shown below:

```
$upload = new Zend_File_Transfer();
// Set a file size with 20000 bytes
$upload->addValidator('Size', false, 20000)
       ->addValidator('Count', false, 2)
       ->addValidator('Filessize', false, 25000);
```

Note

Note that setting the same validator multiple times is allowed, but doing so can lead to issues when using different options for the same validator.

Last but not least, you can simply check the files using isValid().

Example 21.12. Validate the Files

isValid() accepts the file name of the uploaded or downloaded file, the temporary file name and or the name of the form element. If no parameter or null is given all files will be validated

```
$upload = new Zend_File_Transfer();
// Set a file size with 20000 bytes
$upload->addValidator('Size', false, 20000)
       ->addValidator('Count', false, 2)
       ->addValidator('Filessize', false, 25000);
if ($upload->isValid()) {
```

```
        print "Validation failure";
}
```

Note

Note that isValid() will be called automatically when you receive the files and have not called it previously.

When validation has failed it is a good idea to get information about the problems found. To get this information, you can use the methods getMessages() which returns all validation messages as array, getErrors() which returns all error codes, and hasErrors() which returns true as soon as a validation error has been found.

Count Validator

The Count validator checks for the number of files which are provided. It supports the following option keys:

- min: Sets the minimum number of files to transfer.

  ## Note

  When using this option you must give the minimum number of files when calling this validator the first time; otherwise you will get an error in return.

  With this option you can define the minimum number of files you expect to receive.

- max: Sets the maximum number of files to transfer.

  With this option you can limit the number of files which are accepted but also detect a possible attack when more files are given than defined in your form.

If you initiate this validator with a string or integer, the value will be used as max. Or you can also use the methods setMin() and setMax() to set both options afterwards and getMin() and getMax() to retrieve the actual set values.

Example 21.13. Using the Count Validator

```
$upload = new Zend_File_Transfer();
// Limit the amount of files to maximum 2
$upload->addValidator('Count', false, 2);
// Limit the amount of files to maximum 5 and minimum 1 file
$upload->addValidator('Count', false, array('min' =>1, 'max' => 5));
```

Note

Note that this validator stores the number of checked files internally. The file which exceeds the maximum will be returned as error.

Crc32 Validator

The Crc32 validator checks the content of a transferred file by hashing it. This validator uses the hash extension from PHP with the crc32 algorithm. It supports the following options:

- *: Sets any key or use a numeric array. The values will be used as hash to validate against.

You can set multiple hashes by using different keys. Each will be checked and the validation will fail only if all values fail.

Example 21.14. Using the Crc32 Validator

```
$upload = new Zend_File_Transfer();
// Checks whether the content of the uploaded file has the given hash
$upload->addValidator('Crc32', false, '3b3652f');
// Limits this validator to two different hashes
$upload->addValidator('Crc32', false, array('3b3652f', 'e612b69'));
```

ExcludeExtension Validator

The `ExcludeExtension` validator checks the file extension of the specified files. It supports the following options:

- `*`: Sets any key or use a numeric array. The values will be used to check whether the given file does not use this file extension.

- `case`: Sets a boolean indicating whether validation should be case-sensitive. The default is not case sensitive. Note that this key can be applied to for all available extensions.

This validator accepts multiple extensions, either as a comma-delimited string, or as an array. You may also use the methods `setExtension()`, `addExtension()`, and `getExtension()` to set and retrieve extensions.

In some cases it is useful to match in a case-sensitive fashion. So the constructor allows a second parameter called `$case` which, if set to true, validates the extension by comparing it with the specified values in a case-sensitive fashion.

Example 21.15. Using the ExcludeExtension Validator

```
$upload = new Zend_File_Transfer();
// Do not allow files with extension php or exe
$upload->addValidator('ExcludeExtension', false, 'php,exe');
// Do not allow files with extension php or exe, but use array notation
$upload->addValidator('ExcludeExtension', false, array('php', 'exe'));
// Check in a case-sensitive fashion
$upload->addValidator('ExcludeExtension',
                      false,
                      array('php', 'exe', 'case' => true));
$upload->addValidator('ExcludeExtension',
                      false,
                      array('php', 'exe', 'case' => true));
```

Note

Note that this validator only checks the file extension. It does not check the file's MIME type.

ExcludeMimeType Validator

The `ExcludeMimeType` validator checks the MIME type of transferred files. It supports the following options:

- `*`: Sets any key individually or use a numeric array. Sets the MIME type to validate against.

  With this option you can define the MIME type of files that are not to be accepted.

This validator accepts multiple MIME types, either as a comma-delimited string, or as an array. You may also use the methods `setMimeType()`, `addMimeType()`, and `getMimeType()` to set and retrieve the MIME types.

Example 21.16. Using the ExcludeMimeType Validator

```
$upload = new Zend_File_Transfer();
// Does not allow MIME type of gif images for all files
$upload->addValidator('ExcludeMimeType', false, 'image/gif');
// Does not allow MIME type of gif and jpg images for all given files
$upload->addValidator('ExcludeMimeType', false, array('image/gif',
                                                       'image/jpeg');
// Does not allow MIME type of the group images for all given files
$upload->addValidator('ExcludeMimeType', false, 'image');
```

The above example shows that it is also possible to disallow groups of MIME types. For example, to disallow all images, just use 'image' as the MIME type. This can be used for all groups of MIME types like 'image', 'audio', 'video', 'text', etc.

Note

Note that disallowing groups of MIME types will disallow all members of this group even if this is not intentional. When you disallow 'image' you will disallow all types of images like 'image/jpeg' or 'image/vasa'. When you are not sure if you want to disallow all types, you should disallow only specific MIME types instead of complete groups.

Exists Validator

The `Exists` validator checks for the existence of specified files. It supports the following options:

- `*`: Sets any key or use a numeric array to check if the specific file exists in the given directory.

This validator accepts multiple directories, either as a comma-delimited string, or as an array. You may also use the methods `setDirectory()`, `addDirectory()`, and `getDirectory()` to set and retrieve directories.

Example 21.17. Using the Exists Validator

```
$upload = new Zend_File_Transfer();
// Add the temp directory to check for
$upload->addValidator('Exists', false, '\temp');
// Add two directories using the array notation
$upload->addValidator('Exists',
                      false,
                      array('\home\images', '\home\uploads'));
```

Note

Note that this validator checks whether the specified file exists in all of the given directories. The validation will fail if the file does not exist in any of the given directories.

Extension Validator

The `Extension` validator checks the file extension of the specified files. It supports the following options:

- `*`: Sets any key or use a numeric array to check whether the specified file has this file extension.

- `case`: Sets whether validation should be done in a case-sensitive fashion. The default is no case sensitivity. Note the this key is used for all given extensions.

This validator accepts multiple extensions, either as a comma-delimited string, or as an array. You may also use the methods `setExtension()`, `addExtension()`, and `getExtension()` to set and retrieve extension values.

In some cases it is useful to test in a case-sensitive fashion. Therefore the constructor takes a second parameter `$case`, which, if set to true, will validate the extension in a case-sensitive fashion.

Example 21.18. Using the Extension Validator

```
$upload = new Zend_File_Transfer();
// Limit the extensions to jpg and png files
$upload->addValidator('Extension', false, 'jpg,png');
// Limit the extensions to jpg and png files but use array notation
$upload->addValidator('Extension', false, array('jpg', 'png'));
// Check case sensitive
$upload->addValidator('Extension', false, array('mo', 'png', 'case'
    => true));
if (!$upload->isValid('C:\temp\myfile.MO')) {
    print 'Not valid because MO and mo do not match with case
        sensitivity;
}
```

Note

Note that this validator only checks the file extension. It does not check the file's MIME type.

FilesSize Validator

The `FilesSize` validator checks for the aggregate size of all transferred files. It supports the following options:

- `min`: Sets the minimum aggregate file size. This option defines the minimum aggregate file size to be transferred.

- `max`: Sets the maximum aggregate file size.

  This option limits the aggregate file size of all transferred files, but not the file size of individual files.

- `bytestring`: Defines whether a failure is to return a user-friendly number or the plain file size.

  This option defines whether the user sees '10864' or '10MB'. The default value is true, so '10MB' is returned if you did not specify otherwise.

You can initialize this validator with a string, which will then be used to set the max option. You can also use the methods `setMin()` and `setMax()` to set both options after construction, along with `getMin()` and `getMax()` to retrieve the values that have been set previously.

The size itself is also accepted in SI notation as handled by most operating systems. That is, instead of specifying *20000 bytes*, *20kB* may be given. All file sizes are converted using 1024 as the base value. The following Units are accepted: `kB`, `MB`, `GB`, `TB`, `PB` and `EB`. Note that 1kB is equal to 1024 bytes, 1MB is equal to 1024kB, and so on.

Example 21.19. Using the FilesSize Validator

```
$upload = new Zend_File_Transfer();
// Limit the size of all files to be uploaded to 40000 bytes
$upload->addValidator('FilesSize', false, 40000);
// Limit the size of all files to be uploaded to maximum 4MB and mimimum 10kB
$upload->addValidator('FilesSize',
                      false,
                      array('min' => '10kB', 'max' => '4MB'));
// As before, but returns the plain file size instead of a user-friendly string
$upload->addValidator('FilesSize',
                      false,
                      array('min' => '10kB',
                            'max' => '4MB',
                            'bytestring' => false));
```

Note

Note that this validator internally stores the file size of checked files. The file which exceeds the size will be returned as an error.

ImageSize Validator

The `ImageSize` validator checks the size of image files. It supports the following options:

- `minheight`: Sets the minimum image height.

- `maxheight`: Sets the maximum image height.

- `minwidth`: Sets the minimum image width.

- `maxwidth`: Sets the maximum image width.

The methods `setImageMin()` and `setImageMax()` also set both minimum and maximum values, while the methods `getMin()` and `getMax()` return the currently set values.

For your convenience there are also the `setImageWidth()` and `setImageHeight()` methods, which set the minimum and maximum height and width of the image file. They, too, have corresponding `getImageWidth()` and `getImageHeight()` methods to retrieve the currently set values.

To bypass validation of a particular dimension, the relevent option simply should not be set.

Example 21.20. Using the ImageSize Validator

```
$upload = new Zend_File_Transfer();
// Limit the size of a image to a height of 100-200 and a width of
// 40-80 pixel
$upload->addValidator('ImageSize', false,
                         array('minwidth' => 40,
                               'maxwidth' => 80,
                               'minheight' => 100,
                               'maxheight' => 200)
                     );
// Reset the width for validation
$upload->setImageWidth(array('minwidth' => 20, 'maxwidth' => 200));
```

IsCompressed Validator

The `IsCompressed` validator checks if a transferred file is a compressed archive, such as zip or arc. This validator is based on the `MimeType` validator and supports the same methods and options. You may also limit this validator to particular compression types with the methods described there.

Example 21.21. Using the IsCompressed Validator

```
$upload = new Zend_File_Transfer();
// Checks is the uploaded file is a compressed archive
$upload->addValidator('IsCompressed', false);
// Limits this validator to zip files only
$upload->addValidator('IsCompressed', false, array('application/zip'));
// Limits this validator to zip files only using simpler notation
$upload->addValidator('IsCompressed', false, 'zip');
```

Note

Note that there is no check if you set a MIME type that is not a archive. For example, it would be possible to define gif files to be accepted by this validator. Using the 'MimeType' validator for files which are not archived will result in more readable code.

IsImage Validator

The `IsImage` validator checks if a transferred file is a image file, such as gif or jpeg. This validator is based on the `MimeType` validator and supports the same methods and options. You can limit this validator to particular image types with the methods described there.

Example 21.22. Using the IsImage Validator

```
$upload = new Zend_File_Transfer();
// Checks whether the uploaded file is a image file
$upload->addValidator('IsImage', false);
// Limits this validator to gif files only
$upload->addValidator('IsImage', false, array('application/gif'));
```

```
// Limits this validator to jpeg files only using a simpler notation
$upload->addValidator('IsImage', false, 'jpeg');
```

Note

Note that there is no check if you set a MIME type that is not an image. For example, it would be possible to define zip files to be accepted by this validator. Using the 'MimeType' validator for files which are not images will result in more readable code.

Hash Validator

The Hash validator checks the content of a transferred file by hashing it. This validator uses the hash extension from PHP. It supports the following options:

- *: Takes any key or use a numeric array. Sets the hash to validate against.

  You can set multiple hashes by passing them as an array. Each file is checked, and the validation will fail only if all files fail validation.

- algorithm: Sets the algorithm to use for hashing the content.

  You can set multiple algorithm by calling the addHash() method multiple times.

Example 21.23. Using the Hash Validator

```
$upload = new Zend_File_Transfer();
// Checks if the content of the uploaded file contains the given hash
$upload->addValidator('Hash', false, '3b3652f');
// Limits this validator to two different hashes
$upload->addValidator('Hash', false, array('3b3652f', 'e612b69'));
// Sets a different algorithm to check against
$upload->addValidator('Hash',
                      false,
                      array('315b3cd8273d44912a7',
                            'algorithm' => 'md5'));
```

Note

This validator supports about 34 different hash algorithms. The most common include 'crc32', 'md5' and 'sha1'. A comprehesive list of supports hash algorithms can be found at the hash_algos method [http://php.net/hash_algos] on the php.net site [http://php.net].

Md5 Validator

The Md5 validator checks the content of a transferred file by hashing it. This validator uses the hash extension for PHP with the md5 algorithm. It supports the following options:

- *: Takes any key or use a numeric array.

  You can set multiple hashes by passing them as an array. Each file is checked, and the validation will fail only if all files fail validation.

Example 21.24. Using the Md5 Validator

```
$upload = new Zend_File_Transfer();
// Checks if the content of the uploaded file has the given hash
$upload->addValidator('Md5', false, '3b3652f336522365223');
// Limits this validator to two different hashes
$upload->addValidator('Md5',
                      false,
                      array('3b3652f336522365223',
                            'eb3365f3365ddc65365'));
```

MimeType Validator

The `MimeType` validator checks the MIME type of transferred files. It supports the following options:

- `*`: Sets any key or use a numeric array. Sets the MIME type type to validate against.

    Defines the MIME type of files to be accepted.

- `magicfile`: The magicfile to be used.

    With this option you can define which magicfile to use. When it's not set or empty, the MAGIC constant will be used instead. This option is available since Zend Framework 1.7.1.

This validator accepts multiple MIME type, either as a comma-delimited string, or as an array. You may also use the methods `setMimeType()`, `addMimeType()`, and `getMimeType()` to set and retrieve MIME type.

You can also set the magicfile which shall be used by fileinfo with the 'magicfile' option. Additionally there are convenient `setMagicFile()` and `getMagicFile()` methods which allow later setting and retrieving of the magicfile parameter. This methods are available since Zend Framework 1.7.1.

Example 21.25. Using the MimeType Validator

```
$upload = new Zend_File_Transfer();
// Limit the MIME type of all given files to gif images
$upload->addValidator('MimeType', false, 'image/gif');
// Limit the MIME type of all given files to gif and jpeg images
$upload->addValidator('MimeType', false, array('image/gif', 'image/jpeg'));
// Limit the MIME type of all given files to the group images
$upload->addValidator('MimeType', false, 'image');
// Use a different magicfile
$upload->addValidator('MimeType',
                      false,
                      array('image',
                            'magicfile' => '/path/to/magicfile.mgx'));
```

The above example shows that it is also possible to limit the accepted MIME type to a group of MIME types. To allow all images just use 'image' as MIME type. This can be used for all groups of MIME types like 'image', 'audio', 'video', 'text', and so on.

Note

Note that allowing groups of MIME types will accept all members of this group even if your application does not support them. When you allow 'image' you will also get 'image/xpixmap' or 'image/vasa' which could be problematic. When you are not sure if your application supports all types you should better allow only defined MIME types instead of the complete group.

Note

This component will use the `fileinfo` extension if it is available. If it's not, it will degrade to the `mime_content_type` function. And if the function call fails it will use the MIME type which is given by HTTP.

You should be aware of possible security problems when you have whether `fileinfo` nor `mime_content_type` available. The MIME type given by HTTP is not secure and can be easily manipulated.

NotExists Validator

The `NotExists` validator checks for the existence of the provided files. It supports the following options:

- `*`: Set any key or use a numeric array. Checks whether the file exists in the given directory.

This validator accepts multiple directories either as a comma-delimited string, or as an array. You may also use the methods `setDirectory()`, `addDirectory()`, and `getDirectory()` to set and retrieve directories.

Example 21.26. Using the NotExists Validator

```
$upload = new Zend_File_Transfer();
// Add the temp directory to check
$upload->addValidator('NotExists', false, '\temp');
// Add two directories using the array notation
$upload->addValidator('NotExists', false,
                      array('\home\images',
                            '\home\uploads')
                );
```

Note

Note that this validator checks if the file does not exist in all of the provided directories. The validation will fail if the file does exist in any of the given directories.

Sha1 Validator

The `Sha1` validator checks the content of a transferred file by hashing it. This validator uses the hash extension for PHP with the sha1 algorithm. It supports the following options:

- `*`: Takes any key or use a numeric array.

You can set multiple hashes by passing them as an array. Each file is checked, and the validation will fail only if all files fail validation.

Example 21.27. Using the sha1 Validator

```
$upload = new Zend_File_Transfer();
// Checks if the content of the uploaded file has the given hash
$upload->addValidator('sha1', false, '3b3652f336522365223');
// Limits this validator to two different hashes
$upload->addValidator('Sha1',
                      false, array('3b3652f336522365223',
                                   'eb3365f3365ddc65365'));
```

Size Validator

The Size validator checks for the size of a single file. It supports the following options:

- min: Sets the minimum file size.

- max: Sets the maximum file size.

- bytestring: Defines whether a failure is returned with a user-friendly number, or with the plain file size.

  With this option you can define if the user gets '10864' or '10MB'. Default value is true which returns '10MB'.

You can initialize this validator with a string, which will then be used to set the max option. You can also use the methods setMin() and setMax() to set both options after construction, along with getMin() and getMax() to retrieve the values that have been set previously.

The size itself is also accepted in SI notation as handled by most operating systems. That is, instead of specifying *20000 bytes*, *20kB* may be given. All file sizes are converted using 1024 as the base value. The following Units are accepted: kB, MB, GB, TB, PB and EB. Note that 1kB is equal to 1024 bytes, 1MB is equal to 1024kB, and so on.

Example 21.28. Using the Size Validator

```
$upload = new Zend_File_Transfer();
// Limit the size of a file to 40000 bytes
$upload->addValidator('Size', false, 40000);
// Limit the size a given file to maximum 4MB and mimimum 10kB
// Also returns the plain number in case of an error
// instead of a user-friendly number
$upload->addValidator('Size',
                      false,
                      array('min' => '10kB',
                            'max' => '4MB',
                            'bytestring' => false));
```

WordCount Validator

The WordCount validator checks for the number of words within provided files. It supports the following option keys:

- min: Sets the minimum number of words to be found.

- max: Sets the maximum number of words to be found.

If you initiate this validator with a string or integer, the value will be used as max. Or you can also use the methods setMin() and setMax() to set both options afterwards and getMin() and getMax() to retrieve the actual set values.

Example 21.29. Using the WordCount Validator

```
$upload = new Zend_File_Transfer();
// Limit the amount of words within files to maximum 2000
$upload->addValidator('WordCount', false, 2000);
// Limit the amount of words within files to maximum 5000 and minimum
   1000 words
$upload->addValidator('WordCount', false, array('min' => 1000, 'max' =>
   5000));
```

Filters for Zend_File_Transfer

Zend_File_Transfer is delivered with several file related filters which can be used to automate several tasks which are often done on files. Note that file filters are applied after validation. Also file filters behave slightly different that other filters. They will always return the file name and not the changed content (which would be a bad idea when working on 1GB files). All filters which are provided with Zend_File_Transfer can be found in the Zend_Filter component and are named Zend_Filter_File_*. The following filters are actually available:

- Decrypt: This filter can decrypt a encrypted file.

- Encrypt: This filter can encrypt a file.

- LowerCase: This filter can lowercase the content of a textfile.

- Rename: This filter can rename files, change the location and even force overwriting of existing files.

- UpperCase: This filter can uppercase the content of a textfile.

Using filters with Zend_File_Transfer

The usage of filters is quite simple. There are several methods for adding and manipulating filters.

- addFilter($filter, $options = null, $files = null): Adds the given filter to the filter stack (optionally only to the file(s) specified). $filter may be either an actual filter instance, or a short name specifying the filter type (e.g., 'Rename').

- addFilters(array $filters, $files = null): Adds the given filters to the stack of filters. Each entry may be either a filter type/options pair, or an array with the key 'filter' specifying the filter (all other options will be considered filter options for instantiation).

- setFilters(array $filters, $files = null): Overwrites any existing filters with the filters specified. The filters should follow the syntax for addFilters().

- hasFilter($name): Indicates if a filter has been registered.

- getFilter($name): Returns a previously registered filter.

- getFilters($files = null): Returns registered filters; if $files is passed, returns filters for that particular file or set of files.

- `removeFilter($name)`: Removes a previously registered filter.

- `clearFilters()`: Clears all registered filters.

Example 21.30. Add filters to a file transfer

```
$upload = new Zend_File_Transfer();
// Set a new destination path
$upload->addFilter('Rename', 'C:\picture\uploads');
// Set a new destination path and overwrites existing files
$upload->addFilter('Rename',
                   array('target' => 'C:\picture\uploads',
                         'overwrite' => true));
```

Example 21.31. Limit filters to single files

`addFilter()`, `addFilters()`, and `setFilters()` each accept a final `$files` argument. This argument can be used to specify a particular file or array of files on which to set the given filter.

```
$upload = new Zend_File_Transfer();
// Set a new destination path and limits it only to 'file2'
$upload->addFilter('Rename', 'C:\picture\uploads', 'file2');
```

Generally you should simply use the `addFilters()` method, which can be called multiple times.

Example 21.32. Add multiple filters

Often it's simpler just to call `addFilter()` multiple times. One call for each filter. This also increases the readability and makes your code more maintainable. As all methods provide a fluent interface you can couple the calls as shown below:

```
$upload = new Zend_File_Transfer();
// Set a filesize with 20000 bytes
$upload->addFilter('Rename', 'C:\picture\newjpg', 'file1')
       ->addFilter('Rename', 'C:\picture\newgif', 'file2');
```

Note

Note that even though setting the same filter multiple times is allowed, doing so can lead to issues when using different options for the same filter.

Decrypt filter

The `Decrypt` filter allows to decrypt a encrypted file.

This filter makes use of `Zend_Filter_Decrypt`. It supports the `Mcrypt` and `OpenSSL` extensions from PHP. Please read the related section for details about how to set the options for decryption and which options are supported.

This filter supports one additional option which can be used to save the decrypted file with another filename. Set the `filename` option to change the filename where the decrypted file will be stored. If you suppress this option, the decrypted file will overwrite the original encrypted file.

Example 21.33. Using the Decrypt filter with Mcrypt

```
$upload = new Zend_File_Transfer_Adapter_Http();
// Adds a filter to decrypt the uploaded encrypted file
// with mcrypt and the key mykey
$upload->addFilter('Decrypt',
    array('adapter' => 'mcrypt', 'key' => 'mykey'));
```

Example 21.34. Using the Decrypt filter with OpenSSL

```
$upload = new Zend_File_Transfer_Adapter_Http();
// Adds a filter to decrypt the uploaded encrypted file
// with openssl and the provided keys
$upload->addFilter('Decrypt',
    array('adapter' => 'openssl',
          'private' => '/path/to/privatekey.pem',
          'envelope' => '/path/to/envelopekey.pem'));
```

Encrypt filter

The `Encrypt` filter allows to encrypt a file.

This filter makes use of `Zend_Filter_Encrypt`. It supports the `Mcrypt` and `OpenSSL` extensions from PHP. Please read the related section for details about how to set the options for encryption and which options are supported.

This filter supports one additional option which can be used to save the encrypted file with another filename. Set the `filename` option to change the filename where the encrypted file will be stored. If you suppress this option, the encrypted file will overwrite the original file.

Example 21.35. Using the Encrypt filter with Mcrypt

```
$upload = new Zend_File_Transfer_Adapter_Http();
// Adds a filter to encrypt the uploaded file
// with mcrypt and the key mykey
$upload->addFilter('Encrypt',
    array('adapter' => 'mcrypt', 'key' => 'mykey'));
```

Example 21.36. Using the Encrypt filter with OpenSSL

```
$upload = new Zend_File_Transfer_Adapter_Http();
// Adds a filter to encrypt the uploaded file
// with openssl and the provided keys
$upload->addFilter('Encrypt',
    array('adapter' => 'openssl',
          'public' => '/path/to/publickey.pem'));
```

LowerCase filter

The LowerCase filter allows to change the content of a file to lowercase. You should use this filter only on textfiles.

At initiation you can give a string which will then be used as encoding. Or you can use the setEncoding() method to set it afterwards.

Example 21.37. Using the LowerCase filter

```
$upload = new Zend_File_Transfer_Adapter_Http();
$upload->addValidator('MimeType', 'text');
// Adds a filter to lowercase the uploaded textfile
$upload->addFilter('LowerCase');
// Adds a filter to lowercase the uploaded file but only for uploadfile1
$upload->addFilter('LowerCase', null, 'uploadfile1');
// Adds a filter to lowercase with encoding set to ISO-8859-1
$upload->addFilter('LowerCase', 'ISO-8859-1');
```

Note

Note that due to the fact that the options for the LowerCase filter are optional, you must give a null as second parameter (the options) when you want to limit it to a single file element.

Rename filter

The Rename filter allows to change the destination of the upload, the filename and also to overwrite existing files. It supports the following options:

- source: The name and destination of the old file which shall be renamed.

- target: The new directory, or filename of the file.

- overwrite: Sets if the old file overwrites the new one if it already exists. The default value is false.

Additionally you can also use the method setFile() to set files, which erases all previous set, addFile() to add a new file to existing ones, and getFile() to get all actually set files. To simplify things, this filter understands several notations and that methods and constructor understand the same notations.

Example 21.38. Using the Rename filter

```
$upload = new Zend_File_Transfer_Adapter_Http();
// Set a new destination path for all files
$upload->addFilter('Rename', 'C:\mypics\new');
// Set a new destination path only for uploadfile1
$upload->addFilter('Rename', 'C:\mypics\newgifs', 'uploadfile1');
```

You can use different notations. Below is a table where you will find a description and the intention for the supported notations. Note that when you use the Adapter or the Form Element you will not be able to use all described notations.

Table 21.1. Different notations of the rename filter and their meaning

notation	description
addFile('C:\uploads')	Specifies a new location for all files when the given string is a directory. Note that you will get an exception when the file already exists, see the overwriting parameter.
addFile('C:\uploads\file.ext')	Specifies a new location and filename for all files when the given string is not detected as directory. Note that you will get an exception when the file already exists, see the overwriting parameter.
addFile(array('C:\uploads\file.ext', 'overwrite' => true))	Specifies a new location and filename for all files when the given string is not detected as directory and overwrites an existing file with the same target name. Note, that you will get no notification that a file was overwritten.
addFile(array('source' => 'C:\temp\uploads', 'target' => 'C:\uploads'))	Specifies a new location for all files in the old location when the given strings are detected as directory. Note that you will get an exception when the file already exists, see the overwriting parameter.
addFile(array('source' => 'C:\temp\uploads', 'target' => 'C:\uploads', 'overwrite' => true))	Specifies a new location for all files in the old location when the given strings are detected as directory and overwrites and existing file with the same target name. Note, that you will get no notification that a file was overwritten.

UpperCase filter

The UpperCase filter allows to change the content of a file to uppercase. You should use this filter only on textfiles.

At initiation you can give a string which will then be used as encoding. Or you can use the setEncoding() method to set it afterwards.

Example 21.39. Using the UpperCase filter

```
$upload = new Zend_File_Transfer_Adapter_Http();
$upload->addValidator('MimeType', 'text');
// Adds a filter to uppercase the uploaded textfile
$upload->addFilter('UpperCase');
// Adds a filter to uppercase the uploaded file but only for uploadfile1
$upload->addFilter('UpperCase', null, 'uploadfile1');
// Adds a filter to uppercase with encoding set to ISO-8859-1
$upload->addFilter('UpperCase', 'ISO-8859-1');
```

Note

Note that due to the fact that the options for the UpperCase filter are optional, you must give a null as second parameter (the options) when you want to limit it to a single file element.

Migrating from previous versions

The API of Zend_File_Transfer has changed from time to time. If you started to use Zend_File_Transfer and it's subcomponents in earlier versions follow the guidelines below to migrate your scripts to use the new API.

Migrating from 1.6 to 1.7 or newer

Changes when using filters and validators

As noted by users, the validators from Zend_File_Transfer do not work in conjunction with Zend_Config due to the fact that they have not used named arrays.

Therefor, all filters and validators for Zend_File_Transfer have been reworked. While the old signatures continue to work, they have been marked as deprecated, and will emit a PHP notice asking you to fix them.

The following list shows you the changes you will have to do for proper usage of the parameters.

Filter: Rename

- Old method API: Zend_Filter_File_Rename($oldfile, $newfile, $overwrite)

- New method API: Zend_Filter_File_Rename($options) where $options accepts the following array keys: *source* equals to $oldfile, *target* equals to $newfile, *overwrite* equals to $overwrite

Example 21.40. Changes for the rename filter from 1.6 to 1.7

```
// Example for 1.6
$upload = new Zend_File_Transfer_Adapter_Http();
$upload->addFilter('Rename',
                   array('/path/to/oldfile', '/path/to/newfile', true));
// Same example for 1.7
$upload = new Zend_File_Transfer_Adapter_Http();
$upload->addFilter('Rename',
                   array('source' => '/path/to/oldfile',
                         'target' => '/path/to/newfile',
                         'overwrite' => true));
```

Validator: Count

- Old method API: Zend_Validate_File_Count($min, $max)

- New method API: Zend_Validate_File_Count($options) where $options accepts the following array keys: *min* equals to $min, *max* equals to $max,

Example 21.41. Changes for the count validator from 1.6 to 1.7

```
// Example for 1.6
$upload = new Zend_File_Transfer_Adapter_Http();
$upload->addValidator('Count',
                      array(2, 3));
```

```
// Same example for 1.7
$upload = new Zend_File_Transfer_Adapter_Http();
$upload->addValidator('Count',
                      false,
                      array('min' => 2,
                            'max' => 3));
```

Validator:Extension

- Old method API: Zend_Validate_File_Extension($extension, $case)

- New method API: Zend_Validate_File_Extension($options) where $options accepts the following array keys: * equals to $extension and can have any other key, *case* equals to $case,

Example 21.42. Changes for the extension validator from 1.6 to 1.7

```
// Example for 1.6
$upload = new Zend_File_Transfer_Adapter_Http();
$upload->addValidator('Extension',
                      array('jpg,gif,bmp', true));
// Same example for 1.7
$upload = new Zend_File_Transfer_Adapter_Http();
$upload->addValidator('Extension',
                      false,
                      array('extension1' => 'jpg,gif,bmp',
                            'case' => true));
```

Validator: FilesSize

- Old method API: Zend_Validate_File_FilesSize($min, $max, $bytestring)

- New method API: Zend_Validate_File_FilesSize($options) where $options accepts the following array keys: *min* equals to $min, *max* equals to $max, *bytestring* equals to $bytestring

Additionally, the useByteString() method signature has changed. It can only be used to test if the validator is expecting to use byte strings in generated messages. To set the value of the flag, use the setUseByteString() method.

Example 21.43. Changes for the filessize validator from 1.6 to 1.7

```
// Example for 1.6
$upload = new Zend_File_Transfer_Adapter_Http();
$upload->addValidator('FilesSize',
                      array(100, 10000, true));
// Same example for 1.7
$upload = new Zend_File_Transfer_Adapter_Http();
$upload->addValidator('FilesSize',
                      false,
                      array('min' => 100,
                            'max' => 10000,
                            'bytestring' => true));
// Example for 1.6
$upload->useByteString(true); // set flag
// Same example for 1.7
$upload->setUseByteSting(true); // set flag
```

Validator: Hash

- Old method API: Zend_Validate_File_Hash($hash, $algorithm)

- New method API: Zend_Validate_File_Hash($options) where $options accepts the following array keys: * equals to $hash and can have any other key, *algorithm* equals to $algorithm,

Example 21.44. Changes for the hash validator from 1.6 to 1.7

```
// Example for 1.6
$upload = new Zend_File_Transfer_Adapter_Http();
$upload->addValidator('Hash',
                      array('12345', 'md5'));
// Same example for 1.7
$upload = new Zend_File_Transfer_Adapter_Http();
$upload->addValidator('Hash',
                      false,
                      array('hash1' => '12345',
                            'algorithm' => 'md5'));
```

Validator: ImageSize

- Old method API: Zend_Validate_File_ImageSize($minwidth, $minheight, $maxwidth, $maxheight)

- New method API: Zend_Validate_File_FilesSize($options) where $options accepts the following array keys: *minwidth* equals to $minwidth, *maxwidth* equals to $maxwidth, *minheight* equals to $minheight, *maxheight* equals to $maxheight,

Example 21.45. Changes for the imagesize validator from 1.6 to 1.7

```
// Example for 1.6
$upload = new Zend_File_Transfer_Adapter_Http();
$upload->addValidator('ImageSize',
                      array(10, 10, 100, 100));
// Same example for 1.7
$upload = new Zend_File_Transfer_Adapter_Http();
$upload->addValidator('ImageSize',
                      false,
                      array('minwidth' => 10,
                            'minheight' => 10,
                            'maxwidth' => 100,
                            'maxheight' => 100));
```

Validator: Size

- Old method API: Zend_Validate_File_Size($min, $max, $bytestring)

- New method API: Zend_Validate_File_Size($options) where $options accepts the following array keys: *min* equals to $min, *max* equals to $max, *bytestring* equals to $bytestring

Example 21.46. Changes for the size validator from 1.6 to 1.7

```
// Example for 1.6
$upload = new Zend_File_Transfer_Adapter_Http();
$upload->addValidator('Size',
                       array(100, 10000, true));
// Same example for 1.7
$upload = new Zend_File_Transfer_Adapter_Http();
$upload->addValidator('Size',
                       false,
                       array('min' => 100,
                             'max' => 10000,
                             'bytestring' => true));
```

Migrating from 1.6.1 to 1.6.2 or newer

Changes when using validators

As noted by users, the validators from Zend_File_Transfer do not work the same way like the default ones from Zend_Form. Zend_Form allows the usage of a breakChainOnFailure parameter which breaks the validation for all further validators when an validation error has occurred.

So we added this parameter also to all existing validators from Zend_File_Transfer.

- Old method API: addValidator($validator, $options, $files).

- New method API: addValidator($validator, $breakChainOnFailure, $options, $files).

To migrate your scripts to the new API, simply add a false after defining the wished validator.

Example 21.47. How to change your file validators from 1.6.1 to 1.6.2

```
// Example for 1.6.1
$upload = new Zend_File_Transfer_Adapter_Http();
$upload->addValidator('FilesSize', array('1B', '100kB'));
// Same example for 1.6.2 and newer
// Note the added boolean false
$upload = new Zend_File_Transfer_Adapter_Http();
$upload->addValidator('FilesSize', false, array('1B', '100kB'));
```

Chapter 22. Zend_Filter

Introduction

The Zend_Filter component provides a set of commonly needed data filters. It also provides a simple filter chaining mechanism by which multiple filters may be applied to a single datum in a user-defined order.

What is a filter?

In the physical world, a filter is typically used for removing unwanted portions of input, and the desired portion of the input passes through as filter output (e.g., coffee). In such scenarios, a filter is an operator that produces a subset of the input. This type of filtering is useful for web applications - removing illegal input, trimming unnecessary white space, etc.

This basic definition of a filter may be extended to include generalized transformations upon input. A common transformation applied in web applications is the escaping of HTML entities. For example, if a form field is automatically populated with untrusted input (e.g., from a web browser), this value should either be free of HTML entities or contain only escaped HTML entities, in order to prevent undesired behavior and security vulnerabilities. To meet this requirement, HTML entities that appear in the input must either be removed or escaped. Of course, which approach is more appropriate depends on the situation. A filter that removes the HTML entities operates within the scope of the first definition of filter - an operator that produces a subset of the input. A filter that escapes the HTML entities, however, transforms the input (e.g., "&" is transformed to "&"). Supporting such use cases for web developers is important, and "to filter," in the context of using Zend_Filter, means to perform some transformations upon input data.

Basic usage of filters

Having this filter definition established provides the foundation for `Zend_Filter_Interface`, which requires a single method named `filter()` to be implemented by a filter class.

Following is a basic example of using a filter upon two input data, the ampersand (&) and double quote (") characters:

```
$htmlEntities = new Zend_Filter_HtmlEntities();
echo $htmlEntities->filter('&'); // &amp;
echo $htmlEntities->filter('"'); // &quot;
```

Using the static get() method

If it is inconvenient to load a given filter class and create an instance of the filter, you can use the static method `Zend_Filter::get()` as an alternative invocation style. The first argument of this method is a data input value, that you would pass to the `filter()` method. The second argument is a string, which corresponds to the basename of the filter class, relative to the Zend_Filter namespace. The `get()` method automatically loads the class, creates an instance, and applies the `filter()` method to the data input.

```
echo Zend_Filter::get('&', 'HtmlEntities');
```

You can also pass an array of constructor arguments, if they are needed for the filter class.

```
echo Zend_Filter::get('"', 'HtmlEntities', array(ENT_QUOTES));
```

The static usage can be convenient for invoking a filter ad hoc, but if you have the need to run a filter for multiple inputs, it's more efficient to follow the first example above, creating an instance of the filter object and calling its `filter()` method.

Also, the Zend_Filter_Input class allows you to instantiate and run multiple filter and validator classes on demand to process sets of input data. See the section called "Zend_Filter_Input".

Standard Filter Classes

Zend Framework comes with a standard set of filters, which are ready for you to use.

Alnum

Returns the string `$value`, removing all but alphabetic and digit characters. This filter includes an option to also allow white space characters.

Note

The alphabetic characters mean characters that makes up words in each language. However, the english alphabet is treated as the alphabetic characters in following languages: Chinese, Japanese, Korean. The language is specified by Zend_Locale.

Alpha

Returns the string `$value`, removing all but alphabetic characters. This filter includes an option to also allow white space characters.

BaseName

Given a string containing a path to a file, this filter will return the base name of the file

Callback

This filter allows you to use own methods in conjunction with `Zend_Filter`. You don't have to create a new filter when you already have a method which does the job.

Let's expect we want to create a filter which reverses a string.

```
$filter = new Zend_Filter_Callback('strrev');
print $filter->filter('Hello!');
// returns "!olleH"
```

As you can see it's really simple to use a callback to define a own filter. It is also possible to use a method, which is defined within a class, by giving an array as callback.

```
// Our classdefinition
class MyClass
{
    public function Reverse($param);
}
// The filter definition
$filter = new Zend_Filter_Callback(array('MyClass', 'Reverse'));
print $filter->filter('Hello!');
```

To get the actual set callback use `getCallback()` and to set another callback use `setCallback()`.

It is also possible to define default parameters, which are given to the called method as array when the filter is executed. This array will be concated with the value which will be filtered.

```
$filter = new Zend_Filter_Callback(
    'MyMethod',
    array('key' => 'param1', 'key2' => 'param2')
);
$filter->filter(array('value' => 'Hello'));
```

When you would call the above method definition manually it would look like this:

```
$value = MyMethod('Hello', 'param1', 'param2');
```

Note

You should note that defining a callback method which can not be called will raise an exception.

Decrypt

This filter will decrypt any given string with the provided setting. Therefor it makes use of Adapters. Actually there are adapters for the `Mcrypt` and `OpenSSL` extensions from php.

For details about how to encrypt content look at the `Encrypt` filter. As the basics are covered within the `Encrypt` filter, we will describe here only the needed additional methods and changes for decryption.

Decryption with Mcrypt

For decrypting content which was previously encrypted with `Mcrypt` you need to have the options with which the encryption has been called.

There is one emminent difference for you. When you did not provide a vector at encryption you need to get it after you encrypted the content by using the `getVector()` method on the encryption filter. Without the correct vector you will not be able to decrypt the content.

As soon as you have provided all options decryption is as simple as encryption.

```
// Use the default blowfish settings
$filter = new Zend_Filter_Decrypt('myencryptionkey');
// Set the vector with which the content was encrypted
$filter->setVector('myvector');
$decrypted = $filter->filter('encoded_text_normally_unreadable');
print $decrypted;
```

Note

Note that you will get an exception if the mcrypt extension is not available in your environment.

Note

You should also note that all settings which be checked when you create the instance or when you call setEncryption(). If mcrypt detects problem with your settings an exception will be thrown.

Decryption with OpenSSL

Decryption with `OpenSSL` is as simple as encryption. But you need to have all data from the person who encrypted the content.

For decryption with `OpenSSL` you need:

- *private*: Your private key which will be used for decrypting the content. The private key can be eighter a filename with path of the key file, or just the content of the key file itself.

- *envelope*: The encrypted envelope key from the user who encrypted the content. You can eigther provide the path and filename of the key file, or just the content of the key file itself.

```
// Use openssl and provide a private key
$filter = new Zend_Filter_Decrypt(array(
    'adapter' => 'openssl',
    'private' => '/path/to/mykey/private.pem'
));
// of course you can also give the envelope keys at initiation
$filter->setEnvelopeKey(array(
    '/key/from/encoder/first.pem',
    '/key/from/encoder/second.pem'
));
```

Note

Note that the `OpenSSL` adapter will not work when you do not provide valid keys.

Optionally it could be necessary to provide the passphrase for decrypting the keys themself by using the `setPassphrase()` method.

```
// Use openssl and provide a private key
$filter = new Zend_Filter_Decrypt(array(
    'adapter' => 'openssl',
    'private' => '/path/to/mykey/private.pem'
));
// of course you can also give the envelope keys at initiation
$filter->setEnvelopeKey(array(
    '/key/from/encoder/first.pem',
    '/key/from/encoder/second.pem'
));
$filter->setPassphrase('mypassphrase');
```

At last, decode the content. Our complete example for decrypting the previously encrypted content looks like this.

```
// Use openssl and provide a private key
$filter = new Zend_Filter_Decrypt(array(
    'adapter' => 'openssl',
    'private' => '/path/to/mykey/private.pem'
));
// of course you can also give the envelope keys at initiation
$filter->setEnvelopeKey(array(
    '/key/from/encoder/first.pem',
    '/key/from/encoder/second.pem'
));
$filter->setPassphrase('mypassphrase');
$decrypted = $filter->filter('encoded_text_normally_unreadable');
print $decrypted;
```

Digits

Returns the string $value, removing all but digit characters.

Dir

Returns directory name component of path.

Encrypt

This filter will encrypt any given string with the provided setting. Therefor it makes use of Adapters. Actually there are adapters for the Mcrypt and OpenSSL extensions from php.

As these two encryption methodologies work completly different, also the usage of the adapters differ. You have to select the adapter you want to use when initiating the filter.

As these two encryption methodologies work completly different, also the usage of the adapters differ. You have to select the adapter you want to use when initiating the filter.

```
// Use the Mcrypt adapter
$filter1 = new Zend_Filter_Encrypt(array('adapter' => 'mcrypt'));
// Use the OpenSSL adapter
$filter2 = new Zend_Filter_Encrypt(array('adapter' => 'openssl'));
```

To set another adapter you can also use setAdapter(), and the getAdapter() method to receive the actual set adapter.

```
// Use the Mcrypt adapter
$filter = new Zend_Filter_Encrypt();
$filter->setAdapter('openssl');
```

Note

When you do not supply the adapter option or do not use setAdapter, then the Mcrypt adapter will be used per default.

Encryption with Mcrypt

When you have installed the Mcrypt extension you can use the Mcrypt adapter. This adapter supports the following options at initiation:

- *key*: The encryption key with which the input will be encrypted. You need the same key for decryption.

- *algorithm*: The algorithm which has to be used. It should be one of the algorithm ciphers which can be found under PHP's mcrypt ciphers [http://php.net/mcrypt]. If not set it defaults to blowfish.

- *algorithm_directory*: The directory where the algorithm can be found. If not set it defaults to the path set within the mcrypt extension.

- *mode*: The encryption mode which has to be used. It should be one of the modes which can be found under PHP's mcrypt modes [http://php.net/mcrypt]. If not set it defaults to cbc.

- *mode_directory*: The directory where the mode can be found. If not set it defaults to the path set within the mcrypt extension.

- *vector*: The initialization vector which shall be used. If not set it will be a random vector.

- *salt*: If the key should be used as salt value. The key used for encryption will then itself also be encrypted. Default is false.

If you give a string instead of an array, this string will be used as key.

You can get/set the encryption values also afterwards with the `getEncryption()` and `setEncryption()` methods.

Note

Note that you will get an exception if the mcrypt extension is not available in your environment.

Note

You should also note that all settings which be checked when you create the instance or when you call setEncryption(). If mcrypt detects problem with your settings an exception will be thrown.

You can get/set the encryption vector by calling `getVector()` and `setVector()`. A given string will be truncated or padded to the needed vector size of the used algorithm.

Note

Note that when you are not using an own vector, you must get the vector and store it. Otherwise you will not be able to decode the encoded string.

```
// Use the default blowfish settings
$filter = new Zend_Filter_Encrypt('myencryptionkey');
// Set a own vector, otherwise you must call getVector()
// and store this vector for later decryption
$filter->setVector('myvector');
// $filter->getVector();
$encrypted = $filter->filter('text_to_be_encoded');
print $encrypted;
// For decryption look at the Decrypt filter
```

Encryption with OpenSSL

When you have installed the OpenSSL extension you can use the OpenSSL adapter. This adapter supports the following options at initiation:

- *public*: The public key of the user whom you want to provide the encrpted content. You can give multiple public keys by using an array. You can eigther provide the path and filename of the key file, or just the content of the key file itself.

- *private*: Your private key which will be used for encrypting the content. Also the private key can be eighter a filename with path of the key file, or just the content of the key file itself.

You can get/set the public keys also afterwards with the `getPublicKey()` and `setPublicKey()` methods. The private key can also be get and set with the related `getPrivateKey()` and `setPrivateKey()` methods.

```
// Use openssl and provide a private key
$filter = new Zend_Filter_Encrypt(array(
    'adapter' => 'openssl',
    'private' => '/path/to/mykey/private.pem'
));
// of course you can also give the public keys at initiation
$filter->setPublicKey(array(
```

```
    '/public/key/path/first.pem',
    '/public/key/path/second.pem'
));
```

Note

Note that the OpenSSL adapter will not work when you do not provide valid keys.

When you want to encode also the keys, then you have to provide a passphrase with the setPassphrase() method. When you want to decode content which was encoded with a passphrase you will not only need the public key, but also the passphrase to decode the encrypted key.

```
// Use openssl and provide a private key
$filter = new Zend_Filter_Encrypt(array(
    'adapter' => 'openssl',
    'private' => '/path/to/mykey/private.pem'
));
// of course you can also give the public keys at initiation
$filter->setPublicKey(array(
    '/public/key/path/first.pem',
    '/public/key/path/second.pem'
));
$filter->setPassphrase('mypassphrase');
```

At last, when you use OpenSSL you need to give the receiver the encrypted content, the passphrase when have provided one, and the envelope keys for decryption.

This means for you, that you have to get the envelope keys after the encryption with the getEnvelopeKey() method.

So our complete example for encrypting content with OpenSSL look like this.

```
// Use openssl and provide a private key
$filter = new Zend_Filter_Encrypt(array(
    'adapter' => 'openssl',
    'private' => '/path/to/mykey/private.pem'
));
// of course you can also give the public keys at initiation
$filter->setPublicKey(array(
    '/public/key/path/first.pem',
    '/public/key/path/second.pem'
));
$filter->setPassphrase('mypassphrase');
$encrypted = $filter->filter('text_to_be_encoded');
$envelope  = $filter->getEnvelopeKey();
print $encrypted;
// For decryption look at the Decrypt filter
```

HtmlEntities

Returns the string $value, converting characters to their corresponding HTML entity equivalents where they exist.

Int

Returns (int) $value

LocalizedToNormalized

This filter will change any given localized input to it's normalized representation. It uses in Background Zend_Locale to do this transformation for you.

This allows your user to enter informations in his own language notation, and you can then store the normalized value into your database for example.

Note

Please note that normalization is not equal to translation. This filter can not translate strings from one language into another like you could expect with months or names of days.

The following input types can be normalized:

• *integer*: Integer numbers, which are localized, will be normalized to the english notation.

• *float*: Float numbers, which are localized, will be normalized to the english notation.

• *numbers*: Other numbers, like real, will be normalized to the english notation.

• *time*: Time values, will be normalized to a named array.

• *date*: Date values, will be normalized to a named array.

Any other input will be returned as it, without changing it.

Note

You should note that normalized output is always given as string. Otherwise your environment would transfor the normalized output automatically to the notation used by the locale your environment is set to.

Normalization for numbers

Any given number like integer, float or real value, can be normalized. Note, that numbers in scientific notation, can actually not be handled by this filter.

So how does this normalization work in detail for numbers:

```
// Initiate the filter
$filter = new Zend_Filter_LocalizedToNormalized();
$filter->filter('123.456,78');
// returns the value '123456.78'
```

Let's expect you have set the locale 'de' as application wide locale. Zend_Filter_LocalizedToNormalized will take the set locale and use it to detect which sort of input you gave. In our example it was a value with precision. Now the filter will return you the normalized representation for this value as string.

You can also control how your normalized number has to look like. Therefor you can give all options which are also used by Zend_Locale_Format. The most common are:

• *date_format*

• *locale*

• *precision*

For details about how these options are used take a look into this Zend_Locale chapter.

Below is a example with defined precision so you can see how options work:

```
// Numeric Filter
$filter = new Zend_Filter_LocalizedToNormalized(array('precision' => 2));
$filter->filter('123.456');
// returns the value '123456.00'
$filter->filter('123.456,78901');
// returns the value '123456.79'
```

Normalization for date and time

Input for date and time values can also be normalized. All given date and time values will be returned as array, where each date part is given within a own key.

```
// Initiate the filter
$filter = new Zend_Filter_LocalizedToNormalized();
$filter->filter('12.April.2009');
// returns array('day' => '12', 'month' => '04', 'year' => '2009')
```

Let's expect you have set the locale 'de' again. Now the input is automatically detected as date, and you will get a named array in return.

Of course you can also control how your date input looks like with the *date_format* and the *locale* option.

```
// Date Filter
$filter = new Zend_Filter_LocalizedToNormalized(
    array('date_format' => 'ss:mm:HH')
);
$filter->filter('11:22:33');
// returns array('hour' => '33', 'minute' => '22', 'second' => '11')
```

NormalizedToLocalized

This filter is the reverse of the filter Zend_Filter_LocalizedToNormalized and will change any given normalized input to it's localized representation. It uses in Background Zend_Locale to do this transformation for you.

This allows you to give your user any stored normalised value in a localized manner, your user is more common to.

Note

Please note that localization is not equal to translation. This filter can not translate strings from one language into another like you could expect with months or names of days.

The following input types can be localized:

- *integer*: Integer numbers, which are normalized, will be localized to the set notation.

- *float*: Float numbers, which are normalized, will be localized to the set notation.

- *numbers*: Other numbers, like real, will be localized to the set notation.

- *time*: Time values, will be localized to a string.

- *date*: Date values, will be normalized to a string.

Any other input will be returned as it, without changing it.

Localization for numbers

Any given number like integer, float or real value, can be localized. Note, that numbers in scientific notation, can actually not be handled by this filter.

So how does localization work in detail for numbers:

```
// Initiate the filter
$filter = new Zend_Filter_NormalizedToLocalized();
$filter->filter(123456.78);
// returns the value '123.456,78'
```

Let's expect you have set the locale 'de' as application wide locale. Zend_Filter_NormalizedToLocalized will take the set locale and use it to detect which sort of output you want to have. In our example it was a value with precision. Now the filter will return you the localized representation for this value as string.

You can also control how your localized number has to look like. Therefor you can give all options which are also used by Zend_Locale_Format. The most common are:

- *date_format*

- *locale*

- *precision*

For details about how these options are used take a look into this Zend_Locale chapter.

Below is a example with defined precision so you can see how options work:

```
// Numeric Filter
$filter = new Zend_Filter_NormalizedToLocalized(array('precision' => 2));
$filter->filter(123456);
// returns the value '123.456,00'
$filter->filter(123456.78901);
// returns the value '123.456,79'
```

Localization for date and time

Normalized for date and time values can also be localized. All given date and time values will be returned as string, with the format defined by the set locale.

```
// Initiate the filter
$filter = new Zend_Filter_NormalizedToLocalized();
$filter->filter(array('day' => '12', 'month' => '04', 'year' => '2009'));
// returns '12.04.2009'
```

Let's expect you have set the locale 'de' again. Now the input is automatically detected as date, and will be returned in the format defined by the locale 'de'.

Of course you can also control how your date input looks like with the *date_format*, and the *locale* option.

```
// Date Filter
$filter = new Zend_Filter_LocalizedToNormalized(
    array('date_format' => 'ss:mm:HH')
);
$filter->filter(array('hour' => '33', 'minute' => '22', 'second' => '11'));
// returns '11:22:33'
```

StripNewlines

Returns the string $value without any newline control characters.

RealPath

This filter will resolve given links and pathnames and returns canonicalized absolute pathnames. References to '/./', '/../' and extra '/' characters in the input path will be stripped. The resulting path will not have any symbolic link, '/./' or '/../' character.

Zend_Filter_RealPath will return FALSE on failure, e.g. if the file does not exist. On BSD systems Zend_Filter_RealPath doesn't fail if only the last path component doesn't exist, while other systems will return FALSE.

```
$filter = new Zend_Filter_RealPath();
$path   = '/www/var/path/../../mypath';
$filtered = $filter->filter();
// returns '/www/mypath'
```

Sometimes it is usefull to get also paths when they don't exist, f.e. when you want to get the real path for a path which you want to create. You can then eighter give a FALSE at initiation, or use setExists() to set it.

```
$filter = new Zend_Filter_RealPath(false);
$path   = '/www/var/path/../../non/existing/path';
$filtered = $filter->filter();
// returns '/www/non/existing/path' even when file_exists or realpath
   would return false
```

StringToLower

Returns the string $value, converting alphabetic characters to lowercase as necessary.

StringToUpper

Returns the string $value, converting alphabetic characters to uppercase as necessary.

StringTrim

Returns the string $value with characters stripped from the beginning and end.

StripTags

This filter returns the input string, with all HTML and PHP tags stripped from it, except those that have been explicitly allowed. In addition to the ability to specify which tags are allowed, developers can specify which attributes are allowed across all allowed tags and for specific tags only. Finally, this filter offers control over whether comments (e.g., <!-- ... -->) are removed or allowed.

Filter Chains

Often multiple filters should be applied to some value in a particular order. For example, a login form accepts a username that should be only lowercase, alphabetic characters. Zend_Filter provides a simple method by which filters may be chained together. The following code illustrates how to chain together two filters for the submitted username:

```
</// Create a filter chain and add filters to the chain
$filterChain = new Zend_Filter();
$filterChain->addFilter(new Zend_Filter_Alpha())
          ->addFilter(new Zend_Filter_StringToLower());
// Filter the username
$username = $filterChain->filter($_POST['username']);
```

Filters are run in the order they were added to Zend_Filter. In the above example, the username is first removed of any non-alphabetic characters, and then any uppercase characters are converted to lowercase.

Any object that implements Zend_Filter_Interface may be used in a filter chain.

Writing Filters

Zend_Filter supplies a set of commonly needed filters, but developers will often need to write custom filters for their particular use cases. The task of writing a custom filter is facilitated by implementing Zend_Filter_Interface.

Zend_Filter_Interface defines a single method, filter(), that may be implemented by user classes. An object that implements this interface may be added to a filter chain with Zend_Filter::addFilter().

The following example demonstrates how to write a custom filter:

```
class MyFilter implements Zend_Filter_Interface
{
    public function filter($value)
    {
        // perform some transformation upon $value to arrive on $valueFiltered
        return $valueFiltered;
    }
}
```

To add an instance of the filter defined above to a filter chain:

```
$filterChain = new Zend_Filter();
$filterChain->addFilter(new MyFilter());
```

Zend_Filter_Input

Zend_Filter_Input provides a declarative interface to associate multiple filters and validators, apply them to collections of data, and to retrieve input values after they have been processed by the filters and validators. Values are returned in escaped format by default for safe HTML output.

Consider the metaphor that this class is a cage for external data. Data enter the application from external sources, such as HTTP request parameters, HTTP headers, a web service, or even read from a database or another file. Data are first put into the cage, and subsequently the application can access data only by telling the cage what the data should be and how they plan to use it. The cage inspects the data for validity. It might apply escaping to the data values for the appropriate context. The cage releases data only if it can fulfill these responsibilities. With a simple and convenient interface, it encourages good programming habits and makes developers think about how data are used.

- *Filters* transform input values, by removing or changing characters within the value. The goal is to "normalize" input values until they match an expected format. For example, if a string of numeric digits is needed, and the input value is "abc123", then it might be a reasonable transformation to change the value to the string "123".

- *Validators* check input values against criteria and report whether they passed the test or not. The value is not changed, but the check may fail. For example, if a string must look like an email address, and the input value is "abc123", then the value is not considered valid.

- *Escapers* transform a value by removing magic behavior of certain characters. In some output contexts, special characters have meaning. For example, the characters '<' and '>' delimit HTML tags, and if a string containing those characters is output in an HTML context, the content between them might affect the output or functionality of the HTML presentation. Escaping the characters removes the special meaning, so they are output as literal characters.

To use Zend_Filter_Input, perform the following steps:

1. Declare filter and validator rules

2. Create the filter and validator processor

3. Provide input data

4. Retrieve validated fields and other reports

The following sections describe the steps for using this class.

Declaring Filter and Validator Rules

Before creating an instance of Zend_Filter_Input, declare an array of filter rules and and an array of validator rules. This associative array maps a rule name to a filter or validator or a chain of filters or validators.

The following example filter rule set that declares the field 'month' is filtered by Zend_Filter_Digits, and the field 'account' is filtered by Zend_Filter_StringTrim. Then a validation rule set declares that the field 'account' is valid only if it contains only alphabetical characters.

```
$filters = array(
    'month'   => 'Digits',
    'account' => 'StringTrim'
);
$validators = array(
    'account' => 'Alpha'
);
```

Each key in the $filters array above is the name of a rule for applying a filter to a specific data field. By default, the name of the rule is also the name of the input data field to which to apply the rule.

You can declare a rule in several formats:

- A single string scalar, which is mapped to a class name.

```
$validators = array(
    'month'   => 'Digits',
);
```

- An object instance of one of the classes that implement Zend_Filter_Interface or Zend_Validate_Interface.

```
$digits = new Zend_Validate_Digits();
$validators = array(
    'month'   => $digits
);
```

- An array, to declare a chain of filters or validators. The elements of this array can be strings mapping to class names or filter/validator objects, as in the cases described above. In addition, you can use a third choice: an array containing a string mapping to the class name followed by arguments to pass to its constructor.

```
$validators = array(
    'month'    => array(
        'Digits',                  // string
        new Zend_Validate_Int(),   // object instance
        array('Between', 1, 12)    // string with constructor arguments
    )
);
```

Note

If you declare a filter or validator with constructor arguments in an array, then you must make an array for the rule, even if the rule has only one filter or validator.

You can use a special "wildcard" rule key '*' in either the filters array or the validators array. This means that the filters or validators declared in this rule will be applied to all input data fields. Note that the order of entries in the filters array or validators array is significant; the rules are applied in the same order in which you declare them.

```
$filters = array(
    '*'     => 'StringTrim',
    'month' => 'Digits'
);
```

Creating the Filter and Validator Processor

After declaring the filters and validators arrays, use them as arguments in the constructor of Zend_Filter_Input. This returns an object that knows all your filtering and validating rules, and you can use this object to process one or more sets of input data.

```
$input = new Zend_Filter_Input($filters, $validators);
```

You can specify input data as the third constructor argument. The data structure is an associative array. The keys are field names, and the values are data values. The standard $_GET and $_POST superglobal variables in PHP are examples of this format. You can use either of these variables as input data for Zend_Filter_Input.

```
$data = $_GET;
$input = new Zend_Filter_Input($filters, $validators, $data);
```

Alternatively, use the setData() method, passing an associative array of key/value pairs the same format as described above.

```
$input = new Zend_Filter_Input($filters, $validators);
$input->setData($newData);
```

The setData() method redefines data in an existing Zend_Filter_Input object without changing the filtering and validation rules. Using this method, you can run the same rules against different sets of input data.

Retrieving Validated Fields and other Reports

After you have declared filters and validators and created the input processor, you can retrieve reports of missing, unknown, and invalid fields. You also can get the values of fields after filters have been applied.

Querying if the input is valid

If all input data pass the validation rules, the isValid() method returns true. If any field is invalid or any required field is missing, isValid() returns false.

```
if ($input->isValid()) {
  echo "OK\n";
}
```

This method accepts an optional string argument, naming an individual field. If the specified field passed validation and is ready for fetching, isValid('fieldName') returns true.

```
if ($input->isValid('month')) {
  echo "Field 'month' is OK\n";
}
```

Getting Invalid, Missing, or Unknown Fields

- *Invalid* fields are those that don't pass one or more of their validation checks.

- *Missing* fields are those that are not present in the input data, but were declared with the metacommand 'presence'=>'required' (see the later section on metacommands).

- *Unknown* fields are those that are not declared in any rule in the array of validators, but appear in the input data.

```
if ($input->hasInvalid() || $input->hasMissing()) {
  $messages = $input->getMessages();
}
// getMessages() simply returns the merge of getInvalid() and
// getMissing()
if ($input->hasInvalid()) {
  $invalidFields = $input->getInvalid();
}
if ($input->hasMissing()) {
  $missingFields = $input->getMissing();
}
if ($input->hasUnknown()) {
  $unknownFields = $input->getUnknown();
}
```

The results of the getMessages() method is an associative array, mapping a rule name to an array of error messages related to that rule. Note that the index of this array is the rule name used in the rule declaration, which may be different from the names of fields checked by the rule.

The getMessages() method returns the merge of the arrays returned by the getInvalid() and getMissing(). These methods return subsets of the messages, related to validation failures, or fields that were declared as required but missing from the input.

The getErrors() method returns an associative array, mapping a rule name to an array of error identifiers. Error identifiers are fixed strings, to identify the reason for a validation failure, while messages can be customized. See the section called "Basic usage of validators" for more information.

You can specify the message returned by getMissing() using the 'missingMessage' option, as an argument to the Zend_Filter_Input constructor or using the setOptions() method.

```
$options = array(
    'missingMessage' => "Field '%field%' is required"
);
$input = new Zend_Filter_Input($filters, $validators, $data, $options);
// alternative method:
$input = new Zend_Filter_Input($filters, $validators, $data);
$input->setOptions($options);
```

The results of the getUnknown() method is an associative array, mapping field names to field values. Field names are used as the array keys in this case, instead of rule names, because no rule mentions the fields considered to be unknown fields.

Getting Valid Fields

All fields that are neither invalid, missing, nor unknown are considered valid. You can get values for valid fields using a magic accessor. There are also non-magic accessor methods getEscaped() and getUnescaped().

```
$m = $input->month;                 // escaped output from magic accessor
$m = $input->getEscaped('month');   // escaped output
$m = $input->getUnescaped('month'); // not escaped
```

By default, when retrieving a value, it is filtered with the Zend_Filter_HtmlEntities. This is the default because it is considered the most common usage to output the value of a field in HTML. The HtmlEntities filter helps prevent unintentional output of code, which can result in security problems.

Note

As shown above, you can retrieve the unescaped value using the getUnescaped() method, but you must write code to use the value safely, and avoid security issues such as vulnerability to cross-site scripting attacks.

You can specify a different filter for escaping values, by specifying it in the constructor options array:

```
$options = array('escapeFilter' => 'StringTrim');
$input = new Zend_Filter_Input($filters, $validators, $data, $options);
```

Alternatively, you can use the setDefaultEscapeFilter() method:

```
$input = new Zend_Filter_Input($filters, $validators, $data);
$input->setDefaultEscapeFilter(new Zend_Filter_StringTrim());
```

In either usage, you can specify the escape filter as a string base name of the filter class, or as an object instance of a filter class. The escape filter can be an instance of a filter chain, an object of the class Zend_Filter.

Filters to escape output should be run in this way, to make sure they run after validation. Other filters you declare in the array of filter rules are applied to input data before data are validated. If escaping filters were run before validation, the process of validation would be more complex, and it would be harder to provide both escaped and unescaped versions of the data. So it is recommended to declare filters to escape output using setDefaultEscapeFilter(), not in the $filters array.

There is only one method getEscaped(), and therefore you can specify only one filter for escaping (although this filter can be a filter chain). If you need a single instance of Zend_Filter_Input to return escaped output using more than one filtering method, you should extend Zend_Filter_Input and implement new methods in your subclass to get values in different ways.

Using Metacommands to Control Filter or Validator Rules

In addition to declaring the mapping from fields to filters or validators, you can specify some "metacommands" in the array declarations, to control some optional behavior of Zend_Filter_Input. Metacommands appear as string-indexed entries in a given filter or validator array value.

The FIELDS metacommand

If the rule name for a filter or validator is different than the field to which it should apply, you can specify the field name with the 'fields' metacommand.

You can specify this metacommand using the class constant `Zend_Filter_Input::FIELDS` instead of the string.

```
$filters = array(
    'month' => array(
        'Digits',         // filter name at integer index [0]
        'fields' => 'mo'  // field name at string index ['fields']
    )
);
```

In the example above, the filter rule applies the 'digits' filter to the input field named 'mo'. The string 'month' simply becomes a mnemonic key for this filtering rule; it is not used as the field name if the field is specified with the 'fields' metacommand, but it is used as the rule name.

The default value of the 'fields' metacommand is the index of the current rule. In the example above, if the 'fields' metacommand is not specified, the rule would apply to the input field named 'month'.

Another use of the 'fields' metacommand is to specify fields for filters or validators that require multiple fields as input. If the 'fields' metacommand is an array, the argument to the corresponding filter or validator is an array of the values of those fields. For example, it is common for users to specify a password string in two fields, and they must type the same string in both fields. Suppose you implement a validator class that takes an array argument, and returns `true` if all the values in the array are equal to each other.

```
$validators = array(
    'password' => array(
        'StringEquals',
        'fields' => array('password1', 'password2')
    )
);
// Invokes hypothetical class Zend_Validate_StringEquals,
// passing an array argument containing the values of the two input
// data fields named 'password1' and 'password2'.
```

If the validation of this rule fails, the rule key ('password') is used in the return value of `getInvalid()`, not any of the fields named in the 'fields' metacommand.

The PRESENCE metacommand

Each entry in the validator array may have a metacommand called 'presence'. If the value of this metacommand is 'required' then the field must exist in the input data, or else it is reported as a missing field.

You can specify this metacommand using the class constant `Zend_Filter_Input::PRESENCE` instead of the string.

```
$validators = array(
    'month' => array(
        'digits',
        'presence' => 'required'
    )
);
```

The default value of this metacommand is 'optional'.

The DEFAULT_VALUE metacommand

If a field is not present in the input data, and you specify a value for the 'default' metacommand for that rule, the field takes the value of the metacommand.

You can specify this metacommand using the class constant `Zend_Filter_Input::DEFAULT_VALUE` instead of the string.

This default value is assigned to the field before any of the validators are invoked. The default value is applied to the field only for the current rule; if the same field is referenced in a subsequent rule, the field has no value when evaluating that rule. Thus different rules can declare different default values for a given field.

```
$validators = array(
    'month' => array(
        'digits',
        'default' => '1'
    )
);
// no value for 'month' field
$data = array();
$input = new Zend_Filter_Input(null, $validators, $data);
echo $input->month; // echoes 1
```

If your rule uses the `FIELDS` metacommand to define an array of multiple fields, you can define an array for the `DEFAULT_VALUE` metacommand and the defaults of corresponding keys are used for any missing fields. If `FIELDS` defines multiple fields but `DEFAULT_VALUE` is a scalar, then that default value is used as the value for any missing fields in the array.

There is no default value for this metacommand.

The ALLOW_EMPTY metacommand

By default, if a field exists in the input data, then validators are applied to it, even if the value of the field is an empty string (' '). This is likely to result in a failure to validate. For example, if the validator checks for digit characters, and there are none because a zero-length string has no characters, then the validator reports the data as invalid.

If in your case an empty string should be considered valid, you can set the metacommand 'allowEmpty' to `true`. Then the input data passes validation if it is present in the input data, but has the value of an empty string.

You can specify this metacommand using the class constant `Zend_Filter_Input::ALLOW_EMPTY` instead of the string.

```
$validators = array(
    'address2' => array(
```

```
        'Alnum',
        'allowEmpty' => true
    )
);
```

The default value of this metacommand is `false`.

In the uncommon case that you declare a validation rule with no validators, but the 'allowEmpty' metacommand is `false` (that is, the field is considered invalid if it is empty), Zend_Filter_Input returns a default error message that you can retrieve with `getMessages()`. You can specify this message using the 'notEmptyMessage' option, as an argument to the Zend_Filter_Input constructor or using the `setOptions()` method.

```
$options = array(
    'notEmptyMessage' => "A non-empty value is required for field '%field%'"
);
$input = new Zend_Filter_Input($filters, $validators, $data, $options);
// alternative method:
$input = new Zend_Filter_Input($filters, $validators, $data);
$input->setOptions($options);
```

The BREAK_CHAIN metacommand

By default if a rule has more than one validator, all validators are applied to the input, and the resulting messages contain all error messages caused by the input.

Alternatively, if the value of the 'breakChainOnFailure' metacommand is `true`, the validator chain terminates after the first validator fails. The input data is not checked against subsequent validators in the chain, so it might cause more violations even if you correct the one reported.

You can specify this metacommand using the class constant Zend_Filter_Input ::BREAK_CHAIN instead of the string.

```
$validators = array(
    'month' => array(
        'Digits',
        new Zend_Validate_Between(1,12),
        new Zend_Validate_GreaterThan(0),
        'breakChainOnFailure' => true
    )
);
$input = new Zend_Filter_Input(null, $validators);
```

The default value of this metacommand is `false`.

The validator chain class, Zend_Validate, is more flexible with respect to breaking chain execution than Zend_Filter_Input. With the former class, you can set the option to break the chain on failure independently for each validator in the chain. With the latter class, the defined value of the 'breakChainOnFailure' metacommand for a rule applies uniformly for all validators in the rule. If you require the more flexible usage, you should create the validator chain yourself, and use it as an object in the validator rule definition:

```
// Create validator chain with non-uniform breakChainOnFailure
// attributes
$chain = new Zend_Validate();
$chain->addValidator(new Zend_Validate_Digits(), true);
$chain->addValidator(new Zend_Validate_Between(1,12), false);
$chain->addValidator(new Zend_Validate_GreaterThan(0), true);
// Declare validator rule using the chain defined above
```

```
$validators = array(
    'month' => $chain
);
$input = new Zend_Filter_Input(null, $validators);
```

The MESSAGES metacommand

You can specify error messages for each validator in a rule using the metacommand 'messages'. The value of this metacommand varies based on whether you have multiple validators in the rule, or if you want to set the message for a specific error condition in a given validator.

You can specify this metacommand using the class constant `Zend_Filter_Input::MESSAGES` instead of the string.

Below is a simple example of setting the default error message for a single validator.

```
$validators = array(
    'month' => array(
        'digits',
        'messages' => 'A month must consist only of digits'
    )
);
```

If you have multiple validators for which you want to set the error message, you should use an array for the value of the 'messages' metacommand.

Each element of this array is applied to the validator at the same index position. You can specify a message for the validator at position *n* by using the value *n* as the array index. Thus you can allow some validators to use their default message, while setting the message for a subsequent validator in the chain.

```
$validators = array(
    'month' => array(
        'digits',
        new Zend_Validate_Between(1, 12),
        'messages' => array(
            // use default message for validator [0]
            // set new message for validator [1]
            1 => 'A month value must be between 1 and 12'
        )
    )
);
```

If one of your validators has multiple error messages, they are identified by a message key. There are different keys in each validator class, serving as identifiers for error messages that the respective validator class might generate. Each validate class defines constants for its message keys. You can use these keys in the 'messages' metacommand by passing an associative array instead of a string.

```
$validators = array(
    'month' => array(
        'digits', new Zend_Validate_Between(1, 12),
        'messages' => array(
            'A month must consist only of digits',
            array(
                Zend_Validate_Between::NOT_BETWEEN =>
                    'Month value %value% must be between ' .
                    '%min% and %max%',
                Zend_Validate_Between::NOT_BETWEEN_STRICT =>
                    'Month value %value% must be strictly between ' .
                    '%min% and %max%'
            )
```

```
        )
      )
);
```

You should refer to documentation for each validator class to know if it has multiple error messages, the keys of these messages, and the tokens you can use in the message templates.

Using options to set metacommands for all rules

The default value for 'allowEmpty', 'breakChainOnFailure', and 'presence' metacommands can be set for all rules using the $options argument to the constructor of Zend_Filter_Input. This allows you to set the default value for all rules, without requiring you to set the metacommand for every rule.

```
// The default is set so all fields allow an empty string.
$options = array('allowEmpty' => true);
// You can override this in a rule definition,
// if a field should not accept an empty string.
$validators = array(
    'month' => array(
        'Digits',
        'allowEmpty' => false
    )
);
$input = new Zend_Filter_Input($filters, $validators, $data, $options);
```

The 'fields', 'messages', and 'default' metacommands cannot be set using this technique.

Adding Filter Class Namespaces

By default, when you declare a filter or validator as a string, Zend_Filter_Input searches for the corresponding classes under the Zend_Filter or Zend_Validate namespaces. For example, a filter named by the string 'digits' is found in the class Zend_Filter_Digits.

If you write your own filter or validator classes, or use filters or validators provided by a third-party, the classes may exist in different namespaces than Zend_Filter or Zend_Validate. You can tell Zend_Filter_Input to search more namespaces. You can specify namespaces in the constructor options:

```
$options = array('filterNamespace' => 'My_Namespace_Filter',
                 'validatorNamespace' => 'My_Namespace_Validate');
$input = new Zend_Filter_Input($filters, $validators, $data, $options);
```

Alternatively, you can use the addValidatorPrefixPath($prefix, $path) or addFilterPrefixPath($prefix, $path) methods, which directly proxy to the plugin loader that is used by Zend_Filter_Input:

```
$input->addValidatorPrefixPath('Other_Namespace', 'Other/Namespace');
$input->addFilterPrefixPath('Foo_Namespace', 'Foo/Namespace');
// Now the search order for validators is:
// 1. My_Namespace_Validate
// 2. Other_Namespace
// 3. Zend_Validate
// The search order for filters is:
// 1. My_Namespace_Filter
// 2. Foo_Namespace
// 3. Zend_Filter
```

You cannot remove Zend_Filter and Zend_Validate as namespaces, you only can add namespaces. User-defined namespaces are searched first, Zend namespaces are searched last.

Note

As of version 1.5 the function `addNamespace($namespace)` was deprecated and exchanged with the plugin loader and the `addFilterPrefixPath` and `addValidatorPrefixPath` were added. Also the constant `Zend_Filter_Input ::INPUT_NAMESPACE` is now deprecated. The constants `Zend_Filter_Input ::VALIDATOR_NAMESPACE` and `Zend_Filter_Input::FILTER_NAMESPACE` are available in releases after 1.7.0.

Note

As of version 1.0.4, `Zend_Filter_Input::NAMESPACE`, having value `namespace`, was changed to `Zend_Filter_Input::INPUT_NAMESPACE`, having value `input Namespace`, in order to comply with the PHP 5.3 reservation of the keyword `namespace`.

Zend_Filter_Inflector

`Zend_Filter_Inflector` is a general purpose tool for rules-based inflection of strings to a given target.

As an example, you may find you need to transform MixedCase or camelCasedWords into a path; for readability, OS policies, or other reasons, you also need to lower case this, and you want to separate the words using a dash ('-'). An inflector can do this for you.

`Zend_Filter_Inflector` implements `Zend_Filter_Interface`; you perform inflection by calling `filter()` on the object instance.

Example 22.1. Transforming MixedCase and camelCaseText to another format

```
$inflector = new Zend_Filter_Inflector('pages/:page.:suffix');
$inflector->setRules(array(
    ':page'  => array('Word_CamelCaseToDash', 'StringToLower'),
    'suffix' => 'html'
));
$string   = 'camelCasedWords';
$filtered = $inflector->filter(array('page' => $string));
// pages/camel-cased-words.html
$string   = 'this_is_not_camel_cased';
$filtered = $inflector->filter(array('page' => $string));
// pages/this_is_not_camel_cased.html
```

Operation

An inflector requires a *target* and one or more *rules*. A target is basically a string that defines placeholders for variables you wish to substitute. These are specified by prefixing with a ':': `:script`.

When calling `filter()`, you then pass in an array of key/value pairs corresponding to the variables in the target.

Each variable in the target can have zero or more rules associated with them. Rules may be either *static* or refer to a `Zend_Filter` class. Static rules will replace with the text provided. Otherwise, a class matching the rule provided will be used to inflect the text. Classes are typically specified using a short name indicating the filter name stripped of any common prefix.

As an example, you can use any `Zend_Filter` concrete implementations; however, instead of referring to them as 'Zend_Filter_Alpha' or 'Zend_Filter_StringToLower', you'd specify only 'Alpha' or 'StringToLower'.

Setting Paths To Alternate Filters

`Zend_Filter_Inflector` uses `Zend_Loader_PluginLoader` to manage loading filters to use with inflection. By default, any filter prefixed with `Zend_Filter` will be available. To access filters with that prefix but which occur deeper in the hierarchy, such as the various Word filters, simply strip off the Zend_Filter prefix:

```
// use Zend_Filter_Word_CamelCaseToDash as a rule
$inflector->addRules(array('script' => 'Word_CamelCaseToDash'));
```

To set alternate paths, `Zend_Filter_Inflector` has a utility method that proxies to the plugin loader, `addFilterPrefixPath()`:

```
$inflector->addFilterPrefixPath('My_Filter', 'My/Filter/');
```

Alternatively, you can retrieve the plugin loader from the inflector, and interact with it directly:

```
$loader = $inflector->getPluginLoader();
$loader->addPrefixPath('My_Filter', 'My/Filter/');
```

For more options on modifying the paths to filters, please see the PluginLoader documentation.

Setting the Inflector Target

The inflector target is a string with some placeholders for variables. Placeholders take the form of an identifier, a colon (':') by default, followed by a variable name: ':script', ':path', etc. The `filter()` method looks for the identifier followed by the variable name being replaced.

You can change the identifier using the `setTargetReplacementIdentifier()` method, or passing it as the third argument to the constructor:

```
// Via constructor:
$inflector = new Zend_Filter_Inflector('#foo/#bar.#sfx', null, '#');
// Via accessor:
$inflector->setTargetReplacementIdentifier('#');
```

Typically, you will set the target via the constructor. However, you may want to re-set the target later (for instance, to modify the default inflector in core components, such as the `ViewRenderer` or `Zend_Layout`). `setTarget()` can be used for this purpose:

```
$inflector = $layout->getInflector();
$inflector->setTarget('layouts/:script.phtml');
```

Additionally, you may wish to have a class member for your class that you can use to keep the inflector target updated -- without needing to directly update the target each time (thus saving on method calls). `setTargetReference()` allows you to do this:

```
class Foo
{
    /**
     * @var string Inflector target
     */
    protected $_target = 'foo/:bar/:baz.:suffix';
    /**
```

```
 * Constructor
 * @return void
 */
public function __construct()
{
    $this->_inflector = new Zend_Filter_Inflector();
    $this->_inflector->setTargetReference($this->_target);
}
/**
 * Set target; updates target in inflector
 *
 * @param  string $target
 * @return Foo
 */
public function setTarget($target)
{
    $this->_target = $target;
    return $this;
}
}
```

Inflection Rules

As mentioned in the introduction, there are two types of rules: static and filter-based.

Note

It is important to note that regardless of the method in which you add rules to the inflector, either one-by-one, or all-at-once; the order is very important. More specific names, or names that might contain other rule names, must be added before least specific names. For example, assuming the two rule names 'moduleDir' and 'module', the 'moduleDir' rule should appear before module since 'module' is contained within 'moduleDir'. If 'module' were added before 'moduleDir', 'module' will match part of 'moduleDir' and process it leaving 'Dir' inside of the target uninflected.

Static Rules

Static rules do simple string substitution; use them when you have a segment in the target that will typically be static, but which you want to allow the developer to modify. Use the setStaticRule() method to set or modify the rule:

```
$inflector = new Zend_Filter_Inflector(':script.:suffix');
$inflector->setStaticRule('suffix', 'phtml');
// change it later:
$inflector->setStaticRule('suffix', 'php');
```

Much like the target itself, you can also bind a static rule to a reference, allowing you to update a single variable instead of require a method call; this is often useful when your class uses an inflector internally, and you don't want your users to need to fetch the inflector in order to update it. The setStaticRuleReference() method is used to accomplish this:

```
class Foo
{
    /**
     * @var string Suffix
     */
    protected $_suffix = 'phtml';
    /**
     * Constructor
     * @return void
     */
```

```
    public function __construct()
    {
        $this->_inflector = new Zend_Filter_Inflector(':script.:suffix');
        $this->_inflector->setStaticRuleReference('suffix', $this->_suffix);
    }
    /**
     * Set suffix; updates suffix static rule in inflector
     *
     * @param  string $suffix
     * @return Foo
     */
    public function setSuffix($suffix)
    {
        $this->_suffix = $suffix;
        return $this;
    }
}
```

Filter Inflector Rules

Zend_Filter filters may be used as inflector rules as well. Just like static rules, these are bound to a target variable; unlike static rules, you may define multiple filters to use when inflecting. These filters are processed in order, so be careful to register them in an order that makes sense for the data you receive.

Rules may be added using setFilterRule() (which overwrites any previous rules for that variable) or addFilterRule() (which appends the new rule to any existing rule for that variable). Filters are specified in one of the following ways:

- *String*. The string may be a filter class name, or a class name segment minus any prefix set in the inflector's plugin loader (by default, minus the 'Zend_Filter' prefix).

- *Filter object*. Any object instance implementing Zend_Filter_Interface may be passed as a filter.

- *Array*. An array of one or more strings or filter objects as defined above.

```
$inflector = new Zend_Filter_Inflector(':script.:suffix');
// Set rule to use Zend_Filter_Word_CamelCaseToDash filter
$inflector->setFilterRule('script', 'Word_CamelCaseToDash');
// Add rule to lowercase string
$inflector->addFilterRule('script', new Zend_Filter_StringToLower());
// Set rules en-masse
$inflector->setFilterRule('script', array(
    'Word_CamelCaseToDash',
    new Zend_Filter_StringToLower()
));
```

Setting Many Rules At Once

Typically, it's easier to set many rules at once than to configure a single variable and its inflection rules at a time. Zend_Filter_Inflector's addRules() and setRules() method allow this.

Each method takes an array of variable/rule pairs, where the rule may be whatever the type of rule accepts (string, filter object, or array). Variable names accept a special notation to allow setting static rules and filter rules, according to the following notation:

- *':' prefix*: filter rules.

- *No prefix*: static rule.

Example 22.2. Setting Multiple Rules at Once

```
// Could also use setRules() with this notation:
$inflector->addRules(array(
    // filter rules:
    ':controller' => array('CamelCaseToUnderscore','StringToLower'),
    ':action'     => array('CamelCaseToUnderscore','StringToLower'),
    // Static rule:
    'suffix'      => 'phtml'
));
```

Utility Methods

Zend_Filter_Inflector has a number of utility methods for retrieving and setting the plugin loader, manipulating and retrieving rules, and controlling if and when exceptions are thrown.

- setPluginLoader() can be used when you have configured your own plugin loader and wish to use it with Zend_Filter_Inflector; getPluginLoader() retrieves the currently set one.

- setThrowTargetExceptionsOn() can be used to control whether or not filter() throws an exception when a given replacement identifier passed to it is not found in the target. By default, no exceptions are thrown. isThrowTargetExceptionsOn() will tell you what the current value is.

- getRules($spec = null) can be used to retrieve all registered rules for all variables, or just the rules for a single variable.

- getRule($spec, $index) fetches a single rule for a given variable; this can be useful for fetching a specific filter rule for a variable that has a filter chain. $index must be passed.

- clearRules() will clear all currently registered rules.

Using Zend_Config with Zend_Filter_Inflector

You can use Zend_Config to set rules, filter prefix paths, and other object state in your inflectors, either by passing a Zend_Config object to the constructor or setConfig(). The following settings may be specified:

- target specifies the inflection target.

- filterPrefixPath specifies one or more filter prefix/path pairs for use with the inflector.

- throwTargetExceptionsOn should be a boolean indicating whether or not to throw exceptions when a replacement identifier is still present after inflection.

- targetReplacementIdentifier specifies the character to use when identifying replacement variables in the target string.

- rules specifies an array of inflection rules; it should consist of keys that specify either values or arrays of values, consistent with addRules().

Example 22.3. Using Zend_Config with Zend_Filter_Inflector

```
// With the constructor:
$config    = new Zend_Config($options);
$inflector = new Zend_Filter_Inflector($config);
```

```
// Or with setConfig():
$inflector = new Zend_Filter_Inflector();
$inflector->setConfig($config);
```

Chapter 23. Zend_Form

Zend_Form

Zend_Form simplifies form creation and handling in your web application. It performs the following tasks:

- Element input filtering and validation

- Element ordering

- Element and Form rendering, including escaping

- Element and form grouping

- Element and form-level configuration

Zend_Form makes use of several Zend Framework components to accomplish its goals, including Zend_Config, Zend_Validate, Zend_Filter, Zend_Loader_PluginLoader, and optionally Zend_View.

Zend_Form Quick Start

This quick start guide covers the basics of creating, validating, and rendering forms with Zend_Form.

Create a form object

Creating a form object is very simple: simply instantiate Zend_Form:

```
$form = new Zend_Form;
```

For advanced use cases, you may want to create a Zend_Form subclass, but for simple forms, you can create a form programmatically using a Zend_Form object.

If you wish to specify the form action and method (always good ideas), you can do so with the setAction() and setMethod() accessors:

```
$form->setAction('/resource/process')
    ->setMethod('post');
```

The above code sets the form action to the partial URL "/resource/process" and the form method to HTTP POST. This will be reflected during final rendering.

You can set additional HTML attributes for the <form> tag by using the setAttrib() or setAttribs() methods. For instance, if you wish to set the id, set the "id" attribute:

```
$form->setAttrib('id', 'login');
```

Add elements to the form

A form is nothing without its elements. Zend_Form ships with some default elements that render XHTML via Zend_View helpers. These are as follows:

- button

- checkbox (or many checkboxes at once with multiCheckbox)

- hidden

- image

- password

- radio

- reset

- select (both regular and multi-select types)

- submit

- text

- textarea

You have two options for adding elements to a form: you can instantiate concrete elements and pass in these objects, or you can pass in simply the element type and have `Zend_Form` instantiate an object of the correct type for you.

Some examples:

```
// Instantiating an element and passing to the form object:
$form->addElement(new Zend_Form_Element_Text('username'));
// Passing a form element type to the form object:
$form->addElement('text', 'username');
```

By default, these do not have any validators or filters. This means you will need to configure your elements with at least validators, and potentially filters. You can either do this (a) before you pass the element to the form, (b) via configuration options passed in when creating an element via `Zend_Form`, or (c) by pulling the element from the form object and configuring it after the fact.

Let's first look at creating validators for a concrete element instance. You can either pass in `Zend_Validate_*` objects, or the name of a validator to utilize:

```
$username = new Zend_Form_Element_Text('username');
// Passing a Zend_Validate_* object:
$username->addValidator(new Zend_Validate_Alnum());
// Passing a validator name:
$username->addValidator('alnum');
```

When using this second option, you can pass constructor arguments in an array as the third parameter if the validator can accept tem:

```
// Pass a pattern
$username->addValidator('regex', false, array('/^[a-z]/i'));
```

(The second parameter is used to indicate whether or not failure of this validator should prevent later validators from running; by default, this is false.)

You may also wish to specify an element as required. This can be done using an accessor or passing an option when creating the element. In the former case:

```
// Make this element required:
```

```
$username->setRequired(true);
```

When an element is required, a 'NotEmpty' validator is added to the top of the validator chain, ensuring that the element has a value when required.

Filters are registered in basically the same way as validators. For illustration purposes, let's add a filter to lowercase the final value:

```
$username->addFilter('StringtoLower');
```

The final element setup might look like this:

```
$username->addValidator('alnum')
        ->addValidator('regex', false, array('/^[a-z]/'))
        ->setRequired(true)
        ->addFilter('StringToLower');
// or, more compactly:
$username->addValidators(array('alnum',
        array('regex', false, '/^[a-z]/i')
    ))
    ->setRequired(true)
    ->addFilters(array('StringToLower'));
```

Simple as this is, repeating it this for every element in a form can be a bit tedious. Let's try option (b) from above. When we create a new element using Zend_Form::addElement() as a factory, we can optionally pass in configuration options. These can include validators and filters. To do all of the above implicitly, try the following:

```
$form->addElement('text', 'username', array(
    'validators' => array(
        'alnum',
        array('regex', false, '/^[a-z]/i')
    ),
    'required' => true,
    'filters'  => array('StringToLower'),
));
```

Note

If you find you are setting up elements using the same options in many locations, you may want to consider creating your own Zend_Form_Element subclass and utilizing that class instead; this will save you typing in the long-run.

Render a form

Rendering a form is simple. Most elements use a Zend_View helper to render themselves, and thus need a view object in order to render. Other than that, you have two options: use the form's render() method, or simply echo it.

```
// Explicitly calling render(), and passing an optional view object:
echo $form->render($view);
// Assuming a view object has been previously set via setView():
echo $form;
```

By default, Zend_Form and Zend_Form_Element will attempt to use the view object initialized in the ViewRenderer, which means you won't need to set the view manually when using the Zend

Framework MVC. To render a form in a view, you simply have to do the following:

```
<?php echo $this->form ?>
```

Under the hood, Zend_Form uses "decorators" to perform rendering. These decorators can replace content, append content, or prepend content, and can fully introspect the element passed to them. As a result, you can combine multiple decorators to achieve custom effects. By default, Zend_Form_Element actually combines four decorators to achieve its output; setup looks something like this:

```
$element->addDecorators(array(
    'ViewHelper',
    'Errors',
    array('HtmlTag', array('tag' => 'dd')),
    array('Label', array('tag' => 'dt')),
));
```

(Where <HELPERNAME> is the name of a view helper to use, and varies based on the element.)

The above creates output like the following:

```
<dt><label for="username" class="required">Username</dt>
<dd>
    <input type="text" name="username" value="123-abc" />
    <ul class="errors">
        <li>'123-abc' has not only alphabetic and digit characters</li>
        <li>'123-abc' does not match against pattern '/^[a-z]/i'</li>
    </ul>
</dd>
```

(Albeit not with the same formatting.)

You can change the decorators used by an element if you wish to have different output; see the section on decorators for more information.

The form itself simply loops through the elements, and dresses them in an HTML <form>. The action and method you provided when setting up the form are provided to the <form> tag, as are any attributes you set via setAttribs() and family.

Elements are looped either in the order in which they were registered, or, if your element contains an order attribute, that order will be used. You can set an element's order using:

```
$element->setOrder(10);
```

Or, when creating an element, by passing it as an option:

```
$form->addElement('text', 'username', array('order' => 10));
```

Check if a form is valid

After a form is submitted, you will need to check and see if it passes validations. Each element is checked against the data provided; if a key matching the element name is not present, and the item is marked as required, validations are run with a null value.

Where does the data come from? You can use $_POST or $_GET, or any other data source you might have at hand (web service requests, for instance):

```
if ($form->isValid($_POST)) {
    // success!
} else {
    // failure!
}
```

With AJAX requests, you can sometimes get away with validating a single element, or groups of elements. isValidPartial() will validate a partial form. Unlike isValid(), however, if a particular key is not present, it will not run validations for that particular element:

```
if ($form->isValidPartial($_POST)) {
    // elements present all passed validations
} else {
    // one or more elements tested failed validations
}
```

An additional method, processAjax(), can be used for validating partial forms. Unlike isValidPartial(), it returns a JSON-formatted string containing error messages on failure.

Assuming your validations have passed, you can now fetch the filtered values:

```
$values = $form->getValues();
```

If you need the unfiltered values at any point, use:

```
$unfiltered = $form->getUnfilteredValues();
```

Get error status

Did your form have failed validations on submission? In most cases, you can simply render the form again, and errors will be displayed when using the default decorators:

```
if (!$form->isValid($_POST)) {
    echo $form;
    // or assign to the view object and render a view...
    $this->view->form = $form;
    return $this->render('form');
}
```

If you want to inspect the errors, you have two methods. getErrors() returns an associative array of element names / codes (where codes is an array of error codes). getMessages() returns an associative array of element names / messages (where messages is an associative array of error code / error message pairs). If a given element does not have any errors, it will not be included in the array.

Putting it together

Let's build a simple login form. It will need elements representing:

- username

- password

- submit

For our purposes, let's assume that a valid username should be alphanumeric characters only, start with a letter, have a minimum length of 6, and maximum length of 20; they will be normalized to lowercase. Passwords must be a minimum of 6 characters. We'll simply toss the submit value when done, so it can remain unvalidated.

We'll use the power of Zend_Form's configuration options to build the form:

```
$form = new Zend_Form();
$form->setAction('/user/login')
     ->setMethod('post');
// Create and configure username element:
$username = $form->createElement('text', 'username');
$username->addValidator('alnum')
         ->addValidator('regex', false, array('/^[a-z]+/'))
         ->addValidator('stringLength', false, array(6, 20))
         ->setRequired(true)
         ->addFilter('StringToLower');
// Create and configure password element:
$password = $form->createElement('password', 'password');
$password->addValidator('StringLength', false, array(6))
         ->setRequired(true);
// Add elements to form:
$form->addElement($username)
     ->addElement($password)
     // use addElement() as a factory to create 'Login' button:
     ->addElement('submit', 'login', array('label' => 'Login'));
```

Next, we'll create a controller for handling this:

```
class UserController extends Zend_Controller_Action
{
    public function getForm()
    {
        // create form as above
        return $form;
    }
    public function indexAction()
    {
        // render user/form.phtml
        $this->view->form = $this->getForm();
        $this->render('form');
    }
    public function loginAction()
    {
        if (!$this->getRequest()->isPost()) {
            return $this->_forward('index');
        }
        $form = $this->getForm();
        if (!$form->isValid($_POST)) {
            // Failed validation; redisplay form
            $this->view->form = $form;
            return $this->render('form');
        }
        $values = $form->getValues();
        // now try and authenticate....
    }
}
```

And a view script for displaying the form:

```
<h2>Please login:</h2>
<?php echo $this->form ?>
```

As you'll note from the controller code, there's more work to do: while the submission may be valid, you may still need to do some authentication using Zend_Auth or another authorization mechanism.

Using a Zend_Config Object

All Zend_Form classes are configurable using Zend_Config; you can either pass a Zend_Config object to the constructor or pass it in with setConfig(). Let's look at how we might create the above form using an INI file. First, let's follow the recommendations, and place our configurations into sections reflecting the release location, and focus on the 'development' section. Next, we'll setup a section for the given controller ('user'), and a key for the form ('login'):

```
[development]
; general form metainformation
user.login.action = "/user/login"
user.login.method = "post"
; username element
user.login.elements.username.type = "text"
user.login.elements.username.options.validators.alnum.validator = "alnum"
user.login.elements.username.options.validators.regex.validator = "regex"
user.login.elements.username.options.validators.regex.options.pattern =
    "/^[a-z]/i"
user.login.elements.username.options.validators.strlen.validator =
    "StringLength"
user.login.elements.username.options.validators.strlen.options.min = "6"
user.login.elements.username.options.validators.strlen.options.max = "20"
user.login.elements.username.options.required = true
user.login.elements.username.options.filters.lower.filter = "StringToLower"
; password element
user.login.elements.password.type = "password"
user.login.elements.password.options.validators.strlen.validator =
    "StringLength"
user.login.elements.password.options.validators.strlen.options.min = "6"
user.login.elements.password.options.required = true
; submit element
user.login.elements.submit.type = "submit"
```

You would then pass this to the form constructor:

```
$config = new Zend_Config_Ini($configFile, 'development');
$form   = new Zend_Form($config->user->login);
```

and the entire form will be defined.

Conclusion

Hopefully with this little tutorial, you should now be well on your way to unlocking the power and flexibility of Zend_Form. Read on for more in-depth information!

Creating Form Elements Using Zend_Form_Element

A form is made of elements that typically correspond to HTML form input. Zend_Form_Element encapsulates single form elements, with the following areas of responsibility:

- validation (is submitted data valid?)
  - capturing of validation error codes and messages
- filtering (how is the element escaped or normalized prior to validation and/or for output?)

- rendering (how is the element displayed?)

- metadata and attributes (what information further qualifies the element?)

The base class, Zend_Form_Element, has reasonable defaults for many cases, but it is best to extend the class for commonly used special purpose elements. Additionally, Zend Framework ships with a number of standard XHTML elements; you can read about them in the Standard Elements chapter.

Plugin Loaders

Zend_Form_Element makes use of Zend_Loader_PluginLoader to allow developers to specify locations of alternate validators, filters, and decorators. Each has its own plugin loader associated with it, and general accessors are used to retrieve and modify each.

The following loader types are used with the various plugin loader methods: 'validate', 'filter', and 'decorator'. The type names are case insensitive.

The methods used to interact with plugin loaders are as follows:

- setPluginLoader($loader, $type): $loader is the plugin loader object itself, while $type is one of the types specified above. This sets the plugin loader for the given type to the newly specified loader object.

- getPluginLoader($type): retrieves the plugin loader associated with $type.

- addPrefixPath($prefix, $path, $type = null): adds a prefix/path association to the loader specified by $type. If $type is null, it will attempt to add the path to all loaders, by appending the prefix with each of "_Validate", "_Filter", and "_Decorator"; and appending the path with "Validate/", "Filter/", and "Decorator/". If you have all your extra form element classes under a common hierarchy, this is a convenience method for setting the base prefix for them.

- addPrefixPaths(array $spec): allows you to add many paths at once to one or more plugin loaders. It expects each array item to be an array with the keys 'path', 'prefix', and 'type'.

Custom validators, filters, and decorators are an easy way to share functionality between forms and to encapsulate custom functionality.

Example 23.1. Custom Label

One common use case for plugins is to provide replacements for standard classes. For instance, if you want to provide a different implementation of the 'Label' decorator -- for instance, to always append a colon -- you could create your own 'Label' decorator with your own class prefix, and then add it to your prefix path.

Let's start with a custom Label decorator. We'll give it the class prefix "My_Decorator", and the class itself will be in the file "My/Decorator/Label.php".

```
class My_Decorator_Label extends Zend_Form_Decorator_Abstract
{
    protected $_placement = 'PREPEND';
    public function render($content)
    {
        if (null === ($element = $this->getElement())) {
            return $content;
        }
        if (!method_exists($element, 'getLabel')) {
            return $content;
        }
        $label = $element->getLabel() . ':';
        if (null === ($view = $element->getView())) {
```

```
        return $this->renderLabel($content, $label);
    }
        $label = $view->formLabel($element->getName(), $label);
        return $this->renderLabel($content, $label);
    }
    public function renderLabel($content, $label)
    {
        $placement = $this->getPlacement();
        $separator = $this->getSeparator();
        switch ($placement) {
            case 'APPEND':
                return $content . $separator . $label;
            case 'PREPEND':
            default:
                return $label . $separator . $content;
        }
    }
}
```

Now we can tell the element to use this plugin path when looking for decorators:

```
$element->addPrefixPath('My_Decorator', 'My/Decorator/', 'decorator');
```

Alternately, we can do that at the form level to ensure all decorators use this path:

```
$form->addElementPrefixPath('My_Decorator', 'My/Decorator/', 'decorator');
```

After it added as in the example above, the 'My/Decorator/' path will be searched first to see if the decorator exists there when you add a decorator. As a result, 'My_Decorator_Label' will now be used when the 'Label' decorator is requested.

Filters

It's often useful and/or necessary to perform some normalization on input prior to validation. For example, you may want to strip out all HTML, but run your validations on what remains to ensure the submission is valid. Or you may want to trim empty space surrounding input so that a StringLength validator will use the correct length of the input without counting leading or trailing whitespace characters. These operations may be performed using Zend_Filter. Zend_Form_Element has support for filter chains, allowing you to specify multiple, sequential filters. Filtering happens both during validation and when you retrieve the element value via getValue():

```
$filtered = $element->getValue();
```

Filters may be added to the chain in two ways:

* passing in a concrete filter instance

* providing a filter name – either a short name or fully qualified class name

Let's see some examples:

```
// Concrete filter instance:
$element->addFilter(new Zend_Filter_Alnum());
// Fully qualified class name:
$element->addFilter('Zend_Filter_Alnum');
// Short filter name:
$element->addFilter('Alnum');
```

```
$element->addFilter('alnum');
```

Short names are typically the filter name minus the prefix. In the default case, this will mean minus the 'Zend_Filter_' prefix. The first letter can be upper-cased or lower-cased.

Using Custom Filter Classes

If you have your own set of filter classes, you can tell Zend_Form_Element about these using addPrefixPath(). For instance, if you have filters under the 'My_Filter' prefix, you can tell Zend_Form_Element about this as follows:

```
$element->addPrefixPath('My_Filter', 'My/Filter/', 'filter');
```

(Recall that the third argument indicates which plugin loader on which to perform the action.)

If at any time you need the unfiltered value, use the getUnfilteredValue() method:

```
$unfiltered = $element->getUnfilteredValue();
```

For more information on filters, see the Zend_Filter documentation.

Methods associated with filters include:

*   addFilter($nameOfFilter, array $options = null)
*   addFilters(array $filters)
*   setFilters(array $filters) (overwrites all filters)
*   getFilter($name) (retrieve a filter object by name)
*   getFilters() (retrieve all filters)
*   removeFilter($name) (remove filter by name)
*   clearFilters() (remove all filters)

Validators

If you subscribe to the security mantra of "filter input, escape output," you'll should use validator to filter input submitted with your form. In Zend_Form, each element includes its own validator chain, consisting of Zend_Validate_* validators.

Validators may be added to the chain in two ways:

*   passing in a concrete validator instance
*   providing a validator name – either a short name or fully qualified class name

Let's see some examples:

```
// Concrete validator instance:
$element->addValidator(new Zend_Validate_Alnum());
// Fully qualified class name:
$element->addValidator('Zend_Validate_Alnum');
// Short validator name:
$element->addValidator('Alnum');
$element->addValidator('alnum');
```

Short names are typically the validator name minus the prefix. In the default case, this will mean minus the 'Zend_Validate_' prefix. As is the case with filters, the first letter can be upper-cased or lower-cased.

Using Custom Validator Classes

If you have your own set of validator classes, you can tell Zend_Form_Element about these using addPrefixPath(). For instance, if you have validators under the 'My_Validator' prefix, you can tell Zend_Form_Element about this as follows:

```
$element->addPrefixPath('My_Validator', 'My/Validator/', 'validate');
```

(Recall that the third argument indicates which plugin loader on which to perform the action.)

If failing a particular validation should prevent later validators from firing, pass boolean true as the second parameter:

```
$element->addValidator('alnum', true);
```

If you are using a string name to add a validator, and the validator class accepts arguments to the constructor, you may pass these to the third parameter of addValidator() as an array:

```
$element->addValidator('StringLength', false, array(6, 20));
```

Arguments passed in this way should be in the order in which they are defined in the constructor. The above example will instantiate the Zend_Validate_StringLenth class with its $min and $max parameters:

```
$validator = new Zend_Validate_StringLength(6, 20);
```

Providing Custom Validator Error Messages

Some developers may wish to provide custom error messages for a validator. The $options argument of the Zend_Form_Element::addValidator() method allows you to do so by providing the key 'messages' and mapping it to an array of key/value pairs for setting the message templates. You will need to know the error codes of the various validation error types for the particular validator.

A better option is to use a Zend_Translate_Adapter with your form. Error codes are automatically passed to the adapter by the default Errors decorator; you can then specify your own error message strings by setting up translations for the various error codes of your validators.

You can also set many validators at once, using addValidators(). The basic usage is to pass an array of arrays, with each array containing 1 to 3 values, matching the constructor of addValidator():

```
$element->addValidators(array(
    array('NotEmpty', true),
    array('alnum'),
    array('stringLength', false, array(6, 20)),
));
```

If you want to be more verbose or explicit, you can use the array keys 'validator', 'breakChainOnFailure', and 'options':

```
$element->addValidators(array(
    array(
        'validator'             => 'NotEmpty',
        'breakChainOnFailure' => true),
    array('validator' => 'alnum'),
    array(
        'validator' => 'stringLength',
        'options'   => array(6, 20)),
));
```

This usage is good for illustrating how you could then configure validators in a config file:

```
element.validators.notempty.validator = "NotEmpty"
element.validators.notempty.breakChainOnFailure = true
element.validators.alnum.validator = "Alnum"
element.validators.strlen.validator = "StringLength"
element.validators.strlen.options.min = 6
element.validators.strlen.options.max = 20
```

Notice that every item has a key, whether or not it needs one; this is a limitation of using configuration files -- but it also helps make explicit what the arguments are for. Just remember that any validator options must be specified in order.

To validate an element, pass the value to isValid():

```
if ($element->isValid($value)) {
    // valid
} else {
    // invalid
}
```

Validation Operates On Filtered Values

Zend_Form_Element::isValid() filters values through the provided filter chain prior to validation. See the Filters section for more information.

Validation Context

Zend_Form_Element::isValid() supports an additional argument, $context. Zend_Form::isValid() passes the entire array of data being processed to $context when validating a form, and Zend_Form_Element::isValid(), in turn, passes it to each validator. This means you can write validators that are aware of data passed to other form elements. As an example, consider a standard registration form that has fields for both password and a password confirmation; one validation would be that the two fields match. Such a validator might look like the following:

```
class My_Validate_PasswordConfirmation extends Zend_Validate_Abstract
{
    const NOT_MATCH = 'notMatch';
    protected $_messageTemplates = array(
        self::NOT_MATCH => 'Password confirmation does not match'
    );
    public function isValid($value, $context = null)
    {
        $value = (string) $value;
        $this->_setValue($value);
        if (is_array($context)) {
            if (isset($context['password_confirm'])
                && ($value == $context['password_confirm']))
```

```
        {
            return true;
        }
    } elseif (is_string($context) && ($value == $context)) {
        return true;
    }
    $this->_error(self::NOT_MATCH);
    return false;
    }
}
```

Validators are processed in order. Each validator is processed, unless a validator created with a true `breakChainOnFailure` value fails its validation. Be sure to specify your validators in a reasonable order.

After a failed validation, you can retrieve the error codes and messages from the validator chain:

```
$errors   = $element->getErrors();
$messages = $element->getMessages();
```

(Note: error messages returned are an associative array of error code / error message pairs.)

In addition to validators, you can specify that an element is required, using `setRequired(true)`. By default, this flag is false, meaning that your validator chain will be skipped if no value is passed to `isValid()`. You can modify this behavior in a number of ways:

*   By default, when an element is required, a flag, 'allowEmpty', is also true. This means that if a value evaluating to empty is passed to `isValid()`, the validators will be skipped. You can toggle this flag using the accessor `setAllowEmpty($flag)`; when the flag is false and a value is passed, the validators will still run.

*   By default, if an element is required but does not contain a 'NotEmpty' validator, `isValid()` will add one to the top of the stack, with the `breakChainOnFailure` flag set. This behavior lends required flag semantic meaning: if no value is passed, we immediately invalidate the submission and notify the user, and prevent other validators from running on what we already know is invalid data.

    If you do not want this behavior, you can turn it off by passing a false value to `setAutoInsertNotEmptyValidator($flag)`; this will prevent `isValid()` from placing the 'NotEmpty' validator in the validator chain.

For more information on validators, see the Zend_Validate documentation.

Using Zend_Form_Elements as general-purpose validators

`Zend_Form_Element` implements `Zend_Validate_Interface`, meaning an element may also be used as a validator in other, non-form related validation chains.

Methods associated with validation include:

*   `setRequired($flag)` and `isRequired()` allow you to set and retrieve the status of the 'required' flag. When set to boolean `true`, this flag requires that the element be in the data processed by Zend_Form.

*   `setAllowEmpty($flag)` and `getAllowEmpty()` allow you to modify the behaviour of optional elements (i.e., elements where the required flag is false). When the 'allow empty' flag is true, empty values will not be passed to the validator chain.

*   `setAutoInsertNotEmptyValidator($flag)` allows you to specify whether or not a 'NotEmpty' validator will be prepended to the validator chain when the element is required. By default, this flag is true.

- addValidator($nameOrValidator, $breakChainOnFailure = false, array $options = null)

- addValidators(array $validators)

- setValidators(array $validators) (overwrites all validators)

- getValidator($name) (retrieve a validator object by name)

- getValidators() (retrieve all validators)

- removeValidator($name) (remove validator by name)

- clearValidators() (remove all validators)

Custom Error Messages

At times, you may want to specify one or more specific error messages to use instead of the error messages generated by the validators attached to your element. Additionally, at times you may want to mark the element invalid yourself. As of 1.6.0, this functionality is possible via the following methods.

- addErrorMessage($message): add an error message to display on form validation errors. You may call this more than once, and new messages are appended to the stack.

- addErrorMessages(array $messages): add multiple error messages to display on form validation errors.

- setErrorMessages(array $messages): add multiple error messages to display on form validation errors, overwriting all previously set error messages.

- getErrorMessages(): retrieve the list of custom error messages that have been defined.

- clearErrorMessages(): remove all custom error messages that have been defined.

- markAsError(): mark the element as having failed validation.

- hasErrors(): determine whether the element has either failed validation or been marked as invalid.

- addError($message): add a message to the custom error messages stack and flag the element as invalid.

- addErrors(array $messages): add several messages to the custom error messages stack and flag the element as invalid.

- setErrors(array $messages): overwrite the custom error messages stack with the provided messages and flag the element as invalid.

All errors set in this fashion may be translated. Additionally, you may insert the placeholder "%value%" to represent the element value; this current element value will be substituted when the error messages are retrieved.

Decorators

One particular pain point for many web developers is the creation of the XHTML forms themselves. For each element, the developer needs to create markup for the element itself (typically a label) and special markup for displaying validation error messages. The more elements on the page, the less trivial this task becomes.

Zend_Form_Element tries to solve this issue through the use of "decorators". Decorators are simply classes that have access to the element and a method for rendering content. For more information on how decorators work, please see the section on Zend_Form_Decorator.

The default decorators used by `Zend_Form_Element` are:

- *ViewHelper*: specifies a view helper to use to render the element. The 'helper' element attribute can be used to specify which view helper to use. By default, `Zend_Form_Element` specifies the 'formText' view helper, but individual subclasses specify different helpers.

- *Errors*: appends error messages to the element using `Zend_View_Helper_FormErrors`. If none are present, nothing is appended.

- *Description*: appends the element description. If none is present, nothing is appended. By default, the description is rendered in a <p> tag with a class of 'description'.

- *HtmlTag*: wraps the element and errors in an HTML <dd> tag.

- *Label*: prepends a label to the element using `Zend_View_Helper_FormLabel`, and wraps it in a <dt> tag. If no label is provided, just the definition term tag is rendered.

Default Decorators Do Not Need to Be Loaded

By default, the default decorators are loaded during object initialization. You can disable this by passing the 'disableLoadDefaultDecorators' option to the constructor:

```
$element = new Zend_Form_Element('foo',
                           array('disableLoadDefaultDecorators' =>
                               true)
                     );
```

This option may be mixed with any other options you pass, both as array options or in a `Zend_Config` object.

Since the order in which decorators are registered matters- the first decorator registered is executed first- you will need to make sure you register your decorators in an appropriate order, or ensure that you set the placement options in a sane fashion. To give an example, here is the code that registers the default decorators:

```
$this->addDecorators(array(
    array('ViewHelper'),
    array('Errors'),
    array('Description', array('tag' => 'p', 'class' => 'description')),
    array('HtmlTag', array('tag' => 'dd')),
    array('Label', array('tag' => 'dt')),
));
```

The initial content is created by the 'ViewHelper' decorator, which creates the form element itself. Next, the 'Errors' decorator fetches error messages from the element, and, if any are present, passes them to the 'FormErrors' view helper to render. If a description is present, the 'Description' decorator will append a paragraph of class 'description' containing the descriptive text to the aggregated content. The next decorator, 'HtmlTag', wraps the element, errors, and description in an HTML <dd> tag. Finally, the last decorator, 'label', retrieves the element's label and passes it to the 'FormLabel' view helper, wrapping it in an HTML <dt> tag; the value is prepended to the content by default. The resulting output looks basically like this:

```
<dt><label for="foo" class="optional">Foo</label></dt>
<dd>
    <input type="text" name="foo" id="foo" value="123" />
    <ul class="errors">
        <li>"123" is not an alphanumeric value</li>
    </ul>
    <p class="description">
```

```
        This is some descriptive text regarding the element.
    </p>
</dd>
```

For more information on decorators, read the Zend_Form_Decorator section.

Using Multiple Decorators of the Same Type

Internally, Zend_Form_Element uses a decorator's class as the lookup mechanism when retrieving decorators. As a result, you cannot register multiple decorators of the same type; subsequent decorators will simply overwrite those that existed before.

To get around this, you can use *aliases*. Instead of passing a decorator or decorator name as the first argument to addDecorator(), pass an array with a single element, with the alias pointing to the decorator object or name:

```
// Alias to 'FooBar':
$element->addDecorator(array('FooBar' => 'HtmlTag'),
                       array('tag' => 'div'));
// And retrieve later:
$decorator = $element->getDecorator('FooBar');
```

In the addDecorators() and setDecorators() methods, you will need to pass the 'decorator' option in the array representing the decorator:

```
// Add two 'HtmlTag' decorators, aliasing one to 'FooBar':
$element->addDecorators(
    array('HtmlTag', array('tag' => 'div')),
    array(
        'decorator' => array('FooBar' => 'HtmlTag'),
        'options' => array('tag' => 'dd')
    ),
);
// And retrieve later:
$htmlTag = $element->getDecorator('HtmlTag');
$fooBar  = $element->getDecorator('FooBar');
```

Methods associated with decorators include:

* addDecorator($nameOrDecorator, array $options = null)

* addDecorators(array $decorators)

* setDecorators(array $decorators) (overwrites all decorators)

* getDecorator($name) (retrieve a decorator object by name)

* getDecorators() (retrieve all decorators)

* removeDecorator($name) (remove decorator by name)

* clearDecorators() (remove all decorators)

Zend_Form_Element also uses overloading to allow rendering specific decorators. __call() will intercept methods that lead with the text 'render' and use the remainder of the method name to lookup a decorator; if found, it will then render that *single* decorator. Any arguments passed to the method call will be used as content to pass to the decorator's render() method. As an example:

```
// Render only the ViewHelper decorator:
echo $element->renderViewHelper();
```

```
// Render only the HtmlTag decorator, passing in content:
echo $element->renderHtmlTag("This is the html tag content");
```

If the decorator does not exist, an exception is raised.

Metadata and Attributes

Zend_Form_Element handles a variety of attributes and element metadata. Basic attributes include:

- *name*: the element name. Uses the setName() and getName() accessors.

- *label*: the element label. Uses the setLabel() and getLabel() accessors.

- *order*: the index at which an element should appear in the form. Uses the setOrder() and getOrder() accessors.

- *value*: the current element value. Uses the setValue() and getValue() accessors.

- *description*: a description of the element; often used to provide tooltip or javascript contextual hinting describing the purpose of the element. Uses the setDescription() and getDescription() accessors.

- *required*: flag indicating whether or not the element is required when performing form validation. Uses the setRequired() and getRequired() accessors. This flag is false by default.

- *allowEmpty*: flag indicating whether or not a non-required (optional) element should attempt to validate empty values. If it is set to true and the required flag is false, empty values are not passed to the validator chain and are presumed true. Uses the setAllowEmpty() and getAllowEmpty() accessors. This flag is true by default.

- *autoInsertNotEmptyValidator*: flag indicating whether or not to insert a 'NotEmpty' validator when the element is required. By default, this flag is true. Set the flag with setAutoInsertNotEmptyValidator($flag) and determine the value with autoInsertNotEmptyValidator().

Form elements may require additional metadata. For XHTML form elements, for instance, you may want to specify attributes such as the class or id. To facilitate this are a set of accessors:

- *setAttrib($name, $value)*: add an attribute

- *setAttribs(array $attribs)*: like addAttribs(), but overwrites

- *getAttrib($name)*: retrieve a single attribute value

- *getAttribs()*: retrieve all attributes as key/value pairs

Most of the time, however, you can simply access them as object properties, as Zend_Form_Element utilizes overloading to facilitate access to them:

```
// Equivalent to $element->setAttrib('class', 'text'):
$element->class = 'text;
```

By default, all attributes are passed to the view helper used by the element during rendering, and rendered as HTML attributes of the element tag.

Standard Elements

Zend_Form ships with a number of standard elements; please read the Standard Elements chapter for full details.

Zend_Form_Element Methods

Zend_Form_Element has many, many methods. What follows is a quick summary of their signatures, grouped by type:

- Configuration:

    - setOptions(array $options)

    - setConfig(Zend_Config $config)

- I18n:

    - setTranslator(Zend_Translate_Adapter $translator = null)

    - getTranslator()

    - setDisableTranslator($flag)

    - translatorIsDisabled()

- Properties:

    - setName($name)

    - getName()

    - setValue($value)

    - getValue()

    - getUnfilteredValue()

    - setLabel($label)

    - getLabel()

    - setDescription($description)

    - getDescription()

    - setOrder($order)

    - getOrder()

    - setRequired($flag)

    - getRequired()

    - setAllowEmpty($flag)

    - getAllowEmpty()

    - setAutoInsertNotEmptyValidator($flag)

    - autoInsertNotEmptyValidator()

    - setIgnore($flag)

    - getIgnore()

    - getType()

    - setAttrib($name, $value)

- setAttribs(array $attribs)

- getAttrib($name)

- getAttribs()

- Plugin loaders and paths:

  - setPluginLoader(Zend_Loader_PluginLoader_Interface $loader, $type)

  - getPluginLoader($type)

  - addPrefixPath($prefix, $path, $type = null)

  - addPrefixPaths(array $spec)

- Validation:

  - addValidator($validator, $breakChainOnFailure = false, $options = array())

  - addValidators(array $validators)

  - setValidators(array $validators)

  - getValidator($name)

  - getValidators()

  - removeValidator($name)

  - clearValidators()

  - isValid($value, $context = null)

  - getErrors()

  - getMessages()

- Filters:

  - addFilter($filter, $options = array())

  - addFilters(array $filters)

  - setFilters(array $filters)

  - getFilter($name)

  - getFilters()

  - removeFilter($name)

  - clearFilters()

- Rendering:

  - setView(Zend_View_Interface $view = null)

  - getView()

  - addDecorator($decorator, $options = null)

  - addDecorators(array $decorators)

- setDecorators(array $decorators)

- getDecorator($name)

- getDecorators()

- removeDecorator($name)

- clearDecorators()

- render(Zend_View_Interface $view = null)

Configuration

Zend_Form_Element's constructor accepts either an array of options or a Zend_Config object containing options, and it can also be configured using either setOptions() or setConfig(). Generally speaking, keys are named as follows:

- If 'set' + key refers to a Zend_Form_Element method, then the value provided will be passed to that method.

- Otherwise, the value will be used to set an attribute.

Exceptions to the rule include the following:

- prefixPath will be passed to addPrefixPaths()

- The following setters cannot be set in this way:

    - setAttrib (though setAttribs *will* work)

    - setConfig

    - setOptions

    - setPluginLoader

    - setTranslator

    - setView

As an example, here is a config file that passes configuration for every type of configurable data:

```
[element]
name = "foo"
value = "foobar"
label = "Foo:"
order = 10
required = true
allowEmpty = false
autoInsertNotEmptyValidator = true
description = "Foo elements are for examples"
ignore = false
attribs.id = "foo"
attribs.class = "element"
; sets 'onclick' attribute
onclick = "autoComplete(this, '/form/autocomplete/element')"
prefixPaths.decorator.prefix = "My_Decorator"
prefixPaths.decorator.path = "My/Decorator/"
disableTranslator = 0
validators.required.validator = "NotEmpty"
validators.required.breakChainOnFailure = true
```

```
validators.alpha.validator = "alpha"
validators.regex.validator = "regex"
validators.regex.options.pattern = "/^[A-F].*/$"
filters.ucase.filter = "StringToUpper"
decorators.element.decorator = "ViewHelper"
decorators.element.options.helper = "FormText"
decorators.label.decorator = "Label"
```

Custom Elements

You can create your own custom elements by simply extending the `Zend_Form_Element` class. Common reasons to do so include:

- Elements that share common validators and/or filters

- Elements that have custom decorator functionality

There are two methods typically used to extend an element: `init()`, which can be used to add custom initialization logic to your element, and `loadDefaultDecorators()`, which can be used to set a list of default decorators used by your element.

As an example, let's say that all text elements in a form you are creating need to be filtered with `StringTrim`, validated with a common regular expression, and that you want to use a custom decorator you've created for displaying them, 'My_Decorator_TextItem'. In addition, you have a number of standard attributes, including 'size', 'maxLength', and 'class' you wish to specify. You could define an element to accomplish this as follows:

```
class My_Element_Text extends Zend_Form_Element
{
    public function init()
    {
        $this->addPrefixPath('My_Decorator', 'My/Decorator/', 'decorator')
            ->addFilters('StringTrim')
            ->addValidator('Regex', false, array('/^[a-z0-9]{6,}$/i'))
            ->addDecorator('TextItem')
            ->setAttrib('size', 30)
            ->setAttrib('maxLength', 45)
            ->setAttrib('class', 'text');
    }
}
```

You could then inform your form object about the prefix path for such elements, and start creating elements:

```
$form->addPrefixPath('My_Element', 'My/Element/', 'element')
    ->addElement('text', 'foo');
```

The 'foo' element will now be of type `My_Element_Text`, and exhibit the behaviour you've outlined.

Another method you may want to override when extending `Zend_Form_Element` is the `loadDefaultDecorators()` method. This method conditionally loads a set of default decorators for your element; you may wish to substitute your own decorators in your extending class:

```
class My_Element_Text extends Zend_Form_Element
{
    public function loadDefaultDecorators()
    {
        $this->addDecorator('ViewHelper')
            ->addDecorator('DisplayError')
```

```
                 ->addDecorator('Label')
                 ->addDecorator('HtmlTag',
                              array('tag' => 'div', 'class' => 'element'));
        }
    }
```

There are many ways to customize elements. Read the API documentation of Zend_Form_Element to learn about all of the available methods.

Creating Forms Using Zend_Form

The Zend_Form class is used to aggregate form elements, display groups, and subforms. It can then perform the following actions on those items:

- Validation, including retrieving error codes and messages

- Value aggregation, including populating items and retrieving both filtered and unfiltered values from all items

- Iteration over all items, in the order in which they are entered or based on the order hints retrieved from each item

- Rendering of the entire form, either via a single decorator that performs custom rendering or by iterating over each item in the form

While forms created with Zend_Form may be complex, probably the best use case is for simple forms; its best use is for Rapid Application Development (RAD) and prototyping.

At its most basic, you simply instantiate a form object:

```
// Generic form object:
$form = new Zend_Form();
// Custom form object:
$form = new My_Form()
```

You can optionally pass in a instance of Zend_Config or an array, which will be used to set object state and potentially create new elements:

```
// Passing in configuration options:
$form = new Zend_Form($config);
```

Zend_Form is iterable, and will iterate over elements, display groups, and subforms, using the order they were registered and any order index each may have. This is useful in cases where you wish to render the elements manually in the appropriate order.

Zend_Form's magic lies in its ability to serve as a factory for elements and display groups, as well as the ability to render itself through decorators.

Plugin Loaders

Zend_Form makes use of Zend_Loader_PluginLoader to allow developers to specify the locations of alternate elements and decorators. Each has its own plugin loader associated with it, and general accessors are used to retrieve and modify each.

The following loader types are used with the various plugin loader methods: 'element' and 'decorator'. The type names are case insensitive.

The methods used to interact with plugin loaders are as follows:

- setPluginLoader($loader, $type): $loader is the plugin loader object itself, while type is one of the types specified above. This sets the plugin loader for the given type to the newly specified loader object.

- getPluginLoader($type): retrieves the plugin loader associated with $type.

- addPrefixPath($prefix, $path, $type = null): adds a prefix/path association to the loader specified by $type. If $type is null, it will attempt to add the path to all loaders, by appending the prefix with each of "_Element" and "_Decorator"; and appending the path with "Element/" and "Decorator/". If you have all your extra form element classes under a common hierarchy, this is a convenience method for setting the base prefix for them.

- addPrefixPaths(array $spec): allows you to add many paths at once to one or more plugin loaders. It expects each array item to be an array with the keys 'path', 'prefix', and 'type'.

Additionally, you can specify prefix paths for all elements and display groups created through a Zend_Form instance using the following methods:

- addElementPrefixPath($prefix, $path, $type = null): Just like addPrefixPath(), you must specify a class prefix and a path. $type, when specified, must be one of the plugin loader types specified by Zend_Form_Element; see the element plugins section for more information on valid $type values. If no $type is specified, the method will assume it is a general prefix for all types.

- addDisplayGroupPrefixPath($prefix, $path): Just like addPrefixPath(), you must specify a class prefix and a path; however, since display groups only support decorators as plugins, no $type is necessary.

Custom elements and decorators are an easy way to share functionality between forms and encapsulate custom functionality. See the Custom Label example in the elements documentation for an example of how custom elements can be used as replacements for standard classes.

Elements

Zend_Form provides several accessors for adding and removing form elements from a form. These can take element object instances or serve as factories for instantiating the element objects themselves.

The most basic method for adding an element is addElement(). This method can take either an object of type Zend_Form_Element (or of a class extending Zend_Form_Element), or arguments for building a new element -- including the element type, name, and any configuration options.

Some examples:

```
// Using an element instance:
$element = new Zend_Form_Element_Text('foo');
$form->addElement($element);
// Using a factory
//
// Creates an element of type Zend_Form_Element_Text with the
// name of 'foo':
$form->addElement('text', 'foo');
// Pass label option to the element:
$form->addElement('text', 'foo', array('label' => 'Foo:'));
```

addElement() Implements Fluent Interface

addElement() implements a fluent interface; that is to say, it returns the Zend_Form object, and not the element. This is done to allow you to chain together multiple addElement() methods or other form methods that implement the fluent interface (all setters in Zend_Form implement the pattern).

If you wish to return the element instead, use createElement(), which is outlined below. Be aware, however, that createElement() does not attach the element to the form.

Internally, addElement() actually uses createElement() to create the element before attaching it to the form.

Once an element has been added to the form, you can retrieve it by name. This can be done either by using the getElement() method or by using overloading to access the element as an object property:

```
// getElement():
$foo = $form->getElement('foo');
// As object property:
$foo = $form->foo;
```

Occasionally, you may want to create an element without attaching it to the form (for instance, if you wish to make use of the various plugin paths registered with the form, but wish to later attach the object to a sub form). The createElement() method allows you to do so:

```
// $username becomes a Zend_Form_Element_Text object:
$username = $form->createElement('text', 'username');
```

Populating and Retrieving Values

After validating a form, you will typically need to retrieve the values so you can perform other operations, such as updating a database or notifying a web service. You can retrieve all values for all elements using getValues(); getValue($name) allows you to retrieve a single element's value by element name:

```
// Get all values:
$values = $form->getValues();
// Get only 'foo' element's value:
$value = $form->getValue('foo');
```

Sometimes you'll want to populate the form with specified values prior to rendering. This can be done with either the setDefaults() or populate() methods:

```
$form->setDefaults($data);
$form->populate($data);
```

On the flip side, you may want to clear a form after populating or validating it; this can be done using the reset() method:

```
$form->reset();
```

Global Operations

Occasionally you will want certain operations to affect all elements. Common scenarios include needing to set plugin prefix paths for all elements, setting decorators for all elements, and setting filters for all elements. As examples:

Example 23.2. Setting Prefix Paths for All Elements

You can set prefix paths for all elements by type, or using a global prefix. Some examples:

```
// Set global prefix path:
// Creates paths for prefixes My_Foo_Filter, My_Foo_Validate,
// and My_Foo_Decorator
$form->addElementPrefixPath('My_Foo', 'My/Foo/');
// Just filter paths:
$form->addElementPrefixPath('My_Foo_Filter',
                            'My/Foo/Filter',
                            'filter');
// Just validator paths:
$form->addElementPrefixPath('My_Foo_Validate',
                            'My/Foo/Validate',
                            'validate');
// Just decorator paths:
$form->addElementPrefixPath('My_Foo_Decorator',
                            'My/Foo/Decorator',
                            'decorator');
```

Example 23.3. Setting Decorators for All Elements

You can set decorators for all elements. setElementDecorators() accepts an array of decorators, just like setDecorators(), and will overwrite any previously set decorators in each element. In this example, we set the decorators to simply a ViewHelper and a Label:

```
$form->setElementDecorators(array(
    'ViewHelper',
    'Label'
));
```

Example 23.4. Setting Decorators for Some Elements

You can also set decorators for a subset of elements, either by inclusion or exclusion. The second argument to setElementDecorators() may be an array of element names; by default, specifying such an array will set the specified decorators on those elements only. You may also pass a third argument, a flag indicating whether this list of elements is for inclusion or exclusion purposes. If the flag is false, it will decorate all elements *except* those in the passed list. As with standard usage of the method, any decorators passed will overwrite any previously set decorators in each element.

In the following snippet, we indicate that we want only the ViewHelper and Label decorators for the 'foo' and 'bar' elements:

```
$form->setElementDecorators(
    array(
        'ViewHelper',
        'Label'
    ),
    array(
        'foo',
        'bar'
    )
);
```

On the flip side, with this snippet, we'll now indicate that we want to use only the ViewHelper and Label decorators for every element *except* the 'foo' and 'bar' elements:

```
$form->setElementDecorators(
    array(
        'ViewHelper',
        'Label'
    ),
    array(
        'foo',
        'bar'
    ),
    false
);
```

Some Decorators are Inappropriate for Some Elements

While setElementDecorators() may seem like a good solution, there are some cases where it may actually end up with unexpected results. For example, the various button elements (Submit, Button, Reset) currently use the label as the value of the button, and only use ViewHelper and DtDdWrapper decorators -- preventing an additional labels, errors, and hints from being rendered. The example above would duplicate some content (the label) for button elements.

You can use the inclusion/exclusion array to overcome this issue as noted in the previous example.

So, use this method wisely, and realize that you may need to exclude some elements or manually change some elements' decorators to prevent unwanted output.

Example 23.5. Setting Filters for All Elements

In some cases, you may want to apply the same filter to all elements; a common case is to trim() all values:

```
$form->setElementFilters(array('StringTrim'));
```

Methods For Interacting With Elements

The following methods may be used to interact with elements:

- createElement($element, $name = null, $options = null)

- addElement($element, $name = null, $options = null)

- addElements(array $elements)

- setElements(array $elements)

- getElement($name)

- getElements()

- removeElement($name)

- clearElements()

- setDefaults(array $defaults)

- setDefault($name, $value)

- `getValue($name)`

- `getValues()`

- `getUnfilteredValue($name)`

- `getUnfilteredValues()`

- `setElementFilters(array $filters)`

- `setElementDecorators(array $decorators)`

- `addElementPrefixPath($prefix, $path, $type = null)`

- `addElementPrefixPaths(array $spec)`

Display Groups

Display groups are a way to create virtual groupings of elements for display purposes. All elements remain accessible by name in the form, but when iterating over the form or rendering, any elements in a display group are rendered together. The most common use case for this is for grouping elements in fieldsets.

The base class for display groups is `Zend_Form_DisplayGroup`. While it can be instantiated directly, it is usually best to use `Zend_Form`'s `addDisplayGroup()` method to do so. This method takes an array of elements as its first argument, and a name for the display group as its second argument. You may optionally pass in an array of options or a `Zend_Config` object as the third argument.

Assuming that the elements 'username' and 'password' are already set in the form, the following code would group these elements in a 'login' display group:

```
$form->addDisplayGroup(array('username', 'password'), 'login');
```

You can access display groups using the `getDisplayGroup()` method, or via overloading using the display group's name:

```
// Using getDisplayGroup():
$login = $form->getDisplayGroup('login');
// Using overloading:
$login = $form->login;
```

Default Decorators Do Not Need to Be Loaded

By default, the default decorators are loaded during object initialization. You can disable this by passing the 'disableLoadDefaultDecorators' option when creating a display group:

```
$form->addDisplayGroup(
    array('foo', 'bar'),
    'foobar',
    array('disableLoadDefaultDecorators' => true)
);
```

This option may be mixed with any other options you pass, both as array options or in a `Zend_Config` object.

Global Operations

Just as with elements, there are some operations which might affect all display groups; these include setting decorators and setting the plugin path in which to look for decorators.

Example 23.6. Setting Decorator Prefix Path for All Display Groups

By default, display groups inherit whichever decorator paths the form uses; however, if they should look in alternate locations, you can use the addDisplayGroupPrefixPath() method.

```
$form->addDisplayGroupPrefixPath('My_Foo_Decorator', 'My/Foo/Decorator');
```

Example 23.7. Setting Decorators for All Display Groups

You can set decorators for all display groups. setDisplayGroupDecorators() accepts an array of decorators, just like setDecorators(), and will overwrite any previously set decorators in each display group. In this example, we set the decorators to simply a fieldset (the FormElements decorator is necessary to ensure that the elements are iterated):

```
$form->setDisplayGroupDecorators(array(
    'FormElements',
    'Fieldset'
));
```

Using Custom Display Group Classes

By default, Zend_Form uses the Zend_Form_DisplayGroup class for display groups. You may find you need to extend this class in order to provided custom functionality. addDisplayGroup() does not allow passing in a concrete instance, but does allow specifying the class to use as one of its options, using the 'displayGroupClass' key:

```
// Use the 'My_DisplayGroup' class
$form->addDisplayGroup(
    array('username', 'password'),
    'user',
    array('displayGroupClass' => 'My_DisplayGroup')
);
```

If the class has not yet been loaded, Zend_Form will attempt to do so using Zend_Loader.

You can also specify a default display group class to use with the form such that all display groups created with the form object will use that class:

```
// Use the 'My_DisplayGroup' class for all display groups:
$form->setDefaultDisplayGroupClass('My_DisplayGroup');
```

This setting may be specified in configurations as 'defaultDisplayGroupClass', and will be loaded early to ensure all display groups use that class.

Methods for Interacting With Display Groups

The following methods may be used to interact with display groups:

- addDisplayGroup(array $elements, $name, $options = null)

- addDisplayGroups(array $groups)

- setDisplayGroups(array $groups)

- getDisplayGroup($name)

- getDisplayGroups()

- removeDisplayGroup($name)

- clearDisplayGroups()

- setDisplayGroupDecorators(array $decorators)

- addDisplayGroupPrefixPath($prefix, $path)

- setDefaultDisplayGroupClass($class)

- getDefaultDisplayGroupClass($class)

Zend_Form_DisplayGroup Methods

Zend_Form_DisplayGroup has the following methods, grouped by type:

- Configuration:

  - setOptions(array $options)

  - setConfig(Zend_Config $config)

- Metadata:

  - setAttrib($key, $value)

  - addAttribs(array $attribs)

  - setAttribs(array $attribs)

  - getAttrib($key)

  - getAttribs()

  - removeAttrib($key)

  - clearAttribs()

  - setName($name)

  - getName()

  - setDescription($value)

  - getDescription()

  - setLegend($legend)

  - getLegend()

  - setOrder($order)

  - getOrder()

- Elements:

  - createElement($type, $name, array $options = array())

- addElement($typeOrElement, $name, array $options = array())

- addElements(array $elements)

- setElements(array $elements)

- getElement($name)

- getElements()

- removeElement($name)

- clearElements()

- Plugin loaders:

  - setPluginLoader(Zend_Loader_PluginLoader $loader)

  - getPluginLoader()

  - addPrefixPath($prefix, $path)

  - addPrefixPaths(array $spec)

- Decorators:

  - addDecorator($decorator, $options = null)

  - addDecorators(array $decorators)

  - setDecorators(array $decorators)

  - getDecorator($name)

  - getDecorators()

  - removeDecorator($name)

  - clearDecorators()

- Rendering:

  - setView(Zend_View_Interface $view = null)

  - getView()

  - render(Zend_View_Interface $view = null)

- I18n:

  - setTranslator(Zend_Translate_Adapter $translator = null)

  - getTranslator()

  - setDisableTranslator($flag)

  - translatorIsDisabled()

Sub Forms

Sub forms serve several purposes:

- Creating logical element groups. Since sub forms are simply forms, you can validate subforms as individual entities.

- Creating multi-page forms. Since sub forms are simply forms, you can display a separate sub form per page, building up multi-page forms where each form has its own validation logic. Only once all sub forms validate would the form be considered complete.

- Display groupings. Like display groups, sub forms, when rendered as part of a larger form, can be used to group elements. Be aware, however, that the master form object will have no awareness of the elements in sub forms.

A sub form may be a Zend_Form object, or, more typically, a Zend_Form_SubForm object. The latter contains decorators suitable for inclusion in a larger form (i.e., it does not render additional HTML form tags, but does group elements). To attach a sub form, simply add it to the form and give it a name:

```
$form->addSubForm($subForm, 'subform');
```

You can retrieve a sub form using either getSubForm($name) or overloading using the sub form name:

```
// Using getSubForm():
$subForm = $form->getSubForm('subform');
// Using overloading:
$subForm = $form->subform;
```

Sub forms are included in form iteration, although the elements they contain are not.

Global Operations

Like elements and display groups, there are some operations that might need to affect all sub forms. Unlike display groups and elements, however, sub forms inherit most functionality from the master form object, and the only real operation that may need to be performed globally is setting decorators for sub forms. For this purpose, there is the setSubFormDecorators() method. In the next example, we'll set the decorator for all subforms to be simply a fieldset (the FormElements decorator is needed to ensure its elements are iterated):

```
$form->setSubFormDecorators(array(
    'FormElements',
    'Fieldset'
));
```

Methods for Interacting With Sub Forms

The following methods may be used to interact with sub forms:

- addSubForm(Zend_Form $form, $name, $order = null)

- addSubForms(array $subForms)

- setSubForms(array $subForms)

- getSubForm($name)

- getSubForms()

- removeSubForm($name)

- clearSubForms()

- setSubFormDecorators(array $decorators)

Metadata and Attributes

While a form's usefulness primarily derives from the elements it contains, it can also contain other metadata, such as a name (often used as a unique ID in the HTML markup); the form action and method; the number of elements, groups, and sub forms it contains; and arbitrary metadata (usually used to set HTML attributes for the form tag itself).

You can set and retrieve a form's name using the name accessors:

```
// Set the name:
$form->setName('registration');
// Retrieve the name:
$name = $form->getName();
```

To set the action (url to which the form submits) and method (method by which it should submit, e.g., 'POST' or 'GET'), use the action and method accessors:

```
// Set the action and method:
$form->setAction('/user/login')
     ->setMethod('post');
```

You may also specify the form encoding type specifically using the enctype accessors. Zend_Form defines two constants, Zend_Form::ENCTYPE_URLENCODED and Zend_Form::ENCTYPE_MULTIPART, corresponding to the values 'application/x-www-form-urlencoded' and 'multipart/form-data', respectively; however, you can set this to any arbitrary encoding type.

```
// Set the action, method, and enctype:
$form->setAction('/user/login')
     ->setMethod('post')
     ->setEnctype(Zend_Form::ENCTYPE_MULTIPART);
```

Note

The method, action, and enctype are only used internally for rendering, and not for any sort of validation.

Zend_Form implements the Countable interface, allowing you to pass it as an argument to count:

```
$numItems = count($form);
```

Setting arbitrary metadata is done through the attribs accessors. Since overloading in Zend_Form is used to access elements, display groups, and sub forms, this is the only method for accessing metadata.

```
// Setting attributes:
$form->setAttrib('class', 'zend-form')
     ->addAttribs(array(
         'id'       => 'registration',
         'onSubmit' => 'validate(this)',
     ));
// Retrieving attributes:
$class = $form->getAttrib('class');
$attribs = $form->getAttribs();
// Remove an attribute:
$form->removeAttrib('onSubmit');
// Clear all attributes:
$form->clearAttribs();
```

Decorators

Creating the markup for a form is often a time-consuming task, particularly if you plan on re-using the same markup to show things such as validation errors, submitted values, etc. Zend_Form's answer to this issue is *decorators*.

Decorators for Zend_Form objects can be used to render a form. The FormElements decorator will iterate through all items in a form -- elements, display groups, and sub forms -- and render them, returning the result. Additional decorators may then be used to wrap this content, or append or prepend it.

The default decorators for Zend_Form are FormElements, HtmlTag (wraps in a definition list), and Form; the equivalent code for creating them is as follows:

```
$form->setDecorators(array(
    'FormElements',
    array('HtmlTag', array('tag' => 'dl')),
    'Form'
));
```

This creates output like the following:

```
<form action="/form/action" method="post">
<dl>
...
</dl>
</form>
```

Any attributes set on the form object will be used as HTML attributes of the <form> tag.

Default Decorators Do Not Need to Be Loaded

By default, the default decorators are loaded during object initialization. You can disable this by passing the 'disableLoadDefaultDecorators' option to the constructor:

```
$form = new Zend_Form(array('disableLoadDefaultDecorators' => true));
```

This option may be mixed with any other options you pass, both as array options or in a Zend_Config object.

Using Multiple Decorators of the Same Type

Internally, Zend_Form uses a decorator's class as the lookup mechanism when retrieving decorators. As a result, you cannot register multiple decorators of the same type; subsequent decorators will simply overwrite those that existed before.

To get around this, you can use aliases. Instead of passing a decorator or decorator name as the first argument to addDecorator(), pass an array with a single element, with the alias pointing to the decorator object or name:

```
// Alias to 'FooBar':
$form->addDecorator(array('FooBar' => 'HtmlTag'), array('tag' => 'div'));
// And retrieve later:
$form = $element->getDecorator('FooBar');
```

In the addDecorators() and setDecorators() methods, you will need to pass the 'decorator' option in the array representing the decorator:

```
// Add two 'HtmlTag' decorators, aliasing one to 'FooBar':
$form->addDecorators(
    array('HtmlTag', array('tag' => 'div')),
    array(
        'decorator' => array('FooBar' => 'HtmlTag'),
        'options' => array('tag' => 'dd')
    ),
);
// And retrieve later:
$htmlTag = $form->getDecorator('HtmlTag');
$fooBar  = $form->getDecorator('FooBar');
```

You may create your own decorators for generating the form. One common use case is if you know the exact HTML you wish to use; your decorator could create the exact HTML and simply return it, potentially using the decorators from individual elements or display groups.

The following methods may be used to interact with decorators:

- `addDecorator($decorator, $options = null)`

- `addDecorators(array $decorators)`

- `setDecorators(array $decorators)`

- `getDecorator($name)`

- `getDecorators()`

- `removeDecorator($name)`

- `clearDecorators()`

Zend_Form also uses overloading to allow rendering specific decorators. `__call()` will intercept methods that lead with the text 'render' and use the remainder of the method name to lookup a decorator; if found, it will then render that *single* decorator. Any arguments passed to the method call will be used as content to pass to the decorator's `render()` method. As an example:

```
// Render only the FormElements decorator:
echo $form->renderFormElements();
// Render only the fieldset decorator, passing in content:
echo $form->renderFieldset("<p>This is fieldset content</p>");
```

If the decorator does not exist, an exception is raised.

Validation

A primary use case for forms is validating submitted data. Zend_Form allows you to validate an entire form, a partial form, or responses for XmlHttpRequests (AJAX). If the submitted data is not valid, it has methods for retrieving the various error codes and messages for elements and sub forms.

To validate a full form, use the `isValid()` method:

```
if (!$form->isValid($_POST)) {
    // failed validation
}
```

`isValid()` will validate every required element, and any unrequired element contained in the submitted data.

Sometimes you may need to validate only a subset of the data; for this, use

```
isValidPartial($data):

if (!$form->isValidPartial($data)) {
    // failed validation
}
```

isValidPartial() only attempts to validate those items in the data for which there are matching elements; if an element is not represented in the data, it is skipped.

When validating elements or groups of elements for an AJAX request, you will typically be validating a subset of the form, and want the response back in JSON. processAjax() does precisely that:

```
$json = $form->processAjax($data);
```

You can then simply send the JSON response to the client. If the form is valid, this will be a boolean true response. If not, it will be a javascript object containing key/message pairs, where each 'message' is an array of validation error messages.

For forms that fail validation, you can retrieve both error codes and error messages, using getErrors() and getMessages(), respectively:

```
$codes = $form->getErrors();
$messages = $form->getMessages();
```

Note

Since the messages returned by getMessages() are an array of error code/message pairs, getErrors() is typically not needed.

You can retrieve codes and error messages for individual elements by simply passing the element name to each:

```
$codes = $form->getErrors('username');
$messages = $form->getMessages('username');
```

Note

Note: When validating elements, Zend_Form sends a second argument to each element's isValid() method: the array of data being validated. This can then be used by individual validators to allow them to utilize other submitted values when determining the validity of the data. An example would be a registration form that requires both a password and password confirmation; the password element could use the password confirmation as part of its validation.

Custom Error Messages

At times, you may want to specify one or more specific error messages to use instead of the error messages generated by the validators attached to your elements. Additionally, at times you may want to mark the form invalid yourself. This functionality is possible via the following methods.

- addErrorMessage($message): add an error message to display on form validation errors. You may call this more than once, and new messages are appended to the stack.

- addErrorMessages(array $messages): add multiple error messages to display on form validation errors.

- setErrorMessages(array $messages): add multiple error messages to display on form validation errors, overwriting all previously set error messages.

- getErrorMessages(): retrieve the list of custom error messages that have been defined.

- `clearErrorMessages()`: remove all custom error messages that have been defined.

- `markAsError()`: mark the form as having failed validation.

- `addError($message)`: add a message to the custom error messages stack and flag the form as invalid.

- `addErrors(array $messages)`: add several messages to the custom error messages stack and flag the form as invalid.

- `setErrors(array $messages)`: overwrite the custom error messages stack with the provided messages and flag the form as invalid.

All errors set in this fashion may be translated.

Methods

The following is a full list of methods available to `Zend_Form`, grouped by type:

- Configuration and Options:

  - `setOptions(array $options)`

  - `setConfig(Zend_Config $config)`

- Plugin Loaders and paths:

  - `setPluginLoader(Zend_Loader_PluginLoader_Interface $loader, $type = null)`

  - `getPluginLoader($type = null)`

  - `addPrefixPath($prefix, $path, $type = null)`

  - `addPrefixPaths(array $spec)`

  - `addElementPrefixPath($prefix, $path, $type = null)`

  - `addElementPrefixPaths(array $spec)`

  - `addDisplayGroupPrefixPath($prefix, $path)`

- Metadata:

  - `setAttrib($key, $value)`

  - `addAttribs(array $attribs)`

  - `setAttribs(array $attribs)`

  - `getAttrib($key)`

  - `getAttribs()`

  - `removeAttrib($key)`

  - `clearAttribs()`

  - `setAction($action)`

  - `getAction()`

  - `setMethod($method)`

- getMethod()
- setName($name)
- getName()
- Elements:
  - addElement($element, $name = null, $options = null)
  - addElements(array $elements)
  - setElements(array $elements)
  - getElement($name)
  - getElements()
  - removeElement($name)
  - clearElements()
  - setDefaults(array $defaults)
  - setDefault($name, $value)
  - getValue($name)
  - getValues()
  - getUnfilteredValue($name)
  - getUnfilteredValues()
  - setElementFilters(array $filters)
  - setElementDecorators(array $decorators)
- Sub forms:
  - addSubForm(Zend_Form $form, $name, $order = null)
  - addSubForms(array $subForms)
  - setSubForms(array $subForms)
  - getSubForm($name)
  - getSubForms()
  - removeSubForm($name)
  - clearSubForms()
  - setSubFormDecorators(array $decorators)
- Display groups:
  - addDisplayGroup(array $elements, $name, $options = null)
  - addDisplayGroups(array $groups)
  - setDisplayGroups(array $groups)
  - getDisplayGroup($name)

- getDisplayGroups()

- removeDisplayGroup($name)

- clearDisplayGroups()

- setDisplayGroupDecorators(array $decorators)

- Validation

  - populate(array $values)

  - isValid(array $data)

  - isValidPartial(array $data)

  - processAjax(array $data)

  - persistData()

  - getErrors($name = null)

  - getMessages($name = null)

- Rendering:

  - setView(Zend_View_Interface $view = null)

  - getView()

  - addDecorator($decorator, $options = null)

  - addDecorators(array $decorators)

  - setDecorators(array $decorators)

  - getDecorator($name)

  - getDecorators()

  - removeDecorator($name)

  - clearDecorators()

  - render(Zend_View_Interface $view = null)

- I18n:

  - setTranslator(Zend_Translate_Adapter $translator = null)

  - getTranslator()

  - setDisableTranslator($flag)

  - translatorIsDisabled()

Configuration

Zend_Form is fully configurable via setOptions() and setConfig() (or by passing options or a Zend_Config object to the constructor). Using these methods, you can specify form elements, display groups, decorators, and metadata.

As a general rule, if 'set' + the option key refers to a Zend_Form method, then the value provided will be passed to that method. If the accessor does not exist, the key is assumed to reference an attribute, and will be passed to `setAttrib()`.

Exceptions to the rule include the following:

- `prefixPaths` will be passed to `addPrefixPaths()`
- `elementPrefixPaths` will be passed to `addElementPrefixPaths()`
- `displayGroupPrefixPaths` will be passed to `addDisplayGroupPrefixPaths()`
- the following setters cannot be set in this way:
  - `setAttrib (though setAttribs *will* work)`
  - `setConfig`
  - `setDefault`
  - `setOptions`
  - `setPluginLoader`
  - `setSubForms`
  - `setTranslator`
  - `setView`

As an example, here is a config file that passes configuration for every type of configurable data:

```
[element]
name = "registration"
action = "/user/register"
method = "post"
attribs.class = "zend_form"
attribs.onclick = "validate(this)"
disableTranslator = 0
prefixPath.element.prefix = "My_Element"
prefixPath.element.path = "My/Element/"
elementPrefixPath.validate.prefix = "My_Validate"
elementPrefixPath.validate.path = "My/Validate/"
displayGroupPrefixPath.prefix = "My_Group"
displayGroupPrefixPath.path = "My/Group/"
elements.username.type = "text"
elements.username.options.label = "Username"
elements.username.options.validators.alpha.validator = "Alpha"
elements.username.options.filters.lcase = "StringToLower"
; more elements, of course...
elementFilters.trim = "StringTrim"
;elementDecorators.trim = "StringTrim"
displayGroups.login.elements.username = "username"
displayGroups.login.elements.password = "password"
displayGroupDecorators.elements.decorator = "FormElements"
displayGroupDecorators.fieldset.decorator = "Fieldset"
decorators.elements.decorator = "FormElements"
decorators.fieldset.decorator = "FieldSet"
decorators.fieldset.decorator.options.class = "zend_form"
decorators.form.decorator = "Form"
```

The above could easily be abstracted to an XML or PHP array-based configuration file.

Custom forms

An alternative to using configuration-based forms is to subclass Zend_Form. This has several benefits:

- You can unit test your form easily to ensure validations and rendering perform as expected.

- Fine-grained control over individual elements.

- Re-use of form objects, and greater portability (no need to track config files).

- Implementing custom functionality.

The most typical use case would be to use the init() method to setup specific form elements and configuration:

```
class My_Form_Login extends Zend_Form
{
    public function init()
    {
        $username = new Zend_Form_Element_Text('username');
        $username->class = 'formtext';
        $username->setLabel('Username:')
                 ->setDecorators(array(
                     array('ViewHelper',
                           array('helper' => 'formText')),
                     array('Label',
                           array('class' => 'label'))
                 ));
        $password = new Zend_Form_Element_Password('password');
        $password->class = 'formtext';
        $password->setLabel('Username:')
                 ->setDecorators(array(
                     array('ViewHelper',
                           array('helper' => 'formPassword')),
                     array('Label',
                           array('class' => 'label'))
                 ));
        $submit = new Zend_Form_Element_Submit('login');
        $submit->class = 'formsubmit';
        $submit->setValue('Login')
               ->setDecorators(array(
                   array('ViewHelper',
                         array('helper' => 'formSubmit'))
               ));
        $this->addElements(array(
            $username,
            $password,
            $submit
        ));
        $this->setDecorators(array(
            'FormElements',
            'Fieldset',
            'Form'
        ));
    }
}
```

This form can then be instantiated with simply:

```
$form = new My_Form_Login();
```

and all functionality is already setup and ready; no config files needed. (Note that this example is greatly simplified, as it contains no validators or filters for the elements.)

Another common reason for extension is to define a set of default decorators. You can do this by overriding the loadDefaultDecorators() method:

```
class My_Form_Login extends Zend_Form
{
    public function loadDefaultDecorators()
    {
        $this->setDecorators(array(
            'FormElements',
            'Fieldset',
            'Form'
        ));
    }
}
```

Creating Custom Form Markup Using Zend _Form_Decorator

Rendering a form object is completely optional -- you do not need to use Zend_Form's render() methods at all. However, if you do, decorators are used to render the various form objects.

An arbitrary number of decorators may be attached to each item (elements, display groups, sub forms, or the form object itself); however, only one decorator of a given type may be attached to each item. Decorators are called in the order they are registered. Depending on the decorator, it may replace the content passed to it, or append or prepend the content.

Object state is set via configuration options passed to the constructor or the decorator's setOptions() method. When creating decorators via an item's addDecorator() or related methods, options may be passed as an argument to the method. These can be used to specify placement, a separator to use between passed in content and newly generated content, and whatever options the decorator supports.

Before each decorator's render() method is called, the current item is set in the decorator using setElement(), giving the decorator awareness of the item being rendered. This allows you to create decorators that only render specific portions of the item -- such as the label, the value, error messages, etc. By stringing together several decorators that render specific element segments, you can build complex markup representing the entire item.

Operation

To configure a decorator, pass an array of options or a Zend_Config object to its constructor, an array to setOptions(), or a Zend_Config object to setConfig().

Standard options include:

- placement: Placement can be either 'append' or 'prepend' (case insensitive), and indicates whether content passed to render() will be appended or prepended, respectively. In the case that a decorator replaces the content, this setting is ignored. The default setting is to append.

- separator: The separator is used between the content passed to render() and new content generated by the decorator, or between items rendered by the decorator (e.g. FormElements uses the separator between each item rendered). In the case that a decorator replaces the content, this setting may be ignored. The default value is PHP_EOL.

The decorator interface specifies methods for interacting with options. These include:

- setOption($key, $value): set a single option.

- getOption($key): retrieve a single option value.

- getOptions(): retrieve all options.

- `removeOption($key)`: remove a single option.

- `clearOptions()`: remove all options.

Decorators are meant to interact with the various Zend_Form class types: Zend_Form, Zend_Form_Element, Zend_Form_DisplayGroup, and all classes deriving from them. The method setElement() allows you to set the object the decorator is currently working with, and getElement() is used to retrieve it.

Each decorator's render() method accepts a string, $content. When the first decorator is called, this string is typically empty, while on subsequent calls it will be populated. Based on the type of decorator and the options passed in, the decorator will either replace this string, prepend the string, or append the string; an optional separator will be used in the latter two situations.

Standard Decorators

Zend_Form ships with many standard decorators; see the chapter on Standard Decorators for details.

Custom Decorators

If you find your rendering needs are complex or need heavy customization, you should consider creating a custom decorator.

Decorators need only implement Zend_Decorator_Interface. The interface specifies the following:

```
interface Zend_Decorator_Interface
{
    public function __construct($options = null);
    public function setElement($element);
    public function getElement();
    public function setOptions(array $options);
    public function setConfig(Zend_Config $config);
    public function setOption($key, $value);
    public function getOption($key);
    public function getOptions();
    public function removeOption($key);
    public function clearOptions();
    public function render($content);
}
```

To make this simpler, you can simply extend Zend_Decorator_Abstract, which implements all methods except render().

As an example, let's say you want to reduce the number of decorators you use, and build a "composite" decorator to take care of rendering the label, element, any error messages, and description in an HTML div. You might build such a 'Composite' decorator as follows:

```
class My_Decorator_Composite extends Zend_Form_Decorator_Abstract
{
    public function buildLabel()
    {
        $element = $this->getElement();
        $label = $element->getLabel();
        if ($translator = $element->getTranslator()) {
            $label = $translator->translate($label);
        }
        if ($element->isRequired()) {
            $label .= '*';
```

```
        }
        $label .= ':';
        return $element->getView()
                      ->formLabel($element->getName(), $label);
    }
    public function buildInput()
    {
        $element = $this->getElement();
        $helper  = $element->helper;
        return $element->getView()->$helper(
            $element->getName(),
            $element->getValue(),
            $element->getAttribs(),
            $element->options
        );
    }
    public function buildErrors()
    {
        $element  = $this->getElement();
        $messages = $element->getMessages();
        if (empty($messages)) {
            return '';
        }
        return '<div class="errors">' .
               $element->getView()->formErrors($messages) . '</div>';
    }
    public function buildDescription()
    {
        $element = $this->getElement();
        $desc    = $element->getDescription();
        if (empty($desc)) {
            return '';
        }
        return '<div class="description">' . $desc . '</div>';
    }
    public function render($content)
    {
        $element = $this->getElement();
        if (!$element instanceof Zend_Form_Element) {
            return $content;
        }
        if (null === $element->getView()) {
            return $content;
        }
        $separator = $this->getSeparator();
        $placement = $this->getPlacement();
        $label     = $this->buildLabel();
        $input     = $this->buildInput();
        $errors    = $this->buildErrors();
        $desc      = $this->buildDescription();
        $output = '<div class="form element">'
                . $label
                . $input
                . $errors
                . $desc
                . '</div>'
        switch ($placement) {
            case (self::PREPEND):
                return $output . $separator . $content;
            case (self::APPEND):
            default:
                return $content . $separator . $output;
        }
    }
}
```

```
}
```

You can then place this in the decorator path:

```
// for an element:
$element->addPrefixPath('My_Decorator',
                        'My/Decorator/',
                        'decorator');
// for all elements:
$form->addElementPrefixPath('My_Decorator',
                            'My/Decorator/',
                            'decorator');
```

You can then specify this decorator as 'Composite' and attach it to an element:

```
// Overwrite existing decorators with this single one:
$element->setDecorators(array('Composite'));
```

While this example showed how to create a decorator that renders complex output from several element properties, you can also create decorators that handle a single aspect of an element; the 'Decorator' and 'Label' decorators are excellent examples of this practice. Doing so allows you to mix and match decorators to achieve complex output -- and also override single aspects of decoration to customize for your needs.

For example, if you wanted to simply display that an error occurred when validating an element, but not display each of the individual validation error messages, you might create your own 'Errors' decorator:

```
class My_Decorator_Errors
{
    public function render($content = '')
    {
        $output = '<div class="errors">The value you provided was invalid;
            please try again</div>';
        $placement = $this->getPlacement();
        $separator = $this->getSeparator();
        switch ($placement) {
            case 'PREPEND':
                return $output . $separator . $content;
            case 'APPEND':
            default:
                return $content . $separator . $output;
        }
    }
}
```

In this particular example, because the decorator's final segment, 'Errors', matches the same as Zend_Form_Decorator_Errors, it will be rendered *in place of* that decorator -- meaning you would not need to change any decorators to modify the output. By naming your decorators after existing standard decorators, you can modify decoration without needing to modify your elements' decorators.

Rendering Individual Decorators

Since decorators can target distinct metadata of the element or form they decorate, it's often useful to render one individual decorator at a time. This behavior is possible via method overloading in each major form class type (forms, sub form, display group, element).

To do so, simply call render[DecoratorName]() , where "[DecoratorName]" is the "short name" of your decorator; optionally, you can pass in content you want decorated. For example:

```
// render just the element label decorator:
echo $element->renderLabel();
// render just the display group fieldset, with some content:
echo $group->renderFieldset('fieldset content');
// render just the form HTML tag, with some content:
echo $form->renderHtmlTag('wrap this content');
```

If the decorator does not exist, an exception is raised.

This can be useful particularly when rendering a form with the ViewScript decorator; each element can use its attached decorators to generate content, but with fine-grained control.

Standard Form Elements Shipped With Zend Framework

Zend Framework ships with concrete element classes covering most HTML form elements. Most simply specify a particular view helper for use when decorating the element, but several offer additional functionality. The following is a list of all such classes, as well as descriptions of the functionality they offer.

Zend_Form_Element_Button

Used for creating HTML button elements, `Zend_Form_Element_Button` extends Zend_Form_Element_Submit, specifying some custom functionality. It specifies the 'formButton' view helper for decoration.

Like the submit element, it uses the element's label as the element value for display purposes; in other words, to set the text of the button, set the value of the element. The label will be translated if a translation adapter is present.

Because the label is used as part of the element, the button element uses only the ViewHelper and DtDdWrapper decorators.

After populating or validating a form, you can check if the given button was clicked using the `isChecked()` method.

Zend_Form_Element_Captcha

CAPTCHAs are used to prevent automated submission of forms by bots and other automated processes.

The Captcha form element allows you to specify which Zend_Captcha adapter you wish to utilize as a form CAPTCHA. It then sets this adapter as a validator to the object, and uses a Captcha decorator for rendering (which proxies to the CAPTCHA adapter).

Adapters may be any adapters in `Zend_Captcha`, as well as any custom adapters you may have defined elsewhere. To allow this, you may pass an additional plugin loader type key, 'CAPTCHA' or 'captcha', when specifying a plugin loader prefix path:

```
$element->addPrefixPath('My_Captcha', 'My/Captcha/', 'captcha');
```

Captcha's may then be registered using the `setCaptcha()` method, which can take either a concrete CAPTCHA instance, or the short name of a CAPTCHA adapter:

```
// Concrete instance:
$element->setCaptcha(new Zend_Captcha_Figlet());
// Using shortnames:
```

```
$element->setCaptcha('Dumb');
```

If you wish to load your element via configuration, specify either the key 'captcha' with an array containing the key 'captcha', or both the keys 'captcha' and 'captchaOptions':

```
// Using single captcha key:
$element = new Zend_Form_Element_Captcha('foo', array(
    'label' => "Please verify you're a human",
    'captcha' => array(
        'captcha' => 'Figlet',
        'wordLen' => 6,
        'timeout' => 300,
    ),
));
// Using both captcha and captchaOptions:
$element = new Zend_Form_Element_Captcha('foo', array(
    'label' => "Please verify you're a human"
    'captcha' => 'Figlet',
    'captchaOptions' => array(
        'captcha' => 'Figlet',
        'wordLen' => 6,
        'timeout' => 300,
    ),
));
```

The decorator used is determined by querying the captcha adapter. By default, the Captcha decorator is used, but an adapter may specify a different one via its getDecorator() method.

As noted, the captcha adapter itself acts as a validator for the element. Additionally, the NotEmpty validator is not used, and the element is marked as required. In most cases, you should need to do nothing else to have a captcha present in your form.

Zend_Form_Element_Checkbox

HTML checkboxes allow you return a specific value, but basically operate as booleans. When checked, the checkbox's value is submitted. When the checkbox is not checked, nothing is submitted. Internally, Zend_Form_Element_Checkbox enforces this state.

By default, the checked value is '1', and the unchecked value '0'. You can specify the values to use using the setCheckedValue() and setUncheckedValue() accessors, respectively. Internally, any time you set the value, if the provided value matches the checked value, then it is set, but any other value causes the unchecked value to be set.

Additionally, setting the value sets the checked property of the checkbox. You can query this using isChecked() or simply accessing the property. Using the setChecked($flag) method will both set the state of the flag as well as set the appropriate checked or unchecked value in the element. Please use this method when setting the checked state of a checkbox element to ensure the value is set properly.

Zend_Form_Element_Checkbox uses the 'formCheckbox' view helper. The checked value is always used to populate it.

Zend_Form_Element_File

The File form element provides a mechanism for supplying file upload fields to your form. It utilizes Zend_File_Transfer internally to provide this functionality, and the FormFile view helper as also the File decorator to display the form element.

By default, it uses the Http transfer adapter, which introspects the $_FILES array and allows you to attach validators and filters. Validators and filters attached to the form element are in turn attached to the transfer adapter.

Example 23.8. File form element usage

The above explanation of using the File form element may seem arcane, but actual usage is relatively trivial:

```
$element = new Zend_Form_Element_File('foo');
$element->setLabel('Upload an image:')
        ->setDestination('/var/www/upload');
// ensure only 1 file
$element->addValidator('Count', false, 1);
// limit to 100K
$element->addValidator('Size', false, 102400);
// only JPEG, PNG, and GIFs
$element->addValidator('Extension', false, 'jpg,png,gif');
$form->addElement($element, 'foo');
```

You also need to ensure that the correct encoding type is provided to the form; you should use 'multipart/form-data'. You can do this by setting the 'enctype' attribute on the form:

```
$form->setAttrib('enctype', 'multipart/form-data');
```

After the form is validated successfully, you must receive the file to store it in the final destination using `receive()`. Additionally you can determinate the final location using `getFileName()`:

```
if (!$form->isValid) {
    print "Uh oh... validation error";
}
if (!$form->foo->receive()) {
    print "Error receiving the file";
}
$location = $form->foo->getFileName();
```

Default Upload Location

By default, files are uploaded to the system temp directory.

File values

Within HTTP a file element has no value. For this reason and because of security concerns `getValue()` returns only the uploaded filename and not the complete path. If you need the file path, call `getFileName()`, which returns both the path and the name of the file.

Per default the file will automatically be received when you call `getValues()` on the form. The reason behind this behaviour is, that the file itself is the value of the file element.

```
$form->getValues();
```

Note

Therefor another call of `receive()` after calling `getValues()` will not have an effect. Also creating a instance of `Zend_File_Transfer` will not have an effect as there no file anymore to receive.

Still, sometimes you may want to call `getValues()` without receiving the file. You can archive this by calling setValueDisabled(true). To get the actual value of this flag you can call isValueDisabled().

Example 23.9. Explicit file retrievement

First call setValueDisabled(true).

```
$element = new Zend_Form_Element_File('foo');
$element->setLabel('Upload an image:')
        ->setDestination('/var/www/upload')
        ->setValueDisabled(true);
```

Now the file will not be received when you call getValues(). So you must call receive() on the file element, or an instance of Zend_File_Transfer yourself.

```
$values = $form->getValues();
if ($form->isValid($form->getPost())) {
    if (!$form->foo->receive()) {
        print "Upload error";
    }
}
```

There are several states of the uploaded file which can be checked with the following methods:

- isUploaded(): Checks if the file element has been uploaded or not.

- isReceived(): Checks if the file element has already been received.

- isFiltered(): Checks if the filters have already been applied to the file element or not.

Example 23.10. Checking if an optional file has been uploaded

```
$element = new Zend_Form_Element_File('foo');
$element->setLabel('Upload an image:')
        ->setDestination('/var/www/upload')
        ->setRequired(false);
$element->addValidator('Size', false, 102400);
$form->addElement($element, 'foo');
// The foo file element is optional but when it's given go into here
if ($form->foo->isUploaded()) {
    // foo file given... do something
}
```

Zend_Form_Element_File also supports multiple files. By calling the setMultiFile($count) method you can set the number of file elements you want to create. This keeps you from setting the same settings multiple times.

Example 23.11. Setting multiple files

Creating a multifile element is the same as setting a single element. Just call setMultiFile() after the element is created:

```
$element = new Zend_Form_Element_File('foo');
$element->setLabel('Upload an image:')
        ->setDestination('/var/www/upload');
// ensure minimum 1, maximum 3 files
$element->addValidator('Count', false, array('min' => 1, 'max' => 3));
// limit to 100K
$element->addValidator('Size', false, 102400);
// only JPEG, PNG, and GIFs
$element->addValidator('Extension', false, 'jpg,png,gif');
// defines 3 identical file elements
$element->setMultiFile(3);
$form->addElement($element, 'foo');
```

You now have 3 identical file upload elements with the same settings. To get the set multifile number simply call getMultiFile().

File elements in Subforms

When you use file elements in subforms you must set unique names. For example, if you name a file element in subform1 "file", you must give any file element in subform2 a different name.

If there are 2 file elements with the same name, the second element is not be displayed or submitted.

To limit the size of the file uploaded by the client, you can specify the maximum file size by setting the MAX_FILE_SIZE option on the form. When you set this value by using the setMaxFileSize($size) method, it will be rendered with the file element.

```
$element = new Zend_Form_Element_File('foo');
$element->setLabel('Upload an image:')
        ->setDestination('/var/www/upload')
        ->addValidator('Size', false, 102400) // limit to 100K
        ->setMaxFileSize(102400); // limits the filesize on the client side
$form->addElement($element, 'foo');
```

MaxFileSize with Multiple File Elements

When you use multiple file elements in your form you should set the MAX_FILE_SIZE only once. Setting it again will overwrite the previous value.

Note, that this is also the case when you use multiple forms.

Zend_Form_Element_Hidden

Hidden elements inject data that should be submitted, but that should not manipulated by the user . Zend_Form_Element_Hidden accomplishes this with the 'formHidden' view helper.

Zend_Form_Element_Hash

This element provides protection from CSRF attacks on forms, ensuring the data is submitted by the user session that generated the form and not by a rogue script. Protection is achieved by adding a hash element to a form and verifying it when the form is submitted.

The name of the hash element should be unique. We recommend using the salt option for the element-two hashes with same names and different salts would not collide:

```
$form->addElement('hash', 'no_csrf_foo', array('salt' => 'unique'));
```

You can set the salt later using the setSalt($salt) method.

Internally, the element stores a unique identifier using Zend_Session_Namespace, and checks for it at submission (checking that the TTL has not expired). The 'Identical' validator is then used to ensure the submitted hash matches the stored hash.

The 'formHidden' view helper is used to render the element in the form.

Zend_Form_Element_Image

Images can be used as form elements, and you can use these images as graphical elements on form buttons.

Images need an image source. Zend_Form_Element_Image allows you to specify this by using the setImage() accessor (or 'image' configuration key). You can also optionally specify a value to use when submitting the image using the setImageValue() accessor (or 'imageValue' configuration key). When the value set for the element matches the imageValue, then the accessor isChecked() will return true.

Image elements use the Image Decorator for rendering, in addition to the standard Errors, HtmlTag, and Label decorators. You can optionally specify a tag to the Image decorator that will then wrap the image element.

Zend_Form_Element_MultiCheckbox

Often you have a set of related checkboxes, and you wish to group the results. This is much like a Multiselect, but instead of them being in a dropdown list, you need to show checkbox/value pairs.

Zend_Form_Element_MultiCheckbox makes this a snap. Like all other elements extending the base Multi element, you can specify a list of options, and easily validate against that same list. The 'formMultiCheckbox' view helper ensures that these are returned as an array in the form submission.

By default, this element registers an InArray validator which validates against the array keys of registered options. You can disable this behavior by either calling setRegisterInArrayValidator(false), or by passing a false value to the registerInArrayValidator configuration key.

You may manipulate the various checkbox options using the following methods:

- addMultiOption($option, $value)

- addMultiOptions(array $options)

- setMultiOptions(array $options) (overwrites existing options)

- getMultiOption($option)

- getMultiOptions()

- removeMultiOption($option)

- clearMultiOptions()

To mark checked items, you need to pass an array of values to setValue(). The following will check the values "bar" and "bat":

```
$element = new Zend_Form_Element_MultiCheckbox('foo', array(
    'multiOptions' => array(
        'foo' => 'Foo Option',
        'bar' => 'Bar Option',
        'baz' => 'Baz Option',
        'bat' => 'Bat Option',
```

```
        );
));
$element->setValue(array('bar', 'bat'));
```

Note that even when setting a single value, you must pass an array.

Zend_Form_Element_Multiselect

XHTML `select` elements allow a 'multiple' attribute, indicating multiple options may be selected for submission, instead of the usual one. Zend_Form_Element_Multiselect extends Zend_Form_Element_Select, and sets the `multiple` attribute to 'multiple'. Like other classes that inherit from the base Zend_Form_Element_Multi class, you can manipulate the options for the select using:

- `addMultiOption($option, $value)`

- `addMultiOptions(array $options)`

- `setMultiOptions(array $options)` (overwrites existing options)

- `getMultiOption($option)`

- `getMultiOptions()`

- `removeMultiOption($option)`

- `clearMultiOptions()`

If a translation adapter is registered with the form and/or element, option values will be translated for display purposes.

By default, this element registers an InArray validator which validates against the array keys of registered options. You can disable this behavior by either calling `setRegisterInArrayValidator(false)`, or by passing a false value to the `registerInArrayValidator` configuration key.

Zend_Form_Element_Password

Password elements are basically normal text elements -- except that you typically do not want the submitted password displayed in error messages or the element itself when the form is re-displayed.

Zend_Form_Element_Password achieves this by calling `setObscureValue(true)` on each validator (ensuring that the password is obscured in validation error messages), and using the 'formPassword' view helper (which does not display the value passed to it).

Zend_Form_Element_Radio

Radio elements allow you to specify several options, of which you need a single value returned. Zend_Form_Element_Radio extends the base Zend_Form_Element_Multi class, allowing you to specify a number of options, and then uses the `formRadio` view helper to display these.

By default, this element registers an InArray validator which validates against the array keys of registered options. You can disable this behavior by either calling `setRegisterInArrayValidator(false)`, or by passing a false value to the `registerInArrayValidator` configuration key.

Like all elements extending the Multi element base class, the following methods may be used to manipulate the radio options displayed:

- `addMultiOption($option, $value)`

- addMultiOptions(array $options)

- setMultiOptions(array $options) (overwrites existing options)

- getMultiOption($option)

- getMultiOptions()

- removeMultiOption($option)

- clearMultiOptions()

Zend_Form_Element_Reset

Reset buttons are typically used to clear a form, and are not part of submitted data. However, as they serve a purpose in the display, they are included in the standard elements.

Zend_Form_Element_Reset extends Zend_Form_Element_Submit. As such, the label is used for the button display, and will be translated if a translation adapter is present. It utilizes only the 'ViewHelper' and 'DtDdWrapper' decorators, as there should never be error messages for such elements, nor will a label be necessary.

Zend_Form_Element_Select

Select boxes are a common way of limiting to specific choices for a given form datum. Zend_Form_Element_Select allows you to generate these quickly and easily.

By default, this element registers an InArray validator which validates against the array keys of registered options. You can disable this behavior by either calling setRegisterInArrayValidator(false), or by passing a false value to the registerInArrayValidator configuration key.

As it extends the base Multi element, the following methods may be used to manipulate the select options:

- addMultiOption($option, $value)

- addMultiOptions(array $options)

- setMultiOptions(array $options) (overwrites existing options)

- getMultiOption($option)

- getMultiOptions()

- removeMultiOption($option)

- clearMultiOptions()

Zend_Form_Element_Select uses the 'formSelect' view helper for decoration.

Zend_Form_Element_Submit

Submit buttons are used to submit a form. You may use multiple submit buttons; you can use the button used to submit the form to decide what action to take with the data submitted. Zend_Form_Element_Submit makes this decisioning easy, by adding a isChecked() method; as only one button element will be submitted by the form, after populating or validating the form, you can call this method on each submit button to determine which one was used.

Zend_Form_Element_Submit uses the label as the "value" of the submit button, translating it if a translation adapter is present. isChecked() checks the submitted value against the label in order to determine if the button was used.

The ViewHelper and DtDdWrapper decorators to render the element. No label decorator is used, as the button label is used when rendering the element; also, typically, you will not associate errors with a submit element.

Zend_Form_Element_Text

By far the most prevalent type of form element is the text element, allowing for limited text entry; it's an ideal element for most data entry. Zend_Form_Element_Text simply uses the 'formText' view helper to display the element.

Zend_Form_Element_Textarea

Textareas are used when large quantities of text are expected, and place no limits on the amount of text submitted (other than maximum size limits as dictated by your server or PHP). Zend_Form_Element_Textarea uses the 'textArea' view helper to display such elements, placing the value as the content of the element.

Standard Form Decorators Shipped With Zend Framework

Zend_Form ships with several standard decorators. For more information on general decorator usage, see the Decorators section.

Zend_Form_Decorator_Callback

The Callback decorator can execute an arbitrary callback to render content. Callbacks should be specified via the 'callback' option passed in the decorator configuration, and can be any valid PHP callback type. Callbacks should accept three arguments, $content (the original content passed to the decorator), $element (the item being decorated), and an array of $options. As an example callback:

```
class Util
{
    public static function label($content, $element, array $options)
    {
        return '<span class="label">' . $element->getLabel() . "</span>";
    }
}
```

This callback would be specified as array('Util', 'label'), and would generate some (bad) HTML markup for the label. The Callback decorator would then either replace, append, or prepend the original content with the return value of this.

The Callback decorator allows specifying a null value for the placement option, which will replace the original content with the callback return value; 'prepend' and 'append' are still valid as well.

Zend_Form_Decorator_Captcha

The Captcha decorator is for use with the CAPTCHA form element. It utilizes the CAPTCHA adapter's render() method to generate the output.

A variant on the Captcha decorator, 'Captcha_Word', is also commonly used, and creates two elements, an id and input. The id indicates the session identifier to compare against, and the input is for the user verification of the CAPTCHA. These are validated as a single element.

Zend_Form_Decorator_Description

The Description decorator can be used to display a description set on a Zend_Form, Zend_Form_Element, or Zend_Form_DisplayGroup item; it pulls the description using the object's getDescription() method. Common use cases are for providing UI hints for your elements.

By default, if no description is present, no output is generated. If the description is present, then it is wrapped in an HTML p tag by default, though you may specify a tag by passing a tag option when creating the decorator, or calling setTag(). You may additionally specify a class for the tag using the class option or by calling setClass(); by default, the class 'hint' is used.

The description is escaped using the view object's escaping mechanisms by default. You can disable this by passing a false value to the decorator's 'escape' option or setEscape() method.

Zend_Form_Decorator_DtDdWrapper

The default decorators utilize definition lists (<dl>) to render form elements. Since form items can appear in any order, display groups and sub forms can be interspersed with other form items. To keep these particular item types within the definition list, the DtDdWrapper creates a new, empty definition term (<dt>) and wraps its content in a new definition datum (<dd>). The output looks something like this:

```
<dt></dt>
<dd><fieldset id="subform">
    <legend>User Information</legend>
    ...
</fieldset></dd>
```

This decorator replaces the content provided to it by wrapping it within the <dd> element.

Zend_Form_Decorator_Errors

Element errors get their own decorator with the Errors decorator. This decorator proxies to the FormErrors view helper, which renders error messages in an unordered list (<ul>) as list items. The <ul> element receives a class of "errors".

The Errors decorator can either prepend or append the content provided to it.

Zend_Form_Decorator_Fieldset

Display groups and sub forms render their content within fieldsets by default. The Fieldset decorator checks for either a 'legend' option or a getLegend() method in the registered element, and uses that as a legend if non-empty. Any content passed in is wrapped in the HTML fieldset, replacing the original content. Any attributes set in the decorated item are passed to the fieldset as HTML attributes.

Zend_Form_Decorator_File

File Elements have special notation when you use multiple file elements or subforms. The File decorator is used by Zend_Form_Element_File and allows to set multiple file elements with only a single methodcall. It is used automatically and fixes the elements name.

Zend_Form_Decorator_Form

Zend_Form objects typically need to render an HTML form tag. The Form decorator proxies to the Form view helper. It wraps any provided content in an HTML form element, using the Zend_Form object's action and method, and any attributes as HTML attributes.

Zend_Form_Decorator_FormElements

Forms, display groups, and sub forms are collections of elements. In order to render these elements, they utilize the FormElements decorator, which iterates through all items, calling `render()` on each and joining them with the registered separator. It can either append or prepend content passed to it.

Zend_Form_Decorator_FormErrors

Some developers and designers prefer to group all error messages at the top of the form. The FormErrors decorator allows you to do this.

By default, the generated list of errors has the following markup:

```
<ul class="form-errors>
    <li><b>[element label or name]</b><ul>
            <li>[error message]</li>
            <li>[error message]</li>
        </ul>
    </li>
    <li><ul>
        <li><b>[subform element label or name</b><ul>
                <li>[error message]</li>
                <li>[error message]</li>
            </ul>
        </li>
    </ul></li>
</ul>
```

You can pass in a variety of options to configure the generated output:

- `ignoreSubForms`: whether or not to disable recursion into subforms. Default value: false (i.e., allow recursion).

- `markupElementLabelEnd`: Markup to append to element labels. Default value: ''

- `markupElementLabelStart`: Markup to prepend to element labels. Default value: ''

- `markupListEnd`: Markup to append error message lists with. Default value: '</ul>'.

- `markupListItemEnd`: Markup to append individual error messages with. Default value: '</li>'

- `markupListItemStart`: Markup to prepend individual error messages with. Default value: '<li>'

- `markupListStart`: Markup to append error message lists with. Default value: '<ul class="form-errors">'

The FormErrors decorator can either prepend or append the content provided to it.

Zend_Form_Decorator_HtmlTag

The HtmlTag decorator allows you to utilize HTML tags to decorate content; the tag utilized is passed in the 'tag' option, and any other options are used as HTML attributes to that tag. The tag by default is assumed to be block level, and replaces the content by wrapping it in the given tag. However, you can specify a placement to append or prepend a tag as well.

Zend_Form_Decorator_Image

The Image decorator allows you to create an HTML image input (`<input type="image" ... />`), and optionally render it within another HTML tag.

By default, the decorator uses the element's src property, which can be set with the `setImage()` method, as the image source. Additionally, the element's label will be used as the alt tag, and the `imageValue` (manipulated with the Image element's `setImageValue()` and `getImageValue()` accessors) will be used for the value.

To specify an HTML tag with which to wrap the element, either pass a 'tag' option to the decorator, or explicitly call `setTag()`.

Zend_Form_Decorator_Label

Form elements typically have labels, and the Label decorator is used to render these labels. It proxies to the FormLabel view helper, and pulls the element label using the `getLabel()` method of the element. If no label is present, none is rendered. By default, labels are translated when a translation adapter exists and a translation for the label exists.

You may optionally specify a 'tag' option; if provided, it wraps the label in that block-level tag. If the 'tag' option is present, and no label present, the tag is rendered with no content. You can specify the class to use with the tag with the 'class' option or by calling `setClass()`.

Additionally, you can specify prefixes and suffixes to use when displaying the element, based on whether or not the label is for an optional or required element. Common use cases would be to append a ':' to the label, or a '*' indicating an item is required. You can do so with the following options and methods:

- `optionalPrefix`: set the text to prefix the label with when the element is optional. Use the `setOptionalPrefix()` and `getOptionalPrefix()` accessors to manipulate it.

- `optionalSuffix`: set the text to append the label with when the element is optional. Use the `setOptionalSuffix()` and `getOptionalSuffix()` accessors to manipulate it.

- `requiredPrefix`: set the text to prefix the label with when the element is required. Use the `setRequiredPrefix()` and `getRequiredPrefix()` accessors to manipulate it.

- `requiredSuffix`: set the text to append the label with when the element is required. Use the `setRequiredSuffix()` and `getRequiredSuffix()` accessors to manipulate it.

By default, the Label decorator prepends to the provided content; specify a 'placement' option of 'append' to place it after the content.

Zend_Form_Decorator_PrepareElements

Forms, display groups, and sub forms are collections of elements. When using the ViewScript decorator with your form or sub form, it's useful to be able to recursively set the view object, translator, and all fully qualifid names (as determined by sub form array notation). The 'PrepareElements' decorator can do this for you. Typically, you will set it as the first decorator in the list.

```
$form->setDecorators(array(
    'PrepareElements',
    array('ViewScript', array('viewScript' => 'form.phtml')),
));
```

Zend_Form_Decorator_ViewHelper

Most elements utilize `Zend_View` helpers for rendering, and this is done with the ViewHelper decorator. With it, you may specify a 'helper' tag to explicitly set the view helper to utilize; if none is provided, it uses the last segment of the element's class name to determine the helper, prepending it with the string 'form': e.g., 'Zend_Form_Element_Text' would look for a view helper of 'formText'.

Any attributes of the provided element are passed to the view helper as element attributes.

By default, this decorator appends content; use the 'placement' option to specify alternate placement.

Zend_Form_Decorator_ViewScript

Sometimes you may wish to use a view script for creating your elements; this way you can have fine-grained control over your elements, turn the view script over to a designer, or simply create a way to easily override setting based on which module you're using (each module could optionally override element view scripts to suit their own needs). The ViewScript decorator solves this problem.

The ViewScript decorator requires a 'viewScript' option, either provided to the decorator, or as an attribute of the element. It then renders that view script as a partial script, meaning each call to it has its own variable scope; no variables from the view will be injected other than the element itself. Several variables are then populated:

- `element`: the element being decorated

- `content`: the content passed to the decorator

- `decorator`: the decorator object itself

- Additionally, all options passed to the decorator via `setOptions()` that are not used internally (such as placement, separator, etc.) are passed to the view script as view variables.

As an example, you might have the following element:

```
// Setting the decorator for the element to a single, ViewScript,
// decorator, specifying the viewScript as an option, and some extra
// options:
$element->setDecorators(array(array('ViewScript', array(
    'viewScript' => '_element.phtml',
    'class'      => 'form element'
))));
// OR specifying the viewScript as an element attribute:
$element->viewScript = '_element.phtml';
$element->setDecorators(array(array('ViewScript',
                                    array('class' => 'form element'))));
```

You could then have a view script something like this:

```
<div class="<?php echo $this->class ?>">
    <?php echo $this->formLabel($this->element->getName(),
                        $this->element->getLabel()) ?>
    <?php echo $this->{$this->element->helper}(
        $this->element->getName(),
        $this->element->getValue(),
        $this->element->getAttribs()
    ) ?>
    <?php echo $this->formErrors($this->element->getMessages()) ?>
    <div class="hint"><?php echo $this->element->getDescription() ?></div>
</div>
```

Replacing content with a view script

You may find it useful for the view script to replace the content provided to the decorator -- for instance, if you want to wrap it. You can do so by specifying a boolean false value for the decorator's 'placement' option:

```
// At decorator creation:
$element->addDecorator('ViewScript', array('placement' => false));
// Applying to an existing decorator instance:
$decorator->setOption('placement', false);
// Applying to a decorator already attached to an element:
$element->getDecorator('ViewScript')->setOption('placement', false);
// Within a view script used by a decorator:
$this->decorator->setOption('placement', false);
```

Using the ViewScript decorator is recommended for when you want to have very fine-grained control over how your elements are rendered.

Internationalization of Zend_Form

Increasingly, developers need to tailor their content for multiple languages and regions. Zend_Form aims to make such a task trivial, and leverages functionality in both Zend_Translate and Zend_Validate to do so.

By default, no internationalisation (I18n) is performed. To turn on I18n features in Zend_Form, you will need to instantiate a Zend_Translate object with an appropriate adapter, and attach it to Zend_Form and/or Zend_Validate. See the Zend_Translate documentation for more information on creating the translate object and translation files

Translation Can Be Turned Off Per Item

You can disable translation for any form, element, display group, or sub form by calling its setDisableTranslator($flag) method or passing a disableTranslator option to the object. This can be useful when you want to selectively disable translation for individual elements or sets of elements.

Initializing I18n in Forms

In order to initialize I18n in forms, you will need either a Zend_Translate object or a Zend_Translate_Adapter object, as detailed in the Zend_Translate documentation. Once you have a translation object, you have several options:

- *Easiest:* add it to the registry. All I18n aware components of Zend Framework will autodiscover a translate object that is in the registry under the 'Zend_Translate' key and use it to perform translation and/or localization:

  ```
  // use the 'Zend_Translate' key; $translate is a Zend_Translate object:
  Zend_Registry::set('Zend_Translate', $translate);
  ```

  This will be picked up by Zend_Form, Zend_Validate, and Zend_View_Helper_Translate.

- If all you are worried about is translating validation error messages, you can register the translation object with Zend_Validate_Abstract:

  ```
  // Tell all validation classes to use a specific translate adapter:
  Zend_Validate_Abstract::setDefaultTranslator($translate);
  ```

- Alternatively, you can attach to the Zend_Form object as a global translator. This has the side effect of also translating validation error messages:

  ```
  // Tell all form classes to use a specific translate adapter, as well
  ```

```
// as use this adapter to translate validation error messages:
Zend_Form::setDefaultTranslator($translate);
```

- Finally, you can attach a translator to a specific form instance or to specific elements using their `setTranslator()` methods:

```
// Tell *this* form instance to use a specific translate adapter; it
// will also be used to translate validation error messages for all
// elements:
$form->setTranslator($translate);
// Tell *this* element to use a specific translate adapter; it will
// also be used to translate validation error messages for this
// particular element:
$element->setTranslator($translate);
```

Standard I18n Targets

Now that you've attached a translation object to, what exactly can you translate by default?

- *Validation error messages.* Validation error messages may be translated. To do so, use the various error code constants from the `Zend_Validate` validation classes as the message IDs. For more information on these codes, see the Zend_Validate documentation.

  Alternately, as of 1.6.0, you may provide translation strings using the actual error messages as message identifiers. This is the preferred use case for 1.6.0 and up, as we will be deprecating translation of message keys in future releases.

- *Labels.* Element labels will be translated, if a translation exists.

- *Fieldset Legends.* Display groups and sub forms render in fieldsets by default. The Fieldset decorator attempts to translate the legend before rendering the fieldset.

- *Form and Element Descriptions.* All form types (element, form, display group, sub form) allow specifying an optional item description. The Description decorator can be used to render this, and by default will take the value and attempt to translate it.

- *Multi-option Values.* for the various items inheriting from `Zend_Form_Element_Multi` (including the MultiCheckbox, Multiselect, and Radio elements), the option values (not keys) will be translated if a translation is available; this means that the option labels presented to the user will be translated.

- *Submit and Button Labels.* The various Submit and Button elements (Button, Submit, and Reset) will translate the label displayed to the user.

Advanced Zend_Form Usage

`Zend_Form` has a wealth of functionality, much of it aimed at experienced developers. This chapter aims to document some of this functionality with examples and use cases.

Array Notation

Many experienced web developers like to group related form elements using array notation in the element names. For example, if you have two addresses you wish to capture, a shipping and a billing address, you may have identical elements; by grouping them in an array, you can ensure they are captured separately. Take the following form, for example:

```
<form>
```

```
<fieldset>
    <legend>Shipping Address</legend>
    <dl>
        <dt><label for="recipient">Ship to:</label></dt>
        <dd><input name="recipient" type="text" value="" /></dd>
        <dt><label for="address">Address:</label></dt>
        <dd><input name="address" type="text" value="" /></dd>
        <dt><label for="municipality">City:</label></dt>
        <dd><input name="municipality" type="text" value="" /></dd>
        <dt><label for="province">State:</label></dt>
        <dd><input name="province" type="text" value="" /></dd>
        <dt><label for="postal">Postal Code:</label></dt>
        <dd><input name="postal" type="text" value="" /></dd>
    </dl>
</fieldset>
<fieldset>
    <legend>Billing Address</legend>
    <dl>
        <dt><label for="payer">Bill To:</label></dt>
        <dd><input name="payer" type="text" value="" /></dd>
        <dt><label for="address">Address:</label></dt>
        <dd><input name="address" type="text" value="" /></dd>
        <dt><label for="municipality">City:</label></dt>
        <dd><input name="municipality" type="text" value="" /></dd>
        <dt><label for="province">State:</label></dt>
        <dd><input name="province" type="text" value="" /></dd>
        <dt><label for="postal">Postal Code:</label></dt>
        <dd><input name="postal" type="text" value="" /></dd>
    </dl>
</fieldset>
<dl>
    <dt><label for="terms">I agree to the Terms of Service</label>
        </dt>
    <dd><input name="terms" type="checkbox" value="" /></dd>
    <dt></dt>
    <dd><input name="save" type="submit" value="Save" /></dd>
</dl>
</form>
```

In this example, the billing and shipping address contain some identical fields, which means one would overwrite the other. We can solve this solution using array notation:

```
<form>
    <fieldset>
        <legend>Shipping Address</legend>
        <dl>
            <dt><label for="shipping-recipient">Ship to:</label></dt>
            <dd><input name="shipping[recipient]" id="shipping-recipient"
                type="text" value="" /></dd>
            <dt><label for="shipping-address">Address:</label></dt>
            <dd><input name="shipping[address]" id="shipping-address"
                type="text" value="" /></dd>
            <dt><label for="shipping-municipality">City:</label></dt>
            <dd><input name="shipping[municipality]" id="shipping
                -municipality"
                type="text" value="" /></dd>
            <dt><label for="shipping-province">State:</label></dt>
            <dd><input name="shipping[province]" id="shipping-province"
                type="text" value="" /></dd>
            <dt><label for="shipping-postal">Postal Code:</label></dt>
            <dd><input name="shipping[postal]" id="shipping-postal"
                type="text" value="" /></dd>
        </dl>
```

```
        </fieldset>
        <fieldset>
            <legend>Billing Address</legend>
            <dl>
                <dt><label for="billing-payer">Bill To:</label></dt>
                <dd><input name="billing[payer]" id="billing-payer"
                    type="text" value="" /></dd>
                <dt><label for="billing-address">Address:</label></dt>
                <dd><input name="billing[address]" id="billing-address"
                    type="text" value="" /></dd>
                <dt><label for="billing-municipality">City:</label></dt>
                <dd><input name="billing[municipality]" id="billing
                    -municipality"
                    type="text" value="" /></dd>
                <dt><label for="billing-province">State:</label></dt>
                <dd><input name="billing[province]" id="billing-province"
                    type="text" value="" /></dd>
                <dt><label for="billing-postal">Postal Code:</label></dt>
                <dd><input name="billing[postal]" id="billing-postal"
                    type="text" value="" /></dd>
            </dl>
        </fieldset>
        <dl>
            <dt><label for="terms">I agree to the Terms of Service</label>
                </dt>
            <dd><input name="terms" type="checkbox" value="" /></dd>
            <dt></dt>
            <dd><input name="save" type="submit" value="Save" /></dd>
        </dl>
</form>
```

In the above sample, we now get separate addresses. In the submitted form, we'll now have three elements, the 'save' element for the submit, and then two arrays, 'shipping' and 'billing', each with keys for their various elements.

Zend_Form attempts to automate this process with its sub forms. By default, sub forms render using the array notation as shown in the previous HTML form listing, complete with ids. The array name is based on the sub form name, with the keys based on the elements contained in the sub form. Sub forms may be nested arbitrarily deep, and this will create nested arrays to reflect the structure. Additionally, the various validation routines in Zend_Form honor the array structure, ensuring that your form validates correctly, no matter how arbitrarily deep you nest your sub forms. You need do nothing to benefit from this; this behaviour is enabled by default.

Additionally, there are facilities that allow you to turn on array notation conditionally, as well as specify the specific array to which an element or collection belongs:

- Zend_Form::setIsArray($flag): By setting the flag true, you can indicate that an entire form should be treated as an array. By default, the form's name will be used as the name of the array, unless setElementsBelongTo() has been called. If the form has no specified name, or if setElementsBelongTo() has not been set, this flag will be ignored (as there is no array name to which the elements may belong).

  You may determine if a form is being treated as an array using the isArray() accessor.

- Zend_Form::setElementsBelongTo($array): Using this method, you can specify the name of an array to which all elements of the form belong. You can determine the name using the getElementsBelongTo() accessor.

Additionally, on the element level, you can specify individual elements may belong to particular arrays using Zend_Form_Element::setBelongsTo() method. To discover what this value is -- whether set explicitly or implicitly via the form -- you may use the getBelongsTo() accessor.

Multi-Page Forms

Currently, Multi-Page forms are not officially supported in Zend_Form; however, most support for implementing them is available and can be utilized with a little extra tooling.

The key to creating a multi-page form is to utilize sub forms, but to display only one such sub form per page. This allows you to submit a single sub form at a time and validate it, but not process the form until all sub forms are complete.

Example 23.12. Registration Form Example

Let's use a registration form as an example. For our purposes, we want to capture the desired username and password on the first page, then the user's metadata -- given name, family name, and location -- and finally allow them to decide what mailing lists, if any, they wish to subscribe to.

First, let's create our own form, and define several sub forms within it:

```
class My_Form_Registration extends Zend_Form
{
    public function init()
    {
        // Create user sub form: username and password
        $user = new Zend_Form_SubForm();
        $user->addElements(array(
            new Zend_Form_Element_Text('username', array(
                'required'   => true,
                'label'      => 'Username:',
                'filters'    => array('StringTrim', 'StringToLower'),
                'validators' => array(
                    'Alnum',
                    array('Regex',
                        false,
                        array('/^[a-z][a-z0-9]{2,}$/'))
                )
            )),
            new Zend_Form_Element_Password('password', array(
                'required'   => true,
                'label'      => 'Password:',
                'filters'    => array('StringTrim'),
                'validators' => array(
                    'NotEmpty',
                    array('StringLength', false, array(6))
                )
            )),
        ));
        // Create demographics sub form: given name, family name, and
        // location
        $demog = new Zend_Form_SubForm();
        $demog->addElements(array(
            new Zend_Form_Element_Text('givenName', array(
                'required'   => true,
                'label'      => 'Given (First) Name:',
                'filters'    => array('StringTrim'),
                'validators' => array(
                    array('Regex',
                        false,
                        array('/^[a-z][a-z0-9., \'-]{2,}$/i'))
                )
            )),
            new Zend_Form_Element_Text('familyName', array(
                'required'   => true,
```

```
                    'label'        => 'Family (Last) Name:',
                    'filters'      => array('StringTrim'),
                    'validators' => array(
                        array('Regex',
                                false,
                                array('/^[a-z][a-z0-9., \'-]{2,}$/i'))
                    )
                )),
                new Zend_Form_Element_Text('location', array(
                    'required'     => true,
                    'label'        => 'Your Location:',
                    'filters'      => array('StringTrim'),
                    'validators' => array(
                        array('StringLength', false, array(2))
                    )
                )),
            ));
            // Create mailing lists sub form
            $listOptions = array(
                'none'         => 'No lists, please',
                'fw-general'   => 'Zend Framework General List',
                'fw-mvc'       => 'Zend Framework MVC List',
                'fw-auth'      => 'Zend Framwork Authentication and ACL List',
                'fw-services'  => 'Zend Framework Web Services List',
            );
            $lists = new Zend_Form_SubForm();
            $lists->addElements(array(
                new Zend_Form_Element_MultiCheckbox('subscriptions', array(
                    'label'        =>
                        'Which lists would you like to subscribe to?',
                    'multiOptions' => $listOptions,
                    'required'     => true,
                    'filters'      => array('StringTrim'),
                    'validators'   => array(
                        array('InArray',
                                false,
                                array(array_keys($listOptions)))
                    )
                )),
            ));
            // Attach sub forms to main form
            $this->addSubForms(array(
                'user'  => $user,
                'demog' => $demog,
                'lists' => $lists
            ));
        }
    }
}
```

Note that there are no submit buttons, and that we have done nothing with the sub form decorators --
which means that by default they will be displayed as fieldsets. We will need to be able to override these
as we display each individual sub form, and add in submit buttons so we can actually process them --
which will also require action and method properties. Let's add some scaffolding to our class to provide
that information:

```
class My_Form_Registration extends Zend_Form
{
    // ...
    /**
     * Prepare a sub form for display
     *
     * @param  string|Zend_Form_SubForm $spec
     * @return Zend_Form_SubForm
```

```php
     */
    public function prepareSubForm($spec)
    {
        if (is_string($spec)) {
            $subForm = $this->{$spec};
        } elseif ($spec instanceof Zend_Form_SubForm) {
            $subForm = $spec;
        } else {
            throw new Exception('Invalid argument passed to ' .
                                __FUNCTION__ . '()');
        }
        $this->setSubFormDecorators($subForm)
             ->addSubmitButton($subForm)
             ->addSubFormActions($subForm);
        return $subForm;
    }
    /**
     * Add form decorators to an individual sub form
     *
     * @param  Zend_Form_SubForm $subForm
     * @return My_Form_Registration
     */
    public function setSubFormDecorators(Zend_Form_SubForm $subForm)
    {
        $subForm->setDecorators(array(
            'FormElements',
            array('HtmlTag', array('tag' => 'dl',
                                   'class' => 'zend_form')),
            'Form',
        ));
        return $this;
    }
    /**
     * Add a submit button to an individual sub form
     *
     * @param  Zend_Form_SubForm $subForm
     * @return My_Form_Registration
     */
    public function addSubmitButton(Zend_Form_SubForm $subForm)
    {
        $subForm->addElement(new Zend_Form_Element_Submit(
            'save',
            array(
                'label'    => 'Save and continue',
                'required' => false,
                'ignore'   => true,
            )
        ));
        return $this;
    }
    /**
     * Add action and method to sub form
     *
     * @param  Zend_Form_SubForm $subForm
     * @return My_Form_Registration
     */
    public function addSubFormActions(Zend_Form_SubForm $subForm)
    {
        $subForm->setAction('/registration/process')
                ->setMethod('post');
        return $this;
    }
}
```

Next, we need to add some scaffolding in our action controller, and have several considerations. First, we need to make sure we persist form data between requests, so that we can determine when to quit. Second, we need some logic to determine what form segments have already been submitted, and what sub form to display based on that information. We'll use Zend_Session_Namespace to persist data, which will also help us answer the question of which form to submit.

Let's create our controller, and add a method for retrieving a form instance:

```
class RegistrationController extends Zend_Controller_Action
{
    protected $_form;
    public function getForm()
    {
        if (null === $this->_form) {
            $this->_form = new My_Form_Registration();
        }
        return $this->_form;
    }
}
```

Now, let's add some functionality for determining which form to display. Basically, until the entire form is considered valid, we need to continue displaying form segments. Additionally, we likely want to make sure they're in a particular order: user, demog, and then lists. We can determine what data has been submitted by checking our session namespace for particular keys representing each subform.

```
class RegistrationController extends Zend_Controller_Action
{
    // ...
    protected $_namespace = 'RegistrationController';
    protected $_session;
    /**
     * Get the session namespace we're using
     *
     * @return Zend_Session_Namespace
     */
    public function getSessionNamespace()
    {
        if (null === $this->_session) {
            $this->_session =
                new Zend_Session_Namespace($this->_namespace);
        }
        return $this->_session;
    }
    /**
     * Get a list of forms already stored in the session
     *
     * @return array
     */
    public function getStoredForms()
    {
        $stored = array();
        foreach ($this->getSessionNamespace() as $key => $value) {
            $stored[] = $key;
        }
        return $stored;
    }
    /**
     * Get list of all subforms available
     *
     * @return array
     */
    public function getPotentialForms()
```

```
    {
        return array_keys($this->getForm()->getSubForms());
    }
    /**
     * What sub form was submitted?
     *
     * @return false|Zend_Form_SubForm
     */
    public function getCurrentSubForm()
    {
        $request = $this->getRequest();
        if (!$request->isPost()) {
            return false;
        }
        foreach ($this->getPotentialForms() as $name) {
            if ($data = $request->getPost($name, false)) {
                if (is_array($data)) {
                    return $this->getForm()->getSubForm($name);
                    break;
                }
            }
        }
        return false;
    }
    /**
     * Get the next sub form to display
     *
     * @return Zend_Form_SubForm|false
     */
    public function getNextSubForm()
    {
        $storedForms     = $this->getStoredForms();
        $potentialForms = $this->getPotentialForms();
        foreach ($potentialForms as $name) {
            if (!in_array($name, $storedForms)) {
                return $this->getForm()->getSubForm($name);
            }
        }
        return false;
    }
}
```

The above methods allow us to use notations such as "$subForm = $this->getCurrentSubForm();" to retrieve the current sub form for validation, or "$next = $this->getNextSubForm();" to get the next one to display.

Now, let's figure out how to process and display the various sub forms. We can use getCurrentSubForm() to determine if any sub forms have been submitted (false return values indicate none have been displayed or submitted), and getNextSubForm() to retrieve a form to display. We can then use the form's prepareSubForm() method to ensure the form is ready for display.

When we have a form submission, we can validate the sub form, and then check to see if the entire form is now valid. To do these tasks, we'll need additional methods that ensure that submitted data is added to the session, and that when validating the form entire, we validate against all segments from the session:

```
class RegistrationController extends Zend_Controller_Action
{
    // ...
    /**
     * Is the sub form valid?
     *
```

```
 * @param   Zend_Form_SubForm $subForm
 * @param   array $data
 * @return bool
 */
public function subFormIsValid(Zend_Form_SubForm $subForm,
                                  array $data)
{
    $name = $subForm->getName();
    if ($subForm->isValid($data)) {
        $this->getSessionNamespace()->$name = $subForm->getValues();
        return true;
    }
    return false;
}
/**
 * Is the full form valid?
 *
 * @return bool
 */
public function formIsValid()
{
    $data = array();
    foreach ($this->getSessionNamespace() as $key => $info) {
        $data[$key] = $info;
    }
    return $this->getForm()->isValid($data);
}
}
```

Now that we have the legwork out of the way, let's build the actions for this controller. We'll need a landing page for the form, and then a 'process' action for processing the form.

```
class RegistrationController extends Zend_Controller_Action
{
    // ...
    public function indexAction()
    {
        // Either re-display the current page, or grab the "next"
        // (first) sub form
        if (!$form = $this->getCurrentSubForm()) {
            $form = $this->getNextSubForm();
        }
        $this->view->form = $this->getForm()->prepareSubForm($form);
    }
    public function processAction()
    {
        if (!$form = $this->getCurrentSubForm()) {
            return $this->_forward('index');
        }
        if (!$this->subFormIsValid($form,
                                   $this->getRequest()->getPost())) {
            $this->view->form = $this->getForm()->prepareSubForm($form);
            return $this->render('index');
        }
        if (!$this->formIsValid()) {
            $form = $this->getNextSubForm();
            $this->view->form = $this->getForm()->prepareSubForm($form);
            return $this->render('index');
        }
        // Valid form!
        // Render information in a verification page
        $this->view->info = $this->getSessionNamespace();
        $this->render('verification');
```

```
    }
}
```

As you'll notice, the actual code for processing the form is relatively simple. We check to see if we have a current sub form submission, and if not, we go back to the landing page. If we do have a sub form, we attempt to validate it, redisplaying it if it fails. If the sub form is valid, we then check to see if the form is valid, which would indicate we're done; if not, we display the next form segment. Finally, we display a verification page with the contents of the session.

The view scripts are very simple:

```php
<?php // registration/index.phtml ?>
<h2>Registration</h2>
<?php echo $this->form ?>
<?php // registration/verification.phtml ?>
<h2>Thank you for registering!</h2>
<p>
    Here is the information you provided:
</p>
<?
// Have to do this construct due to how items are stored in session
// namespaces
foreach ($this->info as $info):
    foreach ($info as $form => $data): ?>
<h4><?php echo ucfirst($form) ?>:</h4>
<dl>
    <?php foreach ($data as $key => $value): ?>
    <dt><?php echo ucfirst($key) ?></dt>
    <?php if (is_array($value)):
        foreach ($value as $label => $val): ?>
    <dd><?php echo $val ?></dd>
        <?php endforeach;
        else: ?>
    <dd><?php echo $this->escape($value) ?></dd>
    <?php endif;
    endforeach; ?>
</dl>
<?php endforeach;
endforeach ?>
```

Upcoming releases of Zend Framework will include components to make multi page forms simpler by abstracting the session and ordering logic. In the meantime, the above example should serve as a reasonable guideline on how to accomplish this task for your site.

Chapter 24. Zend_Gdata

Introduction

Google Data APIs provide programmatic interface to some of Google's online services. The Google data Protocol is based upon the Atom Publishing Protocol [http://ietfreport.isoc.org/idref/draft-ietf-atompub-protocol/] and allows client applications to retrieve data matching queries, post data, update data and delete data using standard HTTP and the Atom syndication formation. The Zend_Gdata component is a PHP 5 interface for accessing Google Data from PHP. The Zend_Gdata component also supports accessing other services implementing the Atom Publishing Protocol.

See http://code.google.com/apis/gdata/ for more information about Google Data API.

The services that are accessible by Zend_Gdata include the following:

- Google Calendar is a popular online calendar application.

- Google Spreadsheets provides an online collaborative spreadsheets tool which can be used as a simple data store for your applications.

- Google Documents List provides an online list of all spreadsheets, word processing documents, and presentations stored in a Google account.

- Google Provisioning provides the ability to create, retrieve, update, and delete user accounts, nicknames, and email lists on a Google Apps hosted domain.

- Google Base provides the ability to retrieve, post, update, and delete items in Google Base.

- YouTube provides the ability to search and retrieve videos, comments, favorites, subscriptions, user profiles and more.

- Picasa Web Albums provides an online photo sharing application.

- Google Blogger [http://code.google.com/apis/blogger/developers_guide_php.html] is a popular Internet provider of "push-button publishing" and syndication.

- Google CodeSearch allows you to search public source code from many projects.

- Google Notebook allows you to view public Notebook content.

Unsupported services

Zend_Gdata does not provide an interface to any other Google service, such as Search, Gmail, Translation, or Maps. Only services that support the Google Data API are supported.

Structure of Zend_Gdata

Zend_Gata is composed of several types of classes:

- Service classes - inheriting from Zend_Gdata_App. These also include other classes such as Zend_Gdata, Zend_Gdata_Spreadsheets, etc. These classes enable interacting with APP or GData services and provide the ability to retrieve feeds, retrieve entries, post entries, update entries and delete entries.

- Query classes - inheriting from Zend_Gdata_Query. These also include other classes for specific services, such as Zend_Gdata_Spreadsheets_ListQuery and Zend_Gdata_Spreadsheets_CellQuery. Query classes provide methods used to construct a query for data to be retrieved from GData services. Methods include getters and setters like setUpdatedMin(), setStartIndex(), and getPublishedMin(). The query classes also have a method to generate a URL representing the constructed query -- getQueryUrl. Alternatively, the query string component of the URL can be retrieved used the getQueryString() method.

- Feed classes - inheriting from Zend_Gdata_App_Feed. These also include other classes such as Zend_Gdata_Feed, Zend_Gdata_Spreadsheets_SpreadsheetFeed, and Zend_Gdata_Spreadsheets_ListFeed. These classes represent feeds of entries retrieved from services. They are primarily used to retrieve data returned from services.

- Entry classes - inheriting from Zend_Gdata_App_Entry. These also include other classes such as Zend_Gdata_Entry, and Zend_Gdata_Spreadsheets_ListEntry. These classes represent entries retrieved from services or used for constructing data to send to services. In addition to being able to set the properties of an entry (such as the spreadsheet cell value), you can use an entry object to send update or delete requests to a service. For example, you can call $entry->save() to save changes made to an entry back to service from which the entry initiated, or $entry->delete() to delete an entry from the server.

- Other Data model classes - inheriting from Zend_Gdata_App_Extension. These include classes such as Zend_Gdata_App_Extension_Title (representing the atom:title XML element), Zend_Gdata_Extension_When (representing the gd:when XML element used by the GData Event "Kind"), and Zend_Gdata_Extension_Cell (representing the gs:cell XML element used by Google Spreadsheets). These classes are used purely to store the data retrieved back from services and for constructing data to be sent to services. These include getters and setters such as setText() to set the child text node of an element, getText() to retrieve the text node of an element, getStartTime() to retrieve the start time attribute of a When element, and other similiar methods. The data model classes also include methods such as getDOM() to retrieve a DOM representation of the element and all children and transferFromDOM() to construct a data model representation of a DOM tree.

Interacting with Google Services

Google data services are based upon the Atom Publishing Protocol (APP) and the Atom syndication format. To interact with APP or Google services using the Zend_Gdata component, you need to use the service classes such as Zend_Gdata_App, Zend_Gdata, Zend_Gdata_Spreadsheets, etc. These service classes provide methods to retrieve data from services as feeds, insert new entries into feeds, update entries, and delete entries.

Note: A full example of working with Zend_Gdata is available in the demos/Zend/Gdata directory. This example is runnable from the command-line, but the methods contained within are easily portable to a web application.

Obtaining instances of Zend_Gdata classes

The Zend Framework naming standards require that all classes be named based upon the directory structure in which they are located. For instance, extensions related to Spreadsheets are stored in: Zend/Gdata/Spreadsheets/Extension/... and, as a result of this, are named Zend_Gdata_Spreadsheets_Extension_.... This causes a lot of typing if you're trying to construct a new instance of a spreadsheet cell element!

We've implemented a magic factory method in all service classes (such as Zend_Gdata_App, Zend_Gdata, Zend_Gdata_Spreadsheets) that should make constructing new instances of data model, query and other classes much easier. This magic factory is implemented by using the magic __call method to intercept all attempts to call $service->newXXX(arg1, arg2, ...). Based off the value of XXX, a search is performed in all registered 'packages' for the desired class. Here's some examples:

```
$ss = new Zend_Gdata_Spreadsheets();
```

```
// creates a Zend_Gdata_App_Spreadsheets_CellEntry
$entry = $ss->newCellEntry();
// creates a Zend_Gdata_App_Spreadsheets_Extension_Cell
$cell = $ss->newCell();
$cell->setText('My cell value');
$cell->setRow('1');
$cell->setColumn('3');
$entry->cell = $cell;
// ... $entry can then be used to send an update to a Google Spreadsheet
```

Each service class in the inheritance tree is responsible for registering the appropriate 'packages' (directories) which are to be searched when calling the magic factory method.

Google Data Client Authentication

Most Google Data services require client applications to authenticate against the Google server before accessing private data, or saving or deleting data. There are two implementations of authentication for Google Data: AuthSub and ClientLogin. Zend_Gdata offers class interfaces for both of these methods.

Most other types of queries against Google Data services do not require authentication.

Dependencies

Zend_Gdata makes use of Zend_Http_Client to send requests to google.com and fetch results. The response to most Google Data requests is returned as a subclass of the Zend_Gdata_App_Feed or Zend_Gdata_App_Entry classes.

Zend_Gdata assumes your PHP application is running on a host that has a direct connection to the Internet. The Zend_Gdata client operates by contacting Google Data servers.

Creating a new Gdata client

Create a new object of class Zend_Gdata_App, Zend_Gdata, or one of the subclasses available that offer helper methods for service-specific behavior.

The single optional parameter to the Zend_Gdata_App constructor is an instance of Zend_Http_Client. If you don't pass this parameter, Zend_Gdata creates a default Zend_Http_Client object, which will not have associated credentials to access private feeds. Specifying the Zend_Http_Client object also allows you to pass configuration options to that client object.

```
$client = new Zend_Http_Client();
$client->setConfig( ...options... );
$gdata = new Zend_Gdata($client);
```

Beginning with Zend Framework 1.7, support has been added for protocol versioning. This allows the client and server to support new features while maintaining backwards compatibility. While most services will manage this for you, if you create a Zend_Gdata instance directly (as opposed to one of its subclasses), you may need to specify the desired protocol version to access certain server functionality.

```
$client = new Zend_Http_Client();
$client->setConfig( ...options... );
$gdata = new Zend_Gdata($client);
$gdata->setMajorProtocolVersion(2);
$gdata->setMinorProtocolVersion(null);
```

Also see the sections on authentication for methods to create an authenticated `Zend_Http_Client` object.

Common Query Parameters

You can specify parameters to customize queries with `Zend_Gdata`. Query parameters are specified using subclasses of `Zend_Gdata_Query`. The `Zend_Gdata_Query` class includes methods to set all query parameters used throughout GData services. Individual services, such as Spreadsheets, also provide query classes to defined parameters which are custom to the particular service and feeds. Spreadsheets includes a CellQuery class to query the Cell Feed and a ListQuery class to query the List Feed, as different query parameters are applicable to each of those feed types. The GData-wide parameters are described below.

- The q parameter specifies a full-text query. The value of the parameter is a string.

  Set this parameter with the `setQuery()` function.

- The `alt` parameter specifies the feed type. The value of the parameter can be `atom`, `rss`, `json`, or `json-in-script`. If you don't specify this parameter, the default feed type is `atom`. NOTE: Only the output of the atom feed format can be processed using `Zend_Gdata`. The `Zend_Http_Client` could be used to retrieve feeds in other formats, using query URLs generated by the `Zend_Gdata_Query` class and its subclasses.

  Set this parameter with the `setAlt()` function.

- The `maxResults` parameter limits the number of entries in the feed. The value of the parameter is an integer. The number of entries returned in the feed will not exceed this value.

  Set this parameter with the `setMaxResults()` function.

- The `startIndex` parameter specifies the ordinal number of the first entry returned in the feed. Entries before this number are skipped.

  Set this parameter with the `setStartIndex()` function.

- The `updatedMin` and `updatedMax` parameters specify bounds on the entry date. If you specify a value for `updatedMin`, no entries that were updated earlier than the date you specify are included in the feed. Likewise no entries updated after the date specified by `updatedMax` are included.

  You can use numeric timestamps, or a variety of date/time string representations as the value for these parameters.

  Set this parameter with the `setUpdatedMin()` and `setUpdatedMax()` functions.

There is a `get` function for each `set` function.

```
$query = new Zend_Gdata_Query();
$query->setMaxResults(10);
echo $query->getMaxResults();    // returns 10
```

The `Zend_Gdata` class also implements "magic" getter and setter methods, so you can use the name of the parameter as a virtual member of the class.

```
$query = new Zend_Gdata_Query();
$query->maxResults = 10;
echo $query->maxResults;         // returns 10
```

You can clear all parameters with the `resetParameters()` function. This is useful to do if you reuse a `Zend_Gdata` object for multiple queries.

```
$query = new Zend_Gdata_Query();
$query->maxResults = 10;
// ...get feed...
$query->resetParameters();        // clears all parameters
// ...get a different feed...
```

Fetching a Feed

Use the getFeed() function to retrieve a feed from a specified URI. This function returns an instance of class specified as the second argument to getFeed, which defaults to Zend_Gdata_Feed.

```
$gdata = new Zend_Gdata();
$query = new Zend_Gdata_Query(
        'http://www.blogger.com/feeds/blogID/posts/default');
$query->setMaxResults(10);
$feed = $gdata->getFeed($query);
```

See later sections for special functions in each helper class for Google Data services. These functions help you to get feeds from the URI that is appropriate for the respective service.

Working with Multi-page Feeds

When retrieving a feed that contains a large number of entries, the feed may be broken up into many smaller "pages" of feeds. When this occurs, each page will contain a link to the next page in the series. This link can be accessed by calling getLink('next'). The following example shows how to retrieve the next page of a feed:

```
function getNextPage($feed) {
    $nextURL = $feed->getLink('next');
    if ($nextURL !== null) {
        return $gdata->getFeed($nextURL);
    } else {
        return null;
    }
}
```

If you would prefer not to work with pages in your application, pass the first page of the feed into Zend_Gdata_App::retrieveAllEntriesForFeed(), which will consolidate all entries from each page into a single feed. This example shows how to use this function:

```
$gdata = new Zend_Gdata();
$query = new Zend_Gdata_Query(
        'http://www.blogger.com/feeds/blogID/posts/default');
$feed = $gdata->retrieveAllEntriesForFeed($gdata->getFeed($query));
```

Keep in mind when calling this function that it may take a long time to complete on large feeds. You may need to increase PHP's execution time limit by calling set_time_limit().

Working with Data in Feeds and Entries

After retrieving a feed, you can read the data from the feed or the entries contained in the feed using either the accessors defined in each of the data model classes or the magic accessors. Here's an example:

```
$client = Zend_Gdata_ClientLogin::getHttpClient($user, $pass, $service);
$gdata = new Zend_Gdata($client);
$query = new Zend_Gdata_Query(
```

```
        'http://www.blogger.com/feeds/blogID/posts/default');
$query->setMaxResults(10);
$feed = $gdata->getFeed($query);
foreach ($feed as $entry) {
    // using the magic accessor
    echo 'Title: ' . $entry->title->text;
    // using the defined accessors
    echo 'Content: ' . $entry->getContent()->getText();
}
```

Updating Entries

After retrieving an entry, you can update that entry and save changes back to the server. Here's an example:

```
$client = Zend_Gdata_ClientLogin::getHttpClient($user, $pass, $service);
$gdata = new Zend_Gdata($client);
$query = new Zend_Gdata_Query(
        'http://www.blogger.com/feeds/blogID/posts/default');
$query->setMaxResults(10);
$feed = $gdata->getFeed($query);
foreach ($feed as $entry) {
    // update the title to append 'NEW'
    echo 'Old Title: ' . $entry->title->text;
    $entry->title->text = $entry->title->text . ' NEW';
    // update the entry on the server
    $newEntry = $entry->save();
    echo 'New Title: ' . $newEntry->title->text;
}
```

Posting Entries to Google Servers

The Zend_Gdata object has a function insertEntry() with which you can upload data to save new entries to Google Data services.

You can use the data model classes for each service to construct the appropriate entry to post to Google's services. The insertEntry() function will accept a child of Zend_Gdata_App_Entry as data to post to the service. The method returns a child of Zend_Gdata_App_Entry which represents the state of the entry as it was returned from the server.

Alternatively, you could construct the XML structure for an entry as a string and pass the string to the insertEntry() function.

```
$gdata = new Zend_Gdata($authenticatedHttpClient);
$entry = $gdata->newEntry();
$entry->title = $gdata->newTitle('Playing football at the park');
$content =
    $gdata->newContent('We will visit the park and play football');
$content->setType('text');
$entry->content = $content;
$entryResult = $gdata->insertEntry($entry,
        'http://www.blogger.com/feeds/blogID/posts/default');
echo 'The <id> of the resulting entry is: ' . $entryResult->id->text;
```

To post entries, you must be using an authenticated Zend_Http_Client that you created using the Zend_Gdata_AuthSub or Zend_Gdata_ClientLogin classes.

Deleting Entries on Google Servers

Option 1: The Zend_Gdata object has a function delete() with which you can delete entries from Google Data services. Pass the edit URL value from a feed entry to the delete() method.

Option 2: Alternatively, you can call $entry->delete() on an entry retrieved from a Google service.

```
$gdata = new Zend_Gdata($authenticatedHttpClient);
// a Google Data feed
$feedUri = ...;
$feed = $gdata->getFeed($feedUri);
foreach ($feed as $feedEntry) {
    // Option 1 - delete the entry directly
    $feedEntry->delete();
    // Option 2 - delete the entry by passing the edit URL to
    // $gdata->delete()
    // $gdata->delete($feedEntry->getEditLink()->href);
}
```

To delete entries, you must be using an authenticated Zend_Http_Client that you created using the Zend_Gdata_AuthSub or Zend_Gdata_ClientLogin classes.

Authenticating with AuthSub

The AuthSub mechanism enables you to write web applications that acquire authenticated access Google Data services, without having to write code that handles user credentials.

See http://code.google.com/apis/accounts/AuthForWebApps.html for more information about Google Data AuthSub authentication.

The Google documentation says the ClientLogin mechanism is appropriate for "installed applications" whereas the AuthSub mechanism is for "web applications." The difference is that AuthSub requires interaction from the user, and a browser interface that can react to redirection requests. The ClientLogin solution uses PHP code to supply the account credentials; the user is not required to enter her credentials interactively.

The account credentials supplied via the AuthSub mechanism are entered by the user of the web application. Therefore they must be account credentials that are known to that user.

Registered applications

Zend_Gdata currently does not support use of secure tokens, because the AuthSub authentication does not support passing a digital certificate to acquire a secure token.

Creating an AuthSub authenticated Http Client

Your PHP application should provide a hyperlink to the Google URL that performs authentication. The static function Zend_Gdata_AuthSub::getAuthSubTokenUri() provides the correct URL. The arguments to this function include the URL to your PHP application so that Google can redirect the user's browser back to your application after the user's credentials have been verified.

After Google's authentication server redirects the user's browser back to the current application, a GET request parameter is set, called token. The value of this parameter is a single-use token that can be used for authenticated access. This token can be converted into a multi-use token and stored in your session.

Then use the token value in a call to Zend_Gdata_AuthSub::getHttpClient(). This function returns an instance of Zend_Http_Client, with appropriate headers set so that subsequent requests your application submits using that Http Client are also authenticated.

Below is an example of PHP code for a web application to acquire authentication to use the Google Calendar service and create a Zend_Gdata client object using that authenticated Http Client.

```
$my_calendar = 'http://www.google.com/calendar/feeds/default/private/full';
if (!isset($_SESSION['cal_token'])) {
    if (isset($_GET['token'])) {
        // You can convert the single-use token to a session token.
        $session_token =
            Zend_Gdata_AuthSub::getAuthSubSessionToken($_GET['token']);
        // Store the session token in our session.
        $_SESSION['cal_token'] = $session_token;
    } else {
        // Display link to generate single-use token
        $googleUri = Zend_Gdata_AuthSub::getAuthSubTokenUri(
            'http://'. $_SERVER['SERVER_NAME'] . $_SERVER['REQUEST_URI'],
            $my_calendar, 0, 1);
        echo "Click <a href='$googleUri'>here</a> " .
            "to authorize this application.";
        exit();
    }
}
// Create an authenticated HTTP Client to talk to Google.
$client = Zend_Gdata_AuthSub::getHttpClient($_SESSION['cal_token']);
// Create a Gdata object using the authenticated Http Client
$cal = new Zend_Gdata_Calendar($client);
```

Revoking AuthSub authentication

To terminate the authenticated status of a given token, use the
Zend_Gdata_AuthSub::AuthSubRevokeToken() static function. Otherwise, the token is still
valid for some time.

```
// Carefully construct this value to avoid application security problems.
$php_self = htmlentities(substr($_SERVER['PHP_SELF'],
                                0,
                                strcspn($_SERVER['PHP_SELF'], "\n\r")),
                         ENT_QUOTES);
if (isset($_GET['logout'])) {
    Zend_Gdata_AuthSub::AuthSubRevokeToken($_SESSION['cal_token']);
    unset($_SESSION['cal_token']);
    header('Location: ' . $php_self);
    exit();
}
```

Security notes

The treatment of the $php_self variable in the example above is a general security
guideline, it is not specific to Zend_Gdata. You should always filter content you output to
http headers.

Regarding revoking authentication tokens, it is recommended to do this when the user is
finished with her Google Data session. The possibility that someone can intercept the token and
use it for malicious purposes is very small, but nevertheless it is a good practice to terminate
authenticated access to any service.

Using the Book Search Data API

The Google Book Search Data API allows client applications to view and update Book Search content in
the form of Google Data API feeds.

Your client application can use the Book Search Data API to issue full-text searches for books and to retrieve standard book information, ratings, and reviews. You can also access individual users' library collections and public reviews [http://books.google.com/googlebooks/mylibrary/]. Finally, your application can submit authenticated requests to enable users to create and modify library collections, ratings, labels, reviews, and other account-specific entities.

For more information on the Book Search Data API, please refer to the official PHP Developer's Guide [http://code.google.com/apis/books/gdata/developers_guide_php.html] on code.google.com.

Authenticating to the Book Search service

You can access both public and private feeds using the Book Search Data API. Public feeds don't require any authentication, but they are read-only. If you want to modify user libraries, submit reviews or ratings, or add labels, then your client needs to authenticate before requesting private feeds. It can authenticate using either of two approaches: AuthSub proxy authentication or ClientLogin username/password authentication. Please refer to the Authentication section in the PHP Developer's Guide [http://code.google.com/apis/books/gdata/developers_guide_php.html#Authentication] for more detail.

Searching for books

The Book Search Data API provides a number of feeds that list collections of books.

The most common action is to retrieve a list of books that match a search query. To do so you create a VolumeQuery object and pass it to the Books::getVolumeFeed method.

For example, to perform a keyword query, with a filter on viewability to restrict the results to partial or full view books, use the setMinViewability and setQuery methods of the VolumeQuery object. The following code snippet prints the title and viewability of all volumes whose metadata or text matches the query term "domino":

```
$books = new Zend_Gdata_Books();
$query = $books->newVolumeQuery();
$query->setQuery('domino');
$query->setMinViewability('partial_view');
$feed = $books->getVolumeFeed($query);
foreach ($feed as $entry) {
    echo $entry->getVolumeId();
    echo $entry->getTitle();
    echo $entry->getViewability();
}
```

The Query class, and subclasses like VolumeQuery, are responsible for constructing feed URLs. The VolumeQuery shown above constructs a URL equivalent to the following:

```
http://www.google.com/books/feeds/volumes?q=keyword&amp;min-viewability
    =partial
```

Note: Since Book Search results are public, you can issue a Book Search query without authentication.

Here are some of the most common VolumeQuery methods for setting search parameters:

setQuery: Specifies a search query term. Book Search searches all book metadata and full text for books matching the term. Book metadata includes titles, keywords, descriptions, author names, and subjects. Note that any spaces, quotes or other punctuation in the parameter value must be URL-escaped. (Use a plus (+) for a space.) To search for an exact phrase, enclose the phrase in quotation marks. For example, to search for books matching the phrase "spy plane", set the q parameter to %22spy+plane%22. You can also use any of the advanced search operators [http://books.google.com/advanced_book_search] supported by Book Search. For example, jane+austen+-inauthor:austen returns matches that mention (but are not authored by) Jane

Austen.

`setStartIndex`: Specifies the index of the first matching result that should be included in the result set. This parameter uses a one-based index, meaning the first result is 1, the second result is 2 and so forth. This parameter works in conjunction with the max-results parameter to determine which results to return. For example, to request the third set of 10 results—results 21-30—set the `start-index` parameter to `21` and the max-results parameter to `10`. Note: This isn't a general cursoring mechanism. If you first send a query with `?start-index=1&max-results=10` and then send another query with `?start-index=11&max-results=10`, the service cannot guarantee that the results are equivalent to `?start-index=1&max-results=20`, because insertions and deletions could have taken place in between the two queries.

`setMaxResults`: Specifies the maximum number of results that should be included in the result set. This parameter works in conjunction with the start-index parameter to determine which results to return. The default value of this parameter is `10` and the maximum value is `20`.

`setMinViewability`: Allows you to filter the results according to the books' viewability status [http://code.google.com/apis/books/docs/dynamic-links.html#terminology]. This parameter accepts one of three values: `'none'` (the default, returning all matching books regardless of viewability), `'partial_view'` (returning only books that the user can preview or view in their entirety), or `'full_view'` (returning only books that the user can view in their entirety).

Partner Co-Branded Search

Google Book Search provides Co-Branded Search [http://books.google.com/support/partner/bin/answer.py?hl=en&answer=65113], which lets content partners provide full-text search of their books from their own websites.

If you are a partner who wants to do Co-Branded Search using the Book Search Data API, you may do so by modifying the feed URL above to point to your Co-Branded Search implementation. If, for example, a Co-Branded Search is available at the following URL:

```
http://www.google.com/books/p/PARTNER_COBRAND_ID?q=ball
```

then you can obtain the same results using the Book Search Data API at the following URL:

```
http://www.google.com/books/feeds/p/PARTNER_COBRAND_ID/volumes?q=ball+-soccer
```

To specify an alternate URL when querying a volume feed, you can provide an extra parameter to `newVolumeQuery`

```
$query =
    $books->newVolumeQuery('http://www.google.com/books/p/PARTNER
      _COBRAND_ID');
```

For additional information or support, visit our Partner help center [http://books.google.com /support/partner/].

Using community features

Adding a rating

A user can add a rating to a book. Book Search uses a 1-5 rating system in which 1 is the lowest rating. Users cannot update or delete ratings.

To add a rating, add a `Rating` object to a `VolumeEntry` and post it to the annotation feed. In the example below, we start from an empty `VolumeEntry` object.

```
$entry = new Zend_Gdata_Books_VolumeEntry();
$entry->setId(new Zend_Gdata_App_Extension_Id(VOLUME_ID));
$entry->setRating(new Zend_Gdata_Extension_Rating(3, 1, 5, 1));
$books->insertVolume($entry, Zend_Gdata_Books::MY_ANNOTATION_FEED_URI);
```

Reviews

In addition to ratings, authenticated users can submit reviews or edit their reviews. For information on how to request previously submitted reviews, see Retrieving annotations [#zend.gdata.books.retrieving_annotations].

Adding a review

To add a review, add a `Review` object to a `VolumeEntry` and post it to the annotation feed. In the example below, we start from an existing `VolumeEntry` object.

```
$annotationUrl = $entry->getAnnotationLink()->href;
$review        = new Zend_Gdata_Books_Extension_Review();
$review->setText("This book is amazing!");
$entry->setReview($review);
$books->insertVolume($entry, $annotationUrl);
```

Editing a review

To update an existing review, first you retrieve the review you want to update, then you modify it, and then you submit it to the annotation feed.

```
$entryUrl = $entry->getId()->getText();
$review    = new Zend_Gdata_Books_Extension_Review();
$review->setText("This book is actually not that good!");
$entry->setReview($review);
$books->updateVolume($entry, $entryUrl);
```

Labels

You can use the Book Search Data API to label volumes with keywords. A user can submit, retrieve and modify labels. See Retrieving annotations [#zend.gdata.books.retrieving_annotations] for how to read previously submitted labels.

Submitting a set of labels

To submit labels, add a `Category` object with the scheme `LABELS_SCHEME` to a `VolumeEntry` and post it to the annotation feed.

```
$annotationUrl = $entry->getAnnotationLink()->href;
$category      = new Zend_Gdata_App_Extension_Category(
    'rated',
    'http://schemas.google.com/books/2008/labels');
$entry->setCategory(array($category));
$books->insertVolume($entry, Zend_Gdata_Books::MY_ANNOTATION_FEED_URI);
```

Retrieving annotations: reviews, ratings, and labels

You can use the Book Search Data API to retrieve annotations submitted by a given user. Annotations include reviews, ratings, and labels. To retrieve any user's annotations, you can send an unauthenticated request that includes the user's user ID. To retrieve the authenticated user's annotations, use the value me as the user ID.

```
$feed = $books->getVolumeFeed(
            'http://www.google.com/books/feeds/users/USER_ID/volumes');
<i>(or)</i>
$feed = $books->getUserAnnotationFeed();
// print title(s) and rating value
foreach ($feed as $entry) {
    foreach ($feed->getTitles() as $title) {
        echo $title;
    }
    if ($entry->getRating()) {
        echo 'Rating: ' . $entry->getRating()->getAverage();
    }
}
```

For a list of the supported query parameters, see the query parameters [#zend.gdata.books .query_parameters] section.

Deleting Annotations

If you retrieved an annotation entry containing ratings, reviews, and/or labels, you can remove all annotations by calling deleteVolume on that entry.

```
$books->deleteVolume($entry);
```

Book collections and My Library

Google Book Search provides a number of user-specific book collections, each of which has its own feed.

The most important collection is the user's My Library, which represents the books the user would like to remember, organize, and share with others. This is the collection the user sees when accessing his or her My Library page [http://books.google.com/books?op=library].

Retrieving books in a user's library

The following sections describe how to retrieve a list of books from a user's library, with or without query parameters.

You can query a Book Search public feed without authentication.

Retrieving all books in a user's library

To retrieve the user's books, send a query to the My Library feed. To get the library of the authenticated user, use me in place of USER_ID.

```
$feed = $books->getUserLibraryFeed();
```

Note: The feed may not contain all of the user's books, because there's a default limit on the number of results returned. For more information, see the max-results query parameter in Searching for books [#zend.gdata.books.searching_for_books].

Searching for books in a user's library

Just as you can search across all books [#zend.gdata.books.searching_for_books], you can do a full-text search over just the books in a user's library. To do this, just set the appropriate paramters on the VolumeQuery object.

For example, the following query returns all the books in your library that contain the word "bear":

```
$query = $books->newVolumeQuery(
    'http://www.google.com/books/feeds/users' .
    '/USER_ID/collections/library/volumes');
$query->setQuery('bear');
$feed = $books->getVolumeFeed($query);
```

For a list of the supported query parameters, see the query parameters [#zend.gdata.books.query_pParameters] section. In addition, you can search for books that have been labeled by the user [#zend.gdata.books.labels]:

```
$query = $books->newVolumeQuery(
    'http://www.google.com/books/feeds/users/' .
    'USER_ID/collections/library/volumes');
$query->setCategory(
$query->setCategory('favorites');
$feed = $books->getVolumeFeed($query);
```

Updating books in a user's library

You can use the Book Search Data API to add a book to, or remove a book from, a user's library. Ratings, reviews, and labels are valid across all the collections of a user, and are thus edited using the annotation feed (see Using community features [#zend.gdata.books.community_features]).

Adding a book to a library

After authenticating, you can add books to the current user's library.

You can either create an entry from scratch if you know the volume ID, or insert an entry read from any feed.

The following example creates a new entry and adds it to the library:

```
$entry = new Zend_Gdata_Books_VolumeEntry();
$entry->setId(new Zend_Gdata_App_Extension_Id(VOLUME_ID));
$books->insertVolume(
    $entry,
    Zend_Gdata_Books::MY_LIBRARY_FEED_URI
);
```

The following example adds an existing VolumeEntry object to the library:

```
$books->insertVolume(
    $entry,
    Zend_Gdata_Books::MY_LIBRARY_FEED_URI
);
```

Removing a book from a library

To remove a book from a user's library, call deleteVolume on the VolumeEntry object.

```
$books->deleteVolume($entry);
```

Authenticating with ClientLogin

The ClientLogin mechanism enables you to write PHP application that acquire authenticated access to Google Services, specifying a user's credentials in the Http Client.

See http://code.google.com/apis/accounts/AuthForInstalledApps.html [http://code.google.com/apis/accounts/AuthForInstalledApps.html] for more information about Google Data ClientLogin authentication.

The Google documentation says the ClientLogin mechanism is appropriate for "installed applications" whereas the AuthSub mechanism is for "web applications." The difference is that AuthSub requires interaction from the user, and a browser interface that can react to redirection requests. The ClientLogin solution uses PHP code to supply the account credentials; the user is not required to enter her credentials interactively.

The account credentials supplied via the ClientLogin mechanism must be valid credentials for Google services, but they are not required to be those of the user who is using the PHP application.

Creating a ClientLogin authenticated Http Client

The process of creating an authenticated Http client using the ClientLogin mechanism is to call the static function `Zend_Gdata_ClientLogin::getHttpClient()` and pass the Google account credentials in plain text. The return value of this function is an object of class `Zend_Http_Client`.

The optional third parameter is the name of the Google Data service. For instance, this can be 'cl' for Google Calendar. The default is "xapi", which is recognized by Google Data servers as a generic service name.

The optional fourth parameter is an instance of `Zend_Http_Client`. This allows you to set options in the client, such as proxy server settings. If you pass `null` for this parameter, a generic `Zend_Http_Client` object is created.

The optional fifth parameter is a short string that Google Data servers use to identify the client application for logging purposes. By default this is string "Zend-ZendFramework";

The optional sixth parameter is a string ID for a CAPTCHA™ challenge that has been issued by the server. It is only necessary when logging in after receiving a CAPTCHA™ challenge from a previous login attempt.

The optional seventh parameter is a user's response to a CAPTCHA™ challenge that has been issued by the server. It is only necessary when logging in after receiving a CAPTCHA™ challenge from a previous login attempt.

Below is an example of PHP code for a web application to acquire authentication to use the Google Calendar service and create a `Zend_Gdata` client object using that authenticated `Zend_Http_Client`.

```
// Enter your Google account credentials
$email = 'johndoe@gmail.com';
$passwd = 'xxxxxxxx';
try {
    $client = Zend_Gdata_ClientLogin::getHttpClient($email, $passwd, 'cl');
} catch (Zend_Gdata_App_CaptchaRequiredException $cre) {
    echo 'URL of CAPTCHA image: ' . $cre->getCaptchaUrl() . "\n";
    echo 'Token ID: ' . $cre->getCaptchaToken() . "\n";
} catch (Zend_Gdata_App_AuthException $ae) {
    echo 'Problem authenticating: ' . $ae->exception() . "\n";
}
$cal = new Zend_Gdata_Calendar($client);
```

Terminating a ClientLogin authenticated Http Client

There is no method to revoke ClientLogin authentication as there is in the AuthSub token-based solution. The credentials used in the ClientLogin authentication are the login and password to a Google account, and therefore these can be used repeatedly in the future.

Using Google Calendar

You can use the `Zend_Gdata_Calendar` class to view, create, update, and delete events in the online Google Calendar service.

See http://code.google.com/apis/calendar/overview.html [http://code.google.com/apis/calendar/overview.html] for more information about the Google Calendar API.

Connecting To The Calendar Service

The Google Calendar API, like all GData APIs, is based off of the Atom Publishing Protocol (APP), an XML based format for managing web-based resources. Traffic between a client and the Google Calendar servers occurs over HTTP and allows for both authenticated and unauthenticated connections.

Before any transactions can occur, this connection needs to be made. Creating a connection to the calendar servers involves two steps: creating an HTTP client and binding a `Zend_Gdata_Calendar` service instance to that client.

Authentication

The Google Calendar API allows access to both public and private calendar feeds. Public feeds do not require authentication, but are read-only and offer reduced functionality. Private feeds offers the most complete functionality but requires an authenticated connection to the calendar servers. There are three authentication schemes that are supported by Google Calendar:

- *ClientAuth* provides direct username/password authentication to the calendar servers. Since this scheme requires that users provide your application with their password, this authentication is only recommended when other authentication schemes are insufficient.

- *AuthSub* allows authentication to the calendar servers via a Google proxy server. This provides the same level of convenience as ClientAuth but without the security risk, making this an ideal choice for web-based applications.

- *MagicCookie* allows authentication based on a semi-random URL available from within the Google Calendar interface. This is the simplest authentication scheme to implement, but requires that users manually retrieve their secure URL before they can authenticate, doesn't provide access to calendar lists, and is limited to read-only access.

The `Zend_Gdata` library provides support for all three authentication schemes. The rest of this chapter will assume that you are familiar the authentication schemes available and how to create an appropriate authenticated connection. For more information, please see section the Authentication section of this manual or the Authentication Overview in the Google Data API Developer's Guide [http://code.google.com/apis/gdata/auth.html].

Creating A Service Instance

In order to interact with Google Calendar, this library provides the `Zend_Gdata_Calendar` service class. This class provides a common interface to the Google Data and Atom Publishing Protocol models and assists in marshaling requests to and from the calendar servers.

Once deciding on an authentication scheme, the next step is to create an instance of `Zend_Gdata_Calendar`. The class constructor takes an instance of `Zend_Http_Client` as a single argument. This provides an interface for AuthSub and ClientAuth authentication, as both of these require creation of a special authenticated HTTP client. If no arguments are provided, an unauthenticated instance of `Zend_Http_Client` will be automatically created.

The example below shows how to create a Calendar service class using ClientAuth authentication:

```
// Parameters for ClientAuth authentication
$service = Zend_Gdata_Calendar::AUTH_SERVICE_NAME;
$user = "sample.user@gmail.com";
$pass = "pa$$w0rd";
// Create an authenticated HTTP client
$client = Zend_Gdata_ClientLogin::getHttpClient($user, $pass, $service);
// Create an instance of the Calendar service
$service = new Zend_Gdata_Calendar($client);
```

A Calendar service using AuthSub can be created in a similar, though slightly more lengthy fashion:

```
/*
 * Retrieve the current URL so that the AuthSub server knows where to
 * redirect the user after authentication is complete.
 */
function getCurrentUrl()
{
    global $_SERVER;
    // Filter php_self to avoid a security vulnerability.
    $php_request_uri =
        htmlentities(substr($_SERVER['REQUEST_URI'],
                            0,
                            strcspn($_SERVER['REQUEST_URI'], "\n\r")),
                     ENT_QUOTES);
    if (isset($_SERVER['HTTPS']) &&
        strtolower($_SERVER['HTTPS']) == 'on') {
        $protocol = 'https://';
    } else {
        $protocol = 'http://';
    }
    $host = $_SERVER['HTTP_HOST'];
    if ($_SERVER['HTTP_PORT'] != '' &&
        (($protocol == 'http://' && $_SERVER['HTTP_PORT'] != '80') ||
        ($protocol == 'https://' && $_SERVER['HTTP_PORT'] != '443'))) {
        $port = ':' . $_SERVER['HTTP_PORT'];
    } else {
        $port = '';
    }
    return $protocol . $host . $port . $php_request_uri;
}
/**
 * Obtain an AuthSub authenticated HTTP client, redirecting the user
 * to the AuthSub server to login if necessary.
 */
function getAuthSubHttpClient()
{
    global $_SESSION, $_GET;
    // if there is no AuthSub session or one-time token waiting for us,
    // redirect the user to the AuthSub server to get one.
    if (!isset($_SESSION['sessionToken']) && !isset($_GET['token'])) {
        // Parameters to give to AuthSub server
        $next = getCurrentUrl();
        $scope = "http://www.google.com/calendar/feeds/";
        $secure = false;
        $session = true;
        // Redirect the user to the AuthSub server to sign in
        $authSubUrl = Zend_Gdata_AuthSub::getAuthSubTokenUri($next,
                                                             $scope,
                                                             $secure,
```

```
                                                                    $session);
        header("HTTP/1.0 307 Temporary redirect");
        header("Location: " . $authSubUrl);
        exit();
    }
    // Convert an AuthSub one-time token into a session token if needed
    if (!isset($_SESSION['sessionToken']) && isset($_GET['token'])) {
        $_SESSION['sessionToken'] =
            Zend_Gdata_AuthSub::getAuthSubSessionToken($_GET['token']);
    }
    // At this point we are authenticated via AuthSub and can obtain an
    // authenticated HTTP client instance
    // Create an authenticated HTTP client
    $client = Zend_Gdata_AuthSub::getHttpClient($_SESSION['sessionToken']);
    return $client;
}
// -> Script execution begins here <-
// Make sure that the user has a valid session, so we can record the
// AuthSub session token once it is available.
session_start();
// Create an instance of the Calendar service, redirecting the user
// to the AuthSub server if necessary.
$service = new Zend_Gdata_Calendar(getAuthSubHttpClient());
```

Finally, an unauthenticated server can be created for use with either public feeds or MagicCookie authentication:

```
// Create an instance of the Calendar service using an unauthenticated
// HTTP client
$service = new Zend_Gdata_Calendar();
```

Note that MagicCookie authentication is not supplied with the HTTP connection, but is instead specified along with the desired visibility when submitting queries. See the section on retrieving events below for an example.

Retrieving A Calendar List

The calendar service supports retrieving a list of calendars for the authenticated user. This is the same list of calendars which are displayed in the Google Calendar UI, except those marked as "hidden" are also available.

The calendar list is always private and must be accessed over an authenticated connection. It is not possible to retrieve another user's calendar list and it cannot be accessed using MagicCookie authentication. Attempting to access a calendar list without holding appropriate credentials will fail and result in a 401 (Authentication Required) status code.

```
$service = Zend_Gdata_Calendar::AUTH_SERVICE_NAME;
$client = Zend_Gdata_ClientLogin::getHttpClient($user, $pass, $service);
$service = new Zend_Gdata_Calendar($client);
try {
    $listFeed= $service->getCalendarListFeed();
} catch (Zend_Gdata_App_Exception $e) {
    echo "Error: " . $e->getMessage();
}
```

Calling getCalendarListFeed() creates a new instance of Zend_Gdata_Calendar_ListFeed containing each available calendar as an instance of Zend_Gdata_Calendar_ListEntry. After retrieving the feed, you can use the iterator and accessors contained within the feed to inspect the enclosed calendars.

```
echo "<h1>Calendar List Feed</h1>";
echo "<ul>";
foreach ($listFeed as $calendar) {
    echo "<li>" . $calendar->title .
        " (Event Feed: " . $calendar->id . ")</li>";
}
echo "</ul>";
```

Retrieving Events

Like the list of calendars, events are also retrieved using the Zend_Gdata_Calendar service class. The event list returned is of type Zend_Gdata_Calendar_EventFeed and contains each event as an instance of Zend_Gdata_Calendar_EventEntry. As before, the iterator and accessors contained within the event feed instance allow inspection of individual events.

Queries

When retrieving events using the Calendar API, specially constructed query URLs are used to describe what events should be returned. The Zend_Gdata_Calendar_EventQuery class simplifies this task by automatically constructing a query URL based on provided parameters. A full list of these parameters is available at the Queries section of the Google Data APIs Protocol Reference [http://code.google.com/apis/gdata/reference.html#Queries]. However, there are three parameters that are worth special attention:

- *User* is used to specify the user whose calendar is being searched for, and is specified as an email address. If no user is provided, "default" will be used instead to indicate the currently authenticated user (if authenticated).

- *Visibility* specifies whether a users public or private calendar should be searched. If using an unauthenticated session and no MagicCookie is available, only the public feed will be available.

- *Projection* specifies how much data should be returned by the server and in what format. In most cases you will want to use the "full" projection. Also available is the "basic" projection, which places most meta-data into each event's content field as human readable text, and the "composite" projection which includes complete text for any comments alongside each event. The "composite" view is often much larger than the "full" view.

Retrieving Events In Order Of Start Time

The example below illustrates the use of the Zend_Gdata_Query class and specifies the private visibility feed, which requires that an authenticated connection is available to the calendar servers. If a MagicCookie is being used for authentication, the visibility should be instead set to "private-magicCookieValue", where magicCookieValue is the random string obtained when viewing the private XML address in the Google Calendar UI. Events are requested chronologically by start time and only events occurring in the future are returned.

```
$query = $service->newEventQuery();
$query->setUser('default');
// Set to $query->setVisibility('private-magicCookieValue') if using
// MagicCookie auth
$query->setVisibility('private');
$query->setProjection('full');
$query->setOrderby('starttime');
$query->setFutureevents('true');
// Retrieve the event list from the calendar server
try {
    $eventFeed = $service->getCalendarEventFeed($query);
} catch (Zend_Gdata_App_Exception $e) {
```

```
        echo "Error: " . $e->getMessage();
}
// Iterate through the list of events, outputting them as an HTML list
echo "<ul>";
foreach ($eventFeed as $event) {
    echo "<li>" . $event->title . " (Event ID: " . $event->id . ")</li>";
}
echo "</ul>";
```

Additional properties such as ID, author, when, event status, visibility, web content, and content, among others are available within Zend_Gdata_Calendar_EventEntry. Refer to the Zend Framework API Documentation [http://framework.zend.com/apidoc/core/] and the Calendar Protocol Reference [http://code.google.com/apis/gdata/reference.html] for a complete list.

Retrieving Events In A Specified Date Range

To print out all events within a certain range, for example from December 1, 2006 through December 15, 2007, add the following two lines to the previous sample. Take care to remove "$query->setFutureevents('true')", since futureevents will override startMin and startMax.

```
$query->setStartMin('2006-12-01');
$query->setStartMax('2006-12-16');
```

Note that startMin is inclusive whereas startMax is exclusive. As a result, only events through 2006-12-15 23:59:59 will be returned.

Retrieving Events By Fulltext Query

To print out all events which contain a specific word, for example "dogfood", use the setQuery() method when creating the query.

```
$query->setQuery("dogfood");
```

Retrieving Individual Events

Individual events can be retrieved by specifying their event ID as part of the query. Instead of calling getCalendarEventFeed(), getCalendarEventEntry() should be called instead.

```
$query = $service->newEventQuery();
$query->setUser('default');
$query->setVisibility('private');
$query->setProjection('full');
$query->setEvent($eventId);
try {
    $event = $service->getCalendarEventEntry($query);
} catch (Zend_Gdata_App_Exception $e) {
    echo "Error: " . $e->getMessage();
}
```

In a similar fashion, if the event URL is known, it can be passed directly into getCalendarEntry() to retrieve a specific event. In this case, no query object is required since the event URL contains all the necessary information to retrieve the event.

```
$eventURL = "http://www.google.com/calendar/feeds/default/private"
          . "/full/g829on5sq4ag12se91d10uumko";
```

```
try {
    $event = $service->getCalendarEventEntry($eventURL);
} catch (Zend_Gdata_App_Exception $e) {
    echo "Error: " . $e->getMessage();
}
```

Creating Events

Creating Single-Occurrence Events

Events are added to a calendar by creating an instance of Zend_Gdata_EventEntry and populating it with the appropriate data. The calendar service instance (Zend_Gdata_Calendar) is then used to used to transparently covert the event into XML and POST it to the calendar server. Creating events requires either an AuthSub or ClientAuth authenticated connection to the calendar server.

At a minimum, the following attributes should be set:

- *Title* provides the headline that will appear above the event within the Google Calendar UI.

- *When* indicates the duration of the event and, optionally, any reminders that are associated with it. See the next section for more information on this attribute.

Other useful attributes that may optionally set include:

- *Author* provides information about the user who created the event.

- *Content* provides additional information about the event which appears when the event details are requested from within Google Calendar.

- *EventStatus* indicates whether the event is confirmed, tentative, or canceled.

- *Hidden* removes the event from the Google Calendar UI.

- *Transparency* indicates whether the event should be consume time on the user's free/busy list.

- *WebContent* allows links to external content to be provided within an event.

- *Where* indicates the location of the event.

- *Visibility* allows the event to be hidden from the public event lists.

For a complete list of event attributes, refer to the Zend Framework API Documentation [http://framework.zend.com/apidoc/core/] and the Calendar Protocol Reference [http://code.google.com/apis/gdata/reference.html]. Attributes that can contain multiple values, such as where, are implemented as arrays and need to be created accordingly. Be aware that all of these attributes require objects as parameters. Trying instead to populate them using strings or primitives will result in errors during conversion to XML.

Once the event has been populated, it can be uploaded to the calendar server by passing it as an argument to the calendar service's insertEvent() function.

```
// Create a new entry using the calendar service's magic factory method
$event= $service->newEventEntry();
// Populate the event with the desired information
// Note that each attribute is crated as an instance of a matching class
$event->title = $service->newTitle("My Event");
$event->where = array($service->newWhere("Mountain View, California"));
$event->content =
    $service->newContent(" This is my awesome event. RSVP required.");
// Set the date using RFC 3339 format.
$startDate = "2008-01-20";
$startTime = "14:00";
```

```
$endDate = "2008-01-20";
$endTime = "16:00";
$tzOffset = "-08";
$when = $service->newWhen();
$when->startTime = "{$startDate}T{$startTime}:00.000{$tzOffset}:00";
$when->endTime = "{$endDate}T{$endTime}:00.000{$tzOffset}:00";
$event->when = array($when);
// Upload the event to the calendar server
// A copy of the event as it is recorded on the server is returned
$newEvent = $service->insertEvent($event);
```

Event Schedules and Reminders

An event's starting time and duration are determined by the value of its when property, which contains the properties startTime, endTime, and valueString. StartTime and EndTime control the duration of the event, while the valueString property is currently unused.

All-day events can be scheduled by specifying only the date omitting the time when setting startTime and endTime. Likewise, zero-duration events can be specified by omitting the endTime. In all cases, date/time values should be provided in RFC3339 [http://www.ietf.org/rfc/rfc3339.txt] format.

```
// Schedule the event to occur on December 05, 2007 at 2 PM PST (UTC-8)
// with a duration of one hour.
$when = $service->newWhen();
$when->startTime = "2007-12-05T14:00:00-08:00";
$when->endTime="2007-12-05T15:00:00-08:00";
// Apply the when property to an event
$event->when = array($when);
```

The when attribute also controls when reminders are sent to a user. Reminders are stored in an array and each event may have up to find reminders associated with it.

For a reminder to be valid, it needs to have two attributes set: method and a time. Method can accept one of the following strings: "alert", "email", or "sms". The time should be entered as an integer and can be set with either the property minutes, hours, days, or absoluteTime. However, a valid request may only have one of these attributes set. If a mixed time is desired, convert to the most precise unit available. For example, 1 hour and 30 minutes should be entered as 90 minutes.

```
// Create a new reminder object. It should be set to send an email
// to the user 10 minutes beforehand.
$reminder = $service->newReminder();
$reminder->method = "email";
$reminder->minutes = "10";
// Apply the reminder to an existing event's when property
$when = $event->when[0];
$when->reminders = array($reminder);
```

Creating Recurring Events

Recurring events are created the same way as single-occurrence events, except a recurrence attribute should be provided instead of a where attribute. The recurrence attribute should hold a string describing the event's recurrence pattern using properties defined in the iCalendar standard (RFC 2445 [http://www.ietf.org/rfc/rfc2445.txt]).

Exceptions to the recurrence pattern will usually be specified by a distinct recurrenceException attribute. However, the iCalendar standard provides a secondary format for defining recurrences, and the possibility that either may be used must be accounted for.

Due to the complexity of parsing recurrence patterns, further information on this them is outside the scope of this document. However, more information can be found in the Common Elements section of the Google Data APIs Developer Guide [http://code.google.com/apis/gdata/elements.html#gdRecurrence], as well as in RFC 2445.

```
// Create a new entry using the calendar service's magic factory method
$event= $service->newEventEntry();
// Populate the event with the desired information
// Note that each attribute is crated as an instance of a matching class
$event->title = $service->newTitle("My Recurring Event");
$event->where = array($service->newWhere("Palo Alto, California"));
$event->content =
    $service->newContent(' This is my other awesome event, ' .
                         ' occurring all-day every Tuesday from .
                         '2007-05-01 until 207-09-04. No RSVP required.');
// Set the duration and frequency by specifying a recurrence pattern.
$recurrence = "DTSTART;VALUE=DATE:20070501\r\n" .
        "DTEND;VALUE=DATE:20070502\r\n" .
        "RRULE:FREQ=WEEKLY;BYDAY=Tu;UNTIL=20070904\r\n";
$event->recurrence = $service->newRecurrence($recurrence);
// Upload the event to the calendar server
// A copy of the event as it is recorded on the server is returned
$newEvent = $service->insertEvent($event);
```

Using QuickAdd

QuickAdd is a feature which allows events to be created using free-form text entry. For example, the string "Dinner at Joe's Diner on Thursday" would create an event with the title "Dinner", location "Joe's Diner", and date "Thursday". To take advantage of QuickAdd, create a new QuickAdd property set to "true" and store the freeform text as a content property.

```
// Create a new entry using the calendar service's magic factory method
$event= $service->newEventEntry();
// Populate the event with the desired information
$event->content= $service->newContent("Dinner at Joe's Diner on Thursday");
$event->quickAdd = $service->newQuickAdd("true");
// Upload the event to the calendar server
// A copy of the event as it is recorded on the server is returned
$newEvent = $service->insertEvent($event);
```

Modifying Events

Once an instance of an event has been obtained, the event's attributes can be locally modified in the same way as when creating an event. Once all modifications are complete, calling the event's save() method will upload the changes to the calendar server and return a copy of the event as it was created on the server.

In the event another user has modified the event since the local copy was retrieved, save() will fail and the server will return a 409 (Conflict) status code. To resolve this a fresh copy of the event must be retrieved from the server before attempting to resubmit any modifications.

```
// Get the first event in the user's event list
$event = $eventFeed[0];
// Change the title to a new value
$event->title = $service->newTitle("Woof!");
// Upload the changes to the server
try {
    $event->save();
```

```
} catch (Zend_Gdata_App_Exception $e) {
    echo "Error: " . $e->getMessage();
}
```

Deleting Events

Calendar events can be deleted either by calling the calendar service's `delete()` method and providing the edit URL of an event or by calling an existing event's own `delete()` method.

In either case, the deleted event will still show up on a user's private event feed if an `updateMin` query parameter is provided. Deleted events can be distinguished from regular events because they will have their `eventStatus` property set to "http://schemas.google.com/g/2005#event.canceled".

```
// Option 1: Events can be deleted directly
$event->delete();


// Option 2: Events can be deleted supplying the edit URL of the event
// to the calendar service, if known
$service->delete($event->getEditLink()->href);
```

Accessing Event Comments

When using the full event view, comments are not directly stored within an entry. Instead, each event contains a URL to its associated comment feed which must be manually requested.

Working with comments is fundamentally similar to working with events, with the only significant difference being that a different feed and event class should be used and that the additional meta-data for events such as where and when does not exist for comments. Specifically, the comment's author is stored in the `author` property, and the comment text is stored in the `content` property.

```
// Extract the comment URL from the first event in a user's feed list
$event = $eventFeed[0];
$commentUrl = $event->comments->feedLink->url;
// Retrieve the comment list for the event
try {
$commentFeed = $service->getFeed($commentUrl);
} catch (Zend_Gdata_App_Exception $e) {
    echo "Error: " . $e->getMessage();
}
// Output each comment as an HTML list
echo "<ul>";
foreach ($commentFeed as $comment) {
    echo "<li><em>Comment By: " . $comment->author->name "</em><br/>" .
        $comment->content . "</li>";
}
echo "</ul>";
```

Using Google Documents List Data API

The Google Documents List Data API allows client applications to upload documents to Google Documents and list them in the form of Google Data API ("GData") feeds. Your client application can request a list of a user's documents, and query the content in an existing document.

See http://code.google.com/apis/documents/overview.html for more information about the Google Documents List API.

Get a List of Documents

You can get a list of the Google Documents for a particular user by using the getDocumentListFeed method of the docs service. The service will return a Zend_Gdata_Docs_DocumentListFeed object containing a list of documents associated with the authenticated user.

```
$service = Zend_Gdata_Docs::AUTH_SERVICE_NAME;
$client = Zend_Gdata_ClientLogin::getHttpClient($user, $pass, $service);
$docs = new Zend_Gdata_Docs($client);
$feed = $docs->getDocumentListFeed();
```

The resulting Zend_Gdata_Docs_DocumentListFeed object represents the response from the server. This feed contains a list of Zend_Gdata_Docs_DocumentListEntry objects ($feed->entries), each of which represents a single Google Document.

Upload a Document

You can create a new Google Document by uploading a word processing document, spreadsheet, or presentation. This example is from the interactive Docs.php sample which comes with the library. It demonstrates uploading a file and printing information about the result from the server.

```
/**
 * Upload the specified document
 *
 * @param Zend_Gdata_Docs $docs The service object to use for communicating
 *      with the Google Documents server.
 * @param boolean $html True if output should be formatted for display in a
 *      web browser.
 * @param string $originalFileName The name of the file to be uploaded. The
 *      MIME type of the file is determined from the extension on this file
 *      name. For example, test.csv is uploaded as a comma seperated volume
 *      and converted into a spreadsheet.
 * @param string $temporaryFileLocation (optional) The file in which the
 *      data for the document is stored. This is used when the file has been
 *      uploaded from the client's machine to the server and is stored in
 *      a temporary file which does not have an extension. If this parameter
 *      is null, the file is read from the originalFileName.
 */
function uploadDocument($docs, $html, $originalFileName,
                        $temporaryFileLocation) {
  $fileToUpload = $originalFileName;
  if ($temporaryFileLocation) {
    $fileToUpload = $temporaryFileLocation;
  }
  // Upload the file and convert it into a Google Document. The original
  // file name is used as the title of the document and the MIME type
  // is determined based on the extension on the original file name.
  $newDocumentEntry = $docs->uploadFile($fileToUpload, $originalFileName,
      null, Zend_Gdata_Docs::DOCUMENTS_LIST_FEED_URI);
  echo "New Document Title: ";
  if ($html) {
      // Find the URL of the HTML view of this document.
      $alternateLink = '';
      foreach ($newDocumentEntry->link as $link) {
          if ($link->getRel() === 'alternate') {
              $alternateLink = $link->getHref();
          }
      }
      // Make the title link to the document on docs.google.com.
      echo "<a href=\"$alternateLink\">\n";
  }
  echo $newDocumentEntry->title."\n";
```

```
    if ($html) {echo "</a>\n";}
}
```

Searching the documents feed

You can search the Document List using some of the standard Google Data API query parameters [http://code.google.com/apis/gdata/reference.html#Queries]. Categories are used to restrict the type of document (word processor document, spreadsheet) returned. The full-text query string is used to search the content of all the documents. More detailed information on parameters specific to the Documents List can be found in the Documents List Data API Reference Guide [http://code.google.com/apis/documents/reference.html#Parameters].

Get a List of Word Processing Documents

You can also request a feed containing all of your documents of a specific type. For example, to see a list of your work processing documents, you would perform a category query as follows.

```
$feed = $docs->getDocumentListFeed(
    'http://docs.google.com/feeds/documents/private/full/-/document');
```

Get a List of Spreadsheets

To request a list of your Google Spreadsheets, use the following category query:

```
$feed = $docs->getDocumentListFeed(
    'http://docs.google.com/feeds/documents/private/full/-/spreadsheet');
```

Performing a text query

You can search the content of documents by using a Zend_Gdata_Docs_Query in your request. A Query object can be used to construct the query URI, with the search term being passed in as a parameter. Here is an example method which queries the documents list for documents which contain the search string:

```
$docsQuery = new Zend_Gdata_Docs_Query();
$docsQuery->setQuery($query);
$feed = $client->getDocumentListFeed($docsQuery);
```

Using Google Health

The Google Health Data API is designed to enable developers to do two things:

- Read a user's Google Health profile or query for medical records that match particular criteria and then use the results to provide personalized functionality based on the data.

- Add new medical records to a user's profile by including CCR data when sending a notice to a user's profile. Note: The CCR data is stored as an XML blob within the <atom> entry. The library does not provide direct accessors to the object model but it does have helpers for extracting specific fields.

There are three main feeds, each of which requires authentication. Unlike other Google Data APIs, each Google Health feed has a limited set of HTTP operations you can perform on it, depending on which authentication method you are using (ClientLogin or AuthSub/OAuth). For a list of permitted operations, see http://code.google.com/apis/health/reference.html#Authentication.

- *Profile Feed* use the profile feed to query a user's health profile for specific information.

- *Register Feed* use the register feed to reconcile new CCR data into a profile.

- *Profile List Feed* the profile list feed should be used to determine which of the user's Health profiles to interact with. This feed is only available when using ClientLogin.

See http://code.google.com/apis/health [http://code.google.com/apis/health/] for more information about the Google Health API.

Connect To The Health Service

The Google Health API, like all Google Data APIs, is based off of the Atom Publishing Protocol (APP), an XML based format for managing web-based resources. Traffic between a client and the Google Health servers occurs over HTTP and allows for authenticated connections.

Before any transactions can occur, a connection needs to be made. Creating a connection to the Health servers involves two steps: creating an HTTP client and binding a Zend_Gdata_Health service instance to that client.

Authentication

The Google Health API allows programmatic access to a user's Health profile. There are three authentication schemes that are supported by Google Health:

- *ClientLogin* provides direct username/password authentication to the Health servers. Since this method requires that users provide your application with their password, this authentication scheme is only recommended for installed/desktop applications.

- *AuthSub* allows a user to authorize the sharing of their private data. This provides the same level of convenience as ClientLogin but without the security risk, making it an ideal choice for web-based applications. For Google Health, AuthSub must be used in registered and secure mode--meaning that all requests to the API must be digitally signed.

- *OAuth* is an alternative to AuthSub. Although this authentication scheme is not discussed in this document, more information can be found in the Health Data API Developer's Guide [http://code.google.com/apis/health/developers_guide_protocol.html#OAuth].

See Authentication Overview in the Google Data API documentation [http://code.google.com/apis/gdata/auth.html] for more information on each authentication method.

Create A Health Service Instance

In order to interact with Google Health, the client library provides the Zend_Gdata_Health service class. This class provides a common interface to the Google Data and Atom Publishing Protocol models and assists in marshaling requests to and from the Health API.

Once you've decided on an authentication scheme, the next step is to create an instance of Zend_Gdata_Health . This class should be passed an instance of Zend_Gdata_HttpClient. This provides an interface for AuthSub/OAuth and ClientLogin to create a special authenticated HTTP client.

To test against the H9 Developer's (/h9) instead of Google Health (/health), the Zend_Gdata_Health constructor takes an optional third argument for you to specify the H9 service name 'weaver'.

The example below shows how to create a Health service class using ClientLogin authentication:

```
// Parameters for ClientLogin authentication
$healthServiceName = Zend_Gdata_Health::HEALTH_SERVICE_NAME;
//$h9ServiceName = Zend_Gdata_Health::H9_SANDBOX_SERVICE_NAME;
$user = "user@gmail.com";
```

```
$pass = "pa$$w0rd";
// Create an authenticated HTTP client
$client = Zend_Gdata_ClientLogin::getHttpClient($user,
                                                $pass,
                                                $healthServiceName);
// Create an instance of the Health service
$service = new Zend_Gdata_Health($client);
```

A Health service using AuthSub can be created in a similar, though slightly more lengthy fashion. AuthSub is the recommend interface to communicate with Google Health because each token is directly linked to a specific profile in the user's account. Unlike other Google Data APIs, it is required that all requests from your application be digitally signed.

```
/*
 * Retrieve the current URL so that the AuthSub server knows where to
 * redirect the user after authentication is complete.
 */
function getCurrentUrl() {
    $phpRequestUri = htmlentities(substr($_SERVER['REQUEST_URI'],
                                         0,
                                         strcspn($_SERVER['REQUEST_URI'],
                                                 "\n\r")),
                                  ENT_QUOTES);
    if (isset($_SERVER['HTTPS']) && strtolower($_SERVER['HTTPS']) == 'on') {
        $protocol = 'https://';
    } else {
        $protocol = 'http://';
    }
    $host = $_SERVER['HTTP_HOST'];
    if ($_SERVER['SERVER_PORT'] != '' &&
        (($protocol == 'http://' && $_SERVER['SERVER_PORT'] != '80') ||
        ($protocol == 'https://' && $_SERVER['SERVER_PORT'] != '443'))) {
        $port = ':' . $_SERVER['SERVER_PORT'];
    } else {
        $port = '';
    }
    return $protocol . $host . $port . $phpRequestUri;
}
/*
 * Redirect a user to AuthSub if they do not have a valid session token.
 * If they're coming back from AuthSub with a single-use token, instantiate
 * a new HTTP client and exchange the token for a long-lived session token
 * instead.
 */
function setupClient($singleUseToken = null) {
    $client = null;
    // Fetch a new AuthSub token?
    if (!$singleUseToken) {
        $next = getCurrentUrl();
        $scope = 'https://www.google.com/health/feeds';
        $authSubHandler = 'https://www.google.com/health/authsub';
        $secure = 1;
        $session = 1;
        $authSubURL =  Zend_Gdata_AuthSub::getAuthSubTokenUri($next,
                                                              $scope,
                                                              $secure,
                                                              $session,
                                                              $authSubHandler);

        // 1 - allows posting notices && allows reading profile data
        $permission = 1;
        $authSubURL .= '&permission=' . $permission;
        echo '<a href="' . $authSubURL . '">Your Google Health Account</a>';
    } else {
```

```
$client = new Zend_Gdata_HttpClient();
// This sets your private key to be used to sign subsequent requests
$client->setAuthSubPrivateKeyFile('/path/to/your/rsa_private_key.pem'
                                  null,
                                  true);
$sessionToken =
    Zend_Gdata_AuthSub::getAuthSubSessionToken(trim($singleUseToken),
                                               $client);
// Set the long-lived session token for subsequent requests
$client->setAuthSubToken($sessionToken);
}
    return $client;
}
// -> Script execution begins here <-
session_start();
$client = setupClient(@$_GET['token']);
// Create an instance of the Health service
$userH9Sandbox = false;
$healthService = new Zend_Gdata_Health($client,
                                       'googleInc-MyTestAppName-v1.0',
                                       $userH9Sandbox);
```

NOTE: the remainder of this document will assume you are using AuthSub for authentication.

Profile Feed

To query the user's profile feed, make sure your initial AuthSub token was requested with the permission=1 parameter set. The process of extracting data from the profile requires two steps, sending a query and iterating through the resulting feed.

Send a Structured Query

You can send structured queries to retrieve specific records from a user's profile.

When retrieving the profile using the Health API, specifically constructed query URLs are used to describe what (CCR) data should be returned. The Zend_Gdata_Health_Query class helps simplify this task by automatically constructing a query URL based on the parameters you set.

Query The Feed

To execute a query against the profile feed, invoke a new instance of an Zend_Gdata_Health_Query and call the service's getHealthProfileFeed() method:

```
$healthService = new Zend_Gdata_Health($client);
// example query for the top 10 medications with 2 items each
$query = new Zend_Gdata_Health_Query();
$query->setDigest("true");
$query->setGrouped("true");
$query->setMaxResultsGroup(10);
$query->setMaxResultsInGroup(2);
$query->setCategory("medication");
$profileFeed = $healthService->getHealthProfileFeed($query);
```

Using setDigest("true") returns all of user's CCR data in a single Atom <entry>.

The setCategory() helper can be passed an additional parameter to return more specific CCR information. For example, to return just the medication Lipitor, use setCategory("medication", "Lipitor"). The same methodology can be applied to other categories such as conditions, allergies, lab results, etc.

A full list of supported query parameters is available in the query parameters section http://code.google.com/apis/health/reference.html#Parameters] of the Health API Reference Guide.

Iterate Through The Profile Entries

Each Google Health entry contains CCR data, however, using the `digest=true` query parameter will consolidate all of the CCR elements (that match your query) into a single Atom `<entry>`.

To retrieve the full CCR information from an entry, make a call to the `Zend_Gdata_Health_ProfileEntry` class's `getCcr()` method. That returns a `Zend_Gdata_Health_Extension_CCR`:

```
$entries = $profileFeed->getEntries();
foreach ($entries as $entry) {
    $medications = $entry->getCcr()->getMedications();
    //$conditions = $entry->getCcr()->getConditions();
    //$immunizations = $entry->getCcr()->getImmunizations();
    // print the CCR xml (this will just be the entry's medications)
    foreach ($medications as $med) {
        $xmlStr = $med->ownerDocument->saveXML($med);
        echo "<pre>" . $xmlStr . "</pre>";
    }
}
```

Here, the `getCcr()` method is used in conjunction with a magic helper to drill down and extract just the medication data from the entry's CCR. The formentioned magic helper takes the form `getCATEGORYNAME()`, where `CATEGORYNAME` is a supported Google Health category. See the Google Health reference Guide [http://code.google.com/apis/health/reference.html#CatQueries] for the possible categories.

To be more efficient, you can also use category queries to only return the necessary CCR from the Google Health servers. Then, iterate through those results:

```
$query = new Zend_Gdata_Health_Query();
$query->setDigest("true");
$query->setCategory("condition");
$profileFeed = $healthService->getHealthProfileFeed($query);
// Since the query contained digest=true, only one Atom entry is returned
$entry = $profileFeed->entry[0];
$conditions = $entry->getCcr()->getConditions();
// print the CCR xml (this will just be the profile's conditions)
foreach ($conditions as $cond) {
    $xmlStr = $cond->ownerDocument->saveXML($cond);
    echo "<pre>" . $xmlStr . "</pre>";
}
```

Profile List Feed

NOTE: This feed is only available when using ClientLogin

Since ClientLogin requires a profile ID with each of its feeds, applications will likely want to query this feed first in order to select the appropriate profile. The profile list feed returns Atom entries corresponding each profile in the user's Google Health account. The profile ID is returned in the Atom `<content>` and the profile name in the `<title>` element.

Query The Feed

To execute a query against the profile list feed, call the service's `getHealthProfileListFeed()` method:

```
$client = Zend_Gdata_ClientLogin::getHttpClient('user@gmail.com',
                                                'pa$$word',
                                                'health');
$healthService = new Zend_Gdata_Health($client);
$feed = $healthService->getHealthProfileListFeed();
// print each profile's name and id
$entries = $feed->getEntries();
foreach ($entries as $entry) {
    echo '<p>Profile name: ' . $entry->getProfileName() . '<br>';
    echo 'profile ID: ' . $entry->getProfileID() . '</p>';
}
```

Once you've determined which profile to use, call setProfileID() with the profileID as an argument. This will restrict subsequent API requests to be against that particular profile:

```
// use the first profile
$profileID = $feed->entry[0]->getProfileID();
$healthService->setProfileID($profileID);
$profileFeed = $healthService->getHealthProfileFeed();
$profileID = $healthService->getProfileID();
echo '<p><b>Queried profileID</b>: ' . $profileID . '</p>';
```

Sending Notices to the Register Feed

Individual posts to the register feed are known as notices. Notice are sent from third-party applications to inform the user of a new event. With AuthSub/OAuth, notices are the single means by which your application can add new CCR information into a user's profile. Notices can contain plain text (including certain XHTML elements), a CCR document, or both. As an example, notices might be sent to remind users to pick up a prescription, or they might contain lab results in the CCR format.

Sending a notice

Notices can be sent by using the sendHealthNotice() method for the Health service:

```
$healthService = new Zend_Gdata_Health($client);
$subject = "Title of your notice goes here";
$body = "Notice body can contain <b>html</b> entities";
$ccr = '<ContinuityOfCareRecord xmlns="urn:astm-org:CCR">
  <Body>
   <Problems>
    <Problem>
      <DateTime>
        <Type><Text>Start date</Text></Type>
        <ExactDateTime>2007-04-04T07:00:00Z</ExactDateTime>
      </DateTime>
      <Description>
        <Text>Aortic valve disorders</Text>
        <Code>
          <Value>410.10</Value>
          <CodingSystem>ICD9</CodingSystem>
          <Version>2004</Version>
        </Code>
      </Description>
      <Status><Text>Active</Text></Status>
    </Problem>
   </Problems>
  </Body>
</ContinuityOfCareRecord>';
$responseEntry = $healthService->sendHealthNotice($subject,
                                                  $body,
```

```
                                                          "html",
                                                          $ccr);
```

Using Google Spreadsheets

The Google Spreadsheets data API allows client applications to view and update Spreadsheets content in the form of Google data API feeds. Your client application can request a list of a user's spreadsheets, edit or delete content in an existing Spreadsheets worksheet, and query the content in an existing Spreadsheets worksheet.

See http://code.google.com/apis/spreadsheets/overview.html for more information about the Google Spreadsheets API.

Create a Spreadsheet

The Spreadsheets data API does not currently provide a way to programmatically create or delete a spreadsheet.

Get a List of Spreadsheets

You can get a list of spreadsheets for a particular user by using the getSpreadsheetFeed method of the Spreadsheets service. The service will return a Zend_Gdata_Spreadsheets_SpreadsheetFeed object containing a list of spreadsheets associated with the authenticated user.

```
$service = Zend_Gdata_Spreadsheets::AUTH_SERVICE_NAME;
$client = Zend_Gdata_ClientLogin::getHttpClient($user, $pass, $service);
$spreadsheetService = new Zend_Gdata_Spreadsheets($client);
$feed = $spreadsheetService->getSpreadsheetFeed();
```

Get a List of Worksheets

A given spreadsheet may contain multiple worksheets. For each spreadsheet, there's a worksheets metafeed listing all the worksheets in that spreadsheet.

Given the spreadsheet key from the <id> of a Zend_Gdata_Spreadsheets_SpreadsheetEntry object you've already retrieved, you can fetch a feed containing a list of worksheets associated with that spreadsheet.

```
$query = new Zend_Gdata_Spreadsheets_DocumentQuery();
$query->setSpreadsheetKey($spreadsheetKey);
$feed = $spreadsheetService->getWorksheetFeed($query);
```

The resulting Zend_Gdata_Spreadsheets_WorksheetFeed object feed represents the response from the server. Among other things, this feed contains a list of Zend_Gdata_Spreadsheets_WorksheetEntry objects ($feed->entries), each of which represents a single worksheet.

Interacting With List-based Feeds

A given worksheet generally contains multiple rows, each containing multiple cells. You can request data from the worksheet either as a list-based feed, in which each entry represents a row, or as a cell-based feed, in which each entry represents a single cell. For information on cell-based feeds, see Interacting with cell-based feeds.

The following sections describe how to get a list-based feed, add a row to a worksheet, and send queries with various query parameters.

The list feed makes some assumptions about how the data is laid out in the spreadsheet.

In particular, the list feed treats the first row of the worksheet as a header row; Spreadsheets dynamically creates XML elements named after the contents of header-row cells. Users who want to provide Gdata feeds should not put any data other than column headers in the first row of a worksheet.

The list feed contains all rows after the first row up to the first blank row. The first blank row terminates the data set. If expected data isn't appearing in a feed, check the worksheet manually to see whether there's an unexpected blank row in the middle of the data. In particular, if the second row of the spreadsheet is blank, then the list feed will contain no data.

A row in a list feed is as many columns wide as the worksheet itself.

Get a List-based Feed

To retrieve a worksheet's list feed, use the `getListFeed` method of the Spreadsheets service.

```
$query = new Zend_Gdata_Spreadsheets_ListQuery();
$query->setSpreadsheetKey($spreadsheetKey);
$query->setWorksheetId($worksheetId);
$listFeed = $spreadsheetService->getListFeed($query);
```

The resulting `Zend_Gdata_Spreadsheets_ListFeed` object `$listfeed` represents a response from the server. Among other things, this feed contains an array of `Zend_Gdata_Spreadsheets_ListEntry` objects (`$listFeed->entries`), each of which represents a single row in a worksheet.

Each `Zend_Gdata_Spreadsheets_ListEntry` contains an array, `custom`, which contains the data for that row. You can extract and display this array:

```
$rowData = $listFeed->entries[1]->getCustom();
foreach($rowData as $customEntry) {
  echo $customEntry->getColumnName() . " = " . $customEntry->getText();
}
```

An alternate version of this array, `customByName`, allows direct access to an entry's cells by name. This is convenient when trying to access a specific header:

```
$customEntry = $listFeed->entries[1]->getCustomByName('my_heading');
echo $customEntry->getColumnName() . " = " . $customEntry->getText();
```

Reverse-sort Rows

By default, rows in the feed appear in the same order as the corresponding rows in the GUI; that is, they're in order by row number. To get rows in reverse order, set the reverse properties of the `Zend_Gdata_Spreadsheets_ListQuery` object to true:

```
$query = new Zend_Gdata_Spreadsheets_ListQuery();
$query->setSpreadsheetKey($spreadsheetKey);
$query->setWorksheetId($worksheetId);
$query->setReverse('true');
$listFeed = $spreadsheetService->getListFeed($query);
```

Note that if you want to order (or reverse sort) by a particular column, rather than by position in the worksheet, you can set the `orderby` value of the `Zend_Gdata_Spreadsheets_ListQuery` object to `column:<the header of that column>`.

Send a Structured Query

You can set a Zend_Gdata_Spreadsheets_ListQuery's sq value to produce a feed with entries that meet the specified criteria. For example, suppose you have a worksheet containing personnel data, in which each row represents information about a single person. You wish to retrieve all rows in which the person's name is "John" and the person's age is over 25. To do so, you would set sq as follows:

```
$query = new Zend_Gdata_Spreadsheets_ListQuery();
$query->setSpreadsheetKey($spreadsheetKey);
$query->setWorksheetId($worksheetId);
$query->setSpreadsheetQuery('name=John and age>25');
$listFeed = $spreadsheetService->getListFeed($query);
```

Add a Row

Rows can be added to a spreadsheet by using the insertRow method of the Spreadsheet service.

```
$insertedListEntry = $spreadsheetService->insertRow($rowData,
                                                    $spreadsheetKey,
                                                    $worksheetId);
```

The $rowData parameter contains an array of column keys to data values. The method returns a Zend_Gdata_Spreadsheets_SpreadsheetsEntry object which represents the inserted row.

Spreadsheets inserts the new row immediately after the last row that appears in the list-based feed, which is to say immediately before the first entirely blank row.

Edit a Row

Once a Zend_Gdata_Spreadsheets_ListEntry object is fetched, its rows can be updated by using the updateRow method of the Spreadsheet service.

```
$updatedListEntry = $spreadsheetService->updateRow($oldListEntry,
                                                   $newRowData);
```

The $oldListEntry parameter contains the list entry to be updated. $newRowData contains an array of column keys to data values, to be used as the new row data. The method returns a Zend_Gdata_Spreadsheets_SpreadsheetsEntry object which represents the updated row.

Delete a Row

To delete a row, simply invoke deleteRow on the Zend_Gdata_Spreadsheets object with the existing entry to be deleted:

```
$spreadsheetService->deleteRow($listEntry);
```

Alternatively, you can call the delete method of the entry itself:

```
$listEntry->delete();
```

Interacting With Cell-based Feeds

In a cell-based feed, each entry represents a single cell.

Note that we don't recommend interacting with both a cell-based feed and a list-based feed for the same worksheet at the same time.

Get a Cell-based Feed

To retrieve a worksheet's cell feed, use the getCellFeed method of the Spreadsheets service.

```
$query = new Zend_Gdata_Spreadsheets_CellQuery();
$query->setSpreadsheetKey($spreadsheetKey);
$query->setWorksheetId($worksheetId);
$cellFeed = $spreadsheetService->getCellFeed($query);
```

The resulting Zend_Gdata_Spreadsheets_CellFeed object $cellFeed represents a response from the server. Among other things, this feed contains an array of Zend_Gdata_Spreadsheets_CellEntry objects ($cellFeed>entries), each of which represents a single cell in a worksheet. You can display this information:

```
foreach($cellFeed as $cellEntry) {
   $row = $cellEntry->cell->getRow();
   $col = $cellEntry->cell->getColumn();
   $val = $cellEntry->cell->getText();
   echo "$row, $col = $val\n";
}
```

Send a Cell Range Query

Suppose you wanted to retrieve the cells in the first column of a worksheet. You can request a cell feed containing only this column as follows:

```
$query = new Zend_Gdata_Spreadsheets_CellQuery();
$query->setMinCol(1);
$query->setMaxCol(1);
$query->setMinRow(2);
$feed = $spreadsheetService->getCellsFeed($query);
```

This requests all the data in column 1, starting with row 2.

Change Contents of a Cell

To modify the contents of a cell, call updateCell with the row, column, and new value of the cell.

```
$updatedCell = $spreadsheetService->updateCell($row,
                                               $col,
                                               $inputValue,
                                               $spreadsheetKey,
                                               $worksheetId);
```

The new data is placed in the specified cell in the worksheet. If the specified cell contains data already, it will be overwritten. Note: Use updateCell to change the data in a cell, even if the cell is empty.

Using Google Apps Provisioning

Google Apps is a service which allows domain administrators to offer their users managed access to Google services such as Mail, Calendar, and Docs & Spreadsheets. The Provisioning API offers a programmatic interface to configure this service. Specifically, this API allows administrators the ability to create, retrieve, update, and delete user accounts, nicknames, and email lists.

This library implements version 2.0 of the Provisioning API. Access to your account via the Provisioning API must be manually enabled for each domain using the Google Apps control panel. Only certain account types are able to enable this feature.

For more information on the Google Apps Provisioning API, including instructions for enabling API access, refer to the Provisioning API V2.0 Reference [http://code.google.com/apis/calendar/overview.html].

Authentication

The Provisioning API does not support authentication via AuthSub and anonymous access is not permitted. All HTTP connections must be authenticated using ClientAuth authentication.

Setting the current domain

In order to use the Provisioning API, the domain being administered needs to be specified in all request URIs. In order to ease development, this information is stored within both the Gapps service and query classes to use when constructing requests.

Setting the domain for the service class

To set the domain for requests made by the service class, either call `setDomain()` or specify the domain when instantiating the service class. For example:

```
$domain = "example.com";
$gdata = new Zend_Gdata_Gapps($client, $domain);
```

Setting the domain for query classes

Setting the domain for requests made by query classes is similar to setting it for the service class-either call `setDomain()` or specify the domain when creating the query. For example:

```
$domain = "example.com";
$query = new Zend_Gdata_Gapps_UserQuery($domain, $arg);
```

When using a service class factory method to create a query, the service class will automatically set the query's domain to match its own domain. As a result, it is not necessary to specify the domain as part of the constructor arguments.

```
$domain = "example.com";
$gdata = new Zend_Gdata_Gapps($client, $domain);
$query = $gdata->newUserQuery($arg);
```

Interacting with users

Each user account on a Google Apps hosted domain is represented as an instance of `Zend_Gdata_Gapps_UserEntry`. This class provides access to all account properties including name, username, password, access rights, and current quota.

Creating a user account

User accounts can be created by calling the `createUser()` convenience method:

```
$gdata->createUser('foo', 'Random', 'User', '••••••••');
```

Users can also be created by instantiating UserEntry, providing a username, given name, family name, and password, then calling `insertUser()` on a service object to upload the entry to the server.

```
$user = $gdata->newUserEntry();
$user->login = $gdata->newLogin();
$user->login->username = 'foo';
$user->login->password = '••••••••';
$user->name = $gdata->newName();
$user->name->givenName = 'Random';
$user->name->familyName = 'User';
$user = $gdata->insertUser($user);
```

The user's password should normally be provided as cleartext. Optionally, the password can be provided as an SHA-1 digest if login->passwordHashFunction is set to 'SHA-1'.

Retrieving a user account

Individual user accounts can be retrieved by calling the retrieveUser() convenience method. If the user is not found, null will be returned.

```
$user = $gdata->retrieveUser('foo');
echo 'Username: ' . $user->login->userName . "\n";
echo 'Given Name: ' . $user->login->givenName . "\n";
echo 'Family Name: ' . $user->login->familyName . "\n";
echo 'Suspended: ' . ($user->login->suspended ? 'Yes' : 'No') . "\n";
echo 'Admin: ' . ($user->login->admin ? 'Yes' : 'No') . "\n"
echo 'Must Change Password: ' .
    ($user->login->changePasswordAtNextLogin ? 'Yes' : 'No') . "\n";
echo 'Has Agreed To Terms: ' .
    ($user->login->agreedToTerms ? 'Yes' : 'No') . "\n";
```

Users can also be retrieved by creating an instance of Zend_Gdata_Gapps_UserQuery, setting its username property to equal the username of the user that is to be retrieved, and calling getUserEntry() on a service object with that query.

```
$query = $gdata->newUserQuery('foo');
$user = $gdata->getUserEntry($query);
echo 'Username: ' . $user->login->userName . "\n";
echo 'Given Name: ' . $user->login->givenName . "\n";
echo 'Family Name: ' . $user->login->familyName . "\n";
echo 'Suspended: ' . ($user->login->suspended ? 'Yes' : 'No') . "\n";
echo 'Admin: ' . ($user->login->admin ? 'Yes' : 'No') . "\n"
echo 'Must Change Password: ' .
    ($user->login->changePasswordAtNextLogin ? 'Yes' : 'No') . "\n";
echo 'Has Agreed To Terms: ' .
    ($user->login->agreedToTerms ? 'Yes' : 'No') . "\n";
```

If the specified user cannot be located a ServiceException will be thrown with an error code of Zend_Gdata_Gapps_Error::ENTITY_DOES_NOT_EXIST. ServiceExceptions will be covered in the section called "Handling errors".

Retrieving all users in a domain

To retrieve all users in a domain, call the retrieveAllUsers() convenience method.

```
$feed = $gdata->retrieveAllUsers();
foreach ($feed as $user) {
    echo " * " . $user->login->username . ' (' . $user->name->givenName .
        ' ' . $user->name->familyName . ")\n";
}
```

This will create a `Zend_Gdata_Gapps_UserFeed` object which holds each user on the domain.

Alternatively, call `getUserFeed()` with no options. Keep in mind that on larger domains this feed may be paged by the server. For more information on paging, see the section called "Working with Multi-page Feeds".

```
$feed = $gdata->getUserFeed();
foreach ($feed as $user) {
    echo " * " . $user->login->username . ' (' . $user->name->givenName .
        ' ' . $user->name->familyName . ")\n";
}
```

Updating a user account

The easiest way to update a user account is to retrieve the user as described in the previous sections, make any desired changes, then call `save()` on that user. Any changes made will be propagated to the server.

```
$user = $gdata->retrieveUser('foo');
$user->name->givenName = 'Foo';
$user->name->familyName = 'Bar';
$user = $user->save();
```

Resetting a user's password

A user's password can be reset to a new value by updating the `login->password` property.

```
$user = $gdata->retrieveUser('foo');
$user->login->password = '••••••••';
$user = $user->save();
```

Note that it is not possible to recover a password in this manner as stored passwords are not made available via the Provisioning API for security reasons.

Forcing a user to change their password

A user can be forced to change their password at their next login by setting the `login->changePasswordAtNextLogin` property to `true`.

```
$user = $gdata->retrieveUser('foo');
$user->login->changePasswordAtNextLogin = true;
$user = $user->save();
```

Similarly, this can be undone by setting the `login->changePasswordAtNextLogin` property to `false`.

Suspending a user account

Users can be restricted from logging in without deleting their user account by instead *suspending* their user account. Accounts can be suspended or restored by using the `suspendUser()` and `restoreUser()` convenience methods:

```
$gdata->suspendUser('foo');
$gdata->restoreUser('foo');
```

Alternatively, you can set the UserEntry's `login->suspended` property to `true`.

```
$user = $gdata->retrieveUser('foo');
$user->login->suspended = true;
$user = $user->save();
```

To restore the user's access, set the `login->suspended` property to `false`.

Granting administrative rights

Users can be granted the ability to administer your domain by setting their `login->admin` property to `true`.

```
$user = $gdata->retrieveUser('foo');
$user->login->admin = true;
$user = $user->save();
```

And as expected, setting a user's `login->admin` property to `false` revokes their administrative rights.

Deleting user accounts

Deleting a user account to which you already hold a UserEntry is a simple as calling `delete()` on that entry.

```
$user = $gdata->retrieveUser('foo');
$user->delete();
```

If you do not have access to a UserEntry object for an account, use the `deleteUser()` convenience method.

```
$gdata->deleteUser('foo');
```

Interacting with nicknames

Nicknames serve as email aliases for existing users. Each nickname contains precisely two key properties: its name and its owner. Any email addressed to a nickname is forwarded to the user who owns that nickname.

Nicknames are represented as an instances of `Zend_Gdata_Gapps_NicknameEntry`.

Creating a nickname

Nicknames can be created by calling the `createNickname()` convenience method:

```
$gdata->createNickname('foo', 'bar');
```

Nicknames can also be created by instantiating NicknameEntry, providing the nickname with a name and an owner, then calling `insertNickname()` on a service object to upload the entry to the server.

```
$nickname = $gdata->newNicknameEntry();
$nickname->login = $gdata->newLogin('foo');
$nickname->nickname = $gdata->newNickname('bar');
$nickname = $gdata->insertNickname($nickname);
```

Retrieving a nickname

Nicknames can be retrieved by calling the `retrieveNickname()` convenience method. This will return `null` if a user is not found.

```
$nickname = $gdata->retrieveNickname('bar');
echo 'Nickname: ' . $nickname->nickname->name . "\n";
echo 'Owner: ' . $nickname->login->username . "\n";
```

Individual nicknames can also be retrieved by creating an instance of `Zend_Gdata_Gapps_NicknameQuery`, setting its nickname property to equal the nickname that is to be retrieved, and calling `getNicknameEntry()` on a service object with that query.

```
$query = $gdata->newNicknameQuery('bar');
$nickname = $gdata->getNicknameEntry($query);
echo 'Nickname: ' . $nickname->nickname->name . "\n";
echo 'Owner: ' . $nickname->login->username . "\n";
```

As with users, if no corresponding nickname is found a ServiceException will be thrown with an error code of `Zend_Gdata_Gapps_Error::ENTITY_DOES_NOT_EXIST`. Again, these will be discussed in the section called "Handling errors".

Retrieving all nicknames for a user

To retrieve all nicknames associated with a given user, call the convenience method `retrieveNicknames()`.

```
$feed = $gdata->retrieveNicknames('foo');
foreach ($feed as $nickname) {
    echo ' * ' . $nickname->nickname->name . "\n";
}
```

This will create a `Zend_Gdata_Gapps_NicknameFeed` object which holds each nickname associated with the specified user.

Alternatively, create a new `Zend_Gdata_Gapps_NicknameQuery`, set its username property to the desired user, and submit the query by calling `getNicknameFeed()` on a service object.

```
$query = $gdata->newNicknameQuery();
$query->setUsername('foo');
$feed = $gdata->getNicknameFeed($query);
foreach ($feed as $nickname) {
    echo ' * ' . $nickname->nickname->name . "\n";
}
```

Retrieving all nicknames in a domain

To retrieve all nicknames in a feed, simply call the convenience method `retrieveAllNicknames()`

```
$feed = $gdata->retrieveAllNicknames();
foreach ($feed as $nickname) {
    echo ' * ' . $nickname->nickname->name . ' => ' .
        $nickname->login->username . "\n";
}
```

This will create a `Zend_Gdata_Gapps_NicknameFeed` object which holds each nickname on the domain.

Alternatively, call `getNicknameFeed()` on a service object with no arguments.

```
$feed = $gdata->getNicknameFeed();
foreach ($feed as $nickname) {
    echo ' * ' . $nickname->nickname->name . ' => ' .
        $nickname->login->username . "\n";
}
```

Deleting a nickname

Deleting a nickname to which you already hold a NicknameEntry for is a simple as calling `delete()` on that entry.

```
$nickname = $gdata->retrieveNickname('bar');
$nickname->delete();
```

For nicknames which you do not hold a NicknameEntry for, use the `deleteNickname()` convenience method.

```
$gdata->deleteNickname('bar');
```

Interacting with email lists

Email lists allow several users to retrieve email addressed to a single email address. Users do not need to be a member of this domain in order to subscribe to an email list provided their complete email address (including domain) is used.

Each email list on a domain is represented as an instance of `Zend_Gdata_Gapps_EmailListEntry`.

Creating an email list

Email lists can be created by calling the `createEmailList()` convenience method:

```
$gdata->createEmailList('friends');
```

Email lists can also be created by instantiating EmailListEntry, providing a name for the list, then calling `insertEmailList()` on a service object to upload the entry to the server.

```
$list = $gdata->newEmailListEntry();
$list->emailList = $gdata->newEmailList('friends');
$list = $gdata->insertEmailList($list);
```

Retrieving all email lists to which a recipient is subscribed

To retrieve all email lists to which a particular recipient is subscribed, call the `retrieveEmailLists()` convenience method:

```
$feed = $gdata->retrieveEmailLists('baz@somewhere.com');
foreach ($feed as $list) {
    echo ' * ' . $list->emailList->name . "\n";
}
```

This will create a `Zend_Gdata_Gapps_EmailListFeed` object which holds each email list associated with the specified recipient.

Alternatively, create a new `Zend_Gdata_Gapps_EmailListQuery`, set its recipient property to the desired email address, and submit the query by calling `getEmailListFeed()` on a service object.

```
$query = $gdata->newEmailListQuery();
$query->setRecipient('baz@somewhere.com');
$feed = $gdata->getEmailListFeed($query);
foreach ($feed as $list) {
    echo ' * ' . $list->emailList->name . "\n";
}
```

Retrieving all email lists in a domain

To retrieve all email lists in a domain, call the convenience method `retrieveAllEmailLists()`.

```
$feed = $gdata->retrieveAllEmailLists();
foreach ($feed as $list) {
    echo ' * ' . $list->emailList->name . "\n";
}
```

This will create a `Zend_Gdata_Gapps_EmailListFeed` object which holds each email list on the domain.

Alternatively, call `getEmailListFeed()` on a service object with no arguments.

```
$feed = $gdata->getEmailListFeed();
foreach ($feed as $list) {
    echo ' * ' . $list->emailList->name . "\n";
}
```

Deleting an email list

To delete an email list, call the deleteEmailList() convenience method:

```
$gdata->deleteEmailList('friends');
```

Interacting with email list recipients

Each recipient subscribed to an email list is represented by an instance of `Zend_Gdata_Gapps_EmailListRecipient`. Through this class, individual recipients can be added and removed from email lists.

Adding a recipient to an email list

To add a recipient to an email list, simply call the `addRecipientToEmailList()` convenience method:

```
$gdata->addRecipientToEmailList('bar@somewhere.com', 'friends');
```

Retrieving the list of subscribers to an email list

The convenience method `retrieveAllRecipients()` can be used to retrieve the list of subscribers to an email list:

```
$feed = $gdata->retrieveAllRecipients('friends');
foreach ($feed as $recipient) {
    echo ' * ' . $recipient->who->email . "\n";
}
```

Alternatively, construct a new EmailListRecipientQuery, set its emailListName property to match the desired email list, and call `getEmailListRecipientFeed()` on a service object.

```
$query = $gdata->newEmailListRecipientQuery();
$query->setEmailListName('friends');
$feed = $gdata->getEmailListRecipientFeed($query);
foreach ($feed as $recipient) {
    echo ' * ' . $recipient->who->email . "\n";
}
```

This will create a `Zend_Gdata_Gapps_EmailListRecipientFeed` object which holds each recipient for the selected email list.

Removing a recipient from an email list

To remove a recipient from an email list, call the `removeRecipientFromEmailList()` convenience method:

```
$gdata->removeRecipientFromEmailList('baz@somewhere.com', 'friends');
```

Handling errors

In addition to the standard suite of exceptions thrown by `Zend_Gdata`, requests using the Provisioning API may also throw a `Zend_Gdata_Gapps_ServiceException`. These exceptions indicate that a API specific error occurred which prevents the request from completing.

Each ServiceException instance may hold one or more Error objects. Each of these objects contains an error code, reason, and (optionally) the input which triggered the exception. A complete list of known error codes is provided in the Zend Framework API documentation under `Zend_Gdata_Gapps_Error`. Additionally, the authoritative error list is available online at Google Apps Provisioning API V2.0 Reference: Appendix D [http://code.google.com/apis/apps/gdata_provisioning_api_v2.0_reference.html#appendix_d].

While the complete list of errors received is available within ServiceException as an array by calling `getErrors()`, often it is convenient to know if one specific error occurred. For these cases the presence of an error can be determined by calling `hasError()`.

The following example demonstrates how to detect if a requested resource doesn't exist and handle the fault gracefully:

```
function retrieveUser ($username) {
    $query = $gdata->newUserQuery($username);
    try {
        $user = $gdata->getUserEntry($query);
    } catch (Zend_Gdata_Gapps_ServiceException $e) {
        // Set the user to null if not found
        if ($e->hasError(Zend_Gdata_Gapps_Error::ENTITY_DOES_NOT_EXIST)) {
            $user = null;
        } else {
```

```
            throw $e;
        }
    }
    return $user;
}
```

Using Google Base

The Google Base data API is designed to enable developers to do two things:

- Query Google Base data to create applications and mashups.

- Input and manage Google Base items programmatically.

There are two item feeds: snippets feed and customer items feeds. The snippets feed contains all Google Base data and is available to anyone to query against without a need for authentication. The customer items feed is a customer-specific subset of data and only a customer/owner can access this feed to insert, update, or delete their own data. Queries are constructed the same way against both types of feeds.

See http://code.google.com/apis/base [http://code.google.com/apis/base/] for more information about the Google Base API.

Connect To The Base Service

The Google Base API, like all GData APIs, is based off of the Atom Publishing Protocol (APP), an XML based format for managing web-based resources. Traffic between a client and the Google Base servers occurs over HTTP and allows for both authenticated and unauthenticated connections.

Before any transactions can occur, this connection needs to be made. Creating a connection to the base servers involves two steps: creating an HTTP client and binding a Zend_Gdata_Gbase service instance to that client.

Authentication

The Google Base API allows access to both public and private base feeds. Public feeds do not require authentication, but are read-only and offer reduced functionality. Private feeds offers the most complete functionality but requires an authenticated connection to the base servers. There are three authentication schemes that are supported by Google Base:

- *ClientAuth* provides direct username/password authentication to the base servers. Since this scheme requires that users provide your application with their password, this authentication is only recommended when other authentication schemes are insufficient.

- *AuthSub* allows authentication to the base servers via a Google proxy server. This provides the same level of convenience as ClientAuth but without the security risk, making this an ideal choice for web-based applications.

The Zend_Gdata library provides support for all three authentication schemes. The rest of this chapter will assume that you are familiar the authentication schemes available and how to create an appropriate authenticated connection. For more information, please see section the section called "Google Data Client Authentication". or the Authentication Overview in the Google Data API Developer's Guide [http://code.google.com/apis/gdata/auth.html].

Create A Service Instance

In order to interact with Google Base, this library provides the Zend_Gdata_Gbase service class. This class provides a common interface to the Google Data and Atom Publishing Protocol models and assists in marshaling requests to and from the base servers.

Once deciding on an authentication scheme, the next step is to create an instance of
Zend_Gdata_Gbase . This class takes in an instance of Zend_Http_Client as a single
argument. This provides an interface for AuthSub and ClientAuth authentication, as both of these
creation of a special authenticated HTTP client. If no arguments are provided, an unauthenticated
instance of Zend_Http_Client will be automatically created.

The example below shows how to create a Base service class using ClientAuth authentication:

```
// Parameters for ClientAuth authentication
$service = Zend_Gdata_Gbase::AUTH_SERVICE_NAME;
$user = "sample.user@gmail.com";
$pass = "pa$$w0rd";
// Create an authenticated HTTP client
$client = Zend_Gdata_ClientLogin::getHttpClient($user, $pass, $service);
// Create an instance of the Base service
$service = new Zend_Gdata_Gbase($client);
```

A Base service using AuthSub can be created in a similar, though slightly more lengthy fashion:

```
/*
 * Retrieve the current URL so that the AuthSub server knows where to
 * redirect the user after authentication is complete.
 */
function getCurrentUrl()
{
    global $_SERVER;
    // Filter php_self to avoid a security vulnerability.
    $php_request_uri =
        htmlentities(substr($_SERVER['REQUEST_URI'],
                            0,
                            strcspn($_SERVER['REQUEST_URI'], "\n\r")),
                     ENT_QUOTES);
    if (isset($_SERVER['HTTPS']) &&
        strtolower($_SERVER['HTTPS']) == 'on') {
        $protocol = 'https://';
    } else {
        $protocol = 'http://';
    }
    $host = $_SERVER['HTTP_HOST'];
    if ($_SERVER['HTTP_PORT'] != '' &&
        (($protocol == 'http://' && $_SERVER['HTTP_PORT'] != '80') ||
         ($protocol == 'https://' && $_SERVER['HTTP_PORT'] != '443'))) {
        $port = ':' . $_SERVER['HTTP_PORT'];
    } else {
        $port = '';
    }
    return $protocol . $host . $port . $php_request_uri;
}
/**
 * Obtain an AuthSub authenticated HTTP client, redirecting the user
 * to the AuthSub server to login if necessary.
 */
function getAuthSubHttpClient()
{
    global $_SESSION, $_GET;
    // If there is no AuthSub session or one-time token waiting for us,
    // redirect the user to the AuthSub server to get one.
    if (!isset($_SESSION['sessionToken']) && !isset($_GET['token'])) {
        // Parameters to give to AuthSub server
        $next = getCurrentUrl();
        $scope = "http://www.google.com/base/feeds/items/";
        $secure = false;
```

```
        $session = true;
        // Redirect the user to the AuthSub server to sign in
        $authSubUrl = Zend_Gdata_AuthSub::getAuthSubTokenUri($next,
                                                             $scope,
                                                             $secure,
                                                             $session);

        header("HTTP/1.0 307 Temporary redirect");
        header("Location: " . $authSubUrl);
        exit();
    }
    // Convert an AuthSub one-time token into a session token if needed
    if (!isset($_SESSION['sessionToken']) && isset($_GET['token'])) {
        $_SESSION['sessionToken'] =
            Zend_Gdata_AuthSub::getAuthSubSessionToken($_GET['token']);
    }
    // At this point we are authenticated via AuthSub and can obtain an
    // authenticated HTTP client instance
    // Create an authenticated HTTP client
    $client = Zend_Gdata_AuthSub::getHttpClient($_SESSION['sessionToken']);
    return $client;
}
// -> Script execution begins here <-
// Make sure http://code.google.com/apis/gdata/reference.html#Queriesthat
// the user has a valid session, so we can record the
// AuthSub session token once it is available.
session_start();
// Create an instance of the Base service, redirecting the user
// to the AuthSub server if necessary.
$service = new Zend_Gdata_Gbase(getAuthSubHttpClient());
```

Finally, an unauthenticated server can be created for use with snippets feeds:

```
// Create an instance of the Base service using an unauthenticated HTTP client
$service = new Zend_Gdata_Gbase();
```

Retrieve Items

You can query customer items feed or snippets feed to retrieve items. It involves two steps, sending a query and iterating through the returned feed.

Send a Structured Query

You can send a structured query to retrieve items from your own customer items feed or from the public snippets feed.

When retrieving items using the Base API, specially constructed query URLs are used to describe what events should be returned. The Zend_Gdata_Gbase_ItemQuery and Zend_Gdata_Gbase_SnippetQuery classes simplify this task by automatically constructing a query URL based on provided parameters.

Query Customer Items Feed

To execute a query against the customer items feed, invoke newItemQuery() and getGbaseItemFeed() methods:

```
$service = new Zend_Gdata_Gbase($client);
$query = $service->newItemQuery();
$query->setBq('[title:Programming]');
$query->setOrderBy('modification_time');
$query->setSortOrder('descending');
```

```
$query->setMaxResults('5');
$feed = $service->getGbaseItemFeed($query);
```

A full list of these parameters is available at the Query parameters section [http://code.google.com/apis/base/items-feed.html#QueParameters] of the Customer Items Feed documentation.

Query Snippets Feed

To execute a query against the public snippets feed, invoke newSnippetQuery() and getGbaseSnippetFeed() methods:

```
$service = new Zend_Gdata_Gbase();
$query = $service->newSnippetQuery();
$query->setBq('[title:Programming]');
$query->setOrderBy('modification_time');
$query->setSortOrder('descending');
$query->setMaxResults('5');
$feed = $service->getGbaseSnippetFeed($query);
```

A full list of these parameters is available at the Query parameters section [http://code.google.com/apis/base/snippets-feed.html#Parameters] of the Snippets Feed documentation.

Iterate through the Items

Google Base items can contain item-specific attributes such as <g:main_ingredient> and <g:weight>.

To iterate through all attributes of a given item, invoke getGbaseAttributes() and iterate through the results:

```
foreach ($feed->entries as $entry) {
  // Get all attributes and print out the name and text value of each
  // attribute
  $baseAttributes = $entry->getGbaseAttributes();
  foreach ($baseAttributes as $attr) {
    echo "Attribute " . $attr->name . " : " . $attr->text . "<br>";
  }
}
```

Or, you can look for specific attribute name and iterate through the results that match:

```
foreach ($feed->entries as $entry) {
  // Print all main ingredients <g:main_ingredient>
  $baseAttributes = $entry->getGbaseAttribute("main_ingredient");
  foreach ($baseAttributes as $attr) {
    echo "Main ingredient: " . $attr->text . "<br>";
  }
}
```

Insert, Update, and Delete Customer Items

A customer/owner can access his own Customer Items feed to insert, update, or delete their items. These operations do not apply to the public snippets feed.

You can test a feed operation before it is actually executed by setting the dry-run flag ($dryRun) to true. Once you are sure that you want to submit the data, set it to false to execute the operation.

Insert an Item

Items can be added by using the `insertGbaseItem()` method for the Base service:

```
$service = new Zend_Gdata_Gbase($client);
$newEntry = $service->newItemEntry();
// Add title
$title = "PHP Developer Handbook";
$newEntry->title = $service->newTitle(trim($title));
// Add some content
$content = "Essential handbook for PHP developers.";
$newEntry->content = $service->newContent($content);
$newEntry->content->type = 'text';
// Define product type
$itemType = "Products";
$newEntry->itemType = $itemType;
// Add item specific attributes
$newEntry->addGbaseAttribute("product_type", "book", "text");
$newEntry->addGbaseAttribute("price", "12.99 USD", "floatUnit");
$newEntry->addGbaseAttribute("quantity", "10", "int");
$newEntry->addGbaseAttribute("weight", "2.2 lbs", "numberUnit");
$newEntry->addGbaseAttribute("condition", "New", "text");
$newEntry->addGbaseAttribute("author", "John Doe", "text");
$newEntry->addGbaseAttribute("edition", "First Edition", "text");
$newEntry->addGbaseAttribute("pages", "253", "number");
$newEntry->addGbaseAttribute("publisher", "My Press", "text");
$newEntry->addGbaseAttribute("year", "2007", "number");
$newEntry->addGbaseAttribute("payment_accepted", "Google Checkout", "text");
$dryRun = true;
$createdEntry = $service->insertGbaseItem($newEntry, $dryRun);
```

Modify an Item

You can update each attribute element of an item as you iterate through them:

```
// Update the title
$newTitle = "PHP Developer Handbook Second Edition";
$entry->title = $service->newTitle($newTitle);
// Find <g:price> attribute and update the price
$baseAttributes = $entry->getGbaseAttribute("price");
if (is_object($baseAttributes[0])) {
  $newPrice = "16.99 USD";
  $baseAttributes[0]->text = $newPrice;
}
// Find <g:pages> attribute and update the number of pages
$baseAttributes = $entry->getGbaseAttribute("pages");
if (is_object($baseAttributes[0])) {
  $newPages = "278";
  $baseAttributes[0]->text = $newPages;
  // Update the attribute type from "number" to "int"
  if ($baseAttributes[0]->type == "number") {
    $newType = "int";
    $baseAttributes[0]->type = $newType;
  }
}
// Remove <g:label> attributes
$baseAttributes = $entry->getGbaseAttribute("label");
foreach ($baseAttributes as $note) {
  $entry->removeGbaseAttribute($note);
}
// Add new attributes
```

```
$entry->addGbaseAttribute("note", "PHP 5", "text");
$entry->addGbaseAttribute("note", "Web Programming", "text");
// Save the changes by invoking save() on the entry object itself
$dryRun = true;
$entry->save($dryRun);
// Or, save the changes by calling updateGbaseItem() on the service object
// $dryRun = true;
// $service->updateGbaseItem($entry, $dryRun);
```

After making the changes, either invoke save($dryRun) method on the Zend_Gdata_Gbase_ItemEntry object or call updateGbaseItem($entry, $dryRun) method on the Zend_Gdata_Gbase object to save the changes.

Delete an Item

You can remove an item by calling deleteGbaseItem() method:

```
$dryRun = false;
$service->deleteGbaseItem($entry, $dryRun);
```

Alternatively, you can invoke delete() on the Zend_Gdata_Gbase_ItemEntry object:

```
$dryRun = false;
$entry->delete($dryRun);
```

Using Picasa Web Albums

Picasa Web Albums is a service which allows users to maintain albums of their own pictures, and browse the albums and pictures of others. The API offers a programmatic interface to this service, allowing users to add to, update, and remove from their albums, as well as providing the ability to tag and comment on photos.

Access to public albums and photos is not restricted by account, however, a user must be logged in for non-read-only access.

For more information on the API, including instructions for enabling API access, refer to the Picasa Web Albums Data API Overview [http://code.google.com/apis/picasaweb/overview.html].

Authentication

The API provides authentication via AuthSub (recommended) and ClientAuth. HTTP connections must be authenticated for write support, but non-authenticated connections have read-only access.

Connecting To The Service

The Picasa Web Albums API, like all GData APIs, is based off of the Atom Publishing Protocol (APP), an XML based format for managing web-based resources. Traffic between a client and the servers occurs over HTTP and allows for both authenticated and unauthenticated connections.

Before any transactions can occur, this connection needs to be made. Creating a connection to the Picasa servers involves two steps: creating an HTTP client and binding a Zend_Gdata_Photos service instance to that client.

Authentication

The Google Picasa API allows access to both public and private photo feeds. Public feeds do not require authentication, but are read-only and offer reduced functionality. Private feeds offers the most complete functionality but requires an authenticated connection to the Picasa servers. There are three authentication schemes that are supported by Google Picasa :

- *ClientAuth* provides direct username/password authentication to the Picasa servers. Since this scheme requires that users provide your application with their password, this authentication is only recommended when other authentication schemes are insufficient.

- *AuthSub* allows authentication to the Picasa servers via a Google proxy server. This provides the same level of convenience as ClientAuth but without the security risk, making this an ideal choice for web-based applications.

The Zend_Gdata library provides support for both authentication schemes. The rest of this chapter will assume that you are familiar the authentication schemes available and how to create an appropriate authenticated connection. For more information, please see section the Authentication section of this manual or the Authentication Overview in the Google Data API Developer's Guide [http://code.google.com/apis/gdata/auth.html].

Creating A Service Instance

In order to interact with the servers, this library provides the Zend_Gdata_Photos service class. This class provides a common interface to the Google Data and Atom Publishing Protocol models and assists in marshaling requests to and from the servers.

Once deciding on an authentication scheme, the next step is to create an instance of Zend_Gdata_Photos. The class constructor takes an instance of Zend_Http_Client as a single argument. This provides an interface for AuthSub and ClientAuth authentication, as both of these require creation of a special authenticated HTTP client. If no arguments are provided, an unauthenticated instance of Zend_Http_Client will be automatically created.

The example below shows how to create a service class using ClientAuth authentication:

```
// Parameters for ClientAuth authentication
$service = Zend_Gdata_Photos::AUTH_SERVICE_NAME;
$user = "sample.user@gmail.com";
$pass = "pa$$w0rd";
// Create an authenticated HTTP client
$client = Zend_Gdata_ClientLogin::getHttpClient($user, $pass, $service);
// Create an instance of the service
$service = new Zend_Gdata_Photos($client);
```

A service instance using AuthSub can be created in a similar, though slightly more lengthy fashion:

```
session_start();
/**
 * Returns the full URL of the current page, based upon env variables
 *
 * Env variables used:
 * $_SERVER['HTTPS'] = (on|off|)
 * $_SERVER['HTTP_HOST'] = value of the Host: header
 * $_SERVER['SERVER_PORT'] = port number (only used if not http/80,
        https/443)
 * $_SERVER['REQUEST_URI'] = the URI after the method of the HTTP request
 *
 * @return string Current URL
 */
function getCurrentUrl()
{
    global $_SERVER;
    /**
     * Filter php_self to avoid a security vulnerability.
```

```
     */
    $php_request_uri = htmlentities(substr($_SERVER['REQUEST_URI'], 0,
    strcspn($_SERVER['REQUEST_URI'], "\n\r")), ENT_QUOTES);
    if (isset($_SERVER['HTTPS']) && strtolower($_SERVER['HTTPS']) ==
        'on') {
        $protocol = 'https://';
    } else {
        $protocol = 'http://';
    }
    $host = $_SERVER['HTTP_HOST'];
    if ($_SERVER['SERVER_PORT'] != '' &&
        (($protocol == 'http://' && $_SERVER['SERVER_PORT'] != '80') ||
        ($protocol == 'https://' && $_SERVER['SERVER_PORT'] != '443'))) {
            $port = ':' . $_SERVER['SERVER_PORT'];
    } else {
        $port = '';
    }
    return $protocol . $host . $port . $php_request_uri;
}
/**
 * Returns the AuthSub URL which the user must visit to authenticate
     requests
 * from this application.
 *
 * Uses getCurrentUrl() to get the next URL which the user will be
     redirected
 * to after successfully authenticating with the Google service.
 *
 * @return string AuthSub URL
 */
function getAuthSubUrl()
{
    $next = getCurrentUrl();
    $scope = 'http://picasaweb.google.com/data';
    $secure = false;
    $session = true;
    return Zend_Gdata_AuthSub::getAuthSubTokenUri($next, $scope, $secure,
        $session);
}
/**
 * Returns a HTTP client object with the appropriate headers for
     communicating
 * with Google using AuthSub authentication.
 *
 * Uses the $_SESSION['sessionToken'] to store the AuthSub session token
 * after it is obtained. The single use token supplied in the URL when
 * redirected after the user succesfully authenticated to Google is retrieved
 * from the $_GET['token'] variable.
 *
 * @return Zend_Http_Client
 */
function getAuthSubHttpClient()
{
    global $_SESSION, $_GET;
    if (!isset($_SESSION['sessionToken']) && isset($_GET['token'])) {
        $_SESSION['sessionToken'] =
            Zend_Gdata_AuthSub::getAuthSubSessionToken($_GET['token']);
    }
    $client = Zend_Gdata_AuthSub::getHttpClient($_SESSION['sessionToken']);
    return $client;
}
/**
 * Create a new instance of the service, redirecting the user
 * to the AuthSub server if necessary.
```

```
 */
$service = new Zend_Gdata_Photos(getAuthSubHttpClient());
```

Finally, an unauthenticated server can be created for use with public feeds:

```
// Create an instance of the service using an unauthenticated HTTP client
$service = new Zend_Gdata_Photos();
```

Understanding and Constructing Queries

The primary method to request data from the service is by constructing a query. There are query classes for each of the following types:

- *User* is used to specify the user whose data is being searched for, and is specified as a username. If no user is provided, "default" will be used instead to indicate the currently authenticated user (if authenticated).

- *Album* is used to specify the album which is being searched for, and is specified as either an id, or an album name.

- *Photo* is used to specify the photo which is being searched for, and is specified as an id.

A new UserQuery can be constructed as followed:

```
$service = Zend_Gdata_Photos::AUTH_SERVICE_NAME;
$client = Zend_Gdata_ClientLogin::getHttpClient($user, $pass, $service);
$service = new Zend_Gdata_Photos($client);
$query = new Zend_Gdata_Photos_UserQuery();
$query->setUser("sample.user");
```

For each query, a number of parameters limiting the search can be requested, or specified, with get(Parameter) and set(Parameter), respectively. They are as follows:

- *Projection* sets the format of the data returned in the feed, as either "api" or "base". Normally, "api" is desired. The default is "api".

- *Type* sets the type of element to be returned, as either "feed" or "entry". The default is "feed".

- *Access* sets the visibility of items to be returned, as "all", "public", or "private". The default is "all". Non-public elements will only be returned if the query is searching for the authenticated user.

- *Tag* sets a tag filter for returned items. When a tag is set, only items tagged with this value will return.

- *Kind* sets the kind of elements to return. When kind is specified, only entries that match this value will be returned.

- *ImgMax* sets the maximum image size for entries returned. Only image entries smaller than this value will be returned.

- *Thumbsize* sets the thumbsize of entries that are returned. Any retrieved entry will have a thumbsize equal to this value.

- *User* sets the user whose data is being searched for. The default is "default".

- *AlbumId* sets the id of the album being searched for. This element only applies to album and photo queries. In the case of photo queries, this specifies the album that contains the requested photo. The album id is mutually exclusive with the album's name. Setting one unsets the other.

- *AlbumName* sets the name of the album being searched for. This element only applies to the album and photo queries. In the case of photo queries, this specifies the album that contains the requested photo. The album name is mutually exclusive with the album's id. Setting one unsets the other.

- *PhotoId* sets the id of the photo being searched for. This element only applies to photo queries.

Retrieving Feeds And Entries

The service has functions to retrieve a feed, or individual entries, for users, albums, and individual photos.

Retrieving A User

The service supports retrieving a user feed and list of the user's content. If the requested user is also the authenticated user, entries marked as "hidden" will also be returned.

The user feed can be accessed by passing the username to the getUserFeed method:

```
$service = Zend_Gdata_Photos::AUTH_SERVICE_NAME;
$client = Zend_Gdata_ClientLogin::getHttpClient($user, $pass, $service);
$service = new Zend_Gdata_Photos($client);
try {
    $userFeed = $service->getUserFeed("sample.user");
} catch (Zend_Gdata_App_Exception $e) {
    echo "Error: " . $e->getMessage();
}
```

Or, the feed can be accessed by constructing a query, first:

```
$service = Zend_Gdata_Photos::AUTH_SERVICE_NAME;
$client = Zend_Gdata_ClientLogin::getHttpClient($user, $pass, $service);
$service = new Zend_Gdata_Photos($client);
$query = new Zend_Gdata_Photos_UserQuery();
$query->setUser("sample.user");
try {
    $userFeed = $service->getUserFeed(null, $query);
} catch (Zend_Gdata_App_Exception $e) {
    echo "Error: " . $e->getMessage();
}
```

Constructing a query also provides the ability to request a user entry object:

```
$service = Zend_Gdata_Photos::AUTH_SERVICE_NAME;
$client = Zend_Gdata_ClientLogin::getHttpClient($user, $pass, $service);
$service = new Zend_Gdata_Photos($client);
$query = new Zend_Gdata_Photos_UserQuery();
$query->setUser("sample.user");
$query->setType("entry");
try {
    $userEntry = $service->getUserEntry($query);
} catch (Zend_Gdata_App_Exception $e) {
    echo "Error: " . $e->getMessage();
}
```

Retrieving An Album

The service supports retrieving an album feed and a list of the album's content.

The album feed is accessed by constructing a query object and passing it to getAlbumFeed:

```
$service = Zend_Gdata_Photos::AUTH_SERVICE_NAME;
$client = Zend_Gdata_ClientLogin::getHttpClient($user, $pass, $service);
$service = new Zend_Gdata_Photos($client);
$query = new Zend_Gdata_Photos_AlbumQuery();
$query->setUser("sample.user");
$query->setAlbumId("1");
try {
    $albumFeed = $service->getAlbumFeed($query);
} catch (Zend_Gdata_App_Exception $e) {
    echo "Error: " . $e->getMessage();
}
```

Alternatively, the query object can be given an album name with setAlbumName. Setting the album name is mutually exclusive with setting the album id, and setting one will unset the other.

Constructing a query also provides the ability to request an album entry object:

```
$service = Zend_Gdata_Photos::AUTH_SERVICE_NAME;
$client = Zend_Gdata_ClientLogin::getHttpClient($user, $pass, $service);
$service = new Zend_Gdata_Photos($client);
$query = new Zend_Gdata_Photos_AlbumQuery();
$query->setUser("sample.user");
$query->setAlbumId("1");
$query->setType("entry");
try {
    $albumEntry = $service->getAlbumEntry($query);
} catch (Zend_Gdata_App_Exception $e) {
    echo "Error: " . $e->getMessage();
}
```

Retrieving A Photo

The service supports retrieving a photo feed and a list of associated comments and tags.

The photo feed is accessed by constructing a query object and passing it to getPhotoFeed:

```
$service = Zend_Gdata_Photos::AUTH_SERVICE_NAME;
$client = Zend_Gdata_ClientLogin::getHttpClient($user, $pass, $service);
$service = new Zend_Gdata_Photos($client);
$query = new Zend_Gdata_Photos_PhotoQuery();
$query->setUser("sample.user");
$query->setAlbumId("1");
$query->setPhotoId("100");
try {
    $photoFeed = $service->getPhotoFeed($query);
} catch (Zend_Gdata_App_Exception $e) {
    echo "Error: " . $e->getMessage();
}
```

Constructing a query also provides the ability to request a photo entry object:

```
$service = Zend_Gdata_Photos::AUTH_SERVICE_NAME;
$client = Zend_Gdata_ClientLogin::getHttpClient($user, $pass, $service);
$service = new Zend_Gdata_Photos($client);
$query = new Zend_Gdata_Photos_PhotoQuery();
$query->setUser("sample.user");
$query->setAlbumId("1");
$query->setPhotoId("100");
$query->setType("entry");
```

```
try {
    $photoEntry = $service->getPhotoEntry($query);
} catch (Zend_Gdata_App_Exception $e) {
    echo "Error: " . $e->getMessage();
}
```

Retrieving A Comment

The service supports retrieving comments from a feed of a different type. By setting a query to return a kind of "comment", a feed request can return comments associated with a specific user, album, or photo.

Performing an action on each of the comments on a given photo can be accomplished as follows:

```
$service = Zend_Gdata_Photos::AUTH_SERVICE_NAME;
$client = Zend_Gdata_ClientLogin::getHttpClient($user, $pass, $service);
$service = new Zend_Gdata_Photos($client);
$query = new Zend_Gdata_Photos_PhotoQuery();
$query->setUser("sample.user");
$query->setAlbumId("1");
$query->setPhotoId("100");
$query->setKind("comment");
try {
    $photoFeed = $service->getPhotoFeed($query);
    foreach ($photoFeed as $entry) {
        if ($entry instanceof Zend_Gdata_Photos_CommentEntry) {
            // Do something with the comment
        }
    }
} catch (Zend_Gdata_App_Exception $e) {
    echo "Error: " . $e->getMessage();
}
```

Retrieving A Tag

The service supports retrieving tags from a feed of a different type. By setting a query to return a kind of "tag", a feed request can return tags associated with a specific photo.

Performing an action on each of the tags on a given photo can be accomplished as follows:

```
$service = Zend_Gdata_Photos::AUTH_SERVICE_NAME;
$client = Zend_Gdata_ClientLogin::getHttpClient($user, $pass, $service);
$service = new Zend_Gdata_Photos($client);
$query = new Zend_Gdata_Photos_PhotoQuery();
$query->setUser("sample.user");
$query->setAlbumId("1");
$query->setPhotoId("100");
$query->setKind("tag");
try {
    $photoFeed = $service->getPhotoFeed($query);
    foreach ($photoFeed as $entry) {
        if ($entry instanceof Zend_Gdata_Photos_TagEntry) {
            // Do something with the tag
        }
    }
} catch (Zend_Gdata_App_Exception $e) {
    echo "Error: " . $e->getMessage();
}
```

Creating Entries

The service has functions to create albums, photos, comments, and tags.

Creating An Album

The service supports creating a new album for an authenticated user:

```
$service = Zend_Gdata_Photos::AUTH_SERVICE_NAME;
$client = Zend_Gdata_ClientLogin::getHttpClient($user, $pass, $service);
$service = new Zend_Gdata_Photos($client);
$entry = new Zend_Gdata_Photos_AlbumEntry();
$entry->setTitle($service->newTitle("test album"));
$service->insertAlbumEntry($entry);
```

Creating A Photo

The service supports creating a new photo for an authenticated user:

```
$service = Zend_Gdata_Photos::AUTH_SERVICE_NAME;
$client = Zend_Gdata_ClientLogin::getHttpClient($user, $pass, $service);
$service = new Zend_Gdata_Photos($client);
// $photo is the name of a file uploaded via an HTML form
$fd = $service->newMediaFileSource($photo["tmp_name"]);
$fd->setContentType($photo["type"]);
$entry = new Zend_Gdata_Photos_PhotoEntry();
$entry->setMediaSource($fd);
$entry->setTitle($service->newTitle($photo["name"]));
$albumQuery = new Zend_Gdata_Photos_AlbumQuery;
$albumQuery->setUser("sample.user");
$albumQuery->setAlbumId("1");
$albumEntry = $service->getAlbumEntry($albumQuery);
$service->insertPhotoEntry($entry, $albumEntry);
```

Creating A Comment

The service supports creating a new comment for a photo:

```
$service = Zend_Gdata_Photos::AUTH_SERVICE_NAME;
$client = Zend_Gdata_ClientLogin::getHttpClient($user, $pass, $service);
$service = new Zend_Gdata_Photos($client);
$entry = new Zend_Gdata_Photos_CommentEntry();
$entry->setTitle($service->newTitle("comment"));
$entry->setContent($service->newContent("comment"));
$photoQuery = new Zend_Gdata_Photos_PhotoQuery;
$photoQuery->setUser("sample.user");
$photoQuery->setAlbumId("1");
$photoQuery->setPhotoId("100");
$photoQuery->setType('entry');
$photoEntry = $service->getPhotoEntry($photoQuery);
$service->insertCommentEntry($entry, $photoEntry);
```

Creating A Tag

The service supports creating a new tag for a photo:

```
$service = Zend_Gdata_Photos::AUTH_SERVICE_NAME;
$client = Zend_Gdata_ClientLogin::getHttpClient($user, $pass, $service);
$service = new Zend_Gdata_Photos($client);
```

```
$entry = new Zend_Gdata_Photos_TagEntry();
$entry->setTitle($service->newTitle("tag"));
$photoQuery = new Zend_Gdata_Photos_PhotoQuery;
$photoQuery->setUser("sample.user");
$photoQuery->setAlbumId("1");
$photoQuery->setPhotoId("100");
$photoQuery->setType('entry');
$photoEntry = $service->getPhotoEntry($photoQuery);
$service->insertTagEntry($entry, $photoEntry);
```

Deleting Entries

The service has functions to delete albums, photos, comments, and tags.

Deleting An Album

The service supports deleting an album for an authenticated user:

```
$service = Zend_Gdata_Photos::AUTH_SERVICE_NAME;
$client = Zend_Gdata_ClientLogin::getHttpClient($user, $pass, $service);
$service = new Zend_Gdata_Photos($client);
$albumQuery = new Zend_Gdata_Photos_AlbumQuery;
$albumQuery->setUser("sample.user");
$albumQuery->setAlbumId("1");
$albumQuery->setType('entry');
$entry = $service->getAlbumEntry($albumQuery);
$service->deleteAlbumEntry($entry, true);
```

Deleting A Photo

The service supports deleting a photo for an authenticated user:

```
$service = Zend_Gdata_Photos::AUTH_SERVICE_NAME;
$client = Zend_Gdata_ClientLogin::getHttpClient($user, $pass, $service);
$service = new Zend_Gdata_Photos($client);
$photoQuery = new Zend_Gdata_Photos_PhotoQuery;
$photoQuery->setUser("sample.user");
$photoQuery->setAlbumId("1");
$photoQuery->setPhotoId("100");
$photoQuery->setType('entry');
$entry = $service->getPhotoEntry($photoQuery);
$service->deletePhotoEntry($entry, true);
```

Deleting A Comment

The service supports deleting a comment for an authenticated user:

```
$service = Zend_Gdata_Photos::AUTH_SERVICE_NAME;
$client = Zend_Gdata_ClientLogin::getHttpClient($user, $pass, $service);
$service = new Zend_Gdata_Photos($client);
$photoQuery = new Zend_Gdata_Photos_PhotoQuery;
$photoQuery->setUser("sample.user");
$photoQuery->setAlbumId("1");
$photoQuery->setPhotoId("100");
$photoQuery->setType('entry');
$path = $photoQuery->getQueryUrl() . '/commentid/' . "1000";
$entry = $service->getCommentEntry($path);
$service->deleteCommentEntry($entry, true);
```

Deleting A Tag

The service supports deleting a tag for an authenticated user:

```
$service = Zend_Gdata_Photos::AUTH_SERVICE_NAME;
$client = Zend_Gdata_ClientLogin::getHttpClient($user, $pass, $service);
$service = new Zend_Gdata_Photos($client);
$photoQuery = new Zend_Gdata_Photos_PhotoQuery;
$photoQuery->setUser("sample.user");
$photoQuery->setAlbumId("1");
$photoQuery->setPhotoId("100");
$photoQuery->setKind("tag");
$query = $photoQuery->getQueryUrl();
$photoFeed = $service->getPhotoFeed($query);
foreach ($photoFeed as $entry) {
    if ($entry instanceof Zend_Gdata_Photos_TagEntry) {
        if ($entry->getContent() == $tagContent) {
            $tagEntry = $entry;
        }
    }
}
$service->deleteTagEntry($tagEntry, true);
```

Optimistic Concurrency (Notes On Deletion)

GData feeds, including those of the Picasa Web Albums service, implement optimistic concurrency, a versioning system that prevents users from overwriting changes, inadvertently. When deleting a entry through the service class, if the entry has been modified since it was last fetched, an exception will be thrown, unless explicitly set otherwise (in which case the deletion is retried on the updated entry).

An example of how to handle versioning during a deletion is shown by deleteAlbumEntry:

```
// $album is the albumEntry to be deleted
try {
    $this->delete($album);
} catch (Zend_Gdata_App_HttpException $e) {
    if ($e->getMessage()->getStatus() === 409) {
        $entry =
            new Zend_Gdata_Photos_AlbumEntry($e->getMessage()->getBody());
        $this->delete($entry->getLink('edit')->href);
    } else {
        throw $e;
    }
}
```

Using the YouTube Data API

The YouTube Data API offers read and write access to YouTube's content. Users can perform unauthenticated requests to Google Data feeds to retrieve feeds of popular videos, comments, public information about YouTube user profiles, user playlists, favorites, subscriptions and so on.

For more information on the YouTube Data API, please refer to the official PHP Developer's Guide [http://code.google.com/apis/youtube/developers_guide_php.html] on code.google.com.

Authentication

The YouTube Data API allows read-only access to public data, which does not require authentication.

For any write requests, a user needs to authenticate either using ClientLogin or AuthSub authentication. Please refer to the Authentication section in the PHP Developer's Guide [http://code.google.com/apis/youtube/developers_guide_php.html#Authentication] for more detail.

Developer Keys and Client ID

A developer key identifies the YouTube developer that is submitting an API request. A client ID identifies your application for logging and debugging purposes. Please visit http://code.google.com/apis/youtube/dashboard/ to obtain a developer key and client ID. The example below demonstrates how to pass the developer key and client ID to the Zend_Gdata_YouTube [http://framework.zend.com/apidoc/core/Zend_Gdata/Zend_Gdata_YouTube.html] service object.

Example 24.1. Passing a Developer Key and ClientID to Zend_Gdata_YouTube

```
$yt = new Zend_Gdata_YouTube($httpClient,
                             $applicationId,
                             $clientId,
                             $developerKey);
```

Retrieving public video feeds

The YouTube Data API provides numerous feeds that return a list of videos, such as standard feeds, related videos, video responses, user's uploads, and user's favorites. For example, the user's uploads feed returns all videos uploaded by a specific user. See the YouTube API reference guide [http://code.google.com/apis/youtube/reference.html#Video_Feeds] for a detailed list of available feeds.

Searching for videos by metadata

You can retrieve a list of videos that match specified search criteria, using the YouTubeQuery class. The following query looks for videos which contain the word "cat" in their metadata, starting with the 10th video and displaying 20 videos per page, ordered by the view count.

Example 24.2. Searching for videos

```
$yt = new Zend_Gdata_YouTube();
$query = $yt->newVideoQuery();
$query->videoQuery = 'cat';
$query->startIndex = 10;
$query->maxResults = 20;
$query->orderBy = 'viewCount';
echo $query->queryUrl . "\n";
$videoFeed = $yt->getVideoFeed($query);
foreach ($videoFeed as $videoEntry) {
    echo "---------VIDEO----------\n";
    echo "Title: " . $videoEntry->getVideoTitle() . "\n";
    echo "\nDescription:\n";
    echo $videoEntry->getVideoDescription();
    echo "\n\n\n";
}
```

For more details on the different query parameters, please refer to the Reference Guide [http://code.google.com/apis/youtube/reference.html#Searching_for_videos]. The available helper

functions   in   Zend_Gdata_YouTube_VideoQuery
[http://framework.zend.com/apidoc/core/Zend_Gdata/Zend_Gdata_YouTube_VideoQuery.html]   for
each of these parameters are described in more detail in the PHP Developer's Guide
[http://code.google.com/apis/youtube/developers_guide_php.html#SearchingVideos].

Searching for videos by categories and tags/keywords

Searching for videos in specific categories is done by generating a specially formatted URL
[http://code.google.com/apis/youtube/reference.html#Category_search]. For example, to search for
comedy videos which contain the keyword dog:

Example 24.3. Searching for videos in specific categories

```
$yt = new Zend_Gdata_YouTube();
$query = $yt->newVideoQuery();
$query->category = 'Comedy/dog';
echo $query->queryUrl . "\n";
$videoFeed = $yt->getVideoFeed($query);
```

Retrieving standard feeds

The   YouTube   Data   API   has   a   number   of   standard   feeds
[http://code.google.com/apis/youtube/reference.html#Standard_feeds]. These standard feeds can be
retrieved   as   Zend_Gdata_YouTube_VideoFeed
[http://framework.zend.com/apidoc/core/Zend_Gdata/Zend_Gdata_YouTube_VideoFeed.html] objects
using the specified URLs, using the predefined constants within the Zend_Gdata_YouTube
[http://framework.zend.com/apidoc/core/Zend_Gdata/Zend_Gdata_YouTube.html]   class
(Zend_Gdata_YouTube::STANDARD_TOP_RATED_URI for example) or using the predefined helper
methods (see code listing below).

To retrieve the top rated videos using the helper method:

Example 24.4. Retrieving a standard video feed

```
$yt = new Zend_Gdata_YouTube();
$videoFeed = $yt->getTopRatedVideoFeed();
```

There are also query parameters to specify the time period over which the standard feed is computed.

For example, to retrieve the top rated videos for today:

Example 24.5. Using a Zend_Gdata_YouTube_VideoQuery to Retrieve Videos

```
$yt = new Zend_Gdata_YouTube();
$query = $yt->newVideoQuery();
$query->setTime('today');
$videoFeed = $yt->getTopRatedVideoFeed($query);
```

Alternatively, you could just retrieve the feed using the URL:

Example 24.6. Retrieving a video feed by URL

```
$yt = new Zend_Gdata_YouTube();
$url = 'http://gdata.youtube.com/feeds/standardfeeds/top_rated?time=today'
$videoFeed = $yt->getVideoFeed($url);
```

Retrieving videos uploaded by a user

You can retrieve a list of videos uploaded by a particular user using a simple helper method. This example retrieves videos uploaded by the user 'liz'.

Example 24.7. Retrieving videos uploaded by a specific user

```
$yt = new Zend_Gdata_YouTube();
$videoFeed = $yt->getUserUploads('liz');
```

Retrieving videos favorited by a user

You can retrieve a list of a user's favorite videos using a simple helper method. This example retrieves videos favorited by the user 'liz'.

Example 24.8. Retrieving a user's favorite videos

```
$yt = new Zend_Gdata_YouTube();
$videoFeed = $yt->getUserFavorites('liz');
```

Retrieving video responses for a video

You can retrieve a list of a video's video responses using a simple helper method. This example retrieves video response for a video with the ID 'abc123813abc'.

Example 24.9. Retrieving a feed of video responses

```
$yt = new Zend_Gdata_YouTube();
$videoFeed = $yt->getVideoResponseFeed('abc123813abc');
```

Retrieving video comments

The comments for each YouTube video can be retrieved in several ways. To retrieve the comments for the video with the ID 'abc123813abc', use the following code:

Example 24.10. Retrieving a feed of video comments from a video ID

```
$yt = new Zend_Gdata_YouTube();
$commentFeed = $yt->getVideoCommentFeed('abc123813abc');
foreach ($commentFeed as $commentEntry) {
    echo $commentEntry->title->text . "\n";
    echo $commentEntry->content->text . "\n\n\n";
}
```

Comments can also be retrieved for a video if you have a copy of the Zend_Gdata_YouTube_VideoEntry [http://framework.zend.com/apidoc/core/Zend_Gdata/Zend_Gdata_YouTube_VideoEntry.html] object:

Example 24.11. Retrieving a Feed of Video Comments from a Zend_Gdata_YouTube_VideoEntry

```
$yt = new Zend_Gdata_YouTube();
$videoEntry = $yt->getVideoEntry('abc123813abc');
// we don't know the video ID in this example, but we do have the URL
$commentFeed = $yt->getVideoCommentFeed(null,
                                        $videoEntry->comments->href);
```

Retrieving playlist feeds

The YouTube Data API provides information about users, including profiles, playlists, subscriptions, and more.

Retrieving the playlists of a user

The library provides a helper method to retrieve the playlists associated with a given user. To retrieve the playlists for the user 'liz':

Example 24.12. Retrieving the playlists of a user

```
$yt = new Zend_Gdata_YouTube();
$playlistListFeed = $yt->getPlaylistListFeed('liz');
foreach ($playlistListFeed as $playlistEntry) {
    echo $playlistEntry->title->text . "\n";
    echo $playlistEntry->description->text . "\n";
    echo $playlistEntry->getPlaylistVideoFeedUrl() . "\n\n\n";
}
```

Retrieving a specific playlist

The library provides a helper method to retrieve the videos associated with a given playlist. To retrieve the playlists for a specific playlist entry:

Example 24.13. Retrieving a specific playlist

```
$feedUrl = $playlistEntry->getPlaylistVideoFeedUrl();
$playlistVideoFeed = $yt->getPlaylistVideoFeed($feedUrl);
```

Retrieving a list of a user's subscriptions

A user can have several types of subscriptions: channel subscription, tag subscription, or favorites subscription.   A   Zend_Gdata_YouTube_SubscriptionEntry [http://framework.zend.com/apidoc/core/Zend_Gdata/Zend_Gdata_YouTube_SubscriptionEntry.html] is used to represent individual subscriptions.

To retrieve all subscriptions for the user 'liz':

Example 24.14. Retrieving all subscriptions for a user

```
$yt = new Zend_Gdata_YouTube();
$subscriptionFeed = $yt->getSubscriptionFeed('liz');
foreach ($subscriptionFeed as $subscriptionEntry) {
    echo $subscriptionEntry->title->text . "\n";
}
```

Retrieving a user's profile

You can retrieve the public profile information for any YouTube user. To retrieve the profile for the user 'liz':

Example 24.15. Retrieving a user's profile

```
$yt = new Zend_Gdata_YouTube();
$userProfile = $yt->getUserProfile('liz');
echo "username: " . $userProfile->username->text . "\n";
echo "age: " . $userProfile->age->text . "\n";
echo "hometown: " . $userProfile->hometown->text . "\n";
```

Uploading Videos to YouTube

Please make sure to review the diagrams in the protocol guide [http://code.google.com /apis/youtube/developers_guide_protocol.html#Process_Flows_for_Uploading_Videos]   on code.google.com for a high-level overview of the upload process. Uploading videos can be done in one of two ways: either by uploading the video directly or by sending just the video meta-data and having a user upload the video through an HTML form.

In order to upload a video directly, you must first construct a new Zend_Gdata_YouTube_VideoEntry [http://framework.zend.com/apidoc/core/Zend_Gdata/Zend_Gdata_YouTube_VideoEntry.html] object and specify some required meta-data The following example shows uploading the Quicktime video "mytestmovie.mov" to YouTube with the following properties:

Table 24.1. Metadata used in the code-sample below

Property	Value
Title	My Test Movie
Category	Autos
Keywords	cars, funny
Description	My description
Filename	mytestmovie.mov
File MIME type	video/quicktime
Video private?	false
Video location	37, -122 (lat, long)
Developer Tags	mydevelopertag, anotherdevelopertag

The code below creates a blank Zend_Gdata_YouTube_VideoEntry [http://framework.zend.com/apidoc/core/Zend_Gdata/Zend_Gdata_YouTube_VideoEntry.html] to be uploaded. A Zend_Gdata_App_MediaFileSource [http://framework.zend.com/apidoc/core/Zend_Gdata/Zend_Gdata_App_MediaFileSource.html] object is then used to hold the actual video file. Under the hood, the Zend_Gdata_YouTube_Extension_MediaGroup [http://framework.zend.com/apidoc/core/Zend_Gdata/Zend_Gdata_YouTube_Extension_MediaGroup.html] object is used to hold all of the video's meta-data. Our helper methods detailed below allow you to just set the video meta-data without having to worry about the media group object. The $uploadUrl is the location where the new entry gets posted to. This can be specified either with the $userName of the currently authenticated user, or, alternatively, you can simply use the string 'default' to refer to the currently authenticated user.

Example 24.16. Uploading a video

```
$yt = new Zend_Gdata_YouTube($httpClient);
$myVideoEntry = new Zend_Gdata_YouTube_VideoEntry();
$filesource = $yt->newMediaFileSource('mytestmovie.mov');
$filesource->setContentType('video/quicktime');
$filesource->setSlug('mytestmovie.mov');
$myVideoEntry->setMediaSource($filesource);
$myVideoEntry->setVideoTitle('My Test Movie');
$myVideoEntry->setVideoDescription('My Test Movie');
// Note that category must be a valid YouTube category !
$myVideoEntry->setVideoCategory('Comedy');
// Set keywords, note that this must be a comma separated string
// and that each keyword cannot contain whitespace
$myVideoEntry->SetVideoTags('cars, funny');
// Optionally set some developer tags
$myVideoEntry->setVideoDeveloperTags(array('mydevelopertag',
                                           'anotherdevelopertag'));
// Optionally set the video's location
$yt->registerPackage('Zend_Gdata_Geo');
$yt->registerPackage('Zend_Gdata_Geo_Extension');
$where = $yt->newGeoRssWhere();
$position = $yt->newGmlPos('37.0 -122.0');
$where->point = $yt->newGmlPoint($position);
$myVideoEntry->setWhere($where);
// Upload URI for the currently authenticated user
```

```
$uploadUrl =
    'http://uploads.gdata.youtube.com/feeds/users/default/uploads';
// Try to upload the video, catching a Zend_Gdata_App_HttpException
// if availableor just a regular Zend_Gdata_App_Exception
try {
    $newEntry = $yt->insertEntry($myVideoEntry,
                                 $uploadUrl,
                                 'Zend_Gdata_YouTube_VideoEntry');
} catch (Zend_Gdata_App_HttpException $httpException) {
    echo $httpException->getRawResponseBody();
} catch (Zend_Gdata_App_Exception $e) {
    echo $e->getMessage();
}
```

To upload a video as private, simply use: $myVideoEntry->setVideoPrivate(); prior to performing the upload. $videoEntry->isVideoPrivate() can be used to check whether a video entry is private or not.

Browser-based upload

Browser-based uploading is performed almost identically to direct uploading, except that you do not attach a Zend_Gdata_App_MediaFileSource [http://framework.zend.com/apidoc/core/Zend_Gdata /Zend_Gdata_App_MediaFileSource.html] object to the Zend_Gdata_YouTube_VideoEntry [http://framework.zend.com /apidoc/core/Zend_Gdata/Zend_Gdata_YouTube_VideoEntry.html] you are constructing. Instead you simply submit all of your video's meta-data to receive back a token element which can be used to construct an HTML upload form.

Example 24.17. Browser-based upload

```
$yt = new Zend_Gdata_YouTube($httpClient);
$myVideoEntry= new Zend_Gdata_YouTube_VideoEntry();
$myVideoEntry->setVideoTitle('My Test Movie');
$myVideoEntry->setVideoDescription('My Test Movie');
// Note that category must be a valid YouTube category
$myVideoEntry->setVideoCategory('Comedy');
$myVideoEntry->SetVideoTags('cars, funny');
$tokenHandlerUrl = 'http://gdata.youtube.com/action/GetUploadToken';
$tokenArray = $yt->getFormUploadToken($myVideoEntry, $tokenHandlerUrl);
$tokenValue = $tokenArray['token'];
$postUrl = $tokenArray['url'];
```

The above code prints out a link and a token that is used to construct an HTML form to display in the user's browser. A simple example form is shown below with $tokenValue representing the content of the returned token element, as shown being retrieved from $myVideoEntry above. In order for the user to be redirected to your website after submitting the form, make sure to append a $nextUrl parameter to the $postUrl above, which functions in the same way as the $next parameter of an AuthSub link. The only difference is that here, instead of a single-use token, a status and an id variable are returned in the URL.

Example 24.18. Browser-based upload: Creating the HTML form

```
// place to redirect user after upload
$nextUrl = 'http://mysite.com/youtube_uploads';
$form = '<form action="'. $postUrl .'?nexturl='. $nextUrl .
        '" method="post" enctype="multipart/form-data">'.
        '<input name="file" type="file"/>'.
```

```
'<input name="token" type="hidden" value="'. $tokenValue .'"/>'.
'<input value="Upload Video File" type="submit" />'.
'</form>';
```

Checking upload status

After uploading a video, it will immediately be visible in an authenticated user's uploads feed. However, it will not be public on the site until it has been processed. Videos that have been rejected or failed to upload successfully will also only be in the authenticated user's uploads feed. The following code checks the status of a Zend_Gdata_YouTube_VideoEntry [http://framework.zend.com/apidoc/core /Zend_Gdata/Zend_Gdata_YouTube_VideoEntry.html] to see if it is not live yet or if it has been rejected.

Example 24.19. Checking video upload status

```
try {
    $control = $videoEntry->getControl();
} catch (Zend_Gdata_App_Exception $e) {
    echo $e->getMessage();
}
if ($control instanceof Zend_Gdata_App_Extension_Control) {
    if ($control->getDraft() != null &&
        $control->getDraft()->getText() == 'yes') {
        $state = $videoEntry->getVideoState();
        if ($state instanceof Zend_Gdata_YouTube_Extension_State) {
            print 'Upload status: '
                . $state->getName()
                .' '. $state->getText();
        } else {
            print 'Not able to retrieve the video status information'
                .' yet. ' . "Please try again shortly.\n";
        }
    }
}
```

Other Functions

In addition to the functionality described above, the YouTube API contains many other functions that allow you to modify video meta-data, delete video entries and use the full range of community features on the site. Some of the community features that can be modified through the API include: ratings, comments, playlists, subscriptions, user profiles, contacts and messages.

Please refer to the full documentation available in the PHP Developer's Guide [http://code.google.com/apis/youtube/developers_guide_php.html] on code.google.com.

Catching Gdata Exceptions

The Zend_Gdata_App_Exception class is a base class for exceptions thrown by Zend_Gdata. You can catch any exception thrown by Zend_Gdata by catching Zend_Gdata_App_Exception.

```
try {
    $client =
        Zend_Gdata_ClientLogin::getHttpClient($username, $password);
} catch(Zend_Gdata_App_Exception $ex) {
```

```
        // Report the exception to the user
        die($ex->getMessage());
}
```

The following exception subclasses are used by Zend_Gdata:

- Zend_Gdata_App_AuthException indicates that the user's account credentials were not valid.

- Zend_Gdata_App_BadMethodCallException indicates that a method was called for a service that does not support the method. For example, the CodeSearch service does not support post().

- Zend_Gdata_App_HttpException indicates that an HTTP request was not successful. Provides the ability to get the full Zend_Http_Response object to determine the exact cause of the failure in cases where $e->getMessage() does not provide enough details.

- Zend_Gdata_App_InvalidArgumentException is thrown when the application provides a value that is not valid in a given context. For example, specifying a Calendar visibility value of "banana", or fetching a Blogger feed without specifying any blog name.

- Zend_Gdata_App_CaptchaRequiredException is thrown when a ClientLogin attempt receives a CAPTCHA™ challenge from the authentication service. This exception contains a token ID and a URL to a CAPTCHA™ challenge image. The image is a visual puzzle that should be displayed to the user. After collecting the user's response to the challenge image, the response can be included with the next ClientLogin attempt.The user can alternatively be directed to this website: https://www.google.com/accounts/DisplayUnlockCaptcha Further information can be found in the ClientLogin documentation.

You can use these exception subclasses to handle specific exceptions differently. See the API documentation for information on which exception subclasses are thrown by which methods in Zend_Gdata.

```
try {
    $client = Zend_Gdata_ClientLogin::getHttpClient($username,
                                                    $password,
                                                    $service);
} catch(Zend_Gdata_App_AuthException $authEx) {
    // The user's credentials were incorrect.
    // It would be appropriate to give the user a second try.
    ...
} catch(Zend_Gdata_App_HttpException $httpEx) {
    // Google Data servers cannot be contacted.
    die($httpEx->getMessage);}
```

Chapter 25. Zend_Http

Introduction

Zend_Http_Client provides an easy interface for preforming Hyper-Text Transfer Protocol (HTTP) requests. Zend_Http_Client supports most simple features expected from an HTTP client, as well as some more complex features such as HTTP authentication and file uploads. Successful requests (and most unsuccessful ones too) return a Zend_Http_Response object, which provides access to the response's headers and body (see the section called "Zend_Http_Response").

Using Zend_Http_Client

The class constructor optionally accepts a URL as its first parameter (can be either a string or a Zend_Uri_Http object), and an optional array of configuration parameters. Both can be left out, and set later using the setUri() and setConfig() methods.

Example 25.1. Instantiating a Zend_Http_Client Object

```
$client = new Zend_Http_Client('http://example.org', array(
    'maxredirects' => 0,
    'timeout'      => 30));
// This is actually exactly the same:
$client = new Zend_Http_Client();
$client->setUri('http://example.org');
$client->setConfig(array(
    'maxredirects' => 0,
    'timeout'      => 30));
```

Note

Zend_Http_Client uses Zend_Uri_Http to validate URLs. This means that some special characters like the pipe symbol ('|') or the caret symbol ('^') will not be accepted in the URL by default. This can be modified by setting the 'allow_unwise' option of Zend_Uri to 'true'. See the section called "Allowing "Unwise" characters in URIs" for more information.

Configuration Parameters

The constructor and setConfig() method accept an associative array of configuration parameters. Setting these parameters is optional, as they all have default values.

Table 25.1. Zend_Http_Client configuration parameters

Parameter	Description	Expected Values	Default Value
maxredirects	Maximum number of redirections to follow (0 = none)	integer	5
strict	Whether perform valida- tion on header names. When set to false, valid- ation functions will be	boolean	true

Parameter	Description	Expected Values	Default Value
	skipped. Usually this should not be changed		
strictredirects	Whether to strictly follow the RFC when redirecting (see the section called "HTTP Redirections")	boolean	false
useragent	User agent identifier string (sent in request headers)	string	'Zend_Http_Client'
timeout	Connection timeout (seconds)	integer	10
httpversion	HTTP protocol version (usually '1.1' or '1.0')	string	'1.1'
adapter	Connection adapter class to use (see the section called "Zend_Http_Client - Connection Adapters")	mixed	'Zend_Http_Client _Adapter_Socket'
keepalive	Whether to enable keep-alive connections with the server. Useful and might improve performance if several consecutive requests to the same server are performed.	boolean	false
storeresponse	Whether to store last response for later retrieval with getLastResponse(). If set to false getLastResponse() will return null.	boolean	true

Performing Basic HTTP Requests

Performing simple HTTP requests is very easily done using the request() method, and rarely needs more than three lines of code:

Example 25.2. Performing a Simple GET Request

```
$client = new Zend_Http_Client('http://example.org');
$response = $client->request();
```

The request() method takes one optional parameter - the request method. This can be either GET, POST, PUT, HEAD, DELETE, TRACE, OPTIONS or CONNECT as defined by the HTTP protocol [*] . For convenience, these are all defined as class constants: Zend_Http_Client::GET, Zend_Http_Client::POST and so on.

If no method is specified, the method set by the last setMethod() call is used. If setMethod() was never

---

[*] See RFC 2616 - http://www.w3.org/Protocols/rfc2616/rfc2616.html.

called, the default request method is GET (see the above example).

Example 25.3. Using Request Methods Other Than GET

```
// Preforming a POST request
$response = $client->request('POST');
// Yet another way of preforming a POST request
$client->setMethod(Zend_Http_Client::POST);
$response = $client->request();
```

Adding GET and POST parameters

Adding GET parameters to an HTTP request is quite simple, and can be done either by specifying them as part of the URL, or by using the setParameterGet() method. This method takes the GET parameter's name as its first parameter, and the GET parameter's value as its second parameter. For convenience, the setParameterGet() method can also accept a single associative array of name => value GET variables - which may be more comfortable when several GET parameters need to be set.

Example 25.4. Setting GET Parameters

```
// Setting a get parameter using the setParameterGet method
$client->setParameterGet('knight', 'lancelot');
// This is equivalent to setting such URL:
$client->setUri('http://example.com/index.php?knight=lancelot');
// Adding several parameters with one call
$client->setParameterGet(array(
    'first_name'  => 'Bender',
    'middle_name' => 'Bending'
    'made_in'     => 'Mexico',
));
```

While GET parameters can be sent with every request method, POST parameters are only sent in the body of POST requests. Adding POST parameters to a request is very similar to adding GET parameters, and can be done with the setParameterPost() method, which is similar to the setParameterGet() method in structure.

Example 25.5. Setting POST Parameters

```
// Setting a POST parameter
$client->setParameterPost('language', 'fr');
// Setting several POST parameters, one of them with several values
$client->setParameterPost(array(
    'language'  => 'es',
    'country'   => 'ar',
    'selection' => array(45, 32, 80)
));
```

Note that when sending POST requests, you can set both GET and POST parameters. On the other hand, while setting POST parameters for a non-POST request will not trigger and error, it is useless. Unless the request is a POST request, POST parameters are simply ignored.

Accessing Last Request and Response

Zend_Http_Client provides methods of accessing the last request sent and last response received by the client object. `Zend_Http_Client->getLastRequest()` takes no parameters and returns the last HTTP request sent by the client as a string. Similarly, `Zend_Http_Client->getLastResponse()` returns the last HTTP response received by the client as a Zend_Http_Response object.

Zend_Http_Client - Advanced Usage

HTTP Redirections

By default, Zend_Http_Client automatically handles HTTP redirections, and will follow up to 5 redirections. This can be changed by setting the 'maxredirects' configuration parameter.

According to the HTTP/1.1 RFC, HTTP 301 and 302 responses should be treated by the client by resending the same request to the specified location - using the same request method. However, most clients to not implement this and always use a GET request when redirecting. By default, Zend_Http_Client does the same - when redirecting on a 301 or 302 response, all GET and POST parameters are reset, and a GET request is sent to the new location. This behavior can be changed by setting the 'strictredirects' configuration parameter to boolean TRUE:

Example 25.6. Forcing RFC 2616 Strict Redirections on 301 and 302 Responses

```
// Strict Redirections
$client->setConfig(array('strictredirects' => true));
// Non-strict Redirections
$client->setConfig(array('strictredirects' => false));
```

You can always get the number of redirections done after sending a request using the getRedirectionsCount() method.

Adding Cookies and Using Cookie Persistence

Zend_Http_Client provides an easy interface for adding cookies to your request, so that no direct header modification is required. This is done using the setCookie() method. This method can be used in several ways:

Example 25.7. Setting Cookies Using setCookie()

```
// Easy and simple: by providing a cookie name and cookie value
$client->setCookie('flavor', 'chocolate chips');
// By directly providing a raw cookie string (name=value)
// Note that the value must be already URL encoded
$client->setCookie('flavor=chocolate%20chips');
// By providing a Zend_Http_Cookie object
$cookie = Zend_Http_Cookie::fromString('flavor=chocolate%20chips');
$client->setCookie($cookie);
```

For more information about Zend_Http_Cookie objects, see the section called "Zend_Http_Cookie and

Zend_Http_CookieJar".

Zend_Http_Client also provides the means for cookie stickiness - that is having the client internally store all sent and received cookies, and resend them automatically on subsequent requests. This is useful, for example when you need to log in to a remote site first and receive and authentication or session ID cookie before sending further requests.

Example 25.8. Enabling Cookie Stickiness

```
// To turn cookie stickiness on, set a Cookie Jar
$client->setCookieJar();
// First request: log in and start a session
$client->setUri('http://example.com/login.php');
$client->setParameterPost('user', 'h4x0r');
$client->setParameterPost('password', '1337');
$client->request('POST');
// The Cookie Jar automatically stores the cookies set
// in the response, like a session ID cookie.
// Now we can send our next request - the stored cookies
// will be automatically sent.
$client->setUri('http://example.com/read_member_news.php');
$client->request('GET');
```

For more information about the Zend_Http_CookieJar class, see the section called "The Zend_Http_CookieJar Class: Instantiation".

Setting Custom Request Headers

Setting custom headers can be done by using the setHeaders() method. This method is quite diverse and can be used in several ways, as the following example shows:

Example 25.9. Setting A Single Custom Request Header

```
// Setting a single header, overwriting any previous value
$client->setHeaders('Host', 'www.example.com');
// Another way of doing the exact same thing
$client->setHeaders('Host: www.example.com');
// Setting several values for the same header
// (useful mostly for Cookie headers):
$client->setHeaders('Cookie', array(
    'PHPSESSID=1234567890abcdef1234567890abcdef',
    'language=he'
));
```

setHeader() can also be easily used to set multiple headers in one call, by providing an array of headers as a single parameter:

Example 25.10. Setting Multiple Custom Request Headers

```
// Setting multiple headers, overwriting any previous value
$client->setHeaders(array(
    'Host' => 'www.example.com',
    'Accept-encoding' => 'gzip,deflate',
```

```
    'X-Powered-By' => 'Zend Framework'));
// The array can also contain full array strings:
$client->setHeaders(array(
    'Host: www.example.com',
    'Accept-encoding: gzip,deflate',
    'X-Powered-By: Zend Framework'));
```

File Uploads

You can upload files through HTTP using the setFileUpload method. This method takes a file name as the first parameter, a form name as the second parameter, and data as a third optional parameter. If the third data parameter is null, the first file name parameter is considered to be a real file on disk, and Zend_Http_Client will try to read this file and upload it. If the data parameter is not null, the first file name parameter will be sent as the file name, but no actual file needs to exist on the disk. The second form name parameter is always required, and is equivalent to the "name" attribute of an >input< tag, if the file was to be uploaded through an HTML form. A fourth optional parameter provides the file's content-type. If not specified, and Zend_Http_Client reads the file from the disk, the mime_content_type function will be used to guess the file's content type, if it is available. In any case, the default MIME type will be application/octet-stream.

Example 25.11. Using setFileUpload to Upload Files

```
// Uploading arbitrary data as a file
$text = 'this is some plain text';
$client->setFileUpload('some_text.txt', 'upload', $text, 'text/plain');
// Uploading an existing file
$client->setFileUpload('/tmp/Backup.tar.gz', 'bufile');
// Send the files
$client->request('POST');
```

In the first example, the $text variable is uploaded and will be available as $_FILES['upload'] on the server side. In the second example, the existing file /tmp/Backup.tar.gz is uploaded to the server and will be available as $_FILES['bufile']. The content type will be guesses automatically if possible - and if not, the content type will be set to 'application/octet-stream'.

Uploading files

When uploading files, the HTTP request content-type is automatically set to multipart/form-data. Keep in mind that you must send a POST or PUT request in order to upload files. Most servers will ignore the requests body on other request methods.

Sending Raw POST Data

You can use a Zend_Http_Client to send raw POST data using the setRawData() method. This method takes two parameters: the first is the data to send in the request body. The second optional parameter is the content-type of the data. While this parameter is optional, you should usually set it before sending the request - either using setRawData(), or with another method: setEncType().

Example 25.12. Sending Raw POST Data

```
$xml = '<book>' .
       '    <title>Islands in the Stream</title>' .
       '    <author>Ernest Hemingway</author>' .
       '    <year>1970</year>' .
```

```
       '</book>';
$client->setRawData($xml, 'text/xml')->request('POST');
// Another way to do the same thing:
$client->setRawData($xml)->setEncType('text/xml')->request('POST');
```

The data should be available on the server side through PHP's $HTTP_RAW_POST_DATA variable or through the php://input stream.

Using raw POST data

Setting raw POST data for a request will override any POST parameters or file uploads. You should not try to use both on the same request. Keep in mind that most servers will ignore the request body unless you send a POST request.

HTTP Authentication

Currently, Zend_Http_Client only supports basic HTTP authentication. This feature is utilized using the setAuth() method. The method takes 3 parameters: The user name, the password and an optional authentication type parameter. As mentioned, currently only basic authentication is supported (digest authentication support is planned).

Example 25.13. Setting HTTP Authentication User and Password

```
// Using basic authentication
$client->setAuth('shahar', 'myPassword!', Zend_Http_Client::AUTH_BASIC);
// Since basic auth is default, you can just do this:
$client->setAuth('shahar', 'myPassword!');
```

Sending Multiple Requests With the Same Client

Zend_Http_Client was also designed specifically to handle several consecutive requests with the same object. This is useful in cases where a script requires data to be fetched from several places, or when accessing a specific HTTP resource requires logging in and obtaining a session cookie, for example.

When performing several requests to the same host, it is highly recommended to enable the 'keepalive' configuration flag. This way, if the server supports keep-alive connections, the connection to the server will only be closed once all requests are done and the Client object is destroyed. This prevents the overhead of opening and closing TCP connections to the server.

When you perform several requests with the same client, but want to make sure all the request-specific parameters are cleared, you should use the resetParameters() method. This ensures that GET and POST parameters, request body and request-specific headers are reset and are not reused in the next request.

Resetting parameters

Note that non-request specific headers are not reset when the resetParameters method is used. As a matter of fact, only the 'Content-length' and 'Content-type' headers are reset. This allows you to set-and-forget headers like 'Accept-language' and 'Accept-encoding'

Another feature designed specifically for consecutive requests is the Cookie Jar object. Cookie Jars allow you to automatically save cookies set by the server in the first request, and send them on consecutive requests transparently. This allows, for example, going through an authentication request before sending the actual data fetching request.

If your application requires one authentication request per user, and consecutive requests might be performed in more than one script in your application, it might be a good idea to store the Cookie Jar object in the user's session. This way, you will only need to authenticate the user once every session.

Example 25.14. Performing consecutive requests with one client

```
// First, instantiate the client
$client = new Zend_Http_Client('http://www.example.com/fetchdata.php', array(
    'keepalive' => true
));
// Do we have the cookies stored in our session?
if (isset($_SESSION['cookiejar']) &&
    $_SESSION['cookiejar'] instanceof Zend_Http_CookieJar)) {
    $client->setCookieJar($_SESSION['cookiejar']);
} else {
    // If we don't, authenticate and store cookies
    $client->setCookieJar();
    $client->setUri('http://www.example.com/login.php');
    $client->setParameterPost(array(
        'user' => 'shahar',
        'pass' => 'somesecret'
    ));
    $client->request(Zend_Http_Client::POST);
    // Now, clear parameters and set the URI to the original one
    // (note that the cookies that were set by the server are now
    // stored in the jar)
    $client->resetParameters();
    $client->setUri('http://www.example.com/fetchdata.php');
}
$response = $client->request(Zend_Http_Client::GET);
// Store cookies in session, for next page
$_SESSION['cookiejar'] = $client->getCookieJar();
```

Zend_Http_Client - Connection Adapters

Overview

Zend_Http_Client is based on a connection adapter design. The connection adapter is the object in charge of performing the actual connection to the server, as well as writing requests and reading responses. This connection adapter can be replaced, and you can create and extend the default connection adapters to suite your special needs, without the need to extend or replace the entire HTTP client class, and with the same interface.

Currently, the Zend_Http_Client class provides three built-in connection adapters:

*   Zend_Http_Client_Adapter_Socket (default)

*   Zend_Http_Client_Adapter_Proxy

*   Zend_Http_Client_Adapter_Test

*   Zend_Http_Client_Adapter_Curl

The Zend_Http_Client object's adapter connection adapter is set using the 'adapter' configuration option. When instantiating the client object, you can set the 'adapter' configuration option to a string containing the adapter's name (eg. 'Zend_Http_Client_Adapter_Socket') or to a variable holding an adapter object (eg. new Zend_Http_Client_Adapter_Test). You can also set the adapter later, using the Zend_Http_Client->setConfig() method.

The Socket Adapter

The default connection adapter is the Zend_Http_Client_Adapter_Socket adapter - this adapter will be used unless you explicitly set the connection adapter. The Socket adapter is based on PHP's built-in fsockopen() function, and does not require any special extensions or compilation flags.

The Socket adapter allows several extra configuration options that can be set using Zend_Http_Client->setConfig() or passed to the client constructor.

Table 25.2. Zend_Http_Client_Adapter_Socket configuration parameters

Parameter	Description	Expected Type	Default Value
persistent	Whether to use persistent TCP connections	boolean	false
ssltransport	SSL transport layer (eg. 'sslv2', 'tls')	string	ssl
sslcert	Path to a PEM encoded SSL certificate	string	null
sslpassphrase	Passphrase for the SSL certificate file	string	null

Persistent TCP Connections

Using persistent TCP connections can potentially speed up HTTP requests - but in most use cases, will have little positive effect and might overload the HTTP server you are connecting to.

It is recommended to use persistent TCP connections only if you connect to the same server very frequently, and are sure that the server is capable of handling a large number of concurrent connections. In any case you are encouraged to benchmark the effect of persistent connections on both the client speed and server load before using this option.

Additionally, when using persistent connections it is recommended to enable Keep-Alive HTTP requests as described in the section called "Configuration Parameters" - otherwise persistent connections might have little or no effect.

HTTPS SSL Stream Parameters

ssltransport, sslcert and sslpassphrase are only relevant when connecting using HTTPS.

While the default SSL settings should work for most applications, you might need to change them if the server you are connecting to requires special client setup. If so, you should read the sections about SSL transport layers and options here [http://www.php.net/manual/en/transports.php#transports.inet].

Example 25.15. Changing the HTTPS transport layer

```
// Set the configuration parameters
$config = array(
    'adapter'      => 'Zend_Http_Client_Adapter_Socket',
    'ssltransport' => 'tls'
```

```
);
// Instantiate a client object
$client = new Zend_Http_Client('https://www.example.com', $config);
// The following request will be sent over a TLS secure connection.
$response = $client->request();
```

The result of the example above will be similar to opening a TCP connection using the following PHP command:

```
fsockopen('tls://www.example.com', 443)
```

The Proxy Adapter

The Zend_Http_Client_Adapter_Proxy adapter is similar to the default Socket adapter - only the connection is made through an HTTP proxy server instead of a direct connection to the target server. This allows usage of Zend_Http_Client behind proxy servers - which is sometimes needed for security or performance reasons.

Using the Proxy adapter requires several additional configuration parameters to be set, in addition to the default 'adapter' option:

Table 25.3. Zend_Http_Client configuration parameters

Parameter	Description	Expected Type	Example Value
proxy_host	Proxy server address	string	'proxy.myhost.com' or '10.1.2.3'
proxy_port	Proxy server TCP port	integer	8080 (default) or 81
proxy_user	Proxy user name, if required	string	'shahar' or '' for none (default)
proxy_pass	Proxy password, if required	string	'secret' or '' for none (default)
proxy_auth	Proxy HTTP authentication type	string	Zend_Http_Client:: AUTH_BASIC (default)

proxy_host should always be set - if it is not set, the client will fall back to a direct connection using Zend_Http_Client_Adapter_Socket. proxy_port defaults to '8080' - if your proxy listens on a different port you must set this one as well.

proxy_user and proxy_pass are only required if your proxy server requires you to authenticate. Providing these will add a 'Proxy-Authentication' header to the request. If your proxy does not require authentication, you can leave these two options out.

proxy_auth sets the proxy authentication type, if your proxy server requires authentication. Possibly values are similar to the ones accepted by the Zend_Http_Client::setAuth() method. Currently, only basic authentication (Zend_Http_Client::AUTH_BASIC) is supported.

Example 25.16. Using Zend_Http_Client behind a proxy server

```
// Set the configuration parameters
$config = array(
    'adapter'    => 'Zend_Http_Client_Adapter_Proxy',
    'proxy_host' => 'proxy.int.zend.com',
```

```
        'proxy_port' => 8000,
        'proxy_user' => 'shahar.e',
        'proxy_pass' => 'bananashaped'
);
// Instantiate a client object
$client = new Zend_Http_Client('http://www.example.com', $config);
// Continue working...
```

As mentioned, if proxy_host is not set or is set to a blank string, the connection will fall back to a regular direct connection. This allows you to easily write your application in a way that allows a proxy to be used optionally, according to a configuration parameter.

The Test Adapter

Sometimes, it is very hard to test code that relies on HTTP connections. For example, testing an application that pulls an RSS feed from a remote server will require a network connection, which is not always available.

For this reason, the Zend_Http_Client_Adapter_Test adapter is provided. You can write your application to use Zend_Http_Client, and just for testing purposes, for example in your unit testing suite, you can replace the default adapter with a Test adapter (a mock object), allowing you to run tests without actually performing server connections.

The Zend_Http_Client_Adapter_Test adapter provides an additional method, setResponse() method. This method takes one parameter, which represents an HTTP response as either text or a Zend_Http_Response object. Once set, your Test adapter will always return this response, without even performing an actual HTTP request.

Example 25.17. Testing Against a Single HTTP Response Stub

```
// Instantiate a new adapter and client
$adapter = new Zend_Http_Client_Adapter_Test();
$client = new Zend_Http_Client('http://www.example.com', array(
    'adapter' => $adapter
));
// Set the expected response
$adapter->setResponse(
    "HTTP/1.1 200 OK"              . "\r\n" .
    "Content-type: text/xml"       . "\r\n" .
                                     "\r\n" .
    '<?xml version="1.0" encoding="UTF-8"?>' .
    '<rss version="2.0" ' .
    '    xmlns:content="http://purl.org/rss/1.0/modules/content/"' .
    '    xmlns:wfw="http://wellformedweb.org/CommentAPI/"' .
    '    xmlns:dc="http://purl.org/dc/elements/1.1/">' .
    '  <channel>' .
    '    <title>Premature Optimization</title>' .
    // and so on...
    '</rss>');
$response = $client->request('GET');
// .. continue parsing $response..
```

The above example shows how you can preset your HTTP client to return the response you need. Then, you can continue testing your own code, without being dependent on a network connection, the server's response, etc. In this case, the test would continue to check how the application parses the XML in the response body.

Sometimes, a single method call to an object can result in that object performing multiple HTTP transactions. In this case, it's not possible to use setResponse() alone because there's no opportunity to set the next response(s) your program might need before returning to the caller.

Example 25.18. Testing Against Multiple HTTP Response Stubs

```
// Instantiate a new adapter and client
$adapter = new Zend_Http_Client_Adapter_Test();
$client = new Zend_Http_Client('http://www.example.com', array(
    'adapter' => $adapter
));
// Set the first expected response
$adapter->setResponse(
    "HTTP/1.1 302 Found"        . "\r\n" .
    "Location: /"               . "\r\n" .
    "Content-Type: text/html"   . "\r\n" .
                                  "\r\n" .
    '<html>' .
    '  <head><title>Moved</title></head>' .
    '  <body><p>This page has moved.</p></body>' .
    '</html>');
// Set the next successive response
$adapter->addResponse(
    "HTTP/1.1 200 OK"           . "\r\n" .
    "Content-Type: text/html"   . "\r\n" .
                                  "\r\n" .
    '<html>' .
    '  <head><title>My Pet Store Home Page</title></head>' .
    '  <body><p>...</p></body>' .
    '</html>');
// inject the http client object ($client) into your object
// being tested and then test your object's behavior below
```

The setResponse() method clears any responses in the Zend_Http_Client_Adapter_Test's buffer and sets the first response that will be returned. The addResponse() method will add successive responses.

The responses will be replayed in the order that they were added. If more requests are made than the number of responses stored, the responses will cycle again in order.

In the example above, the adapter is configured to test your object's behavior when it encounters a 302 redirect. Depending on your application, following a redirect may or may not be desired behavior. In our example, we expect that the redirect will be followed and we configure the test adapter to help us test this. The initial 302 response is set up with the setResponse() method and the 200 response to be returned next is added with the addResponse() method. After configuring the test adapter, inject the HTTP client containing the adapter into your object under test and test its behavior.

The cURL Adapter

cURL is a standard HTTP client library that is distributed with many operating systems and can be used in PHP via the cURL extension. It offers functionality for many special cases which can occur for a HTTP client and make it a perfect choice for a HTTP adapter. It supports secure connections, proxy, all sorts of authentication mechanisms and shines in applications that move large files around between servers.

Example 25.19. Setting cURL options

```
$config = array(
    'adapter'    => 'Zend_Http_Client_Adapter_Curl',
    'curloptions' => array(CURLOPT_FOLLOWLOCATION => true),
);
$client = new Zend_Http_Client($uri, $config);
```

By default the cURL adapter is configured to behave exactly like the Socket Adapter. You can change the cURL options by either specifying the 'curloptions' key in the constructor of the adapter or by calling setCurlOption($name, $value). The $name key corresponds to the CURL_* constants of the cURL extension.

Example 25.20. Transfering Files by Handle

You can use cURL to transfer very large files over HTTP by filehandle.

```
$putFileSize   = filesize("filepath");
$putFileHandle = fopen("filepath", "r");
$adapter = new Zend_Http_Client_Adapter_Curl();
$client = new Zend_Http_Client();
$client->setAdapter($adapter);
$adapter->setConfig(array(
    'curloptions' => array(
        CURLOPT_INFILE => $putFileHandle,
        CURLOPT_INFILESIZE => $putFileSize
    )
));
$client->request("PUT");
```

Creating your own connection adapters

You can create your own connection adapters and use them. You could, for example, create a connection adapter that uses persistent sockets, or a connection adapter with caching abilities, and use them as needed in your application.

In order to do so, you must create your own adapter class that implements the Zend_Http_Client_Adapter_Interface interface. The following example shows the skeleton of a user-implemented adapter class. All the public functions defined in this example must be defined in your adapter as well:

Example 25.21. Creating your own connection adapter

```
class MyApp_Http_Client_Adapter_BananaProtocol
    implements Zend_Http_Client_Adapter_Interface
{
    /**
     * Set the configuration array for the adapter
     *
     * @param array $config
     */
    public function setConfig($config = array())
    {
        // This rarely changes - you should usually copy the
        // implementation in Zend_Http_Client_Adapter_Socket.
```

```
}
/**
 * Connect to the remote server
 *
 * @param string  $host
 * @param int     $port
 * @param boolean $secure
 */
public function connect($host, $port = 80, $secure = false)
{
    // Set up the connection to the remote server
}
/**
 * Send request to the remote server
 *
 * @param string        $method
 * @param Zend_Uri_Http $url
 * @param string        $http_ver
 * @param array         $headers
 * @param string        $body
 * @return string Request as text
 */
public function write($method,
                      $url,
                      $http_ver = '1.1',
                      $headers = array(),
                      $body = '')
{
    // Send request to the remote server.
    // This function is expected to return the full request
    // (headers and body) as a string
}
/**
 * Read response from server
 *
 * @return string
 */
public function read()
{
    // Read response from remote server and return it as a string
}
/**
 * Close the connection to the server
 *
 */
public function close()
{
    // Close the connection to the remote server - called last.
}
}
// Then, you could use this adapter:
$client = new Zend_Http_Client(array(
    'adapter' => 'MyApp_Http_Client_Adapter_BananaProtocol'
));
```

Zend_Http_Cookie and Zend_Http_CookieJar

Introduction

Zend_Http_Cookie, as expected, is a class that represents an HTTP cookie. It provides methods for parsing HTTP response strings, collecting cookies, and easily accessing their properties. It also allows checking if a cookie matches against a specific scenario, IE a request URL, expiration time, secure connection, etc.

Zend_Http_CookieJar is an object usually used by Zend_Http_Client to hold a set of Zend_Http_Cookie objects. The idea is that if a Zend_Http_CookieJar object is attached to a Zend_Http_Client object, all cookies going from and into the client through HTTP requests and responses will be stored by the CookieJar object. Then, when the client will send another request, it will first ask the CookieJar object for all cookies matching the request. These will be added to the request headers automatically. This is highly useful in cases where you need to maintain a user session over consecutive HTTP requests, automatically sending the session ID cookies when required. Additionally, the Zend_Http_CookieJar object can be serialized and stored in $_SESSION when needed.

Instantiating Zend_Http_Cookie Objects

Instantiating a Cookie object can be done in two ways:

- Through the constructor, using the following syntax: new Zend_Http_Cookie(string $name, string $value, string $domain, [int $expires, [string $path, [boolean $secure]]]);

  - $name: The name of the cookie (eg. 'PHPSESSID') (required)

  - $value: The value of the cookie (required)

  - $domain: The cookie's domain (eg. '.example.com') (required)

  - $expires: Cookie expiration time, as UNIX time stamp (optional, defaults to null). If not set, cookie will be treated as a 'session cookie' with no expiration time.

  - $path: Cookie path, eg. '/foo/bar/' (optional, defaults to '/')

  - $secure: Boolean, Whether the cookie is to be sent over secure (HTTPS) connections only (optional, defaults to boolean FALSE)

- By calling the fromString() static method, with a cookie string as represented in the 'Set-Cookie' HTTP response header or 'Cookie' HTTP request header. In this case, the cookie value must already be encoded. When the cookie string does not contain a 'domain' part, you must provide a reference URI according to which the cookie's domain and path will be set.

Example 25.22. Instantiating a Zend_Http_Cookie object

```
// First, using the constructor. This cookie will expire in 2 hours
$cookie = new Zend_Http_Cookie('foo',
                               'bar',
                               '.example.com',
                               time() + 7200,
                               '/path');
// You can also take the HTTP response Set-Cookie header and use it.
// This cookie is similar to the previous one, only it will not expire, and
// will only be sent over secure connections
$cookie = Zend_Http_Cookie::fromString('foo=bar; domain=.example.com; ' .
                                        'path=/path; secure');
// If the cookie's domain is not set, you have to manually specify it
$cookie = Zend_Http_Cookie::fromString('foo=bar; secure;',
                                       'http://www.example.com/path');
```

Note

When instantiating a cookie object using the Zend_Http_Cookie::fromString() method, the cookie value is expected to be URL encoded, as cookie strings should be. However, when using the constructor, the cookie value string is expected to be the real, decoded value.

A cookie object can be transferred back into a string, using the __toString() magic method. This method will produce a HTTP request "Cookie" header string, showing the cookie's name and value, and terminated by a semicolon (';'). The value will be URL encoded, as expected in a Cookie header:

Example 25.23. Stringifying a Zend_Http_Cookie object

```
// Create a new cookie
$cookie = new Zend_Http_Cookie('foo',
                               'two words',
                               '.example.com',
                               time() + 7200,
                               '/path');
// Will print out 'foo=two+words;' :
echo $cookie->__toString();
// This is actually the same:
echo (string) $cookie;
// In PHP 5.2 and higher, this also works:
echo $cookie;
```

Zend_Http_Cookie getter methods

Once a Zend_Http_Cookie object is instantiated, it provides several getter methods to get the different properties of the HTTP cookie:

- string getName(): Get the name of the cookie

- string getValue(): Get the real, decoded value of the cookie

- string getDomain(): Get the cookie's domain

- string getPath(): Get the cookie's path, which defaults to '/'

- int getExpiryTime(): Get the cookie's expiration time, as UNIX time stamp. If the cookie has no expiration time set, will return NULL.

Additionally, several boolean tester methods are provided:

- boolean isSecure(): Check whether the cookie is set to be sent over secure connections only. Generally speaking, if true the cookie should only be sent over HTTPS.

- boolean isExpired(int $time = null): Check whether the cookie is expired or not. If the cookie has no expiration time, will always return true. If $time is provided, it will override the current time stamp as the time to check the cookie against.

- boolean isSessionCookie(): Check whether the cookie is a "session cookie" - that is a cookie with no expiration time, which is meant to expire when the session ends.

Example 25.24. Using getter methods with Zend_Http_Cookie

```
// First, create the cookie
$cookie =
    Zend_Http_Cookie::fromString('foo=two+words; ' +
                                 'domain=.example.com; ' +
                                 'path=/somedir; ' +
                                 'secure; ' +
                                 'expires=Wednesday, 28-Feb-05 20:41:22
                                     UTC');
echo $cookie->getName();    // Will echo 'foo'
echo $cookie->getValue();   // will echo 'two words'
echo $cookie->getDomain();  // Will echo '.example.com'
echo $cookie->getPath();    // Will echo '/'
echo date('Y-m-d', $cookie->getExpiryTime());
// Will echo '2005-02-28'
echo ($cookie->isExpired() ? 'Yes' : 'No');
// Will echo 'Yes'
echo ($cookie->isExpired(strtotime('2005-01-01') ? 'Yes' : 'No');
// Will echo 'No'
echo ($cookie->isSessionCookie() ? 'Yes' : 'No');
// Will echo 'No'
```

Zend_Http_Cookie: Matching against a scenario

The only real logic contained in a Zend_Http_Cookie object, is in the match() method. This method is used to test a cookie against a given HTTP request scenario, in order to tell whether the cookie should be sent in this request or not. The method has the following syntax and parameters: boolean Zend_Http_Cookie->match(mixed $uri, [boolean $matchSessionCookies, [int $now]]);

- mixed $uri: A Zend_Uri_Http object with a domain name and path to be checked. Optionally, a string representing a valid HTTP URL can be passed instead. The cookie will match if the URL's scheme (HTTP or HTTPS), domain and path all match.

- boolean $matchSessionCookies: Whether session cookies should be matched or not. Defaults to true. If set to false, cookies with no expiration time will never match.

- int $now: Time (represented as UNIX time stamp) to check a cookie against for expiration. If not specified, will default to the current time.

Example 25.25. Matching cookies

```
// Create the cookie object - first, a secure session cookie
$cookie = Zend_Http_Cookie::fromString('foo=two+words; ' +
                                       'domain=.example.com; ' +
                                       'path=/somedir; ' +
                                       'secure;');
$cookie->match('https://www.example.com/somedir/foo.php');
// Will return true
$cookie->match('http://www.example.com/somedir/foo.php');
// Will return false, because the connection is not secure
$cookie->match('https://otherexample.com/somedir/foo.php');
// Will return false, because the domain is wrong
$cookie->match('https://example.com/foo.php');
// Will return false, because the path is wrong
$cookie->match('https://www.example.com/somedir/foo.php', false);
// Will return false, because session cookies are not matched
$cookie->match('https://sub.domain.example.com/somedir/otherdir/foo.php');
// Will return true
```

```
// Create another cookie object - now, not secure, with expiration time
// in two hours
$cookie = Zend_Http_Cookie::fromString('foo=two+words; ' +
                                        'domain=www.example.com; ' +
                                        'expires='
                                        . date(DATE_COOKIE, time() + 7200));
$cookie->match('http://www.example.com/');
// Will return true
$cookie->match('https://www.example.com/');
// Will return true - non secure cookies can go over secure connections
// as well!
$cookie->match('http://subdomain.example.com/');
// Will return false, because the domain is wrong
$cookie->match('http://www.example.com/', true, time() + (3 * 3600));
// Will return false, because we added a time offset of +3 hours to
// current time
```

The Zend_Http_CookieJar Class: Instantiation

In most cases, there is no need to directly instantiate a Zend_Http_CookieJar object. If you want to attach a new cookie jar to your Zend_Http_Client object, just call the Zend_Http_Client->setCookieJar() method, and a new, empty cookie jar will be attached to your client. You could later get this cookie jar using Zend_Http_Client->getCookieJar().

If you still wish to manually instantiate a CookieJar object, you can do so by calling "new Zend_Http_CookieJar()" directly - the constructor method does not take any parameters. Another way to instantiate a CookieJar object is to use the static Zend_Http_CookieJar::fromResponse() method. This method takes two parameters: a Zend_Http_Response object, and a reference URI, as either a string or a Zend_Uri_Http object. This method will return a new Zend_Http_CookieJar object, already containing the cookies set by the passed HTTP response. The reference URI will be used to set the cookie's domain and path, if they are not defined in the Set-Cookie headers.

Adding Cookies to a Zend_Http_CookieJar object

Usually, the Zend_Http_Client object you attached your CookieJar object to will automatically add cookies set by HTTP responses to your jar. If you wish to manually add cookies to your jar, this can be done by using two methods:

- `Zend_Http_CookieJar->addCookie($cookie[, $ref_uri])`: Add a single cookie to the jar. $cookie can be either a Zend_Http_Cookie object or a string, which will be converted automatically into a Cookie object. If a string is provided, you should also provide $ref_uri - which is a reference URI either as a string or Zend_Uri_Http object, to use as the cookie's default domain and path.

- `Zend_Http_CookieJar->addCookiesFromResponse($response,   $ref_uri)`: Add all cookies set in a single HTTP response to the jar. $response is expected to be a Zend_Http_Response object with Set-Cookie headers. $ref_uri is the request URI, either as a string or a Zend_Uri_Http object, according to which the cookies' default domain and path will be set.

Retrieving Cookies From a Zend_Http_CookieJar object

Just like with adding cookies, there is usually no need to manually fetch cookies from a CookieJar object. Your Zend_Http_Client object will automatically fetch the cookies required for an HTTP request for you. However, you can still use 3 provided methods to fetch cookies from the jar object: getCookie(), getAllCookies(), and getMatchingCookies(). Additionnaly, iterating over the CookieJar will let you retrieve all the Zend_Http_Cookie objects from it.

It is important to note that each one of these methods takes a special parameter, which sets the return type of the method. This parameter can have 3 values:

- `Zend_Http_CookieJar::COOKIE_OBJECT`: Return a Zend_Http_Cookie object. If the method returns more than one cookie, an array of objects will be returned.

- `Zend_Http_CookieJar::COOKIE_STRING_ARRAY`: Return cookies as strings, in a "foo=bar" format, suitable for sending in a HTTP request "Cookie" header. If more than one cookie is returned, an array of strings is returned.

- `Zend_Http_CookieJar::COOKIE_STRING_CONCAT`: Similar to COOKIE_STRING_ARRAY, but if more than one cookie is returned, this method will concatenate all cookies into a single, long string separated by semicolons (;), and return it. This is especially useful if you want to directly send all matching cookies in a single HTTP request "Cookie" header.

The structure of the different cookie-fetching methods is described below:

- `Zend_Http_CookieJar->getCookie($uri, $cookie_name[, $ret_as])`: Get a single cookie from the jar, according to its URI (domain and path) and name. $uri is either a string or a Zend_Uri_Http object representing the URI. $cookie_name is a string identifying the cookie name. $ret_as specifies the return type as described above. $ret_type is optional, and defaults to COOKIE_OBJECT.

- `Zend_Http_CookieJar->getAllCookies($ret_as)`: Get all cookies from the jar. $ret_as specifies the return type as described above. If not specified, $ret_type defaults to COOKIE_OBJECT.

- `Zend_Http_CookieJar->getMatchingCookies($uri[, $matchSessionCookies[, $ret_as[, $now]]])`: Get all cookies from the jar that match a specified scenario, that is a URI and expiration time.

  - $uri is either a Zend_Uri_Http object or a string specifying the connection type (secure or non-secure), domain and path to match against.

  - $matchSessionCookies is a boolean telling whether to match session cookies or not. Session cookies are cookies that have no specified expiration time. Defaults to true.

  - $ret_as specifies the return type as described above. If not specified, defaults to COOKIE_OBJECT.

  - $now is an integer representing the UNIX time stamp to consider as "now" - that is any cookies who are set to expire before this time will not be matched. If not specified, defaults to the current time.

You can read more about cookie matching here: the section called "Zend_Http_Cookie: Matching against a scenario".

Zend_Http_Response

Introduction

Zend_Http_Response provides easy access to an HTTP responses message, as well as a set of static methods for parsing HTTP response messages. Usually, Zend_Http_Response is used as an object returned by a Zend_Http_Client request.

In most cases, a Zend_Http_Response object will be instantiated using the factory() method, which reads a string containing an HTTP response message, and returns a new Zend_Http_Response object:

Example 25.26. Instantiating a Zend_Http_Response Object Using the Factory Method

```
$str = '';
$sock = fsockopen('www.example.com', 80);
$req =      "GET / HTTP/1.1\r\n" .
            "Host: www.example.com\r\n" .
            "Connection: close\r\n" .
            "\r\n";
fwrite($sock, $req);
while ($buff = fread($sock, 1024))
    $str .= $sock;
$response = Zend_Http_Response::factory($str);
```

You can also use the contractor method to create a new response object, by specifying all the parameters of the response:

```
public function __construct($code, $headers, $body = null, $version =
'1.1', $message = null)
```

- $code: The HTTP response code (eg. 200, 404, etc.)

- $headers: An associative array of HTTP response headers (eg. 'Host' => 'example.com')

- $body: The response body as a string

- $version: The HTTP response version (usually 1.0 or 1.1)

- $message: The HTTP response message (eg 'OK', 'Internal Server Error'). If not specified, the message will be set according to the response code

Boolean Tester Methods

Once a Zend_Http_Response object is instantiated, it provides several methods that can be used to test the type of the response. These all return Boolean true or false:

- Boolean isSuccessful(): Whether the request was successful or not. Returns TRUE for HTTP 1xx and 2xx response codes

- Boolean isError(): Whether the response code implies an error or not. Returns TRUE for HTTP 4xx (client errors) and 5xx (server errors) response codes

- Boolean isRedirect(): Whether the response is a redirection response or not. Returns TRUE for HTTP 3xx response codes

Example 25.27. Using the isError() method to validate a response

```
if ($response->isError()) {
  echo "Error transmitting data.\n"
  echo "Server reply was: " . $response->getStatus() .
      " " . $response->getMessage() . "\n";
}
// .. process the response here...
```

Accessor Methods

The main goal of the response object is to provide easy access to various response parameters.

- int getStatus(): Get the HTTP response status code (eg. 200, 504, etc.)

- string getMessage(): Get the HTTP response status message (eg. "Not Found", "Authorization Required")

- string getBody(): Get the fully decoded HTTP response body

- string getRawBody(): Get the raw, possibly encoded HTTP response body. If the body was decoded using GZIP encoding for example, it will not be decoded.

- array getHeaders(): Get the HTTP response headers as an associative array (eg. 'Content-type' => 'text/html')

- string|array getHeader($header): Get a specific HTTP response header, specified by $header

- string getHeadersAsString($status_line = true, $br = "\n"): Get the entire set of headers as a string. If $status_line is true (default), the first status line (eg. "HTTP/1.1 200 OK") will also be returned. Lines are broken with the $br parameter (Can be, for example, "<br />")

- string asString($br = "\n"): Get the entire response message as a string. Lines are broken with the $br parameter (Can be, for example, "<br />")

Example 25.28. Using Zend_Http_Response Accessor Methods

```
if ($response->getStatus() == 200) {
   echo "The request returned the following information:<br />";
   echo $response->getBody();
} else {
   echo "An error occurred while fetching data:<br />";
   echo $response->getStatus() . ": " . $response->getMessage();
}
```

Always check return value

Since a response can contain several instances of the same header, the getHeader() method and getHeaders() method may return either a single string, or an array of strings for each header. You should always check whether the returned value is a string or array.

Example 25.29. Accessing Response Headers

```
$ctype = $response->getHeader('Content-type');
if (is_array($ctype)) $ctype = $ctype[0];
$body = $response->getBody();
if ($ctype == 'text/html' || $ctype == 'text/xml') {
   $body = htmlentities($body);
}
echo $body;
```

Static HTTP Response Parsers

The Zend_Http_Response class also includes several internally-used methods for processing and parsing HTTP response messages. These methods are all exposed as static methods, which means they can be used externally, even if you do not need to instantiate a response object, and just want to extract a specific part of the response.

- `int Zend_Http_Response::extractCode($response_str)`: Extract and return the HTTP response code (eg. 200 or 404) from $response_str

- `string Zend_Http_Response::extractMessage($response_str)`: Extract and return the HTTP response message (eg. "OK" or "File Not Found") from $response_str

- `string Zend_Http_Response::extractVersion($response_str)`: : Extract and return the HTTP version (eg. 1.1 or 1.0) from $response_str

- `array Zend_Http_Response::extractHeaders($response_str)`: Extract and return the HTTP response headers from $response_str as an array

- `string Zend_Http_Response::extractBody($response_str)`: Extract and return the HTTP response body from $response_str

- `string Zend_Http_Response::responseCodeAsText($code = null, $http11 = true)`: Get the standard HTTP response message for a response code $code. For example, will return "Internal Server Error" if $code is 500. If $http11 is true (default), will return HTTP/1.1 standard messages - otherwise HTTP/1.0 messages will be returned. If $code is not specified, this method will return all known HTTP response codes as an associative (code => message) array.

Apart from parser methods, the class also includes a set of decoders for common HTTP response transfer encodings:

- `string Zend_Http_Response::decodeChunkedBody($body)`: Decode a complete "Content-Transfer-Encoding: Chunked" body

- `string Zend_Http_Response::decodeGzip($body)`: Decode a "Content-Encoding: gzip" body

- `string Zend_Http_Response::decodeDeflate($body)`: Decode a "Content-Encoding: deflate" body